DECODING ANDEAN MYTHOLOGY

Decoding
Andean
MYTHOLOGY

~~

Margarita B. Marín-Dale

The University of Utah Press

Salt Lake City

The Defiance House Man colophon is a registered trademark
of the University of Utah Press. It is based on a four-foot-tall
Ancient Puebloan pictograph (late PIII) near Glen Canyon, Utah.

20 19 18 17 16   1 2 3 4 5

LIBRARY OF CONGRESS CATALOGING-IN-PUBLICATION DATA
Name: Marín-Dale, Margarita B., 1958–author.
Title: Decoding Andean Mythology / Margarita B. Marín-Dale.
Description: Salt Lake City : The University of Utah Press, 2016. | Includes
bibliographical references and index.
Identifiers: LCCN 2016014223| ISBN 9781607815082 (pbk. : alk. paper) |
ISBN 9781607815099 (ebook)
Subjects: LCSH: Indian mythology—Andes Region. | Indians of South
America—Andes Region—Folklore.
Classification: LCC F2230.1.R3 M28 2016 | DDC 398.20898—dc23
LC record available at http://lccn.loc.gov/2016014223

Cover painting by Sairy Tupak Lligalo.

Printed and bound by Edwards Brothers Malloy, Inc., Ann Arbor, Michigan.

contents

acknowledgments

They say it takes a village to raise a child. Many generous and talented people helped me to raise this child, my book, from infancy to maturity over a period of twenty years. In many ways this book wanted to be born. As I was writing another book, this one branched off and took on a life of its own, growing into something greater than I had imagined. But I could not have done it alone; this work benefitted from many caregivers.

My understanding of Native Andean cultures and traditions was greatly enriched through my discussions with Ricardo Sánchez, Elmer Herrera, and my many friends and colleagues at Quechua Network and Jach'a Uru. There is an indigenous renaissance taking place in the Andes, and their work with native and immigrant communities is an integral part of that effort.

I would also like to thank my fellow professors and colleagues at American University, especially the late Jack Child, who took a chance with me more than a decade ago by letting me teach the subjects that I love and influencing me beyond measure. Jack not only shared his office but also created the space for me to teach in innovative ways. He leaves behind no shortage of friends at AU; he is always with us in spirit.

I am also indebted to my wonderful students, some of whom are now working in the Andes and other parts of Latin America, who over the years have posed interesting questions, helped me to refine my thoughts, and filled my academic life with their idealism and inquisitiveness. Because of them I believe the future of our planet is very bright; theirs will be a kinder and more just world.

Many friends have supported me through the years, including John Mackenzie, Marco Antonio Ribeiro, Kathleen Manning, Doreen Kinashi, Teresa Rogovsky, the late Elizabeth Rogovsky, and Karen Fall. Together we mulled over book ideas, fueled by pastries and countless cups of coffee. Their warmth, good humor, and encouragement inspired and sustained me.

A special thank you goes to Lynette Yetter and Tamara Trownsell, who helped me obtain obscure reference materials from Andean bookstores and libraries, and to Tim O'Hagan, who read the first draft of my work and made some very useful comments and suggestions.

I also express gratitude to my editor, John Alley, and the editorial board of the University of Utah Press for taking an interest in my manuscript and accepting it for publication. I especially appreciate John's willingness to answer all my queries, no matter how small, and to provide much-needed guidance, which has sharpened the focus of my book.

I am also beholden to two anonymous readers for the Press, later revealed to be John Bierhorst and Paul R. Steele, who provided useful insights and thoughtful recommendations that improved the quality of my manuscript. Their comments were very valuable to me, and I appreciate the time and effort they expended in carefully reviewing my work.

I thank the publishing companies and authors in Latin America and the United States who granted me permission to translate stories and long excerpts from their published works: the heirs of José María Arguedas, the heirs of Antonio-Paredes Candia, Ruth Moya, Ricardo Sánchez, José Yánez del Pozo, Gerald Taylor, César Itier, Johnny Payne, Editorial Abya-Yala, and Waveland Press. And I owe many thanks to Martín Moscoso Villacorta, Alejandra Bernal, and David Mora Navarro for assisting me with this process.

This book would not have been possible without the love and support of my family. My beloved husband, Thomas Dale, gave me the courage to forge ahead, even when faced with the most challenging obstacles. My wonderful and intellectually curious sons, Philip and William (my expert grammarians), and my dear stepson, Brian, celebrated every milestone along this long journey. My brilliant mother, Mercedes Paz Arauco-Carty, a writer in her own right, instilled in me not only a passion for words, but also a passion for justice. I also count my five siblings among my closest friends and advisors: María Eugenia Marín, Mónica Marín Rein, María Ximena Marín, María Inés Marín, and Edward Andrews. I cannot thank them enough for their faith and encouragement in what seemed, at times, like a never-ending project.

Finally, I express my deep appreciation for the people of my *llaqta*, Bolivia, and for the Quechua caregivers of my childhood, who left me the priceless legacy of stories, traditions, and languages upon which this book is based. I dedicate this work to them and hope it honors their lives and memories.

A NOTE ON PRONUNCIATION

To facilitate the reading of the italicized terms in the text and glossary, a general pronunciation guide is provided hereinafter. However, please keep in mind that these brief guidelines merely provide rough phonetic approximations for English speakers; they do not capture the proper native pronunciations, which are highly variable and complex.

It is important to mention that most monolingual Quechua and Aymara speakers use only three vowels, *a*, *i*, and *u*, whereas Spanish speakers recognize five. The consonants *b, c, d, f, g, v*, and *z* do not exist in either Quechua or Aymara and are found only in borrowed spellings. Aymara also makes use of the letter *x*, whereas Quechua does not.

The letter *h* exists in both Quechua and Aymara in certain consonant combinations, such as *ch, kh, qh*, and so forth. However, an initial *h* occurs only in Quechua; in Aymara it appears only in variant spellings. In both languages an initial *h* may also indicate a borrowed spelling from Spanish.

- *a* as in the English words "f<u>a</u>ther" or "<u>a</u>h" (ex: *Apu*, a divinized mountain or mountain peak);

- *e* as in the English words "m<u>e</u>n" or "t<u>e</u>n" (ex: *eqeqo*, an Andean idol of good fortune). The vowel *e* is phonemic in Spanish but not in Quechua or Aymara, where it is heard as a variant form of the vowel sound *i*;

- *i* is pronounced as in the English double *ee* or the ending *ey*, as in the words "s<u>ee</u>" or "k<u>ey</u>" (ex: *Inti*, the Andean Sun god);

- *o* as in the English words "<u>o</u>r" or "m<u>o</u>re," without the following *r* sound (ex: *oca*, an Andean tuber). The vowel *o* is phonemic in Spanish but not in Quechua or Aymara, where it is heard as a variant form of the vowel sound *u*;

- *u* as in the English double *oo* used in "st<u>oo</u>l" or "c<u>oo</u>l" (ex: *ukuku*, meaning "bear," and also the "Boy-Bear" of Andean folktales and dances);

- the letter *h* appearing at the beginning of a word is silent in Spanish (ex: *hombre*, meaning "man" or "humankind") and in Quechua and Aymara words transcribed into Spanish spelling (ex: [Q] *huaca*, a sacred place, object, animal, or person venerated by a Native Andean religion; [A and Q] *huari*, meaning "vicuña");

- the vowel *u* is silent in Spanish words beginning with *qu*, and the initial *q* is pronounced like a soft English *k*. Thus, *que* is pronounced like the *ke* sound in the English word "<u>ke</u>g," and *qui* is pronounced like the English word "<u>key</u>" (exs: *quena*, the traditional Andean flute; *quinoa*, an Andean crop);

- the letter *q* in Quechua and Aymara has no English equivalent. When it appears at the end of a Quechua word, it sounds like the soft English *k* in "sul<u>k</u>" or "sil<u>k</u>" but pronounced further back in the throat (ex: *atoq*, meaning "fox"). However, when it appears at the beginning or in the middle of a word in either Quechua or Aymara, it sounds more like a depressed *g* or *c*, originating in the back of the throat. Try depressing the tongue with the index finger and then saying a word such as "go," "caw," or "cocoa" to re-create this sound (exs: [Q] *qori*, meaning "gold"; *orqo*, meaning "mountain"; [A] *qawra*, meaning "llama"; *quqa*, meaning "tree").

1

INTRODUCTION

Voices of the Andean World

Living in the highlands between earth and sky, the indigenous peoples of the Andes have developed a rich oral tradition and a body of mythology spanning millennia, which expresses their deep connection to the earth, the mountains, the animals, and the celestial bodies that influence their life cycles. Their stories describe not only their beliefs, rituals, and individual cultures, but also their collective wounds and struggles, and their hopes for the future.

In the last several decades, many international scholars have compiled and analyzed aspects of Andean mythology and made valuable contributions to this growing field. With few exceptions, these works generally take two forms: written compilations of oral stories collected, transcribed, and translated by the researchers while living and interacting with Native Andean communities; or scholarly analyses intended to shed new light on the cultural context, content, or significance of these stories. These studies generally focus on one or more discreet stories, or a distinct corpus of stories, as a means of developing theories and advancing our understanding of contemporary Andean culture and society. In both cases, investigators typically rely on close observation of the sociocultural context in which these stories occur. Often the researchers are immersed in the culture and gain knowledge about it through informants and what community members articulate about their culture.

In this work, I approach Andean mythology from the perspective of both observer and participant in the culture, with personal knowledge of many of the stories and belief systems described herein.[1] So in many

1

respects this book builds a bridge between the two bodies of research previously described. Although this book is scholarly, it is also meant to educate and entertain the reader, providing a panoramic view of many wonderful folk narratives derived from both contemporary and ancient Native Andean cultures.

This survey of Native Andean mythology from across various regions of the Andes offers new interpretations from an interdisciplinary perspective. Previous scholarship has focused primarily on Inca origin and creation myths derived from the Spanish colonial chronicles, or modern Quechua stories from the Cuzco region of Peru. This book is wider in scope, presenting a comprehensive analysis of Native Andean oral tradition spanning five centuries, from pre-Hispanic myths, recorded during the Spanish colonial period, to modern times. It is also a departure from the Cuzco-centered focus of many Andean narratives and includes full translations of myths, stories, and folktales from other Andean ethnic groups, including the Aymaras, Wankas, and Cañaris, and from Quechua/Quichua-speaking regions outside of Cuzco. Yet, this is not an anthropological or ethnographic work; rather, it is intended to provide the reader with various theoretical tools, derived from diverse fields of knowledge, to decipher meaning and deepen an understanding of this rich oral tradition.

For almost two decades I have analyzed hundreds of Native Andean myths, legends, and folktales from various theoretical perspectives and have uncovered some of the recurring elements and themes which, like interwoven threads, form the intricate tapestry of Andean folklore. This work will principally highlight the following elements and themes: Andean animism (chap. 2); intermediaries (chap. 3); *pachacuti* (inversion or revolution of time-space; chap. 4); *huacas* (sacred objects, animals, people, and places; chap. 5); the origin of culture (chap. 6); sexuality and guilt (chap. 7); supernatural beings (chap. 8); and social protest (chap. 9). Each will be addressed in greater detail in a separate chapter. However, the material presented here is by no means exhaustive; rather, it is a starting point for those who wish to unlock the secrets of this living mythology and explore a non-Western, indigenous world that offers a vision and cosmological perspective very unlike our own.

Regrettably, it is virtually impossible to recount in a single manuscript all of the colorful and captivating stories of the hundreds of Native Andean cultures that inhabit the Andean region of South America today. In my native land of Bolivia alone, various indigenous groups, each with its own distinctive community and tradition, speak more than thirty indigenous languages. For this reason, most of the legends, myths, and folktales selected for inclusion in this text derive from the Quechua and Aymara peoples of the Andean region. These two ethnic groups are the largest and most predominant in the area.

Recent statistics indicate that there are an estimated ten million speakers of the Quechua language in the Andes, most of whom live in Peru, Bolivia, Ecuador, Colombia, Chile, and Argentina. Additionally, between two and three million people speak the Aymara language in the Andean *altiplano*—the high plateau between the eastern and western mountain ranges of the Peruvian and Bolivian Andes—and in parts of Argentina and northern Chile. There are also numerous regional variations of each of these languages[2] and many cultural variations from one community to another. Moreover, in certain regions of the Andes, Quechuas and Aymaras have lived side by side for centuries, contributing to linguistic and cultural exchanges.

The Quechuas are the modern-day descendants of the mighty Inca civilization of the past, which reached its apogee in the Andes between 1438 and 1532 AD, the Empire Period.[3] The Incas did not develop independently but rather represented the culmination of thousands of years of Native Andean statecraft, culture, and tradition.[4] The empire was the largest in the Americas, extending north to south for over twenty-five hundred miles, from the border of present-day Ecuador and Colombia to central Chile, and east to west for five hundred miles, from the Pacific Ocean to the Amazonian piedmont.

The Incas were formidable warriors. Using a variety of methods, including conquest and peaceful incorporation, they subjugated a large portion of western South America. In a period of some fifty-five years (1438–1493), under the leadership of two military geniuses, Pachacuti Inca Yupanqui and his son, Tupac Inca Yupanqui, the Incas conquered most of the territory of *Tawantinsuyu* ("The Four Parts United or Integrated Together"), the name they ascribed to their nation. Tupac's son, Huayna Capac (1493–1525), conquered the remainder of *Tawantinsuyu* and then presided over the largest Native American empire ever to develop in the Americas. A vast system of roads and highways traversed the empire, connecting every region.[5] All along such roads were storehouses (*collca*) and lodgings (*tampu*) for the traveling armies. Spanish conquerors who looted these storehouses during the Conquest of Peru reported that some held a ten-year reserve of food and supplies. The Incas also developed a highly efficient communication system in which they employed short-distance runners, called *chasquis*, posted every few miles along the Inca roads. These runners relayed oral messages and messages recorded on the *khipu*—the Inca recording system—from one region of the empire to another. According to many colonial accounts, this relay network of Inca messengers was so effective, messages could travel even over challenging terrain as far as 250 miles a day!

The Incas also achieved major advancements in architecture, engineering, astronomy, medicine (including cranial surgery or trepanation), tax (tribute) administration, terrace cultivation, and numerous other fields. As did some pre-Inca cultures, they also freeze-dried potatoes (*chuño*) to permit storage for extended periods. Additionally, one of their most noteworthy accomplishments was their fine stone masonry that, according to some architects, stands unrivaled by any world culture, past or present. Of major significance is that such masonry was accomplished without the use of mortar or draft animals and without knowledge of the wheel. Yet the Spanish chroniclers observed that adjoining blocks of stones were so closely fitted that not even a coin could be forced between the blocks. Great mystery is attached to how such formidable constructions could have been accomplished at such great altitudes and in some of the most inhospitable regions of the world. Many structures still stand in quiet elegance today, towering over hilltops, valleys, precipices, and rugged mountainous terrain. In their harmonious and aesthetic unity with the landscape, they almost appear to be born out of the mountain rock. These are testaments to the once-glorious Incas, who always performed their tasks—great or small—deliberately, precisely, practically, and artistically.

Of special interest is that Inca history is interposed with mythology. Legend has it, for instance, that the Sun god, *Inti*, appeared to Pachacuti Inca Yupanqui and foretold that he would lead his people to victory over their adversaries[6] and conquer innumerable lands. As a result, Pachacuti launched the Incas' greatest period of expansion and turned what might otherwise have been a local chiefdom into a magnanimous empire. The gods also intervened when Pachacuti went to war with his most challenging adversary, the Chanca confederation, which threatened to overcome Cuzco, the Inca capital. The turning point of the war came when Pachacuti's forces were nearly depleted and he called upon the Sun god (some versions say the Creator god) to come to his aid. According to the legend, the Inca Sun god caused the very stones on the ground to turn into phantom warriors, who fought alongside the Incas and secured their victory over the Chancas.[7] Afterward, Pachacuti gathered the stones—called *pururaucas*—and gave them a place of honor in the *Coricancha* ("Golden Enclosure"), the Incas' most sacred shrine, located in Cuzco.[8]

The Incas also believed in signs and omens, much like their modern-day Quechua descendants. For instance, during the reign of Huayna Capac, the Inca diviners predicted the future fall of their empire. According to the half-Inca colonial chronicler, Garcilaso de la Vega, one clear night the diviners observed three rings encircling the moon. The inner ring was red, the color of blood; the middle ring was black with a tinge of green; the outer ring was gray and hazy like smoke. The diviners entered the chamber of Huayna Capac and advised the Inca emperor that after his death there would be (red) blood shed among his relatives; then, (black) darkness would envelop the empire through warfare and the destruction of their religion; and, finally, everything would go up in (gray) smoke as the days of the empire came to an end.[9] These signs apparently foreshadowed the Inca civil wars between Huayna Capac's sons, Huascar and Atahualpa, which divided and weakened the empire, and also prophesied the ultimate death of the empire at the hands of the conquering Spaniards.

The Incas practiced various divination rituals, the most important of which was *calpa*, performed to determine whether an heir to the throne was suitable to rule[10] or to determine the outcome of an important military undertaking. They performed this ritual by killing an animal and examining its extracted organs, especially the heart, and blowing on its pulmonary veins, the protrusions of which were used to determine an outcome's favorability.[11] The Incas also had priests trained to read coca leaves, corn kernels, llama dung, and smoke emitted from sacrificial fires.[12]

The practice of divination and prognostication is still carried out today among the Quechuas, Aymaras, and many other Native Andean cultures in ways similar to those of their ancestors. Most Native Andeans, especially in rural areas, practice a syncretistic religion that includes many elements of their animistic pre-Columbian rituals, customs, and traditions—including divination—interwoven with Christian elements introduced by the Spanish conquerors. This cultural and religious syncretism figures prominently in Native Andean tales.

Storytelling in the Andes is also an expression of multiculturalism. It is a living, breathing, ever-changing tradition that has not developed in isolation. The Native Andean oral tradition continues, much as in pre-Columbian times, articulating indigenous values and themes handed down from one generation to the next. Yet many modern Native Andean folktales incorporate various European elements, reflecting the indelible influence of the European conquerors and their modern-day descendants on indigenous cultures for nearly five hundred years. As such, they may be rightfully described as *mestizo*, or culturally mixed stories, that today are shared among non-Native Andeans as well. Similarly, Andean indigenous groups, especially those living in close proximity such as the Quechuas and Aymaras, have also influenced one another, both in language and the living oral tradition. To this multicultural tapestry one must add the African influence that has contributed to Andean culture since the arrival of the colonial Spaniards with their African servants and slaves. Although this study focuses primarily on the indigenous perspective, the modern Native Andean story is an intricate *lliklla*—an Andean mantle—woven from indigenous, African, and European threads.

With respect to contemporary Native Andean societies, in addition to Quechua stories, this work also highlights legends of the Aymara people. The Aymaras (also known as "Kollas" or "Collas") trace their origins to the region of *Collasuyu*, the southeast quadrant of *Tawantinsuyu*, the Inca state, which was conquered (and reconquered) by the Incas in the late fifteenth century. Contemporary Aymaras believe they are descendants of the Tiwanaku culture (also spelled "Tiahuanaco"), a complex pre-Inca civilization that emerged in the Andean *altiplano* and served as the dominant political and religious force in that region from about 500 to 1000 AD.[13] In addition to modern Aymara tales, this book recounts a few pre-Columbian origin myths from the region surrounding Lake Titicaca that, centuries ago, was the cornerstone of Tiwanaku culture.

Furthermore, this work incorporates a variety of myths, legends, and folktales of the Cañari peoples of Ecuador. The Cañaris are an ancient Quichua-speaking people (a regional variant of Quechua) who inhabit the southern highland region of Ecuador known as Cañar. Their ancestors founded an impressive city known as *Guapondeleg* ("Land as Large as Heaven"), circa 500 AD, that was subsequently conquered by the Incas some fifty years before the arrival of the Spanish conquerors. During the Inca civil wars, which divided the empire shortly before the arrival of the Spaniards, the Cañaris allied with Huascar Inca, who was defeated by his half brother, Atahualpa. In retribution, they were massacred by the victor and barely survived as a people.[14] Accounts of their origin myths are among some of the earliest indigenous stories recorded by the Spanish colonial chroniclers.[15]

Of special interest is an ancient origin myth of the Wanka (also spelled "Huanca") people of the central highlands region of Peru. The Wanka culture rose to prominence in the thirteenth century in the valley of Jauja or Mantaro, in the central Andes, and was subsequently conquered by the Incas around 1460. The forebears of the Wankas constructed an important temple called *Wariwilka* (also spelled *Wariwillka* or *Huarivilca*, meaning "Native Shrine" or "Liquid [Water] Shrine")[16] that contained a sacred spring with accompanying staircase, two or three Andean pepper trees (*molle*), and a purification pool. The Wankas to this day believe that their ancestors emerged from this sacred spring. Spanish priests destroyed the temple of Wariwilka in 1534, but the sacred spring survives and continues to supply water to the residents of the Jauja valley. It is presumed that prior to the Inca Conquest, the Wankas had their own local language; however, today they speak a variant of Quechua called *Wanka Quechua* that has several regional dialects and is spoken by approximately three hundred thousand people.[17]

At this point, I would like to clarify the use of certain terminology. Generally speaking, Western classical mythology often distinguishes among myth, legend, and folktale. A myth tends to expose and explain the practices and beliefs of a culture and may also expound on its cosmology, particularly with respect to natural phenomena and space-time relations. Often, as in Greek and Roman myths, for instance, the story concerns gods, heroes, and other mythical creatures who embody and represent natural forces that exert their influence on humankind. In Western terms, legends also often include fantastic or exaggerated events but generally concern human beings or specific places. Legends may also have a historical basis, although such basis is often disprovable and unreliable. Folktales are "anonymous tale[s] circulated orally among a people,"[18] with a primary purpose to entertain or communicate a moral lesson concerning "human follies and weaknesses."[19] I am not a classical mythologist, so these guidelines are merely intended to provide a thumbnail sketch of how these terms are generally described.

Still, I believe many mythologists would agree that myth, legend, and folktale are not rigid distinctions, but rather, flexible terms that bend, stretch, and often overlap. However, in Native Andean mythology these terms appear to be meaningless, and for all practical purposes, irrelevant. As will be fairly evident from a close reading of this text, it is nearly impossible to discern the differences among myth, legend, and folktale in Andean mythology. Andean legends often incorporate mythical figures and describe natural forces, and myths often contain allegedly historical as well as cosmological information. Moreover, myths and legends of the past may also be relayed in contemporary Andean society for entertainment purposes or moral value, further blurring the distinctions among these genres. Consequently, I have employed these three terms interchangeably throughout the text. Use (or misuse!) of these terms is not intended to communicate any significant distinction.

Another curious point is that Andean stories often do not assign names to the protagonists and antagonists, except for deities or *huacas*.[20] They are simply described as "the boy," "the condor," "the llama," and so forth. I speculate that this is a function of the great importance Native Andean cultures place on the concept of community. Leaving the main characters nameless has the effect of minimizing individuality and individual differences, and preserving the power of the collective in the story. Unlike our Western European tradition, which places considerable emphasis on individualism, Native Andean peoples take great pride in their communal way of life. In the countryside each community has its own particular native dress, with its own unique style and distinctive coloring, and everyone dresses fairly much the same, in accordance with gender and locality distinctions. Furthermore, each Native Andean ethnic group has its own stories, rituals, and traditions. Nonetheless, with a few exceptions, there is a great deal of cultural, economic, and informational exchange among communities, and between urban and rural areas; thus, it is often difficult to discern the origin of particular stories and beliefs and to ascribe them specifically to one Native Andean group or another.

Another very important Native Andean concept, which bears upon the individual's relationship with the community, is the *ayllu*. Generally, the *ayllu* is a Native Andean organizational or administrative unit that binds the individual to the community in a number of ways. The solidarity of the *ayllu* may arise "by religious and territorial ties [*llaqta ayllu*], by permanent claim to land and lineage [*hatun ayllu*], by affinal ties [*masi ayllu*],…by [communal] work [*mitmaq ayllu*],"[21] and even by symbolic ties to the communal land. The *ayllu* is a non-Western concept that dates back to Inca and pre-Inca times. However, it is still relevant today in that it describes the strong bond between Native Andeans and their community at various levels. The importance of communal values and the strong sense of community figure prominently in Andean stories.

Another non-Western notion that emerges in Native Andean myths is *pachacuti*, a cycle of creation and destruction generally described as an "inversion" or "revolution" of time-space. In many such myths, *pachacuti* commences with a cataclysmic event that destroys the existing world and gives rise to a new creation. Native Andeans since ancient times have believed in many creations and destructions of the world; for this reason, their stories often describe, in symbolic and suggestive ways, their ever-present fear of another *pachacuti* threatening to overcome the world and extinguish humanity. More recently, the Native Andeans have also developed and embraced the notion of a historical or symbolic *pachacuti*, which refers to a transformational historical or sociocultural event that drastically alters their lives. For instance, the Quechua and Aymara peoples believe that the election of Evo Morales, the first indigenous president of Bolivia, is a historical milestone and a *pachacuti*, marking the beginning of a new age that promises to radically alter the status quo and dramatically change the course of their lives.

Aside from *pachacuti*, Native Andean stories address many topics that are very close to the hearts and minds of indigenous peoples. Some of these tales have roots in the pre-Columbian past and date back hundreds, if not thousands, of years. These ancient stories often communicate cultural, traditional, cosmological, or religious beliefs, as, for example, in creation and origin myths. Other Andean stories describe, literally or symbolically, the strong bond between Native Andeans and their immediate environment, particularly their deep attachment to the land, divinized as *Pacha Mama*, the Andean "Earth Mother." Like their pre-Columbian ancestors, many Native Andeans believe the landscape is imbued with life, energy, and spirit. For this reason they often personify mountains, rocks, lakes, rivers, and other aspects of nature, and attribute to them human qualities and characteristics, a doctrine known as *Andean animism*. A number of their tales also concern animals, persons, and supernatural or anthropomorphic beings that live in distinctive "worlds," are caught "in between" worlds, or serve as intermediaries between one world and another. Such tales contain (in our eyes) magical and fantastic elements, and they are consistent with the vivified and dynamic view of nature shared by most Native Andean peoples.

Native Andean mythology also describes certain places, animals, ancestors, and idols, called *huacas*, which are considered sacred in the native traditions. The many customary definitions and interpretations of *huaca* will be investigated in a subsequent chapter. However, there are some Andean stories that identify gateways, or portals, especially in mountains, that open and close between different realities or worlds. So in this work I propose that the Andean notion of *huaca* also aptly describes a portal between the natural and supernatural worlds, or pinpoints a sacred space that exists simultaneously in both worlds. This idea has already been raised based on a linguistic interpretation of *huaca*,[22] and I have found corroborative support for this proposition based on mythological evidence and a review of certain Andean rituals.

As with many other folktales from around the world, Native Andean tales communicate moral lessons and values, such as generosity and hard work, that are important to the survival and integrity of indigenous communities. They also address social taboos, such as incest, although mostly in terms of disguised sexual imagery. It is important to emphasize the pairing of sexuality and guilt in many Andean stories, which I attribute to the conflict between indigenous and European notions of morality in the Andes—the discrepancy between the permissive sexual attitudes and practices of pre-Columbian Andean cultures and the repressive sexual mores introduced by the Catholic Church after the Spanish Conquest, especially with regard to female sexuality. These inconsonant views of sexuality are evident in many Native Andean tales and in some surviving pre-Columbian sexual customs and dances.

Andean stories are also acceptable avenues for making social and political commentaries about the powerful external forces that impinge on Native Andean life. It is not uncommon for Andean stories to criticize white foreigners, the Catholic Church, and Western values in often humorous and satirical ways. Some of these folktales might also be characterized as stories of social protest against the systematic racism, abuse, and oppression endured by Native Andeans over the course of five centuries following the Conquest. At the end of this book, we will examine many of the historical and social roots of racism in the Andes and discuss how contemporary Andean storytellers use the oral tradition as an effective medium for voicing their grievances and criticizing unjust social and political institutions.

THE STORY KEEPERS

Native Andean stories are transmitted orally from one generation to the next, with some measure of variation. Many of these stories have never been recorded, except in the minds and memories of the Andean storytellers. Today, especially in urban and affluent areas, storytelling has been supplanted by other forms of entertainment, such as television and computers, especially among the young. Also, some indigenous languages, even those as widely spoken as Quechua, are slowly heading toward extinction. Some linguists attribute this demise to the marginalization of the Native Andean in Andean society. According to Rodolfo

Cerrón Palomino, a Quechua language expert, "As the dominating culture extends its influence further into the zones where these languages have taken refuge, their role will disappear, and Spanish will be placed on the throne forever."[23] Thus, unless some systematic effort is made to compile and record these indigenous stories in the native languages, many will be lost to future generations.

In this respect, the world is greatly indebted to the renowned Peruvian humanist José María Arguedas (1911–1969) for his compilations, in collaboration with other scholars, of a great number of Native Andean stories. Prior to his death in 1969, Arguedas was considered the principal spokesperson for the Peruvian indigenous literary movement. Although Arguedas was not a Native Andean by birth, after his mother died, his stepmother relegated him to the kitchen to eat and sleep with the household servants, Quechua Indians, who raised and cared for him. By his own admission, he spent his childhood living in the kitchen with these Quechua caregivers, for whom he later expressed profound affection. In his later years, he spent a great deal of time among the native people in the countryside. Fluent in the native Quechua language, Arguedas spent most of his life teaching, compiling, translating, writing, and preserving the oral tradition of the Quechuas, and calling for greater appreciation and acceptance of indigenous cultures in Andean society. He also contributed his own stories, plays, and novels, which realistically portrayed the racial stratification of Andean society, and openly criticized the unjust and deplorable treatment of the native peoples by their white and *mestizo* overlords.[24]

During his early career as a high school teacher, Arguedas asked his students to help him compile legends and stories from communities in all regions of Peru, which he would later edit and publish. The result was more successful than anyone could have anticipated. It became one of the most popular compilations of Native Andean folklore and was subsequently published, in collaboration with Francisco Izquierdo Ríos, as *Mitos, leyendas y cuentos peruanos* ("Peruvian Myths, Legends, and Folktales").[25] Arguedas and Ríos also produced an educational version (*edición escolar*) under the same title, designed as a reader for younger Peruvian students.[26] Arguedas went on to publish several other compilations, including *Canciones y cuentos del pueblo quechua* ("Songs and Stories of the Quechua People"),[27] and contributed to another produced by Andean historian Luis Valcárcel, entitled *Narraciones y leyendas incas* ("Inca Narrations and Legends").[28] The latter collection incorporated a number of modern Quechua folktales, as well as numerous pre-Columbian myths.

For his prolific work and efforts to preserve the culture, traditions, and folklore of the Native Andean peoples, Arguedas was appointed to several governmental and cultural posts during his lifetime, aimed at conserving Peru's historical and cultural heritage. In November 1969, only a few years after resigning as director of the National Museum of History of Peru, Arguedas committed suicide in his small, dark office. His masterpiece, *El zorro de arriba y el zorro de abajo* ("The Fox from Above and the Fox from Down Below"), which sets forth his ideological framework, was published posthumously in 1971.[29]

Arguedas also had a counterpart in my own native land of Bolivia in the humanist and scholar Jesús Lara (1898–1980). Lara was born in Cochabamba of a Quechua-speaking mother and a white father. He learned Quechua at home and was equally fluent in Spanish and Quechua. As a child, his schoolteachers often beat him for speaking in his mother's tongue. This strengthened his resolve to become one of Quechua's leading scholars. Lara began his career as a journalist and later studied all aspects of Quechua culture. He also embarked on a political career as a candidate for the Bolivian vice presidency in 1956, representing the Communist Party. His political loss, however, was literature's gain. Lara wrote prolifically, publishing numerous plays, poems, and novels in Quechua and Spanish. Later, he also developed a well-respected dictionary of the Quechua language.[30] Like Arguedas, he also published various compilations of Native Andean myths, legends, and folktales, as well as Quechua poetry and song.[31] Lara is also renowned for his elegant and poetic translation of a seventeenth-century Quechua document concerning the tragic last days of the Inca emperor Atahualpa.[32]

This gallery of Andean folklorists and writers would not be complete without the inclusion of the Bolivian Goliath, Antonio Paredes-Candia (1923–2004). This Andean giant singlehandedly published more than one hundred books during his lifetime, most of which recount Andean stories, legends, traditions, and customs. Although born into a literary family in La Paz (his father was a distinguished ethnographer), Paredes-Candia was mostly self-taught, and he later became one of the most passionate investigators of Andean popular culture. Most of all, he insisted that his people "must read" and take pride in their cultural heritage. Paredes-Candia never married, dedicating his entire life to compiling, recording, and keeping alive in the collective memory of his people the customs and oral tradition of the Andes. He traveled throughout all regions of Bolivia observing and systematically documenting "national folklore," mostly the indigenous and *mestizo* customs, stories, and traditions, that many of his contemporaries considered unworthy and inferior to "Europeanized" and Western literature and culture.

Paredes-Candia identified with the *runa*, the humble common person of indigenous or mixed ancestry who, in his perception, suffered grave injustices. He was known to sell his books on the street, in a makeshift bookstand, and at public book fairs, accessible to all. Some of his friends described him walking down the street, laden with books, looking like an *eqeqo*, an Aymara idol of good fortune, carrying on his body all kinds of household belongings. Yet, despite his eccentric manner and lashing tongue (he was known to have offended numerous politicians), Paredes-Candia transported not only his books but also nearly eight decades of systematic research on his elderly shoulders. He, perhaps more than any other Andean scholar, elevated the status of the Andean oral tradition and promoted a revival of Andean popular culture. His 112 publications[33] are a testament to his unyielding dedication and a tribute to our rich Andean culture and heritage.

Today, I am heartened that many Andean scholars throughout the world have followed in the footsteps of Arguedas, Lara, and Paredes-Candia, making every effort to record and conserve the Native Andean oral tradition. I also admire the wave of appreciation of indigenous cultures that is sweeping through many universities in the Andean region, some of which are making courageous strides in promoting bilingual education in primary schools; conserving Native Andean languages, stories, and folklore; and promoting the dignity and pride of the Native Andean peoples. Most of the contemporary stories included in this text derive from the written compilations of those who have sought to honor the Andean oral tradition.

Where applicable, my analyses of these stories are supported by anthropological studies, historical works, ethnohistorical documents, psychological writings, theories of mythology, and contemporary Native Andean writings, which provide the theoretical basis for many of my observations. However, as with any study of mythology, there is always room for subjectivity and interpretation, especially in the realm of symbolism. I believe that through a careful reading of these myths and tales, the reader will arrive at the conclusion that Andean stories have multiple layers of meaning. Perhaps in this respect I depart from the teachings of the Belgian-French mythologist and anthropologist, the father of structuralism, Claude Lévi-Strauss, who, by studying the "invariant elements" of myth, attempted to turn the study of mythology into a precise science such as physics and mathematics.[34]

Nonetheless, after nearly two decades of rigorous examination, I concur with Lévi-Strauss that certain universal structures and themes do emerge from Andean mythology. This will become fairly evident to readers as they see the similarity and coincidence among various regional and ethnic Andean myths. Although, arguably, these concurrences may be attributable in part to informational and cultural exchanges among the various Andean regions, communities, and ethnic groups, in most instances they also suggest a high degree of concordance, independent of time and space. However, more in accord with Carl G. Jung's flexible notion of unconscious "archetypes," I believe these structures are flexible and malleable, and not as rigid and fixed as the term "structure" seems to imply.

Moreover, from Sigmund Freud I have borrowed the notion of unconscious psychic processes that reveal themselves through symbols in a disguised and latent form. But, in this respect, my interpretation of Native Andean symbols is more akin to Freud's theories concerning the interpretation of dreams[35] than those comparing "primitive" cultures to the mental life of neurotics in his controversial work *Totem and Taboo*.[36] In some instances I also refer to the writings of Carl Jung, father of analytic psychology and onetime follower of Freud, who maintained that psychic libido, which gives rise to collective symbol, is a much more generalized "creative life force... that underlies myths" and encompasses the entire arena of human activity.[37] Although I recognize that all these theories have some limitations,[38] they are offered here as instruments of analysis—tools in the toolbox, so to speak—to give the reader various methods by which to analyze and interpret the meaning of these stories.

In addition, with respect to Andean pre-Columbian myths, scholars are limited by the many constraints posed by the Spanish colonial narratives, collectively known as the "chronicles." Unfortunately, we are still very dependent on these colonial documents because (to our knowledge) the ancient Andean peoples left no written record of their history and culture. Such chronicles reveal that the Incas, and some of their predecessors, had developed a system of recording mathematical, narrative, and historical information on the *khipu*, a complex recording system comprised of knotted strings and cords of different colors.[39] Modern scholars have deciphered the code of the mathematical *khipu*, but they have neither decoded nor located a narrative khipu that may provide a key to an Inca writing system. Nonetheless, recent studies have proposed various hypotheses as to how such a *khipu* may have encoded narrative information.[40] However, in the absence of any existing literary *khipu*, the primary sources for these pre-Columbian myths remain the colonial writings of the Spaniards, often rife with inaccuracies and limitations.[41]

The colonial chroniclers transcribed and recorded many ancient Native Andean myths but often tried to interpret them in a manner consistent with their own Western European concepts and values. The chroniclers were also Christian, so they attempted to describe and explain Native Andean cosmologies and religions in terms that were concordant with their Christian ideology. For instance, it is not uncommon in chroniclers' accounts to find timelines of Native Andean history described in terms of biblical chronology. Moreover, these Bible-based chronologies fail to account for cyclical concepts of time-space, which form the foundation of Native Andean cosmologies. The colonial chronicles were also written in the language of the conquerors and not in those of the conquered. Although some of the native and *mestizo* chroniclers inserted the Quechua language at intervals in the Spanish narratives, few colonial documents were written entirely in Quechua or any other Native Andean language of the past.

It is also quite evident that most Spanish colonial chroniclers believed that their own culture, beliefs, and ways of life were superior to those of the Native Andeans; as such, their writings are imbued with Eurocentric views and disparaging remarks about the native peoples. Within this framework hinging on cultural biases, they presented conflicting information, couched as history, but often intended as propaganda—they used the power of the pen to justify the Spanish Conquest and forced Christianization of the Native Andeans. In their writings they also incorporated European concepts, such as primogeniture and illegitimacy, which had little, if any, significance in Native Andean societies. On the other hand, some chroniclers, such as Garcilaso de la Vega, tried to overcompensate for this imperious view by depicting idealized portrayals of the Native Andeans. In so doing, however, they sometimes furnished erroneous or misleading information, particularly with respect to Native Andean religions.

Concerning Native Andean religions, the *Manuscript of Huarochirí* is of paramount importance, for it "alone of all colonial sources records a [pre-Columbian] religious tradition of the Andes in [a Native] Andean language."[42] This colonial document, composed at the turn of the seventeenth century, was probably written by indigenous informants from the highland region of Huarochirí, to the east of present-day Lima, Peru. It appears the document was compiled by order of the Spanish extirpator and priest, Francisco de Avila,[43] during the Extirpation of Idolatries, the period during which the Roman Catholic Church and the Spanish colonial authorities tried to systematically destroy the Native Andean religions and supplant the belief systems of the vanquished with the Christian faith of the victors.

But, as the Andean humanist José María Arguedas explains, "It is not [Francisco de] Avila who tells [the stories contained in the manuscript], but rather, the practitioner of the ancient religion, the believer in the ancient gods and heroes."[44] According to Arguedas, who collaborated on a translation of the document from Quechua into Spanish, its tone and style is primarily oral and consistent with the Native Andean oral tradition "as we [Andeans] uniquely feel in the Quechua folktales we have heard since childhood."[45] Hence, the stories in the *Huarochirí Manuscript* provide a rare glimpse into the pre-Columbian oral tradition of a distinct region of the Andes. As such, some of these stories will be featured in this book.

In weaving this Andean tapestry of colorful and symbolic threads, I have also relied on the works of numerous colonial chroniclers for other pre-Columbian myths. Among them, the most notable are El Inca Garcilaso de la Vega (1609 and 1617), Cristóbal de Molina (el "Cuzqueño") (1573), Bernabé Cobo (1653), Juan de Betanzos (1551), Pedro Sarmiento de Gamboa (1572), Felipe Guaman Poma de Ayala (circa 1615), Pedro de Cieza de León (1550 and 1553), and Joan de Santacruz Pachacuti Yamqui Salcamaygua (1613).

In reading the translations of these pre-Columbian stories, it is important to keep in mind that all of these colonial chroniclers were Christian, or converts to Christianity, and all but two—Guaman Poma and Santacruz Pachacuti Yamqui Salcamaygua—were of Spanish, or mixed Spanish and Native Andean, ancestry. As previously noted, one major limitation is that these chroniclers had ulterior reasons for writing and compiling information about the indigenous peoples. The priest-chroniclers Cobo and Molina, for instance, participated in the colonial Extirpation of Idolatries. Their main reason, possibly, for collecting stories and data about Native Andean religions, was to further the Church's attempt to Christianize the Indians and destroy all vestiges of the ancient Andean cults. Likewise, the Spanish colonial viceroy Francisco de Toledo commissioned the explorer and chronicler Sarmiento to write an Inca history justifying the Spanish Conquest. In order to legitimize the Conquest, Sarmiento portrayed the Incas as "tyrants," "infidels," and "barbarians."[46]

By contrast, the *mestizo* chronicler Garcilaso de la Vega was an ardent advocate of Inca culture and achievement. Garcilaso was born in Cuzco,

Peru, in 1539 to an Inca princess, Chimpu Ocllo (baptized Isabel Palla), and a Spanish captain, Sebastián Garcilaso de la Vega y Vargas. He was educated both in Cuzco and Europe. In his writings, Garcilaso had a tendency to idealize the Incas. In an effort to persuade his European audience that the Incas were "civilized" and stood apart from other indigenous (New World) cultures, Garcilaso sometimes distorted Inca religion and beliefs in an effort to make the Incas appear more Christian-like than they actually were.[47]

Notwithstanding these limitations, there is great merit in his masterwork, *Comentarios reales de los incas* ("Royal Commentaries of the Incas"), published in two volumes in the early seventeenth century. His *Comentarios* elegantly present a menagerie of topics, including Inca history, culture, religion, and administration. In my view, the hidden gems in Garcilaso's writings are the anecdotal tidbits intertwined in his text: the rich details about his personal upbringing with an Inca mother; the linguistic subtleties of the Quechua language, which he claimed the Spaniards had trouble mastering; and his cultural observations, such as how the older Incas spat on the ground whenever they saw one of their own begging for change (laziness was considered a crime in the former Inca Empire). Most importantly, I value the way Garcilaso came to appreciate and learn Inca myth—the very mechanism that is still being used today to transmit stories from one generation to the next—through the oral tradition of the Andes.

In this book I have included my translation of Garcilaso's version of the founding of the Inca Empire by the mythical rulers, Manco Capac and Mama Ocllo. According to this legend, Manco Capac and Mama Ocllo were brother and sister, husband and wife, and children of the Sun and the Moon. By his own account, Garcilaso heard this legend in his youth at a gathering of relatives at his mother's house. It was relayed by an elderly uncle, an Inca nobleman who lived in the city of Cuzco and had survived the Spanish Conquest of Peru.[48]

This work also draws attention to another colonial chronicler of great importance in the study of Andean mythology. His name is Felipe Guaman Poma de Ayala, and he can be considered one of the first "voices of protest" in Latin American colonial society. Unlike most other colonial chroniclers, Guaman Poma was a full-blooded Indian by birth and a "*mestizo* by culture."[49] He was probably born around 1534 in Suntunto, in the province of Lucanas, in what is today the Peruvian region of Ayacucho.[50] By his own account, he descended from the Yerovilca Indians of Huánuco. After the Incas conquered the Yerovilcas, his father, Martín

Guaman Mallqui de Ayala, presumedly was named "*capac apo*...prince of the Chincha Suyos and second person of the Inca in this kingdom of Peru."[51] His mother was Juana Curi Ocllo, whom he claims was a daughter of the Inca emperor Tupac Inca Yupanqui.[52]

Guaman Poma wrote a lengthy manuscript entitled *Nueva corónica y buen gobierno* ("New Chronicle and Good Government"), totaling over one thousand pages, intended as a letter to King Philip III of Spain. In the first part of his voluminous "letter," Guaman described life during the Inca Empire before the arrival of the Europeans; in the second part, he openly criticized the Spanish colonial authorities and members of the Catholic clergy for abusing and exploiting the Native Andean people.[53]

As one instructed in the Christian faith (his half brother was a priest), Guaman Poma admonished "the Spanish authorities for their ambition and corruption; the clergy for their materialism and lasciviousness; and any Indian who betrayed his own people."[54] In his manuscript, Guaman Poma envisioned a Christian state, led by Native Andean rulers, who would honor the values and communal integrity of the Inca past.[55] Consistent with these principles, his treatise made a series of recommendations to the Spanish king about how to reform and improve the Spanish colonial government.

Guaman Poma also adorned his manuscript with remarkably detailed drawings depicting Inca and Spanish colonial life. These drawings have been popularized in many Andean texts. In many ways his drawings and text express the cultural and religious syncretism still prevalent in the Andes—a world in which past and present meld together in a delicate and synchronic dance at each telling, and retelling, of a Native Andean story. As anthropologist Lévi-Strauss explains, "Each telling of a myth draws upon [the] rags and bones [of previous myths], and each piece has its own previous life history that it brings to the story."[56]

In recent years Guaman Poma's work has been called into question for lack of historical accuracy; nevertheless, it provides a wealth of information about Native Andean culture and belief systems, which has influenced my analysis, and resonates strongly with the worldview of many Native Andean peoples of today. Guaman Poma speaks to the ages of the world, ritual offerings, agricultural cycles, Andean dualism, *huacas*, communal values, loss of indigenous identity, and various other themes that permeate Andean mythology. Moreover, one could make the case that this chronicler paved the way for social protest against the dominant white and *mestizo* culture that, to this day, marginalizes the Native Andean. This theme also underlies many contemporary Andean stories.

This book is my humble effort to honor and preserve the Native Andean stories that are written, and rewritten, in the palimpsest of human memory. As previously stated, this work synthesizes and draws from various fields of knowledge, including history, psychology, literature, anthropology, languages, cosmology, and, of course, mythology. It is also one of the first endeavors to interpret the oral tradition of various Native Andean ethnic groups from across several Andean regions primarily from an interdisciplinary perspective, with due regard for the cultural and religious syncretism of these cultures and the pluralism of contemporary Andean society. In the forthcoming chapters, my aim is to identify those recurring elements and themes that imbue the everyday life of Native Andeans and reveal themselves through myth. Like precious archaeological artifacts unearthed from the ground, these elements uncover the richness and complexity of this millennial oral tradition.

Finally, these are stories of Native Andean peoples whose voices have been silenced for nearly five hundred years since the trauma of the European Conquest. It is my strongest desire that through these compelling stories, we shall hear their muted voices; we shall respect their traditions and beliefs; we shall acknowledge their cries and protests; and we shall share in their hopes and dreams.

2

Andean Animism

The Vivified Landscape

Anyone who has traveled to the Andes has paused to admire the grandiose mountains that tower over the landscape and pierce the hovering clouds. The mountains dressed in royal robes of purple and bluing violet clearly dominate the landscape and stand together as proud and uncontested rulers of the vast Andean world. It is no wonder, then, that the indigenous peoples of the Andes continue the ancient traditions of their forebears and venerate and make offerings to these lofty peaks.

Just as their pre-Columbian ancestors, the Quechuas, the Aymaras, and other Native Andean peoples believe that the landscape they inhabit is *alive*, and is imbued with consciousness, spirit, and life-giving energy. A vivifying essence not only animates the landscape, but also infuses all material things, such as handwoven textiles and the bones of the ancestors.[1]

Many Native Andean communities continue the practice of worshipping *huacas*, or animas of nature, associated with their surrounding environment, including certain rocks, mountains, springs, rivers, lakes, caves, and so forth. They also conceive, especially in rural areas, that weather and meteorological phenomena, such as rain, thunder, snow, lightning, and wind, are created by supernatural beings and forces that share their dynamic landscape.

By far one of the strongest remnants of pre-Columbian cosmology is the widespread veneration of *Pacha Mama*, the Andean Earth Mother, which survives in the highland regions of Peru, Ecuador, Bolivia, northern Chile, and northwest Argentina. *Pacha Mama* is worshipped at all major agricultural festivals and receives community and family offerings of all kinds, including coca leaves, *chicha* (maize beer), llama wool, incense, candies, llama fetuses, llama fat, animal blood, cigars, ritual foods, dances, and prayers, among other things. It is also customary that before an alcoholic beverage is consumed, a person flick or sprinkle a portion of his or her beverage on the ground—a ritual act called *ch'allakuy* (sometimes also known as *challa*)—as a thanksgiving offering to *Pacha Mama*.

Many propitiatory rituals are also dedicated to the mountains and mountain peaks. The Quechuas, for instance, believe that the *Apus* or *Wamanis*, spirits of the mountains and high mountain lakes, are the most powerful and influential deities of the region.[2] Their power is also presumably based on the relative height of their peaks—the higher the mountain, the more powerful its guardian spirit. Similarly, the Aymaras who live in the *altiplano*[3] have an intimate relationship with the mountains. They regard the mountains surrounding their villages, called *Achachilas* or *Mallkus*, as the ancestors or godparents of their people.[4] In Native Andean belief systems, mountain deities are responsible for the production and dispensation of life-giving water needed for irrigation and other community uses. They are also considered to be the guardians of people, animals, and crops inhabiting their territories.

Interestingly, in Native Andean mythology, mountain spirits have distinct personalities and display human characteristics. For instance, they may show anger and jealousy, have parties and socialize with other mountains, and even play musical instruments. They may also assume human, and sometimes animal, form. In some Andean communities the mountain spirits also "have an organizational hierarchy likened to provincial government structure," with more powerful spirits dominating others of lesser rank.[5] If angered, the mountain spirits may cause death, illness, and tragedy, which is why ritual offerings are necessary to prevent such misfortunes. The mountain spirits must also be treated with affection and respect, leading some communities to address the masculine mountain spirits as *Tayta* (also spelled *Taita* or *Tata*), meaning "father," and the feminine mountain spirits as *Mama*, meaning "mother" in the Quechua language.

The following is a legend from Ecuador based on the stories the Cañari people tell about one of their favorite mountains, named Cerro Buerán, situated in the proximity of the canton of Cañar, in the province of the same name.

The Legend of Taita Buerán

~~~~~~~

(Cañari)

The mountain named Buerán is located two kilometers from the canton of Cañar and is at the crossroads between two mountain ranges: the eastern and the western.

It is the clock of time and the home of the gods for the *campesinos* [country people] living in the communities of our canton.

This mountain is full of fantastic stories and legends that are told by many old people.

When they describe this mystical character—Taita Buerán—they describe him as a person short in stature, dressed with indigenous clothing from the Cañar, with a woolen hat and blond hair.

They say that by chance some people have come across him, which is a sign of good fortune. There are some who describe him as an expert *curandero* [healer or medicine man], and as a Juan Tenorio[6] since he likes single women.

Many people believe that "el Buerán" is an enchanted mountain; that in its interior there is an orchard with all kinds of fruits, from the highlands as well as from the coast.

They say that Taita Buerán is divorced from the mountain that is in front of him, whose name is Mama Zhinzhona, and that it's been some time since their divorce. Taita Buerán lives with his sons, and Mama Zhinzhona with her daughters. They're in the habit of living in constant discord, because Mama Zhinzhona keeps a close eye on Taita Buerán with the [female] mountain Mama Charón Ventanas.

They say that on desolate nights they insult one another. And that is why there is a belief that when it's cloudy over Taita Buerán, that's because he is angry and the day [weather] will turn out badly.

Many people from our region tell this story.[7]

~~~~

It is clear from these descriptions of Taita Buerán and Mama Zhinzhona that the Cañari people have assigned human characteristics and personalities to their mountains. Taita Buerán dresses as an indigenous person from Cañar and wears a woolen hat. He is short in stature and has blond hair. Some regard him as an expert healer or medicine man. He is a male who was once wed to, and is now divorced from, a female mountain named Mama Zhinzhona. Just as the notorious character in José Zorilla's play, "Don Juan Tenorio," he is partial to single women, which is a source of constant friction between him and Mama Zhinzhona who, despite their divorce, is jealous of his interactions with other female mountains, especially Mama Charón Ventanas.

Consistent with the animistic traditions of the Andean peoples, these mountains also experience human emotions: anger, love, lust, jealousy, and so forth. They are not perfect beings; they have virtues and shortcomings, just like us. For example, Taita Buerán's emotions seemingly affect the weather. When he is angry, clouds hover over the mountain, and this portends bad weather. He also possesses supernatural qualities. His interior is believed to house an enchanted orchard that grows a multiplicity of fruits from different regions and climates. These human and superhuman qualities are also characteristic of Andean *huacas*—"animas" or spirits associated with individual aspects of nature.

In order to understand Native Andean animism, it is important to suspend our enduring and unwavering adherence to certain Western European philosophical suppositions. For instance, our Western tradition operates within the framework of Cartesian dualism, which dictates a separation between mind and body (the mental and physical) and between subject and object. As such, within this paradigm the Native Andeans would view the personified landscape described in their mythology and cosmology as separate and distinct from themselves.

However, a number of anthropological studies have observed that some Native Andean communities view themselves as inseparable—and possibly, indistinguishable—from their immediate environment. According to anthropologist Alan Kolata, who lived among the Aymara people of the altiplano, the Aymaras "project themselves, their sense of identity, on the physical reality around them ... [and this is] an essential step toward understanding and appreciating the [Aymaras'] and their ancestors' special vision of the world."[8] Contrary to our perceived separation of subject and object, these Native Andeans view their mountainous landscape as an integral part of themselves, and vice versa. Kolata likens the Aymaras' experience with their surrounding mountains as direct and immediate, as if they were living relatives. He vividly describes how they

beseech and cajole the *achachilas* [mountain deities] to bring the rains and to protect their growing crops from frost and hail. And, like any family, the Aymara argue among themselves and with the *achachilas*. They hurl insults at, curse, and threaten the *achachilas* if they do not respond to their pleas for help.... To the Aymara, the geography of the world is a projection of the family, and time is a dialogue with the dead.[9]

Similarly, the neighbors of the Aymaras, commonly called the Urus,[10] who live on human-made floating islands atop Lake Titicaca, refer to themselves as *Kot'suñs* ("People of the Lake"); and the land-dwelling Chipaya describe them as *Jas-shoni*, "water people," inhabiting an aqueous environment, conceptually and metaphorically different from the "dry people" who live and farm on the land.[11] In these cultures, therefore, we also see another example of the concurrence between the geographical environment and the cosmological and perceptual mapping of an Andean people.

Additionally, in the Native Andean community of Kaata, a mountain in midwestern Bolivia to the northeast of Lake Titicaca, anthropologist Joseph Bastien observed that the villagers who lived on the mountain personified the mountain as a human body, with all locations on the body being "organically united."[12] According to Bastien, locations on the mountain-body are named after different parts of the human anatomy. For instance, "*Apacheta*...is the head, *Kaata* is the bowels and the heart, and *Niñokorin* is the legs of the body."[13] Throughout the year, different parts of the mountain-body are "fed" ritualistic offerings from the three major levels of the mountain, each of which also has ecological and cosmological significance.[14] These offerings are made at specific shrines and are intended to circulate blood and fat to the mountain-body, which are considered the "life principle" and the "energy principle" of the community.[15]

Of special interest here is that Kaatans believe that what happens to or on the mountain is also reflected in the bodies of the individuals who actually reside on the mountain. In one instance, for example, one of the *curanderos* or medicine men determined that a woman's "blood was weak because a landslide [on the mountain] had taken it and replaced it with water."[16] Thus, the physical loss of land on the mountain caused by the landslide, which had replaced land with water, was manifested metaphorically in the woman's bloodstream, where blood was also determined to be "taken away" or diluted by water.

What these various studies suggest is that for many Native Andean communities, the people and the landscape comprise a "gestalt"—a totality, unity, and completeness[17]—that cannot be readily apprehended in our Western dualistic framework. Consequently, it is imperative to seek to understand Andean myths in the context of a much broader and integrated definition of animism that considers the immediate, interactive, and intimate relationship between the Native Andeans and their surroundings, as well as the integration, or projection, of the person, the family, the community, and the landscape onto a unified, indivisible, and dynamic vision of the cosmos.

The following Kolla,[18] or ancient Aymara, origin myth illustrates the Native Andeans' vivified view of nature and the dynamic interplay between human beings and natural elements. Moreover, it also projects human qualities onto natural forces, including human virtues and shortcomings.

Kolla Legend of the Creation of the World
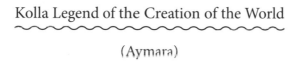

(Aymara)

Persistent sadness engulfed the world. All was night, darkness, silence. The earth was desolate without any form of life. Neither man nor animals existed.

Wiracocha, the god of the gods, lamented that darkness enveloped the world; so he created two suns to light up the world from on high.

The two sons were named Inti and Pajsi. They say that the two were equally beautiful, strong, and skillful, except that Pajsi shined more brightly than his brother.

Wiracocha ordered them to climb up to the sky from where they would illuminate the earth. As obedient children, the two set out to climb to *Alaj Pacha* [the World Above].

But Inti was being eaten up with envy because of Pajsi's brilliance. He wasn't happy that Pajsi shined more brightly and better, or that the heat he radiated was more easily exhausted than Pajsi's. Recklessly, he picked up a handful of ashes and threw it at Pajsi's face, darkening it forever.

Since then, Pajsi shines more faintly and only likes to go out at night. The sun, Inti, on the other hand, shines his haughty light and radiates heat that burns, destroys, and even kills when he's angry.

Wiracocha ignored the incident. He was very busy creating the world. He worked the granite rock from Komanche and created humankind. Every night, he carefully sculpted hundreds of people in all kinds of positions—sitting, standing, lying down—and engaged in different occupations—cooking, weaving, singing, and dancing. When he thought he had a sufficient number of people to populate the earth, he distributed them in the highlands and the lowlands, and later brought them to life with his divine breath.

This is how different peoples came to populate the earth, and build houses and found cities.

At the beginning, these peoples observed the teachings that had been dictated to them by Wiracocha. They were good. They worked with enthusiasm. The men worked the land, and the women cooked and wove beautiful mantles. During their spare time, they played *zampoñas* [Andean wind instruments] and danced their [native] dances.

Until one day, the peoples whom Wiracocha had created with so much love turned bad, envious, and lazy under the influence of Supay, Mekhala, and Anchanchu, evil deities who had managed to capture the human heart. The stronger peoples began to dominate the weaker ones and turn them into slaves. They stole the food from the weaker ones and forced them to perform the most arduous work, so that they could live a life of drinking and dancing. The weaker peoples cried out in desperation because the arms of the powerful ones never ceased flogging them and leaving welts on their backs.

The clamor of the weak turned into a single scream, which reached the cracks and crevices of the rocks and ascended into the mountains. And, finally, it reached the ears of Wiracocha.

Wiracocha, who was a just and magnanimous god, looked sadly upon his people and deep was his despair. The woes of the oppressed wounded his caring heart.

Suddenly, in a fit of divine rage, he summoned Wayra Tata, the god of the wind. He ordered Wayra Tata to "Run, run, run with all your strength through the earth, and knock down every object standing in your way. Turn the rivers rough and stormy, cause the mountains to crumble, agitate the lake, and return to my side only when the ancient silence flaps over the earth, as a tired bird looking for its nest."

Wayra Tata carried out the order of the god Wiracocha. He ran with his outstretched tail dragging along everything that lay in his path. The strongest trees buckled over, like *quinua* stems [a high-altitude grain] snapping at the roots. The houses built of stone were destroyed as easily as if they were made out of clay. The rivers burst their banks and giant boulders rolled down the hills.

Wayra Tata's strength was uncontrollable! And it was aroused even more with each destruction. He roared, howled, shook, and delighted in devastating enthusiasm.

The terrified people ran into caves in search of salvation, but all of the caves were already filled with pumas, wild animals, and other beasts that were also looking for refuge.

Exhausted from all the running and destroying, Wayra Tata returned and appeared before Wiracocha. Resting at the god's side, Wayra Tata begged: "I have carried out your order as far as my strength would allow. But now I am tired of these comings and goings without any end. Let me rest for a moment, so that I may have enough strength to begin running again; or else, relieve me of this burden."

"Rest!" shouted the god angrily. Then he summoned Kjunu, the venerable god of snow, so that he could continue inflicting punishment on the people who had not known how to value his teachings.

Wiracocha spoke: "Let the snow from your *espallas* [Andean bags] cover those wicked peoples who enslave their own brothers. Freeze their blood and cover them with snow."

Then he disappeared into infinity.

Kjunu carried out the command, just as his father Wiracocha had requested. Stealthily, he emptied snow from his bags, completely covering the earth and killing off any remaining survivors with his white mantle of death.

That is how Wiracocha ended his creation, and how the Andes [mountains] were born.[19]

~~

Many Andean myths describe multiple creations, and this Aymara myth is no exception. In this powerful story of creation and destruction (a cycle known in Native Andean cosmology as *pachacuti*), the Andean Creator god, *Wiracocha* (also spelled *Viracocha*, meaning "Sea Foam" or "Sea Fat"), destroys the existing world through various natural catastrophes, precipitated by wind and snow. Nevertheless, the death of the existing creation paves the way for a new birth and a new creation. As the world ends, the Andes Mountains are born, which in time become the birthplace of a subsequent creation. We speculate that this is perhaps one reason why the Aymaras consider the *Achachilas* (deified mountains) the ancestors or godparents of their people. In another age of the world, in primordial times, their ancestors emerged from the earth out of the death and sacrifice of the previous creation.

In this myth Wiracocha also exhibits a wide range of human qualities and emotions. At first he laments that darkness has enveloped the world and takes pity upon the lifeless earth. In what might be described as an act of compassion, he creates two suns to illuminate the world, *Inti* (meaning "Sun") and *Pajsi* (also spelled *Phaxsi*, meaning "Moon"). Later, he shows industry and artistry by creating humankind out of granite rock and sculpting it into various forms, depicting human movements and occupations. Finally, he populates the world with his human creations, bringing "them to life with his divine breath."

Wiracocha also appears to have dictated some laws or principles, guiding the manner in which his people should live. This revelation in the myth could be interpreted as the origin of culture or civilization. This is suggested in the story when the narrator observes that "At the beginning, these men observed the teachings that had been dictated by Wiracocha." These teachings required human beings to be kind, to be "good," and to work "with enthusiasm." They also allocated labor between men and women: men "worked the land," while "women cooked and wove beautiful mantles." Wiracocha also did not rule out entertainment. In their "spare time" his people enjoyed music and dance.

In his role as creator, Wiracocha may be viewed as the benevolent god, ending desolation in the world by introducing heat and light and giving his peoples rules by which to live and prosper. In this respect he reminds us of a caring and loving father, who wants the best for the world and for his children. Further in the story he is also deeply moved by the cries of his people. When the "scream" of the oppressed and the weak reaches "the ears of Wiracocha," his caring heart is depressed and wounded. He looks "sadly upon his people" and "deep [is] his despair." He then sets out to punish those who enslaved others and those "who had not known how to value his teachings." Therefore, one aspect of this myth demonstrates that the Aymaras may be projecting onto Wiracocha many of their own virtues and community values: affection, benevolence, generosity, concern, creativity, artistry, industry, and imagination, among others.

But, as is characteristic of many Andean deities, Wiracocha is not perfect. He also displays negative characteristics and, in some cases, indifference toward his creation. During the conflict between Inti and Pajsi, in which Inti intentionally hurts Pajsi by throwing ashes at his face and "darkening it forever," Wiracocha ignores the incident. "He was [too] busy creating the world" and could not bother to intervene. As a result, Pajsi is victimized and permanently damaged by his brother. The storyteller also explains that from that moment on, Pajsi "shine[d] more faintly" than Inti and only went out at night. Hence, the creation of the moon in this myth is the by-product of sibling rivalry and the result of a cruel and reckless act that might have been prevented by Wiracocha, had he decided to intervene.

At times, Wiracocha also appears to be a demanding, angry, and unreasonable god. When *Wayra Tata* ("Father Wind") requests a short break from his whirlwind of destruction to regain his strength, Wiracocha shouts at him angrily. He also humiliates Wayra Tata by summoning the god of snow, *Kjunu* (also spelled *Khunu*, meaning "Snow"), to continue the task of inflicting punishment on humankind. He does not have the patience to wait until Wayra Tata recovers his strength. He also fails to acknowledge or give credit to Wayra Tata for the extraordinary work he has already performed.

In many respects, Wiracocha is not only a creator but also a destroyer. When his anger is unleashed, he wreaks havoc on humankind. He summons Wayra Tata "in a fit of divine rage" after hearing the cries of the oppressed peoples. He instructs the god of wind to initiate a series of cataclysmic events in the rivers, mountains, and lakes that will inevitably destroy the world and all of humankind. His instructions to Kjunu are equally merciless: "Let the snow from your [bags] cover those wicked peoples.... Freeze their blood and cover them with snow."

It is curious that Wiracocha does not spare anyone from the impending destruction. He does not differentiate between good and evil peoples, or between the oppressors and the oppressed, or between animals and humans. His punishments are not selective—they apply equally to all. Although at first the storyteller leads one to believe that only the "wicked peoples who enslave their own brothers" will be subjected to the intense snow, at the end of the story one learns that Kjunu's white mantle of death completely "covers the earth and [kills off] any remaining survivors," leading to the end of this creation. Thus, Wiracocha's cruel punishment is meted out to all, without regard to virtue or wrongdoing.

In this respect, this mythical character typifies the duality that is often present in Native Andean gods (*huacas*) and personifications of nature. Wiracocha is both benevolent and malevolent, just and unjust, humane and inhumane, creative and destructive. This is also consistent with the notion that the Aymaras experience certain aspects of nature and geography as extensions of their own human family, as well as projections of their own qualities and values, including strengths and weaknesses.

Similarly, the other characters in the story—Inti, Pajsi, Wayra Tata, and Kjunu—are also endowed with human and superhuman qualities. Wayra Tata, the wind, is a great "runner." With his "outstretched tail" he can knock down trees, destroy houses, burst riverbanks, and push boulders. He roars, howls, shakes, and destroys. At times, his strength is "uncontrollable" and has a devastating effect on humankind. Kjunu, the snow, is also a menace to humankind. When he empties too much snow from his bags, he can cover the earth with his "white mantle of death."

Inti, the Sun god, is usually portrayed in Native Andean stories as a benevolent and beneficent being; however, in this myth he is characterized as an envious and reckless god who injures and destroys. He not only blemishes and diminishes the light of his brother, but he also shines "his haughty light and radiates heat that burns, destroys, and even kills when he's angry."

This negative depiction of the forces of nature is understandable, given the often unpredictable and harsh environmental conditions in which the Aymaras live and work every day. Much of the Aymara land is dry and uninhabitable. When the rains do come they are often severe, causing mudslides, flooding, and other forms of devastation. Many Aymaras live in areas over two miles high in elevation where they are subjected to minimal oxygen, extreme sun, extreme cold, extreme wind, recurring lighting, frost, snow, and other variable and capricious "moods" of nature. In the altiplano, diurnal temperatures also fluctuate dramatically, and differences between nighttime lows and daytime highs may be as great as 30°C (86°F) or more.[20] The Aymara land is one of ecological extremes and encompasses some of the most inhospitable places on earth. For this reason it is not surprising that in this creation myth the people are nameless, faceless, and expendable, inhabiting an unforgiving environment and subject to the whims and caprices of the nature gods.

MULTIPLE WORLDS AND THE INCA COSMOS

In the creation myth of the Aymaras we have just examined, Inti and Pajsi climb to the World Above, or *Alaj Pacha* (also spelled *Araj Pacha* or *Alax Pacha*), from which they illuminate the earth. One indigenous belief infused into Andean mythology is the existence of multiple worlds inhabited by different kinds of beings. In Aymara cosmology the sun and the moon are "sky beings" that dwell in *Alaj Pacha*. Although in most Andean myths these worlds are generally not mentioned by name, they nevertheless constitute the cosmological underpinning in which mythical events take place.

To illustrate, the Aymaras believe in three worlds: *Alaj Pacha* (The World Above), *Aca Pacha* (also spelled *Aka Pacha*, or "This World"), and *Manqha Pacha* (the "World Below" or the "Interior World").[21] For the Aymaras, *Alaj Pacha*, or the World Above, is the space of luminosity occupied by the foreign Inca and Christian deities, including the Sun god *Inti* (more or less identified with the Inca Creator god, *Wiracocha*), the Inca Moon goddess *Killa*, the Thunder and Lightning god *Illapa*, the Stars, God the Father, Jesus Christ, the Virgin Mary, the Apostles, the Saints, and the Patron Saints of the community.[22]

By contrast, *Manqha Pacha*, or the World Below, is often associated with darkness, interior spaces like caves and mines ("the bowels" or "entrails" of the earth), and the black arts (*brujería*).[23] In modern times it has also come to be associated with the Christian inferno, the devil, condemned souls, and other malevolent spirits and demons.[24] But at one time, in the autochthonous pre-Columbian religion, it may have simply been the subterranean space occupied by minerals and their guardian spirits.[25] In some Aymara communities, the World Below is also associated with the cult of the ancestors and ancestral deities, which were demonized and vilified after the Spanish Conquest in an effort to convert the Native Andeans to Christianity.[26]

Finally, the *Aca Pacha*, or This World, encompasses the surface of the earth and all its inhabitants, including flora, fauna, and humanity. According to Kolata, it is "the space in-between, the here and now, the place and time where creatures, including humans, exist in life."[27] *Aca Pacha* is a neutral space that is neither good nor bad, neither beneficent nor maleficent. It "forms a complete and finished universe, without heaven or hell."[28]

The association of the World Above and the World Below with maleficent or beneficent forces, or with God and the devil, may be a fairly recent development in Native Andean cosmology. In the case of the Aymaras, some speculate that the notions of superior and inferior, and good and evil, with respect to religion, were imposed on their culture by a succession of invaders—first the Incas, and then the Spaniards—in order to establish cultural and religious supremacy.[29] If that is the case, then the contemporary cosmology of the Aymaras has subsumed and internalized this hierarchy, which expresses an ideology of domination that is also mirrored by the modern political and social structures that exercise control over the Aymaras.[30]

In a similar manner, the tripartition of the cosmos is also found among the Quechuas, whose three worlds—*Hanan Pacha* (also spelled *Janaq Pacha*, meaning "Upper World"),[31] *Kay Pacha* ("This World"), and *Ukhu Pacha* (also spelled *Uk'u Pacha*, meaning "Lower World," "Inner World," or "Interior World")[32]—are roughly analogous to the three Aymara worlds. In the autochthonous (pre-Columbian) cosmology of the Quechuas, it is likely that the sky beings that populated *Hanan Pacha* resembled the deities worshipped by the Incas,[33] the forebears of the contemporary

Quechuas. However, after the Spanish Conquest the pantheon of *Hanan Pacha* expanded to include the three aspects of the Christian God, in addition to the Virgin Mary, the Apostles, and the Catholic Saints.

In an interesting drawing experiment involving some fifty Quechua children, anthropologist Billie Jean Isbell attempted to capture their conception of *Hanan Pacha* (Upper World) and other cosmological entities.[34] Then she sought to compare those results to the Inca model of the cosmos depicted in a colonial manuscript entitled *Relación de antigüedades deste reyno del Pirú* ("Recounting of Antiquities from this Kingdom of Peru"), recorded in 1613 by the Native Andean chronicler Joan de Santacruz Pachacuti Yamqui Salcamaygua. The chronicler maintained that such a model was etched on a gold plate housed in the *Coricancha* ("Golden Enclosure"), the Incas' most important temple, in the city of Cuzco.[35]

The Inca diagram reproduced by Santacruz Pachacuti was divided into two halves, with the right side representing the male elements of the cosmos and the left side the female elements (Fig. 2.1). The masculine elements included (1) the sun; (2) the morning star (Venus) as "grandfather"; (3) the stars of summer (associated with the dry season, May–October); (4) thunder or lightning; (5) Lord Earth (*Camac Pacha*) with an arching rainbow; (6) a human male figure, probably representing the Inca ruler; and (7) the "eyes of abundance" (*ymaymana ñauraycunañawin*).

Lord Earth represented the world in its totality and was depicted as a circle with an arching rainbow above it. Like thunder and lightning, the rainbow conjoins the earth and the sky, or This World and the Upper World, so it may have functioned as a mediating agent in Inca cosmology. Santacruz Pachacuti labeled the *inside* of the circle (the "inner earth") as *Pacha Mama*, the venerated Andean Earth Mother. *Pacha Mama* was pictured with three Andean mountains inside, from which descended the *Pillcumayu*,[36] a river associated with the legendary origin of the Incas. The river exited the inner earth, or circle, in a downward direction like "flowing" or "running" water, suggesting the movement of symbolic semen and "water that inseminates and germinates."[37] Moreover, the "eyes of abundance have been compared to little stones called *inqaychus* [also known as *inqa, illa,* or *conopa*] that modern communities believe contain generative powers."[38] In Inca religion, the Sun god (*Inti*), the Rainbow (*Cuichu* or *Cuychi*), and the Thunder–Lightning (*Illapa*) were strongly associated with the Inca ruler;[39] so, in conjunction with the image of the Inca on the center-right side of the diagram, it is fair to say that the right side of the Inca plate strongly connoted maleness and the masculine procreative principle.

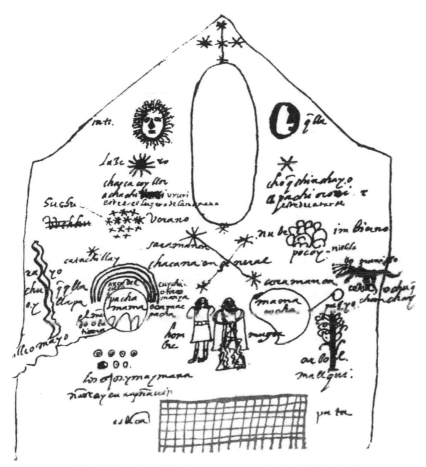

FIGURE 2.1. Colonial drawing of the Inca cosmos, as depicted by the indigenous chronicler Joan de Santacruz Pachacuti Yamqui Salcamaygua (1613).

Complementing the masculine right side, the feminine left side of the plate incorporated (1) the moon; (2) the evening star (Venus) as "grandmother"; (3) the clouds of winter (associated with the rainy season, November–April); (4) a mythological cat called *choquechinchay*, also described as a *ccoa* or *qoa* cat, which is believed to mediate between the Lower World and the Upper World;[40] (5) Mother Sea or Mother Lake (*Mama Cocha*) feeding, or being fed by, an upward spring; (6) a human female figure, probably representing the Inca queen or *Coya*; and (7) a young tree or sapling called a *mallqui*, a Quechua word synonymous with "ancestor."[41]

"Still" or "standing" water, such as found in lakes and springs, is often associated with femininity and nurturance in Andean cosmology;

moreover, in Inca times *Mama Cocha* was a female deity considered to be "the mother of lakes and water."[42] Here, the image of the sapling evokes notions of fertility and new life, as does the symbolic reference to Mother Sea (Lake) in relation to the feminine activities of feeding and nurturing (still or standing water). The Inca queen, or *Coya*, directed the cult of the Moon in the Inca religion, and only women priestesses could care for the idol of the Moon in the Inca Temple of the Sun in Cuzco.[43] As sister-wife of the Sun, the Moon was an important deity and "held sway over [all] divine and mortal beings of like sex."[44] Therefore, in parallel with the right side, the left side of the Inca plate conjures notions of femininity in relation to fertility and regeneration.

Additionally, at the top center of the Inca diagram there was a gold elliptical plaque representing the Inca Creator god, *Viracocha*, with five connected stars above it, possibly portraying Orion. The placement of Viracocha at the midpoint between the masculine and feminine elements led anthropologist Tom Zuidema to conclude that Viracocha may have been viewed as an androgynous "supreme creator god, father-mother of the sun, moon, man, woman, and all creation."[45] Santacruz Pachacuti's handwritten notes, placed alongside his elliptical drawing of this Inca deity, also confirm this supposition. "Above [its] image [the chronicler] inscribed the words 'whether it be male, whether it be female,'"[46] clearly affirming the sexual duality embodied by Viracocha.

Opposite Viracocha, at the bottom center of the diagram, below the human couple, there was also a graphic representation of storehouse terraces (*collcapata*), or an Inca storehouse (*collca*), that the Incas used to house agricultural products and other items that were collected as taxes and later redistributed to the people by the state. It is probably no accident that Santacruz Pachacuti placed the *collcapata* in direct and complementary opposition to the elliptical image of Viracocha. According to Isbell, "The creator god [Viracocha] is the origin and generator of all and the *collcas* represent abundance in the real world, the end product of the procreative process. Together they form a closed system—the beginning and the end of the reproductive cycle."[47]

In conformity with Quechua notions about the existence of three worlds, we would expect the children in Isbell's study to include in their drawings some of the same or similar cosmological elements that Santacruz Pachacuti portrayed in his drawing of the Inca plate representing the Andean cosmos. And that indeed was the case. For example, one young girl's vision of *Hanan Pacha*, the Upper World, included the sun and moon and two stars below them, which she labeled as *abuelo* and *abuela*, meaning "grandfather" and "grandmother" in Spanish.[48] In the Inca diagram all four of the same elements appeared and were similarly labeled.[49] The girl also drew a picture of a woman, which she identified as her mother,[50] and added a picture of *Kay Pacha* ("This World"), which was divided in half and painted black on one side and white on the other. Isbell speculated that the girl's division of This World into halves might represent sexual symbolism and the same male/female duality reflected in the Inca diagram.[51]

Of special interest to us dealing in mythical symbols is that some of the children also produced drawings of a synthetic nature, combining, metaphorically, more than one image to represent a single concept. For example, one young boy combined the image of "a cross and a condor as manifestations of the *Wamanis* [Quechua mountain spirits], and a cat and a tree (or *mallqui*) as [his] non-Christian ancestors," commonly known in the Andes as *gentiles*.[52] The cross is evocative of Christianity, but a square-shaped cross, which is often made of twigs and accompanies Andean offerings, is a male fertility symbol associated with the *Apus or Wamanis*. In Native Andean cosmology and ritual, the condor also acts as a mediator between This World and the Upper World. With respect to the boy's depiction of a cat and a tree, Isbell observed that

> *Mallqui* signifies both sapling, or branch, and ancestor [in Quechua]. The boy is expressing the duality of the forces of the ancestors, the non-Christian *gentiles* of the Underworld, and the procreative energy of the Wamanis that results in progeny (the sapling).... The boy's cat (*choquechinchay*) in its role as the mediator of the Underworld, the residing place of the ancestors, and his tree are clearly related to the dual concepts of ancestors and progeny shown by the noble [seventeenth-century] chronicler.[53]

Thus, the Andean concept of multiple worlds expresses a complex interaction among beings inhabiting these worlds, represented, in the children's drawings, by symbolic and synthetic elements. The following story, entitled "The Young Man Who Flew Up to the Sky," is a well-known Quechua folktale about a young man who journeys to the sky world in search of his star-wife on the wings of a mighty condor. The condor figures prominently in Andean mythology and is often viewed as an intermediary between This World and the Upper World.[54]

The Young Man Who Flew Up to the Sky

(Quechua)

Once upon a time there was a married couple who had only one son. The father sowed the most beautiful potatoes on a parcel of land that was located far from the house in which they lived. The potatoes that he planted in that land grew lush and luxuriant. Only he, the father, owned this sublime kind of seed.

Every night, however, thieves would come, pull out the tufts from the sown field, and rob its beautiful fruits. So the father and mother called their young son and told him: "It shouldn't happen that with a son as young and as strong as you, thieves should come and steal all of our potatoes. Go and keep watch over our field. At night, sleep next to the field and intercept the thieves."

The young man did as he was told and set off to look after the sown field.

Three nights went by. On the first night, the young man stayed awake all night watching over the potatoes. However, at daybreak he was overcome by sleep and fell asleep. At that very instant, the thieves entered the field and picked the potatoes. In view of his failure, the young man was forced to go home to his parents' house and tell them about what had occurred. Upon hearing his account his parents answered, "We'll forgive you this time. Go back to the field and keep better watch."

The young man returned to the field. He intended to watch over the sown field, with his eyes wide open, until dawn. But at midnight he blinked for an instant. In that instant, the thieves came into the field. The young man stayed awake and guarded the field until the morning. He didn't see any thieves. But at dawn he again had to go to his parents' house and tell them about the new robbery. He said to them, "Even though I remained watchful all night, the thieves deceived me in a single instant at midnight in which I closed my eyes."

Upon hearing this account the parents replied, "Is that so? Who's going to believe that they robbed you while you were looking? You must have gone out to look for women! You must have gone out to have fun!" As they said this, they beat him and insulted him for a long time.

The next day they sent the young man, all beaten up, back to the field again. "Now you'll understand how we want you to keep watch," they said.

The young man returned to his task. From the moment he arrived at the edge of the sown field he stood motionless and attentive, watching the field. That night, the moon was brilliant. He continued contemplating the perimeter of the potato field until daybreak. As he watched, his eyes trembled, and he dozed off for a few instants. In the brief moments of sleep that he snatched, while the young man blinked, a multitude of beautiful young women, princesses and fair-skinned girls, populated the field. Their faces were like flowers; their hair shone like gold; they were dressed in garments of silver. Hurriedly, all together, they began to steal the potatoes. They were stars that came down from the highest sky, assuming the appearance of princesses.

Just then the young man woke up and surveyed the cultivated field. Gazing at the beautiful maidens he exclaimed, "Oh! How I would like to snatch one of these beautiful girls for myself! And how could such beautiful and radiant maidens devote themselves to such a lowly task?"

As he said this, his heart almost exploded with love. And he thought to himself, "Couldn't I, perhaps, keep at least a pair of these beauties for myself?"

And he very quickly lunged on top of the beautiful thieves. Only at the last minute, and at great pains, did he manage to capture one of the beautiful maidens. The rest of them ascended to the sky, as lights that fade and die in the distance.

Angrily, the young man said to the star that he was able to capture, "So you were the thieves that robbed from the sown fields of my father!" Having said this, he took her to his hut and said nothing else about the theft. But later he added, "Stay with me; become my wife!"

The young woman did not accept his proposal. She was full of fear and begged the young man to release her. She said, "Release me, release me! Take pity on me! My sisters will tell my parents. I will return all the potatoes that we robbed. Don't force me to live on the earth!"

The young man didn't listen to the pleas of the beautiful girl. He held her firmly in his hands. But he decided not to return to his parents' house. He remained with the star-girl in the hut that was next to the sown field.

Meanwhile, the parents speculated, "I bet they've robbed the potatoes again from that good-for-nothing boy. There can be no other reason why he hasn't shown up here." And, since he took so long, the mother decided to take him some food. She went to the field to check on him.

From the hut the young man and the star-girl watched the road. As soon as they saw the mother, the star-girl said to the young man, "There is no way that you can introduce me to either your father or your mother."

So the young man ran to meet up with his mother, and from a distance he shouted, "No, Mom, don't come any closer! Wait for me out back! Back!" He received the food in a place behind the hut and took the food in to the star-princess.

The mother returned home soon after she delivered the food. When she arrived at the house she told her husband, "So, our son has imprisoned one of the potato thieves that came down from the sky. He takes care of her in the hut. And he says he plans to marry her. He doesn't let anyone come near the hut."

Meanwhile, the young man pretended to trick the maiden. He would say to her, "Now that it's nighttime, let's go to my parents' house." But the princess insisted, "There is no way that your parents should see me, nor can I meet with them."

Nevertheless, the young man deceived her. He said to her, "I have another house." So during the night he took her on the road.

In this way, against her wishes, he had her enter the home of his elders and showed her to his parents. The parents received her and were dazzled by this creature whose luminosity and beauty were beyond description. They took care of her and raised her, showering her with love. But they did not let her out. Nobody outside ever got to know her or to see her.

The star-princess lived with the young man's parents for a long time. She became pregnant and gave birth, but the baby mysteriously died; nobody knew why.

The shiny clothing that belonged to the star-girl was kept locked. They dressed her in ordinary clothing, and that's how they raised her.

One day the young man went to work far away from the house, and while he was away, the star-girl went out, pretending that she would stay nearby. And she returned to the sky.

The young man returned home and asked for his wife. But he couldn't find her. Since he could see that she had disappeared, he began to cry.[55]

They say that he roamed about the mountains, crying like crazy, sleepwalking, out of control, walking everywhere. Finally, he arrived at a solitary mountaintop and found a divine Condor.

The Condor said to him, "Young man, why are you crying in this way?"

And the young man told him his life's story. "So it is, sir. The most beautiful woman in the world was mine. Now I don't know which way she went. I am lost without her. I fear that she escaped to the skies from where she came."

When he said this the Condor responded, "Don't cry, young man. It is true; she has returned to the upper sky. But if your misery is as great as you describe, if you wish I will carry you up to that world. All I ask is that you bring me two llamas to eat—one I will consume right here; the other, along the way."

"Very well, sir," replied the young man, "I will bring you the two llamas that you request. I ask that you wait for me at this same spot."

Immediately, the young man headed home in search of the llamas. Shortly after he arrived, he said to his parents, "Dear Father and Mother, I am going to look for my wife. I have found someone who can take me to the place where she is. All he asks is two llamas in return for doing me this great favor. I will take the llamas to him right now."

And he carried off the two llamas for the Condor. The Condor devoured one of them immediately, up to the bone, tearing out the meat with his own beak. He had the young man slit the other one's throat so that he could eat its meat along the way. Then he had the young man carry the decapitated animal on his back. Afterward, the Condor ordered the young man to climb on a rock and mount him. Then he issued this warning: "You have to close your eyes and shut your eyelids very tightly. You cannot open your eyes for any reason. And every time that I say 'Meat!' you must put a piece of llama meat in my beak."

Then the Condor took flight.

The young man obeyed and did not open his eyes at any time. He had his eyelids shut tightly and firmly. "Meat!" requested the *Mallku* [Condor], and the young man cut a piece of llama meat and inserted it in the Condor's beak. [And so the young man continued to feed the Condor meat every single time he requested it.]

But in the swiftest part of the journey, the meat ran out. Before taking flight, the Condor had warned the young man, "If when I say 'Meat!' you don't put any meat in my beak, I will let you drop, wherever we might be."

Fearing this might happen, the young man began to cut pieces of his own calf [muscle] to feed the Condor. Every time that the Condor asked for meat, he served the Condor small portions of his own flesh. So, at the cost of his own blood, he managed to have the Condor take him up to the sky. It is said that it took them one year to ascend to such a great height.

When they arrived, the Condor rested a bit. Then, again, he carried the young man and flew to the edge of a distant sea. There he said, "Now, dear young man, bathe in this sea." The young man bathed immediately. And the Condor also bathed.

Both had arrived at the sky dirty, with full-grown beards, and old. But when they stepped out of the bath, they were beautifully rejuvenated. Then the Condor said to the young man, "At the edge of this sea there is a great shrine. A ceremony will take place there. Go there and wait at the door of that beautiful temple. The young women of the sky will attend that ceremony. There are a multitude of them, and all of them have the same face as your wife. When they are marching next to you as they enter the temple, do not speak to any of them. Yours will be the last one to enter and will give you a shove. When this happens, seize her and do not let her go for any reason."

The young man obeyed the Condor. He arrived at the door of the great enclosure and waited, standing. An infinite number of young women arrived, and all of them had an identical face. They entered and entered, one behind the other. All of them looked impassively at the man. He could not recognize which one was his wife among so many of them. And when the last ones finally entered, suddenly one of them gave him a push on the arm as she entered the large temple.

It was the resplendent temple of the Sun and the Moon. The Sun and the Moon were the father and mother of all of these stars and of all the luminous beings. There, in the temple, the celestial beings gathered. The luminous beings came there to worship the Sun every day. These young white stars sang melodiously for the Sun like countless princesses, luminous beings.

When the ceremony finished, the young women began to leave. The young man continued waiting at the door. The young women continued to look at him with the same indifference as before. And once again it was impossible to distinguish among all of them which one was his wife. Suddenly, just as the first time around, one of the princesses gave him a push on the arm and then tried to flee. But the young man was able to clasp her in his arms and didn't let her go.

She guided him to her house and said, "Why have you come? I was going to return to where you were anyway."

When they arrived at her home, the young man's body was cold due to hunger. Upon seeing him like this she told him, "Take this bit of quinua and cook it." She gave him a meager tablespoon of quinua. Meanwhile, the young man was observing everything and noticed from where she was taking the quinua. When he saw the few grains that he had in his hands, he said to himself, "Look at the pittance of quinua that she has given me! How can this meager amount satisfy the hunger I have endured for one year?"

The young woman told him, "I have to go for a moment over to my parents' house. You cannot show yourself to them. Until I return, make a soup with the quinua that I have given you."

Just as soon as she left, the young man stood up and headed for the storeroom where the quinua was kept. He brought a good portion of quinua and threw it in the pot. Suddenly, the soup that was boiling began to overflow and spew out in all directions over the brim of the pot. He consumed everything that he could and filled his stomach with quinua until it could hold no more; then he buried the remainder of the soup. Yet even from underneath the earth, the quinua continued to burst out. At this critical moment the princess returned and said, "This is not the way you're supposed to eat our quinua! Why did you add to the portion that I gave you?"

Then she helped the young man hide the overflowing quinua so that her parents wouldn't discover it. In the meantime, she warned, "My parents should not see you. You may stay here only if you hide."

And that's what happened. He lived in hiding, and the beautiful star brought him food at his place of refuge.

The young man lived with his wife in this sad condition for a year. And just as soon as the year was up, she forgot to bring him food. One day she left, saying, "The time has come for you to leave." And she never appeared in the house again. She abandoned him.

So, with a face full of tears, the young man headed once again toward the edge of the sea that was in the sky. When he arrived there, he saw the Condor rising at a distance. He ran to catch up with him. The Condor flew and alighted next to him. The young man observed that the divine *Mallku* had aged. At the same time, the Condor also noticed that the young man had grown old and withered. When they met, they both cried out at the same time, "How have you been?"

The young man again told the Condor his story and complained, "So you see, sir, in this sad way, my wife has abandoned me. She has left me forever."

The Condor lamented the young man's misfortune.

"How is it possible that things could have turned out this way? My poor friend!" he said. And he drew closer to his friend, caressing him, sweetly, with his wings.

As in their first encounter, the young man pleaded with him, "Sir, lend me your wings. Take me back to the earth, to the house of my parents."

And the Condor responded, "All right. I will take you. But first, let's bathe in this sea."

And they both bathed and were rejuvenated.

As they came out of the water, the Condor said, "Once again, you'll have to give me two llamas for all the work required in carrying you home."

"Sir, when I return to my home, I will hand over two llamas to you."

The Condor accepted. He threw the young man over his wings and embarked upon his flight. For a year they flew toward the earth. And upon their arrival, the young man kept his promise and handed over two llamas to the Condor.

The young man entered his parents' house and found that they had grown old, very old. They welcomed him full of tears and sadness. The Condor said to the elderly couple, "I have returned your son to you safe and sound. Now you should treat him with affection."

The young man said to his parents, "Dear Father, dear Mother, it is impossible for me now to love any other woman. It is impossible to find a woman like the one who was mine. So I have decided to live alone until I die."

And his elders replied, "Very well. As you wish, dear son. We will bring you up alone, if it is your desire not to take another wife."

And the young man lived in this way with great agony in his heart.

Here lies this heart that loved a woman so. I have roamed about, suffering all the pain. And now I will give myself over to my weeping.[56]

~~~

In this Quechua story of a love lost, one sees the underlying Andean theme of multiple worlds binding mythical events together. The star-woman belongs to *Hanan Pacha* (Upper World); the young man to *Kay Pacha* (This World). The Condor is the intermediary that travels in both worlds, providing safe passage to and from the Upper World in exchange for a *pago* (payment) of two llamas. The *pago* in the story is suggestive of the *pagos* or ritual offerings that the Native Andeans make to their *huacas* (holy objects, places, and animals) in the hope that the *huacas* will be gratified with these gifts and reciprocate by bestowing good fortune, abundant crops, and other blessings upon the community.

In keeping with the animistic tradition of the Andes, the Condor in this story is a personified and sentient being—he speaks and issues instructions and warnings, but he also displays human emotions, such as concern and pity. Similarly, the star-woman is both celestial and human, endowed with the beauty and luminosity of the sky beings and the physical form and emotions—even negative ones—of a human being. In some respects she is also an intermediary who transcends the duality of the Upper World and This World. However, it is clear in the story that she can only live (happily) in the sky world to which she originally belongs. Similarly, the young man is a being of This World and cannot survive in the Upper World without a great deal of sacrifice and pain. Theirs is an "improper" union of two worlds, which is symbolically represented by their baby—an infant "which mysteriously died; [yet] nobody knew why." The subject of prohibited unions between worlds will be addressed at length in a subsequent chapter.

This story is also reminiscent of the pre-Columbian religion of the Incas, who practiced Sun worship before the Spanish Conquest. They also worshipped the Moon, the Stars, the Morning and Evening Star (Venus), the Thunder–Lightning, the Rainbow, and other celestial phenomena. According to the colonial chronicler Garcilaso de la Vega, the stars were considered by the Incas to be "the ladies and attendants of the house and court [of the Sun and Moon]."[57] The Inca ruler himself was considered the "son of the Sun" (*intip churin*)[58] and, therefore, a divine being. Much like the stars and the luminous beings in this Quechua story, the Inca ruler also gathered with his relatives in the temple of the Sun in Cuzco to pay homage to his celestial father, the Sun.

In order to apprehend the Andean concept of multiple worlds and their mythical dimension, as in this folktale, it is beneficial to keep in mind that we are limited by language and our Western European orientation. The boundaries and limits that we perceive, or presume to exist, among these mythical worlds merely function as useful linguistic markers to help us describe these "spaces" and the "beings" that populate them. In our cultural tradition we observe a separation between the material world and the spiritual realm; we also distinguish among the past that we keep in memory, the present world of the here and now, and the future world to come. Classical Western cosmology and mythology separate space and time, and this separation is also reflected in the semantic and grammatical structure of our Indo-European languages.[59]

Yet in Native Andean cultures, these distinctions do not exist in the same way that they do in Western cultures. Generally speaking, there is no time-space distinction and no linear chronology in Native Andean mythology. But to describe Andean time as "cyclical" is also an oversimplification. For the Aymaras, Quechuas, and many other Native Andean cultures, multiple notions converge in the Andean concept of *pacha*, which signifies time, space, and world at the same time. Anthropologist Sarah Lund Skar describes the Andean concept of time-space, or *pacha*, in the following manner:

> The most lengthy discussion of the term *pacha* is found in Cesar Guardia Mayorga's (1971) short, but detailed, dictionary of the Cuzco

[Quechua] dialect. Guardia specifically states that *pacha* refers to 'the animated world as a totality, a universe from beginning to end, boundary to boundary.' *Pacha* as time is not to be understood as being abstract or isolated but as it is unified with the earth (*mundo*).... [Guardia] introduces 'space/time' (*'mundo/tiempo'*) as the best translation of the word *pacha*. Though we feel uncomfortable with this combination, it is important to remind ourselves that to the Runa [Native Andean person or people] time and space are not two separate abstractions but are only aspects of one and the same phenomenon.[60]

Similarly, anthropologist Frank Salomon describes *pacha* in reference to the colonial Huarochirí manuscript as "an untranslatable word that simultaneously denotes a moment or interval in time and a locus or extension in space—and does so, moreover, at any scale."[61] Therefore, from a Native Andean perspective, *pacha* expresses a concurrence or a convergence of space and time, with no distinct boundaries or separations.

Within the Andean framework of *pacha*, Western European chronology and time-space distinctions are inappropriate. In fact, some studies indicate that in the Aymara language, the order of time-space is reversed. The future is "behind" the observer; whereas the past is "in front."[62] Just as gazing into the night sky allows us to catch a glimpse of the past, millions of light years away, for many Native Andeans the past is standing "in front" of them, etched in the ancient and vivified landscape that melds into their experience of the present. The future, however, is more tenebrous, for it is hidden "behind" the line of sight. Therefore, it is knowable only through the appropriate rituals of divination and prognostication.

CHAPTER SUMMARY

In this chapter we have discussed the doctrine of animism, the belief shared by many Native Andean peoples that the landscape they inhabit is imbued with life, consciousness, and spirit. For this reason the Quechuas, Aymaras, and other Native Andean groups worship and make offerings to Mother Earth (*Pacha Mama*), insuring the success of agriculture, and venerate the surrounding mountains and mountain peaks (*Apus* or *Wamanis* in Quechua; *Achachilas* or *Mallkus* in Aymara), which dispense the life-giving waters needed to irrigate and fertilize their fields. In concordance with their animistic beliefs, the Native Andean peoples attribute personalities, emotions, and human characteristics to these nature spirits, also known as *huacas*.

Among some Native Andean groups, the people and the landscape comprise a gestalt—a totality, unity, and completeness—that is not readily comprehended in our Western philosophical framework. For them, physicality may be illusory because in their worldview the material world and the spiritual world converge in one integrated reality. For the Aymaras in particular, aspects of nature and their geography are perceived as extensions of their own human family. The Aymaras project their sense of identity, including inner qualities and values, onto their surrounding landscape.

Starting with a description of the Inca cosmos, we have also explored the Native Andean belief in multiple worlds, each inhabited by different kinds of beings. The Quechuas and Aymaras divide the cosmos into three worlds or *pachas*: the Upper World (or World Above); This World; and the Lower, or Interior, World (or World Below). Due to the influence of Christianity brought by the Spanish Conquest, the Upper and Lower Worlds are now associated with beneficent and maleficent forces, incorporating the Christian notions of heaven and hell.

In Andean mythology, the concept of multiple worlds expresses a complex interaction among beings proceeding from different worlds. Time is also not to be understood as a linear or chronological concept, or as separate and isolated from This World; on the contrary, it exists in the integrated concept of *pacha*—which expresses the concurrence of space, time, and world—and has no counterpart in our Western philosophical tradition.

3

intermediaries

Anthropomorphic Intermediaries

Claude Lévi-Strauss, the father of structural mythology,[1] theorizes that every myth presents a duality or opposition that produces tension and conflict in the story. The introduction of an intermediary element or a mediating factor seeks to resolve such duality by attempting to transcend the opposition or conflict, or bridge the disjunction presented in the story. The intermediary element may, for instance, be a person, an animal, an object, a cultural activity, or even a personal characteristic exhibited by one of the mythical characters.[2]

In concordance with the theories of Lévi-Strauss, intermediaries figure prominently in Native Andean mythology. They appear in the form of animals, people, cultural activities, and, most importantly, anthropomorphic beings (part human, part animal). These intermediaries seek to reestablish a conjunction between opposing or complementary elements and transcend a duality presented in the myth. Often, they try to bridge the gap between different "worlds," such as earth (This World) and sky (Upper World or World Above), and unite complementary or opposing elements, such as nature and culture, life and death, or *hanan* ("upper" or "above") and *hurin* ("lower" or "below").[3]

Also central to the notion of intermediaries in Andean mythology is the ability to function in, or to possess characteristics or qualities belonging to, different worlds. For example, the *ukuku*, the Andean "Boy-Bear," belongs both to the animal world and to the human world, and, therefore, both to nature and to culture. Consequently, aside from the mixed human and animal physical characteristics, the Boy-Bear also possesses other real and imaginary qualities that can be ascribed to each of these worlds. For example, just as a human male, the *ukuku* of Andean folktales may have the ability to talk, to walk on two legs, to go to school or to work, and to engage in sexual relations with women; yet, like a wild animal, he may show a propensity for extreme violence and aggression or steal large domesticated animals—cows, horses, sheep, and pigs—for his voracious consumption. Since bears do not act like humans, nor do they eat large animals in the wild, these aspects of the *ukuku* exist only in the storyteller's imagination.[4]

Interestingly, although the *ukuku* is celebrated in many Andean festivals and dances in which highland men wear colorful costumes and masks representing the spirit of the Boy-Bear, very few Andeans have ever seen a bear. The only species native to South America is the "spectacled bear" (*Tremarctos ornatus*), a docile and primarily vegetarian animal whose diet consists of roots, leaves, fruits, corn, small rodents, and insects. Less than five percent of its diet consists of meat.[5] Thus, the excessive meat-eating habits of the Boy-Bear are part of his mythological dimension.

The following two stories present two very different portrayals of the *ukuku* (sometimes also called *jukumari* or *ucumari*), a common intermediary in many Andean folktales. The first story is more typical in that it depicts an innocent Boy-Bear trying to do his best to please his elders and to fit into human society; yet, society disdains him. In fact, the village priest is constantly conjuring up ways to try to kill the Boy-Bear. The second story, which is less common, portrays an angry Boy-Bear, intent on killing and fighting against society. This Boy-Bear is aggressive, brazen, and dismissive of societal rules. He is a threat and a menace to his community.

The Bear's Son

(Quechua)

They say that a bear took a young woman to his cave. There she lived, locked up for a long time, and had a son. She lived a long time that way, a long time.

The son became strong and large. One day, the son said to his mother, "Mom, where is your home? Let's leave this place!"

Then when the father bear came home, the mother pointed to [a cow grazing at the foot of] a mountain in front of their cave and told him,

"Bring me that cow over there. We'll eat it."

The mother waited a while until the bear was some distance away and escaped with her child. The opening of the cave was sealed off with a giant rock, but the Boy-Bear easily opened it with a push.

They were quite a distance away, but the large father bear managed to catch up with them. The mother and the child proposed that the father bear live with them in the village. [He agreed.] So they made a bridge by pulling out large tree branches and crossed the river. The Boy-Bear was walking behind his parents. When they were halfway across the river, the Boy-Bear grabbed his father and pushed him into the water. The river swept him away.

The son and his mother reached her village by themselves. She took him into her home. But the Boy-Bear grew too much. The kid grew, and grew quickly.

The village priest had been named his godfather. So just as soon as the Boy-Bear was baptized, the priest put him in school. But the Boy-Bear killed many children just by playing marbles. So the mother handed her child over to the priest, who was put in charge of the Boy-Bear.

One day the priest told some men, "When the Boy-Bear goes to ring the church bells, you will push him off the bell tower." Then he ordered the Boy-Bear to climb the tower to ring the bells. But when the men were about to push him off, the Boy-Bear caught them and threw them off the tower. As they fell down, they looked like frogs.

Later, the Boy-Bear told the priest, "I don't know why I did it, father. I felt like some flies were bothering me, and I threw them down one by one." The men died instantly. It's just that the Boy-Bear was too strong.

After that, the priest looked for another solution. He gathered some old mules and told the Boy-Bear, "Go fetch some firewood on the mountain." The Boy-Bear asked if the priest could prepare him a cold lunch to take with him. The priest made the lunch and ordered that little bells be hung around the necks of all the mules. But, truth be told, the priest had brought him [old and sick] mules and old, useless horses. He was hoping some wild animals would devour the Boy-Bear on the mountain.

The Boy-Bear left and did as he was told, but the mules became very weak and couldn't make it the rest of the way. So the Boy-Bear carried the mules up the mountain. There he released them, and while they grazed he went to fetch firewood. When he finished his task and returned to round up the mules there weren't any left. The wild beasts had devoured them all. So he went to gather some bears, tigers, and other wild animals, loaded the firewood on their backs, hung bells around their necks, and brought them back to the priest.

"Why did you do that?" asked the priest.

"Father, the wild animals ate our mules," he answered innocently.

"Hurry and take them back immediately to where you found them!" ordered the priest. So the Boy-Bear took them to the entrance of the village and, using his whip, sent them running off.

The Boy-Bear continued living there, in the village. One day, the priest learned that in another village a condemned soul[6] was devouring the people and was about to depopulate the whole town. So he ordered the Boy-Bear to go to that village. Before he left, the Boy-Bear requested, "Father, please have a wooden doll made for me."

The priest had the doll made and gave the Boy-Bear a man from their village as a helper.[7] He also made the Boy-Bear a cold lunch, and the Boy-Bear set off for the other village. In fact, by then the condemned soul had killed off the entire village and devoured all the people.

The Boy-Bear arrived and knocked on someone's door, but no one answered. He knocked on another door, and there was nothing. He knocked on still another door, and there he found a young woman, the only person left in the town. The young woman invited him in. She might have made him some food, I don't really know.

Later that evening, at nightfall, the Boy-Bear went to the church tower to ring the bells. There the condemned soul attacked him. They fought long and hard. At times the condemned soul was about to win, but at other times the Boy-Bear had the condemned soul retreating. While the Boy-Bear rested, the wooden doll fought in his place. Finally, when the rooster crowed at dawn, the condemned soul admitted defeat. He said, "You are my savior. You will kill me.[8] But before you do, let me hand you these keys." And he handed some keys to the Boy-Bear.[9]

At the crack of dawn the Boy-Bear killed the condemned soul. Later, he might have buried him, I don't know. The Boy-Bear returned to his mother's village and took her and the priest to his new village, where they stayed to live. The story ends there.[10]

Juan Bear

(Quechua)

I am going to tell you a story about something that happened in the olden days. In this life we can't say whether it's true or not. But I'll tell you the story anyway.

They say that in the olden days a bear lived with a Christian, a woman. While living like that, it happened that the woman became pregnant. When their son was born, they say that the bear regretted what he had done. He asked himself how he, as an animal, would be able to take care of the baby. But the bear was brave and proud, so he recognized the child as his own.

The child grew, and since he was a wild animal, he was disrespectful and brazen; that's what they say. He never minded his parents. After his father punished him twice, the child obeyed him. But when he got bigger, he hung on to his father's neck, and they pushed one another. After that, his father gave him his freedom [and asked him to leave the house].

The Boy-Bear was so daring that they say he caused trouble everywhere, everywhere he went. He killed anyone who bothered him, with a single blow. He was so terrible that the authorities got involved, and they prohibited him from behaving like that. But then he killed the governor. As he killed him, he said, "Why are you messing in my business?" So after that everyone left him alone.

The Boy-Bear had the bad habit of climbing the bell tower of the church to ring the bells. He had this bad habit of going to play up there. He was so brazen that he frightened the authorities, who said, "We can't prevent him from doing that. The best thing is to scare him. We'll put a man at the top of the stairwell leading up to the tower, a man dressed up as a corpse! That's the only way we will frighten him!"

In fact, the Boy-Bear returned to play in the bell tower. Suddenly, bong! He ran into him. The man was standing at the stairwell. The man dressed up as a corpse was standing there.

The Boy-Bear stopped and said, "Get out of my way!" The man, pretending to be dead, didn't answer him.

The Boy-Bear repeated, "Get out of my way!" The corpse remained silent.

The Boy-Bear rolled the man dressed as a corpse this way and that. He pushed him down the stairs and continued climbing up to the bell tower. The poor man just lay there. The Boy-Bear rang the bells until he had his fill.

Way up there, the Boy-Bear had the urge to urinate. So he said, "Let's see if you're dead or alive!" The Boy-Bear urinated on top of the man... and when he urinated on his head, the man became uncomfortable. "Whizz!" he moved.

When the corpse moved to avoid the urine, the Boy-Bear was put on alert. "Ah, I see now. It looks like you're not dead!" he said. And bop! He gave the man a blow and killed him, too.

The Boy-Bear continued to behave this way, and on one occasion he ran into his father while visiting his mother's house. When he saw his father, the Boy-Bear said to him, "Now one of us will die!" His father, who was a very clever bear, tried to gain the upper hand by rolling a huge boulder into the inside of the cave and closing it off. But the Boy-Bear effortlessly picked up the boulder and whoosh! threw it at his father and killed him. And the Boy-Bear continued to live.

The Boy-Bear continued acting bold and proud and continued his brazen behavior. So to get rid of him, the authorities sent him as a messenger to a *pascana* [a lodging along an Inca road]. As he was sleeping, the Boy-Bear heard a voice that said, "I will fall." And the voice kept on repeating, "I will fall, I will fall." The bear was angry. "Who are you?" he asked. No one answered.

The voice was following him around, saying, "I will fall, I will fall," and was getting closer and closer. Finally, the Boy-Bear shouted, "Shut up once and for all!" Clang, clang, clang! A whole bunch of bones fell to the floor. Remembering how much anger the voice had caused him, the Boy-Bear started crushing all the bones that had fallen on the ground.

When he finally reduced them to dust, the bones came together again and transformed into a whole human being. Then, the Boy-Bear took out an iron bar and broke up the body and threw it. Then, a little dove came out and the body went up to heaven.[11]

That way, the Boy-Bear was saved from his misdeed. He didn't kill the man anymore. It is said that upon dying they didn't stay[12] in that place.[13]

~~~

Although these two folktales paint different portraits of the Andean *ukuku*, they nevertheless have much in common. In both cases, the *ukuku* is the offspring of a male bear and a human female. In both instances, the Boy-Bear kills his father in the company of his mother. And, in both stories, the Boy-Bear has a confrontation that leads to the death of his adversary, the condemned soul.

On the surface, these tales appear to be about an adolescent misfit who is trying to find his place in the world. In the story of The Bear's Son, the Boy-Bear is on the verge of being "human": he tries to obey the priest, follow societal rules (as best he can), perform his chores dutifully and thoughtfully, and adapt to community life. He is trying to conform to the established rules of culture. In the tale of Juan Bear, the Boy-Bear's behavior is more like that of a wild "animal": he is reckless, destructive, unruly, and dangerous, causing trouble everywhere he goes. Juan Bear openly rejects and defies the rules of society and prefers to live on the edge, marginalized and excluded from the human community. Both of these characterizations of the *ukuku* describe a range of behaviors often associated with human adolescence, the stage of life in which a young person struggles to find a balance between fitting in and adapting to the prescribed rules of society or rebelling and ignoring those rules in an attempt to assert nonconformity and independence.

Consistent with these observations, anthropologist Gary Urton describes *ukukus* as "animals on the verge of becoming human beings."[14] Although bears demonstrate some human abilities, such as walking on two legs, perhaps mating ventro-ventrally, and eating "domesticated animals and corn and squash" (bears are omnivorous), their behavior is believed to resemble that of human adolescents: "[t]hey are unruly, destructive, sexually aggressive, and they do not have language. They are, like adolescents, on the verge of becoming humans."[15]

Moreover, in terms of membership in an *ayllu*—a Native Andean community—the *ukuku*, part human adolescent and part bear, "best defines the boundary across which one must pass in order to be transformed into a mature human being: a member of an *ayllu*."[16] According to Urton, one typically becomes an adult member of an *ayllu* when one marries, works the land, contributes to the community, and eventually becomes a parent.[17] Since adolescents cannot yet marry or assume the responsibilities of marriage and parenthood, they are not full-fledged "human beings" in the eyes of the Native Andean community; they are simply on the edge of becoming a human being, just like the *ukuku*.

Another way to look at the status of the Andean Boy-Bear in these stories is to recognize that he is acting as a mediating agent between childhood and adulthood, and also as an intermediary between the world of nature (animals/bears) and the world of culture (humans/*ayllu*). His plight may also be emblematic of the struggle to mediate between two different cultural identities in Andean society. Anthropologist Catherine Allen suggests that "the awkward yet powerful *ukuku* provides a metaphorical expression of the contradictions faced by Indian men in a Hispanic-oriented society."[18] So, on deeper examination, the *ukuku* must also overcome and relinquish his anthropomorphic intermediary status (part animal, part human) in order to successfully join the human world and integrate himself into the larger culture. In both stories this is accomplished by the symbolic "killing" of his adversary, the condemned soul.

Before examining the significance of the killing of the condemned soul, let us discuss the psychological dimensions of these Andean stories, based on the theories of Sigmund Freud. The images and details of these *ukuku* tales are highly suggestive of the Oedipus complex,[19] a constellation of sexual desires and emotions that, according to Freud, are experienced universally during childhood. Freudian theory assumes that at the climactic midpoint of a male child's psychosexual development, the child becomes unconsciously enamored with his mother and harbors secret unconscious desires to kill his father, who stands in the way of possessing his mother. This is demonstrated in both tales when the *ukuku* kills his father in the presence of his mother. In The Bear's Son, the Boy-Bear pushes his father off a bridge on the way to his mother's village, and the river carries his father away. In the story of Juan Bear, the Boy-Bear is visiting his mother's house and confronts his father—"Now one of us will die!" he says—and kills his father.

The Boy-Bear fantasizes that if he kills his rival father, this will leave his mother for himself. These sexual desires are revealed through certain symbolic images in these stories. According to Freud, enclosed spaces, such as caves and rooms—just as those in which the mother and the *ukuku* typically dwell—are associated with the female sexual organ.[20] Thus, the references describing how easily the Boy-Bear "opened [the cave] with a push," or how "effortlessly [he] picked up the boulder" blocking the entrance of the cave, are, from a classical psychoanalytic perspective, symbolic allusions to the sexual act that confirm the sexual/sensual nature of this mother-child relationship.

However, the Boy-Bear's erotic feelings toward his mother are usually accompanied by anxiety, shame, and moral guilt that threaten to overpower the ego, or conscious personality. Consequently, these unacceptable impulses and anxiety-provoking sexual desires lead to repression, a psychological process designed to protect the conscious personality from the conflict of this sexual trauma. According to Freud, repression is the mechanism by which unacceptable desires and feelings, usually sexual in nature, are dispatched to the unconscious mind and kept out of conscious awareness, because they cause too much anxiety and threaten to overwhelm the ego.[21] So repression enables the Boy-Bear to keep his ego intact while erasing the unacceptable thoughts from his conscious awareness.

The priest and the authorities in these *ukuku* tales may symbolically represent the mechanism of repression. The Catholic Church has a long history in the Andes of trying to categorize, suppress, and control sexual desires deemed as "sinful";[22] therefore, it seems reasonable that when the Boy-Bear is about to reach adolescence and attain full sexual maturity, he is taken, or driven, away from the home and separated from his mother (the object of his preadolescent affection) and turned over to the control (repression) of the village priest. Similarly, in the story of Juan Bear the *ukuku* is hunted down by the authorities, whose prime intention is to rid the community of this hairy misfit.

The priest "usually puts the Boy-Bear through a series of labors which he accomplishes in unexpected fashion, much to the priest's vexed chagrin."[23] In The Bear's Son, for example, the village priest attempts to kill the Boy-Bear in various ways, and symbolically destroy the adolescent's "animal" nature, in much the same way as the psyche tries to extinguish the adolescent's sexual desires through the mechanism of repression. Likewise, in the tale of Juan Bear the authorities try to hunt the Boy-Bear down, intending to frighten him but not necessarily kill him, as in the first story. However, neither the priest nor the authorities succeed in destroying or capturing the Boy-Bear, and this, too, is analogous to the mechanism of repression. Repression does not destroy the anxiety-provoking material; it simply conceals it and stashes it away in the unconscious.[24] So by repressing unacceptable feelings and desires, they are banished to, but not deleted from, the unconscious mind. They are merely kept at bay and out of the individual's conscious awareness.

Another curious aspect in both *ukuku* stories is the Boy-Bear's preoccupation with climbing the bell tower and ringing the bells. In The Bear's Son, for instance, the Boy-Bear "climb[s] the tower to ring the bells" shortly before he is attacked by the village men. In Juan Bear the storyteller tells us that the Boy-Bear "had the bad habit of climbing the bell tower of the church to ring the bells. He had this bad habit of going to play up there." According to classical psychoanalytic theory, these passages also connote the Boy-Bear's budding sexuality.

According to Freud, upon reaching puberty the boy experiences a reawakening of sexual urges similar to, but broader than, those of early childhood, which include greater sexual exploration and experimentation. The goal of the adolescent male, from a psychoanalytic perspective, is not only to derive sexual pleasure, but also to "discharge sexual products."[25] This increased sexual activity is suggested in the *ukuku* stories through images that conjure sexual experimentation.

The phallic symbol of the bell tower, in conjunction with the pealing of the church bells, connotes a variety of sexual activities that the Boy-Bear is unwilling to cease from doing. In the first story, the village priest, intent on killing the Boy-Bear, hires some men to "push him off the bell tower" when the Boy-Bear "climb[s] the tower to ring the bells," but the men fall to their deaths instead. In the second story, the Boy-Bear's behavior prompts the authorities to place a man, dressed as a corpse, at the stairwell leading up to the tower in order to "prevent him from doing that." The man is unable to stop the Boy-Bear, who climbs up to the bell tower and rings "the bells until he [has] had his fill." Later, the Boy-Bear urinates on the man, suggesting, perhaps, that he is flaunting his male member.

Finally, as is typical of many Andean *ukuku* tales, the Boy-Bear kills his adversary, the condemned soul. In the tale of The Bear's Son, the Boy-Bear defeats the condemned soul at a church tower in a depopulated village. In the story of Juan Bear, the Boy-Bear overcomes the condemned soul, described as a "whole bunch of bones," at a *pascana*, a lodging along an Inca road.

Much like the Boy-Bear, the condemned soul (*alma condenada*) is an intermediary being. In Andean lore, condemned souls are wandering spirits or supernatural beings that can adopt a variety of forms and are forced to walk the earth in order to expiate a grave sin (typically incest) committed during their lifetime. Condemned souls are neither living nor dead, and can neither enter heaven nor hell.[26] One way a condemned soul may be "saved" in Andean *ukuku* tales is if he battles the Boy-Bear (generally, the condemned soul is male in these stories) and is finally freed from his intermediary status. If this occurs, the condemned soul will no longer be forced to live "in between" worlds, and his punishment will be deemed served.

By fighting and killing an intermediary in the bell tower, the Boy-Bear is also defeating and overcoming his own intermediary status. One might call this event a rite of passage from childhood into adulthood, and from the world of nature (animal) into the world of culture (human). The victory over the condemned soul implies transcendence and independence (sexual and otherwise), and, by analogy, "saving" the condemned soul makes the *ukuku* his own "savior." This is implicit in the story of The Bear's Son, when the condemned soul offers the Boy-Bear some keys after his defeat. The keys appear to give the Boy-Bear ownership of the condemned soul's property in the depopulated village. This is clearly implied in the story when, after receiving the keys, the Boy-Bear "returned to his mother's village, and took her and the priest to his new village, where they stayed to live." In similar *ukuku* tales, the Boy-Bear also typically marries the daughter or the widow of the condemned soul, who is often the sole survivor of the depopulated village. This is suggested when the Boy-Bear finds a young woman, "the only person left in the town," who invites him into her home. In the end, the Boy-Bear (now Man-Bear) usually "lives happily ever after as lord of the manor."[27]

As previously discussed, an adolescent becomes an adult member of the *ayllu*, or Native Andean community, when he marries and assumes the responsibilities of marriage, work, and parenthood. The keys the condemned soul gives to the Boy-Bear may also symbolize the keys to the Boy-Bear's nascent adulthood. By possessing the keys, the *ukuku* can now lay claim to land and, foreseeably, be able to work that land. He may now also be able to marry the young woman and assume his marital and parental obligations. In this way, the *ukuku* is no longer an intermediary adolescent on the verge of becoming human; he can now earn his rightful place as an adult member of the *ayllu*.

The Boy-Bear in Juan Bear also successfully makes the passage into adulthood and human society. The narrator tells us that, in the end, the Boy-Bear is "saved from his misdeed," because neither the condemned soul he killed at the *pascana* nor he (presumably after his own death) "stayed in that place" as attached souls.[28] In Andean lore, souls may come to dwell and become "attached" to certain places if their death is unresolved or if they have left unfinished business on earth before they died. But the storyteller clearly indicates this did not happen. Again, this strongly suggests that the Boy-Bear does not stagnate ("stay in place") but triumphs over his intermediary status.

One might also argue that the Boy-Bear has reemerged from this transitory adolescent experience as a more complete and integrated human being. The "voice" that haunts the Boy-Bear at the end of Juan Bear may typify the guilt related to his sexual desires that followed him into adolescence; however, after he crushes the bones associated with the voice, the bones come together and "transform into a whole human being," denoting transcendence. Even after the body is cut up with an iron bar, the soul-body is "saved" nonetheless. A little dove—an Andean symbol for the soul—leaves the body, and then the body itself goes up to heaven, presumably with the dove (soul). The body and soul are no longer at odds. This may be emblematic of the Boy-Bear overcoming his sexual guilt, arriving at sexual maturity, and reconciling body and spirit. By defeating his adversary, he has overcome his intermediary status and earned the rite of passage into adulthood and the human community.

In many respects, the Boy-Bear is an ideal symbolic adversary for the condemned soul. In Andean folktales, the Boy-Bear is born of an exogamous relationship between a bear and a human, which are very distant species, biologically speaking, whereas the condemned soul is usually accused of having had an endogamous, incestuous relationship with a blood relative or close family relation, for which he is being punished.

Therefore, some argue that the Boy-Bear and the condemned soul are complementary or opposing characters in the Andean dualistic paradigm.[29] For this reason, it is often the case in Andean tales that the condemned soul engages the Boy-Bear, his antithesis, in single combat in an effort to be "saved" from his unfortunate intermediary condition. Through this struggle, the Boy-Bear is also saved from his own intermediary status.

The intermediary nature of the *ukuku*, Boy-Bear, is also celebrated in Native Andean ritual. One such ritual takes place at the Sinakara Valley in the Cuzco region of Peru during the three-day festival of *Qoyllur Rit'i* (meaning "Starry Snow" or "Shining Snow"), which typically takes place in late May or early June, one week prior to the Christian celebration of Corpus Christi. As part of the celebration, young Andean men gather, dressed in costume as *ukukus*, sporting shaggy dark coats and woolen masks that cover their face and head, except for their eyes. They speak in high-pitched voices and play pranks but also act as policemen directing the crowd of pilgrims, which number in the thousands. The *ukukus* prepare to embark on a climb to the summit of *Monte Colquepunku* ("Mount Silver Gate"), home of an important *Apu*, or mountain spirit, considered a healer and guardian of the local native people. According to the locals, due to their special intermediary status and supernatural strength the *ukukus* protect the pilgrims from the condemned souls that wander at night among the glaciers.

The pilgrimage to the top of the mountain starts at an altitude of 4,800 meters, that is, over 15,700 feet. From there, the *ukukus* climb for several hours to the snow-capped peak, hitting each other and slipping and sliding along the way. Once they reach the glacier at the summit, they stay the night, fighting or warding off condemned souls, or *kukuchis*, which are believed to haunt the glacier.[30] In the morning they chisel off blocks of ice and bring them down to the foot of the mountain.[31] These ice blocks are believed to contain special healing properties due to their sacred source at the top of the mountain, and they must be shared among the many pilgrims. Local custom also dictates that these blocks of ice be used as offerings to the spirit of the mountain to help sinners gain entry into heaven; otherwise, they may suffer the same fate as the condemned souls which, after death, wander about aimlessly in the world.

The Boy-Bear, who brings back the ice and offers a means to salvation, is acting as an intermediary between This World and the Upper World of the *Apu*, and between the human and supernatural worlds. As designated guardian of the pilgrims, the *ukuku* is also bridging the divide between the world of the living and the world of the dead. It is because of his special status as a mediating agent that he is capable of fighting and warding off the condemned souls, which are allegedly neither living nor dead.

In addition to the Andean Boy-Bear, other anthropomorphic beings also appear in Native Andean folktales, including the Calf-Girl (or She-Calf), the Frog-Girl (or She-Frog), the Bull-Boy, the Lizard-Boy, the Macaw-Woman, and others. In each case, the character functions in, or inhabits, more than one world and possesses certain attributes or characteristics belonging to each. As such, much like the *ukuku*, each character functions as an intermediary, bridging the disjunction between disparate worlds.

As with the Boy-Bear, most of these anthropomorphic intermediaries are generally considered outcasts and misfits in human society. For instance, in the Quechua story of "*Wakacha*" ("The Calf-Girl," "Little Cow," or "She-Calf"),[32] a She-Calf is born from a pregnant mother who loves cats and dogs and wishes her baby could be just like them. The birth of the child, who is part human and part animal, infuriates the father, who banishes his child to the highlands. A boy, who is in love with the She-Calf, follows her from one village to another and eventually to "the heart of the jungle."[33] There the boy passes a test set up by a group of condors, and he makes an offering to the mountain god that eventually breaks the spell that has enchanted the She-Calf. He reunites with his beloved, who changes back into human form and marries her faithful rescuer. The young couple is transported back to a village where they marry and live in a beautiful palace.

Similarly, in the tales of the Bull-Boy and the Lizard-Boy, the intermediary is considered a misfit in human society because of his insatiable "appetites." The Bull-Boy gores and kills his wives, one after another, and the Lizard-Boy devours his wives, one by one, after sleeping with them.[34] These are further examples of the prevalence of sexual symbolism in Andean folktales. The anthropomorphic beast "consumes" each wife, usually on his wedding night, to the horror and dismay of his parents and community. In the end, however, the Bull-Boy and Lizard-Boy (sometimes also referred to as "Bull-Man" and "Lizard-Man") generally find a benevolent and intelligent woman who, not wanting to be consumed, either outsmarts the beast and learns to manage him or genuinely cares for him and treats him like a human being instead of an animal. In some cases she may even "save" him and help him "transform" physically back into a human being.[35]

Like the Boy-Bear, these anthropomorphic beings represent the intermediary stage of adolescence, the confusing and sometimes violent passage between the innocence and immaturity of childhood and the experience and responsibility of adulthood. Perhaps it is not coincidental that most of these intriguing characters are characterized as part girl or part boy. Adolescence is a time of sexual discovery in which the sexual "beast" becomes unleashed and expresses its animal instincts, sometimes voraciously and indiscriminately. As mentioned previously, in some Andean folktales the boy-animal "devours" several members of the opposite sex before finally settling down with a single, caring partner. In most cases, the boy-animal settles down with the woman who finally "tames" or "manages" the savage beast.

Although girl-animal intermediaries are less common in Andean mythology, sexual symbolism also infiltrates these tales. In the tale of the She-Calf, for example, the She-Calf climbs out of her animal skin and sleeps with a boy, concealing her identity. When the boy tries to sneak a peek and light a candle to see her face, he inadvertently drops a little wax on her face.[36] Novelist and folklorist Johnny Payne, who has transcribed and translated a version of this story into English, observes that the Quechua storyteller who recorded this tale "clearly appears to say *esperma* (sperm)," when she recounts this passage, although later the storyteller self-corrects and "says the Spanish word *cera* (wax)" instead.[37] This sexual imagery is also consistent with other parts of the story in which the She-Calf requests that her mother set up an elaborate, possibly nuptial, offering in the bedroom, consisting of "the first loaves of bread to come out of the oven... the first cup of wine from the bottle... flowers, and holy water... [and] an innocent boy waiting for me."[38]

SHAPE-SHIFTERS

Another important intermediary figure in the realm of Native Andean mythology is the deceptive shape-shifter. This intermediary is usually male and presents himself as an animal or deity—capable of altering his shape or appearance and adopting a human form (or vice versa)—for the purpose of romancing a woman, a potential human sexual partner, and avoiding detection by others. The shape-shifter walks a fine line between the animal and human worlds, between nature and culture, and between the natural and supernatural worlds.

For instance, in the Quechua folktale of "The Mouse Husband," a mouse falls in love with a beautiful young woman and changes "himself into a slender young man, quite long-faced, with tiny bright eyes... [and] a thin, whistling voice."[39] After being sexually intimate with the woman, she gives birth to a tiny boy nine months later. Like his mouse-father, the boy also has a shrill and squeaky voice. The mouse has a cat-faced mother-in-law, however, who discovers the true identity of her son-in-law and ultimately kills the boy. Grief-stricken, the mouse buries his child under a *kantuta* plant (also spelled *khantuta*), a bell-shaped Andean wildflower that he waters every day with his tears. Bathed with the mouse-father's tears, the *kantuta* never dies; it flourishes with the tears of love and never withers. The mouse then enlists the help of his fellow mice and storms the house of the cat-faced mother-in-law. They empty all her food bins, surround her, and gnaw her to death. Finally, the mice devour her remains, "leaving nothing but a skeleton."[40] The shape-shifting mouse runs off, never to return to the human world.

The shape-shifting mouse is often portrayed in Quechua folktales as "a courageous, well-prepared, and very hard working animal," whose family benefits from his diligence and resourcefulness.[41] He is an excellent family man and a good provider, but, due to his tiny size, he often falls victim to heavy rains, larger predatory animals, and other misfortunes. His stories are often used to teach Andean children moral lessons about the value of hard work and the merit of using intelligence and industry to survive under difficult circumstances.

In addition to the mouse, another famous shape-shifter in the Andes is the *Runa-Tigre*, or Andean Man-Tiger.[42] There are many Native Andean beliefs concerning the Man-Tiger, the most important of which is that he is really a man who has the power of transfiguration and can change himself into a feline.[43] Some Native Andeans have told me they would never dare hurt a *tigrecito*, "a little wild cat," for fear that he may be a shaman from a neighboring village who is simply guarding his territory or coming to spy on them. Among many legends of the *Runa-Tigre* is one that he possesses an extraordinary sense of smell and can discern between cowardly and valiant men.

> They say that he has respect for dignified men. He recognizes the brave through his sense of smell, and if he encounters one, he cedes the way, letting him continue without bothering him. [However,] that is not the case when a coward crosses his path. He pursues [the coward] and stalks him, then, if opportunity strikes, he hypnotizes him and swipes at him with the mortal blow of his paw. Then [he] leaves his bones as exemplary trophies.[44]

Much like other anthropomorphic intermediaries, the Man-Tiger also has a predilection for women, especially the "soft parts" of a woman.[45]

According to legend, the Man-Tiger often rapes women and then "fills his stomach with the flesh of the terrorized [victims]."[46] In many parts of the Andes, they also say that he especially enjoys feasting on the breasts and tongues of women after he has sexually violated them.

However, by far the most renowned shape-shifter in Andean folklore is the mighty condor. The condor in the Andes is a symbol linked to the lofty mountains and to *Hanan Pacha* (Upper World) for the Quechuas and *Alaj Pacha* (World Above) for the Aymaras.[47] In his role as intermediary, he mediates between This World and the World Above. In fact, in some Native Andean legends the condor is believed to be the child of a male and a female mountain.[48] He is also connected with the glory of the former Inca Empire and is often considered a messenger from the Sun god, *Inti*.[49] Sometimes he is portrayed as a wise and benevolent intermediary who intercedes with the gods on behalf of humanity. Occasionally, one hears tales about human beings becoming condors. The Aymaras, for instance, relay the story of a mountain named *Condor Jipiña* (the "Condor's Nest") where, allegedly, at one time a prince who could shape-shift into a condor had been wounded and turned into stone.[50] But by far an overwhelming number of Quechua folktales portray the condor as a trickster and lover of women.[51] In this role, he employs his personal charm and shape-shifting ability to further his sexual exploits.

In the following Andean folktale, entitled "The Condor's Lover," a gallant and elegantly dressed condor adopts the form of a man to entice a beautiful young shepherdess to become his lover. After she returns his love and becomes pregnant with his child, the condor lifts his lover on his wings and carries her off to his cave, amidst the mountain rocks and cliffs, where he leaves her alone for extended periods while he scavenges for carcasses.

The Condor's Lover

(Quechua)

There lived a young woman whose parents were still alive. She was a young woman with a beautiful face.

One day her parents sent her to take care of their flock of sheep. Seeing that she could do it, from then on they sent her every day to carry out this task.

One day a man approached her while she was watching over the sheep. This gentleman was elegantly dressed, wearing riding attire. He sported his trousers with an energetic and masculine air. He wore gaiters (*kkarawatanas*) that protected his legs like the livestock farmers from the steppes. He wore a gold necklace fitted around his neck and the most beautiful *chullo* [a woven Andean woolen hat] on top of his head.

The dashing traveler said to the young woman, "Be my lover."

"Sure," answered the young woman.

So the young woman accepted the traveler at his word. And they made love.

From then on, the gentleman came to look for her at the same place for many days. But she didn't tell her father or her mother about the visits from this gentleman stranger. Only her heart kept this secret.

In this way, without anyone knowing, she became pregnant.

The man dressed as a traveler was the Condor, who had assumed the appearance of an elegant gentleman to win the young woman's heart. For that reason the young woman only saw in him a *werakkocha*, an honorable gentleman.

When she found herself pregnant, the young woman said to him, "I have conceived your child. Now we should go to either your house or mine. But I don't want my parents to see me in this state, or to meet you, because I have been with you without their knowledge."

Upon hearing this the gentleman replied, "I will take you to my home. Tomorrow I will carry you there. Now go home. Tomorrow bring your things without telling your parents. Just herd and bring along the sheep as you always do."

"Fine," said the young woman, and she walked down the mountain toward her home.

At nightfall she silently gathered her belongings, and at dawn she herded and walked the sheep toward the mountain where her lover was waiting. She did this furtively, without her parents becoming aware of her departure. Loaded with all of her personal belongings, she waited at the top of the mountain for the Condor.

The Condor had her waiting there until midday. At about that time he appeared with his usual attire of a gentleman. He said to the young woman, "So you're here already?" And he asked, "Did you remember to bring all your things?"

"Yes, I arrived, and I brought everything I have," she responded. Then they agreed to leave.

"Now scare the sheep back toward the house. Your parents will see the animals and bring them back. Step lively! Do what you are told, and return immediately!" ordered the Condor.

The young woman obeyed. She ran toward the flock of sheep and took them as far as the lower slope of the mountain within view of her parents' home. There she scared away the animals toward the house and ran back as fast as she could.

Just as soon as she returned the Condor said, "Now I will carry you."

He led the young woman to some rocks, and there he warned, "Do not open your eyes for any reason. Shut them tightly. If you open them, I will let go."

So shutting her eyes tightly, the young woman mounted her lover's back. Then the Condor took flight. She couldn't see anything. The only thing she could hear was the rushing of the wind against some large wings. She couldn't feel anything that resembled walking, because she was already too high up in the skies. She perceived only a smooth and balanced ride, as though she were floating with her lover in a dream.

They flew and flew up to the skies. In the afternoon they arrived at a frightening cliff made of rocks. The Condor had made his den there. The young woman dismounted and opened her eyes and found herself in a solitary cave. She looked above her and saw that the summit of the mountain was very far away, overlooking a precipice of granite rock. When she contemplated the base of the cliff, she saw a dark abyss of silent and dark depth, filled with horror.

When she discovered that she was alone at the entrance of the cave, in such a horrible place, she started to cry. "Why in the world did I come?" she asked herself.

She found only bones around her, with some of the flesh gnawed away, and some pieces of meat scattered about the interior of the cave.

The Condor and the young woman slept there together. The following morning the Condor said to her, "Sit here and wait for me." Then he got off the ground and took off.

Abandoned in this great silence, the young woman cried inconsolably. She didn't have anything to cook or eat in the cave. She had to remain seated and wait for the arrival of the Condor.

"Oh, what will become of me! Had I known about this, I would never have come, never!" she cried.

In the late afternoon the Condor arrived, bringing some meat, which she had to cook. Near the cave the young woman noticed that there was a small stream of water. The water trickled down from a spring that was crystal clear, forming a clean pool of water among the rocks. From there, the Condor's lover fetched the water.

Every day was the same. The Condor would always leave, and many times he would not return for three or four days. When he came back, he brought back meat to cook from dead animals and decomposed flesh.

The young girl lived, crying, until she gave birth. Afterward, she washed the child's diapers and clothing in the little pool of water at the foot of the crystalline spring. She cooked the meat that was brought by the Condor, and some days she didn't even eat because she didn't have any leftovers from the remains of the dead animals.

Meanwhile, the parents of the young woman also cried incessantly. "We wonder what happened to our daughter! Where, oh where could she be?" they asked. Nobody knew that the unfamiliar traveler, the Condor, had abducted her.

"The earth must have taken her,[52] or someone must have lost her," the parents lamented and cried.

One day, when the mother was sobbing behind the orchard of her home, a Hummingbird (*kkenti*) appeared. He started flying in circles around her head. He sang:

Reúú, flyer, reú[53] ... *kkenti* Hummingbird!
I wonder whose daughter, whose [daughter] is crying among the rocks.
I wonder whose daughter is crying among the rocks.

He sang, and returned, and whirled around.

Then the woman responded, "Hummingbird, nobody knows how often and how much I cry and grieve for my daughter! And here you come with these tales!"

She picked up a rock and threw it at the Hummingbird and broke one of his little legs. Wounded, the Hummingbird flew away over the rooftops. The mother, grieving and crying, continued to wait for her daughter. Again the Hummingbird returned. He flew around in circles, singing:

Reúú ... flyer, reúú ... *kkenti* Hummingbird!
I wonder whose daughter is crying among the rocks.
I wonder whose daughter is crying among the rocks.

Then the woman thought, "Maybe he knows where my daughter is." So she asked aloud, "Hummingbird, Hummingbird, the color of emerald, perhaps you know where my daughter can be found?"

The Hummingbird answered, "Of course I know where she can be found! If only you hadn't broken my little leg! But if you treat it with *chancaca* [a hard block of molasses] and give me some sweets, I will tell you where she is."

"I'll give you what you ask for. I'll give you some *chancaca* to cure your little broken leg."

The woman brought some *chancaca* and some sweets and put them over his little leg.

The emerald-colored Hummingbird perched on a rock and licked the sweets. He treated his little leg with the *chancaca* and wrapped a bandage around it. Then he said, "Your daughter is crying among some very high rocks, overlooking a precipice."

"Bring her to me, Hummingbird! Please carry her here!" begged the woman.

"If you give me some more sweets, I can carry her and bring her here tomorrow," replied the Hummingbird.

"Yes, Hummingbird, I will give you lots of honey until you're full!" offered the mother.

"Very well. I will go right now." And having said this, he flew away over the rooftops.

He flew up to the great cave and waited until the Condor departed. The Condor set sail; his black body disappeared in the distant sky.

After the Condor disappeared, the Hummingbird flew up to the young woman, singing:

Reú, flyer, reú *kkenti* Hummingbird!
I wonder whose mother, whose father
are crying in their empty house.
I wonder whose mother, whose father
are crying, pleading,
"Hummingbird, save my daughter!"
If you wish, if you wish,
I, Hummingbird, flyer, reú *kkenti*, flyer,
I could carry you there.
I could take you there.

And he flew, whirling around over the abyss, next to the cave.

Then the young woman spoke to him, "Emerald Hummingbird, save me! Can you carry me back to my parents' house?"

"Yes, I will save you! I will carry you—you and your child. Hurry! Get ready quickly!"

The Condor's lover made a small bundle with all of her and the baby's belongings and mounted the back of the Hummingbird.

The Hummingbird flew up, carrying the young woman and her child. She arrived at the house of her parents, and the Hummingbird sang over the rooftops:

Reú, flyer, reú *kkenti* Hummingbird!
I am arriving with your daughter!

"Emerald Hummingbird, great Hummingbird," said the parents, "You have brought us back our daughter!" And they gave him sweets and honey.

"Lock up your daughter," ordered the Hummingbird. "Your son-in-law will come. Don't let him see her. Lock her up with the child. Tomorrow I will return before the Condor arrives. I will return with news."

"We'll do whatever you request," replied the parents.

The parents locked up the daughter. And they had her tell them how and where she had lived, how and with whom she had been, and how and in what way she had managed to have a child.

The young woman confessed everything. She explained, "This gentleman tricked me and took me to his house. There he had me, and there I gave birth to this child. It was the Condor who assumed the appearance of a gentleman and seduced me. He carried me off to his den. He is the father of my child."

Meanwhile, the Hummingbird flew back to the Condor's cave. He looked for the Frog that lived in the crystalline pool of water among the rocks, and said to him, "When the Condor returns, you will change yourself into a woman and pretend to be washing the child's clothes at the edge of the pool."

"Fine," said the Frog.

Since the Frog accepted the assignment, the Hummingbird continued with his instructions. He said, "Just as soon as he arrives, he will ask you, 'What are you doing over there?' And you will answer, 'I am washing clothes.' Then he will say, 'Hurry! Hurry!' And when he asks you, 'Have you finished the wash?' you will respond, 'No, not yet.' And when he calls you over and says, 'Come quickly, come quickly,' you will submerge in the water. Then you will hide and not come out again."

After saying this, the Hummingbird hopped over and hid behind the rocks, and the Frog changed himself into a woman.

The woman began washing clothes. The Condor had just returned. The Hummingbird, hidden in a cranny, watched from behind the rocks.

The Frog looked very busy, washing and washing. The Condor perched near the pool. "What are you doing?" he asked the woman.

"I am still washing, my husband," she replied.

"Hurry, hurry," said the Condor.

"Yes, I will," replied the woman.

The Condor headed toward his den and entered the cave. He looked all over for his child but couldn't find him. Then he thought, "I wonder where she took the child."

He came out of the cave and asked the woman in a loud voice, "Where's our son?"

"He must be over there," she answered.

"Hurry, hurry! I've brought some meat. Come and cook it."

"Right away, right away," replied the woman.

"Enough already! Enough already!" shouted the Condor, as he lifted up his neck to take a look. "Enough already! Enough already!" he called out again. Finally, he jumped up in the air and shouted, "I'm going to kick you, if you don't come inside!"

Suddenly, the Frog submerged in the water, and his body gurgled in the crystalline pool of water. Nothing remained on the edge of the pool, neither clothes nor diapers belonging to the child. Only a small rock remained there.

But the eyes of the Condor had seen the woman washing. Motionless, he looked at the pool of water. "She'll come up, she'll come up," he said. But nothing appeared on the surface of the water.

The Hummingbird watched the Condor attentively from his hiding place. Seeing the Condor perplexed and confused, he sang to him:

Jajaulla![54] Reúú *kkenti*! I am the flying Hummingbird!
How dumb you are!
How dumb you are!
Reúú, flyer, reúú, flyer.
Jajaulla!
Your wife is already at home.
She is already in her town.
Ajaujaulla! Jajaulla![55]

Infuriated, the Condor responded, "You have carried her off! You have kidnapped my wife! Now you're going to get it! Now you're going to get it! I will swallow you whole! I will gobble you up!"

Jajay![56] What kind of a Hummingbird can carry a woman?

Singing, the Hummingbird disappeared in the air. The Condor flew after him. He followed the Hummingbird and tried to encircle him. He went round and round but couldn't trap him. The Hummingbird slipped away and disappeared.

Since he couldn't catch up with the Hummingbird, and the Hummingbird escaped him, the Condor flew toward the woman's house.

He arrived at the door transformed into an elegant and handsome gentleman. A gold chain adorned his neck. His flaky and dirty legs were covered with brilliant gaiters. He entered the house and said, "My dear sir and my dear madam, kindly let me in. If your daughter has returned, please return her to me, for she is mine."

"No, sir. Nobody has come here. Nobody has arrived in this house," replied the mother.

So the Condor walked away, pondering.

The next day the Hummingbird returned to the woman's house.

"I am going to save your daughter," he told the mother. "Tomorrow your son-in-law will return. But tomorrow you will boil water and fill a vat with boiling water all the way up to the brim. When your son-in-law comes to the door, you will cover up the vat with a mantle. But for now, give me a little hot chili pepper. I'll be back." He received the hot chili pepper and left.

The Condor was looking for the Hummingbird in the sky. The Hummingbird flew toward the Condor's cave carrying the hot chili pepper. They met along the way.

The Condor shouted out to him, "Now you'll have it! I'm going to eat you!" And he followed him round and round, round and round, encircling the Hummingbird in order to trap him.

The two arrived at some large rocky cliffs. The Hummingbird flew across the air and slid inside a crag in the rocks, into a very small hole. Then the Condor stuck his beak as deeply as possible into the hole. "I'm going to take him out," he said. But he couldn't reach him.

"Come out, Hummingbird! Come out now!" he shouted from outside.

"Right away, right away, my great sir," replied the Hummingbird. "But you'll have to wait a moment until I finish putting my socks on."

The Condor waited with his beak half open, preparing to gobble up his morsel. The Hummingbird spoke to him again from his hiding place, "Right away! Right away! I'm about to come out! Open your mouth, and also your anus. Both openings, great sir."

The Condor opened his beak some more. So with his mouth open, he waited.

The Hummingbird suddenly came out and went inside the Condor's mouth. He slid along his windpipe, escaping through his anus. He flew away swiftly, losing himself in the air.

The Condor was in a daze. "I should have chewed him up!" he lamented. "How could he have slipped away like this, in one go?!"

He took flight, chasing after the Hummingbird again. "I have to chew him up!" he said.

Searching and searching in the highlands, he caught up with him. "You got all the way up to here? Now you'll see! You won't escape me this time! I will eat you right now!" shouted the Condor.

"Of course, of course! There's no reason not to! Of course, you will eat me!" answered the Hummingbird.

The Condor whirled around, following him and encircling him. He took the Hummingbird all the way up the cliffs. And again the Hummingbird hid inside a small hole in the rocks.

"Where did you put yourself? Come out, because in any event I'm going to eat you!" shouted the Condor.

"Right away, right away, great sir! I'm not opposed to you eating me. Of course you will eat me, dear sir. But wait just a moment. I'm grinding a little hot chili pepper to lick."

"Enough already, enough already! Come out now!" called out the Condor, as he watched the exit hole vigilantly.

"Woe is me!...takk...takk...takk! Woe is me!...takk...takk..takk!" [bemoaned the Hummingbird.]

The Hummingbird ground the hot chili pepper in the interior of the hole. He painstakingly ground the hot chili pepper. Then he said to the Condor, "I can escape. Look, I can escape. Open your eyes wide, Mr. Condor, open them wide and look at me well. Don't stop looking at me."

The Condor opened his eyes. With his large pupils, he carefully watched the hole. That instant, the Hummingbird violently threw the ground hot chili pepper at the Condor's eyes. And after forcing the Condor to shut his eyes with the sting of the red-hot chili pepper, the Hummingbird flew away toward the home of the Condor's lover. Meanwhile, the Condor rolled around in the air, rubbing his eyes hard for a long time.

The Hummingbird arrived at the home of the young woman. He called to the mother. "Reúú, flyer, reú *kkenki* Hummingbird!" he sang. "What can you say? What will you say? I have burned the eyes of your son-in-law with hot chili pepper! Now you will boil the water that I told you to. Your son-in-law comes already; he comes already! It is time to kill him. Now you will kill him!

"Fill the vat to the brim with boiling water. Cover the top with many garments of clothing. When your son-in-law arrives, he will ask you, 'Your daughter must be here. I know that she came back.' You will answer, 'I haven't seen my daughter, dear sir.' But he will continue asking, 'Where's your daughter? Where is she? You have to give her back to me!' Then you will say, 'Come in, sir, rest a while. Have a seat under the shade of my roof.' And you will invite him in. You will guide him. And when he's about to sit on the stone bench, you will direct him to the vat and have him sit on top of it instead, because that's what he'll do. When he falls into the vat, you will push him down with a large stick and make him sink. Then you will throw more boiling water over his body. And that way you will drown your daughter's husband! Like a chicken, you will pluck his feathers. Remember that under no circumstances can he see your daughter. He's coming already; he's coming already! Put the water to boil!" said the Hummingbird and left.

The woman obeyed the little bird. She filled the vat with boiling water. Then she covered the opening with a mantle. The vat looked like a comfortable seat.

At that moment the Condor arrived at the door. It was true; his eyes were irritated, red, and burning. But he still acted haughty, ostentatious, and dignified.

"Please permit me to enter and pay you a visit," he said. "Has your daughter arrived? Are you aware that she has returned?" he asked.

"No, dear sir. My daughter has not returned to this house. She hasn't even arrived," the mother responded.

"No!" insisted the Condor. "She's here! I know she has arrived!" He made the mother feel guilty.

The woman kindly allowed him to enter and said to him, "Yes, dear sir. It is true. In a moment, I will return her to you. But please come in, rest and sit with us for a bit." Having said this, she guided him toward the sitting room. The Condor entered the house.

The woman led the Condor to the vat and said to him, "Please take a seat on this humble bench, on top of this mantle."

The Condor sat down and sunk into the vat! His body made a loud sound as it dropped into the water. Then the woman pushed him down even more with a large stick; she stuffed him to the bottom of the vat. Then she covered him with many large pitchers of boiling water.

The Condor looked like a poor chicken. Not even his feathers were feathers anymore. His body was bare and whitish; his legs, his wings, his neck, and his stomach were devoid of plumes. He looked like an old, naked rooster. His semblance of a great gentleman had been a mere appearance; but his true form was that of a condor.

After the death of the Condor, the parents, the daughter, and the child could finally live together peacefully. Their anguish and pain turned into joy, into real happiness.

And in this way, even today, this happiness endures in a village very far away, very far away.[57]

~~~

In this entertaining yet complex Andean folktale, the Condor and the Frog are intermediary shape-shifters who can assume the guise of a human being at will. The Condor changes his semblance to appeal sexually to the young woman, and the Frog adopts the form of the young woman in order to trick the Condor. The Andean condor (in Quechua, *kuntur*; scientific name, *Vultur gryphus*) is an inhabitant of the towering mountain peaks and the skies, the domain of the Upper World; yet, in this story, he deftly assumes a human disguise and walks in This World as an elegant gentleman, connecting both cosmological worlds. Similarly, the Andean highland frog (in Quechua, *k'ayra*, *k'ayrankulli*, or *ch'eqlla*) is often linked to rainwater and to the common Andean toad, *hanp'atu* (scientific name, *Bufo spinulosus Wiegmann* or *Rhinella spinulosa*).[58] The *hanp'atu* is thought to be a "chthonic earth-born creature"[59] of the Lower World, which hibernates underground during the dry season, starting in May, and reemerges above ground during the rainy season, starting in August.[60] Because of its dual nature of living above and below the ground, the *hanp'atu* is an inhabitant of both the Lower World (underworld) and This World and an effective mediator between the two.

With respect to the condor, it is worth noting that, unlike the stories about the imaginary *ukuku* (the Andean Boy-Bear), the tales about the mythological condor are quite accurate, in particular regarding its nesting and eating practices. Just as in the story of The Condor's Lover, the immense Andean condor nests among crevices and caves on the rocky Andean cliffs but does not make a nest for its egg. The female generally lays her egg at the edge of a cliff in a site similar to the one the Condor takes the young woman to in this story. The Andean condor is also a scavenger that feasts on carrion, the remains of large dead animals. Just as in The Condor's Lover, the condor gorges on the carcasses of dead animals but then may go several days without eating until it finds more food. This too is described in the story when the narrator comments that the young woman goes without food for several days until the Condor returns with more carcasses "from dead animals and decomposed flesh." This acute perception about the ways of the condor bears witness to the Native Andean peoples' intimate connection with this imposing bird that has lived side by side with them for millennia.

The indigenous peoples of the pre-Columbian Andes venerated the condor. The Incas dedicated a temple to this bird at *Machu Picchu* (meaning "Ancient Peak") with a carved rock on the floor in the form of a condor head and ruff, with natural boulders flaring above the rock shaped carefully to resemble the condor's outstretched wings. Due to the somewhat flattened surface and positioning of the condor rock, the Incas may have used it at Machu Picchu for making sacrificial offerings. Condors also appear in the iconography of other ancient Andean civilizations. For example, the ancient Chachapoyas, or People of the "Cloud Forest,"[61] who thrived in the dense cloud forest of the Amazonian region of the northern Peruvian Andes, carved a monolith in the image of a condor deity at their monumental fortress at Kuelap.[62] It is said that after they were conquered by the Incas, their representatives traveled to Cuzco and dressed as condors during the Inca feast of *Inti Raymi*, a solstice festival dedicated to the Sun god.[63]

Likewise, zoomorphic and anthropomorphic condor figures are also featured in the woven mantles of Paracas, the stonework of Chavín, and even in the Sun Gate at Tiwanaku, where forty-eight winged "condor-men" were carved around the central figure of the "staff" god holding two scepters. In similar fashion, the Nazca culture often depicted in its ceramics an "anthropomorphic, raptorial bird," denominated "Horrible Bird," which seemed to combine aspects of the condor and the hawk, both powerful birds of the Andean skies.[64] Sometimes the condor is also depicted, in a more recognizable form, on Nazca plates and painted ceremonial textiles.[65] Just as in many other Andean pre-Columbian cultures, it is likely the Nazcas viewed the condor "as a powerful spirit or force, the lord of the skies or a messenger to the mountain and water spirits."[66] In this role as messenger to the mountain deities and water spirits of the high mountain lakes, the condor acts as an intermediary between the human world and the world of the *Apus* or *Achachilas* (mountain gods); or between This World and the Upper World.[67]

Some contemporary Native Andean peoples still venerate the condor and include it as a participant in their festivals and rituals. For example, in Aymara propitiatory rituals directed at the *Achachilas* or *Mallkus* (mountain deities), the diviner asks the condor, which is closely affiliated with the spirit of the mountains, to "speak for" the mountain, possibly as an intermediary or as the physical embodiment of the mountain itself.[68] In Aymara the honorific for the condor and the mountain deity are the same—*Mallku.*

With respect to the other shape-shifter in our story, the Andean highland frog (*k'ayra*), the distinction between frog and toad is somewhat murky in the Quechua language. For example, the dictionary of the *Academia Mayor de la Lengua Quechua*, a collaborative work of numerous Quechua scholars, defines the generic term *hanp'atu* ("toad") as "toad and other [anuran] species," including varieties of "green frog[s]" (*k'ayra*) and "small, agile, mottle-colored toad[s]" (*ch'eqlla*) found in the Cuzco region.[69] Moreover, in the Andean oral tradition the frog is also thought to be related to the common toad.[70] So for purposes of this discussion, and coincident with Quechua usage, the use of the terms frog and toad is not intended to communicate any significant distinction.

Some Spanish chroniclers report that during the colonial period Andean healers and sorcerers used "live and dead toads" among the many "instruments and materials" for practicing their arts.[71] Some of these ancient practices continue to this day among native priests who practice white or black magic, or *brujería*.[72] Interestingly, in the case of the black arts, the sorcerers use the amphibian body in substitution for the human body. In many cases they dismember or disembowel the amphibian to transfer the "injury" to the intended human victim, who allegedly will die from the same injury or a related condition.[73] In such cases, the frog or the toad is being used as an intermediary agent or a medium between the sorcerer and his victim.[74]

In the Andes, black sorcerers are believed to derive their power from the devil (in Quechua, *saqra* or *supay*), *Santiago* (Spanish for "St. James" but now refers to the Andean god of "lightning"),[75] or from malevolent beings called *malignos*; thus, animals used in their practices are also now associated with the "diabolical" space of the Lower World. Anthropologist Jan van Kessel presumes that for the Aymaras, in particular, the puma, the lizard, and the toad may have been sacred symbols in their pre-Columbian religion, formerly associated with the grazing fields, or "second [ecological] zone" of the mountains, but that after the Conquest, with the arrival of the Christian missionaries, these animals were considered pagan idols and relegated to the Christian inferno, which the contemporary Aymaras synonymously identify with the Lower World.[76] Further, the Andean toad "has for a long time been associated with ill fortune; it is seen as a bad omen, and it is said that it was created by the devil."[77] The fact that the toad is also sometimes referred to as *saqra* ("devil")[78] is evidence that it is now strongly linked with the Lower World.

For both the Quechuas and the Aymaras, the frog and toad are strongly correlated with the presence or absence of water. Some Aymaras share the belief that if one removes a frog from a mountain spring or the alpine tundra, "the water could dry up, because it is said that this aquatic animal attracts water. That is why one must always take care of the frog."[79] As previously discussed, the *hanp'atu* toad burrows in the earth during the cold, dry season and later resurfaces during the warm, wet season. Because of this cyclical behavior pattern, the Quechuas call them *pacha-wawa*, "children of the earth."[80] When the toads reappear during the wet season, farmers observe their croaking patterns to forecast the future of their crops. "If in the months of September and October they croak day and night in great numbers, it is an augury that there will be much rain and, as a consequence, the crops will be abundant; but, if during these months they croak only a little and softly, it is a sign that it will not rain and that the frosts will be strong."[81]

Because drought and lack of water are ongoing concerns in many parts of the Andes, the appearance of these toads—which often reemerge in armies of thousands—symbolizes renewal, rebirth, and the return of water for agriculture. In much the same way as for the Quechuas, the toad for the Aymaras is a divinatory sign that rainwater is, or is soon to become, available. Anthropologist Alan Kolata describes an Aymara rain-calling ritual called *ch'uwa khiwxata* ("calling for rain, or clear liquid, from afar"), in which the community's religious leaders climb to the top of a hill where three springs meet. At the summit, they make offerings to *Pacha Mama*, the Andean Earth Mother, and to the guardian spirit of irrigation (*qarpa achachila*), pleading, crying, and imploring the spirit to bring them rains.[82] If the rains do not come, as a final resort the *yatiri* (diviner-priest) goes to a mountain peak known for its underground water and places a jar of three toads, swimming in freshwater, on top of the peak. Because of the burning sun, the toads croak and "cry" until the waters evaporate. The irrigation spirit allegedly takes pity on the toads and brings the much-needed rainwater to the community.[83]

The importance of water is particularly salient in the story of The Condor's Lover when the narrator makes a point of telling us that the young woman finds a spring of water in the vicinity of the cave. Effectively, he is telling us she can survive on the edge of the abysmal cliff, in a virtually uninhabitable region of the world, because there is life-giving water at her disposal. Moreover, the shape-shifting Frog lives in this mountain spring. Since the Frog (or toad) is associated with renewal, life-giving water, and rebirth, it is not surprising that shortly after discovering the spring the woman gives birth to a child. Renewal, rebirth, fertility, and fecundity are closely interrelated in Andean mythology.

The shape-shifting Frog in this story plays only a secondary role. He plays the part of the young woman to deceive the Condor into thinking his diligent wife is at home and is busy washing laundry. Then he gives the Condor the shock of his life as his alleged "wife" submerges in a pool and doesn't float up to the surface. The Frog picks the opportune moment to "drown" when the impatient Condor threatens to kick his wife for not responding to his needs immediately. The Frog's presence in the story also suggests he is connected with the arrival of the water that guaranteed the woman's survival among the barren cliffs—water she needed for drinking, cooking, and washing. Later, he shape-shifts into *her*, suggesting a strong symbolic identification with the young woman.

Unlike the Condor and the Frog, the Hummingbird is not an intermediary shape-shifter. He does not alter his avian appearance in the story. Nonetheless, like the Condor, the Hummingbird is also an intermediary traveler between the Upper World and This World, as exemplified by his comings and goings between the sky world—the realm of the mountain peaks and the Condor—and the home of the young woman's family. In many respects, the Hummingbird, like the Condor and the Frog, is also a trickster. Far from being altruistic, he has his own selfish reasons for helping the young woman and her family. At first he extorts sweets and *chancaca* from the young woman's mother in exchange for telling her where her daughter is. Later, he requisitions more sweets to bring her back home. By helping the young woman escape, the Hummingbird also sees another opportunity to create mischief. He goads the Condor into playing chase games in the sky by letting the Condor know, in very patent ways, that he is the one who carried the young woman back to her parents' home. The Hummingbird is also the character that orchestrates the deceptive incident with the Frog and coordinates the sequence of events that ultimately lead to the Condor's death.

The hummingbird of Andean folktales appears to have had some symbolic or religious significance in the pre-Columbian Andes. For example, figures of hummingbirds appear in the battle scenes of ancient Moche iconography, either "naturalistically, flying among Moche warriors, or as anthropomorphic warriors themselves."[84] It is also well known that one of the figures depicted in the ancient Nazca lines[85] of Peru is a hummingbird, so it is likely that at one time the hummingbird was worshipped or symbolically linked with Nazca ritual. Figures of hummingbirds also appear on Nazca ceramics.[86]

In view of this history, we should attach some importance to the fact that the hummingbird was chosen in this Quechua narrative to be the rescuer and savior of the young woman, and the medium through which she returns to her earthly home (*Kay Pacha* or "This World"). A recurring theme in Native Andean mythology is that except in some origin and creation myths, the dualism of the cosmos must be preserved, and different worlds must remain separate and distinct so as not to violate the cosmic order. In other words, the beings of the Upper World and Lower World must not cohabit, interfere, alter, or permanently conjoin with beings from This World; otherwise, dire consequences will ensue, owing to this cosmic violation.

In The Condor's Lover, the Condor violates this prohibition by seeking to bring a woman, a being from This World, to live permanently in the Upper World of the mountains and sky. He kidnaps her to live with him amidst the rocky cliffs and fathers a (human?) child destined to live in his altitudinous world. The Condor, for his own selfish objectives, disturbs the established order of the cosmos and suffers the ultimate punishment for his violation—he precipitates his own death. Likewise, we saw in the previous chapter that a man's efforts to cohabit with a star-girl, a being from the Upper World, also results in the death of their child "for unknown reasons" and the permanent loss of his star-wife, who decides to remain in the Upper World. There also exist a number of Andean stories in which beings from the Lower World, usually *gentiles* (ancestors) or demonic snakes, violate the cosmic order by bedding and impregnating human women. Their offspring usually die at birth, are born abnormal in some way, or are subsequently killed by the human world.[87]

Viewed from this cosmological perspective, it is perfectly understandable why the hummingbird was chosen as the designated intermediary in the story, to restore balance to the cosmos. The hummingbird is one of the smallest of birds; the condor is one of the largest in the Western hemisphere. The emerald hummingbird has colorful plumage; the condor has, for the most part, only black plumage. The hummingbird feeds on the sweet nectar of flowers; the condor feeds on the flesh of dead animals. The hummingbird makes its cuplike nest in trees, where it lays two small eggs. The condor has no nest and lays its egg on rocky cliffs. The hummingbird prefers to spend its time flying among the flowers, trees, and gardens of

This World. The condor favors the solitary existence of the Upper World among the mountains, rocks, and cliffs.

Yet both the hummingbird and condor are great flyers and travel easily between worlds. The hummingbird can travel astounding distances in its migrations; the condor often travels more than one hundred miles a day in search of its next meal. Whereas in the story the Condor threatens to eat the Hummingbird (a very real possibility given that large, hungry birds sometimes prey on small birds), the Hummingbird plays several tricks on the Condor to show that he is "not food." Although the Hummingbird travels the length of the Condor's digestive tract (from mouth to anus), he demonstrates to the Condor that he is a *nonfood*. Within the dualistic framework of Andean mythology and cosmology, the Hummingbird is everything that the Condor is not, and he is also not what the Condor purports him to be (food or prey); thus, in this story, the Hummingbird is the most suitable character to mediate between worlds and reinstitute the cosmic equilibrium the Condor has disturbed.

In addition to stories about the mouse, the condor, and the frog or toad, there are numerous other Native Andean folktales that depict other animals as shape-shifters. Among the Aymaras, for instance, the fox is best known for his shape-shifting antics and usually goes by the name *Antonio* (Anthony). In the typical Aymara folktale, a fox assumes the form of a human being and falls in love with a beautiful woman. Later, he uses trickery and deception to win her affection, and then he asks the woman's parents for her hand in marriage. Sometimes the ruse is not discovered until shortly before or during the wedding, when the groom inadvertently transforms back into a fox and scurries away in humiliation,[88] and sometimes his secret is uncovered after the marriage is underway and he misbehaves.[89] There are also a few rare tales in which the fox entices a married woman to commit adultery, but then he gets his just deserts.[90]

For example, in "The Fox Who Changed into a Man,"[91] the fox is an animal by day and a handsome young man by night. One evening he meets a beautiful young woman at a dance, and he falls head over heels in love with her. The fox, disguised as a man, asks for the woman's hand in marriage, and she introduces him to her parents, who take a liking to him and consent to the proposal. Assuming his human form, the fox starts courting the young woman and sleeps at her house every night. However, the fact that he always leaves before daybreak arouses the family's suspicions, so they decide to lock all the doors and windows to see what will happen the next day. When daylight comes and the fox cannot escape, he reverts back to his animal form. Everyone is astonished to see the transformation and the fox runs away, never to return. In the end, the fox dies of heartbreak and sadness.

What these shape-shifting intermediaries of Andean stories have in common is that they function in, and possess characteristics belonging to, other worlds and This World, including the animal and human worlds, as well as the worlds of nature and culture. In a manner similar to the anthropomorphic intermediaries, each shape-shifter is endowed with animal and human characteristics, as well as human and supernatural qualities. This combination of attributes allows the intermediary free movement and liberal access to more than one world or cosmological realm. However, as previously discussed, a recurring tenet in Native Andean stories is that the dualism of the cosmos must be preserved, and different worlds must remain separate and distinct so as not to disturb the cosmic balance.

If one examines these stories in symbolic terms, the sexual act may represent the symbolic union or integration of two distinct worlds, such as the earth (This World) and the sky (Upper World), the animal world and the human world, nature and culture, and *hanan* ("upper") and *hurin* ("lower"). Such a union or integration often produces fertility, as evidenced by the birth of a living child. However, in cosmological terms this union violates the notion of Andean dualism, which is premised on maintaining the separate coexistence of opposing or complementary elements and principles, unless they are "properly" united in Andean ritual. (Origin and creation myths are an exception that will be discussed more fully in a subsequent chapter.) When this prescription is violated, this alters the existing order of the cosmos, often producing disastrous results. In the story of The Mouse-Husband, a child dies on account of the forbidden union. In the tale of The Condor's Lover, the Condor is killed in a vat of boiling water. In The Fox Who Changed into a Man, the fox dies of heartbreak, and so forth. These "deaths" or "sacrifices" could be viewed as the negative effects of disrupting and creating an imbalance in the cosmic order.

Nevertheless, in some stories the balance may be restored if the characters return to their respective worlds or states of being. For instance, in the tale of The She-Calf the young man who loves the She-Calf symbolically ventures to the edge of civilization, the boundary between the human world (villages, representing culture) and the animal world (the jungle, representing nature) in order to find his beloved, an intermediary who travels in both worlds. Once he satisfies the gatekeepers of the animal world (the condors) by passing a test and making an offering to a mountain god, the young man is allowed to enter the animal world to claim her. However, to come back into the human world she must, by necessity, change form, discarding her calf-like appearance in the animal world (thereby breaking the spell) and transforming herself back into a woman to live with her husband in the human world.[92]

THE PRESERVATION OF DUALISM

The Native Andeans divide the cosmos into opposite or complementary elements such as masculine and feminine, day and night, earth and sky, still water and rapidly moving water, wet and dry, high and low, sweet and salty, upper and lower, and many other such dualities. This dualism forms the structure and foundation of the Native Andean belief systems and penetrates almost every aspect of life. The concept that dualism must be preserved is also a recurring theme in Andean mythology. My many discussions with Native Andeans lead me to believe that this concept is related to their notion that everything has its own place in the cosmological world, as prescribed by their ancient customs and traditions. Moreover, humanity cannot violate the order without creating an imbalance in the cosmos. Viewed in this way, life is a fragile process of trying to maintain harmony between opposing or complementary elements—such as feminine and masculine principles—and maintaining the integrity of what the cosmos originally intended. In other words, what these stories prescribe is preserving the balancing principles that structure and govern our world, a concept known as *yanantin* in Quechua and *yanani* in Aymara. I might add that some Native Andeans also express disdain for what they perceive as our blatant Western disregard for this sacred balance.

Yanantin has been described as "complementary duality,"[93] "two equal but complementary elements that are always found together,"[94] and "a relation of mirrored symmetry [making] it possible to envisage an ideal of unity between the sexes."[95] With respect to the relation of *hanan* (upper) and *hurin* (lower) in the colonial Huarochirí Manuscript, it has also been conceptualized as "two halves [comprising] a firm totality, sanctioned by myths that are repeated from one generation to the next."[96] The word ending *–ntin* also denotes inclusion, totality, and union:

> The term *yanantin* is made up of the stem *yana-* ("help-"; cf. *yanapay*, "help") and the termination *–ntin*: according to Solá (1978), *–ntin* is "inclusive in nature, with implications of totality, spatial inclusion of

one thing in another, or identification of two elements as members of the same category." Yanantin can thus be strictly translated as "helper and helped united to form a single category."[97]

Moreover, from our reading of Andean mythology, it is not enough to "couple" or bring together two opposing or complementary principles or elements without regard to cosmic balance and order. For there to be *yanantin*, there must also be a "proper" and harmonious pairing of opposites/complements, as observed in Andean rites, rituals, and traditions.

The doctrines of preservation of dualism and cosmic balance permeate almost every aspect of Native Andean life. This is an ancient notion that is expressed in Andean indigenous cultures of both the past and the present. For example, during the colonial period the Quechua language distinguished between masculine and feminine words, as determined by the gender of the speaker. In his colonial chronicle, the half-Inca chronicler Garcilaso de la Vega explains that an Inca father would address his children as *churi*, whereas a mother could only use the word *huahua* (also spelled *wawa* or *guagua* and pronounced "wah-wah"). In this manner, clarifies Garcilaso, the language differentiated between words that were "appropriate for men and others for women," so that they could utilize them without confusion.[98] Put differently, the duality and separateness of the sexes, as manifested by the use of appropriate gender-based language, was considered important and duly preserved in Inca culture. Some of these gender-based distinctions are still observed in contemporary Quechua.[99]

Even the daily tasks of Native Andean people express this duality. For instance, in the town of Misiminay, Peru, Gary Urton observed that "men attempt to increase their capital by bringing *trago* [hard liquor from outside the community], while women do so by preparing and selling *chicha* [maize beer made within the community]."[100] He adds that it would be inappropriate for men and women to perform the task of the other because of the gender-based nature of each task. "[A] substance . . . *made* within the community and sold," would be considered a female task, whereas one "*bought* outside the community and sold," would be considered strictly a male task.[101]

Likewise, among the Quechua-speaking Macha of northern Potosí, Bolivia, anthropologist Tristan Platt observed *ecological* duality. According to Platt, the Macha culture adheres to "regional segmentation" between puna ("cold region" or "high country") and valley ("hot region" or "low country").[102] This affects various aspects of their economy and culture, including the division of products. For instance, Macha farmers could not conceive of producing *chuño* (freeze-dried potatoes) in the valley, even though it was technically feasible to do so, because *chuño*, in their estimation, could "only [be] made in the puna."[103] There was also universal agreement among the farmers that failure to uphold this dual distinction in their ecological exchange might cause their other crops to fail.[104]

Dualism also formed the foundation of Inca religion. According to some Inca origin myths, the first mythological Inca rulers, Manco Capac and Mama Ocllo Huaco, were children of the Sun (*Inti*) and the Moon (*Killa* or *Quilla*), male and female celestial deities, respectively, who were also siblings and spouses. Consequently, the Inca ruler and his queen, the Coya, were the male and female progeny and counterparts of these gods on earth. One of the honorary titles of the Inca was *intip churin*, meaning "son of the Sun," and the Inca presided over all major festivals dedicated to the Sun god, including the solstice festivals of *Inti Raymi* ("Feast of the Sun") and *Capac Inti Raymi* ("Great or Royal Feast of the Sun"). The Coya, in like manner, was closely associated with the Moon and oversaw the major festivals honoring the Moon goddess, including *Coya Raymi Killa* ("Month of the Feast of the Queen"), celebrated during the September equinox.[105]

Today, the same duality holds true in many Native Andean cultures and communities. Among the Quechua and Aymara communities, for example, Mother Earth, *Pacha Mama*, is a personified female deity and is generally paired with the male celestial divinities associated with meteorological phenomena, such as lightning, rain, thunder, hail, and snow, known by a variety of names across the Andes.[106] *Pacha Mama* is also sometimes partnered with the masculine spirits of the mountains and mountain peaks, called *Apus* or *Wamanis* in Quechua, and *Achachilas* or *Mallkus* in Aymara. She represents the divinized earth, mother of people and crops, as well as the feminine occupations, such as spinning, weaving, and pottery,[107] whereas her male partner is usually associated with mountain heights and the heavens, which in much of Andean mythology and cosmology (except Amazonian) are considered masculine elements. This is also consistent with the findings of anthropologist Frank Salomon with respect to the colonial Huarochirí Manuscript, written in the Quechua language. Salomon concludes that in the Manuscript, the "earth has predominantly female associations and water predominantly male... [and that also] altitude and motion connote maleness, while depth and stability are associated with femaleness."[108]

Another salient example of Andean dualism, and the proper pairing of *Pacha Mama* with her male "groom," is found in the Quechua canal-cleaning festival of *Yarqa Aspiy*, which generally takes place in September, at the time of the spring equinox in the southern hemisphere.[109] In one such festival in the town of Chuschi, Peru, the Quechua people clean and clear the irrigation canals of debris, rocks, sedimentation, and weeds, and "open" and plough the land in preparation for planting. Groups of Quechua men climb to the mountaintops, the home of the resident *Wamanis*, or male mountain spirits, where they make offerings of coca leaves and *chicha*, a maize beer. Then they descend to the valley, carrying heavy "crosses," perhaps as phallic reminders of the fertility of the *Wamanis*, who will be the generous benefactors of the much-needed irrigation waters. In time, the "open" furrows of *Pacha Mama* will receive the foamy irrigation waters (symbolic semen) of the *Wamanis*, culminating in a symbolic sexual act of conception between the male and female elements[110] of the high mountains and the earth. The proper and symbolic union of the two will fertilize the land and yield abundant crops for the community.

Interestingly, in the belief system of the Macha of Potosí, *Pacha Mama* is coupled with *Pacha Tata* ("Father Earth"), and the culture also recognizes other cosmological pairs: male mountain peaks (*jurq'us*) with certain female mountain springs (*warmi jurq'us*), who are considered their "wives"; the sun (*Tata Inti*, "father sun") is coupled with the moon (*Mama Killa*, "mother moon"); and certain male rocks are partnered with certain female rocks (collectively considered *huacas* or *wak'as*).[111] Duality is even observed in their prognostications. If a fox is spotted "going uphill in September (sowing time)," the Macha predict "the year will be productive on the puna [high country]; but if the fox is seen going downhill, the year will be good in the valley."[112] In marriage, the Macha also demonstrate a strong "preference for interregional marriage between puna and valley."[113]

This insistence on preserving duality, and properly bringing male and female aspects together, is also observed in Andean ritual. It is important to note that in the Andes, the fertility of the earth and the fecundity of women are strongly associated with the "proper" union of the masculine and feminine elements, as prescribed by ritual. For instance, in the Quechua festival of *Yarqa Aspiy*, anthropologist Billie Jean Isbell notes that "women are purified and [made] ready for conception" in much the same way that the earth (the feminine principle) is prepared to receive the life-giving waters of the *Wamanis*, or male mountain spirits.[114] In like manner, anthropologist Olivia Harris describes the "ritual insistence" on male-female coupling at a symbolic level in the rituals performed by the Laymi, an Aymara-speaking people who are close neighbors of the Macha.

They must perform most ritual acts together, and in cases where a ritual sponsor has no spouse, he or she must find a sexual complement from among his or her close kin in order for the ritual to be performed properly. At a central moment in many rituals the pair stand together in between the seated women and men of the community, the man on the right and the woman on the left, and together pour libations for the ongoing fertility of all: the crops, livestock, and human beings. The survival of the community is thus symbolically incarnated in the conjugal pair, who both directly reproduce its members and whose labor brings earth and animals to fruit.[115]

This symbolic pairing of complementary elements is also evident in Andean mythology. In various Native Andean stories, we have seen that the "improper" union of complementary elements or worlds results in calamitous consequences such as death, violence, and sacrifice. Yet another undesirable consequence—one of paramount importance in the Andes—is infertility. Many, if not most, of the Native Andean rural communities, including those of the Quechuas and the Aymaras, are agricultural, pastoral, and/or mining economies, heavily dependent on the physical labor of both parents and children. In such communities, infertility is viewed as a sign of grave misfortune and is sometimes even considered a curse upon the ill-starred family. In the following Quechua story of "The Eagles Who Raised a Girl," the punishment of infertility is meted out by the sky-dwelling eagles in response to an improper union of earth and sky.

The Eagles Who Raised a Girl

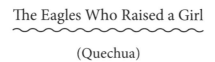

(Quechua)

There was once a postman who delivered letters to all the villages. Letters to different villages, here and there. One time, while on one of his delivery trips, the calf of his leg started feeling very heavy. The calf grew and grew, and finally the postman said, "What's happening with my leg? I wonder what I have?" Well, even in that state, he continued walking and walking, but his calf started dragging closer and closer to the ground.

Then the man said, "Jeez, what on earth do I have here? I can't even walk!" He sat down alongside the road. "I wonder what I have here," he said and took out his knife. "Maybe it's pus. Who in the hell knows?" So he cut it open. When he cut his calf open, there was a baby girl inside. What rubbish! No wonder it felt so heavy. He took the baby out and threw her into some thorny bushes nearby. He stood up and continued quickly along the road.

The little girl stayed in the bush, crying. One could hear her newborn cry, "Unggaah, unggaah, unggaah."

An eagle and her mate were circling around those parts and saw the little girl. When they saw her they said, "What should we do here?"

"Come on, let's take her," said the female eagle.

"Take her?" replied the [other] eagle. "Ah, but what do we have to feed this little baby?"

"It doesn't matter," answered the female eagle. "We're going to find some way to raise her. Look how pretty she is!"

So they took her and made a hole for her in the cliffs, a pretty big hole. That's where they took the little girl. But as she grew, the eagles had to make the hole larger and larger. She learned to walk very well. She eventually became a lady, a young woman.

The eagles traveled all over to get her food. They gathered all kinds of food. They made every effort to raise her well. Then she became a lady, a grown up young woman.

They brought a little parrot to play with her. They also brought a kitten and other little animals to play with her. They made a little fence so that she wouldn't fall into the river. There the young woman had a very, very good time. The eagles raised the young woman with a lot of affection.

The hair on one side of the young woman's head was gold; on the other side, silver. The eagles counted all her strands of hair and combed her hair with their beaks. They counted the strands of hair one by one, and they would leave her there until they came back.

She was already fairly grown up, and she would watch the river below. But there was no way to get down. The son of a king always went there, to that spot, to bathe. One day, he was bathing. As he bathed, he had to put his face close to the water to wash it. When he looked at the water, he saw a pretty face. "But how? Is this my face?" he asked, touching it. But no, it was not his. It belonged to someone else. "What could this be?" he asked himself. It didn't occur to him to look above.

The next day, he returned to the same place to bathe. While he was bathing, he saw the same face again. As he washed himself, he said, "How beautiful! How beautiful she is!" He looked above him and immediately realized that there was a pretty young lady watching him. "It can't be! I will do whatever it takes to get her out. I'll take her with me, and this young lady and I will get married! We will get married! But why is she there? Is she enchanted or what?" he asked himself. "How did she climb up there? The cliff is extremely high!"

He brought over a ladder and climbed up. Once he got there he asked, "At what time is your mother usually home?"

"My parents leave at such and such time," answered the young woman, "so come at such and such time."

At the designated time, the young man climbed the ladder, and the two went to the back to talk. The young woman was quite pretty, beautiful really.

"How did you get here?" he asked.

"[The eagles brought me here.] I don't know how my parents would have raised me. I don't know my parents. The eagles are my parents, but they're terribly mean," she said, "really mean. My father is terribly mean."

"What a shame," said the young man.

Then they played together. While they were playing by the window, he pulled out a strand of her hair. So she said to him, "Get down! Go now! My parents are about to arrive!" He climbed down as quickly as he could and folded his ladder. He hid the ladder in some bushes so he could return the next day.

Another day, they were talking. The young man again pulled out a strand of hair from the other side of her head and took it with him. Later, when the eagles counted the strands of hair, one was missing. "Where is your strand of hair? Who pulled it out?" they asked.

"We were playing around, and my little parrot cut it off," she replied. The eagles killed the little parrot.

"You've killed him!"

"Do you think that we've raised you with all this affection for this? So that a little parrot can cut off strands of your hair? Where is the strand now?"

"The wind blew it down to the river," she replied.

Well, then, on the following day the same thing happened. The young man took one of her strands of hair from the other side this time, one made of silver.

When the eagles returned the next day to comb her hair with their beaks, another strand was missing. "Where is your strand of hair?" they asked.

"I was playing with my kitten," she responded. And so the eagles took the kitten and threw it off the cliff. They killed it.

There was no one left for her to blame if the young man climbed up and took another strand of her hair. "Now what do I do?" the young woman asked herself. Then she thought, "It doesn't matter. I'm going to get married anyway. I'm already getting my wedding dress and everything ready. Tomorrow at dawn, I'm going to leave."

The young man set a wedding date with his parents. The parents of the boy said, "Our son is going to get married well. A beautiful young woman is going to marry a prince." So they arranged everything to look very pretty. They swept the streets and placed flowers all over the town. A very good band went to receive her.

"The bride will arrive soon," said the townspeople. Everyone in the whole town had already heard the news. "It's lovely that the groom's father has prepared everything for her arrival!" they said. They walked and walked as far as a distant prairie. "Where is she? Has she shown up yet? Where is she? Has she shown up yet?" everyone asked.

They had rolled out a carpet for her for when she entered the town. There was a carpet and baskets of flowers everywhere. But the girl failed to appear.

When the bride and groom were about to enter the town, the eagle appeared. "What? Did I raise you for this?" the eagle shouted. Whack! She slapped the young woman across one side of her face, and that side turned into a donkey. Whack! She slapped her across the other side, and that side turned into a horse. Nothing was left of her face, not even her hair, nothing. One side of her face was a horse, and the other, a donkey.

The young man took her looking like that to his town. When the king saw her, he said, "How ugly! Is this what I have worked so hard to prepare for? With so much fanfare?"

"He's planning on marrying this one? The son of our king? The son of our king is marrying this one? The one with the donkey face?" mocked the townspeople. Everyone was insulting them. The girl was crying; her tears were falling like drops of hail.

The young man wanted to take her to his home, but the father threw them out. "Look how much shame you have caused me! You were planning to marry this one? What would the other kings say? How could I introduce my friends to this one!"

How sad! He threw them out, and they made a little hut for themselves outside the town. That's where they lived. They slept in a tiny bed. They bought only a single little pot. She didn't even know how to cook. She didn't know how to do anything. The boy had to bring everything to the house. He had to be a day laborer because his parents had kicked him out of their home with only the shirt on his back.

The wives of his older brothers, on the other hand, were— wow!— elegant. One time, the king's birthday was approaching. And the wives said, "Should we go? Let's go to the donkey woman's place. Let's see what she's making for our father-in-law! We've ordered some beautiful shirts to be made. And what could she possibly give him? Should we see?" They went inside the little hut. "Sister, sister, we've come to visit. Sister," they asked, "so what are you making for our father-in-law's birthday?"

"It's nothing. I'm just sewing this shirt by hand, of coarse cotton cloth. I don't even have a sewing machine. I hope he will accept it. I hope he will, hope he will, but I doubt it." She was making him a little shirt out of coarse cotton cloth.

When the wives stepped out they said, "How ugly!" And they spat on the ground. "How ugly! Our father-in-law is going to put that shirt on? How ugly! I bet he'll just throw that cotton shirt right back at her face!" And they continued laughing like that all the next day up until the party.

Oh, you wouldn't believe! The sisters-in-law doused their shirts in perfume and sent them to their father-in-law on a tray. They were competing with one another.

The couple had a servant, a young *cholito* [mestizo]. The young woman said to the servant, "Take this. Give it to the king." She had folded her handmade shirt in a little matchbox. "Give him this," she instructed.

Meanwhile, the father-in-law had tried on one of the other shirts. For heaven's sake! It wasn't made for his body. He tried on another one. That one didn't fit him either. He got wrapped up inside of it. When he put on yet another one, he said, "These good-for-nothing women don't even know how to sew!" When he saw the young servant, he asked, "And you? What do you want?"

"Sir, my mistress sent me to bring you this. The lady with the donkey face sent me with this."

"Ahhhh! What tacky thing are you bringing me? Bring it over, let's see." He received the little matchbox. Inside the box was a beautiful shirt, nicely folded, the size of a little thumbnail. "Oh, it's beautiful!" He put it on. The neck, the body, the sleeves fit him perfectly. He put it on.[116]

In the hut, the couple was talking. The young man said, "What if we invite them over?"

"If you want to," she replied.

"Come on, then, let's go," said the young man.

"No. I don't want to cause your parents any more embarrassment. I don't ever want to go there again."

"Come on, let's go, just in case. [I don't mean my parents.] Let's ask your parents for forgiveness." Then the two started walking toward that place, arm in arm.

They found the eagle circling around. Crying, they asked the eagle for forgiveness.

"So, this is what you wanted, right? This is what I raised you for? This is why I pulled you out of the thorny bushes? I raised you with so much sacrifice, so that you would do this to me? [But still,] I forgive you," she said.

Whack! The eagle slapped her across the face on one side with all her strength, and the young woman became beautiful again. Whack! She slapped her across the face again, on the other side, and the same thing happened: she changed back into a beautiful young woman. Her hair shone again of gold and silver. Both sides shone.

She said, "Ahhh!" Even her clothes were beautiful. She put on the bride's dress she had made. She also had another dress made for the king's party.

After she had changed back, the young man asked his father, "Dad, may I bring my fiancée over?"

"Yuck! You're really going to bring that donkey-faced woman into this house?"

"No, Dad," he replied, "she has already asked her parents for forgiveness."

"It's probably better that you invite her parents."

"Couldn't she just come in?" he asked.

"Bring her in, then."

Then the young man brought her in. Wow! The girl was beautiful!

The wives of the older brothers were green with envy. "Did he like our shirts, or what? Let's see. He's wearing the shirt that she sent him, and ours are just thrown away anywhere!"

The father of the young man said, "Well, now you can get married." When the party was finished, they prepared the young woman for the wedding.

Once again, they sent out invitations. They ordered dresses to be made for the bride one by one. Ah! And there was a ball. While everyone danced, pearls dropped from the bosom of the young woman. The wives of the brothers-in-law were picking them up off the floor. "How could this be?" they asked.

So they took the bride's servant to the kitchen. "Hey, you! Hey, you! What kind of makeup is your mistress wearing?"

"I don't think she's wearing any," he replied. "She took a handful of peeled potato skins and put them down her neck. She put them in her bosom, inside her dress."

So the sisters-in-law did the same thing. They put potato skins inside their dresses, and as they started dancing, the potato skins were falling off of them.

Their husbands said, "What are these women doing?" They grabbed them and took them outside. "What kind of trick are you trying to pull?"

"We haven't put anything on."

"And this? And this? What is this? What is it?" Each one of them hit his wife. Meanwhile, the bride looked beautiful.

Finally, when all of this ended, they got ready for the wedding. They made all the preparations for the wedding. Every single one of the guests came. They called for the best priest, everything. Finally, they were married.

I was making the rounds at the wedding too, helping out. And I was bringing you back some lunch—some stew—but the dog ate it.[117]

～～

This remarkable Andean story highlights the "improper" union between the earthly prince, an inhabitant of This World, and the eagle's daughter, who was adopted by the Upper World. Andean dualism also comes into play as girl meets boy, high meets low, and the upper (*hanan*) sky encounters the lower (*hurin*) terrestrial world below. (Here *hanan* and *hurin*, lowercased, are used as relative terms. They should not be confused with *Hanan Pacha* and *Ukhu Pacha*, meaning Upper and Lower Worlds.)

The young girl's nascent fertility is also captured in the image of the gold and silver hair. Gold, in some Native Andean societies, is correlated with the male sun, and silver is associated with the female moon.[118] Together, the masculine sun and feminine moon coexist in the young woman's hair in perfect balance, harmony, and equality (*yanantin*), until the prince disrupts that fragile balance by "plucking" the strands of her hair, which has obvious sexual connotations.

Due to the illicit affair, the earth and the sky have formed an improper union. Likewise, male and female, nature and culture, the human world and the animal world, and *hanan* and *hurin* have come together and integrated in an improper fashion, breaching the cosmic prohibition against the improper union of complementary elements. Dualism has not been preserved, and this leads to the eagle's punishment—the girl's symbolic infertility, signified by the horse-donkey face, which together comprise an infertile "mule." However, once the girl has been pardoned by her adoptive parents—the sky eagles—and the balance of the cosmos is reestablished, the girl is allowed to return to This World, the place of her beginnings. She relinquishes her adoption into the Upper World and reclaims her position in This World, thereby gaining readmission into human culture and reinstating her rightful place in human society. Then, with the blessing of the sky elements, the girl regains her beauty and fertility. Her female body, teeming with fecundity, is reaffirmed as the pearls, or symbolic ova, spill out from her youthful bosom at the prenuptial celebration.

CHAPTER SUMMARY

In this chapter we have introduced the concepts of intermediaries, dualism, and preservation of dualism, which are fundamental ideas and recurring themes in Andean mythology and cosmology. Each Andean myth presents a duality, an opposition, or a disjunction that produces tension and conflict in the story. However, each myth also presents an intermediary character, such as an anthropomorphic being or a shape-shifter, who attempts to bridge such duality or disjunction. For example, the Andean Boy-Bear (*ukuku*) is an anthropomorphic being, part boy and part bear, who figures prominently in Andean folktales, festivals, and rituals. He expresses a range of behaviors associated with human adolescence and acts as a mediating agent between childhood and adulthood, and between the world of nature and the world of culture. Many Andean intermediary tales also evince strong sexual symbolism and aspects of the Oedipus complex.

Intermediary characters in Andean mythology also have the ability to function in, or to possess characteristics belonging to, different worlds. For instance, in many Quechua stories the shape-shifting condor, a creature of the skies and Upper World, typically has the ability to disguise himself as a human and interact in This World. Andean dualism, however, is premised on the notion that opposing or complementary elements must remain separate and distinct unless "properly" united in Andean ritual. This harmonious and complementary pairing, which denotes inclusion, totality, and integration, is called *yanantin* in Quechua and *yanani* in Aymara. Except in some origin myths, the "improper" union of complementary or opposing elements produces dire consequences in Andean stories. It is for this reason that intermediaries—such as condors, frogs, lizards, bulls, and other beings of the animal world—can alter the cosmic balance by having sexual relations with (human) women. Theirs is an improper union, occurring outside of ritual, which violates Andean balancing principles and the preservation of dualism. These prohibited relationships often produce dire consequences such as death, sacrifice, infertility, violence, and other calamities in the story.

4

$\sim$

pachacuti

The Cycle of Pachacuti

Modern and pre-Columbian Native Andean myths describe many creations or ages of the world. This idea stems from an ancient Andean belief that the world has been created and destroyed many times, and that following each destruction, or cataclysmic event, a new world is born out of the chaos. In the Quechua language of many Native Andeans, this cyclical concept of successive destructions and creations of the world is called *pachacuti*, from the union of the word *pacha*, signifying time-space, age, world, or earth; and *cuti* (also spelled *kuti*), meaning inversion, revolution, or turning over, around, or upside down. In essence, *pachacuti* expresses the inversion of time-space within a cyclical framework of destruction and creation.

The ancient Andean peoples greatly feared the prospect of a *pachacuti*, because it signified the end of the existing world and the destruction of humanity. Many pre-Columbian creation myths describe the end of the world by fire, deluge, petrification, earthquake, or other cataclysm,[1] usually brought on by angry deities, and invariably followed by a new creation, a new age of the world, or a new "sun." However, the end of the world is not a theme confined to pre-Columbian mythology; it also permeates contemporary Native Andean myths.

In recent decades, Native Andeans have also embraced the concept of a historical or symbolic *pachacuti*, which refers to a cataclysmic historical or cultural transformation that drastically alters the lives of the Native Andean people. For example, the Spanish Conquest of Peru, the indigenous insurrections against the Spanish colonial authorities in the late eighteenth

91

century, and the Bolivian Revolution and land reform of 1952–1964[2] are some of the historical events that, from an Andean indigenous perspective, dramatically transformed the lives of the Native Andean people and are strongly identified with *pachacuti*.[3] Some also view the election of Evo Morales, the first indigenous president of Bolivia, as a historical milestone and *pachacuti* for all the native peoples of the Americas.[4]

In pre-Columbian times, *pachacuti* concerned the destruction of this world. The writings of the colonial Spanish and mestizo chroniclers indicate that even after the Spanish Conquest, Native Andeans continued to practice certain ancient rituals and customs to prevent the occurrence of a *pachacuti*. In the seventeenth century the Spanish colonial priest-chronicler Bernabé Cobo witnessed firsthand the Incas' response to a lunar eclipse, which they equated with a potential *pachacuti*. Of this custom Cobo wrote:

> They said that when there was an eclipse of the Moon a [mountain] lion or a serpent was attacking in order to tear her apart, and for that reason they shouted at the top of their voices and whipped their dogs so that they would bark and howl. The men made ready for war by blowing their trumpets, beating their drums, and yelling as loud as they could. They hurled arrows and spears at the Moon, and they made menacing gestures with their spears, as if they were going to wound the lion and the serpent. They said that this was done to frighten the lion and the serpent so that they would not tear the Moon apart. This they did because they understood that if the lion accomplished his aim, the world would be left in darkness.[5]

The mestizo chronicler Garcilaso de la Vega elaborated on the significance of this event. He explained that during a lunar eclipse the Incas believed the moon "was ill" and that if she darkened completely, "she would die and fall from the sky, killing everyone below; and the world would come to an end."[6]

Nearly four centuries after these accounts, during my childhood in Bolivia I witnessed similar events in my hometown of Cochabamba. During a lunar eclipse I saw Native Andeans beating on metal pots and pans with an assortment of kitchen utensils. The object was to make as much noise as possible to chase away the imaginary animal or illness threatening to overtake the moon. The men and women blew on whistles, shouted at the top of their voices, and sometimes tied their dogs to posts and whipped them until they howled.[7] At the time I did not understand the reason behind this practice, but my observations were remarkably similar to those of Garcilaso and Cobo during the early Spanish colonial period. Now I realize the Native Andeans of my childhood were continuing the ancient custom of their ancestors, attempting to forestall an impending *pachacuti*, which they believed might annihilate this world and all its inhabitants.

Similarly, the Incas and other pre-Columbian Andean peoples made sacrificial offerings, including human offerings, to their deities in order to appease them and to prevent them from meting out punishments that might result in a *pachacuti*. For example, according to Garcilaso de la Vega, the Incas believed that during a solar eclipse the Sun god was angry at them for some transgression committed against him, and that is why "his face darkened... [revealing] that some grave punishment would befall them."[8] Likewise, the indigenous colonial chronicler Felipe Guaman Poma de Ayala explained that the Incas made offerings such as gold, silver, llamas, guinea pigs, rabbits, shells, crops, coca leaves, fine textiles, and even "innocent children" to their deities during important religious festivals in order to prevent flooding, hunger, pestilence, disease, and drought, among other ills.[9] Bernabé Cobo cited similar reasons for such offerings.[10] From the perspective of the Incas, any of these pernicious events might obliterate the empire and initiate a *pachacuti*.

Making offerings to the deities or *huacas* to gain their favor was a daily task in the Inca Empire. In this respect, much like other pre-Columbian Andean peoples, the Incas were a very devout religious people who took great care in their sacrifices. By all accounts, even the smallest shrines always received devotional offerings.

Even the Christian extirpators, who overtly condemned the "pagan" practices of the Incas, could not deny the Incas' profound devotion to their religion and the rigorous discipline with which they practiced it.[11] However, it appears that the Incas adhered very strictly to their religious practices, at least in part, to keep their deities placated, thereby avoiding the possibility of a *pachacuti*.

The following Inca creation myth illustrates the Andean concept of *pachacuti* and depicts the kind of cataclysmic event the Incas might have feared. It was recorded in 1573 by the colonial priest Cristóbal de Molina ("El Cuzqueño") in his chronicle *Fábulas y ritos de los incas* ("Fables and Rites of the Incas"). The narrative explains how the Creator god, whom the Incas named *Viracocha* (also spelled *Wiracocha* or *Wiraqucha*, meaning "Sea Fat" or "Sea Foam" in Quechua), created the many peoples and nations of the world on the shores of Lake Titicaca at the ancient site of Tiahuanaco.[12] In this myth, the cycle of *pachacuti* commences when a powerful deluge destroys the existing world, and "in it [perish] all peoples and all creation"; thereafter, the Creator molds a new creation out of clay, completing the cycle of *pachacuti* and marking a new age for humankind.

Origin of the Incas

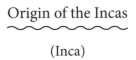

(Inca)

During the life of Mango Capac, who was the first Inca, when they began boasting and calling themselves Children of the Sun, and at the inception of idolatry and adoration of the Sun, they received news of the deluge. They say that in it perished all peoples and all creation. The deluge occurred in such a way that the waters rose above the highest mountains in the world, so that nothing remained alive except for one man and one woman who remained [hidden] in the box of a drum. After the waters receded, the wind blew these two to Tiahuanaco, which is located about seventy leagues, more or less, from Cuzco. Of all things, the Creator ordered them to stay there as *mitima[e]s* [transplants or colonists].

From there, at Tiahuanaco the Creator began to create the peoples and nations that exist in this land today. He made every nation out of clay and painted the garments and clothing each one was to have and wear. And those that were to have hair he painted with hair, and those with cut hair he painted with cut hair. And when his creation was finished, he gave to each nation the language it would speak, the songs it would sing, and the seeds and foods it would sow. And when he finished painting and creating the said nations and bundles of clay, he gave each one life and spirit, to men and women alike, and ordered them to sink beneath the ground, each nation by itself.

Then he told them that from there each nation would emerge from the parts and places of the earth that he instructed. And, in that way, they say that some emerged from caves, others from mountains, others from fountains, others from lakes, others from the bottoms of trees, and other such places in that manner. And after emerging and [their people spreading and] multiplying from the said locations, each such place was designated as the origin of each lineage. They constructed *guacas* [shrines or holy places] and temples on those sites, in memory of the first of their lineage who had proceeded from there.

For that reason, and in that manner, every nation dresses and wears the garment with which its guaca [ancestor] was dressed. And they say that the first one who was born from each such place turned into rock, and others into hawks and condors and other animals and birds. And for that reason, the guacas that they worship and use [in their native rituals] assume different forms.[13]

~~~

This pre-Columbian creation myth effectively illustrates the Andean cyclical concept of *pachacuti* precipitated by a cataclysmic event—in this case, a deluge—that destroys the existing world and later gives rise to a new creation. However, it must be noted that in this depiction of the myth, some passages appear to be reinterpreted by the chronicler in a manner consistent with his Christian and Western European beliefs. For instance, Molina refers to "the deluge" (as opposed to *a* deluge) in the Inca story of creation as if he were referring to "the Deluge," or "the Flood," a singular event described in the Old Testament of the Bible.[14] Just as Noah in that telling was spared from the Flood, so too are "one man and one woman" in this story, "who remained [hidden] in the box of a drum."

Also, according to the origin story in the Bible, God "formed man out of the clay of the ground and blew into his nostrils the breath of life, and so man became a living being."[15] Similarly, in this Inca creation myth the Creator also makes humankind out of clay, and "when he [finishes] painting and creating the said nations and bundles of clay, he [gives] each one life and spirit." It is worth noting that although it was fairly common during the colonial period for chroniclers to apply Biblical chronology to Andean historical and mythical events, including creation and origin myths, some colonial chroniclers, such as Pedro de Cieza de León, argued that Andean origins had to have occurred *after* the Deluge, because in the Bible only Noah and his relatives survived the Flood; the rest of humanity was utterly destroyed.[16]

As stated in the Inca origin myth, the Creator god molds each nation out of clay and begins to "paint" and endow each one with certain visible physical characteristics (e.g., hair and cut hair); then he assigns to each nation its unique language, song, clothing, and seeds for cultivation. Thus, this passage could be interpreted as the origin of language, music or oral history (which was sometimes sung in the ancient Andes), and agriculture—arts essential to the formation and development of a culture. Subsequently, the Creator orders humankind "to sink beneath the ground" and instructs each nation to emerge from a distinct place on earth, whether cave, mountain, fountain (spring), lake, tree, or other natural location. In

Andean cosmology, each of these locations is called a *paqarina*, a sacred place of origin venerated by each locality or ethnic group. In this myth, the Creator god designates the site of each *paqarina*, and thereafter each nation constructs shrines or temples on those sites "in memory of the first of their lineage who had proceeded from there." In that manner, each Andean nation establishes its own lineage and religion, based on the worship of its ancestors and its sacred place of origin.

The cyclical concept of *pachacuti* also encompasses the Andean notions of dualism and intermediaries, so prevalent in Native Andean mythology, and previously discussed in other chapters. In this Inca creation myth, water—which surely fell from the sky in torrents and caused the deluge— serves as a mediating element between the sky "above" (*hanan*) and the earth "below" (*hurin*, relative to the sky), and between a former and a new creation.[17] The survivors of the deluge, a man and a woman, are also intermediaries between the prediluvial and postdiluvial ages of the world. Furthermore, there are many dualities presented in this myth: destruction paves the way for a new creation; peoples and nations emerge from both the highlands and the lowlands; people appear above ground after having been ordered to "sink beneath the ground"; and the Creator himself is both a creator, the maker of humankind, and a destroyer, if he caused the deluge.

Additionally, there is a distinction made between the age of the ancestors and the age of humans. The first ancestors emerged and "turned into rock...hawks...condors and other animals and birds" and presumably formed the world of nature; their descendants turned into men and women, who constituted "nations" and created the world of culture. Therefore, as with many other Native Andean myths, the concept of *pachacuti* also embraces the Andean notions of dualism and mediating and transitional elements (intermediaries) that attempt to transcend the dualities presented in each myth.

In this story Molina also blames the Incas for "the inception of idolatry and adoration of the Sun." His contention that the Incas were responsible for introducing idolatry strongly resonates with arguments made by the indigenous colonial chronicler Felipe Guaman Poma de Ayala, that prior to the advent of the Incas, the Native Andeans were monotheistic and practiced Christian values, even though they had not yet been introduced to the Gospel of Christ.[18] Yet this argument seems contradictory, because elsewhere in the myth Molina acknowledges that "the peoples and nations that exist in this land today"—which likely included non-Inca peoples subjugated by the Incas—practiced ancestor worship. From a Christian perspective, such practice would also be considered idolatrous. Regarding the latter, he recounts, "every nation dresses and wears the garment with which its *guaca* [ancestor] was dressed. And they say that the first one who was born in such place [their sacred place of origin, or *paqarina*] turned into rock, and others into hawks and condors and other animals and birds. And for that reason, the *guacas* that they worship and use [in their native rituals] assume different forms." The same held true for the Incas. In much the same way as other pre-Columbian Andean peoples, the Incas also worshipped their mythical ancestors and their sacred place of origin. According to a number of colonial sources, their *paqarina* was a cave called *Tampu T'oqo* (also spelled *Tambotoco*) at *Pacariqtambo* (also spelled *Paqariq Tanpu*),[19] meaning "Lodging [of That Which] Awakens, Is Created, or Is Born" in Quechua.

Perhaps one way to resolve this inconsistency is to view this myth as one continuous myth of creation and Inca origin, which is clearly fused with pre-Inca or regional mythical elements, that survived well into the sixteenth century when this account was recorded. It was a common practice in the Inca Empire to have the local or regional cults exist side by side with the solar cult of the Inca. Classics scholar Sabine MacCormack informs that by the sixteenth century the Spanish campaigns of extirpation had destroyed or disrupted the Inca mythology and belief systems. She posits that "in many parts of the [former] Inca empire, the myths and cults that the Incas brought with them constituted little more than a veneer that disappeared within a generation of the Spanish invasion."[20] So while the Inca myths and beliefs "had receded to the past," what did persist were the older pre-Inca myths and religious practices "punctuating the agricultural calendar, and cults of ancestors, of mythic founders, of the Sun, and of the atmospheric deities."[21]

A salient example of the persistence of these pre-Inca beliefs may be the cult of *Viracocha* itself. The ancient cult of Viracocha, the Andean Creator god, may have predated the Incas. Anthropologist Arthur Demarest argues quite convincingly that Viracocha may have first appeared in the form of a generalized creator-sky-god complex worshipped by the common people in various regions of the pre-Columbian Andes.[22] For instance, Viracocha is reminiscent of the god *Pachacamac*, worshipped by the pre-Columbian Pachacamac cult of coastal Peru, and the deity *Thunapa*, venerated by the ancient Aymara religion in the region of Collao, today encompassing the Lake Titicaca basin and vicinity. Demarest contends that the Incas may have modified the concept of a generalized creator-sky god and created an artificial dichotomy between the Creator and the Sun, personified as Viracocha and *Inti*, respectively, to enhance the prestige of their empire and aggrandize the lineage of the Inca elite. This notion is concordant with some Spanish colonial chronicles that maintain the Incas altered elements of their religion from time to time to suit their political and administrative purposes.

The Inca origin myth we have examined also incorporates information about regional or local cults, which included the veneration of ancestors at their respective *paqarinas*, and whose deified idols assumed the forms of rocks, animals, and birds in their native rituals. The story also mentions the mythical Inca founder, Mango Capac (also spelled "Manco Capac"), who introduced the cult of the Sun. And although the cause of the deluge is left unexplained, it is reasonable to surmise that either the Creator god or atmospheric deities, such as the Thunder or Lightning god, responsible for bringing rain, precipitated the deluge, in which "perished all peoples and all creation." Taken together, these elements leave little doubt that this is an Inca origin myth that is combined with regional or local (pre-Inca) elements, which would also explain its apparent inconsistencies.

It is also not uncommon in pre-Columbian or contemporary Andean myths for the gods to initiate a *pachacuti* and set in motion a cataclysmic event that punishes and destroys the inhabitants of a certain creation for not obeying their laws. In concordance with this idea, we find an implicit threat in this story that the Creator may well punish the Inca people *again* for worshipping the false god of the Sun and practicing idolatry, because "when they began boasting and calling themselves Children of the Sun, and at the inception of idolatry and adoration of the Sun, they received news of the deluge."

If so, from the perspective of Molina, who was a Christian priest and longtime resident of Cuzco, this leaves room for the introduction of Christianity as a means of saving the native peoples from their wayward idolatry and legitimizing the Spanish Conquest. The Catholic Church made similar arguments during the Spanish colonial period justifying the evangelization of the Native Andean peoples and its aggressive campaigns of extirpation of idolatry. It argued that the devil had tricked the Indians into worshipping false gods and paying homage to pagan idols, and that the only way to save their misguided souls from the eternal fires of hell was by destroying their *huacas* and all instruments of their idolatry and convincing them to embrace Christianity.[23] Nonetheless, from a Native Andean perspective, the Spanish Conquest of Peru and the forced Christianization of the indigenous peoples were nothing less than a *pachacuti*—a "turning around" or "inversion" of the world—that dramatically altered the course and character of their lives.

From a cosmological viewpoint, *pachacuti* marks the destruction of the existing world and the elimination of humanity, but it also triggers a return to a primordial, chaotic world. In Andean mythology, the primordial periods of destruction and chaos in the cycle of *pachacuti* are characterized by uninterrupted states of darkness, light, water, fire, or petrification, followed by the advent of a new creation. The following Wanka[24] origin myth, collected from the Valley of Jauja in Peru, alludes to a primordial state of water, inhabited by two unruly mythical serpents called *Amaru*, which struggle over supremacy of their world. Their perpetual state of water is interrupted by the appearance of two human beings, named *Mama* and *Taita*, who have been hiding underneath the earth for fear of the powerful *Amaru*.

The Appearance of the First Human Beings on Earth

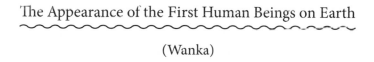

(Wanka)

Long ago, the present-day valley of Jauja or Mantaro was covered by the waters of a great lake, from the center of which protruded a great rock called Wanka, which was the resting place of the Amaru, a horrible monster with the head of a llama, two small wings, and the body of a batrachian [amphibian], which ended in a serpent's tail. Later, Tulunmaya, the Rainbow, planted another Amaru in the lake to serve as a companion to the first. This Amaru was darker in color and never reached the same size as the first one, which had acquired a whitish color on account of its greater age. The two monsters fought over the supremacy of the lake, whose rock, though of great dimension, did not have enough room for both of them to rest upon. The violence of these frequent battles caused the waters of the lake to rise, creating whirlwinds of water, agitating the lake. In one of these battles, the large Amaru lost a great chunk of its tail while furiously attacking the smaller one.

Irritated by these disturbances, the god Tiksi [a meteorological god] discharged a tempest over them and sent lightning bolts that struck and killed both serpents. The two Amaru fell in pieces, along with the diluvial rain, over the agitated lake, increasing the volume of the lake to the point of rupturing its rim and causing it to empty its waters in the south.

In this way the valley was formed, and the first human beings, Mama and Taita, were launched out of a *Warina* or *Wari-puquio*, or spring.[25] Until then, the two had remained underneath the earth for a long time for fear of the Amaru. The descendants of this couple later constructed the Temple of Wariwilka, the ruins of which still exist today.

Today, it is widely believed among the Wankas that the Amaru is a serpent that, hidden in a cave, has grown to an enormous size. And taking advantage of the great winds that develop during thunderstorms, it attempts to climb up to the sky but is destroyed by thunderbolts striking down through the clouds. And, based on its color, be it white or black, the figure of the Amaru appearing in the sky portends a good or a bad year.[26]

~~~

In this Wanka origin myth, the storytellers explain the circumstances surrounding the appearance of their ancestors, *Mama* and *Taita* (meaning "Mother" and "Father" in Quechua), ostensibly the first woman and man on earth. The arrival of these human beings and the newly formed valley, with its encompassing landscape, fracture and dismantle the primordial world of the lake with its terrifying inhabitants, the *Amaru*. In the primordial world, the violent behavior of the serpents infuriates the meteorological god Tiksi, who discharges a tempest and sends lightning bolts to kill them. The torrential rains and broken body parts of the *Amaru* cause the lake to overflow and create the topography of the valley, leading to the formation of a new world. The broken rim of the lake gives birth to the valley, with rivulets or rivers sprouting from the south side of the lake where the lake empties its waters. There is also some suggestion of the creation of waterspouts as, according to the myth, the serpents' "frequent battles caused the waters of the lake to rise, creating whirlwinds of water, agitating the lake."

More importantly, the destruction of the *Amaru* and the disruption of the great lake, the creatures' habitat, signify the end of the primordial water world in which the *Amaru* had reigned supreme. The creation of topography and the appearance of *Mama* and *Taita* designate the beginning of a new creation in the repeating cycle of *pachacuti*. In this creation, humankind reigns. The descendants of *Mama* and *Taita* construct the first temple at *Wariwilka* ("Native Shrine" or "Liquid [Water] Shrine"[27]), implying the origin of the Wanka religion, and possibly culture. Their descendants also learn to look to the skies for the ominous figure of the *Amaru* and use its darkened or whitish color to forecast the future. This could also be interpreted as the origin of divination, a Native Andean ritual still practiced in this region today.

As with many ancestral religions of the Andes, this myth identifies the site of the *paqarina*, the sacred place on earth from which the ancestors of the Wankas are believed to have emerged. In this case, the first couple is launched out of a sacred spring, a *warina* or *wari-puqio* (also spelled *wari pukyu*, meaning "native spring"), considered the holy birthplace of the Wanka people. This is evocative of the Inca creation myth at the beginning of the chapter, in which the Creator god, *Viracocha*, orders the first people on earth to emerge from "caves, others from mountains, others from fountains, others from lakes, others from the bottoms of trees, and other such places." Like the Wankas, many Native Andean cultures believe that their first ancestors emerged from below the ground and appeared at one of these natural sites. Today, as in ancient times, offerings are made at the *paqarina* sites, honoring and commemorating the ancestors of each local indigenous group or community. These offerings may include coca leaves, crops, *chicha* (maize beer), food, sweets, llama fat, shells, figurines, wool, feathers, and other items available to the community. As in the case of the Wankas, the origin myth of each locality usually pinpoints the precise location and nature of the *paqarina*.

In most Native Andean origin myths, the introduction of the first human beings, and the establishment of a new creation, fracture and destroy the continuous state of water, fire, darkness, petrification, or other condition in which primordial beings, such as the *Amaru*, live. According to theologian Lawrence E. Sullivan, "the protean beings of the early primordia still appear but now become subject to temporal periodicity and spatial bounds: light by day alone, darkness by night alone, primordial stone only in the *huacas*."[28] In other words, the primordial world of the mythical creatures, which is of unbroken duration, gives way to the world of humans, where change, periodicity, and finiteness rule. The totality and uninterrupted state of chaos is replaced by a bounded and finite human world where the sun rises and sets, birth begins and death terminates the life cycle, and the land receives offerings and yields fruits in exchange for community offerings. In short, as perpetuity terminates, periodicity commences within the framework of *pachacuti*.

However, in many Native Andean belief systems the continued existence of this world, which embodies change, finiteness, and periodicity, depends on the performance of appropriate rites and rituals. From this perspective, the lack of ritual constitutes inappropriate behavior, which "may have disastrous consequences for the cosmos—famine, flood, death, disease, infertility, prolonged eclipse. In a sense, the continued fruitful interplay of cosmogonic elements in the cosmos is dependent upon the history of proper human action, which relies, in turn, on observance of cosmic order."[29]

The observance of cosmic order within a dualistic paradigm may explain the origin and function of ritual among Native Andean peoples. As in the Wanka origin myth and the Inca practices associated with eclipses, many Native Andean communities live in fear of another destructive *pachacuti* that looms menacingly on the horizon. Therefore, from a mythological and cosmological perspective, one of the primary functions of Andean ritual may be to avert a *pachacuti*.

To illustrate this point, let us examine a myth from the northern Andes. In the northern Andean volcanic belt in the vicinity of the Colombian peaks known as Nevado del Ruiz, Tolima, and Santa Isabel,[30] its inhabitants relay an ancient myth about a mighty condor that introduced sunlight to the world.[31] According to several versions of this myth, the first peoples of the world lived in total darkness, except the gold metal they worked gave off some light and allowed them to produce works of great refinement. Weary of living in an endless night, these ancients went in search of a "golden ball" (the sun), which the Lord of the Peaks, a mighty condor, had placed next to a rocky outcrop, where he frequently appeared. The ancients found the golden ball and, using a very forceful breath, blew it up to the sky, where it became permanently attached. From then on, the golden ball illuminated the world and put an end to the interminable darkness that had previously enveloped a world inhabited by wandering night spirits. Later, the elders took the gold in their possession and made molds of animals and plants to populate the world. To give thanks to the condor for bringing light to the world and for allowing the sun to appear each day, the people made the condor daily offerings of gold at the foot of the rocky outcrop. "The women, every day, at daybreak, deposited golden offerings at the foot of the cliff; the children, at midday, brought him panpipes made of thick golden plumes; at sunset, the men offered him pieces of solid gold bearing the likeness of condors, vultures, and all sorts of birds."[32]

But when the Spanish Conquest began, the people who worshipped the condor hid all their gold in mountain lakes, waterfalls, and volcanoes to keep it away from the Spaniards. Some worshippers sacrificed themselves to take care of this gold on behalf of their people. Acting as guardians for the gold, they performed their rituals and then threw themselves, along with the gold, into these lakes, waterfalls, and volcanoes. Today, their Andean descendants believe that these treasures continue to travel underground "on Holy Fridays, at midnight, and whenever the moon is full," and will one day reemerge and reappear in the mountain peaks.[33] When a bright light appears, they say it is the light of the "golden condor," the owner of these enchanted treasures, who will resurface and ascend when the end of the world arrives. On that day, "the Condor will come out flying from the peaks, and [all] the treasures will fuse together into an immense ball of fire that will go round the earth burning everything in its path. That is how life will be erased, fulfilling the [prophetic] words of the ancients."[34]

It is easy to conceptualize and interpret this story in terms of the repeating cycle of *pachacuti*. In its preliminary and creative phase the "golden ball," representing the sun, which the condor had placed next to a rocky outcrop, brings light to a dark world (except for the glimmer of gold), much like the advent of a *pachacuti* fragments an uninterrupted state of darkness and introduces periodicity and change in the world. After the golden ball adheres to the sky, the sun rises and sets; day appears, as opposed to night; and the condor worshippers make their offerings at daybreak, at midday, and at sunset (i.e., at specific intervals). The debut of the golden ball also introduces fertility and new life: the elders create golden molds of animals and plants, thereby populating the light-filled world previously inhabited by wandering spirits of the dark. In thanksgiving, the worshippers make offerings at the foot of the condor's cliff, the dwelling place of the Lord of the Peaks.

By contrast, in its final and destructive phase, the return of the golden condor with its burning ball of fire, forged from the stream of "treasures" and sacrificial offerings, conjures images of a *pachacuti*, marking the end of the world and obliterating all signs of creation. The once-isolated offerings made at the foot of the cliff become fused and resurface at the mountain peak(s), where the golden condor ascends with its burning ball of fire, destroying everything in its path. The gleaming golden ball, which inaugurated the creation of animals and plants and brought forth light into this world, becomes the scorching golden ball that sets this creation aflame and extinguishes all life. Put differently, the rise of the golden condor and the blazing ball of fire complete the cycle of creation and destruction that characterizes *pachacuti*; from the ashes of the old creation a new world, and a new cycle, will begin anew.

However, it is important to emphasize that in this story the golden condor has not yet ascended; it only *threatens* to ascend when the end of the world arrives, just like the *Amaru* in the Wanka myth hides in a cave, where it is growing, and *threatens* to come out and climb the sky, possibly launching another *pachacuti*. Even after the appearance of *Mama* and *Taita*, the *Amaru* is "hidden in a cave [and] has grown to an enormous size. And taking advantage of the great winds that develop during thunderstorms, it attempts to climb up to the sky." The *Amaru* hiding in the cave is, therefore, an ever-present yet "contained" symbolic representation of a potential *pachacuti*. If the *Amaru* were unleashed, this creation could end, and the world would likely return to the primordium. Metaphorically, the creature's enormous growth and very presence threaten our human existence and raise the possibility of another cataclysmic event that could destroy the existing world, just as such an event destroyed the previous creation in the Wanka origin myth.

The appearance of the *Amaru*, a mythical creature of the primordium, poses a threat to humankind in a manner similar to the golden condor, another mythical creature whose reemergence is associated with destruction and the end of the world. In the legend of the golden condor, ritual offerings are made to the condor to allow the sun to appear each day and, therefore, to preserve the finiteness and the order of this existing creation. In concordance with Sullivan's observations, it would be understandable and appropriate for the condor worshippers to appease the golden condor and preserve the existing world through the proper observance of rites and rituals ("proper human action"); otherwise, from their perspective the sun might disappear and the world would return to primordial darkness. Moreover, in adopting this outlook, proper human behavior might delay the appearance of the golden condor with its fatal and destructive ball of fire, marking the death of this "sun" (age of the world) in the progressive cycles of *pachacuti*. In a like manner, proper ritual might contain the menacing *Amaru* and avert the possibility of another world destruction.

AMARU AND UNBALANCED FORCES

In the Wanka myth we determined that the *Amaru* may symbolize the lingering threat of a potential *pachacuti*. In many parts of the Andes, the *Amaru* (also known as *Katari*) is also associated with *pachacuti*-like explosive events, emerging from the underground, and the presence and provision of irrigation water.

In the contemporary cosmology of the Aymaras of Tarapacá in northern Chile, the *Amaru* is "the serpent that is linked to the economy of water [and to] the rivers and irrigation canals of agricultural lands [situated] at 2,000–3,000 mts. [meters of elevation]"[35] (approximately 6,500 to 9,800 feet above sea level), an ecological zone described as the *precordillera*.[36] Anthropologist Jan van Kessel explains that most of the rituals and festivals dedicated to the *Amaru* in this area concern the cleaning and opening of irrigation canals prior to the beginning of a new agricultural cycle.[37] He speculates that the customs and rituals belonging to the cult of the *Amaru* are vestiges of some of the most ancient and authentic religious practices of the Andes that concern the flow of river water through canals and the provision of irrigation water for agriculture.[38]

Similarly, anthropologists John Earls and Irene Silverblatt have determined that among some contemporary Quechuas, the *Amaru* is identified with "explosive force" and the presence of water.[39] Although it is not always represented as a serpent, it always assumes a zoomorphic form.[40] As discussed earlier, the *Amaru* is sometimes affiliated with *pachacuti*-like events; for example, in certain communities the Native Andeans describe it as an animal "tunneling under the lands of [a] community" and speculate that "one day it will cause the community to collapse."[41] In other communities, the villagers report that the *Amaru* "explodes out of the mountain springs" and slithers down "through the irrigation canals, dragging with it lots of water, mud, and rocks."[42] According to Earls and Silverblatt, some Native Andeans also attribute certain topographical formations to former *Amaru* "explosions," but accounts vary as to whether the *Amaru* bursts out of lakes, mountains, or springs. The *Amaru's* connection to sudden, explosive force in relation to water has led Earls and Silverblatt to conclude that the *Amaru* "manifests in the sudden burst of unbalanced forces" striving for readjustment and equilibrium.[43]

The portrayal of explosive, unbalanced forces trying to reach equilibrium is reminiscent of the battle of the mythical serpents fighting over supremacy of the lake in the Wanka origin myth. In terms of the cycle of *pachacuti*, the *Amaru* may be depicting the primordial world of chaos and violence as it struggles to find a new order (creation) and regain its balance. This view is consistent with the often violent and explosive cataclysmic events that tend to initiate the cycle of *pachacuti* and cause irreversible destruction. "In an even more metaphorical sense, *amaru* is perceived as a revolutionary force that dismantles a system which is out of equilibrium and then helps to bring back balance, harmony, and peace within a new system."[44]

The Wanka origin myth about the *Amaru* also describes how the descendants of the Wankas use the figure of the *Amaru*, as it appears in the skies, in divination and prognostication rituals to make predictions about the future. The form or figure of the *Amaru* depicted in this myth may be referring to one of the "dark cloud constellations" ("*yana phuyu*" in Quechua) described by anthropologist Gary Urton in his study of

Quechua astronomy and cosmology in Misminay, Peru.[45] Dark cloud constellations are not recognized in Western astronomy, but they are very much a part of the Native Andean sky.

According to Urton, dark cloud constellations are patches of interstellar dust situated between or among star constellations in the Milky Way, which the Native Andeans call *Mayu*, or "[Celestial] River."

> Dark cloud constellations are located in that portion of the Milky Way where one sees the densest clustering of stars and the greatest surface brightness, and where the fixed clouds of interstellar dust (dark cloud constellations) which cut through the Milky Way therefore appear in sharper contrast. From the earth these dark spots appear to be huge shadows or silhouettes pasted against the Milky Way.[46]

The ancient Andeans and some modern Native Andean communities assign forms and names to these dark cloud constellations, much as we do in Western astronomy to star-to-star constellations. However, whereas star-to-star constellations are generally "inanimate, geometrical or architectural figures," dark cloud constellations often assume the form of living animals, such as "Toad" (*Hanp'átu*), "Fox" (*Atoq*), "Tinamou" (*Yutu*), "Llama" (*Llama*), "Baby Llama" (*Uñallamacha*), and "Serpent" (*Mach'ácuay*).[47]

Urton suggests that the dark cloud constellation *Mach'ácuay* may be related to the *Amaru*.[48] It is also strongly correlated with rain, as his Quechua informants observed that in the highlands "the dark cloud Serpent" (*Mach'ácuay*) is visible at night during the rainy season, but not during the dry season.[49] According to some Spanish colonial chroniclers, the Incas worshipped *Mach'ácuay* as the patron of "snakes, serpents, and vipers."[50] Bernabé Cobo maintained that the Incas, especially those from Chinchasuyu (the northwest quadrant of the Inca Empire), carried snakes as weapons and venerated them as *huacas*, or deities.[51] The Incas also constructed a temple called *chacara*, dedicated to the worship of snakes, suggesting that snakes played a significant role in Inca religion.[52] This fact is also corroborated by the Spanish colonial priest and Catholic extirpator, Cristóbal de Albornoz, who wrote that the Incas used serpents in their religious rituals and assigned the names of *Amaru* and *Mach'ácuay* to their principal Incas.

> There is another kind of *guaca* [or *huaca*] that is a certain kind of snake of different forms. They adore and serve them. The principal

Incas adopted their names. They called themselves *Machacuay* and *Amaru*. They put these hungry, living [snakes] in large vats and nourish them for many years with the blood of guinea pigs and with plants. And they dedicate many festivals and sacrifices to them.[53]

In pre-Columbian Andean iconography the *Amaru* is sometimes represented as a giant two-headed serpent with one head rising from a spring, its body arching across the sky, and its second head, at the opposite end of its body, reentering the earth through another spring. According to Urton, the image created by the two-headed serpent is a giant rainbow that also coincides with one of the Quechua meteorological terms for rainbow, which is *Amaru*.[54] The two-headed rainbow-serpent is also a recurring motif in the pre-Columbian iconography of the Moche (or Mochica)[55] and the Chimor (or Chimú)[56] cultures of the Peruvian north coast. Moreover, the two-headed serpent appears in 3,000-year-old sculptures discovered on the shores of Lake Titicaca belonging to a little-known religious tradition called *Yayamama* (meaning "Father-Mother" or "Man-Woman" in Quechua), which predated the Tiahuanaco culture and religion by about 1,500 years.[57] These images are still worshipped today as *huacas* by the local indigenous communities.

The rainbow aptly represents the intermediary nature of the *Amaru*. The Incas also worshiped the rainbow[58] as an entity that links the sky and the earth, the world of the celestial gods and the human world. According to Garcilaso, the Incas believed the rainbow "came from the Sun"[59] and, therefore, had a divine origin. The Inca ruler, also considered a divine being, used the rainbow as one of his royal insignias,[60] and serpents as another.[61] Even after the Spanish Conquest, "indigenous artists often depicted ancestral Incas under the arch of a rainbow emerging from the mouth of two felines."[62]

Urton postulates that the representation of the *Amaru* rising out of a spring correlates with the behavior patterns of Andean terrestrial snakes that emerge from underground hibernation at the beginning of the rainy season and then, much like the two-headed *Amaru*, reenter the earth during the dry season.[63] Since rainbows usually only appear during the rainy season and disappear during the dry season, their activity cycle mirrors that of these terrestrial snakes.[64] This suggests that the appearance of the *Amaru*, both above ground and in the sky, is closely aligned with the cycle of Andean rainfall and the arrival of irrigation water used in agriculture.

From a psychoanalytic perspective, it is impossible to ignore the image of the serpent or snake as a phallic symbol. This is particularly poignant in the Inca ritual described by Albornoz, in which animal blood and plants were used to nourish the deified snakes living in the vat. Sigmund Freud identified images of enclosed spaces as vaginal symbols;[65] hence, the vat could represent a female womb or the female sexual organ. The blood fed to the snakes may also represent menstrual flow, and the concomitant menstrual cycle, which in the Andes is strongly associated with femininity, fecundity, and fertility. Similarly, the plants—offspring of Mother Earth (*Pacha Mama*)—may also represent the feminine principle. Therefore, the snakes living in the vat, sustained and nourished by the "feminine" elements in this Inca ritual, may have represented the conjugal union of male and female or the merger of masculine and feminine principles, which together embodied the necessary integration and proper pairing of vital forces to ensure the fertility of the land, fecundity of women, and cosmic equilibrium.[66]

We speculate that the mythical *Amaru* embraces all of the aforementioned characteristics and more. In its mythical dimension, the *Amaru* may represent the destructive, explosive, or unbalanced primordial forces that threaten our world with a *pachacuti* until order and balance are restored. In its metaphoric or divinized aspect, the *Amaru* may represent the mediating rainbow and serpents, which graced the insignia of the Inca rulers, considered deities here on earth. In its earthly expression, the *Amaru* may be the Andean snake, which burrows under the ground during the dry season, only to reemerge during the rainy season. In its celestial form, it may arise as the dark shadow constellation of *Mach'ácuay*, which appears in the Andes during the rainy season, and which the Incas believed guarded the snakes, vipers, and serpents of this world. All these attributes link the powerful *Amaru* to the presence (or absence) of water in the cycle of Andean rainfall, and to the economy and provision of water in contemporary Aymara ritual. Behind all these manifestations is the elusive figure of the *Amaru*, an intermediary being, that connects the primordial world to this one, and the earth to the underworld and the sky.

INVERSION OF TIME-SPACE IN THE HUAROCHIRÍ MANUSCRIPT
In studying the oral traditions of the pre-Columbian Andean peoples, investigators are limited by the many constraints posed by the narratives of the Spanish colonial chroniclers, who compiled and transcribed these stories and often tried to interpret Andean notions in a manner consistent with Western European constructs. Many of the colonial chroniclers awkwardly tried to describe and explain an alien world they had just conquered in terms that were concordant with their European and Christian

ideologies but, in fact, were far removed from a true understanding of the Native Andean belief systems and cosmology.

The colonial chronicles inform that the Incas had developed a system of recording mathematical, narrative, and historical information on the *khipu*, a three-dimensional recording system composed of knotted strings and cords of different colors.[67] They also furnish various clues that have since helped modern scholars decode the mathematical *khipu*;[68] surprisingly, however, they give little indication of how to decipher or "read" a narrative *khipu*, which one day may provide a key to an Inca writing system.[69] To date, archaeologists and other scholars have not been able to locate, let alone decipher, a narrative *khipu*. Thus, in the absence of any existing literary *khipu*, the primary sources for pre-Columbian Andean myths are the colonial writings of the Spaniards, which are often riddled with inaccuracies and limitations.[70]

One of the most problematic issues raised by the Spanish colonial chronicles is that they were written in the language of the conquerors and not of the conquered. Although some writings of the colonial mestizo and Native Andean chroniclers interspersed the Inca language of *Runa Simi* (literally, "People's Speech," today known as "Quechua") at intervals in their Spanish narratives, few colonial documents were written entirely in Quechua or in any Native Andean language of the past.

In a sea of rough and imperfect stones, however, *The Manuscript of Huarochirí* is a precious gem. It alone of all colonial sources records a pre-Columbian Andean religious tradition in a Native Andean language, Quechua; it alone of all Andean colonial narratives offers a complete, coherent picture of a pre-Hispanic religion,[71] along with its rites and rituals. *The Manuscript* also presents a view of society and daily life in a province of the former Inca Empire, unlike the perspective offered in most Andean colonial chronicles, informed by the Inca elite residing in the city of Cuzco.[72]

The account described in *The Manuscript of Huarochirí* was recorded at the turn of the seventeenth century and was probably compiled by order of the Spanish extirpator and priest, Francisco de Avila,[73] during the colonial Extirpation of Idolatries. The Extirpation was the period in Andean history during which the Roman Catholic Church, with the support of the Spanish colonial authorities, sought to systematically dismantle and destroy pre-Columbian religions and convert Native Andeans to Christianity. Part of this effort was to locate all the *huacas* "in order to dismantle them... [or] burn them before the community...and also burn the remains of any garments found [belonging to any idol]"; because, according to the Spanish colonial priests, "if one should leave [behind] a single seed, they will worship it as the seed of the devil."[74]

In addition to discrediting and destroying the *huacas* (temples, shrines, idols, and sacred natural formations), the extirpators also sought to learn the stories and beliefs associated with each pre-Columbian religion in an effort to rupture the spiritual, emotional, and historical connection the Native Andeans had with their past and, more specifically, with their revered ancestors. The Church also tried to sever the attachment the Indians had to their deities and to demonstrate that the Christian God was more powerful than the Andean gods. According to Cristóbal de Albornoz, "A community does not hold in high regard a *guaca* [*huaca*] that has been vanquished."[75]

Against the backdrop of this volatile, tumultuous, and conflicting period of Christianization and Extirpation (a subject on which we will elaborate in a subsequent chapter), indigenous scribes from the highland region of Huarochirí, to the east of present-day Lima, Peru, wrote a powerful and compelling testament to the ancient beliefs of their people. These informants were probably converts to Christianity who recorded this information to further the efforts of the Extirpation; however, we shall never know whether this record was made voluntarily or under coercion by the Catholic Church.

The Manuscript also appears to be annotated and edited, probably by Francisco de Avila.[76] Nonetheless, the Peruvian humanist José María Arguedas explains, "It is not Avila who tells [the stories contained in the Manuscript], but rather, the practitioner of the ancient religion, the believer in the ancient gods and heroes."[77] According to Arguedas, who collaborated on a translation of the document from Quechua into Spanish, the tone and style of the Manuscript is primarily oral and consistent with the Native Andean oral tradition, and the simplicity of the language is free from European-style rhetoric.[78] Even so, according to anthropologist Frank Salomon, another Huarochirí scholar and translator, "the way the people recalled their ancient tradition... could not but be influenced by the seventy preceding years of colonial turbulence, during which one potent innovation was the art of writing itself."[79] Thus the oral tradition presented in the Manuscript is likely to have been altered by the very process of writing, limiting, and editing the text, not to mention the human drama that unfolded behind the scenes: extirpation, forced conversion, conflict, persecution, subjugation, and even death.

In spite of its limitations, the *Huarochirí Manuscript* furnishes a unique view of a pre-Columbian religion interlaced with non-Western, and uniquely Andean, concepts, including the cyclical concept of *pachacuti*. The storytellers of Huarochirí recount instances in ancient times in which the world "wanted to come to an end."[80] In one tale the storytellers describe a time when the ocean overflowed, then dried, retreated, and "exterminated all the people."[81] In another, "the sun died."[82] This latter cataclysmic event caused rocks to bang against one another, and inverted the order of the world: "Mortars and grinding stones began to eat people; llamas started to drive men."[83] In yet another story, the storytellers expressed fear that if their deity *Pacha Camac* ("World Shaker" or "World Maker") should get angry, he would cause an earthquake to occur; and, "if he ever rolled over" in his sleep, "the world would end."[84]

The *Manuscript of Huarochirí* distinguishes between two epochs of the world. The first, called *Ñawpa Pacha* (also spelled *Naupa Pacha*), describes the pre-Christian world before the arrival of the Spaniards, from which the scribes of Huarochirí claimed they derived their rites, rituals, and customs.[85] This epoch coincides with the mythic times of the Huarochirí peoples. The second is the Christian epoch after the arrival of the Spaniards—the state of the indigenous world during the early colonial period, contemporaneous with the writing of the manuscript.[86] The *Ñawpa Pacha* is characterized by successive cycles of creation and destruction, which rightfully could fall under the category of *pachacuti*, an inversion of time-space. In the following story from the Manuscript, a deluge destroys the existing world, initiating the cycle of *pachacuti*, and paving the way for the creation of a new world, thus completing the cycle.

What Happened to the Indians in the Olden Days
When the Sea Overflowed
(In this part we shall return to those matters
that ancient men talked about)

(Quechua with possible Jaqi/Aymara influence)[87]

What they tell us is this: In ancient times, the world wanted to come to an end. A male llama that grazed on a mountain with excellent grass knew that Mother Sea had wished (and decided) to overflow, and pour down in torrents. The llama became sad and cried, "In, in," and didn't eat.

Angered, the owner of the llama hit it with a corncob. "Eat, dog!" he said. "You rest over the best grass!"

Then the llama, speaking like a man, told him, "Pay attention and remember what I am going to tell you. Five days from now, the sea will overflow and the whole world will come to an end." That's what he said.

And the owner became frightened; he believed him.

"Let's go somewhere where we can escape. Let's go to Mount Huill-cacoto.[88] There we will save ourselves. Take food for five days," the llama ordered.

And so, that instant, the man started to walk, taking along his family and his llama.

When the man was about to reach Mount Huillcacoto, he found that all the animals had gathered there: the puma, the fox, the guanaco, the condor, and all the species of animals. And no sooner had the man arrived than the water began to pour down in torrents. Then the men and the animals from everywhere huddled closely together in a very small space on Mount Huillcacoto.

The summit was the only place where the water could not reach them. But the water managed to soak the tip of the fox's tail. That's why [to this day] it has remained blackened.

At the end of the five days, the water began to recede and dry up. The dry part grew; the sea retreated some more, and as it retreated and dried it killed all the people. Only the man [and his family] survived on the mountain. And because of him, the number of people multiplied, and because of him, people still exist until today.

And now, we bless this account. We Christians bless the time of the Flood, just as they tell, and bless the way in which they were able to save themselves on Mount Huillcacoto.[89]

~~

As is typical of many contemporary and ancient Andean myths, this Huarochirí myth incorporates the doctrine of Andean animism in which anima, life, consciousness, and spirit are attributed to the natural elements. It is important to highlight that the Native Andeans of the past, as well as the present, live in a vivified landscape, alive with the breathing and pulsating rhythms of a dynamic, interactive *natura viva*. To the Native Andean peoples, caves, waterfalls, trees, mountains, rivers, fountains, and every other aspect of Mother Earth (*Pacha Mama*) are sentient, living entities that exhibit volition, consciousness, and intentionality.

One of the trappings of Western culture is that we are often unable to escape the philosophical paradigm that we have been taught from birth and that frames every aspect of our lives. This is the paradigm of Cartesian dualism—the division between mind and body, or the mental and the material—that serves as our foundation for science, philosophy, psychology, cosmology, and almost every other discipline. I had a difficult time with this myself as I struggled to understand the Native Andean view of the natural elements as living, sentient, and conscious entities. So to help me better understand nature from this perspective, I received experiential training in an ancient pre-Columbian cosmology taught by the Q'ero[90] people of Peru called *Kausay Puriq* (also spelled *Kawsay Puriq*, meaning "Circulating Life"; often translated as "Path of Living Energy").

From this experience I learned that the Q'eros, like many other Native Andean peoples, do not make a distinction between mind and body, or material and immaterial. When the Q'ero priest speaks to a rock (and vice versa!), he or she does not distinguish between the body/form of the rock and the "spirit" or "anima" of the rock. Conceptually, many Westerners envisage the Native Andean *huacas* as animas or spirits inhabiting a "thing" or an aspect of nature; however, this is not true for the Q'eros, and it is probably also inaccurate when describing many other Native Andean belief systems. The body and spirit (mind or immaterial aspect) of the rock are indistinguishable; the rock is a unified entity, and a conscious and sentient being. It is a body-spirit (my term, not theirs) with its own "living energy" just as every other plant, animal, mountain, person, community, or *huaca* in the universe of *Kausay Pacha* ("The World of Living Energies"). There is no independent, immaterial spirit, mind, or soul inhabiting or finding expression in a material body. The experience of the rock and every other aspect of nature is direct, immediate, and personal—an interaction or exchange between one unified body-spirit and another, between one living energy and another.

That is perhaps why in the myth about "The Olden Days When the Sea Overflowed," the Huarochirí storytellers ascribe to Mother Sea choices and desires that are generally attributed to animate beings. Through her *desire* and *choice* to overflow and inundate the world with water, Mother Sea precipitates the calamitous deluge, which destroys everything on earth save for the people and animals that have retreated to the summit of Mount Huillcacoto. This cataclysmic event initiates the cycle of *pachacuti* that culminates in the destruction of that creation and which, after an interim period of disorder, leads to the advent of a new creation. The last passage of the myth also dutifully reminds us that the Huarochirí scribes were converts to Christianity. As with the Inca myth concerning the Inca Creator god *Viracocha* and the creation of the world, it is clear that the storytellers associate the deluge in this story with the Flood in the Christian Bible.

Much like the *Amaru* in the Wanka myth, in this myth we also see the appearance of an intermediary character that mediates between the supernatural world and This World, and between the old and the new creation. In this case, the male llama acts not only as an intermediary, but also as an oracle prophesying the future of humankind. He forewarns his master about the approaching flood and advises him on what he must do to save himself and his family. The oracle also makes it possible for humanity to survive the cataclysm, as the man who takes refuge at the summit of Mount Huillcacoto is also instrumental in repopulating the earth. The water could also be viewed as a mediating element between the previous creation and this one, as could the man who survived the destruction of the old world.

In the following myth from the *Huarochirí Manuscript*, the storytellers describe the state of chaos in the primordial world, which generally precedes a new creation in the recurring cycle of *pachacuti*. In this myth, time-space has become inverted, or turned upside down, and the rules of a bounded, finite world no longer apply. The sun disappears, initiating the cycle of *pachacuti*, and the world returns to the primordium and enters an uninterrupted state of darkness and chaos. In this primordial world of unbroken darkness, the world's order is inverted: rocks bang against each other, stone implements come to life, and mortars and grinding stones begin to eat people. This appropriately describes the period of chaos and destruction that immediately follows a cataclysmic event in the repeating cycle of *pachacuti*. At the end of the passage, again we observe a syncretistic reference to the three hours of darkness during Christ's crucifixion, which is mentioned in the New Testament of the Bible.[91]

How the Sun Disappeared for Five Days
(And now we shall tell how daylight died)

(Quechua with possible Jaqi/Aymara influence)

In ancient times they say the sun died.

And, [once] the sun [was] dead, it turned into night for five days. The stones then banged against each other.

From that time on, those [implements] called *mortars* were formed, that is to say *muchcas*,[92] and also the grinding stones.[93] Mortars and grinding stones began to eat people; llamas started to drive men.

We Christians now bless this, saying: "Perhaps the world darkened on account of the death of our almighty Lord Jesus Christ."

And it is possible that it occurred that way.[94]

~~~

In subsequent sections of the Manuscript, *pachacuti* culminates in a new creation and the birth of one the most important deities of the Huarochirí religion, whose name is *Pariacaca* (also spelled *Pariya Qaqa*, meaning "Igneous Rock"[95]). *Pariacaca* is born of five eggs on Mount *Condorcoto* (meaning "Condor Mountain").[96] Later, the five eggs are transformed into five falcons or hawks[97] that are transformed into five men, who walk the earth and are worshipped as living gods.[98]

According to the Manuscript, *Pariacaca's* son, *Huatya Curi* (also spelled *Watiya Curi*, meaning "Baked Potato Picker" or "Baked Potato Gleaner"), subsisted as a poor man by baking potatoes, or eating leftover potatoes, found in earth pits beneath the ground. While he was sleeping, *Huatya Curi* overheard two foxes, one from above and one from down below, speaking about a certain rich man from the highlands named *Tamta Ñamca* (also spelled *T'anta Nanka*), who owned yellow, blue, and red llamas and had married a corn woman from the lowlands, becoming their Corn Leader. Corn Leader claimed to be a healer and diviner, but he was deathly ill and could not cure himself. In fact, no one could ascertain the cause of his disease. One of the foxes explained that the cause was an infected penis—a corn kernel had popped from his wife's griddle and penetrated her vagina. The wife picked out the kernel and gave it to another man to eat, an act tantamount to adultery. The fox also explained that a snake and a two-headed toad had made their nests in Corn Leader's house and were robbing him of his energy.

After learning this information, Baked Potato Picker made his way to Corn Leader's home and offered to cure him in exchange for his youngest daughter's hand in marriage. At first the rich man and his wise men laughed at Baked Potato Picker, but Corn Leader was so desperate to get well that he agreed to Baked Potato Picker's proposal. Following the poor man's instructions, Corn Leader dismantled his house, found the snake and the two-headed toad, and killed them. After that, his wife also confessed to the adultery. The ailing man got well and recovered from his illness. Baked Potato Picker had Corn Leader promise that he would worship his father *Pariacaca*, who would soon be born on Condor

Mountain. After Corn Leader's recovery, Baked Potato Picker traveled to Condor Mountain for the first time and saw his father, who still dwelled there in the form of five eggs.[99]

According to anthropologist Joseph Bastien, in this myth "marriage between highlanders and lowlanders at first resulted in a feuding mountain, that is an infected penis."[100] However, *Pariacaca* "is born again when the llama, corn, and potato people [different lineage groups and ecological levels within a community] come together in kinship and ritual. [*Pariacaca*] is the mountain, but he is also a body. He is formed by the parts of the mountain."[101]

Pariacaca still comes alive today in certain highland regions of the Andes. Just as in the *Huarochirí Manuscript*, in which *Pariacaca* appeared in the world in the form of five eggs, five hawks, and five humans symbolizing "the unity of the levels and communities of the mountain,"[102] so too does he arise in a Kallawaya agricultural ritual, called New Earth, which brings about a similar rebirth for the mountain-body of Kaata located in the Bolivian altiplano. Bastien describes this ritual as follows:

> New Earth, an important agricultural ritual, effects a similar rebirth for the body of the mountain. Apachetans, Kaatans, and Niñokorins [communities that live on different ecological levels of the mountain] come together during New Earth to recreate the mountain's body. The lower and upper communities send leaders to Kaata for this rite, each bringing his zone's characteristic product, a llama and chicha. The llama's heart and bowels are buried in the center fields, and blood and fat are sent by emissaries to feed the earth shrines of the mountain. The body awakes to become the new earth.[103]

And, as in the corresponding number of eggs, falcons, and men in the Huarochirí myth, ritual offerings in the Kaatan community also involve the number five, or the grouping of offerings by five, representing *Tawantinsuyu* (the name of the former Inca Empire), *Pariacaca*, and the mountain-body of Kaata.[104]

The significance of the number five was also proposed by Andean anthropologist George Urioste, who was a transcriber and, along with Frank Salomon, a co-translator of the *Huarochirí Manuscript*. Urioste focuses on the Andean suffix *"ntin"* as in *Tawantin-suyu*, the name the Incas ascribed to their empire or nation. Urioste contends that this suffix denotes integration or completeness and that the number five represents the four quarters of the former Inca Empire, in addition to the organic body.[105]

In regard to the notion of *pachacuti*, one can also observe that in the *Huarochirí Manuscript* the god *Pariacaca* emerges in mythic time-space during the fifth cycle, or fifth age of the world. In the first remote age a cannibal fire deity named *Huallallo Carhuincho* (also spelled *Wallallo Carwancho*, the "Man Eater" or "Man Drinker") preys on one of every two children born of immortal humans. In the second age, the principal deity is *Cuniraya Viracocha*, whose myth we will analyze in a subsequent chapter. The third age describes the deluge depicted earlier. And during the fourth age the sun dies and night falls upon the earth, paving the way for the luminous *Pariacaca* to make his appearance during the fifth age of the world.[106]

Viewed from this perspective, the five eggs from which *Pariacaca* emerges may be symbolic of each of these five mythical ages. The concept of five ages of the world is also concordant with the notion presented in the colonial chronicle *Nueva corónica* [*crónica*] *y buen gobierno* ("New Chronicle and Good Government") by Felipe Guaman Poma de Ayala, a convert to Christianity, and one of the few Native Andean chroniclers of the Spanish colonial period. According to Guaman Poma, four ages of the world had passed before the ascent of the Inca during the fifth age or "sun."[107]

In Guaman Poma's chronicle, the first age of the world was called *Wari Wira Cocha Runa* ("Primitive People [who descended from the] Wira Cocha"[108]). According to Guaman Poma, this "first generation of Indians descended from the Spaniards whom God brought to this kingdom of the Indies; those who came out of Noah's ark [after the] Deluge."[109] They were coupled in male and female pairs. The *Wari Wira Cocha Runa* did not know how to make clothing, so they dressed like Adam and Eve, covering themselves with the leaves of trees and wild straw. They did not know how to make houses; they lived in caves and in large crags among the rocks. They were not idolatrous and did not worship any *huacas*, "not even the sun, the moon, the stars, nor the demons."[110] They worshipped the Creator god, who went by several different names, including *Ticsi Wira Cocha* ("Fundamental or Primary Lord") and *Runa Rurac* ("Maker of Man"), and they prayed to him. After a while, they forgot their origins but still remembered the (biblical) Deluge, which they called *unu yaku pachacuti* ("*pachacuti* or cataclysm caused by sacred water").[111] Guaman Poma claimed that "from these descended the rest of the generations of Indians called *Pacarimoc Runa*"[112] ("People of the Dawning," or the Original Peoples).

The second age of the world was simply called *Wari Runa* ("Primitive People"), and it was populated by Indians who continued to worship the Creator as well as three aspects of the Thunder or Lightning god (*IIapa* or *Yllapa*)—the "father," the "middle son," and the "younger son," whom Guaman Poma equated with the Christian Trinity because "these ancient Indians had knowledge of the fact that there was only one God, [in] three persons."[113] For this reason, Guaman Poma alleged that they too were not idolatrous, for "they did not worship idols or *huacas*."[114] The *Wari Runa* dressed in animal skins, lived in houses that looked like ovens, and developed primitive agriculture. They started cultivating the land, built rudimentary irrigation canals, developed agricultural terraces (singularly called *pata* in Quechua and *andén* in Spanish), and, according to Guaman Poma, kept the laws and commandments of the Creator.

The third age of the world was called *Purun Runa* ("Uncivilized People" or "People of the Wilderness"[115]), and it was inhabited by people who adhered to the law of the Creator and fought to defend the laws of their lords and king.[116] During this age, they improved their agricultural methods, raised camelids such as llamas and alpacas, and learned to spin yarn, dye wool, and weave colorful clothing. They also built roads, constructed walls and enclosures out of stone, created dances and songs, mined "native" silver and gold (*purun cullque* and *purun cori*), and set forth rules and laws for the population to follow.[117] According to Guaman Poma, these people suffered from a devastating pestilence in which "very many people died. [It is said that] for six months the condors [and] the vultures ate the [decomposed bodies of the] people, and all the vultures of this kingdom could not even finish [them all]."[118]

The fourth age of the world produced the bellicose *Auca Runa* or *Auca Pacha Runa* ("Warlike People" or "People of the Age of War") who, by force of arms, caused "much death and bloodshed."[119] The *Auca Runa* waged war with more advanced weapons such as lances, slings, clubs, and hatchets, and they were led into battle by brave captains and princes, who dressed as and allegedly transformed into animals such as pumas, jaguars, foxes, hawks, vultures, and others during battle.[120] According to Guaman Poma, these people moved out of the lowlands and started populating the highlands and built fortresses (*pucara*) to protect themselves. They pillaged and stole lands, clothing, gold, silver, and copper from other groups of people and accumulated wealth. They imposed severe penalties for crimes such as thievery and adultery, and they continued worshipping the Creator and performing acts of charity. Each community celebrated its military victories with dances and songs, "without engaging in idolatry, without prostrating themselves before the *huacas*, without any ceremonies. They ate and drank and enjoyed themselves without [succumbing to] the devils' temptations; neither did they kill nor become inebriated like in this time of the Spanish Christians."[121] The *Auca Runa* continued to rule the land, each community with its own king, until the fifth age of the world when the Incas conquered them. During the fifth age the mighty Inca ruler came to power and declared himself "son of the Sun" (*intip churin*) and also son "of the moon, and brother of the Evening and Morning Star."[122]

At the heart of Guaman Poma's vision of the five ages of the world is the underlying Andean cyclical and nonlinear concept of *pachacuti*, which contemplates dramatic changes, inversions, or revolutions—a "turning around" of the world—precipitated by cataclysmic forces and events that change the existing order. This notion confounded the colonial chroniclers. "Neither Garcilaso [de la Vega] nor any of the chroniclers intuited [its meaning], and the inassimilable myths of the New World were [examined] with a Judeo-Christian lens of the ancient 'ages' and stages of the universe. They viewed the Aztec *sun*, the Andean *pachacuti*, as [linear] patterns of time comparable to a century, 500 years, [or] a millennium perhaps."[123] Although Guaman Poma presents what appears to be a historical chronology of the Native Andean peoples, "the description of different world epochs separated by catastrophes . . . is, though, an Andean perception of time."[124]

One clear illustration of the nonlinear, nonchronological aspect of Andean time-space, singularly called *pacha* (from which the word *pachacuti*, "inversion of time-space," is derived), is found in the fifth chapter of the *Huarochirí Manuscript*. The indigenous storytellers introduce a mythical character called *Huatyacuri*, described as a poor "potato eater."[125] This potato eater was the first to witness the birth of his *father*, the deity *Pariacaca*, born of five eggs on Condorcoto.[126] The myth acknowledges that in a nonlinear, mythical epoch of space and time, a son may be born *before* his father. Similarly, in the Wanka origin myth the two *Amaru* are killed in the primordial world by the meteorological god *Tiksi*; nonetheless, the storyteller maintains that the *Amaru* (it is not clear whether there are still one or two) continues to live in a cave during *this creation*, which presumably followed the destruction of its world. So the *Amaru* is, paradoxically, both dead and alive, or, alive after death, within the framework of Andean time-space.

RETURN OF THE INCA

The vision of *pachacuti* "today [also] revolve[s] around the millenarian theme of the return of the Inca."[127] This body of myths concerns a messianic hero, known in the Andes as *Inkarrí* ("Inca King"),[128] whose legend foretells that he will one day return to reinstate the power of the Inca and put an end to "European" (white and mestizo) domination.[129] There are many versions of the myth which, in part, have a historical basis. In 1572 the last Inca king, Tupac Amaru, was captured and beheaded by the colonial Spaniards. His death ended forty years of guerrilla warfare that the Incas had waged against the Spaniards from their secret refuges in the mountains. The struggle began in 1532 when the Spanish conquistador, Francisco Pizarro, ambushed the Inca emperor, Atahualpa, at Cajamarca and later garroted him, despite the payment of an extraordinary ransom for the emperor's release and freedom. Forty years later the last Inca king, Tupac Amaru, suffered the same fate at the hands of the Spaniards at the tender age of fifteen.

Felipe Guaman Poma de Ayala describes the last Inca's arrival in Cuzco, the former capital of the Inca Empire:

> They brought Tupac Amaru Inca as a prisoner, as a child Inca king, crowned as a king and lord of this kingdom. And Captain Martín García de Oyola brought him barefoot and handcuffed and tied with a gold chain around his neck. And the other captain walked in front, carrying the Inca's idol of the Sun god, made from the finest gold, and the idol of Huanacauri, with all of the Inca's arms and captains, and male and female children. They paraded them along the street of their neighbor, Diego de Silva, where the said [Viceroy] Don Francisco de Toledo was lodging. The Viceroy came to the window and saw everything. And they imprisoned Tupac Amaru Inca and also Don Carlos Paullo Tupac Inca and Don Alonso Atauchi and the rest of the Incas of the city of Cuzco.... Tupac Amaru Inca was beheaded by order of Don Francisco de Toledo. [Viceroy Toledo] sentenced the child Inca king, and he died, baptized as a Christian, at the age of fifteen years old. On account of his death, all the Inca women of royal blood and the Indians of this kingdom cried and wept loudly throughout the city, and rang the [church] bells. And all the most important people and women and important Indians went to the burial, and the clergy accompanied them, and they buried him in the largest church of the City of Cuzco. And then Don Francisco de Toledo ceased [his relentless pursuit].[130]

After the execution, Tupac Amaru's head was displayed on a pike as a warning to all who might consider rebelling against the Spaniards. But since the Inca ruler was considered a deity, the son of the Sun god on earth, his people came to worship his head at night. Legend has it that the handsome head of the young Inca became even more beautiful every day, as his subjects came to venerate it in secret.[131] To put an end to this clandestine ritual, the Spanish viceroy ordered that the head be buried in a remote location.[132]

Some Andeans believe that the *Inkarrí* myth alludes to another historical event—the execution of the revolutionary hero José Gabriel Condorcanqui, who earlier had assumed the name of José Gabriel Tupac Amaru, or Tupac Amaru II, in honor of the last Inca ruler, from whom he claimed descent.[133] The rebel leader, Condorcanqui, had been educated by Jesuits and was the *cacique* (chieftain or local indigenous leader) of Surinamá, Tungasuca, and Pampamarca, Peru. Proclaiming that he was the legitimate Inca ruler of the Peruvian people, including Indians, mestizos, and African slaves (he was one of the first leaders in the Americas to call for an abolition of slavery and signed an edict declaring all slaves free), Condorcanqui sent envoys to other Andean regions and led numerous uprisings against the Spanish colonial authorities. In 1780 he solidly defeated the Spanish army in the vicinity of Cuzco, but in 1781 one of his own betrayed him and turned him over to the Spaniards. The Spanish sentenced him to death and, after being forced to witness the execution of his wife and sons, he was drawn and quartered in the square of Cuzco. Afterward, the Spanish viceroy sent each of his body parts to every Andean region supporting the insurgency. But this did not completely quell the rebellion. Under the leadership of the surviving relatives of Condorcanqui, including his brother Diego Cristóbal and his nephew Andrés, as well as another relative named Tupac Catari, the insurgency spread beyond the Viceroyalty of Peru to the Viceroyalties of Río de la Plata and Nueva Granada. By the end of the year, however, the wave of rebellion subsided as rebel leaders (real or imagined by the colonial authorities) were captured, tortured, and executed. Many were decapitated; some were drawn and quartered; others were burned alive.

Since that time, according to the *Inkarrí* myth, the head of the Inca has been looking for its body. When the two are reunited a *pachacuti* will take place, and the Inca will be born again, initiating "a radical transformation for the benefit of the descendants of the Inca."[134] In some versions of the myth, the buried head is growing and sprouting underneath the ground.[135] So when the body regenerates and becomes whole again, then *Inkarrí* will return, ushering in a new age for the descendants of the Inca.

The following is one of many Native Andean myths prophesying the return of *Inkarrí*.

The Myth of Inkarrí

~~~~~~

(Quechua)

The *Wamanis* [mountain spirits or spiritual embodiment of the mountain peaks] exist; like our own. They were put there by our ancient Lord, by Inkarrí.

The *Wamani* is, you know, our second God.

All the mountains have *Wamani*. In all the mountains is the *Wamani*.

The *Wamani* gives us grass for [grazing] our animals, and for us, his vein, the Water.[136]

God placed the cloud[s], the rain; we receive all of this as a blessing from Him.

And from our parents, the *Wamanis*, we receive the *unu* water,[137] because that's what God has settled and ordered. But everything was placed here by our ancient Inkarrí. He created everything that exists.

So, when he worked he told his father, the Sun, "Wait for me." And with iron cinches he tied up the Sun to the mountain at Osqonta, next to Wanakupampa.[138]

The father of Inkarrí was the Sun.

Inkarrí has an abundance of gold. They say that now he is in Cuzco.

We don't know who took him to Cuzco. They say they took his head, only his head. And so, they say that his head of hair is growing; his body is growing downward [toward his feet]. When it becomes whole, Judgment will be carried out perhaps.

When Inkarrí was about to die, he said, "Oh, silver and gold!" All the silver disappeared in the entire world. "Hide the gold and silver in our seven states," he ordered.

We don't know who killed him; perhaps the Spanish killed him and took his head to Cuzco.

That's why the birds on the coastline sing: "The king is in Cuzco. Go to Cuzco," they sing.[139]

~~~~~~

In this Andean myth *Inkarrí* is not only a savior but also a creator who "created everything that exists." The *Wamani*, who this Quechua storyteller refers to as "our second God," was also "put there by our ancient Lord, by Inkarrí." Whereas the Christian God created the clouds and the rain, which the narrator considers "a blessing from Him," *Inkarrí* created the *Wamanis*, or mountain deities, whose vein (waterways and mountain springs) produces the fertilizing blood of the earth, or sacred water, known as *yaku unu*, *unu agua*, or *aguay unu*.[140] Just as the Inca rulers of the pre-Columbian past, *Inkarrí* is also the son of the Sun, who ties his father to the mountain of *Osqonta*[141] while he goes about his work. Perhaps this is a reference to the sacred *intiwatana* (also spelled *intihuatana*, "the hitching post of the Sun") that the Incas constructed as a sundial or astronomical calendar from the bedrock at Machu Picchu, and at other Inca sites,[142] to ensure the permanence of the Sun and, conceivably, to prevent a *pachacuti*.

The syncretistic juxtaposition of pre-Columbian and Christian elements in the myth suggests that the storyteller acknowledges that both legacies, indigenous and Western European, exist side by side in contemporary Andean culture and society; still, he expresses ambivalence, if not anger, about the effects of colonialism, for colonialism killed the indigenous hero *Inkarrí*. He gingerly alludes to the subject of decapitation ("They say they took his head, only his head") and the plundering that took place during the Spanish Conquest ("Hide the gold and silver in our seven states, ordered [Inkarrí]"); yet, he does not strongly acknowledge who orchestrated the Inca's heinous execution ("We don't know who took him to Cuzco" and "perhaps the Spanish killed him, and took his head to Cuzco"). Nonetheless, the narrator predicts that when the body of *Inkarrí* becomes whole again, "Judgment will be carried out perhaps."

The conflict between indigenous and European legacies is portrayed in various ingenious ways in Andean stories. In some *Inkarrí* myths, *Inkarrí* and *Españarrí* (a play on the Spanish words *España*, meaning "Spain," and *rey*, meaning "king") are brothers who misunderstand one another.

Españarrí went looking [for Inkarrí] and left him a written letter. When Inkarrí returned, he found the written message and shouted angrily, "What kind of bird, what kind of animal could have stained this white paper with its paws?" But Inkarrí was aware of [the existence] of his brother. That's why he left him some *khipus* [records made of knotted cords] made out of thread. [Upon finding these, Españarrí inquired,] "What kind of miserable man would own these tattered rags [and] these frayed threads?"[143]

Although the conflict presented here is allegedly between *Españarrí's* use of "pen and paper," a Western mode of communication, and *Inkarrí's* employment of *"khipu,"* an Inca recording device made of knots and colored threads, Andean listeners readily understand that the conflict is much deeper and is being playfully disguised in the story as something more trivial and inconsequential.

In other Andean myths, the conflict and mistrust generated by the historical or symbolic *pachacuti*—the European Conquest and subsequent colonization and Christianization of the Andes—is personified in the character of an ancient being called *Ñawpa Machu* (also spelled *Ñaupa Machu*, meaning "Ancient Old Man") from the "Dark or Previous Age" of the world (*Ch´awaq Pacha*). Legend has it that *Ñawpa Machu* "lived in a mountain called School," and he "was delighted to learn that the Inca [ruler] was dead."[144] In his desire to dishearten and ultimately "eat" the children of the Inca and *Pacha Mama*, he told the children, "Pacha Mama doesn't love the Inca anymore. The Inca has befriended Jesus Christ and now they live together as little brothers."[145]

Just as in the story concerning the *Wamani* and *Inkarrí*, Andean narrators of the *Ñawpa Machu* stories are expressing their misgivings about the Europeanization of Native Andean cultures. The antagonist in these stories lives in the mountain of "School"—a salient reference to writing, literacy, and Christianity—which the colonists imported to the New World from Europe. Many scholars have already commented that in Latin American colonial society, the quill was always the companion of the sword and was used as an instrument of power and cultural domination.[146] For that reason, to this day, some Native Andeans are suspicious and mistrustful of books and Westernized schooling in general.[147]

THE BODY AS UNIFYING METAPHOR

The corpus of *Inkarrí* myths in the Andes predicts that one day the body of *Inkarrí* will be restored, and the Native Andeans will be made whole at the dawning of a new Indigenous Age, or symbolic *pachacuti*. Metaphorically, when the head and the body reconnect, the present-day Andeans will reconnect with the teachings and traditions of their pre-Columbian past. Moreover, the symbolic body of *Inkarrí* will reestablish the bond between the Native Andeans and their ancestors, a vital link that was abruptly ruptured by the European Extirpation in an effort to break the attachment between the native lineages and their ancestral religions.

The body of *Inkarrí*, however, is also a metaphor for the Native Andean communities at many different levels. In many respects, the "body" represents the unifying metaphor for the relationship between the individual and his or her Native Andean community, and between the community and the cosmos of time-space. In fact, the organization of the world into a body form has a long history in the Andes.

For example, some archaeologists maintain that the Inca capital of Cuzco was constructed in the form or symbolic body of a puma.[148] The lavish Temple of the Sun in Cuzco was located in the "tail" of the puma; the great fortress of Sacsahuman was situated at the "head." Aside from the symbolic representation of physical space, the Inca emperor, Pachacuti Inca Yupanqui, also referred to the whole of his city as a "puma's body," where he was the "head" of the puma and his people were the puma's "limbs."[149]

Similarly, some modern Native Andean communities envision themselves as both a collective and a physical body. For example, as previously discussed, anthropologist Joseph Bastien, who studied the highland communities living on the Bolivian mountain of Kaata, concluded that the Quechua and Aymara communities living there perceive themselves as one unified and integrated body.[150] Further, the mountain itself is also considered a body with a distinct head, mouth, heart, limbs, and other body parts, and each part of the mountain-body is "fed" ritual offerings in order to maintain the integrity and life force of the community.[151] There is also a correspondence among the three parts of the mountain, the three ecological zones in which the inhabitants live, and the three "worlds" (*pachas*) of the Kaatan cosmos. Thus, the body serves as a unifying metaphor, connecting the community, the cosmos, and the land (mountain) itself.

Likewise, centuries ago the Incas adopted the body metaphor in their religious rites and rituals. They performed a ritual called *pirac* or *pirani* (derived from the Quechua verb *piray*, meaning "to mark with blood") in which the faces of people or religious idols (*huacas*) were marked with animal or human blood, creating a symbolic facial geometry. For instance, as part of a monthlong ceremony associated with male maturity rites (*huarachico* or *warachicuy*), an Inca priest, or the initiates, would smear a horizontal line of animal blood across their faces, "with much reverence...from ear to ear,"[152] crossing the natural vertical axis of the face, and essentially dividing the facial surface into four regions or quarters. This facial geometry is believed to replicate, in this case, the quadripartite division of Cuzco, the Inca imperial capital, and to mirror the four (political) quarters, or *suyus*, into which the Inca Empire was divided.[153] In essence, the facial geometry outlined in blood depicted the symbolic "body" of Cuzco and also that of the Empire.

Cristóbal de Molina also described a similar ritual that took place during the coronation of a new Inca ruler. According to Molina, during the coronation Inca children were offered as sacrifices to the Inca Creator god. After the children were killed, the priests used their blood to mark the idol from "ear to ear" and also offered up the bodies of the victims, which were later interred along with other offerings.[154] The Spanish colonial chronicler Juan de Betanzos also described a similar ceremony performed by the Inca ruler and his lords to bless and consecrate the Inca Temple of the Sun. In that ceremony the Inca ordered that the blood of sacrificed animals be used to draw lines on the temple walls. Later, the Inca used the same blood to draw a line on the face of the priest, "who was designated as caretaker of this temple, and he did the same to those three lords his friends and to the *mamaconas*, nuns [who worked] in the service of the Sun."[155] So then, in a manner similar to the sacred facial geometry created by the lines drawn during the male maturity rites, these Inca ceremonies strongly suggest that this symbolic geometry of the "body" (city/Empire) was also replicated in other important rituals.

The present-day Aymaras also practice a comparable ritual in a rite of passage ceremony called *sucullu*, which takes place during the potato harvest and is intended to incorporate children into the social order. In preparation, all mothers who have given birth in the preceding year gather with their babies in the center of the village. According to anthropologist Thérèse Boysse-Cassagne, on the first day of the *sucullu* festival each child's maternal uncle (*lari*) collects the blood from a dead vicuña and smears it horizontally across the face of the child, making "a transversal mark from cheek to cheek."[156] In much the same way it was done in the Inca *pirac* or *pirani*, this horizontal mark not only divides the face of the child into two symmetrical halves (left and right of the vertical axis through the nose) but also creates a symbolic and unifying body, establishing *yanantin* or *yanani* (complementary duality).

> Their convergence (*taypi*) establishes a new facial geometry... [consisting of] four *tawantin* sectors (right above, left above, right below, left below), a symbolic quadripartition that can be related to the layout

of the village. A mutual confirmation is achieved, as it were, between the body of the child and the body politic.[157]

Hence, as in the Inca rituals, the facial division in the Aymara *sucullu* ritual also appears to represent both the physical layout of the land and the metaphoric, integrated "body" of the community.

Given the importance of the body as a unifying metaphor for Native Andean society, land, and cosmos, it is readily apparent why The Myth of *Inkarrí* and the union of the head and body in particular will, from a Native Andean cosmological perspective, bring about a *pachacuti*. The reconstituted body of *Inkarrí* may be viewed as a basic organizing principle, or a paradigm, for a new age of "wholeness" where the Native Andeans are realigned with their land, community, and vision of the cosmos.

As some scholars have recognized, however, the return of the Inca, as posited by the myth, may be an idealization.[158] From the perspective of some Native Andeans, The Myth of *Inkarrí* embodies romantic and positive memories associated with the Inca past and calls for a return to the greatness and magnanimity of Inca rule. With respect to this view, sometimes called *incarismo,* anthropologist José Yánez del Pozo maintains that in the memory of the Native Andeans "the Andean past has been reconstructed and transformed... as an alternative to the present," where they imagine themselves living "without hunger, without exploitation, and where [Native] Andean people once again govern, [marking] the end of disorder and obscurity."[159] He contends that the myth must be reconceptualized to incorporate the new realities of a mixed, multicultural, and multiethnic Andean culture and society.

> More than a return to a paradisiacal and monolithic [past] Inca realm, it must be understood that our [Andean] past is like a true palimpsest.... We have to finally convince ourselves that the Andean reality at the time of the Inca was a multi-regional, multi-ethnic, multi-lordly, and multi-social reality.... If we manage to recover this multiplicity as an organizing principle... we [Andeans] shall be able to confront many of our problems at the same time.[160]

Although the search for wholeness embodied by the *Inkarrí* myth can probably not be achieved by a return to a foregone Andean past, by the same token the present state of affairs of Native Andeans cannot be maintained in a society that purports to recognize and value its ethnic and racial diversity and multiculturalism. In many instances, Andean societies (including mine) silently condone racism and marginalize Native Andeans from the mainstream of society. This theme also recurs in many Andean stories and will be discussed more fully in a subsequent chapter regarding social protest.

According to some sources, between 1953 and 1972, fifteen different versions of the *Inkarrí* myth took root in the Andes.[161] As Manuel Espinoza Tamayo observed, "Among the common people and among the poor mestizos, there are no negative memories, images, or feelings related to the Inca conquest[s]. As much for the *cholos* [mestizos], as for the *runas* [common indigenous people], everything Inca is associated with positive values, and especially with the ideals of liberty and liberation."[162] As this passage aptly illustrates, the *Inkarrí* myth creates an idyllic view of the Inca past that may or may not coincide with historical reality. However, in the final analysis the facts may be inconsequential. What appears to be expressed in the myth, and another possible interpretation, is that the restored body of *Inkarrí* represents the desire or longing for certain fundamental rights and freedoms that would result from reintegration or reincorporation of Native Andeans into the mainstream of Andean society.

Metaphorically, the head of *Inkarrí*, associated with the Native Andean people, is still divided and separated from its "body," the collective representation of Andean culture and society. When colonial Spaniards beheaded the last Inca rulers, the head of the mythical hero *Inkarrí* was also severed; it was purposely cut off by repressive colonial policies and their modern progeny that alienated and fractured the indigenous population from the whole of Andean society. Nevertheless, the myth recognizes that the head cannot function without its body (and vice versa); thus, according to the legend, the head persists in its search for unification and reintegration with the body, to make its body "whole" again. Conceivably, therein lies an underlying expression of hope: *pachacuti* will usher in a new age when this separation ends and the Native Andean peoples will be reconnected with the traditions and positive values of their illustrious ancestors, and reintegrated into the body politic of Andean society.

Until that day, the Native Andeans await the return of the formidable *Inkarrí*, the mythical indigenous king whose return will precipitate an inversion of time-space and mark the arrival of a new *pachacuti*. A Native Andean storyteller expressed this sentiment well:

The Moon and the Sun came together, the bull and the Amaru. The world progressed. The Earth trembled, and the head of Inkarrí was hidden by his brother. Since then, the decapitators have risen to power. [But] the blood of Inkarrí is alive in the innards of Mother Earth. It is affirmed that there will come a day when his head, his blood, and his body will reunite. On that day, the day will dawn as night; the reptiles will fly. The Parinacochas Lake will become dry. Then the beautiful and great culture that our Inkarrí could not complete will be visible once again.[163]

CHAPTER SUMMARY

This chapter introduced the Andean cyclical concept of *pachacuti* in relation to origin myths that describe the creation and destruction of the world and the inversion or "turning around" of time-space. In this context we have also discussed the importance of the *Manuscript of Huarochirí*, one of the few colonial documents written in the Quechua language, which provides a rare opportunity to read a coherent account of a pre-Columbian religion, recorded by native Christian scribes, who at one time had probably been practitioners of this ancient religion. Their narration distinguishes between different ages of the world and presents successive cycles of creation and destruction consistent with the Andean view of *pachacuti*.

With regard to *pachacuti*, we also discussed the significance of the Andean mythological serpent, *Amaru*, which is identified with explosive forces, the presence of water, and *pachacuti*-like events. In terms of Andean mythology, its appearance points to the struggle of unbalanced primordial forces striving to regain stability and equilibrium.

Finally, using various examples we have described the Andean notion of the body as a unifying metaphor, expressing the integrity and whole-ness of the land, cosmos, and Native Andean community. Within that framework, we have explored the significance of the *Inkarrí* myths, which focus on the millenarian theme of the return of the Inca and the reconstitution of the symbolic "body" of the Inca. These myths may be expressing a longing for a symbolic *pachacuti* or "turning over" of the European Age to pave the way for a new Indigenous Age, where the Native Andeans—in actuality or metaphorically—will return to the magnificence and glory of the former Inca Empire. However, it is more likely that such myths express a desire to be reconnected with the traditions and positive values of the pre-Hispanic past that were severed and dismantled by the Spanish colonial system, and are calling for a reintegration of the Native Andean people into the collective body of Andean culture and society.

5

~~

huacas

The Many Definitions of Huaca

The meaning and description of the non-Western concept of *huaca* (also spelled *waka* or *guaca*) has preoccupied the minds of many Andean scholars. In its most general definition a *huaca* is an object, animal, person, or place venerated by the Native Andean religions of the past and present. Many describe *huacas* as "animas" or spirits associated with individual aspects of nature—mountains, caves, lakes, springs, rivers, streams, and rocks; others simply describe *huacas* as indigenous "places of worship [where] offerings" are made.[1] *Huacas* may be natural or human-made. Temples, shrines, idols, sepulchers, and other holy objects and places worshipped by the Native Andean peoples are also considered *huacas*.

Anthropologist Frank Salomon describes a whole host of *huacas* that appear in the colonial *Huarochirí Manuscript*. For example, there are *huacas* that lodge in nature, such as "mountains, springs, lakes, rock outcrops, ancient ruins, caves, and any number of humanly made objects in shrines: effigies, mummies, oracles and so forth."[2] *Huacas* are also deities such as the Huarochirí god *Pariacaca* or the Andean Earth Mother *Pacha Mama*, and material things that exhibit "superhuman" characteristics such as a mountain peak that stands above the rest, or an anomaly of nature such as a twinned cob of maize or a double-yolked egg.[3] *Huacas* can also include mummies and ancestors worshipped by the native peoples. They may even include victims of human sacrifice, called *capac cocha* or *capac hucha* ("opulent prestation"),[4] who, in some ancient pre-Columbian Andean societies, were deified after their deaths.

130

One of the most extensive explanations of the meaning of the term *huaca* was furnished by the colonial mestizo chronicler, Garcilaso de la Vega, in the first volume of his *Comentarios reales de los incas* ("Royal Commentaries of the Incas"), published in 1609. He wrote:

> *Huaca*... means "sacred thing," as were all those things through which the devil spoke to them. These are the idols, the rocks, the great stones, or trees in which the enemy [Satan] entered to make them believe that he was a god. Likewise, they apply the name *huaca* to those things that they had offered to the Sun [god], such as figures of men, birds and animals, made of gold or of silver or of wood, and any other offerings that they considered sacred because they had been received by the Sun as offerings and were his.... They also give the name *huaca* to any temple, large or small, and to the sepulchers that they had in the fields and in the corners of the houses where the devil spoke to [their] priests and other individuals.... They also give the same name to all those things that in their beauty and excellence stand above others of their same species, such as a rose, apple, or pippin, or any other fruit that is better or more beautiful than all the others of the same tree. On the other hand, they apply the name *huaca* to ugly and monstrous things that cause horror and fright. And thus, they gave this name to the great snakes of the Antis [Andes], which measure from 25 to 30 feet in length. They also give the name *huaca* to all things that are out of the ordinary course of nature, such as a woman who gives birth to twins... [or] sheep that give birth to twins.... And similarly, they apply the name *huaca* to a double-yolked egg. And the same name is given to children who are born breach or bent or with six toes or fingers in their feet or hands.... Likewise, they give this name to the mighty fountains that spray like rivers... [and] to the great range of the Sierra Nevada that runs through Peru.... They give the same name to high mountains that stand above the others... and to steep mountain slopes... that the Indians worshipped, and to which they gave offerings.[5]

Garcilaso also described the kinds of offerings that were made to the *huacas*. These included animals, large and small, such as llamas, rabbits, and birds; and also food, coca leaves, animal fat, *chicha* (maize beer), gold and silver objects, and fine woven garments, called *cumbi*, that were ceremoniously burned.[6] Although Garcilaso disputed the notion that the Incas had practiced human sacrifice, other colonial writers affirmed that the

Incas did engage in this practice, as did some of their conquered peoples.[7]
Today there is a large body of archaeological evidence that supports the
contention that the Inca and other ancient Andean civilizations made
human offerings to their gods on special occasions,[8] such as the coronation of an emperor, in response to a cataclysmic event or natural disaster,
during the most important festivals dedicated to the Sun god, and before
important military expeditions and conquests. They considered human
sacrifice to be the most precious offering that could be made to the gods.

Today in the Andes, human sacrifice is no longer practiced. However,
the custom of offering smaller sacrifices to the *huacas* still continues as part
of many syncretistic Native Andean rituals, which combine Christian and
pre-Columbian elements. Modern offerings, similar to those of Andean
antiquity, include food, coca, *chicha*, figurines, crops, shells, animals
(principally guinea pigs, sheep, rabbits, and llamas), mineral powders,
candies, animal fat, llama dung, wool, flowers, and many other items
available to each community. These offerings and *pagos* ("payments"),
also called *despachos* ("remittances"), are customarily made to the *huacas*
during every stage of the life cycle which is accompanied by ritual: the
celebration of a birth; the first haircutting and baptism of a child; marriage
(to assure a couple's fecundity and success); and funerary rites (to assure
the deceased's safe passage to the afterlife). There are also gifts, such as
food and clothing, that are offered up to the dead so they may receive
and partake of them in the afterlife. In *Mountain of the Condor*, Joseph
Bastien describes offerings of food and clothing made in preparation
for the burial of a member of an Andean (Kaatan) community named
Guillermo.

> In preparation for [Guillermo's] burial...friends and relatives paid
> their respects by praying Hail Marys and Our Fathers and by putting
> coca into his bag for the journey [of the dead]....Refilda filled his
> medicine bag with cooked potatoes, oca [an Andean tuber], charqui
> [meat jerky], hot sauce, and llama fat, enough for a long day's journey.
> She wrapped his blankets and poncho around him, for it would be
> cold inside of the earth as he traveled the underground waterways
> toward the highlands.[9]

Offerings are also made to ensure the health and well-being of the
community. Specific rituals and sacrifices are offered to alleviate illness,
dispel misfortune and bad luck, and to maintain the integrity of the

community. Ritual offerings also coincide with the agricultural cycle and are generally characterized as "feedings" for Pacha Mama, who in turn is expected to reciprocate with her gift of a bountiful harvest.[10] These ritual offerings are made at designated *huacas*, or holy sites, venerated by the Native Andean community.

Sometimes *huacas* also appear in the form of animals. In his narrative *Relación de antigüedades deste reyno del Pirú* ("Recounting of Antiquities from this Kingdom of Peru"), written in 1613, the Native Andean chronicler Joan de Santacruz Pachacuti Yamqui Salcamaygua described an encounter between the Inca emperor Pachacuti Inca Yupanqui and the *huaca* of a province called Cañacuay of the Condesuyos, a people who inhabited the region southwest of the Inca capital of Cuzco. In this passage one recognizes the *huaca* as an animal when it appears to the Inca emperor in the form of a frightening serpent. It also represents the *huaca* as a willful and sentient being that attempts to prevent the Inca army from entering and conquering its province. Later the Inca had a stone idol made in the form of a serpent to commemorate his miraculous victory over the enemy *huaca*. He also assigned a name to the idol and commanded that it be placed strategically overlooking the cultivated terraces, where it was likely to be seen and worshipped by farmers. Both of these measures suggest that to the Inca, the stone idol was also a *huaca*.

> Finally, Pachacuti Inca Yupanqui made his entry to conquer the Condesuyos with one hundred thousand men. [But] then the *huaca* of Cañacuay burst into frightening flames and did not allow [Pachacuti's] people to enter [its province]. And finally it appeared as a frightening serpent and they say that it consumed many people, which caused [the Inca Pachacuti] great sorrow. And grieving, [the Inca] raised his eyes to heaven, asking the Lord of heaven and earth for help, with great sadness and weeping. Then came from the sky an *auancana*, or eagle, [which] with frightening fury and loud whirring, snatched the serpent and raised it by its head and later let it drop to the ground. And they say that it burst. The same thing happened to another companion [serpent that also] burst while climbing a tree to catch the Inca captain, Ttopa Capac, the bastard brother of the Inca [Pachacuti]. And then they say the Indians [Incas] all came out alive. Finally, in memory of that miracle, said Inca ordered that a serpent be made out of stone and placed in the graded cultivated terraces of that province. [This stone serpent] is called Uatipirca.[11]

In some cases *huacas* also assume human form. Unlike the Western European concept of an invisible God, *huacas* eat, walk, play music, engage in sexual relations, and occasionally appear and talk to human beings. The human characteristics of *huacas* are evident in numerous Native Andean myths and legends.[12] The following is the story of two famous ancient Andean *huacas*, *Cuniraya Viracocha* and *Cauillaca*. The story is translated from the colonial *Manuscript of Huarochirí*, one of the few colonial documents recorded in the Quechua language.

THE ILL-FATED LOVE OF TWO HUACAS, CUNIRAYA VIRACOCHA AND CAUILLACA

How Cuniraya Viracocha Behaved in His Own Time, and How Cauillaca Gave Birth to His Child and What Occurred The Life of Cuniraya Viracocha

(Quechua with possible Jaqi/Aymara influence)

This Cuniraya Viracocha, long, long ago, walked, wandered, and assumed the appearance of a miserably poor man. His cloak and his tunic were ripped and tattered. Some, who didn't know him, murmured upon seeing him, "You lousy wretch!" This man had power over all the villages. Just by saying so, he managed to construct well-finished agricultural terraces, sustained by fine walls. He also taught the people how to build irrigation canals by throwing the flower of a reed, called *pupuna*, on the ground. He taught them how to make the canals channeling out from their source. In this way, doing this and that, he walked about humiliating the *huacas* from other villages with his cleverness.

And so, in that time, there was a *huaca* named Cauillaca. She was a maiden, of course. She was so beautiful that all the *huacas*, one by one, would say, "I want to sleep with her." They longed for her and desired her. But none of them got what he wanted. Cauillaca never allowed anyone to have sex with her. One day, she was weaving under a *lúcuma* tree.[13] At that moment Cuniraya, who was clever, changed himself into a bird and climbed up into the tree. He took a fruit from one of the tree branches, put his semen into it, and dropped it in front of the woman. She swallowed it down contentedly.

In this way, Cauillaca became pregnant without ever having relations with any man. Like any woman, she gave birth to a baby girl after nine months. For one year she breast-fed the little girl, wondering, "Whose child could this be?" When her daughter turned exactly one, and could crawl on all fours, the mother summoned all the *huacas* from all the regions, hoping that one of them would recognize her daughter as his child. When the *huacas* heard the news, they dressed in their finest clothing. "It's me she'll love, it's me she'll love," they each would say, as they heeded the call from Cauillaca.

The gathering was held in Anchicocha, where the woman lived. Then, when all the sacred *huacas* were seated, Cauillaca said to them, "Behold, gentlemen, powerful chiefs, come forth and acknowledge this child. Which of you made me pregnant with your seed?" And one by one she asked each one of them, "Was it you? Was it you?" But none of them answered, "It is mine."

Then, Cuniraya Viracocha, the one we spoke about before, sat down humbly. He appeared to be a beggar, so the woman did not question him. "My baby cannot be the child of a wretched beggar," she thought, nauseated by the sight of the man dressed in rags, surrounded by men who were handsomely dressed.

Since no one had affirmed "The child is mine," Cauillaca spoke to her child and said, "Go and identify your father." And she addressed the *huacas,* "If one of you is the father, my daughter will climb up into your arms."

The baby began crawling on all fours up to the place where the beggar sat. Along the way, she did not climb up on any other *huacas* in attendance. But as soon as she reached the beggar, she instantly brightened up and hugged her father's legs. When the mother witnessed this, she became indignant and exclaimed, "How repulsive! How could I possibly give birth to the child of such a wretched man?" She picked up her child and ran in the direction of the ocean. Witnessing what had transpired, Cuniraya Viracocha asserted, "Soon she will desire me."

Cuniraya put on his golden gown and scared away all the other *huacas.* And since they were so frightened, he drove them away. He called after Cauillaca, "Sister Cauillaca, turn around and look at me! See how beautiful I am now!" He stood very erect, making his garment sparkle. But she never turned around to look at Cuniraya. She continued to flee, heading toward the ocean.

"Because I've given birth to the filthy child of a despicable man, a mangy beggar, I will disappear," she said, and threw herself into the ocean. Just as soon as they fell into the sea, both mother and daughter turned into stone. And there, to this day, in the deep sea of Pachacamac, one can see very clearly two stones living there, shaped like human beings.[14]

Cuniraya insisted, "My sister will see me; she will [re]appear." And he moved away from that place [called Anchicocha], saying, calling, and shouting out her name.

Along the way, he encountered an old condor. He asked the condor, "Brother, where did you run into my woman?"

"Very near here," replied the condor. "You will find her."

Cuniraya spoke to him and said, "You will live a long life. When wild animals die [on the slopes]—whether guanacos or vicuñas, or any other animal—you will eat their flesh. And if anyone should kill you, he will also die." That's what he said to him.

Later, he encountered a skunk. Cuniraya asked him, "Brother, where did you encounter my woman?" The skunk replied, "You will never find her now. She is too far away."

Cuniraya cursed him, "For giving me such bad news, you will not be able to walk about in the daytime, because men will detest you. You will walk only at night, hated by men, and stinking disgustingly. You will suffer from man's contempt for you."

Further on, he met up with a puma. The puma said to Cuniraya, "She is very close by. You will soon reach her."

Cuniraya responded, "You will be well loved. You will eat the llamas of guilty men.[15] If they should kill you, men will drape your head over their heads [as a headdress] during great festivals and make you dance. Every year they will bring you out and sacrifice a llama [in your honor] and set you dancing."

Next, he met up with a fox. The fox said to him, "She's already far away. You won't find her."

Cuniraya replied, "You will be hated and pursued by men, even when you keep your distance from them. They will call you 'wretched fox,' and, dissatisfied with just killing you, they'll pass your hide around and mistreat it."

Later, he came across a falcon. The falcon said, "She is very nearby. You will find her." Cuniraya responded, "You will be very happy. You will have hummingbirds for lunch and then dine on all kinds of other birds. And if you should die, or be killed, men will offer up a llama [in your honor]. And when they dance and sing they will drape you over their heads, and there you will be perched beautifully."

Right after that, he met up with a parakeet. The parakeet said to him, "She has already covered a great distance. You will not find her."

"You will walk around always shrieking ceaselessly. When you say to men, who'll despise you, 'I'll ruin your crops!', they will locate you by your shrieks. They will chase you away, and you will live in suffering."

And, in that way, Cuniraya conferred blessings upon those who gave him good news, and as he traveled he cursed those who tried to dissuade him with bad news.

He continued walking and reached the edge of the sea. Just as soon as he reached the seashore, he entered the water and made it swell and increase [in volume]. And about this occurrence, people say today that he [was headed for] Castile. "The old world also goes to another world," they say.

Then he turned back toward Pachacamac. There he arrived at the place where the two young daughters of [the god] Pachacamac[16] lived, who were guarded by a serpent. Shortly before Cuniraya's arrival, the mother of the two young women went to visit Cauillaca at the bottom of the sea into which she had thrown herself. The name of that woman was Urpayhuachac.

While Urpayhuachac was away on her visit, Cuniraya Viracocha made the elder of the daughters sleep with him. But when he tried to sleep with the other daughter, she changed herself into a dove and flew away. That is why the mother [Urpayhuachac] is called "She Who Gives Birth to Doves."

At that time, they say, there wasn't a single fish in the sea. Only Urpayhuachac used to breed them in a small water well she had at home. Cuniraya asked, "Why does this woman have to visit Cauillaca at the bottom of the sea?" Angrily, he emptied all of Urpayhuachac's fish into the ocean. Ever since then, fish have bred and multiplied in the ocean.

Then he whom they called Cuniraya traveled along the seashore. And the woman, Urpayhuachac, was told how her daughters had been seduced. Furious, Urpayhuachac chased after Cuniraya. As she pursued and called out to him, he answered, "Yes?" and remained in place. Then she spoke to him and said, "Cuniraya, I just want to remove your lice!" And she started delousing him. As she was picking off his lice, she caused a steep precipice to rise up in that spot [next to Cuniraya]. She thought, "I'll knock him over the edge and make him fall." But in his cleverness, Cuniraya realized the woman's intentions. "Sister, I have to go for a while and urinate," he said and fled toward these villages. He remained in these villages, on their outskirts and vicinities, for a long time, subjecting men and villages to his trickery.[17]

~

This intriguing myth about two *huacas*, *Cuniraya Viracocha*[18] (hereinafter Cuniraya) and *Cauillaca*,[19] reveals both the human and supernatural qualities often attributed to Native Andean deities. Cuniraya displays an array of human qualities and emotions that are very much like our own—lust, love, anger, vengefulness, arrogance, cleverness, and so forth. Likewise, Cauillaca engages in human tasks, such as weaving, and gives birth to a child, like any ordinary woman. She also exhibits anger, disdain, confusion, desperation, and maybe even fear. In an act akin to suicide, she throws herself, babe in arms, into the sea to escape Cuniraya's advances.

However, both *huacas* are also more than human. Cuniraya adopts the form of a bird in order to inseminate a fruit, which Cauillaca consumes, causing her to become pregnant. "In this way," the narrative explains, "Cauillaca became pregnant without ever having relations with any man." This image is reminiscent of the Roman Catholic notion of the Immaculate Conception of Jesus, and it is also evocative of certain Aztec and North American Indian myths concerning goddesses or women impregnated by unusual means.[20] Cauillaca also has the supernatural ability to live submerged under the sea in petrified form. The myth relates that "just as soon as they fell into the sea, both mother and daughter turned into stone. And there, to this day, in the deep sea of Pachacamac, one can see very clearly two stones living there, shaped like human beings." Thus, both Cuniraya and Cauillaca concurrently manifest human and superhuman characteristics in a manner consistent with the animistic tradition of the Andes.

Additionally, Cuniraya may be viewed as both an intermediary and a shape-shifter. Aside from his physical transformation into a bird, Cuniraya also displays other shape-shifting abilities. The story informs that he travels about assuming the disguise of a wretched beggar and, later, changes into a resplendent being whose garments glimmer as radiantly as the sun. He also dupes others with his trickery and is not beyond "humiliating the *huacas* from other villages with his cleverness." Even at the end of the story when he takes refuge in the villages, according to the narrative, he continues to subject others to his trickery. In this respect, Cuniraya embodies the Jungian archetype of the trickster—a deceptive mythical character that plays mischievous and often malicious pranks, exhibiting a dual nature.[21]

In Jungian analysis, "Trickster is a figure whose physical appetites dominate his behavior; he has the mentality of an infant. Lacking any purpose beyond the gratification of his primary needs, he is cruel, cynical, and unfeeling... [and] passes from one mischievous exploit to another."[22] This description aptly describes Cuniraya, whose mischievous exploits seem focused primarily on his sexual appetites. First, his lust for Cauillaca leads him to alter his appearance in order to impregnate her without her knowledge or consent. His emotional reaction to her flight also suggests that he did not properly consider the consequences of his deceitful act. Next, he takes advantage of the two daughters of Urpayhuachac while the latter is away. The narrative suggests that the first daughter was raped (he "made the elder of the daughters sleep with him") and that the second daughter narrowly escaped his sexual advances by assuming the form of a dove.

However, Cuniraya's deceptions are not strictly limited to his sexual exploits. He also roams about in ragged and tattered clothes, leading people to believe he is a lousy beggar. Gods wearing tattered clothes, in the guise of beggars, often infested with lice, are recurring characters in ancient Andean myths.[23] And in some modern syncretistic Andean stories even Jesus appears dressed as a beggar "wearing a poncho full of lice and fleas."[24] The significance of this is unknown, but in some regions of the Andes lice are associated with the duality of life and death, and with appropriate or inappropriate lovemaking.[25] Concerning the latter, anthropologist Marie-France Souffez explains:

> The selfish and dispersed sexual relationship, outside of the [ap-propriate] order, favors the propagation and increase of lice. [By contrast,] sexual acts performed within the framework of a durable union, and [as] a couple, are associated with [the act of] mutual and tender delousing."[26]

It is clear in this myth that Cuniraya, although probably capable of a mature and durable union, is rather selfish and immature in his sexual pursuits. In this respect, he embodies the dual nature of a trickster. Yet this trickster is also a creator, thus fitting the model of this archetype. Although this aspect of the *huaca* is not well developed in the story, Cuniraya works for the advancement of humankind. He teaches people how to build irrigation canals; he orders the construction of well-finished agricultural terraces sustained by fine masonry. He is also credited with populating the ocean with fish when he dumped Urpayhuachac's well water containing fish into the ocean. He also endows certain animals with positive or negative characteristics, depending on whether they predict that Cauillaca, the object of his affection, is close by or far away. On the one hand, Cuniraya curses those animals that predict Cauillaca is far away and beyond his reach; on the other hand, he blesses those animals that forecast she is nearby and within his grasp. In this respect, the myth suggests that Cuniraya, in his capacity as creator, is responsible for the origin of certain distinguishing characteristics in animals.

The pairing of trickery and creation is one example of the dual nature and intermediary status of this *huaca*. There are numerous other examples in the narrative. Cuniraya is clearly a resplendent deity with supernatural powers, but he also walks among humans dressed as a beggar and displays human appetites. Moreover, he impregnates Cauillaca but is unable to marry her. He also seduces the daughters of Pachacamac and Urpayhuachac. Further, both he and Cauillaca in many respects also embody the intermediary characteristics of adolescents who, like adults, are sexually mature enough to marry and start a family, yet, like children, engage in childish behaviors that stop short of demonstrating full maturity.

The mythologist John Bierhorst theorizes that this "is also a myth about growing up."[27] Bierhorst states that Cauillaca reminds us of a pubescent maiden who is able to conceive a child and is thus biologically capable of marrying; yet, she has not engaged in sexual contact with any man or *huaca* and, therefore, is technically still a virgin. However, when faced with the possibility of starting a family with a man she finds repugnant, Cauillaca flees to the sea "and becomes immobilized in a world inhabited by her own sex."[28]

Both *huacas* also shirk their adult responsibilities. Cauillaca has given birth to a child and knows the art of weaving. Thus, she has proven that she is capable of providing for a family.[29] Similarly, Cuniraya, "for his part, has fathered a child... [and has also] filled the sea with fish," demonstrating that he could also be a provider.[30] However, in each case the *huacas* return to their intermediary status as adolescents. Although they are capable of performing sexually as adults, and of assuming their respective roles as providers of the family, nevertheless, the *huacas* reject the adult obligations in favor of the more irresponsible and childlike behavior that characterizes adolescence. And to the extent that the sexes remain separate, their adult responsibilities cannot be met.

Bierhorst draws a parallel between the flight of Cauillaca to the lowlands and the Inca male puberty rites of *huarachico* (also spelled *guarachico* or *warachikuy*), a part of which involved "boys [racing] down from a mountaintop in pursuit of young women (who would await them with jars of an alcoholic beverage called chicha)."[31] He notes, however, that in the second part of the story, Cuniraya departs from the lowlands— metaphorically "the world of women"—and "returns to the highlands, where... the men are actors."[32] In both instances, the *huacas* return to the safety of their own sex and revert to their childlike condition.

The physical separation of Cuniraya and Cauillaca, male and female, is a critical element in this story. Consistent with the notion of Andean dualism, Cuniraya personifies the masculine principle often associated with the sun (in Quechua, *Inti*), the sky, the mountain peaks *(Wamanis* or *Apus* in Quechua, or *Achachilas* or *Mallkus* in Aymara), and *hanan* (a Quechua term meaning "above"). Likewise, Cauillaca and, later, the other female characters in the story represent the feminine principle often associated with the earth (*Pacha Mama*), the moon (*Mama Killa or Quilla*), the ocean (*Mama Cocha*), and *hurin* (a Quechua term meaning "below," relative to another point or position that is "higher"). Therefore, another interpretation of the story suggests that the underlying structure of this myth concerns the appropriate distancing between masculine and feminine elements and, more particularly, between the earth and the sun.[33] This is based on the concept that several themes are repeated in the myth, which point to the proper separation of the masculine and feminine principles.

Bierhorst observes that this is a double myth, "a myth that repeats itself… [and] tells the same story twice."[34] The structural anthropologist Claude Lévi-Strauss explains the process of theme duplication in the following manner.

> The question has often been raised why myths, and more generally oral literature, are so much addicted to duplication, triplication, or qua-druplication of the same sequence. If our hypotheses are accepted, the answer is obvious: The function of repetition is to render the structure of the myth apparent.…A myth exhibits a "slated" structure, which comes to the surface, so to speak, through the process of repetition.[35]

In this case, one of the themes duplicated in the myth pertains to the opposing elements of "close or far away."[36] We first noted an obvious reference to this pairing in relation to the animals Cuniraya encountered on his journey. The animals that predicted Cauillaca was "close by" were blessed by Cuniraya; those that foretold distance (i.e., "far away") were cursed by Cuniraya. Yet this opposition may also be applicable to the movements of Cuniraya himself as a measure of the appropriate distancing of the sun in relation to the earth. If the sun were too close to the earth, it would lead to a "burnt world" (a phrase coined by Lévi-Strauss) where nothing would grow or thrive in the sweltering heat. If the sun were too far away from the earth, this would give way to a "world of rottenness,"[37] where nothing would grow or thrive due to the frigid cold.

Based on his physical description in the myth, Cuniraya is closely associated with the resplendent Sun god, on whom the ancient Andeans depended for their survival. In an effort to get the fleeing Cauillaca to turn around and look at him, Cuniraya appears in a sparkling golden gown that is so intimidating it drives away the other *huacas*. His movements also mimic the daily path of the sun, appearing first in the eastern highlands and then proceeding in a westwardly direction toward the sea (in Peru, the Pacific Ocean) in pursuit of Cauillaca. Upon reaching the seashore, Cuniraya enters the water and makes it swell. This is reminiscent of an Inca belief that the sun followed a course from east to west and then submerged in the ocean at the end of the day. From there, it continued its swim underneath the earth and reappeared in the east the next day, reemerging at its point of origin. Garcilaso de la Vega described how the Incas observed this daily cycle of the sun.

> When the Sun set, [the Incas], watching it cross over the water (because the entire length of Peru has the ocean to the west), said that the Sun entered the ocean and dried a large portion of it with his fire and heat; and that, as he was a great swimmer, he [the Sun] would swim underneath the earth to come out the next day in the east, for it was understood that the earth was situated over the water.[38]

The sun's trajectory is also apparent in the rich imagery of the myth. At the beginning of the story, Cuniraya appears as a lowly beggar, much like the sun, which appears low and close to the earth at daybreak. Later in the story Cuniraya appears in full regalia—wearing a golden garment that radiates like the sun—showing himself as the luminous and dazzling *huaca* that he really is. This is analogous to the sun reaching its zenith, the highest point of its orbit in the sky. Then Cuniraya reaches the coastline where he enters the home of the god Pachacamac, which is guarded by a serpent. In the Andean world, the serpent *Amaru* (also known as *Katari*) is usually associated with the lower subterranean world ("Lower World" or "World Below").

At the home of Pachacamac, Cuniraya pauses to have sexual relations with Pachacamac's daughters, whose mother, Urpayhuachac, is away on a visit to the bottom of the sea. The sun at this point is dangerously close to the earth, suggested by the sexual act, where male and female are in intimate proximity. Cuniraya rapes the eldest daughter, accentuating the notion that the sun is so close to the earth that it effectively "rapes" the land. The low position of the sun is also emphasized by the flight of the youngest daughter, who transforms into a dove to avoid being raped like her older sister. At this point the sun is lower than the dove-woman, who takes to the skies, accentuating the sun's lowly position relative to the earth. These images are evocative of the setting sun described by Garcilaso, in close proximity to the earth before it enters the sea. The presence of the guardian serpent is also a sign that the sun is about to embark on its journey into the lower (aquatic and subterranean) world beneath the earth, only to resurface and be reborn in the highlands the next day.

In addition to the sun following its daily course from east to west, and then beneath the ocean, the myth also hints at a north–south movement of the sun over the course of the year.[39] In the story Cuniraya arrives at the home of the god Pachacamac and his wife Urpayhuachac on the Peruvian coast.[40] As shown, Cuniraya rapes the eldest daughter and nearly takes advantage of the younger daughter, who escapes. Later, Cuniraya continues his travels along the coastline, but Urpayhuachac, upon learning of her daughters' predicament, pursues him, presumably up the coast. Cuniraya's movement along the coast in a north–south direction could also be associated with the sun's seasonal movement, most northerly at the June solstice and most southerly at the December solstice.

The appropriate distancing between the sun and the earth is depicted at various points in the story. First Cuniraya, in the form of a bird, deposits his seed in the fruit of the *lúcuma* tree; Cauillaca eats the fruit and becomes pregnant. In this instance Cuniraya, the symbolic male Sun, fertilizes Cauillaca, the symbolic female Earth, because he has maintained a proper distance. Perched in the tree, the Sun (bird/Cuniraya) is high, and the Earth (Cauillaca) is properly below. The duality and complementarities of high and low, sky and earth, and masculine and feminine principles are respected and preserved, and the Sun brings fertility to the Earth. However, when Cuniraya visits the home of Pachacamac and Urpayhuachac, he commits a violation by forcing the eldest daughter to have sexual relations with him, failing to maintain an appropriate distance. The symbolic Sun, in the form of Cuniraya, is *too close* to the Earth, represented, in this case, by another female character, the eldest daughter. The symbolism does not elude us—in this instance, the sun produces *too much* heat, thereby violating the Earth. No doubt the ancient Andeans observed what too much sun could do— rob and deprive the earth of its abundance and fertility, creating a burnt world. The coastal desert is a poignant example of this cosmic violation. When the sun fails to keep a safe distance from the earth, it scorches and injures the land. This inappropriate union of earth and sky, feminine and masculine principles, produces death and destruction.

Death and destruction could also occur due to the absence of sun. This might occur if the sun failed to return to the frigid mountain peaks of the east, the origin of its trajectory. This would create a world so cold that ice and snow would cover the land and crops would fail to grow. This would yield what Lévi-Strauss described as a "world of rottenness," a world too distant from the sun. This possibility becomes apparent at the end of the story when Urpayhuachac causes "a steep precipice to form," next to Cuniraya, scheming to "knock him over the edge and make him fall" as she picks off his lice. Cleverly, Cuniraya realizes her intentions and escapes by pretending to go relieve himself. He then makes his getaway to the eastern highlands, symbolically returning to the sun's point of origin, and avoiding the creation of a world of rottenness.

In the same manner, the opposing elements of "close by" and "far away"—illustrated by the various encounters between Cuniraya and different animals—also resonate with the theme of the appropriate distancing between the earth and the sun. If the masculine sun (Cuniraya) is too far away from the feminine earth (Cauillaca), the earth is deprived of life-giving light and warmth, which are essential to its fertility, growth, and regeneration. This is analogous to Cuniraya punishing the skunk, the fox, and the parakeet for predicting he is too far away from *Cauillaca*. In both cases the "curse" is caused by too much distance between the earth (Cauillaca, the feminine principle) and the sun (Cuniraya, the masculine principle). Nevertheless, Cuniraya blesses the condor, the puma, and the hawk for predicting that he is "close" to finding and reaching the beautiful Cauillaca. In much the same way, the appropriate "closeness" between the earth and the sun produces fertility and fecundity. However, too much or too little closeness is akin to a cosmic violation, which ruptures the delicate balance and separation between masculine and feminine elements, thereby resulting in infertility and destruction.

HUACAS AS PORTALS BETWEEN THE NATURAL AND SUPERNATURAL WORLDS

As previously discussed, the Andean concept of *huaca* has numerous definitions and myriad interpretations. The colonial Quechua dictionary of Diego González Holguín (1608) defines the term *huac* as "double, other, or apart" in Quechua.[41] The term *huaca* signifies "a split" (in relation to body parts).[42] Based on these definitions, cultural historian Constance Classen proposed that *huaca* may signify a sacred place that is also "a crack or mediating space between the supernatural and the natural, or else something that exists on both levels at once and thus is double."[43]

From a mythological and cosmological perspective, an examination of various Andean myths supports this interesting proposition.

To illustrate this point, let us examine a corpus of legends from the southern highland region of Ecuador known as Hatun Cañar that give credence to the notion that a *huaca* is a mediating space or a "crack" between the natural and supernatural worlds, or a space that exists simultaneously in both worlds.

The Legend of Shishu

(Cañari)

Shishu ["Pregnant Mountain"][44] is a mountain located to the west of the top region of the canton of Cañar, down toward the subtropical region. The distance between Cañar and this place is approximately two kilometers.

Many popular stories about this mountain circulate among the villagers from the surrounding districts. These relate that in the interior of the mountain is an area with a coastal climate.

In the wintertime, amid the fog, a door appears on the mountain, through which one can observe a considerable range of fruit trees, such as orange trees, banana trees, mango trees, etc., which are native to the coastal region. According to what they say, whoever manages to enter into the interior of the mountain and gather some fruit will reap good fortune.[45]

The Legend of Mount Curitaqui

(Cañari)

The small mountain of Curitaqui ["Granary of Gold"][46] is located next to the mountain of Huahual Shumi, which is near the towns of Nulti, Paccha, and Jadán.

The elders tell us that in the interior of Mount Curitaqui are gardens of red peppers and flowers and gold corncobs, which are all guarded by a black dog, and that the owner of all this is Mama Huaca.

Some people say they have received gold in exchange for leaving a young child, who hasn't been baptized yet, at Mount Curitaqui.

It is said that at one time a very poor family, who could barely make ends meet, lived in that region. One time they experienced such dire need that with great sadness they left their child at the entrance of the cave at Mount Curitaqui. Immediately after leaving the child, an imperfect-looking dog with extremely long ears came out and devoured the child, tearing it limb from limb. Afterward, a person came out and handed them some gold corncobs.

The family took the corncobs and returned home with a fortune. Eventually they became rich. The money they deposited always tended to increase. They became slaves of Mama Huaca and of their wealth.

They say that after the family died, their souls went straight to hell and all their wealth disappeared.[47]

The Legend of Mount Tepal

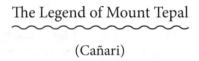

(Cañari)

Many people who live in these parts comment that Mount Tepal[48] is enchanted. Many different comments are made with regard to this point, but we have selected those that are most important.

It is said that in the interior of Mount Tepal is an enchanted lagoon guarded by a blonde huaca who dresses in a blue tunic. Her hair is the color of gold and comes down to her heels. They also say that various persons have seen her come out in the misty or early hours of the morning.

[The villagers] also remark that previously they had heard the blows produced by the surging waves of the lagoon as they crashed against the banks, and that as they approached the mountain, they could hear sounds resembling deep and mournful sighs.

They say that back then, if someone left something behind [accidentally], next to the mountain as they took their animals to graze, the object would immediately disappear. That's because, according to them, Mama Huaca would hide it.

There are also people who believe that inside Mount Tepal are mines of gold.[49]

Each of these Native Andean legends highlights the intermediary role of the *huaca* as an opening or a crack between the natural and the supernatural worlds,[50] or as a mediating space where these worlds converge or exist together. In each case the supernatural world *inside* the *huaca*-mountain is inhabited by supernatural beings, such as *Mama Huaca* (loosely translated as "Divine Mother" or "Mother Divinity") and the child-eating dog, who both clearly belong to the supernatural realm. In The Legend of Mount Tepal, Mama Huaca is further characterized as a blonde who can also be physically differentiated from the typically dark-haired Native Andean people living outside the *huaca*-mountain.

Inside each *huaca*-mountain the villagers speculate there are, or claim to have seen, extraordinary conditions that defy the reality of the natural world. For instance, in contrast to the foggy and cold winter landscape depicted in The Legend of Shishu outside of the *huaca*-mountain, some people claim that *inside* the mountain is an area with a warm coastal climate and fruit trees indigenous to the coastal region. Another example is the presence of an enchanted lagoon inside the *huaca*-mountain of Tepal. According to that legend, the lagoon is guarded by a *huaca*-woman with "hair the color of gold" and "who dresses in a blue tunic." The surging waves of the enchanted lagoon also seem to make sounds that resemble "deep and mournful sighs" to the approaching villagers. In some respects the sounds of the lagoon appear to take on "human" emotional qualities, consistent with the Andean animistic tradition. Likewise, in The Legend of Mount Curitaqui the inside of the mountain-*huaca* grows gardens of gold corncobs, which are guarded by a black dog. This dog is presumably the same one that later receives and consumes the child sacrifice offered at the entrance of the mountain cave. The gold corn produced inside the mountain also has supernatural properties: it can make the recipients of the corn slaves to wealth and "slaves of Mama Huaca."

Critical to the discussion of these three Andean legends is the "crack" or mediating space between the natural and supernatural worlds. In The Legend of Shishu, "a door appears on the mountain" through which the villagers can observe the supernatural phenomena taking place within, namely, the presence of the warm coastal zone and the luscious fruit trees. The door, therefore, represents the passage or portal between the two worlds, as one must peer through it in order to catch a glimpse of the supernatural world inside. In similar fashion, The Legend of Mount Curitaqui also identifies the entrance of the cave that marks the boundary between the natural and supernatural worlds. It is at the cave entrance that the imperfect-looking dog receives the "offering" of the child and devours it. Shortly thereafter, a person comes "out [of the mountain or cave] and hand[s] them some gold corncobs." More than likely, this person—who has the power to enslave individuals—is either *Mama Huaca* or her agent. In either case, it is a supernatural being who dwells on the *other side* of the entrance to the cave; that is, a being from the supernatural world who is *inside* the mountain-*huaca*.

In some respects, the offering of the child at the entrance of the mountain-*huaca* is reminiscent of the human sacrifice rituals that were performed in various pre-Columbian Native Andean cultures. As in this story, in some cases the human offerings were left on the *huaca*-mountains to die.[51] Interestingly, according to the indigenous colonial chronicler Felipe Guaman Poma de Ayala, children and dogs figured prominently in the ancient cult of the Chinchasuyos, the inhabitants of the northwest region of the Inca Empire, which roughly corresponds to the area where these present-day stories originate.[52]

In the third story, The Legend of Mount Tepal, the mediating space between the natural and supernatural worlds is not as clearly demarcated. However, in this particular narrative we learn that the supernatural beings that inhabit the mountain-*huaca* cross the mediating space and enter this world from time to time. For example, in this legend various persons claim to have seen Mama Huaca "come out in the misty or early hours of the morning." They also allege that "if someone left something behind [accidentally]," while grazing on the mountain, Mama Huaca "would hide it" and make it disappear. These descriptions suggest that, on occasion, Mama Huaca comes out of her supernatural world inside the mountain-*huaca* and sets foot in this world, the "human space" outside of the mountain-*huaca*, where human beings take their animals to pasture.

Similar legends exist throughout the Andes in which a crack or a portal opens between the natural and supernatural worlds, permitting the *huacas* to interact with humans in both malevolent and benevolent ways.[53] In each case the worlds interact with one another through an opening or "split" (*huaca*) between the two; alternatively, they could also be perceived as mediating spaces where the two worlds unite or converge, essentially making them "double" (*huac*).

The notion of mediating spaces where worlds converge is not unique to Andean mythology; it also characterizes Native Andean ritual. For example, the *mesa* ("table") rituals of many Native Andean religions are emblematic of the union between the natural and supernatural worlds that may underlie the significance of the term *huaca*. Typically, a *mesa* ritual involves the division of a table—often called "the altar"—into three distinct parts or levels. In most cases one part signifies "a positive, right side associated with the golden sun, man, day, good"; another part represents "a negative, left side associated with the silver moon, woman, night, evil; and [the third part,] a mediating middle zone containing the *axis mundi* and combining the opposites of left and right."[54] The goal is to bring the left and right parts together "into [a] meaningful and complementary interaction through the mediation of the middle zone."[55]

In the same manner, in an Aymara and Kallawaya syncretistic ritual called the *Muxsa Misa* or *Muxsa Mesa* ("Sweet Table"[56]), different cosmological worlds converge on the ritual surface of the table. The purpose of the ritual is to make sweet offerings and recite prayers, invoking the protection of Pacha Mama, the Virgin Mary, the Christian saints, the mountain dcities, and the spirits of the earth and sky against natural and supernatural threats.[57] It is also an opportunity to thank the *huacas* for the blessings conferred on the community.[58]

The celebrants of the *Muxsa Misa* place the offerings on a special kind of paper, reserved for this purpose, which is laid out on a blanket or the ground. Some of the most important offerings include multicolored chalky rectangular candies called *misterios* ("mysteries") embossed with images of the sun, moon, stars, planets, signs of the Zodiac, the Virgin Mary, and other beings that correspond to the Upper World, or the celestial sphere, of Aymara and Kallawaya cosmology (*Alaj Pacha* or *Alax Pacha* for the Aymaras; *Gloria* for the Kallawayas[59]). The Kallawayas also add a circular cookie known as *pan de San Nicolás* ("bread of Saint Nicholas") at the center of which appears an image of a star or the Virgin Mary.[60] As part of the ritual, the priest or his assistants place the sun, the moon, and a six-pointed star in the upper right-hand corner, the upper left-hand corner, and the center of the *mesa*, respectively.[61] Just as the sun and moon in Andean cosmology are considered complementary pairs, in the ritual surface of the *mesa* the "figurative objects must always be paired; there should never be one without its corresponding partner."[62]

Beneath the celestial *misterios*, the celebrants also place handmade effigies of llama fat mixed with an intensely aromatic herb known as *q'uwa*—shaped in the form of little llamas with eyes, feet, and other details—along with green and perfectly shaped coca leaves, incense, puma skin (*titi*), cigarettes, a white or grayish mineral (stone) powder called *mullu*, and tiny tin and lead figurines that are "schematic representations of people, houses, plants, trees, animals, tools, plates, cups, forks and spoons."[63] These figurines, contained in envelopes, are called *chiwchi* and are distributed across the surface of the *mesa*, adding sparkle to the offering when covered with thin pieces of gold and silver-colored foil.[64] Whereas the *misterios* "[call] down the power and abundance of the sky," the other ingredients placed below them in the *mesa* are "emblematic of the earth's fertility."[65] They represent images symbolic of This World (*Aca*

Pacha) and the fertilizing powers of Pacha Mama and of earthly spirits. The mineral and metal ingredients might also symbolize the power of the Lower World or Interior World (*Manqha Pacha*), the realm of the caves, mines, minerals, and their guardian spirits.

At the conclusion of the ritual the *mesa* is ceremoniously burned "in a bonfire fueled by llama dung and eucalyptus leaves soaked in alcohol."[66] Although to the untrained eye the scattering of these offerings appears to be random, to the trained Aymara and Kallawaya shamans and their "lieutenants" (assistants), the placement of these ingredients on "specific locations in the sacred geography of the *misa* [or *mesa*]" is part of the "microcosmic landscape" of the ritual.[67] Thus, the ritual surface of the *Muxsa Misa* unites the cosmological worlds of the Aymaras and the Kallawayas in a ceremony that "would channel their fertilizing power on behalf of the community."[68]

Just as these ritual tables are emblematic of sacred spaces where various "worlds" meet, so too could certain sacred locations in the Andes be considered mediating spaces or portals between the natural and supernatural worlds. Some of these sacred locations, generally called *paqarinas*, are *huacas* from which the mythical ancestors of a community are believed to have emerged. Although this topic will be discussed more fully in a subsequent chapter, *paqarinas* could also be considered cracks or mediating spaces between this world and the supernatural world of the ancestors.

A salient example of *paqarinas* as cracks or portals between the natural and supernatural worlds may be found in Inca myths recounting the origin of three lineage groups, including the Incas, who were native to the valley of Cuzco. These three groups emerged from one of three distinct "windows" or caves[69] (in Quechua, *t'oqo*) in the mountain or hill of *Tampu T'oqo* (also spelled *Tambotoco*), located in a place called *Pacariqtambo*.[70] One such group emerged from a cave called *Marastoco* and engendered the lineage of the Maras. Another group emerged from a second cave named *Sutictoco* and begat the lineage of the Tambos. Yet a third group emerged from the largest cave called *Capactoco* (also spelled *Qhapaq t'oqo*),[71] and this group, comprised of four women and four men, became the ancestors of the Incas. According to legend, these men and women appeared fully grown, had supernatural and divine powers, and were siblings "spontaneously generated" without parents.[72] They were summoned to emerge by *Ticci Viracocha*, the Creator god of the Incas.[73] Consequently, the Incas worshipped the cave at *Pacariqtambo* and considered it a sacred *huaca*.[74]

Many such myths still abound in the Andes and speak of the birth of different ethnic groups and communities. Each of these myths pinpoints the location of the *huaca,* or sacred site, venerated by the group or community. At each of these *huacas* the community makes offerings and recites devotional prayers to the Andean divinities, which are expected to be received in the supernatural or "other" (*huac*) world. As in the origin myth of the Incas, the *paqarina* could be viewed as a portal or mediating space between this world and that of the ancestors. And just as in the stories analyzed concerning the supernatural beings living "inside" a cave or "behind a door" in a sacred mountain, the ancestors of the Incas who came out of the cave, fully formed and endowed with supernatural qualities, must also have crossed through an opening or crack between the Other World and this one. Afterward, they went on to settle the valley of Cuzco.

It is important to point out that in the Quechua language even secular terms such as earth and water, seemingly of "This World," can be elevated to the status of "Other World"—and therefore, *huaca,* also meaning "other"—depending on the context. For instance, the notion of earth is often referred to in Quechua as *allpa* in a nonreligious or secular context and as *pacha* in a religious context.[75] Similarly, the term water used for secular purposes, such as irrigation, is called *yaku,* whereas in a cosmological or religious context it is referred to as *unu.*[76] Thus the Western distinction between the natural and the supernatural is somewhat illusory from a Native Andean perspective, as both belong to a single and unified reality of multiple levels that coexist, or merge together, in a single object, event, or aspect of nature. This notion may also be embodied in the term *huaca* itself, which connotes the existence of two levels at once and is thus appropriately also defined as "double."

Another way *huacas* may conjoin the natural and the supernatural is by allowing a return to the primal matrix from which creation and life began. Such a journey is chronicled by anthropologist Douglas Sharon in his description of the northern Peruvian pilgrimage to Las Huaringas, a lowland coastal region of Peru.[77] According to Sharon, on the first day of the pilgrimage the pilgrims travel to the home of the *curandero* ("healer" or "shaman"), who resides in the highland region near a sacred lagoon. The pilgrims are required to refrain from eating salt, peppers, and beans, from bathing and washing, and from engaging in sexual activity. On the second day the pilgrims begin their journey to the sacred lagoon, guided by the *curandero.* The passage to the lagoon, which is "only apparent to the shaman," is "narrow, steep, and muddy...and is considered...a dangerous activity, [requiring] elaborate rituals performed by the curer."[78] Upon arrival, the pilgrims enter the lagoon at high noon and are essentially "reborn" into This World. They nasally imbibe a hallucinogen made from the San Pedro cactus that represents their "first food" after their ritualistic bath. Afterward, they return to the *curandero's* home for an all-night curing session, which involves sleep deprivation and consuming more San Pedro cactus and other herbal remedies that cause hallucinations and regurgitation. In the interim the shaman sings religious songs, performs a *mesa* ritual, and swordfights with "the devil." At daybreak each pilgrim receives advice from the healer, and the session ends with a purification ritual, after which the restrictions on sexual activity, washing, and ingesting salt are lifted.

Sharon views the ritual bath in the lagoon as a symbolic "return to origins."

> The bath itself . . . can be seen as a symbolic *regresum ad uterum* [return to the womb] followed by rebirth. This "return to origins" manifests in terms that are rooted in Peruvian prehistory. For Pachamama, Earth Mother, was—and is—one of the principal deities in the Indian pantheon. Lagoons, springs, and caves—the orifices of Pachamama—were the places where mankind emerged during the Creation, as well as the channels of communication with the Earth Mother. Entering the lagoon, then, represents the "reversal" of ordinary reality and return to the paradisiacal First Times before the World and man were born.[79]

Moreover, one could add that the dangerous trail leading to the lagoon, which "is only apparent to the shaman," could be viewed as the boundary between This World and the Other (supernatural) World. Symbolically, this dangerous passage is the mediating space or portal which the pilgrims must cross, guided by the *curandero*, to enter the sacred lagoon and the "paradisiacal First Times" where they will symbolically be reborn.

ENCHANTED WATER, LAKES, AND LAGOONS

In many parts of the Andes, some lakes and lagoons are believed to be enchanted and to house superhuman *huacas* and magical realms below the surface of the water. This was alluded to in The Legend of Mount Tepal where the storyteller describes the existence of an enchanted lagoon, guarded by a *huaca*-woman in the interior of a mountain. Water *huacas* have a mythology of their own. They are supernatural beings who are sometimes kind and benevolent toward human beings,[80] yet often coldhearted and malevolent. In their malevolent aspect they often kidnap innocent people or entice them with their beauty, food, or drink, and force them to live inside the lake or lagoon against their will. In these situations, the sequestered person is believed to be bewitched by the water *huaca* and, in most cases, must be rescued in order to be freed from the spell of the captor. Water *huacas* may be male or female and typically assume the form of animals (snakes or serpents, pumas, bulls, toads, or frogs), zoomorphic creatures, or beautiful women (sirens).

Peruvian authors José María Arguedas and Franciso Izquierdo Ríos compiled many stories from various regions of Peru about enchanted lakes and lagoons housing supernatural *huacas*. In one such story from the department of Ayacucho, villagers claim that in the evening a golden bull appears at Lake *Yanacocha* ("Black Lake") pulled by a beautiful siren with golden hair.[81] The bull tries to come out of the lake, but the siren yanks a gold chain tied around its neck and prevents the bull from escaping. They say the bull is really a young man who became enchanted, and that every night he cries out, "I am a young man who came looking for treasure, but now I have been taken prisoner and have been transformed into a bull. If you break the spell, you can still save me."[82] But legend has it that whoever tries to save the youth from his capturer will disappear in the dark waters of the lake forever.

In yet another story from the vicinity of Lima, residents allege to have seen a lion emerge out of a whirlpool of water at the lagoon of *León Cocha* ("Lion Lagoon").[83] They say that in ancient times the mountains surrounding the lagoon were made of gold, but after the Spaniards came, the captors took all the gold and left the mountains arid and bare. Today nothing grows there, not even a wildflower. In this desolate landscape, many a villager has observed that from the depths of the dark lagoon a lion comes out of an eddy or a whirlpool in the middle of the water. In fact, they claim it left its giant footprint on a smooth, almost polished, rock adjacent to the water. The lion materializes and roars, and then vanishes without a trace.

The townspeople also inform that in *La laguna de las campanas encantadas* ("The Lake of the Enchanted Bells"), also on the outskirts of Lima, a silver bull comes out every day at midnight. When the silver bull steps on the rocks and stones along the shores of the lake, the stones assume the forms of little animals. A shepherd who finds one of these stones is considered incredibly lucky, because it is a sure sign that his animals will be fertile and that his herds will multiply.[84]

Elsewhere, in the nearby department of Pasco to the east of Lima, the villagers explain that the thermal baths at Piquilhuanca, which at one time were used exclusively by the Inca, are guarded by a zoomorphic water spirit who also possesses shape-shifting abilities. Those who claim to have seen this spirit describe it as "a toad with the fins of a fish, but when he sees people, he turns into a bat."[85] The Native Andeans who inhabit this region believe that "spirits bathe [in the waters] of Piquilhuanca, and that is the reason they have curative powers."[86]

There are countless other stories about water *huacas* with magical powers throughout the Andean region. However, the strength of this Andean belief was recently brought home to me while watching a TV program about a young Peruvian woman who gave birth to a baby girl with a rare congenital disease known as "sirenomelia," or "mermaid syndrome." The little girl, named Milagros, was born with legs fused from her thighs to her ankles, giving her legs a fishlike appearance. During the program several people interviewed from the mother's hometown outside of Lima were convinced that the reason little Milagros was born with this condition was because her mother had "napped" next to an enchanted lake. Although the townspeople did not elaborate, the suggestion was that somehow the water *huaca* inhabiting the lake had caused or created this condition in the child. Luckily, baby Milagros underwent extensive surgery in Lima with a team of medical specialists, and, by all accounts, she appears to be doing well.

This example highlights the pervasiveness of the belief in enchanted lakes and water *huacas* even among contemporary Andean communities. Although this may surprise some Westerners who strictly adhere to the principles of reason and science, these beliefs (some would even say "superstitions") are still very much alive, especially in the rural communities of the Andes. It is fair to say that many Native Andeans in these communities have a perception of reality much broader than our own, which may include encounters with "beings" and *huacas* from the Other World, or in-between worlds. From their perspective, meetings of this kind, although unusual, are readily accepted and part of the natural experience.

On occasion, male water *huacas* are also believed to have sexual relations with women, who fall under their spell, and animal or animal-like offspring result from these unions.[87] The following is a typical example of an Andean story featuring a woman impregnated by a water *huaca*, who gives birth to live snakes. In the contemporary Andes, snakes are often symbolically associated with the Lower World or the World Below and with the element of water; they are also strongly connected "with the infrastructure related to the distribution of water."[88]

The Legendary Lagoon of the Little Snakes

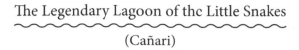

(Cañari)

A long time ago a married couple camped near a lagoon. It was twelve o'clock on a magnificent day, and the couple agreed that they would eat their food while contemplating the calm and brilliant surface of the lagoon. They calmly sat down.

Within a few minutes, the husband got up and wandered a short distance away from the lagoon, while his wife [stayed behind and] arranged and got everything ready for lunch.

No more than fifteen minutes had passed since the husband had left, when he returned to find his wife missing. He called and searched everywhere, but it was all in vain. His wife had mysteriously disappeared, leaving no trace for him to follow.

Thousands of thoughts crossed the husband's mind; then he had an idea. He thought that maybe his wife had gone ahead of him. But at the same time, he asked himself: Why? And where could she have gone?

In any event, confused and worried, he walked speedily back home, asking the few travelers he encountered whether or not they had seen his wife. But nobody had a clue.

When he returned home, he told his relatives what had happened. But instead of believing him, they started to suspect that perhaps for some reason he had attempted something violent against his wife.

In the sorrow of his loneliness and the unexplained absence of his dear wife, the man became very weak, as much in spirit as in health. He couldn't sleep because he was tormented by horrible nightmares in which he saw his wife desperately asking for his help.

One afternoon while he sat contemplating the lagoon that had swallowed his dear wife, a traveler arrived asking for lodging. In those days, one never turned down a person who asked for a place to stay and rest from an exhausting journey. So the man gave him a place to stay.

As usual, night arrived and the unfortunate husband, while sleeping, started to scream desperately in the middle of his dream. The next morning, after waking up, he told the stranger that he had seen his wife in the middle of a llama herd, unable to find her way out.

Then the stranger asked of the poor man, "Why do you torture yourself so much?"

The relatives of the man told the stranger everything that had occurred. The stranger listened attentively without interrupting. Afterward he asked, "How was the woman dressed when she disappeared?"

After receiving information about how the woman was dressed at the moment she disappeared, the stranger made the following remark: "With your permission, let me start by saying that I take regular walks, and always around these parts. For that reason, I will tell you that on more than one occasion I have seen in the lagoon the vision of a woman dressed in the same clothing that you have described. She always spends her time sleeping with a snake wrapped around her leg. This vision appears every day more or less at noon."

The stranger also indicated to them at which angle they should place themselves [in relation to the water] in order to better contemplate the vision in the Lagoon of the Little Snakes, which, [he added], he found very strange.

Without a moment to lose, the relatives who lived in the house, along with various other relatives, got ready to travel to the lagoon, hoping they might find the woman who had disappeared such a long time ago.

They reached the site indicated by their guest. They waited patiently. Indeed, the woman came out of the water and a snake descended slowly from her leg and then lay on the sand to bask in the burning midday sun.

Stealthily, the relatives approached the spot where the snake was lying. Then, with good aim, they clobbered the head of the animal. As the snake took the hit, it became ferociously agitated, lunged forward, and wriggled on the sand.

They also say that the water followed the snake, which disappeared in a surprising and mysterious way.

Since then, the lagoon has been called *Leoquina*, which means "snake." This is the way they rescued the woman who had been held captive by the snake. They rescued her in the midst of a hurricane, with wind so turbulent and uncontrollable its fury agitated the water, and turned this side of the lagoon into rough water. The lagoon was calm before this incident occurred on its banks.

They say that the Lagoon of the Little Snakes has the same characteristics to this day. Its waters agitate suddenly, bursting its normal banks.

A few days after her rescue, the woman gave birth to twelve little snakes at home. For that reason, our elders used to call the lagoon *Leoquinillas Cocha*, which means "water of little snakes" or simply "little snakes."[89]

~~

As is readily apparent, this Andean *huaca* legend has strong sexual overtones. The snake is a powerful masculine symbol, as is the moving

force of foamy water, or symbolic semen, which often describes the movements or habitat of a water *huaca* in Andean stories.[90] In the colonial
Huarochirí Manuscript, "Water is often male, especially storm water and
downward-flowing water."[91] However, little is written concerning still or
unmoving water, which may embody femaleness. In the Huarochirí myths,
"altitude and motion connote maleness, while depth and stability are associated with femaleness."[92] If such is the case in other regions of the Andes,
then a snake submerged in still water, or physically bringing a woman into
still or deep water, may be envisioned as sexual intercourse. This notion is
consistent with the imagery found in some Andean origin myths in which
human beings are considered the offspring of water and snakes.[93]

From a classical psychoanalytic perspective a snake is a phallic symbol,
and a woman giving birth to snakes is also strongly suggestive of the
concept of "penis envy," which Sigmund Freud attributed to women.[94]
According to Freud, at a certain point in a woman's psychosexual development, she longs for a penis; recognizing that she does not have one,
and never will, she settles for a "penis substitute"—a baby. In the case of
Andean legends, however, the "baby" is even more like a penis than a
human being. The baby is a "little snake," or a little penis, dramatizing the
connection between the offspring and the masculine sex organ.

In some respects, one could also draw a parallel between water
huacas and other magical beings of Andean lakes with the power of the
unconscious mind. In the legendary Lagoon of the Little Snakes, the water
huaca may represent the great power or force of the unconscious mind
that, according to Freud, often "steals" or "abducts" (by the mechanism
of repression) unacceptable and erotic (sexual) desires, threatening to
overcome the ego.[95] The unconscious maintains these in a dreamlike state,
just as the kidnapped victim was completely unaware that she had spent
"her time sleeping with [the] snake wrapped around her leg." Metaphorically, when the repressed desires are submerged in the water, they are
immersed in the lagoon of forgetfulness and oblivion, the "enchantment"
which generally characterizes unconscious processes.

For Carl G. Jung, the father of analytical psychology, the snake
emerges from the waters of the collective unconscious, the impersonal and
transpersonal part of the psyche containing primordial images and ideas,
which he called "archetypes," that all human beings have shared since the
beginning of time.[96] This is the universal psychic realm inherited from
our collective experience that, according to Jung, gives birth to dreams
and myths that transcend our personal experience. And, according to
Jung, the snake is the "commonest dream symbol of transcendence."[97]

From a Jungian perspective, a water *huaca* may be one of those "creatures, figuratively coming from the depths of the ancient Earth Mother, [which] are symbolic denizens of the collective unconscious. They bring into the field of consciousness a special chthonic (underworld) message that is somewhat different from the spiritual aspirations symbolized by the birds ... [and other winged creatures]."[98] This view might emphasize the intermediary status of the water *huaca* as a creature inhabiting the collective "underworld" of the unconscious—in other words, the unknown—while concurrently trying to penetrate its phallus into the "known world" of conscious activity through sexual conjunction with a human.[99]

From a cosmological perspective, Andean dualism permeates every aspect of this story. The woman, feminine principle, is a creature of the dry land, whereas her captor, the water *huaca*, exemplifying the masculine principle, is a creature of the wet lagoon. There is also a separation between those who live on the land and the creature who lives below the surface of the water. The water *huaca*, which takes the woman by force, might also represent the unpredictable forces of nature, such as storms, floods, the El Niño effects, and other atmospheric phenomena, which exert great influence over the daily lives of Native Andeans. Note that when the victim's relatives clobber the head of the snake in a rescue attempt, this provokes "a hurricane, with wind so turbulent and uncontrollable its fury agitated the water, and turned this side of the lagoon into rough water. The lagoon was calm before this incident occurred on its banks." The legend also reminds us that land and water, nature and culture, and masculine and feminine principles must remain separate, except when united by proper Andean ritual. Otherwise, the improper union of complementary pairs violates the cosmic order and produces dire outcomes. In the case of the water serpent, the breach results in violence against its body; for the kidnapped woman, the violation produces symbolic infertility, for she gives birth to little snakes, or creatures that are less than human.

Sacred Water as the Symbolic Blood and Creative Life Principle of the Huaca

It is remarkable to observe the dual nature of water as both a creative and a destructive power in Native Andean mythology. In many pre-Columbian Andean myths, water is the primal matrix, the universal womb, from which the world is created and humankind originates. By contrast, water is also a destructive force which may initiate a cataclysmic event, marking the end of an existing world or age and the commencement of a new one, an

Andean cyclical concept known as *pachacuti*. We have already seen an example of the destructive power of water in the form of *Mama Cocha* ("Mother Sea") in the Huarochirí myth, What Happened to the Indians in the Olden Days When the Sea Overflowed. In that story, Mother Sea decides to overflow and creates a devastating flood that inundates and destroys the existing world, save the animals and a man and his family who escape to the summit of a very high mountain. The same theme has been addressed in other Andean stories. These two contrasting yet complementary aspects of water—destruction and creation—are recurring leitmotifs in Andean mythology.

For purposes of this discussion, we shall examine one aspect of this complementary duality—the creative capacity of "sacred water," which is also considered a *huaca*. The following is an ancient Inca myth recorded by the Spanish colonial chronicler Juan de Betanzos in 1551. In this and other similar Inca myths the Creator god *Viracocha* emerges from the waters of Lake Titicaca, which is considered one of the Incas' most important *huacas*, or sacred sites.

Concerning Con Tici Viracocha,
Whom They Consider the Creator,
and How He Created The Sky and the Earth
and the Indian Peoples of These Provinces of Peru

(Inca)

In ancient times, they say that the land and provinces of Peru were dark, and that there was no light or day. And in that time, there were certain people who inhabited the land who were ruled over by a certain lord and to whom they were subject. They do not remember the name of these people or of the lord who ruled over them.

In those days, when this land was as night [covered in darkness], they say that a certain lord, whom they called Con Tici Viracocha,[100] came out of a lake that is in this land of Peru, in the province they call Collasuyo. They say that he emerged with a great number of people, which number they cannot remember. He came out of the lake, and from there went to a place next to the lake, where today there is a town called Tiaguanaco [Tiahuanaco] in that province, the aforementioned province of Collao (another name for Collasuyo). There he and the others went.

Then they say that there he created the sun and the day, and ordered the sun to follow its [present] course. Then they say that he created the stars and the moon.

They say that this Con Tici Viracocha had come out once before, and on that occasion he had created the sky and the earth and had left everything dark. He then created those people who lived in the time of darkness.

These people had done a disservice to Viracocha. This angered him, and he determined that this would be the last time [that they would do so]. So he came out, just as before, and turned the first people and their lord into stone as punishment for having angered him.

Then, as we have said before, he came out at that [second] time and created the sun and the day and the moon and the stars.

Having done this, he made certain people out of stone at the site of Tiaguanaco [Tiahuanaco] and perfected the manner in which he was to produce others in the same fashion. He made a certain number of people out of stone, and a lord to govern them and rule over them, and many women [some] pregnant and others having given birth, with their babies in cradles according to the custom.

Everything he created out of stone he set aside in a designated place. Then he created another province [nation] of people in the same manner, and this continued until he created all the peoples of Peru, molding the stone in the manner just described.

Once he had finished creating, he ordered that all the people [who had emerged with him from the lake] depart, except for two in his company to whom he assigned the task of watching over the stone bundles.

[To these two] he relayed the names he had given to each kind of people. To them he indicated and said, "These people will be called so-and-so, and will emerge from such and such fountain in such and such province and will populate it, and multiply. These others will come out of such and such cave and will be called so-and-so and will populate such and such [region]; and just as I have painted them and created them out of stone, they will come out of fountains and rivers and caves and mountains in the provinces that I have so said and named. Then you will go in the direction (pointing them toward the sunrise), and you will divide them up, each with their own [group], and indicate to them the direction they are to take."[101]

～～

In this Andean origin myth it is clear that the location of the *huaca* or sacred lake from which the Inca Creator god emerged is Lake Titicaca, situated on the border of present-day Bolivia and Peru. On its banks stand the proud ancient ruins of Tiahuanaco (also spelled "Tiwanaku" or "Tiahuanacu"), an advanced pre-Inca civilization that reached its apogee between 300 and 500 AD and maintained its economic and political clout in the Andes for some five hundred years. The Incas conquered the Lake Titicaca basin and called this part of their empire *Collasuyo* ("Province or Quadrant of the *Colla*"), after the principal inhabitants of this region, a warrior nation known as the *Colla*. For various reasons it is difficult to determine the antiquity of this myth, of which there are several versions.[102] However, suffice it to say that the Incas worshipped Tiahuanaco and Lake Titicaca as *huacas*, as do the contemporary Native Andean peoples who live in the vicinity of the lake.[103]

As depicted in the myth, Tiahuanaco is also the seat of a great many stone monoliths, whose significance has yet to be fully understood. Perhaps it is these monolithic creations that inspired the Incas to believe that their Creator god *Viracocha* molded and fashioned humankind out of the stone at Tiahuanaco. Likewise, the first mythological Inca rulers, *Manco Capac* and *Mama Ocllo*, according to one Andean legend appeared on Lake Titicaca,[104] further enhancing the sacredness and significance of the lake. According to this legend, it is from Lake Titicaca that the first mythological rulers of the Incas embarked on a journey by land to civilize the Andean world. Thus, for the Incas of the pre-Columbian Andes, as well as for some contemporary Native Andean peoples, the Creator and the founding rulers of their culture emerged from this sacred water. The Creator formed the sun, the moon, the stars, and "all peoples of Peru," breathing life into this creation. And, pursuant to the legend, the mythological rulers *Manco Capac* and *Mama Ocllo* introduced the civilizing arts in this region of the world. These beings, who are glorified in Andean mythology, are linked to the creative capacity of this sacred water or *huaca*.

This link between sacred water and creation might be further extended to characterize sacred water as the blood (in Quechua, *yawar*), or the creative life principle, of certain *huacas* associated with fertility, birth, death, and regeneration. In previous chapters we discussed the significance of *unu* water, which is considered the sacred, fertilizing blood flowing through the "veins" or waterways of the *Wamanis*, mountain deities that guard the Native Andean communities. For instance, a study conducted by Peruvian anthropologist Juan Ossio reveals that the Quechua elders of Chaupi, Peru, believe that the water flowing from the mountains—the sacred a*guay unu* that fertilizes their fields—is the fertilizing blood of the *Wamanis*.[105] In keeping with the syncretistic tradition of the Andes, these

Native Andeans differentiate between normal water and sacred water. On the one hand, normal water (in Quechua, *yaku*) may arise in the form of rain and is considered "the work of [the Christian] God"; on the other hand, sacred water (*aguay unu*) "is the water that flows from the vein of Father mountain" and is "a gift from the *Wamanis*."[106]

It is this sacred water, or symbolically this "fertilizing blood" of the *huacas*, which these Native Andeans believe give rise to crops needed to sustain their communities and to plants indigenous to their landscape. Accordingly, the blood of the *huacas* in this case is also synonymous with "sacred water," just as *unu* water is believed to flow from the "veins" (symbolic blood vessels) of the Andean mountain deities.

Numerous Andean myths about the origin of maize, potatoes, yucca, and other crops draw a parallel between blood—death, burial, or human sacrifice—and the birth of certain crops and plants.[107] It is as if the blood from the body parts or sacrifice of the victims *becomes* the sacred *unu* water, the fertilizing blood or creative life principle which gives rise to agriculture and native flora. To illustrate, let us examine an ancient Native Andean myth recounting the origin of agriculture that was recorded during the colonial period by the Augustinian monk Antonio de la Calancha (1637).[108] This myth was well known all along the western Andean coast from northern Peru to northern Chile.

The story relates that in the beginning of the world, the god *Pachacamac*, who was the son of the Sun god, created the first man and woman but did not provide them with any food or source of nourishment. After a while, the man died due to lack of food, and the woman was forced to go out every day in search of roots and herbs among the thorny bushes so that she could sustain herself in the wild. Weary of her daily struggle to survive, the woman raised her eyes toward the heavens, and with tears running down her face, she pleaded to the Sun god to save her from this predicament. The Sun came down from the sky and kindly tried to console the woman. He told her that soon her situation would change and that she had no need to worry. The next day, as she went about gathering wild roots, the Sun impregnated her with his rays, and four days later the woman gave birth to a beautiful boy. This boy, who was a child of the Sun god, was, therefore, also the brother of Pachacamac.

Jealous and enraged, the god Pachacamac took his brother away from the woman and killed him, tearing him into pieces. And so that no one would ever complain about the lack of food again, Pachacamac used his brother's dismembered body parts to create food in the world. He scattered his brother's teeth, and from them maize sprang up. He sowed his brother's

PLATE 1. Mount Illimani overlooking La Paz. Illimani is considered an Achachila, a mountain deity and ancestor of the Aymara people, and is the second-highest peak in the Bolivian Andes.

PLATE 2. Village of Puka Wayra on the Island of the Sun in Lake Titicaca, Bolivia. According to some origin myths, the mythical ancestors of the Incas, Manco Capac and Mama Ocllo, first appeared on this island on Lake Titicaca.

PLATE 3. Quechua family. The Quechua language, or Runa Simi (People's Speech), has more than 40 regional variations and is spoken by more than 10 million people in Peru, Bolivia, Ecuador, Colombia, Chile, and Argentina. Las Rayas, between Puno and Cuzco regions, Peru.

PLATE 4. Quechua priest preparing a despacho, a devotional offering or remittance to Pacha Mama (the Andean Earth Mother), the Apus (mountain deities), and other Andean huacas. Cuzco, Peru. *Photo courtesy of Ricardo Sánchez.*

PLATE 5. Underground chamber at
Q'enqo, one of the largest Inca huacas,
or holy sites, in the Sacred Valley of the
Incas. Cuzco region, Peru.

PLATE 6. Aymara-speaking Uru woman selling her wares. Uru women, living on floating human-made islands on Lake Titicaca, have adopted the Aymara language and an Aymara mode of dress while also intermarrying with Aymaras, creating a composite ethnic identity and syncretistic culture. Off the shore of Puno, Peru.

PLATE 7. Titi Qala, Rock of the Puma, is
a huaca on the Island of the Sun in Lake
Titicaca, Bolivia. It was one of the Incas'
most sacred and important pilgrimage
destinations.

PLATE 8. Floating island Uru women. The land-dwelling Aymaras refer to their island-dwelling neighbors, the Urus, as haqi huaca (human huacas), because the Uru people are believed to have survived since primordial times. Lake Titicaca, off the shore of Puno, Peru.

PLATE 9. Traditional view of Machu
Picchu, an Inca palace complex con-
structed by the Inca ruler Pachacuti Inca
Yupanqui in the fifteenth century. In 2007
Machu Picchu was recognized as one of
the New Seven Wonders of the World.
Cuzco region, Peru.

PLATE 10. Urubamba River, also known as the Willkamayu or Vilcanota in its upper course, traverses the Sacred Valley of the Incas. Inca pilgrims traveled along this river in a course that mirrored the path taken by their Creator god, Wiracocha. Cuzco region, Peru.

PLATE 11. Hatun Rumiyoc, the twelve-sided
Inca stone, gracing an Inca wall in Cuzco,
Peru. The Incas are widely known for their fine
masonry, which was accomplished without the
use of mortar.

PLATE 12. Serpentine rock formation at the Inca
citadel of Saksaywaman. According to some colonial accounts, the Incas had a temple dedicated
to the worship of snakes, and their principals
adopted names such as Amaru and Mach'acuay
in honor of these serpent huacas. Cuzco, Peru.

PLATE 13. Aymara woman gazing at the dry altiplano, the high Andean plateau situated between the eastern and western mountain ranges of the Peruvian and Bolivian Andes, as well as parts of northern Chile and Argentina. La Paz Department, Bolivia.

PLATE 14. Aymara boat craftsmen from the Island of Suriki. These master craftsmen assisted Thor Heyerdahl, the Norwegian adventurer and ethnographer, in constructing reed boats for his successful Ra II, transatlantic expedition from Morocco to Barbados. Lake Titicaca, Bolivia.

PLATE 15. Modern replica of the Inca diagram of the cosmos, as described by the native colonial chronicler Joan de Santacruz Pachacuti Yamqui Salcamaygua. The original gold plate was housed in the Qoricancha (Golden Enclosure), the most important and sacred Inca temple. Qoricancha-Museo del Convento de Santo Domingo, Cuzco, Peru.

PLATE 16. Pre-Hispanic agricultural terraces, called andenes by the Spaniards and pata pata by Quechua speakers. The Incas and their ancestors constructed these on the Andean slopes to create cultivable hillsides and maximize agriculture. Many are still in use today. Chinchero, Cuzco region, Peru.

PLATE 17. Large stone monolith at the pre-Inca site of Tiwanaku. Statues such as these may have inspired Andean creation myths about primordial giants who were turned into stone in a prior creation of the world. La Paz Department, Bolivia.

PLATE 18. Gateway god holding two staffs atop the Sun Gate at Tiwanaku. His headdress consists of sunrays, suggesting he is a solar deity or a Creator deity, such as Wiracocha. La Paz Department, Bolivia.

PLATE 19. Capac Colla dancer, representing the highland merchants from Potosí who traveled during the colonial period to trade their products in Cuzco. They perform during the Catholic festival of St. Joseph. Cuzco, Peru.

PLATE 20. Andean yatiri blessing a colorfully decorated van to protect it against accidents and misfortune. Copacabana, Manco Kapac Province, Bolivia.

PLATE 21. Lone boatman on Lake Titicaca, Bolivia. The Aymaras still venerate and address the lake as Mama Cocha in honor of the Inca Mother of the Sea who was believed to have dominion over all bodies of water, including oceans, lakes, and lagoons.

PLATE 22. Highflying condor, guardian of the Andes. In Andean cosmology, the condor acts as an intermediary between earth and sky and often possesses the power of transfiguration. Colca Canyon, Arequipa region, Peru. *Photo courtesy of Ricardo Sánchez.*

ribs and bones, and from them sprouted yucca (manioc or cassava) and other tubers. He planted his brother's flesh, and soon cucumber plants and guava trees were born, along with all the other vegetables and fruit trees. Even though the world was now blessed with an abundance of food, the mother could not help but remember her son in every morsel of food; each one was a constant reminder of her deep anguish. Again she called upon the Sun god for help, and the Sun asked for the dead child's "vine" (symbolic penis) and navel (umbilical cord). From these, the Sun god created another handsome child named *Vichama* (or *Villama*), who grew to travel the world, just like his father, and later even revived his mother, who had been killed and dismembered by his brother Pachacamac.[109]

The link between blood and the emergence of agriculture is evident in this tale, as the deity Pachacamac uses the body parts of his dismembered brother to generate food in the world. Another way to look at this myth is to view the death of the child as a symbolic sacrifice for the benefit of humankind (which is created later in the story): the blood of the innocent child, whose body parts are sown, becomes the sacred *unu* water or creative life principle that bathes the barren land, making it fertile ground for the cultivation of grains, fruits, vegetables, and other crops that are essential for human survival. It is as if the body parts themselves, as symbolic seeds, are scattered and planted in the furrows of Mother Earth, activated by the "fertilizing blood" of the Sun child (*huaca*).

A very similar theme is presented in another well-known Quechua myth from the Cuzco area of Peru. In that myth, the Creator god *Con Ticsi Viracocha*[110] created the Andes Mountains and populated the skies with all species of birds. During that time there were no plants or animals, and no food for the birds to eat. So the god sent the *huaca Mama Raywana* ("Mother Furrow") to explore ways to produce food from the land, since after creating the birds the god also intended to create people, and people, no doubt, would eat more than birds. Mama Raywana became pregnant and gave birth to a beautiful boy. One day she went off to wash his clothes and left the child in the care of the birds. After a while the boy began to cry, and the birds did not know how to console him. Every time he cried, they tried to stroke him with their pointy beaks. But instead of comforting him, the beaks started piercing and wounding his flesh, and peck after peck, they accidentally killed him. Frightened, the birds held a meeting and decided they had to make the body disappear before Mama Raywana returned. They tore the boy's body into pieces, and each bird took a piece, lifted it away, and buried it with its beak. That way, the boy's body parts were scattered all over the earth.

Mama Raywana returned, but when she could not find her child she cried and screamed in desperation. Finally, when she could search no longer, she stopped and turned into stone in the highest part of the Andes. But over time, something miraculous happened. From every one of the body parts the birds had buried, a plant began to grow. Peas sprouted from the boy's eyes; broad beans from his nails; corn from his teeth; potatoes from his heart and kidneys; *olluco* (an Andean tuber) from his testicles; oca from his penis; yucca from his bones; and fruit from his flesh. They say the birds were alarmed and confused, swirling around in the air, hopelessly disoriented. So *Con Ticsi Viracocha* turned them into snow, the ageless snow that you see today, resting on the rocks of the Andean peaks.[111]

In yet another plant myth from the Bolivian altiplano, an Inca *ñusta*, a virgin betrothed to the Sun god, broke her vow of chastity and breached Inca law by falling in love with a young commoner with whom she conceived a child. The Inca sentenced them both to death, and the priests buried and burned the couple alive in a bed of coca leaves as offerings to the Sun god. Soon calamity befell the empire, and the Inca priests decided to unearth the bodies for fear that the Sun god had been displeased with their offering. For months they searched for the charred bodies of the couple, but they always came up empty. One day they finally discovered the burnt bed of coca leaves, upon which the couple had been laid, but the priests were astounded to find no human remains. Instead, a wondrous and beautiful plant was taking root in the scorched and lifeless soil. It had soft blue flowers and round bulbous tubers growing from its roots. On that day, they claim, the potato plant was born.[112]

Again, these complex Andean myths allude to the intimate connection between blood from death or interment—which sometimes includes dismemberment—and the origin of agriculture in the Andes. The blood of the sacrifice, in a manner analogous to the sacred blood or sacred *unu* water of the mountain spirits (*huacas*), nourishes the lifeless earth, allowing for the emergence of cultigens and plants. Hence, the fertilizing capacity of blood, as sacred water, might be viewed as the creative life principle activating the earth and leading to the birth and regeneration of crops, plants, and fruitage needed for our survival.

This theme of fertilizing blood as sacred *unu* water is also played out in another familiar Andean legend belonging to the Aymara people of the altiplano. In that legend two warring kings, one from the north and another from the south, were mortally wounded in battle. Each one had a young son who was reluctant to go to war, but each father on his deathbed ordered his son to wage war on the opposing kingdom and defend his honor. A bloody battle ensued and both young princes were violently injured. As they fell to the ground, the young monarchs embraced and forgave one another and forsook the pride of their fathers, which had instigated the violence. The youths died together in an eternal embrace and were buried together in a single tomb. Yet "amid the debris of the bloody earth, [a] flower of conciliation was born"; from the blood of the two fallen princes sprouted a graceful, tricolored wildflower—the *khantuta* (also spelled *kantuta* or *qantuta*).[113]

In keeping with the theme of blood sacrifice as sacred water, there are also several Andean myths about the origin of the sacred coca plant, in which human death or human sacrifice precedes the appearance or birth of the plant.[114] In one of the oldest versions of this legend, recorded in the sixteenth century, the death, or symbolic sacrifice, of a promiscuous woman gives rise to the coca plant.

According to this account, in the distant past a beautiful but loose young woman lived in a village. The inhabitants of the village plotted against her and gathered an assembly of elders, who passed judgment against her for her crimes and sentenced her to death. After the sentence was carried out, and as a greater penalty, they ordered that her body be cut in half before being buried. To everyone's amazement, in the same spot where her body parts were scattered grew a coca shrub, which the villagers named *Mamacoca* or *Cocamama* ("Mother Coca").[115] This is yet one more illustration of the connection among blood, dismemberment, and the origin of a native plant, energized by sacred water (in this case the "blood" of the executed woman).

One might then speculate why the Incas called human sacrifice *capac cocha* (also spelled *qhapaq qocha*) and considered it the most precious offering that could be made to their *huacas*. In Quechua, *capac* means rich, noble, or powerful, and *cocha* means sea, lake, or lagoon.[116] This would suggest that the "rich lake" of human blood, resulting from human sacrifice, was akin to the sacred *unu* water (*yaku unu* or *aguay unu*) or the life-giving principle of creation. Therefore, one way to interpret this ceremony might be to view it as a reciprocal and mutually beneficial exchange where the blood of the human victim was being offered in exchange for the symbolic blood (sacred water/life-giving principle) of the *huaca*.[117] This arrangement would also have preserved the duality and complementarity of the cosmos: the destruction of the human offering would have given way to creation, and the death of the sacrificial victim would have paved the way for birth, life, fertility, and regeneration.

CHAPTER SUMMARY

Throughout this chapter we have explored the various definitions of *huacas*, including objects, animals, persons, or places venerated by Native Andean religions; animas or spirits associated with individual aspects of nature such as mountains, caves, springs, rivers, rocks, and so forth; temples, shrines, idols, and other holy human-made objects; deities that exhibit superhuman qualities or characteristics; and sacred places where offerings are made. From Garcilaso de la Vega we have also derived the notion that *huacas* may be anomalies of nature, such as a double-yolked egg or children born with six toes. Additionally, they may be ugly or monstrous things, or specimens that in beauty or excellence stand above others of their same species.

We have also set forth the proposition that a *huaca* may represent a portal or an opening between the natural and supernatural worlds, or, alternatively, a mediating space where these worlds converge. This is based on an analysis of numerous Native Andean legends in which mountains are described with "doors" and "openings" leading to a magical or supernatural world in their interior. The notion of a *huaca* as a mediating or converging space is also consistent with Native Andean *mesa* (table) rituals that bring together complementary elements through the mediation of a middle zone or unite cosmological words in the sacred geography of the *mesa*. Also, in some Andean pilgrimages, such as the Huaringas pilgrimage, a person must traverse certain mediating passages connecting the natural and supernatural worlds, demonstrating the dual notion of a *huaca* as both a "crack" or portal between worlds or a space where these worlds converge.

In Andean mythology *huacas* may also assume human and sometimes animal forms. Unlike the Western concept of an invisible God, *huacas* eat, walk, talk, and engage in sexual relations with humans and other *huacas*. Among the Cañari people of Ecuador, *Mama Huaca* is believed to live in the interior of many mountains. And in many parts of the Andes, some lakes and lagoons are believed to be enchanted and to house *huacas*, which live in magical realms below the surface of the water. On occasion, male water *huacas* are also believed to have sexual relations with women, who fall under their powerful spell. These water *huaca* myths, often associated with mythological serpents, are strongly evocative of sex and fertility.

Finally, we have discussed the notion that "sacred water" (*aguay unu*) symbolically represents the blood and creative life principle of Andean *huacas*, such as mountain deities, which distribute and carry the life-giving *unu* water through their "veins" (waterways), thereby fertilizing the earth for agriculture. This is analogous to the flow of blood from a sacrifice—which in Andean myth may include death, dismemberment, or interment of a human—that, as symbolic sacred water, bathes and vitalizes the land, giving rise to certain crops and plants that are important to the survival of the Native Andean community.

6

The Origin of Culture

Origin Myths

Some of the most intricate and beautiful myths of the Andes concern the creation of the world and the origin of culture. Almost every Native Andean community has its own myth about how the world began, how the heavenly bodies were created, and how its own culture came into being. These stories, which are transmitted orally from one generation to the next, are deeply rooted in the pre-Columbian traditions and belief systems of the past, and yet they have evolved to incorporate the present-day realities of the indigenous peoples of the Andes. As such, these stories are not simply nostalgic remembrances of the past, but rather, living and breathing entities that present an ever-changing portrait of the psychology and cosmology of each Andean people.

Andean origin myths generally try to explain how a particular indigenous group came into being. They also usually identify the sacred place of origin—known in Quechua as *paqarina*—from which the group's first ancestors are believed to have emerged. This sacred place of origin may be a particular mountain, fountain, lake, cave, or any other natural site closely associated with the group. The myth may also explain the origin of agriculture and particular crops upon which the group depends for its subsistence. Often the myths also describe the origin of certain rituals and customs, and how the group came to venerate certain gods, nature spirits, or animals.

One of the most intricate and elegant origin myths of the Andes comes from a region known as Cañar in Ecuador, which is inhabited today by the Quichua-speaking[1] Cañari people. The Cañaris are a highland people whose religious practices incorporate elements of both Roman Catholicism and their own ancestral animistic traditions. Their indigenous legacy includes the worship of the Andean Creator god, *Pachacaman* (also spelled *Pachacamac, Pachakamak,* or *Pachacamaq*); the Earth Mother, *Pacha Mama*; and the mountain deities, *Urcu-Yayas*.[2] Cañari writer Luis Bolívar Zaruma describes their beliefs:

> The gods and destiny abandoned men and the incapable [European] colonists. But for the Cañaris, the God *Pachacaman* lives; *Pacha Mama* is within us, young and beautiful. She is also in all that surrounds us—in the breath of the day, in the immense breathing of all of nature, in the tenderness of the sky. He [*Pachacaman*] formed our body, molded our heart[s] as human beings.[3]

The Cañaris are an ancient people whose forebears were contemporaries of the Incas.[4] After the Spanish Conquest, colonial chroniclers, intent on Christianizing the native communities, recorded various versions of the Cañaris' origin myth. One of the earliest versions of this myth was recorded in 1573 by the colonial priest chronicler, Cristóbal de Molina ("el Cuzqueño").

The Myth of Origin of the Cañaris

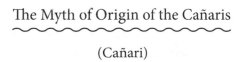

(Cañari)

In the province of Quito there is a province called Cañaribamba, and that is why they call the Indians Cañaris, because of the name of the province. Of these they say that at the time of the deluge, in a very high mountain called Huacayñan[5] ["Trail of Tears"] located in that province, two brothers escaped [and found refuge there from the flood]. And they say in the fable that as the waters began to rise, the mountain began to grow, such that the waters could not reach them. After the deluge, the brothers used up all the food they had previously gathered. They walked through the hills and valleys in search of more food, and they made a small hut in which to live. They sustained themselves by eating roots and weeds, expending great effort and experiencing hunger.

One day, after having gone in search of food, they returned to their hut and found cooked food to eat and chicha [maize beer] to drink. They did not know from where [the food had come] or who had prepared or brought it there. The food lasted about ten days, at the end of which the brothers discussed it among themselves and decided to find out who had done them such a favor in such a time of great need. And so the eldest of them agreed to hide [to discover the identity of their benefactors].

From his hiding place, the elder brother saw two female birds arrive. The Cañaris call them aguaque, and torito by another name. In our language they call them macaws. They came dressed as Cañaris, with hair on their heads, and a band tied around their foreheads, just like those the Cañari women wear today. When they arrived at the hut, the eldest of the macaw-women saw the man hiding; nonetheless, she took off her lliclla, which is the mantle that they use, and started to prepare the food they had brought. When the man saw how beautiful they were, and that they had the faces of women, he came out of his hiding place and attacked them. The macaw-women saw the Indian enraged, so they quickly departed and flew away, without making or leaving anything to eat that day.

The younger brother returned from the countryside where he had gone in search of something to eat. Since he found nothing prepared [to eat], as he was accustomed to finding on other days, he asked his brother what had occurred. His brother explained what had happened. The brothers fought over this, and so the younger brother decided that this time he would remain hidden to see if the macaw-women would return.

After three days, the macaw-women returned and began to make something to eat. The younger brother saw this as an opportune moment to catch them, and he entered the hut just as they had finished making the food. He charged toward the door and locked it, capturing the macaw-women inside. The macaw-women showed great anger. And as the younger brother held on to the younger macaw, the older macaw fled, leaving behind the younger one. And with this younger one, they say he had sexual intercourse.

And in the course of time, the macaw-woman had six sons and daughters with whom the brothers lived on the mountain for a long time. They sustained themselves with the seeds they sowed, which they say were brought by the macaw-woman. These sons and daughters, children of the macaw-woman, distributed themselves throughout the province of Cañaribamba. [From her], they say, descend all of the Cañaris. And that is why they have as their huaca [sacred place of origin] the mountain named Huacayñan, and they hold the macaws in great veneration, and have a high regard for their plumes in their festivals.[6]

~~

This intriguing myth speaks to the origin of the Cañari people and their culture. Their sacred place of origin, or *paqarina*, is identified as Mount *Huacayñan*, or Mount "Trail of Tears," where the brothers escaped during the deluge. As in many other Andean origin myths, the deluge is the catastrophic event that initiates the Andean cycle of *pachacuti*, leading to the destruction of the existing world and the creation of a new one. It is also on Mount *Huacayñan* that the younger brother impregnates the macaw-woman, and together they beget six offspring who populate the province of Cañaribamba and become the progenitors of the Cañari nation.

This myth may also explain the origin of some elements of the autochthonous religion of the Cañaris, which other colonial writings observe included the worship of two copper female macaws perched on top of a small column.[7] Additionally, in the nineteenth century a tomb was discovered in Huapan, in the vicinity of Azoguez, the capital of the Cañar province, in which hundreds of copper axes were unearthed, including many in the shape of macaws,[8] suggesting that the macaws had a strong religious significance for the Cañari people.

The origin myth of the Cañaris also credits the macaw-women with the introduction of agriculture. It is clear from the myth that before the arrival of the macaw-women, the two brothers were surviving on "roots and weeds." At the outset the brothers were "gatherers" who collected wild roots and other plants for their subsistence and survival. However, afterward, the macaw woman and her family "sustained themselves with the seeds they sowed, which . . . were brought by the macaw-woman." This indicates that after the capture of the macaw-woman, the culture transformed into an agricultural society by planting the seeds the macaw-woman introduced. The crops produced by the seeds provided sustenance for the macaw-woman's family and, ultimately, ensured the survival of her Cañari descendants.

The origin of agriculture is a recurring theme found in many Andean origin myths, especially highland myths, which Peruvian anthropologist Maria Rostworowki describes as follows.

Perhaps it is the mythical remembrance of ancient famines that devastated the [region], whose distant memory persists in the mythical narrative. Perhaps these deeds also [bring to mind memories] of a population that was ignorant about agriculture, [and] dedicated itself to hunting, fishing, or gathering, and was exposed to natural phenomena, such as avalanches, rains, drought, and frost in the highlands, and changes and climatic fluctuations in the plains caused by sporadic deviations of the ocean currents. . . . All these disasters were caused by the inclemency of natural forces [that] affected the [ancient] indigenous peoples, even more so when they had no knowledge of agriculture, nor the technology necessary for the preservation and conservation of foodstuffs.[9]

The Cañari myth also suggests that, in addition to introducing agriculture, the macaw-women introduced the art of cooking, which naturally implies the use of fire. In the story it is evident the brothers had no knowledge of fire, for they foraged for food every day and subsisted on the "raw" resources of the earth. The brothers depended on roots and weeds for their nourishment, and possibly (although the myth does not expressly state it) wild grasses and lumber for the construction of their dwelling. Yet the generosity of the macaw-women allowed the men to savor the palatable pleasures of cooked food. And it was also the absence of cooked food that generated fraternal conflict in the story, after the elder brother's assault scared away the macaw-women.

The anthropologist Claude Lévi-Strauss maintains that cooking or "culinary operations" may be viewed as "mediatory activities between heaven and earth, life and death, nature and society."[10] In his analysis of certain Amazonian myths of the Ge and Tupi-Guaraní peoples, Lévi-Strauss concludes that myths relating to cooking and the origin of fire "function in terms of a double contrast . . . between what is raw and what is cooked, and . . . between the fresh and the decayed."[11] With respect to the former, Lévi-Strauss contends that the "raw/cooked axis is characteristic of culture . . . since cooking brings about the cultural transformation of the raw."[12] This is particularly appropriate when applied to the Cañari myth of origin, as the macaw-women are not only the introducers of fire, but also the mothers of agriculture—two activities closely associated with the origin of culture.

It is interesting to note that in a number of Amazonian myths considered by Lévi-Strauss, the secret of fire, inextricably linked to cooking, is in the possession of the animal kingdom.[13] These myths generally attribute the origin of fire to an animal, such as a jaguar, a vulture, or as in the Cañari myth, the macaw, who voluntarily shares the gift with humankind, or to a human being who intentionally steals it from an animal.[14] It is readily apparent at the beginning of the Cañari myth that the macaw-women freely share the gift of cooking, and thus fire, with the human brothers to help them survive. Therefore, consistent with the findings of Lévi-Strauss, cooking functions as an intermediary activity between the world of nature and the world of culture, and it is linked to a societal transformation set in motion by the arrival and intervention of an animal, or as in this case, two anthropomorphic beings who are part human and part macaw.

As in many Andean stories concerning anthropomorphic beings, the macaw-women in this myth are part human and part bird and exhibit characteristics belonging to both the animal kingdom (nature) and humankind (society/culture). So, like other anthropomorphic beings, they too may be characterized as intermediaries between earth and sky, the animal world and the human world, and nature and culture. Although they are birds that can fly and are covered with feathers, they are also women who can cook, display emotion, and have sexual relations with men. They also possess knowledge that is essential, but initially unavailable, to the human brothers; yet, this knowledge has the power to transform their circumstances and introduce them to the civilizing arts of cooking (fire), planting, and sowing (agriculture). In this respect, the macaw-women in the Cañari origin myth are similar to other Andean intermediaries that embody aspects of more than one reality, or more than one "world," and attempt to bridge the disjunction between worlds. They also resemble Andean *huacas* ("animas" of nature) in that they are able to walk the earth as human beings but are also endowed with supernatural or superhuman characteristics.

Previously, we have argued that the general rule in Native Andean myths is that different worlds must remain separate and distinct for the dualism of the cosmos to be preserved. For instance, we have observed in other stories that when two worlds, such as the sky world and the terrestrial world, come together in an improper or unsanctioned union, violence and tragedy inevitably ensue.[15] Often, in such cases, one of the mythical characters dies, physically or symbolically, as a consequence of that union, as for instance a child born from the sexual union of an animal and a human, or the offspring of an undead ancestor and a human.[16] The origin myth, however, sometimes presents an exception to that general rule. In contrast to non-origin myths, some Andean origin myths view creation and the origin of culture as the products of an improper sexual union, a cultural taboo, which results in fecundity.

Some might argue that Native Andean communities, as many other indigenous groups from around the world, have observed the physical, mental, and debilitating effects of inbreeding,[17] and therefore favor exogamy—marriage outside of one's community, tribe, clan, ecological zone, or ethnic group. This view would suggest that this custom or practice is prescribed, symbolically, in Andean origin myths, when a member of one species (e.g., human) in the story has sexual relations with another species (e.g., bird); however, this analysis is far from complete.[18]

In the Cañari myth, for example, the first inhabitants of the new creation after the deluge are products of bestiality—sexual relations between a human and an animal—which in the Andes, as elsewhere, is a cultural taboo. There are very few studies about the actual incidence of bestiality among Native Andean communities, but the implication is that the act itself is considered dehumanizing to the perpetrator. In a study about the effects of alcohol on sexuality and sexual identity in Andean festivities, anthropologist Céline Geffroy Komadina explains that the excessive consumption of alcohol in some Native Andean communities gives members a certain license to engage in sexual practices, such as homosexuality and bestiality, which would otherwise be condemned by the community. In such instances, the person is believed to be "possessed" by the spirit of the alcohol and is, therefore, not personally responsible for the behavior.

> The change of identity [due to excessive alcohol consumption] permits all kinds of possible combinations, and so, rumor has it, that some persons [in an inebriated state] even abuse animals. Zoophilia is totally condemned; it reduces the man to the status of an animal; he loses his humanity and he loses it twice, they say, when a man commits this act (because I never heard them speak of women [in this regard]). He is totally inebriated and his intense drunkenness is another way in which to dehumanize himself. In the face of such a despicable act, the people try to protect themselves as a group and justify what the man did in some way: he was not in control of his actions; the devil [spirit of the alcohol] took control of him and convinced him . . . he was a male sheep[;] . . . Not only do they treat [the man] as an animal; he is an animal.[19]

Likewise, incestuous relationships are uniformly condemned throughout the Andes, and there are many beliefs, especially in rural communities, regarding perpetrators of incest turning into condemned souls after their deaths or supernatural animals at night.[20] Nonetheless, in the following Inca origin myth, we will see that the first Incas rulers, mythical forebears of the Inca people, were believed to be the offspring of an incestuous relationship between the Sun god and the Moon, who also happened to be brother and sister, and husband and wife in the celestial sphere. Mirroring the relationship of their "divine" parents, the first Inca overlords were also thought to be brother and sister, and husband and wife on the earthly plane, a belief that legitimated the practice of incest among the Inca elite.[21]

The following is a legend about the founding of the Inca Empire and the origin of Inca culture, as retold by the colonial (half Inca) chronicler Garcilaso de la Vega in his *Comentarios reales de los incas* ("Royal Commentaries of the Incas"), first published in Lisbon, Portugal, in 1609. It recounts the tale of a brother and a sister who were sent by their father, the Sun god, to civilize the Andean world. Garcilaso heard this elegant account of the founding of Cuzco, the former capital of the Inca Empire, when he was about sixteen or seventeen years old. His maternal uncle, Francisco Huallpa Tupac Yupanqui, an Inca nobleman who had survived the Spanish Conquest of Peru, told it to him at a family gathering. According to Garcilaso, this conversation took place at his mother's home in Cuzco, which was frequented by a number of Inca relatives who gathered to reminisce about the former glories of their vanquished empire. Garcilaso recounts how his dignified uncle shared this story with him in his native Quechua tongue, insisting that he "hear it and keep it in his heart."[22]

Part I. The Origin of the Incas, Kings of Peru

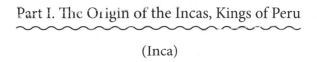

(Inca)

In the first ages of the world, this region of the earth that you see was covered with wilderness and scrub. And people in those days lived like beasts and wild animals, without religion or government, without towns or houses, without tilling or sowing of the earth. There was no clothing or covering for the body, because people did not know how to weave cotton or wool to make clothing. They lived in twos and threes, howsoever they chose to be together in caves, crannies in cliffs, and underground caverns. Like beasts they ate wild plants, roots of trees, and uncultivated fruit; [they also ate] human flesh. They covered their bodies with leaves and the bark of trees, and animal skins. Others went naked. In sum, they lived like deer and other wild game. And even in their intercourse with women they behaved like beasts, for they did not know how to have their own and [separate wives].

Observing what I have described, our father, the Sun, took pity upon humankind and sent down from the sky to the earth his own son and daughter to teach the people his knowledge, so that they might worship him and have him as their god, and to give them rules and laws by which to live as men of reason and courtesy; and so that they may [learn] to dwell in houses and villages, learn how to plough the soil, cultivate plants and grains, breed livestock, and delight in these [things] and in the fruits of the earth, as rational men and not as beasts.

With this, his command and mandate, the Sun god set his two children down on Lake Titicaca, which is located eighty leagues from here. He also entrusted them with a golden staff, which measured about half a yard in length and two fingers in thickness.[23] And he told them to go where they willed, and that wherever they should stop to eat or sleep, they should try to thrust the golden staff into the ground. This he gave them as a sign and proof that wherever the said staff should sink into the ground with a single thrust, there he wanted them to stop and found their city and [establish] their [royal] court.

Lastly, the father Sun said to his children: "When these people become our subjects, you shall rule them with reason and justice, with mercy, clemency, and mildness, always acting as devout parents of [our] tender and beloved children. In this, try to imitate and resemble me, for it is I who brings good to the world. I give light and brightness so that my people might see and do their work; I warm them when they are cold; I grow their pastures and their cultivated lands; I bring fruits to their trees and multiply their livestock; I bring rain and fair weather; and I take care to go round the world every day to observe the needs [of my people], and provide and help them as their sustainer and benefactor.

As you are my children, I want you to follow my example, for you are being sent down to earth to teach and benefit those men who live like beasts. And, of course, I constitute and proclaim you rulers and lords over all the peoples that you instruct with sound reason, [good] works, and [orderly] government."

After making his will known, our father, the Sun god, bade his children farewell. They left Lake Titicaca and walked northward. Wherever they stopped along the way, they thrust the golden staff into the ground, but it did not sink in. At last, the couple entered a shelter or small dormitory [resting place], situated seven or eight leagues south of this city, which today they call Pacárec Tampu (meaning "Shelter or Rest House of the Dawn"). The Inca gave it this name because he set out from that rest house at daybreak. It is one of the towns that the Inca ordered to be populated later on. Now its inhabitants boast enormously about its name, because it was given by our first Inca. From there, he and his [sister-]wife, our queen, [proceeded and] arrived at this valley of Cuzco, which was then covered by wilderness.[24]

Part II. The Founding of Cuzco, Imperial City

(Inca)

The first stop that they made in this valley was in the hill named Huanacauri [meaning "Rainbow"]. There they tried to thrust the golden staff into the earth and it easily sank in on the first blow, and was seen no more. Then the Inca said to his sister-wife, "Our father orders us to remain in this valley and to found our city and our residence in fulfillment of his will. Therefore, let us each go out to [gather] and summon the people together in order to teach them, and bring them good [living], as our father has ordered."

Our first king and queen set out from the hill of Huanacauri, each in a different direction, to call the peoples together. [Huanacauri] is the first place that we know of from which our forebears set foot, and from where they departed to do good toward men; so there we built a temple, as is well known, for the worship of the Sun, in memory of the mercy and beneficence that he had shown the world.

The [lord Inca] went north, and the [queen] went south. They spoke to all the men and women they found in the wilderness. They told them that their father the Sun had sent them down from the sky to be the teachers and benefactors of the inhabitants of that entire region. [They also explained that they were there to] save them from the wild lives that they were leading and to show them how to live as civilized people. In fulfillment of the mandate given to them by their father the Sun, they summoned the peoples together and brought them out of the wild, [to relieve their] ills, and [teach] them how to live in populated villages and give them the proper food for humans and not for beasts.

Our king and queen said these and similar things to the first savages they found living in these mountains and hills. The people were amazed to see two persons clothed and adorned with garments that our father, the Sun, had given them, a mode of dress very different from their own. [They saw that the Inca's] ears were pierced open and stretched, in the same manner that we, their descendants, are also accustomed to wearing. They realized that the [gentle] words and [beautiful] faces [of the Inca and his queen] showed that they were indeed children of the Sun, and that they had come to give them towns in which to live and food for sustenance. The peoples marveled at what they saw, and came to believe the promises that the Incas had made to them. They believed all they had been told. Then they worshipped and revered the strangers as children of the Sun, and obeyed them as rulers.

[Thereafter], the same peoples gathered others and repeated the wonders of what they had seen and heard. A great number of men and women assembled and set out to follow our first Inca rulers, wherever they might go.

When our Incas saw the great crowd they had gathered, they ordered that some of their followers provide food from the countryside for all of them, so hunger would not drive them to disperse through the hills. Others were ordered to work on building huts and houses according to plans specified by the Inca on how they should be made.

In this way our imperial city [of Cuzco] began to be settled. [The great city] was divided into halves, called Hanan Cuzco (meaning, as you know, "Upper Cuzco") and Hurin Cuzco (meaning "Lower Cuzco"). The Inca settled those he had summoned in Hanan Cuzco, which is why they call it "Upper Cuzco," and those that the queen had summoned in Hurin Cuzco, which is why they call it "Lower Cuzco."

The division of the city did not occur so that the inhabitants of the upper half [of the city] should have any advantage over those of the lower half, or enjoy any greater privileges or superior treatment[25] than those of the lower half. Both were to be considered as equals, as brother and sister, children of the same father and mother. The Inca wanted this division of people and the difference in name, upper and lower, only so that the people would always remember that some of the inhabitants had been gathered by the Inca and others by the Coya [queen]. He ordered that the only difference and acknowledgement of superiority between them be that those of Hanan Cuzco be respected and considered as firstborn elder children, and those of Hurin Cuzco be considered as second-born children. In sum, they were to be as right and left arm in any preeminence [matter of position] concerning place and office, for those of Upper Cuzco were summoned by the male, and those of Lower Cuzco by the female.

Similarly, all imperial towns, great and small, [which were founded later], imitated this division. They were divided by district or by lineage as Hanan aillu and Hurin aillu,[26] which mean "upper lineage" and "lower lineage," [and] Hanan suyu and Hurin suyu, which mean "upper district" and "lower district."

Once the city had been jointly established, the Inca showed all the Indian men the tasks pertaining to the male gender, such as breaking and tilling the soil, and sowing crops, seeds, and vegetables. He also showed them that these were edible and nutritious. For this purpose, he taught them how to make foot ploughs and other tools they would need. He also taught them the manner and form in which they were to divert streams that ran through the valley of Cuzco to create irrigation ditches. He even showed them how to make the footwear we use today.

On the other hand, the queen instructed the Indian women in the feminine occupations, [such as] spinning and weaving cotton and wool, and making clothing for themselves and their husbands and children. She also showed them how to perform all the other duties of service in the home.

In sum, there was nothing relating to human life that our Incas failed to teach their first subjects. The Inca was the king and master of men, and the Coya was the queen and mistress of women.[27]

Part III. What Manco Capac Inca Brought Under His Dominion

(Inca)

The same Indians, thus brought under the dominion of the Inca, realized then that they had changed and had received [great] benefits. So, filled with great contentment and joy, they took to the mountains, the hills, and the wilderness to look for other Indians and spread the news about the [arrival] of the children of the Sun in their land for the benefit of them all. They recounted the many benefits they had received and [all the things they had learned from our first rulers]. And, so that they would be believed, they showed them the new clothes they wore and the new foods they ate. [They also described] how now they lived in houses and villages. When the peoples of the wilderness heard all these things, they came in great numbers to behold the wonders they were told about and were publicized concerning our first parents, kings, and lords. They confirmed everything with their own eyes and remained to serve and obey [the Inca and the Coya].

In this manner they summoned one another and spread the word about the arrival of the Incas from this one to that one, such that in a few years many peoples had gathered. So many peoples had gathered that after six or seven years the Inca had enough warriors armed and trained to defend themselves against any attackers who went against the Inca, and [they created an army] strong enough to bring in by force those who would not join willingly. The Inca taught these men how to make defensive weapons such as bows and arrows, lances, clubs, and other weapons that are still being used today.

And to sum up the deeds of our first Inca, I tell you that he subdued the territory to the east of the valley of Cuzco as far as the river Paucartampu [meaning "House of Many Colors"], and to the west he conquered eight leagues up to the river Apurimac [meaning "Great Speaker"], and to the south nine leagues to Quequesana. In this district he commanded that more than one hundred villages be settled, the largest with one hundred houses, and others with less, according to what the land could support.

These were the first beginnings of our city [of Cuzco], how it was founded and settled to become what it is today. These were the beginnings of our great, rich, and famous empire of the Incas, which your [Spanish] father and his companions took away from us. These were our first Incas and kings, who appeared in the first ages of the world, and from whom all the rest of our kings descend. And from these same Incas, all of us descend.

I cannot say precisely how many years have passed since our father, the Sun, sent his first children [to our lands]. They are so many that my memory has not been able to keep track of them all; [however,] we believe that more than 400 [years have passed]. Our [first] Inca was named Manco Capac and our first Coya, Mama Ocllo Huaco. They were, as I said, brother and sister, children of our parents, the Sun and the Moon.[28]

~~~

In 1609, Garcilaso de la Vega published the first tome of his master-work, *Royal Commentaries of the Incas*, in Lisbon, and brought to life the story and history of his mother's Inca culture to European audiences. The *Royal Commentaries* included this elegant recapitulation of the origin myth of the Incas and the founding of their capital city of Cuzco. The publication of this work may have been a personal attempt by Garcilaso to reclaim his indigenous culture and identity in the face of racial and oppressive Spanish colonial polices.[29] Although Garcilaso's father was Spanish by birth, and Garcilaso had embraced his father's language, culture, and religion, nevertheless, his *Royal Commentaries* present a conflicting portrait of the Spaniards. It is as though pride and bitterness were "working in the young man's soul like grits in the bosom of the oyster," and this dissonance would "ultimately produce the twin pearls of the *Royal Commentaries*."[30]

Meanwhile, back in Peru, the colonial authorities, fearing that the dispossessed *mestizos* (persons of mixed heritage) would join forces with the Indians to usurp their power, sought "to break down the last vestiges of Inca power and destroy their imperial legend."[31] By contrast, Garcilaso, then living in Spain, reaffirmed and rendered homage to his Inca heritage and exalted the accomplishments of the Inca rulers. The origin myth of the Incas and the founding of Cuzco, as set forth in the *Royal Commentaries*, portrays the first Inca rulers as the architects of Andean civilization. Although not historically accurate,[32] this was an attempt by Garcilaso to dispel the European myth prevalent at the time that the Native Andeans were ignorant savages who were "prevented by their 'short capacity' from grasping what the rational basis of [Christian] religious practice ought to be."[33] Moreover, because Garcilaso was perfectly fluent in both Quechua and Spanish and had a profound understanding of both Inca and Spanish cultures, his *Royal Commentaries* may be viewed as an effort to mediate between two discrepant world visions and cultures—that of the Christian Spaniard and the Sun-worshipping Inca.[34] Through his writings, Garcilaso eloquently presented a strong case for "restoring the credit and revising the fortunes both of his mother's race and the new breed of *mestizos* [to] which Garcilaso himself belonged."[35]

As with many Andean myths and legends, this account of the origin of the Inca culture begins with an incestuous relationship, a cultural taboo—the pairing of a brother and sister as husband and wife, each with a designated role to play in the formation of the culture. Woven throughout the story, we also see the thread of Andean dualism stitching together almost every major element of the myth. First, one notes the genders of the two mythological rulers, Manco Capac and Mama Ocllo Huaco, as male and female and that of their parents, the (masculine) Sun and the (feminine) Moon. One also observes the duality of the earth and sky; it is from the sky that the Sun god sends his children to disseminate his knowledge and establish a solar cult here on earth. The myth also contrasts the sound reason, good works, and rational "ordering" of civilization (culture) that the first Inca rulers allegedly initiated, with the prior "disorder" of life to which the "savages" had become accustomed in the wilderness (nature). Next, the origin myth describes the creation of two Cuzco moieties, *Hanan* and *Hurin*, and the division of their respective lineages into Upper and Lower. Then, it delineates the gender-specific tasks and obligations of the Inca king and queen and their respective male and female followers. Finally, the myth makes several metaphoric references that characterize the two Cuzco moieties as "elder" and "younger" children, "brother and sister" of the same father and mother, and also as a symbolic body with "right and left" arms.

The incestuous relationship between the Inca ruler and his sister-queen has a mythological basis but is less certain in historical terms. In his *Royal*

Commentaries, Garcilaso explains that the Incas believed that the Moon was the sister and wife of the Sun god, and that the Inca nobility descended from these deities.[36] He contends that "the first Incas and their children established a law that the first-born son of the Inca...was to marry his own full-blooded sister, in imitation of the Sun [god]."[37] According to Garcilaso, this rule was intended to keep the divine bloodline of the Sun from mixing with mere "human" blood.[38] However, many historians today believe that such a marriage was merely ceremonial in nature,[39] and that the first Inca rulers, Manco Capac and Mama Ocllo Huaco, did not institute this practice, as purported by the Inca origin myth recorded by Garcilaso. Instead, other colonial writings maintain that this practice was initiated either during the reign of the ninth Inca emperor, Pachacuti Inca Yupanqui (1438–1471), or that of his son, Tupac Inca Yupanqui (1471–1493), the magnanimous rulers who launched the Incas into their greatest period of expansion.[40] By some accounts Tupac's son, Huayna Capac (reigned 1493–1525), "appears to be the only Inca ruler who came from the union of brother and sister."[41] But other accounts also suggest that Huayna Capac's son, Huascar Inca (reigned 1527–1532), was also the offspring of siblings, the emperor and his full-blooded sister, Raua Ocllo.[42]

As in the Cañari myth about the macaw-women, this origin myth of the Incas also portrays the first Inca rulers as teachers of the civilizing arts. For example, Manco Capac instructs his male followers in the art of agriculture. He shows them how to plant, plow, and cultivate the land, and how to use a foot plough and other farming implements. He also shows them how to divert streams and build irrigation ditches, tasks essential to the success of agriculture.

The Inca leader also teaches his followers how to make footwear. In the Inca Empire, making footwear was an important step toward becoming a responsible male adult. During the Inca maturity rites ceremony of *huarachico* (also spelled *guarachico* or *warachikuy*), the initiates, adolescent boys, were required to make their own sandals,[43] called *usuta* or *ojota*, as part of their rite of passage into adulthood. Given that the Incas were formidable warriors, often traveling hundreds, even thousands of miles in their expeditions of conquest, it was imperative for an Inca soldier to learn how to make his own footwear in the event that his military ventures outlasted the life of his shoes. It is no wonder, then, that the art of making footwear was also incorporated in this Inca myth of origin as one of the essential male-specific tasks.

Regarding the tasks assigned to women, the *Coya*, or Inca queen, instructed her female followers in the arts of spinning, weaving, and making clothing out of cotton and wool. According to the myth, the responsibilities of a woman included the obligation of making clothing for herself and her family and attending to all other duties pertaining to the home. Elsewhere in his chronicle, Garcilaso explains that in the everyday life of the Inca Empire, women took these responsibilities very seriously.

> The Indian women were friends of [the art of] spinning [yarn] and such enemies of wasting even a small amount of time, that coming and going from the villages to the cities, or even going from one neighborhood to another to visit on unavoidable occasions, they carried [with them bundles of yarn] for two different ways of spinning, that is to say, for spinning and winding. Along the way, they wound what they were carrying that was already spun, because this job was easier. And during their visits, they took out their distaff and spun [the yarn] in the course of good conversation.[44]

Idleness in the empire was strictly prohibited and was considered a criminal offense against the state, punishable either by death, flogging, or other humiliating punishments.[45] This was particularly important for maintaining control, because at the height of the empire, the Incas governed over ten million subjects and more than eighty political provinces with distinct ethnic and local identities and strong separatist tendencies. Therefore, it was essential to keep every man, woman, and child occupied with work and other activities in order to avoid rebellion and avert the risk of fracturing the nation.[46]

Since there are numerous colonial accounts of the Inca origin myth, Peruvian scholar María Rostworowski de Diez Canseco speculates whether this was the "official" version of the Inca origin myth disseminated by the Inca royalty in order to enhance their lineage and prestige, or whether Garcilaso dreamed up this version of the myth in order to endear the Inca culture to European audiences.[47] She urges researchers to investigate earlier versions of the Inca origin myth and search for those which, at least on the surface, appear to be "more [authentically] Andean."[48]

There are, in fact, earlier recorded versions of the Inca origin myth, many of which differ from the Garcilascan version presented here.[49] Typically, these myths begin at *Pacariqtambo*,[50] southwest of Cuzco, where Manco Capac (also known as "Ayar Mango"), the first Inca ruler, and his brothers, each with a sister-wife, emerge from three caves (or in some versions a single cave) in the mountain of *Tampu T'oqo*[51] and set out to find a homeland. One of the brothers, Ayar Cachi, is so strong and powerful that he can destroy mountains and reshape the landscape by hurling rocks with his sling. Some versions describe him as thoughtful and brave; others purport he is troublesome and wreaks havoc with his sling. In most versions Ayar Cachi's brothers and sisters find a pretext to lure him inside a cave at *Capac Toco* ("Window or Cave of the Powerful or the Noble") and block the entrance. The earth rumbles and shakes as Ayar Cachi attempts to escape, but he eventually dies. Another brother, Ayar Uchu, is transformed into stone on the slopes of a hill about eight miles from Cuzco. The hill on which he petrifies—*Huanacauri* or *Guanacauri* (meaning "Rainbow")—becomes one of the holiest of Inca shrines. A third brother, Ayar Auca, sprouts wings and reaches Cuzco ahead of Manco Capac and becomes the community stone. Manco Capac and his sister-wife, Mama Ocllo or Mama Huaco, reach Cuzco and build the *Coricancha* or *Qurikancha* ("Golden Enclosure"), the first Inca temple dedicated to the Sun god.

It is important to point out that the names of the brothers *Ayar* are directly linked to agriculture and the introduction of dietary supplements, which were critical to the development of early Andean cultures. According to the Quechua dictionary of Diego González Holguín (1608), *ayar* refers to a form of "wild quinua"[52] (*chenopodium quinoa*), which was later widely cultivated at high altitudes in the former Inca Empire.[53] This nutritious Andean grain, which is a species of goosefoot, is strongly connected with Andean origins, as there was an Inca *huaca* named *Capi* (meaning "Quinoa Root"), located on a mountain named Quisco, that according to Rostworowski symbolically "represented the origin of Cuzco."[54]

In like manner, the Quechua term *uchu*, as in the name of the brother *Ayar Uchu*, is the fruit of any of the "different herbaceous plants...generally called chili peppers [genus *capsicum*], widely utilized in the [Andean] diet as a flavoring in foods."[55] Hence both terms, *ayar* and *uchu*, are associated with the ontogeny of significant Andean crops. In addition, the word *manco* or *mango*, as in the name of the Inca founder *Manco Capac* (also spelled *Mango Capac*) or *Ayar Mango*, may be related to an ancient Andean grain, technically a grass (scientific name *bromus mango*), that until recently was considered extinct.[56] The seed of this plant was toasted to make flour, and it was also used to make *chicha*, a Native Andean beverage made from several different grains.

Uchu, the fruit of the chili pepper plant, which today exists in more than twenty-five varieties in the Andes, is commonly used to make numerous spicy Andean sauces and flavorings, generally called *ajíes* (or *ají* in the singular). According to traditional Andean lore, the chili pepper is also believed to have medicinal and curative properties against some diseases.[57] In Quechua terminology, *cachi*, as in the name of the brother *Ayar Cachi*, signifies "salt," which aside from being an important Andean (and universal) condiment also has enormous significance in Native Andean rituals. During purification and fasting rituals, the Incas were prohibited from consuming salt and chili pepper, and this practice continues to this day among some Native Andean communities. The name of the only remaining *Ayar* brother, *Ayar Auca*, derives from the Quechua word *auca* (also spelled *auka* or *awqa*), which has multiple meanings, including enemy, adversary, rival, or traitor, and also warrior, rebel, or savage. Its significance appears to be independent of the others.

These earlier accounts of the Inca origin myth, which were recorded in the mid to late sixteenth century, differ in many respects from the Garcilascan version, published in 1609. In the earlier versions, the first Incas emerge from three caves, or a single cave, at *Paqaritambo*, instead of making their appearance at Lake Titicaca. In some cases the mythological ruler *Manco Capac* is also one of several brothers and sisters who emerge from the sacred cave(s), and he does not carry a golden staff. Curiously, in one version of the myth it is *Mama Huaco* ("Vigorous Woman," "Great Grandmother," or "Mother Who Shows Her Teeth"[58]) who launches two golden staffs into the air, one of which sinks in the fertile lands near Cuzco.[59] Also, in some versions the first Incas have no known parents and spontaneously appear dressed in fine woolen garments, woven with gold, and wielding powerful gold weapons. The women carry golden pots and plates and drinking tumblers with which to serve and cook for their husbands. There is also precious little in the earlier myths about Manco Capac and Mama Ocllo ("Plump" or "Shapely" Woman or Mother[60]) teaching the native peoples the civilizing arts.

Still, there are some common elements between the Garcilascan origin myth and these earlier myths. In all cases, Manco Capac and his sister-wife (or sister-wives) are considered the founders of the Inca culture. In all cases Manco Capac, with or without his brothers, wanders about in search of a suitable homeland. In every version of the myth the characters display supernatural powers, or at a minimum appear to be more technologically advanced than the people of the surrounding territories. And in each case the Inca culture arises from an incestuous relationship between brother and sister. Oddly, in a subsequent version of the Inca origin myth relayed by the Native Andean chronicler Felipe Guaman Poma de Ayala (circa 1615), Mama Huaco is considered the mother and wife of Manco Capac, and not his sister.[61] Thus, according to one analysis, "one does not find [in these myths] the two fundamental prohibitions [against] incest and parricide, rather, what becomes manifest is the existence of a network of fraternal relations in which incest appears as a given.... The conjugal pair does not exist, only the coupling of mother/son or brother/sister... [while] the father is absent from the interior of the triangle."[62]

As is evident in both the Cañari origin myth about the macaw-women and the Inca origin myth about the children of the Sun, prohibited relations are at the heart of many Native Andean myths concerning the origin of culture—be they conjugal relations between brother and sister, mother and child (the Guaman Poma version of the Inca myth), and even animal (or anthropomorphic being) and human. Hence, both sets of cultural parents may be viewed as intermediaries between the world of nature that existed before their arrival and the world of culture subsequent to their arrival; more importantly, they may also be seen as mediators between the supernatural or divine world of the gods and the terrestrial world of human beings. Both ethnic groups also arose from incestuous unions that resulted in fertility; each couple begat numerous descendants, and these descendants multiplied and developed their culture.

This is intriguing, given that there were, and still are, strong social prohibitions against incest and other taboos in the Andes. Some colonial chroniclers contend that incest was a crime punishable by death in the Inca Empire;[63] "the Inca ordained that no one could have their own sister as their wife, except for the Inca."[64] In this respect we know very little about the ancient Cañaris for lack of a historical record; however, we do know that incest was permitted among the elite of other ancient South American cultures, such as the Chibchas, who lived in the central highlands of the Eastern Andes of Colombia and were contemporaries of the Incas. Like the Incas, the ancient Chibchas had similar restrictions for the common people, but "rulers were excepted from incest rules, marrying full sisters and other close relatives."[65]

Why the Inca and Chibcha rulers fell outside the purview of their own laws, and possibly their own cultural concepts of morality, probably implicated politics, economics, and religion; as described by Garcilaso, the prohibition was lifted for the sovereigns or rulers who claimed their lineage from the gods. It is also possible that as intermediaries or deities, these mythological ancestors were not considered human; they belonged to neither, or both, the human world and the supernatural/divine world, or the world of culture and the world of nature, and as such were exempt from the customary prohibitions against incest and other cultural taboos.

COSMIC VIOLATIONS AND DEATH OF THIS CREATION

As we have noted previously with respect to non-origin myths, one of the recurring themes in Native Andean mythology is that dualism must be preserved in the world and in the cosmos. Anthropologist Billie Jean Isbell sums up this concept: "One of their principal concerns is to maintain equilibrium and order in a world in which dual forces are balanced against one another."[66] Therefore, the separation between male and female, day and night, sky and earth, high and low, upper and lower, wet and dry, and any other opposing or complementary elements, principles, and forces must never cease to exist, because this dualism constitutes the basic foundation of the cosmos, the community, and ultimately humankind itself. In cosmological terms, as discussed in previous chapters, any attempt to unite these dualities, except in appropriate rites and rituals, is tantamount to a universal transgression, a violation of the cosmic order that inevitably brings about violence, injury, and destruction.

By extension—except for some origin myths—any attempt to unite characters, elements, species, or beings from separate "worlds" through the conjugal act produces disastrous results. Implicit in this is a general prohibition in Andean mythology that forbids sexual union between animals and humans or the symbolic union of nature and culture. In some cases the violation of this taboo is so egregious that it threatens the world with a *pachacuti*— an inversion or "turning" of the world, instigated by a cataclysmic event that results in the total annihilation of this creation. The following is a popular Quechua story designed to illustrate this concept in symbolic form.

The Snake's Lover

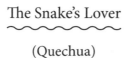

(Quechua)

She was her parents' only child. Every day she went up the mountain and watched over their flock. Her father and mother had no other children but her. And that's why they sent her day after day to graze the flock. The young woman was already of marrying age, well developed and lovely.

One day, on a mountaintop, an elegant, very slender young man approached her.

"Be my lover," he said. And he continued speaking to her of love.

Seeing that he was tall and strong, the young woman accepted his offer. From then on, they met up on the mountain, where they made love.

"I would like you to always bring me some cooked wheat meal," the young man said to the shepherdess.

She complied with her lover's request, and she took him cooked wheat meal every day. They ate together, each one serving the other.

They lived like this for a long time. The young man walked and ran with his face down; he dragged his body as if he had many small feet. That's because he wasn't a man; he was a snake. But to her eyes he appeared as a slim and tall young man.

The young woman became pregnant, and she said to the young man, "I'm pregnant. When my parents find out, they will punish me and ask me who the father is. We must decide whether we will go to your house or mine."

The young man replied, "We will have to go to your house. But I will not be able to enter openly; it's not possible. Tell me if there is a hole in the wall next to the grinding stone of your house. Isn't there always a hole next to the grinding stones to keep the scouring rag used to clean the stone?"

"Yes, next to the grinding stone there's a hole."

"Then you will take me there," said the young man.

And the young woman asked, "What could you possibly do in that hole?"

"I will live there day and night."

"You wouldn't fit. It's impossible. It's a very small hole."

"[You'll see], I'll fit. And it will serve as my home. Now, I'd like to know where you sleep: in the kitchen or in the granary?"

"I sleep in the kitchen," said the young woman, "next to my parents."

"And where is the grinding stone?"

"The grinding stone is in the granary."

"When I'm at your house, you will sleep on the floor, next to the grinding stone."

"And how will I be able to separate myself from my parents? They will not want me to sleep alone."

"You'll pretend to be afraid that thieves will steal from the granary. You'll tell them, 'I'll sleep there to guard it.' And only you will go in to use the grinding stone. You won't allow your parents to do it. Each time you grind flour, you'll toss a little bit into my dwelling hole. I'll live solely on that and won't eat anything else. And so that they won't see me, you'll carefully cover up the hole with the scouring rag."

Then the woman asked, "Can't you openly introduce yourself to my parents?"

"No, no, I can't," he replied. "Little by little, I will begin appearing to them."

"And how are you going to live in that hole? It's very small, hardly big enough for a tuft of wool."

"You'll have to enlarge it on the inside."

"Very well," she said, "I trust that you can figure out how to fit in there."

"But you'll have to take me and leave me behind the wall of your house. And at night, you'll have to lead me to the granary."

"Fine," replied his lover.

That night the young woman went home alone. Furtively, she entered into the granary and enlarged the hole next to the grinding stone. The next day she headed to the mountain to graze her flock. She met her lover at the customary spot. "I've already widened the hole where we put the scouring rag," she told him. So at nightfall they headed together toward the snake lover's home.

She left the young man in the livestock corral behind the house. That night she went out to fetch him, and took him to the hole next to the grinding stone. "Impossible! There's no way he'll fit," the young woman said to herself as the young man headed toward the hole. [But surprisingly], the young man slipped gently into the hole.

That same night the young woman said to her parents, "Mom and Dad, I'm worried that thieves will come during the night and steal all the things we have in the granary. From now on, I'm going to sleep there."

"Go ahead, dear daughter," assented the parents.

The young woman took her bed to the granary and laid it out on the floor, next to the grinding stone. The serpent slipped into the bed, and the lovers slept together. They slept together every night from then on.

When it was time to grind food using the grinding stone, the young woman wouldn't let anyone else do it. She always went [in by herself] and tossed a few handfuls of flour into the hole used to hold the scouring rag. Before leaving, she made sure to cover the hole with a shred of animal hide that was used to clean the grinding stone. In this way neither her parents nor anyone else could see what was inside the hole. Her parents didn't suspect anything. It never occurred to them to uncover the hole and look inside it. Only when they realized that their daughter was pregnant did they grow worried and decided to talk to her.

"It looks like our daughter is pregnant," they said. "We have to ask her who the father is."

They called her in and interrogated her. "You're [obviously] pregnant. Who's the father of your child?"

But she didn't answer.

And so her father and her mother took her aside to talk to her alone, first one and then the other. But the girl remained silent.

Night after night, the young woman felt labor pains. Her parents looked after her. And on those nights, the serpent couldn't slip into the young woman's bed.

The serpent no longer lived in the hole. He grew a lot and became so enormous that he could no longer fit into the hole in the wall. He had grown fat from sucking on the young woman's blood and had become swollen and reddish. He burrowed under the base of the grinding stone, made a hole there, and moved his dwelling. There was a kind of cave beneath the grinding stone, a great nest: the serpent's new home. He had grown fat and rounded in girth; he was plethoric. But to his lover's eyes, he was not a snake, but a young man—a young man who had robustly fattened up.

The lovers could no longer cover up the cave that they had opened beneath the grinding stone. For that reason, every morning, the young girl folded her bedcovers and laid them one on top of the other at the base of the grinding stone. This way they could hide the serpent's nest from her mother and father when her parents entered the granary.

In the face of their daughter's unyielding silence, the parents decided to make some inquiries. They asked the people of their ayllu [community], "Out of thin air, our daughter has turned up pregnant. Have you seen her somewhere talking to someone? Perhaps in the fields where she puts the flock out to pasture?"

But everyone answered, "No, we haven't seen anything."

"Where do you have her sleep?" some asked.

The parents replied, "At first she slept next to us in the same room. But now she insists on sleeping in the granary. She has her bed there on the floor, next to the grinding stone. And only she wants to go in there and use the grinding stone; she doesn't let anyone else near it."

"And why is she opposed to you going near the grinding stone? What does she say?" they probed.

"She says, 'Don't get near the grinding stone, dear parents. You might soil my bed. I'll go use the grinding stone by myself.'"

"And why doesn't she want you to get near the grinding stone?" they asked.

[The parents didn't have an answer.] "She has already experienced her first labor pains," they [added].

[So their friends suggested], "Go visit the seer. Ask him to see and find out what's going on. We common folk can't figure out what's happening.

Wonder what it is?"

The mother and the father went in search of the seer. They took with them a small bundle of coca leaves. They asked him to look into their daughter's case.

"Our daughter doesn't feel well. We don't know what she has," they told him.

The seer asked, "What's the matter with your daughter? What's ailing her?"

"She's turned up pregnant. We don't know by whom. Night after night, she has been suffering labor pains for quite some time now. But she can't give birth. She doesn't want to tell us who the father is," said the mother.

The seer consulted the coca leaves and said, "Something...there is something underneath the grinding stone in your house! And that is the father. Because the father is not a person; he is not a man."

"And what could it be?" inquired the old people fearfully. "Tell us everything you see; see well, we beg of you!"

So the seer continued to speak, "Inside there is a serpent! It is not a man!"

"And what should we do?" asked the parents.

The seer meditated for a few moments and then began to speak again, directing himself toward the father. "Your daughter will be opposed to you killing the serpent. 'Kill me first before killing my lover!' she will say to you. Send her far away, to any place that is a day's march from here. And even then she will refuse to go. But address her in this way: Tell her the name of a particular town. Tell her you know that in this town there is a medicine for giving birth. Tell her, 'Go and buy this medicine and bring it to me. If you don't obey me this time, I'll beat you! I'll beat you until you die!' In the meantime, you'll hire some people armed with sticks, machetes, and strong clubs. Then you'll send your daughter to carry out your mandate. And when she is already far away, all of you will enter into the granary and push aside the grinding stone. There, underneath, you will find the great serpent. You will beat it until it is dead! Be careful that the serpent doesn't lunge toward you, because if it lunges, it will kill you. Make sure you cut off its head really well, then dig a grave for it and bury it."

"Very well, sir. We'll follow your instructions," said the father, and he left, followed by his wife.

The father immediately went to seek out some people, strong men who would help him kill the beast. He hired ten men, well armed with clubs and sharp machetes.

"Tomorrow, after my daughter departs, you'll come to my house on foot, making sure nobody sees you," he said.

The next morning the parents ordered the young woman to cook some lunch. They had her wake up early. They gave her money, pretending [they were sending her on a real] errand, and told her, "With this money, you will buy the medicine that will help you to give birth. In Sumakk Marka, the town that's on the other side of the river, you will find the medicine."

But the young woman didn't wish to obey. "I can't go," she said, "I don't want to." So her parents threatened her. "If you don't go and bring back the medicine, we'll beat you to death! We'll hit you so hard that we'll destroy the [child] you're carrying inside your womb!"

Frightened, the young woman started walking.

They watched her walk away until she disappeared from view. Once she had disappeared in the distance, the hired men headed toward the parents' house. They gathered on the patio. They distributed rations of coca leaves, chewed them for a while, and then entered the granary. They moved everything that was in there out onto the patio, and finally, they took out the young woman's bed.

And they armed themselves. With their clubs on their shoulders and clutching their machetes, they entered the granary, surrounded the grinding stone, and waited. They pushed aside the grinding stone; a thick serpent lay there. It had a giant head, similar to that of a man; it had been growing fatter. "Wat'akk!" the serpent lunged out upon being discovered, its heavy body making a loud noise as it straightened. The ten men beat it and wounded it. They cut it up into several pieces. They tossed its head outside, into the open air. And there it began to struggle. It jumped and seethed upon the ground. The men followed it and crushed it [at every turn]. They went wherever it fell and tried to take it down. They hit it from above. The serpent's blood gushed from its mutilated body and ran across the ground. But it wouldn't die.

And at the very moment that they were beating the serpent's head, the young woman, the serpent's lover, arrived. When she saw people gathered on the patio, she ran into the granary, toward the grinding stone. The stone was bathed in blood. The serpent's nest was empty. She turned her head around toward the patio and saw several men beating the head of her lover with clubs. Then she emitted a scream, a scream of death.

"Why, why are you destroying my lover's head? Why are you killing him?" she exclaimed. "This is my husband! This is the father of my child!"

She screamed again, her voice filling the house. She looked at all the blood and shuddered in fear. And on account of all the effort she exerted in screaming, she aborted. A multitude of little snakes were twisting on the ground, covering the entire floor of the patio, jumping and dragging their bodies.

At last, they killed the giant snake. They also killed the baby snakes. They followed each one of them, and squashed them. Later, some of the men dug a hole in the ground, while others swept up the blood. They swept the blood from the entire house, gathered it near the hole, and then buried the serpents and the bloody mud. Then they took the young woman to her parents' room, and there they cured her. They returned everything to the granary, to its original spot. They cleaned and straightened out the house. They carried the grinding stone to a waterfall in the river; they placed the stone beneath the jet of water and left it there. And when everything was in order, the parents of the young woman paid each man his fair share for the work. The men received their wages and left.

Later, the parents asked their daughter, "How, just how could you live with a serpent? Your husband was not a man; he was a demon!"

Only then did the young woman divulge her story. She told the tale starting from her first meeting with the serpent. And everything came to be known and explained. The parents cured their daughter; they took care of her and healed her body and soul. And later, much later, the young woman married a good man. And she led a happy life.[67]

~~~

This unreserved and intricate Andean tale of The Snake's Lover is gory in its detail and yet is laden with symbolic and cosmological significance. The prohibited relationship between the deceptive serpent and the naïve young woman not only breaches the taboo against bestiality, which symbolically prohibits the union of separate "worlds," but also metaphorically alerts the Native Andeans to the looming threat of a *pachacuti*. Let us now proceed to unravel the various symbolic layers of this daedal myth from various theoretical perspectives.

At the heart of the story is the grinding stone, which in the Andes is called a *batán*. In my native land of Bolivia almost every home has one, irrespective of one's social or economic status, and the women usually prefer it to any other modern grinding appliance. This type of grinding stone was first described in the Spanish colonial chronicles[68] four hundred years ago, and to this day it remains virtually unchanged in the Andean region. The Andean grinding stone usually consists of two separate pieces—a flat rectangular stone slab, which forms the base of the grinding stone, and a second stone, sometimes called the *una*, usually shaped like a thick crescent moon, that rests over the base and is flat and smooth underneath. The user typically begins by placing the seed or grain on the surface of the base slab. Then she places her hands in the corners of the "moon stone" and rocks the stone back and forth repeatedly over the seed, occasionally wiping off some of the grounds, or flour, that adhere to the stone underneath. The *batán* has been the preferred method for grinding maize, quinoa, chili peppers, and other foods in the Andes for hundreds, if not thousands, of years. The grinding may be done dry or wet with water or cooking oil.

This *batán* is particularly significant in the interpretation of this story, because it is associated with the fertile young woman, who becomes the serpent's lover. She is the only one allowed to use the grinding stone, while the serpent nests underneath the stone. The grinding stone also provides a means to feed the snake—every time the young woman grinds some flour, she tosses a few handfuls of it in the snake hole to nourish her oversized lover. Typically in the Andes, only women use the *batán* in connection with food preparation; thus, it is strongly associated with a woman's cooking activities in the home.

The moon-shaped component of the grinding stone is also strongly suggestive of a woman's sexuality, because since ancient times the cycles of the moon have been observed to correlate with a woman's natural menstrual cycle and her potential fecundity. In this story, the snake grows thick and swollen from "sucking" on the young woman's blood (presumably at night) just as it is also revealed that the woman has conceived and is carrying her snake lover's offspring. In this instance, the image of the blood-sucking snake may be metaphorically describing the cessation of menstruation that occurs after conception and continues for the remainder of a woman's pregnancy.

The moon-shaped grinding stone is also noteworthy, for there are various Andean stories that describe the moon as the reluctant object of someone else's affection in the context of a prohibited relationship. For example, in his *Royal Commentaries*, Garcilaso de la Vega tells the tale of an amorous fox who falls in love with the beautiful moon. The fox is so enamored with the moon that he climbs up to the sky, intending to steal her. But just as he extends his hand to reach for the moon, the moon embraces the fox, whose body adheres to hers. According to Garcilaso, this is how the ancient Andeans explained the origin of the dark spots on the moon.[69]

By trying to steal the moon, the fox in this Inca tale is guilty of violating the Andean principles of duality and cosmic order. He leaves his rightful place in the lower terrestrial world (*hurin*, relative to the sky—not to be confused with the Andean concept of *Hurin* or *Ukhu Pacha*, Lower World) and becomes a trespasser in the sky, or Upper World (*hanan*), in an attempt to steal one of the beautiful sky beings. In doing so, he is violating the notion of Andean dualism by ignoring the rules of complementarity and cosmic balance. Like the serpent in The Snake's Lover who impregnates a human, the amorous fox is attempting to enter into a prohibited relationship that could alter the balance of forces in the universe and produce dire consequences in the cosmos.

Even more troubling is a violation considered so egregious that it precipitates a cataclysmic event—a *pachacuti*—leading to the destruction of the existing world. The ancient Andeans were terrified of natural catastrophes—floods, volcanic eruptions, earthquakes, drought, famine, and pestilence, to name a few—because to them it indicated that the correct balance of the cosmos had been altered. And if that balance were not restored, the gods and *huacas* might destroy the existing creation, marking the end of humankind as we know it; moreover, the world would return to the chaos and disorder of the primordium, which the ancient Andeans believed existed between different ages, or epochs, of the world.[70] These primordial states were considered static and unchanging, characterized by unbroken periods of darkness, illumination (perpetual light), or petrification.[71] They were also inconsistent with the dynamic, cyclic, and changing elements of human life. In a perpetual state of darkness or light, for example, there would be no place for the rising and setting of the sun, or the waxing and waning of the moon. There would be no fertility, death, or regeneration; no seasons of the year; no human life cycle; no changing weather. In sum, there would be no "finiteness," "boundedness," or "change" in a state where only totality and chaos existed;[72] such an event would signify the end of the present world and mark the end of human existence.

Since catastrophic (and sometimes inexplicable) events were perceived as a misalignment or disequilibrium in the cosmos, to make up for this deficiency the ancient Andeans offered sacrifices and offerings—including human offerings—to their deities, both greater in number and in kind during such times. For instance, the Moche people of the northern coast of Peru (200–700 AD) engaged in ritual warfare and offered the losing warriors as human offerings to the gods. Their iconography depicts an elaborate human sacrifice ceremony in which the losers were taken prisoner and bled, killed, and dismembered. Their blood was collected in a special goblet and subsequently consumed by the ceremonial priests and priestesses.[73]

The Incas (1438–1532) also practiced human sacrifice—which they called *capac cocha* or *capac hucha*—to a more limited extent. According to the Andean colonial chronicles, *capac cocha* was reserved for times of great distress, such as when the Inca ruler became ill, or when natural catastrophes such as earthquakes, volcanic eruptions, pestilence, famine, and drought occurred or needed to be averted.[74] Thus the Incas, like other ancient Andean societies, also feared the onset of a *pachacuti*, a cataclysmic event that would mark the end of one epoch of the world and the beginning of a new one. As described in previous chapters, the Incas believed this cycle of destruction and creation represented an "inversion" or "turning over" of time-space, which undoubtedly would bring misfortune and possible death to the world. Garcilaso de la Vega describes the Incas' reaction to a lunar eclipse in terms very similar to the threat of an impending *pachacuti*.

> During a lunar eclipse, as [the Incas] saw that the moon darkened, they said that the moon was ill, and that if she darkened completely, she would die and fall from the sky on top of everyone below, killing them, and that the world would come to an end. On account of their fear, whenever the moon began to eclipse, they would play their trumpets, coronets, conch shells, kettledrums and drums, and all available instruments that produced noise. They tied up their dogs, large and small, and beat them so that they would howl and call to the moon, [because] based on a certain fable that they tell, they said that the moon was fond of dogs because of a certain service they had rendered for her. [They believed] that if she were to hear the dogs crying, she would feel pity for them, and this would cause her to wake up from the slumber that her illness was causing her.[75]

In expressing their fear that the moon would die, the Incas were also expressing their apprehension that the world would end in a *pachacuti*. We commented on a similar phenomenon in an earlier chapter when analyzing the Wanka creation myth of The Appearance of the First Human Beings on Earth, which featured two dueling serpents or *Amarus* fighting for supremacy over a lake. In that instance we observed that the mythical *Amaru* lurking in the cave symbolically represented the looming threat of a *pachacuti*, waiting for an opportune moment to make its reappearance and wreak havoc upon humankind. We also noted that the Amaru is closely associated with the primordium—the unbroken and static state of chaos and disorder—that precedes the creation of a new world and is linked to the cycle of *pachacuti*. By unleashing destructive, explosive, and violent primordial forces, the Amaru threatens our world until its balance is reestablished.

Like its mythological counterpart, the Amaru, the serpent in The Snake's Lover hides under the grinding stone, threatening to change the order of the cosmos. Clearly, this character is a trickster, a shape-shifting intermediary from another world—whether animal, chthonic, primordial, or supernatural—who has entered into a prohibited sexual relationship with a human from this world, who is carrying (in cosmological terms) his illicit serpentine offspring. By his actions, he has violated the notion of Andean dualism and the separation of worlds. In other words, his conjugal relations with a human and his attempts to conjoin opposing worlds, outside of appropriate rites and rituals, is tantamount to a cosmic violation, threatening to produce dire consequences. At a minimum, his disregard for proper human relations portends calamity and misfortune for the girl's community. His breach could also assume cosmic proportions and alter the time-space continuum. If this creature were not killed, his fury would be unleashed upon an unsuspecting human world caught in the grips of a *pachacuti*. Therefore, one possible interpretation of the murder of the menacing serpent is that it represents a symbolic attempt by the Native Andeans to avert a potential *pachacuti*, a threat that is growing and threatening to appear like the serpent nesting beneath the grinding stone.

The death of this world, implicit in this story, is the same death the Incas feared five hundred years ago—death by eclipse. Felipe Guaman Poma de Ayala, in his chronicle *Nueva Corónica y Buen Gobierno* ("New Chronicle and Good Government"), comments on this Andean belief.

> The philosophers and ancient astrologers...knew that the sun was at a higher level than the moon, and that [he] would place himself on top of her and she would get stained with blood, and thus darken. And they believed that she would die and darken and fall on the earth [during] the eclipse of the moon. And so they made the people and the dogs yell, and they played drums, and the people made a racket. They still do it to this day and continue [this practice].[76]

The image of the bloody moon during an eclipse in Guaman Poma's colonial account is reminiscent of the bloody moon-shaped grinding stone, or *batán*, in this modern tale. In both cases the feminine "moon" gets stained with blood after the sexual encounter with the masculine entity (sun or serpent). In Guaman Poma's account, the moon becomes stained with blood during sexual intercourse, which is suggested by the masculine sun positioning himself "on top of her." In the second case, the moon-shaped grinding stone gets bathed in the blood gushing from the male snake as the armed men attempt to kill it. Earlier in the story, the snake is also "feeding" on the woman's blood and thereby becoming physically engorged.

The menacing threat of the moon falling upon the earth and the grave fear the Incas experienced upon witnessing the eclipse are similar in both Guaman Poma's and Garcilaso's descriptions; in both accounts, the death of the moon would bring about the end of the world in concordance with *pachacuti*. Guaman Poma's dark and bloody imagery of the sexual encounter between the moon and the sun is also suggestive of rape, because the sun "was at a higher level than the moon," metaphorically suggesting dominance; furthermore, the Incas believed that the sun and the moon were brother and sister, so their sexual union was also tantamount to incest.

Similarly, in The Snake's Lover the storyline points to a prohibited sexual relationship between a male entity and a female entity that ultimately results in a bloodstained "moon" (grinding stone), which is closely associated with female sexuality. As in the colonial account, the reference to the bloodstained moon suggests the occurrence of an eclipse, a disruption in the cosmic order equivalent to a *pachacuti* threatening to destroy the existing world. In The Snake's Lover, the killing of the beast is necessary to thwart this cataclysmic cycle that may potentially annihilate humankind. This is analogous to the imaginary war the Incas waged against an illusive lion or serpent, which was allegedly attacking the moon during a lunar eclipse.

> They said that when there was an eclipse of the Moon a [mountain] lion or a serpent was attacking in order to tear her apart, and for that reason . . . they hurled arrows and spears at the Moon, and they made menacing gestures with their spears, as if they were going to wound the lion and the serpent. They said that this was done to frighten the lion and serpent so they would not tear the moon apart. This they did because they understood that if the lion [or serpent] accomplished its aim, the world would be left in darkness.[77]

Hence, the perceived threat of a *pachacuti* was *real* to the Incas, and, as in this story, the beast had to be overcome to assure the continuance of this creation.

From a psychoanalytic perspective, The Snake's Lover is also saturated with sexual symbolism. Most salient is the phallic symbol of the snake, together with the orifice housing the snake, which resonates with the image of sexual conjugation. Likewise, the snake hole is in the granary, serving as a storage room for maize kernels and other "seeds," which may also be symbolic of sexual gametes (ova or sperm).

The young woman in the story is also carrying a litter of "baby snakes" in her womb, which Freud would no doubt find suggestive of "penis envy," associated with the Electra complex, the female counterpart of the Oedipus complex.[78] According to Freud, at a certain stage in a young woman's psychosexual development she comes to the (unconscious) realization that, unlike a man, she doesn't have a penis. In order to satisfy her desire for a penis, the young woman develops unconscious sexual desires for her father, who has a penis that may satisfy her, or she may search for a "penis substitute" in the form of a baby. In the story of The Snake's Lover, the young woman is carrying several "penis-babies" in her womb in the form of snakes, demonstrating the force and effect of the Electra complex. In addition, the young woman witnesses the brutal death of her snake-lover, and the emotional trauma of this experience causes her to abort the "penis-babies." Thereafter, her family home is bathed in the blood of the mutilated serpent and his offspring, reminiscent of the resumption of menstrual flow of a woman who is no longer pregnant.

In a final Freudian twist, the blood, borne of conflict and trauma, is gathered and buried in the earth, and the young woman's house is "swept," "cleaned," and "straightened" to reveal no trace of the forbidden sexual relationship. Freud maintained that unacceptable impulses and erotic sexual desires causing overwhelming conflict and guilt are automatically and unconsciously "forgotten" through the mechanism of repression and hidden in the unconscious mind.[79] Like the blood that is swept away and disposed of in this tragic tale, these desires are swept away and cleared from our conscious memories, only to be "buried" in the deeper levels of the unconscious.

CHAPTER SUMMARY

A Native Andean origin myth typically explains how a particular indigenous group came into being. The origin myth usually identifies the group's sacred place of origin, or *paqarina*, from which the first ancestors are believed to have emerged. This sacred place of origin is often a natural site closely associated with the group, such as a particular mountain, lake, spring, cave, or other aspect of nature. The origin myth may also describe the origin of agriculture and particular crops upon which the group depends for its subsistence. It may also give an account of the origin of culture, including religion, and explain how the group came to venerate certain gods, nature spirits, celestial bodies, animals, or ancestors, including the mythological first rulers.

In some Andean origin myths the first ancestors or mythological rulers are also the first teachers of the civilizing arts. In the Garcilascan version of the Inca origin myth, the first rulers, Manco Capac and Mama Ocllo, teach their subjects the arts of agriculture, irrigation, spinning and weaving, and even making footwear. Similarly, in the origin myth of the Cañaris, the people sustain themselves with the seeds brought by their ancestral mother, the macaw-woman, who first introduces agriculture and the art of cooking.

In this chapter we have also analyzed several Andean origin myths within the framework of cultural taboos and prohibited relationships. We have demonstrated that some Andean origin myths, such as those of the Cañaris and Incas, view creation and the origin of culture as the products of impermissible sexual unions, such as incest and bestiality. Nonetheless, these prohibited relationships give rise to fecundity, as evidenced by the birth of progeny and the birth of certain indigenous plants.

By contrast, we have also explored how prohibited unions in *non-origin* myths violate Andean notions of dualism and proper separation of worlds. Any attempt to unite or conjoin opposing elements or worlds, outside the scope of appropriate rites and rituals, amounts to a cosmic transgression that may lead to a *pachacuti* and the destruction of our world. This looming threat of a *pachacuti* appears symbolically in some Native Andean stories and resonates with ancient Andean beliefs about real or perceived cataclysmic events, such as eclipses, which, unless properly averted, could mark the end of this creation and human existence on earth.

7

SEXUALITY AND GUILT

A More Permissive View of Sexuality

One of the topics that most preoccupied the Spanish chroniclers after the Spanish Conquest of Peru was the alleged immorality and sexual deviancy of the pre-Columbian peoples. The colonial chronicler Pedro Sarmiento de Gamboa, addressing King Philip of Spain in the introduction to his *Historia de los incas* ("History of the Incas"), commented:

> [Through the Conquest] your Majesty and your most holy royal ancestors have stopped [the Inca and his lords] from sacrificing innocent men, eating human flesh, [committing] the cursed and abominable sin of indiscriminate concubinage with sisters and mothers [alike], abominable use of beasts, and [other] nefarious and heinous customs.[1]

Similarly, the Spanish chronicler Pedro de Cieza de León, in his *Crónica del Perú* ("Chronicle of Peru"), criticized the sexual habits of certain native peoples living on the outskirts of Quito and Tumibamba (in present-day Ecuador).

> They waste the entire day drinking chicha [a maize beer] and a wine which they make out of maize, a glass of which they always carry in their hand. They take great care in performing their festivals and songs in an orderly manner. The men and women hold hands and dance in a circle to the sound of a drum, remembering in their songs and their laments the things of the past and always drinking to the point of intoxication. When they are out of their senses, some of

them take whichever women they want and take them back to some house, where they use them to satisfy their lustfulness. They don't regard it as a bad thing, because they don't understand the quality of [modesty] that underlies shamefulness.[2]

Ironically, the Spaniards themselves were often the worst sexual offenders. For example, the indigenous chronicler Felipe Guaman Poma de Ayala furnished detailed accounts of how the Spanish colonial officials and members of the Catholic clergy raped, impregnated, and even sexually enslaved native women.[3]

Regrettably, the colonial narratives seldom mentioned the sexual abuses committed by the Spaniards. Instead, the colonial chroniclers were intent on revealing the Native Andeans' alleged sexual promiscuity and dishonorable ways of living (*malas costumbres*) that, in their eyes, contravened Christian doctrine and undermined the civilizing process. Notwithstanding these biases, the colonial sources present ample evidence that the pre-Columbian peoples of the Andes had a more relaxed view of sexuality than their European conquerors. For example, in many regions of the Andes polygamy was a common custom among the elite and was a symbol of rank and privilege.[4] The Inca, for instance, offered women as remuneration for services rendered on behalf of the empire.[5] Some chroniclers also condemned the "barbarian and immoral" practice of certain indigenous groups of assigning servant women to young boys. These women would clean, cook, and serve until the boys reached the age of maturity, and afterward would teach them the art of making love.[6] Also, in many regions of the Andes couples entered into "trial marriages" for a designated period of time before making a permanent commitment to each another.[7] This practice continues to this day and is called *sirwanakuy* (or *sirvinakuy*) in Quechua and *tincarjaciña* (or *sirvisiña*) in Aymara.[8]

The colonial writings also suggest that virginity was not as highly prized in the Andes as in European societies. With respect to the chastity of Native Andean women, the Spanish priest-chronicler Bernabé Cobo observed in his chronicle, *Historia del nuevo mundo* ("History of the New World"):

They never knew the splendor and the beauty of chastity [that would have allowed them] to appreciate it.... They found virginity of women offensive because they said that it indicated that such maidens had never been loved.... [Women] easily allowed themselves to be de-flowered. They were so far from calling this a crime that they didn't even reprimand any excess in this regard. In accordance with this depraved custom, when an Indian sets his eyes on a woman in order to take her as his own, he doesn't inquire or seek information about whether she has lived as an honest woman.... Above all, he looks at what property she has, and secondly, whether she is hardworking and will be able to serve him well and give to him.[9]

Thus, the more permissive approach to sexuality among the Native Andean peoples simultaneously interested and offended the colonial Spaniards, whose attitudes toward sexual relations, driven by the teachings of the Catholic Church, were far more conservative. Moreover, the Spaniards were obsessed with the notion of "legitimacy" and "primogeniture,"[10] which in Europe and the Spanish colonies had a direct bearing on an individual's rights to inherit familial property. In large measure this may have been a primary reason why the Catholic Church and Spanish colonial society promoted "Christian" (contractual) marriages and regulated sexual conduct so closely. The colonial chroniclers had assumed that these concepts also existed in pre-Columbian societies; however, these European notions were probably unfamiliar to the Inca and other native groups.[11]

With the forced Christianization of the Native Andean peoples during the colonial period, the Catholic Church also introduced a much more restrictive view of sexual relations and a systematic plan to redefine the propriety of certain "carnal acts" in terms of moral Christian values.[12] However, it is clear that almost five centuries after the Conquest and the introduction of Christianity, a tension lurks beneath the surface of many Andean stories, which strives to reconcile the desire for sexual freedom on one hand with Christian morality on the other. Nevertheless, in a culture that is still predominantly Roman Catholic, it is impossible to discern whether such conflict is borne from a longing for the sexual freedom enjoyed by their pre-Columbian ancestors—a sexual outlook that contravenes the teachings of the Catholic Church—or whether such a conflict is more universal and arises from what Freud called the "renunciation of instinct," central to the development of any society, "the cause of the hostility against which all civilizations have to struggle."[13]

In support of this notion of cultural conflict, there are still pre-Columbian traditions in the Andes where sexual freedom is expressed in a manner that Christian ethics would undoubtedly characterize as immoral. For example, in certain communities of Potosí, Bolivia, the indigenous inhabitants have a sexual custom called *rumitankhay*, which literally means "stone pushing" in Quechua, associated with a dance called *Caja Rueda*

("Box Wheel" or "Box Round"). *Caja Rueda* is a nocturnal circle dance that takes place every night during the carnival season in February. After the dance, it is customary for adolescent males to go in search of young females and to "take them" with or without their consent. According to Bolivian folklorist Antonio Paredes-Candia, this sexual practice is suggestive of drilling and blasting through hard rock and the physical, masculine, and collaborative force required to push and break through the boulders and stones.[14] In other words, raping and sexually overcoming the women is analogous to drilling through, pushing, and overcoming the stones. It is interesting to note that young Andean women do not refer to this practice as "rape" but as "pushing."[15]

In some respects this dance is also similar to another Quechua dance called *tuta qhaswa* (also spelled *tuta kashwa* or *tuta q'ashua*, signifying "night dance") of pre-Columbian origin, in which young men and women join hands and dance in a circle or a ring, much like in the *Caja Rueda*. In the Canas province of the Cuzco Department, as well as in some other areas of southern Peru, this dance usually takes place during the feast of Saint Andrew (*San Andrés*) on December 3 and the feast of the Holy Cross (*Santa Cruz*) on May 3. It represents the culmination of an elaborate courting custom in which single young men try to lure young women of marriageable age to participate in the dance.[16] Many months before the dance, young men stroll through the marketplace and other public places, strumming their *charangos* (Andean stringed instruments) and searching for single and eligible women. Even though some musicians are better than others, most prospective courtiers attempt to play a repetitive melody, also known as the *tuta qhaswa*, which acts as an invitation to courtship and lovemaking. Like the flamboyant plumage displays of some male birds, designed to attract the attention of the female, the young men dress in their Sunday best and decorate their instruments with colorful pendants to attract the eye of a prospective partner. The music itself acts as a nonverbal call to love, which is played repeatedly in the company of the desired or "chosen" woman, if she seems receptive. On the day of the dance, the young man usually stands near the woman's house and plays the same recognizable melody on his *charango*; the music acts as a signal inviting her to join the *tuta qhaswa* dance that evening.

The night dance usually takes place in a rural or remote location, known as the *qhaswapata* (or *kashwapata*, meaning "the place where one dances the *qhaswa* or *kashwa*"), and inevitably leads to a sexual encounter between the couple. For part of the dance, the men form a separate ring around the circle of women and flirt, tease, and shower the women with compliments as they dance. Even though the *tuta qhaswa* is not a couple's dance, each participant identifies his or her partner long before the dance occurs. In this way, as the dance progresses, couples slip away to make love and consummate the *tuta qhaswa*. The dance ends at daybreak with participants reuniting for some more singing and dancing.

These sexual customs are not unique to the Quechuas. Among the Aymaras, ritual robbing of women of marriageable age, a sexual custom called *quispia*, takes place during the first harvest and animal marking festival of *Anata* (meaning "Game") or *Marqha Phajjsi*, beginning February 16 and ending March 17, which marks the transition into autumn and the Andean dry season (*Awti*). In Aymara cosmology the dry season is considered "male" and is associated with traditionally masculine tasks. During this time the community makes offerings to Mother Earth, musicians play "masculine" musical instruments such as *quenas* (also spelled *kenas*, the traditional flutes of the Andes) and *pinkuyllus*,[17] and community members engage in "male-oriented" activities such as harvesting, shearing and marking animals, and constructing housing and agricultural works.

Perhaps for fear of judgment or reprisals, adherents of these sexual customs have permitted few Westerners to witness, let alone participate in, *tuta qhaswa, quispia*, or *rumitankhay*.[18] Thus, for a brief period in the lives of these Native Andeans, they are free to carry on the traditions of their pre-Columbian ancestors and disregard the mores of their European counterparts.

In some Andean communities, sexual relations before marriage are also well received, even encouraged. According to Bolivian ethnographer Rigoberto Paredes, the Aymaras "place no importance on the virginity of a woman; on the contrary, prolonged virginity is considered depressing, [and is viewed] as a sign that a woman has been scorned by men."[19] Note that this perception coincides with Cobo's observation, made during the colonial period, that virginity among native women was considered offensive because "it indicated that such maidens had never been loved." Because rural Aymaras engage in animal husbandry, Paredes maintains that men and women forge close bonds from the time they are very young. From the ages of six or seven years old Aymara children are entrusted with the responsibility of caring for their family's animals and putting them out to pasture. Naturally, as they mature sexually, these youth prefer pasturelands for sexual encounters.[20] From these playful courtships a couple may decide to take their relationship one step further and enter into a "trial marriage" for a certain period of time, a custom which is known as *tincarjaciña* or *sirvisiña* in Aymara.[21]

As in Cobo's colonial account, Paredes also confirms that a mate's ability to perform physical work is of prime importance to a prospective Aymara spouse.[22] After the trial period, the couple may enter into matrimony, sealed with a civil or religious ceremony, provided that both the man and the woman agree to the union (one party is not enough) and both their families acquiesce in the plan. If the families do not favor the union, a man may "steal" his prospective wife and live with her for a time, even several years, until the couple attains economic stability and social acceptance in the community. The Quechuas call this "theft" *suanaku* and cohabitation *tantanaku*; the Aymaras refer to these practices as *irpakaña* or *irpaka*.[23] It is not uncommon for a couple to have several children before their marriage is legally recognized in the presence of civil or religious authorities. Having children and formalizing the marriage is viewed as the final consolidation of the family.[24]

Many of these sexual customs seem to derive from pre-Columbian traditions that predated the Spanish Conquest. And it is interesting to observe that women in pre-Columbian Andean myths are not de-sexualized in any way. Peruvian historian María Rostworowki observes that "the women of these narratives ... present a sexuality that one could consider 'natural' ... fresh and ingenuous. The amorous game[s] [of] gods and men unfold with these characteristics, far from the torturous and twisted sexuality associated with Spanish [colonial] repression and ... Western [culture] in general."[25] Likewise, men are also recognized for their sexual prowess and at times even for the size of their penis.[26] However, since (to our knowledge) the pre-Columbian peoples of the Andes left no written record of their history and mythology, we must keep in mind that the colonial documents in existence today were recorded *after* the native peoples had already been exposed to the teachings of Christianity. Moreover, some narratives were employed in the Extirpation of Idolatries to facilitate the conversion of indigenous peoples and to condemn their pre-Columbian practices as "instruments of the devil." Therefore, the colonial scribes had a vested interest in describing pre-Columbian sexual practices as deviant, and it would be foolish to accept without question the reliability and veracity of these documents.

Notwithstanding these limitations, in many pre-Columbian Andean myths the characters engage in sexual activities that even today might be described as promiscuous; however, the attitude of the storytellers toward these activities appears to be less disparaging, less guilt-ridden, and less critical than in modern Andean myths. In fact, one might even say that in some cases the narrators take a certain delight in describing these sexual exploits. To illustrate, in the *Manuscript of Huarochirí* the female *huaca* Chaupi Ñamca—variously characterized as the daughter of Tamta Ñamca, or the daughter or sister of Paria Caca, and wife of Huatya Curi—adopts the form of a human being and has multiple sexual encounters with male *huacas* (deities) who do not completely satisfy her. Finally, she settles on a male *huaca* named Rucana Coto—whose name means "Finger-Shaped Mountain"—because his penis is the only one large enough to satisfy her needs. According to the *Manuscript*, the men of Huarochirí used to pray to Rucana Coto in the hope of enlarging the size of their penises. There was also a religious cult dedicated to the female deity Chaupi Ñamca, who was depicted in worship as a five-armed stone. Chaupi Ñamca's feast was celebrated in June and was associated with several sensual dances, including one called *Casa Yaco* in which the people danced naked and showed their private parts to please her. "After they danced this dance," the indigenous scribes contended, "a fertile season would follow."[27]

There is little doubt that Christianity, and Roman Catholicism in particular, has had a strong and pervasive influence upon the culture and religion of the Native Andean peoples since the onset of the Conquest. Today, as during the colonial period, many of the sexual activities described in the Chaupi Ñamca myth and other such pre-Columbian Andean myths would be considered "mortal sins" under the modern catechism of the Catholic Church.[28] This conflict between sexual freedom and guilt is often played out in Andean stories and may be a result of these sociocultural and historical factors.

Additionally, in the following sections we will explore the psychological dimension of sexuality and guilt, as evidenced in some Andean stories. The classical psychoanalytic (Freudian) view of sexuality maintains that guilt is often a by-product of repressed sexual desires. As guilt and repressed sexual desires are central to this analysis, I will briefly explain how some of Freud's theories on the origin of guilt, and also on the symbolic content of dreams, may be used to uncover the hidden sexual content of these stories.

THE MASKED PRETENDERS: LATENT IMAGERY IN ANDEAN MYTH
According to classical psychoanalysis, guilt is the result of a developmental process that begins in early childhood when a child engages in behavior, usually sexual or aggressive, which his or her parents or caretakers find reprehensible. The child fears loss of love from the person(s) upon whom he or she depends for survival, and this is enough for the child to avoid engaging in the unacceptable behavior, even if the ego finds it desirable.[29]

Later, as a youth the person habitually engages in the unacceptable behavior, "which promises enjoyment, so long as… the authority [including the external community] will not know anything about it or cannot blame [the youth] for it."[30] Finally, the youth reaches the stage when the "authority is internalized" through the formation of the psychic structure known as the "super-ego." At this point, the super-ego is much more effective at controlling the person's behavior, because "nothing can be hidden from the super-ego, not even thoughts."[31] The person no longer needs external moral authority to guide the ego—the part of the psyche that deals with external reality—because the super-ego (now internalized) torments the "sinful ego" whenever the ego acts on its "unacceptable" impulses and desires. This gives rise to feelings of anxiety, guilt, and sometimes shame.[32]

Sexual desires and guilt are also revealed in dreams. Freud postulates that dream images have a *latent* (hidden) content and a *manifest* (overt) content.[33] The manifest content of a dream is the conscious "story" the dream professes to tell. However, the real significance of the dream is buried in the latent content where sexual, aggressive, and other "unacceptable" wishes and desires are lurking around as "masked criminals" pretending to be other things.[34]

One might ask why the dream symbols appear in disguised, indirect form instead of revealing themselves directly in the "story" of the dream. This is because, according to Freudian theory, they represent wishes, desires, impulses, and notions that are unacceptable to the conscious mind of the individual. For this reason these "undesirables" are censored, distorted, and excluded from conscious awareness, because their appearance causes too much conflict and dissonance in the conscious mind. Thus they are transformed "into an alternate form that does not clash with the conscious ethical standards,"[35] morals, and values of the individual. According to Freud, this conversion occurs because the once-pleasurable desires now cause too much trauma, conflict, guilt, or pain for the conscious personality; consequently, they must be repressed.[36]

However, according to Freud, the real meaning of the censored material does not simply disappear. It still resides in a reduced form in the realm of the unconscious mind, the portion of the psyche outside of conscious awareness. This material has simply been "rejected by the censorship [mechanism and] is in a state of repression."[37] However, through dream work an analyst may help the individual "undo" this process, "unmask the manifest content and reveal the more fundamental latent content" of his or her dreams.[38]

Applying an analogous process, the same theoretical concepts can be used to unravel the hidden content of a sexual myth. Freud himself stated that "symbolism does not appertain especially to dreams, but rather to the unconscious imagination, … and it is found in a more developed condition in folklore, myth, legends, idiomatic phrases, proverbs, and … current witticisms."[39] This will become more apparent through a detailed analysis of the following Andean story.

The Islands of Pachacamac

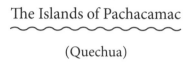

(Quechua)

[Long ago,] there were two curacas [chieftains] who hated one another. They each had children. The son of one of the curacas fell in love with the daughter of the other one. The father of the young woman became aware of their attraction and locked the girl in a palace to prevent the son of the other curaca from seeing her. So the young man changed himself into a beautiful bird so that he could penetrate the castle.

One day, when the girl was in the garden with her handmaidens, she saw an [unusual] bird. The bird was so beautiful the girl wanted to capture it. When she discovered she couldn't, she called on her handmaidens to help her. Together they managed to catch it.

The girl locked the bird in a cage and put it in her room. A few days passed, and the bird transformed into the son of the curaca. He became who he really was.

After many months, the girl's father noticed she was pregnant. So he asked his daughter how this could have happened. She replied that she had once had a dream in which the bird in her room changed itself into a man.

Realizing his daughter had been the victim of a ruse, the father ordered that she be killed. The girl tried to flee, but when she turned around she saw something very surprising. The same bird was pursuing her, [but this time] his appearance was repugnant.

She then threw herself into the ocean with her child to keep the bird from catching up with her. As she fell into the sea, the child transformed into a small island, and she into a large island.

And that is how the islands of Pachacamac were formed.[40]

This straightforward and unadorned Andean myth may rightfully be called an "origin myth" because it explains the mythical origin of two Andean islands, the islands of Pachacamac, situated off the coast of present-day Peru. However, its manifest simplicity belies the complexity of its latent sexual imagery. These sexual symbols are disguised as socially acceptable, almost childlike images, such as "castle" and "bird," confirming Freud's contention that "erotic wishes can succeed in appearing innocently nonsexual in [their] manifest content."[41]

According to Freud, the prince or the princess in a dream is generally the dreamer himself or herself;[42] therefore, one could say that the princess in this story, as the main protagonist, represents the "ego," or the conscious part of the personality. Kings and queens, according to Freud, represent authority figures, such as parents.[43] Although the *curaca* (chieftain or minor king) is the girl's actual father and not her symbolic father, nevertheless, he may also play a symbolic role as the "super-ego" in the story. In this respect, it is beneficial to point out that the establishment of the "super-ego" in Freudian analysis takes place only after the child has internalized the moral code of parents and society.[44] In other words, the punishment, humiliation, censorship, or withdrawal of love that constitutes the fear of external authority for the child becomes internalized and is replaced by the super-ego, which exerts its internal authority over the child in much the same fashion. However, according to Freud, a sense of guilt must precede the development and establishment of the super-ego.[45] This guilt arises from the conflict between the child's desire to satisfy his or her primary instincts and the desire to earn the love and approval of authority figures.[46] We shall return to the subject of the super-ego after a brief discussion of the sexual imagery.

From a classical psychoanalytic perspective, animals have interesting symbolic interpretations. According to Freud, animals in dreams generally represent genital symbols.[47] Although the snake has long been regarded as a phallic symbol, fish, snails, cats, and mice are also sexual symbols, the latter because of "the hairiness of [their] genitals."[48] Although Freud is silent on the issue of birds, it is well known that they, like human beings, engage in sexual reproduction. Much like humans, male birds have testes within their body cavity, and also a cloaca (an opening at the end of the reproductive tract) through which they deposit semen inside the female bird. When reproduction takes place, the male bird will mount the female in what is described as a "cloacal kiss." Interestingly, in the Andes and other parts of Latin America, the names of birds are often used as slang terms denoting the male sexual organ.[49] Thus, the image of the (prince) bird in this story strongly suggests a male sexual symbol.

Confirming the sexual nature of the bird's image, the myth also relates that the prince adopts the form of a bird to "penetrate the castle" where the princess is being held. Enclosed objects, according to Freud, represent the female sexual organ, and an enclosed room generally represents "a woman."[50] Thus, the most obvious interpretation of this passage is that the castle—as an enclosed space—represents the woman's sexual opening, or vagina. It follows that the prince's transformation into a bird in order to "penetrate the castle" is symbolic of his yearning to have sexual intercourse with the princess. Interestingly, the girl's father has his daughter in a "locked" palace, symbolically representing his desire to keep her sexuality "locked up" and her virginity intact.

The garden scene of the princess and her (same-sex) handmaidens is also reminiscent of pre-adolescence. Freud describes this period as the latency stage, when sexual urges are building up but are still repressed and children play with mostly same-sex peers. This period paves the way for the subsequent genital stage, starting at puberty, when the person experiences a sexual reawakening and, as in this story, becomes more open to sexual encounters.[51]

The turning point of the story appears to be when the princess and her handmaidens capture the beautiful bird—an object of (sexual) admiration—and, finally, the princess locks it in a cage and puts it her "room" (female body/female sexual organ). The performance of the sexual act, however, is transformed by the reality principle. Metaphorically, one might say that the innocence and freedom that the princess associates with the small, winged bird turns into the "reality" of a man sharing his sexual organ with her in the bedroom. In other words, from the princess' perspective, the sexual act takes away her childhood innocence and paves the way for the reality principle, which allows her to recognize the act and the man for what and who they really are.

After many months, the girl's father notices she is pregnant. Curiously, the girl alters reality and reverts back to the "dream" in which the bird in her room changed itself into a man. This is akin to the dream state in which Freud contended that "even the most mature adult[s] [regress] to primary process thought as the unconscious system gains control of the mental apparatus."[52] Instead of comforting and reassuring his daughter, the father orders that she be killed. In this case, the father's actions are similar to the role the "super-ego" plays in the human psyche, torturing and humiliating the ego for pursuing pleasure and violating its internalized code of morality.[53] Hence, at this critical juncture in the story, the father's outward condemnation of his daughter is analogous to the super-ego's internal condemnation of the ego.

From this unbearable torment, guilt—personified by the "repugnant" bird—takes wing. What the ego (princess) once perceived as a beautiful bird and the source of immense sexual pleasure now becomes a repugnant bird of guilt in pursuit of the princess and her child. It is not clear from the story whether guilt itself is personified as the repugnant bird or if it is the super-ego, newly formed, which assumes the form of the frightening pursuer.

Finally, the fearful princess takes the child and throws herself into the ocean. According to Freud, flinging oneself into water is an act of "parturition," or giving birth.[54] In this myth, two islands emerge from the depths of the sea after the princess and her child throw themselves into the water—"the child is transformed into a small island, and she into a large island." So arguably, this seems to confirm Freud's theory of parturition, because the water is "giving birth" to something new, much like a mother gives birth to a child from uterine waters.

From another perspective this same deed may be viewed as an act of desperation instead of a symbolic act of renewal. The guilt—embodied by the repugnant bird—threatens to overcome the ego (princess/child). This creates such dissonance, conflict, and pain in the conscious personality that the ego sees no alternative but to *repress* these "unacceptable" sexual desires and banish them to the "ocean" of oblivion, symbolically representing the unconscious.

In his characterization of neurotic defenses, Freud acknowledges that conflicting sexual experiences are often repressed.[55] Additionally, when these instinctual desires "no longer produce an affect of pleasure, but one of pain, [this results in a] conversion of affect that constitutes the essence of what we call 'repression.'"[56] Thus, the act of the princess throwing herself into the ocean with her child is most likely symbolic of the mechanism of repression. This symbolic expression of repression is also evident in other Andean tales[57] and also appears in the following story of "Mama Little Skin."

MAMA LITTLE SKIN: THE INCEST TABOO

There are a number of contemporary Andean stories that link guilt and sexuality in the context of a societal taboo. Unlike the tales that explore the conflict between sexual urges and moral inhibitions, these stories disguise the painful and agonizing trauma of incest. Remarkably, these stories are surprisingly similar in detail throughout the Andes, and generally involve a young girl who runs away from home and hides behind a costume or disguise or, alternatively, steps inside an enclosed container of some kind, such as a doll case or wooden box. In each case, the girl runs away to escape the sexual advances of her father or another close male relative.

In most Andean incest stories, the incestuous act is not overtly disclosed, and in some cases is not even acknowledged. Instead, the incest is disguised and expressed in symbolic form. Generally, the incestuous act is converted into an innocent and "acceptable" image, such as a ring, a dress, a button, and so forth.[58] Sometimes it is also presented as something that *might have happened*, in which case the listener or reader is misled to believe that the sexual trauma was averted altogether. However, it often becomes clear as the story progresses that the young girl continues to live with the residual guilt of the trauma that allegedly *never happened*.

The history of incest in the Andes is an ambiguous one. In the pre-Columbian era, for example, the mythological ancestors of some ethnic groups were considered to be an incestuous couple. As discussed in a previous chapter, the Incas, for instance, believed their first ancestors and rulers were Manco Capac and Mama Ocllo (or in some versions, Ayar Manco and Mama Huaco), who were brother and sister, husband and wife, and children of the Sun and Moon.[59] Sometimes, as with the Inca, the incestuous union of the mythological rulers also reflected the incestuous union of the celestial parents, who gave them birth. For example, Inca religion dictated that the Sun, considered the father of the Inca, was also the husband and brother of the Moon.[60] It was this "divine" origin that gave the Inca rulers the moral and religious authority to preside over the cult of the Sun god, and which became a primary impetus for conquest and expansion.[61]

According to Inca mythology (not history), Manco Capac, the first ruler, legitimated the practice of incest among the Inca elite.[62] The Inca king was obliged to marry his full-blooded sister, and the Inca royal family was allowed to participate in varying degrees of incest.[63] According to the colonial chronicler Garcilaso de la Vega, this practice was intended to keep "the blood of the Sun pure," as the Inca and his royal family were considered to be direct descendants of the Sun god.[64] However, some chroniclers assert that this custom did not become established in the formative years of Cuzco, but rather during the Empire Period to serve the political purposes of the Inca and his royal family.[65] It also appears that most marriages between the Inca and his sister-queen were merely ceremonial, as the Inca rulers "had numerous secondary wives for their sexual pleasure."[66] However, some colonial documents provide evidence to the contrary.[67]

It is important to point out that today incest is a strong cultural taboo among the Native Andean peoples in most regions of the Andes. In many areas the indigenous peoples believe that when a perpetrator of incest dies, he or she will be forced to wander as a "condemned soul" (*alma condenada*). Condemned souls are neither living nor dead and can neither enter heaven nor hell. They are forced to walk the earth after their physical death in order to expiate their sins. Condemned souls usually cannot eat or sleep, and they walk about with open wounds on their hands and feet. The blood from their wounds serves as a constant reminder that they must beseech God for forgiveness. In fact, according to the law of *ayni* (Andean reciprocity), some Native Andeans ascertain that the pain the condemned souls endure after death is directly proportional to the pain they caused their victims in life.

In some parts of the Andes condemned souls are believed to have skulls for heads and animal hooves instead of feet.[68] In some cases they don red boots made of burning fire. Perhaps as a subtle criticism of the Catholic Church, condemned souls may also appear dressed as monks or priests, sometimes wearing long black or white tunics. A few indigenous groups also believe that condemned souls *can* eat but that their diet is limited to some unsavory foods. Among certain Aymara groups, for example, the condemned souls are believed to swallow children whole and to have a predilection for the "soft parts" of the human body, namely the tongue and breasts of women.[69] By contrast, in some Quechua-speaking regions of Peru, children are considered to act as "repellants" that ward off the condemned soul, as do other objects, such as the Christian crucifix, llama wool, bread, salt, and soap, among others.[70]

There is also another interesting belief in Southern Peru and other regions of the Andes concerning the origin of some supernatural beings known as *qarqarias* (also called *jarjarias, joljolias,* and *qarqachas*). *Qarqarias* are similar to shape-shifters in their capacity to assume both human and animal forms. According to the Native Andeans who live in these communities, these creatures are the spirits of *incestuosos* (persons who commit incest) who roam the earth at night, assuming the forms of various animals.[71] The spirits of the perpetrators of incest apparently turn into goats, chickens, pigs, llamas, mules, and other animals that wander about at night, terrorizing and terrifying the villagers. During the day, however, these spirits repossess their bodies and reassume their human form.

It is worth mentioning that although strong prohibitions against incest occur in many Native Andean cultures, the lines are drawn slightly differently than they are in Western cultures. For instance, among some Native Andean communities, the strongest prohibitions against incest involve father and daughter, father and goddaughter, mother and son, and mother and godson. The taboo is less stringent with respect to brother and sister, uncle and niece, aunt and nephew, and cousins, although incestuous relationships between these pairs are still grounds for censure and damnation. So, much like in Western society, most Native Andean communities consider the bond between parent and child the most inviolable and sacred; however, equally strong are the sacrosanct bonds based on religious or spiritual affinity (i.e., godparents and godchildren).[72]

The following Andean story was originally written in Quichua or Kichwa (Ecuadorian Quechua) and follows the pattern of some of the incest stories told in the Andes in which the incest victim takes refuge behind an ugly disguise, usually that of an old beggar woman. It is yet another example where sexuality and guilt are paired in an Andean story, and where the trauma of a distressing sexual event triggers the mechanism of repression.

Mama Little Skin

(Cañari)

A landowning gentleman had a beautiful daughter named Bernarda. Just as the daughter reached marriageable age, she lost her mother.

The rich man wanted to marry his daughter at all costs. But, naturally, the girl suffered and rejected him. "This is not right, Dad!" she would say. "Look for another woman!" But the rich man insisted to the point that it frightened the girl, and she began to refuse the father.

One day, as she was strolling alone near the river, thinking about her problem, she ran across one of her neighbors, who tried to comfort her.

"You look sad and lonely. May I ask why?"

"My father wants to make me his wife. Now you understand why I'm suffering."

"Don't be foolish. Tell him you accept. But ask him for something impossible to get, and then he'll stop bothering you.

"Listen, if I were in your shoes, I would ask him for three dresses: one would be the color of heaven; the other would be the color of purgatory;

the other would be the color of hell. You'll see that it's impossible to meet this demand. No one has ever done it."

Bernarda returned to her house looking very pleased. At the first sign that her father was coming on to her, she asked for the three dresses, as her friend had advised.

The rich man went away silently. He was absent for many days. [Then,] one day, what a surprise! The servants arrived with the three dresses.

"And my father?" asked the young girl.

"He said he'll return tomorrow. He's away with his friends, some strangers we don't know."

Bernarda took the dresses and ran out of the house. Her plan had failed. "Never again will I see my father," she thought. "I may have to fight against poverty and loneliness, but it's better to run away."

Time passed and she saw the sun set in the abyss of its resting place.

One day, the girl found the corpse of an old beggar woman on the road. She carried it with the help of some of her neighbors. Then she dried it and put on its skin. Everyone was amazed! [Bernarda looked like an old beggar woman,] and her neighbors followed her around in disbelief. The servants and her father were also looking for her, [but they couldn't find her].

Bernarda was skillful; she managed to get used to wearing the skin. She also learned to feign her voice and took to the road dressed as a beggar. In her adventures, she got to know many towns.

[One day] she approached a kingdom that was celebrating its feast days. [There] she encountered an old woman who talked to her for a long while. The old woman told Bernarda her story.

"They call me Mama Little Skin. I am the servant of the king and queen. But there is a very mean prince who hits me and mistreats me. I try to avoid him because I'm afraid of him.

"At night I go to the castle to sleep in the cellar. I serve my queen and my lord when the prince is away and busy doing other things. And you? What do you do?"

Bernarda told the old woman her story.

"I'm going to help you," said the old woman, "but first you must take off that ugly costume. You're young and I think the prince would like you."

"No, Mama Little Skin. I don't want my father to discover where I am. He's liable to kill me!"

"What do you want to do then, dear?"

"I'll stay for a few hours in the village begging for money."

"No, that won't be good for you. You look too much like me. If the prince, who is in charge of the feast, sees you, he's likely to lock you up. He'll mistreat you, thinking that you are me, Mama Little Skin, as they call me. Come, I'll take you to a hiding place. What are you carrying in your sack?"

"The dresses my father bought for me."

"I see, I see. We'll take a look at them later."

Once they were in the cellar of the palace, Mama Little Skin accommodated Bernarda. She realized that two old ladies in the palace would be a problem.

"Don't move from here, dear," said Mama Little Skin. "I'll bring you some food. Maybe you can keep me company for a little while. That way I won't have to spend the nights alone."

"But Mama Little Skin, you'll be in the palace, and I'll be imprisoned here."

"Don't worry. I'll come up with a plan to save you."

That same day, the servants of the king invited Mama Little Skin to a ball. "You fools, I'm an old woman. I need to get my sleep!" she responded.

Back at the hiding place, Mama Little Skin told Bernarda about the ball. "They say that there will be a ball tonight in the palace. Do you want to go, dear?"

"No, I'll be found out."

"Then let me look at your dresses."

"Go ahead, take them and try them on. I've never been able to use them anyway."

Mama Little Skin tried on the dress from hell. And at that moment, she transformed into a beautiful maiden.

Bernarda exclaimed, "Oh, what a miracle! Go to the ball with that dress on, and you will impress everyone!"

"How do I look?" asked Mama Little Skin.

"Beautiful and young! It's incredible!"

So Mama Little Skin departed and headed for the ball.

The prince saw the woman stranger and instantly fell in love with her. He danced with her; he held her close; he fell in love at first sight. But when the ball ended, Mama Little Skin fled from the palace.

The following day, everyone was commenting about the beautiful unknown woman. The others even told Mama Little Skin, who [pretended she] didn't go to the ball, that the prince had been captivated by a maiden of unsurpassed beauty.

"Stop making things up," said Mama Little Skin.

[The servants also informed Mama Little Skin that there would be another ball that evening. They asked her if she planned to go.]

"Parties are for young people," she responded. "How can I go when I'm about to fall asleep?"

That night, Mama Little Skin went to the ball wearing the dress from purgatory.

Prince Philip couldn't resist such a beauty. He asked his servants to follow her and find out where she lived.

Just as the day before, when the music ended the woman wearing the dress from purgatory fled the palace, but the servants caught up with her. Realizing she had been discovered, she threw some coins on the ground. While her pursuers fought over the money, she ran as fast as lightning.

The pursuers returned to the palace looking glum. [They said,] "Prince, we were just about to capture her but she vanished into thin air."

On the third day, rumors were abuzz and the prince was even more deeply in love. [That evening,] the beautiful lady wearing the dress from heaven arrived at the ball, but the prince had a plan ready to capture her.

The ball ended, and before anyone could notice, the lady vanished into thin air. The servants looked for her along the road but couldn't find her. [All they knew was that] the beautiful woman was wearing a ring that the prince had placed on her finger. [Finding the woman with the ring] was their only hope.

At the hiding place, Mama Little Skin told Bernarda the whole story, step by step.

"Now what am I going to do with this ring?" remarked the old woman. "Bernarda, if I were you, I would introduce myself to the prince. You are young. You are the lady who drove the prince mad. This is yours. Take off that skin and go and visit the prince. He is very ill."

They talked for a long while and made a plan.

"The prince will die if he doesn't find you, Bernarda. He is in love with you. He has a high fever and doesn't want to see a doctor. He has asked that they look for you in all the neighboring kingdoms. He's looking for the ring. I'll send him some water mixed with a [healing] remedy and drop the ring inside the bottle."

[Just then they heard some steps. Bernarda hid, and the servants of the prince approached Mama Little Skin.]

"Mama Little Skin," said the servants, "please prepare a remedy for the prince."

"Gladly, right away," responded the old woman.

A short while later, the prince was feeling better, having found the ring inside the cup of remedy.

"Who prepared this water?" he asked.

"Mama Little Skin," the servants answered.

"Have her appear before me at once!"

"She won't want to come," said the servants, "because she's afraid Your Majesty will punish her. She is afraid of you, Your Majesty."

"Tell her I order her to come! Tell her I need her!"

[A servant approached Mama Little Skin.] "Mama Little Skin, the prince wants to see you."

"He's not going to hit me, is he?"

"No, no," answered the servant.

"I'll go," replied the old woman.

A bit later, Mama Little Skin disappeared. "Bernarda! Bernarda!" she shouted. "The prince is looking for me and I can't go. You go and find out what he wants!"

"No, Mama Little Skin, I don't want to go!"

"You ought to go. I am an old woman."

"But I'm also disguised as an old woman," replied Bernarda.

"Please get me out of this tight spot, Bernarda, even if he treats you badly."

"And what do I say to him?"

"Tell him you don't know anything."

"What? He'll be furious!"

"You're right. So what should we do?"

A short while later, they heard the queen's voice. "Little Skin, Little Skin, come, I wish to speak to you."

Bernarda decided to impersonate Mama Little Skin. She was curious to find out what the prince wanted, and she also wanted to meet him.

"Where are you hiding, woman?" asked the queen. "My son wants to ask you a few questions."

Bernarda nervously entered Prince Philip's bedroom, pretending to be Mama Little Skin. She kept a prudent distance away.

As soon as the prince saw her, he leaped out of bed and pounced on her. He shook her without saying anything.

From the shaking, the skin that covered Bernarda tore to shreds, revealing the body and face of a beautiful young woman underneath.

Astonished, Prince Philip calmed down. "That's she! That's she!" he exclaimed.

The prince got over his illness, and arrangements were made for the wedding. In this way, Bernarda was finally free of her depraved father and married the prince.[73]

This complex Andean folktale is amenable to various interpretations. In the discussion that follows, we shall briefly analyze the story from various theoretical perspectives, including psychoanalytic (Freudian) theory, interpersonal psychology, analytic (Jungian) psychology, Andean symbolism, and structuralism.

In the curious tale of Mama Little Skin, the incest, at first, appears to be only a threat. The storyteller describes the death of the young girl's mother and the father's desire "to marry his daughter at all costs." Then the storyteller discloses that the daughter rejects the father and understands the wrongfulness of the act ("This is not right, Dad! Look for another woman!"). Finally, the consummation of the incest is clear from the simple follow-up statement—"she began to refuse the father"—implying that the forbidden sexual act has already taken place and that Bernarda is now refusing to sleep with her father. Moreover, as a consequence of the trauma, the young woman is "suffering" and has become depressed.

In an effort to run away from her father and the incestuous relationship, Bernarda finds "the corpse of an old beggar woman on the road." She removes and dries the skin and wears it as a disguise. This is reminiscent of the mechanism of repression, which, according to Freud, can result from childhood sexual trauma.[74] The separation between the girl and her disguise is evocative of the psychic cleavage between conscious and unconscious mental activity that occurs when the mechanism of repression comes into play, and the traumatic sexual experience is relegated to the realm of the unconscious. According to Freud, "the essence of repression lies simply in turning something away, and keeping it at a distance from the conscious."[75] Therefore, one possible interpretation of Bernarda's wearing of the disguise is that it represents the polarity of her mental life: her traumatic and painful memories and feelings about the incest are separated and buried *underneath* her costume in the deep lower layers of her unconscious. On the other hand, her "disguise" is what remains of the incest on the conscious level: the distorted remnants of an ugly and painful sexual experience.

However, according to the theorist Harry Stack Sullivan, the father of interpersonal psychology,[76] Bernarda's disguise may represent those disassociated thoughts and feelings that "have been split off from waking consciousness and thereby freed from control by the ego."[77] In other words, instead of submerging in the unconscious, Bernarda's unacceptable feelings about the incest have been separated from the ego, or her sense of "self" (represented by Bernarda herself), but are still in her awareness as isolated and disassociated fragments. In other words, the disguise is the personification of all the aspects of Bernarda that she considers "Not-Me" (as opposed to "Me"), because it "embodies all the unacceptable behaviors that are accompanied by 'uncanny' feelings of anxiety."[78] Presumably, this would include all the anxiety-provoking ideas and guilt feelings about the incest. Sullivan developed this "Not-Me" concept from his study of schizophrenic patients. According to Sullivan, the "Not-Me" is not unique to schizophrenics but is "part of the ordinary experience of . . . personality development in all of us."[79]

Another interpretation of Bernarda's disguise is based on psychologist Carl G. Jung's analytic psychology. At this point, we will digress and explain Jung's theories of archetypes and the collective unconscious, which are important in understanding Bernarda's disguise as a possible manifestation of the archetype of the Persona.

Jung, initially one of Freud's followers, later parted company due to personal and theoretical disagreements. Jung formulated a notion of the unconscious that was much broader than Freud's[80] and included two levels of the unconscious: the personal unconscious and the collective unconscious. For Jung, the personal unconscious is "a more or less superficial layer of the unconscious [that] is undoubtedly personal."[81] However, "this personal unconscious rests upon a deeper level which does not derive from personal experience and is not a personal acquisition but is inborn. This deeper layer [is called] the *collective unconscious.*"[82]

According to Jung, the collective unconscious is universal, transpersonal, and "constitutes a common psychic substrate . . . which is present in every one of us."[83] Additionally, it is from this common universal substrate—the collective unconscious—that Jung believed myths, legends, fairytales, and religion ("esoteric teachings") developed in every society and culture.[84] In many respects, one could say that mythology for Jung was the symbolic expression of the collective psyche, the unconscious drama taking place in the theater of the collective unconscious.

Jung postulated that the collective unconscious contains primordial images, called *archetypes*, which are often (mistakenly) interpreted as universal symbols. These archetypes are not fixed and rigid symbols, but rather malleable and "unknowable" psychological or instinctual structures.

> Psychologically . . . the archetype as an instinct is a spiritual goal toward which the whole of nature strives; it is the sea toward which all rivers wend their way, the prize which the hero wrests from the fight with the dragon. . . . The archetypal representations (images and ideas) mediated to us by the unconscious [through projection

into the conscious mind] should not be confused with the archetype as such. [The former] are varied structures which all point back to one essentially "irrepresentable" basic form ... [that] can be grasped only approximately. The archetype ... does not appear, in itself, to be capable of reaching consciousness.[85]

Once the archetype surfaces and is perceived in the conscious mind, according to Jung, it is essentially changed. "It takes its colour from the individual consciousness in which it happens to appear."[86] Hence, the unconscious archetype itself is unknowable and irrepresentable, but, nonetheless, it produces images and ideas in the conscious mind that make visualizations of it possible.[87]

The notion of universal archetypes may account for why mythologies and religions throughout the world employ similar symbolic language and images. Although these images and ideas vary slightly from one culture to the next, they also share considerable similarities, which suggest a common origin. For Jung, these *conscious* mythological and esoteric images ("conscious" because each culture fashions its own) point back to an *unconscious* origin in the form of the primordial archetypes found in the collective unconscious. They are conscious emanations of the primordial unconscious archetypes shared by all humanity. Thus, according to Jung, "myths are first and foremost psychic phenomena" that reveal the content of the collective unconscious.[88]

Among the various archetypes that Jung identified in the collective unconscious is the archetype of the Persona. In Greek and Roman drama, "persona" was the term used to describe the mask worn by an actor, identifying the role he played. Therefore, one explanation of the archetype of the Persona is that it represents the public mask behind which an individual hides his or her true, inner self.[89] However, according to Jung, the Persona is not totally created by the individual.

We make the mistake of accepting [the Persona] *in toto* as something "individual." But, as its name shows, it is only a mask for the collective psyche, a mask that *feigns individuality*, and tries to make others and oneself believe that one is an individual, whereas one is simply playing a part in which the collective psyche speaks.[90]

So although the archetype of the Persona on the surface appears to be an individual creation, Jung explains that it is acting as a mask for the collective unconscious. Nonetheless, Jung recognized that the Persona incorporates individual characteristics, for "there is, after all, something individual in the peculiar choice and delineation of the persona," which makes one's individuality always felt, either directly or indirectly.[91]

In the case of Bernarda, the young woman in the story who runs away from her sexually abusive father, the wearing of the disguise puts a mask or shield between her and other people, thus illustrating the Persona archetype. One might say Bernarda is putting on the public mask (in this case the "skin") of the Persona in response to the trauma of incest. However, although Bernarda walks about in the skin of an old beggar woman, she never completely loses sight of "herself," or who she really is underneath the costume. This is consistent with what Jung recognized as a characteristic of the Persona—in the absence of any evidence of psychosis, the person adopting the mask of the Persona never represses the self or "ego-consciousness" to the point of extinction.[92]

Yet throughout the story, one cannot escape the feeling that it is the old beggar woman—the Persona—and not Bernarda who becomes progressively more in charge of Bernarda's life. Bernarda gets "to know many towns" dressed as a beggar woman; she also learns to "feign her voice" so she sounds like an old woman; and in response to Mama Little Skin's question about what she intends to do in the town, she imagines she will stay "in the village begging for money" disguised as an old woman. Even when she has a chance to temporarily rid herself of the disguise by attending the prince's ball and wearing one of her fabulous dresses, Bernarda refuses to for fear she will be "found out" and taken away by her father or his servants.

What seems to be happening to Bernarda is similar to what Jung describes as the growing influence of the collective unconscious over the conscious personality in a state which he characterizes as "psychic disequilibrium."[93] Jung depicts instances in which the influence of the collective unconscious threatens to overpower the conscious personality. In such cases, he explains, "imperceptibly, [the conscious mind] becomes the led, while an unconscious and impersonal process gradually takes control."[94] Hence, in this process it is the collective unconscious that gains control over the fate of the individual, relegating the conscious mind to the position of pawn in a game of psychic chess.

In a counterintuitive revelation, Jung maintains that this state is sometimes necessary to promote a person's healing. He contends that as the unconscious forces gain predominance over the conscious personality, this also enables the disintegration of the Persona and the dismantling of the conscious personality, which is struggling "to master the difficulty by force of will."[95] (In this case, the difficulty being mastered, or overcome, is the trauma of the incest.) According to Jung, the result of this effort is that more psychic energy is freed up from the conscious personality and directed toward the unconscious. In time, this energy will be used to replace a "defective consciousness by the automatic and instinctive activity of the unconscious, which is aiming all the time at the creation of a new balance."[96] However, this is a fragile process, for if the conscious mind is incapable of assimilating and processing the material introduced by the collective unconscious, it runs the risk of "simply [riding] roughshod over the conscious mind, [and] a psychotic condition develops."[97]

With respect to Bernarda, one must assume that her ego, or conscious mind, survives this delicate process, because at the end of the story she sheds the old woman's skin, albeit inadvertently, when it is "torn to shreds" by the shaking of the prince. However, the story also affirms that the shedding of the disguise reveals "the body and face of a beautiful young woman underneath." This suggests that Bernarda finally discards the fake mask of the Persona and reveals her true inner self. This may symbolically represent a process that Jung calls *individuation*, where an individual "harmonizes his unconscious with his ego."[98]

In New Age parlance, individuation has sometimes been characterized as a spiritual process at the end of which one attains Oneness or Wholeness. Jung, however, views individuation as a goal-directed process that all human beings share in common. It is a slow striving toward psychic growth and integration of the Self (capital "S"), as distinguished from the smaller self—the ego—that constitutes only a small fragment of the whole Self.[99] For individuation to occur, the individual must coalesce all parts of the psyche, embracing both the positive and the negative aspects (the "Shadow"),[100] and reconcile opposites and discordant elements. Most importantly, in much the same way that Bernarda finally divests herself of the old woman's skin, individuation requires "nothing less than to divest the self of the false wrappings of the persona on the one hand, and the suggestive power of primordial images [of the collective unconscious] on the other."[101] In this way, a state of equilibrium is reached, which balances both conscious and unconscious processes.

Let us now turn our attention to another important character in the story, Mama Little Skin. In this tale, Mama Little Skin may be characterized as a wise old woman. She provides food and shelter in the castle for Bernarda, and, more importantly, she guides Bernarda's behavior by telling her what to do and what not to do. For example, Mama Little Skin insists that Bernarda appear before the prince. Although Bernarda is reluctant to do so, it is this encounter at the end of the story that inevitably leads to her shedding the disguise and the symbolic dismantling of the Persona. Mama Little Skin also has other special skills consistent with those of a wise old woman. For instance, it is she who is asked by the queen's servants to prepare the remedy for the prince's illness; and it is she who finds a way to reveal to the prince that his ladylove is not lost, but is nearby, by dropping the ring inside his medicine cup. She also has powers of transformation, for she changes herself into a beautiful young woman to attend the royal balls. However, it is not clear whether *she* is directly responsible for this transformation or if it takes place because she is wearing Bernarda's "magical" dresses.

In Jungian theory, a wise old woman is a feminine personification of the archetype of the Self.[102] Like all other archetypes, the Self archetype originates in the collective unconscious. According to Jungian scholar M. L. von Franz, the archetype of the Self generally appears in the psyche when

> the individual has wrestled seriously enough and long enough with the anima (or animus) [also archetypes] problems so that he, or she, is no longer partially identified with it. [In such a case,] the unconscious again changes its dominant character and appears in a new symbolic form, representing the Self, the innermost nucleus of the psyche. In the dreams of a woman this center is usually personified as a superior female figure.[103]

It is interesting to note that Mama Little Skin invites Bernarda to stay with her in "the cellar of the castle." This image is suggestive of the collective unconscious, which, at least metaphorically, exists below the surface of the conscious mind.

The Animus and the Anima are also archetypes of the collective unconscious, which are shared by both men and women. The Animus is "the male personification of the unconscious in a woman," and conversely, the Anima is the "female personification" of the unconscious in a man.[104] These internalized images of femininity and masculinity are shaped by the individual's real experiences with the parent (and other close relatives) of the opposite sex, and by the collective unconscious experiences of humankind as a whole.[105] Both the Animus and the Anima archetypes have positive and negative aspects.

As noted, the archetype of the Self (represented by Mama Little Skin) does not appear in a woman, such as Bernarda, until she has "wrestled" long and hard with the Animus—the "inner man" in her unconscious—and, moreover, she "no longer partially identifie[s]" with it.

But who is the Animus in this Andean story?

One possible response is that Bernarda's father is the personification of the Animus, but in its negative aspect. Bernarda's father is physically abusive. By forcing his daughter to have sex with him, he is luring her away from normal human relationships, depriving her of a normal feminine sexuality, and keeping her from having normal relations with men. These are some of the characteristics of a type of negative Animus portrayed in mythology as a "death-demon."[106] The death-demon often isolates the woman, who is the target of his affection, from other human relationships—especially with men—and imposes his desires "about how things 'ought to be,' which cut the woman off from the normal reality of life."[107] In many cases he also kills the woman in the end. In this case, the father's desire that his daughter replace his dead wife cuts Bernarda off from the reality of a normal life. Moreover, one could also argue that by putting on the skin of a dead old woman, the "real" Bernarda is symbolically being killed off (or at least subordinated) and replaced by the façade of the beggar woman. Bernarda herself relays to Mama Little Skin that if her father finds her, "he's liable to kill me!"

The archetype of the negative Animus may also express unconscious opinions that lead to a woman's feelings of unworthiness, passivity, emotional paralysis, deep sense of insecurity, or even nullity or annihilation.[108] The force of the negative Animus is so powerful it can take control of a woman's mind to the point where her ego identifies with these negative feelings so strongly that it is no longer able to detach itself from them.[109] This is another possible interpretation of what may have occurred with Bernarda. Her sexually abusive interaction with her father may have caused so much guilt, insecurity, and feelings of unworthiness—possibly even feelings of annihilation—that she can no longer separate herself from those self-deprecating thoughts and feelings. Consequently, the wearing of the dead woman's skin could also symbolize the "carrying" of these unconscious tormenting feelings, generated by the negative Animus, which are mistakenly identified with the ego. Moreover, these feelings are linked to a "dead" woman—from whom she obtained the "skin"—metaphorically representing the nullity of the conscious personality. This may also have been the skin of a dead old *wise* woman, metaphorically representing the apparent death of the Self.

PLATE 23. Quechua woman freeze-drying potatoes to make chuño. Using the wide night-and-day temperature fluctuations in the highlands, Andean pre-Hispanic cultures developed a method of alternate freezing and drying potatoes to permit potato storage for extended periods of time. Chinchero, Cuzco region, Peru.

PLATE 24. Aymara woman selling produce at the farmers' market in Copacabana. The emergence of agriculture and of particular crops is a recurring theme in Andean origin myths. Manco Kapac Province, Bolivia.

PLATE 25. Domesticated llama and some alpacas. The llama has been used as a beast of burden and source of wool, and to a lesser extent meat, in the Andes since pre-Inca times. Llama fat and blood are also used as offerings in Andean agricultural and fertility rituals. Island of the Sun, Lake Titicaca, Bolivia.

PLATE 26. Coca plant, native to the Andean region. Legend has it that the Sun god Inti gave the coca plant as a sacred gift to his people, and that he also foretold that it would be misused by the white invaders. Cuzco region, Peru.

PLATE 27. Huacaypata, the main square in Cuzco, Peru, now called Plaza de Armas, was considered the heart of Tawantinsuyu, the name the Incas ascribed to their state. Four roads departed from the city square to each of the four regions, or suyus, of the Empire.

PLATE 28. Cooperative of Quechua
women textile weavers. Communal work
is embodied in the Andean notion of
ayllu, a Native Andean organizational
unit that binds the individual to his or
her community in a number of ways,
including reciprocal obligations. Chinchero, Cuzco region, Peru. *Photo courtesy
of Ricardo Sánchez.*

PLATE 29. Quechua paqos or ritual specialists, also known as altomisayuqkuna, are in charge of making offerings and performing rituals and healings. They may also be diviners who make prognostications using coca leaves and other methods. Raqchi, Cuzco region, Peru. *Photo courtesy of Thomas Miller.*

PLATE 30. Quechua women weavers from Chinchero. Notice the eqeqo doll, an Andean idol of prosperity and abundance, in the background niche along the wall. Cuzco region, Peru. *Photo courtesy of Ricardo Sánchez.*

PLATE 31. Quechua boy in Ollantaytambo wearing a traditional multicolored poncho and a chullo, a woven woolen Native Andean hat worn only by men, with dangling earflaps covering the ears. Cuzco region, Peru. *Photo courtesy of Ricardo Sánchez.*

PLATE 32. Aymara man rowing a reed boat on Lake Titicaca, Bolivia. The Aymaras are at the vanguard of political activism in Bolivia and have formed numerous movements for greater social equality and political power.

PLATE 33. Quechua schoolgirl in
Huilloc. Perhaps criticizing Western-style
education, some Andean myths portray a
character named Ñawpa Machu (Ancient
Old Man) who lives in a mountain called
School and confuses native children with
"writing." Cuzco region, Peru. *Photo
courtesy of Ricardo Sánchez.*

PLATE 34. Llama herder in the Andean altiplano. Andean legend has it that llamas came from the stars or emerged from high mountain springs. Bolivian altiplano, La Paz Department.

PLATE 35. Baby condor or mallku. In some Native Andean rituals, the condor acts as a mediator that "speaks for" the mountain or embodies the spirit of the mountain. Saksaywaman, Cuzco, Peru.

PLATE 36. School-age children heading to a dance performance in Cuzco, Peru. While Quechua and other native languages are still stigmatized in Andean society, studies indicate that children enrolled in bilingual education programs in Quechua and Spanish express more positive attitudes toward speaking Quechua.

PLATE 37. Native Andeans waiting for a bank to open in El Alto. El Alto is the second-largest and fastest-growing city in Bolivia, and 85 percent of its population is indigenous (Aymara and Quechua). La Paz Department, Bolivia.

PLATE 38. Quechua woman cooking food at an Andean open-air market. The consumption of cooked food, as opposed to raw, is one of the dualities presented in Andean myths concerning the origin of culture. Cochabamba, Bolivia.

PLATE 39. Entrance to the Basilica of
Our Lady of Copacabana, a Spanish
colonial church that houses the Virgin
of Copacabana, Patron Saint of Bolivia.
Christianity was imported from Europe
during the Spanish Conquest, and today
many Native Andeans practice a syncretistic religion, blending Christian and
pre-Columbian elements. Copacabana,
Manco Kapac Province, Bolivia.

PLATE 40. Intiwatana, hitching post of the sun, a multifaceted stone that served as an Inca sundial or astronomical calendar. The Incas believed that when the sun appeared directly above the stone, casting no shadow, it was tied or hitched to the rock. In modern Inkarrí myths, the Inca hero also ties or cinches his father, the Sun, to the mountain rock. Machu Picchu, Cuzco region, Peru.

PLATE 41. Vestiges of the Qoricancha, the most sacred Inca temple, the foundations of which were used to build the colonial Church of Santo Domingo in Cuzco. During the colonial Extirpation of Idolatries, it was common practice to build Catholic churches on top of native shrines to facilitate the Christianization of the native peoples. Cuzco, Peru.

PLATE 42. Quechua couple extracting salt from the salt pond terraces at Maras. Using pre-Inca technology, the salt ponds are fed by an underground stream that contains highly salted water, which is allowed to evaporate and dry, leaving behind a precipitate of salt. Maras, Cuzco region, Peru.

PLATE 43. Urban Aymara woman in traditional dress. Native Andeans who move to cities struggle to preserve their traditional customs, languages, and beliefs, as they and their children are encouraged to speak Spanish and adopt a Western manner and mode of dress. La Paz, Bolivia.

PLATE 44. Student protest in the late 1980s. Andean indigenous peoples joined social movements in the 60s and 70s, but they later launched their own indigenous organizations to promote their own interests, such as preserving their languages and territorial integrity. Cochabamba, Bolivia.

However, the Animus in this case is not completely negative. Bernarda's "inner man," the Animus-father, buys her three stunning dresses that her neighbor had predicted would be impossible to obtain. Through this act he demonstrates some generosity and an element of kindness. As in the story of "Beauty and the Beast," which expresses a universal myth, Bernarda may be both repelled by and attracted to her father (Animus), in much the same way as the Beauty is repelled by and attracted to the Beast.[110] In this case the father, like the Beast, may represent both cruelty and kindness. As in Beauty and the Beast, Bernarda needs to reconcile her feelings for the "Beast." She needs to redeem her ego (self) and rehabilitate her internal image of the masculine (Animus) to release herself from the psychic hold of the negative Animus. Only in this way can she allow for the appearance of the Self archetype, embodied by Mama Little Skin.

The rehabilitation process begins in the story when Mama Little Skin learns that the prince, who "hits and mistreats" her, is ill. The queen's servants request that Mama Little Skin "prepare a remedy for the prince." In addition to preparing a medicinal mixture, Mama Little Skin also proposes another "remedy"—that Bernarda appear before the prince. At this point in the story, the reader or listener observes a curious merger of identities. Mama Little Skin unmistakably identifies herself as Bernarda. Even though *Mama Little Skin* is the woman who attended the three palace balls, and *she* is the one who wore the three dresses, and *she* is the one who captured the prince's attention, leading to his infatuation and subsequent illness, Mama Little Skin declares, "The prince will die if he doesn't find you, Bernarda. He is in love with you."

This is quite a change from earlier when Mama Little Skin and Bernarda are outwardly similar—they both appear to be old women—but are clearly distinguishable from one another. For example, at the outset Mama Little Skin expresses some reservation about Bernarda remaining in the village. She says, "You look too much like me. If the prince . . . sees you, he's likely to lock you up. He'll mistreat you, thinking that you are me." Also, when Bernarda is finally hiding in the cellar of the castle, Mama Little Skin recognizes "that two old ladies in the palace would be a problem." For this reason, she recommends that Bernarda remain hidden in the cellar.

The identification of Mama Little Skin with Bernarda marks the emergence of the Self archetype in the form of the wise old woman. This archetype dwells in the "cellar" of the castle, which metaphorically represents the collective unconscious, and surfaces in its most beautiful and radiant form at the prince's ball, presumably in the castle, which metaphorically represents the "conscious" level. This is also the Self that at one time was "abused" by the negative Animus, personified in this section of the story by the abusive prince, who now replaces the image of the abusive father as the Animus in the story.

However, in this part the negative Animus is "ill" because he has lost the beautiful maiden whom he loves, represented by Bernarda and the "young and beautiful" version of Mama Little Skin. He has also given his ladylove a ring, which in many parts of the world, including the Andes, represents a betrothal or bond of marriage. This would indicate that symbolically the ring represents Bernarda's experience with incest—a position in which she is acting as the betrothed or symbolic "wife" of her father. In another symbolic and possibly healing ritual, Mama Little Skin drops the ring in the cup of "medicine" administered to the prince. Thus, one interpretation might be that the presence of the ring in the cup symbolically represents the healing of the incestuous wound. This signifies that Bernarda is no longer "bound" by the ring (symbolic marriage or betrothal) to the negative Animus, and she no longer identifies with its disparaging opinions. The long "wrestling" with the negative Animus is coming to an end and is facilitating the emergence of the Self archetype.

In the fortuitous uncovering of the "inner" Bernarda (ego) by the destruction of the outer disguise (Persona), Bernarda also unveils a more positive Animus, who instantly recognizes the true Bernarda. The healthier Animus (prince) exclaims, "That's she! That's she!" upon setting his eyes on the beautiful Bernarda. At the end of the tale, the prince gets "over his illness, and arrangements [are] made for the wedding." This intimates that a more positive aspect of the Animus is integrated into the psyche (symbolic "wedding"), and "Bernarda [is] finally free of her depraved father" (the negative Animus). This may also mark the culmination of the process of individuation in which the ego harmonizes with the unconscious, embracing all opposing and complementary aspects of the psyche.

Another way this Andean tale communicates the theme of integration is through the symbolic image of the "three dresses" from hell, purgatory, and heaven. Mama Little Skin wears each of the three dresses to the royal balls, and each time she puts one on she becomes the young and beautiful Bernarda. The notion of three possible alternatives in the afterlife—hell, purgatory, and heaven—obviously derives from Roman Catholic doctrine, but it is also evocative of the Native Andean concept of Three Worlds deeply rooted in pre-Columbian traditions: the Lower (or Interior) World, This World, and the Upper World. As discussed in previous chapters, these three worlds come together in contemporary

Native Andean ritual, denoting union and integration. Consequently, the act of wearing all three dresses is analogous to the merger of the three Andean worlds, thereby affirming the Jungian concept of integration, or individuation.

It is important to note that the association of the Upper World and the Lower World with the Christian notions of heaven and hell is a fairly recent development in Andean cosmology.[111] Studies suggest that in the pre-Columbian Andes, the conception of This World was probably as a "neutral space."[112] For this reason, one should not be surprised that this story incorporates the Catholic notion of purgatory. As previously discussed, the Native Andeans practice an admixture of Christian and pre-Hispanic beliefs. Therefore, from a native storyteller's perspective, "purgatory," the state or place where the soul is purified and sometimes punished to expiate its sins and gain entry into heaven, is probably the closest analogy to the Andean notion of This World as a neutral and temporary space.

The reader may observe that this story exemplifies religious syncretism but also cultural syncretism in the Andes. For instance, the story is reminiscent of various European stories of Cinderella.[113] It also awkwardly incorporates Europeanized characters and settings such as the prince, the queen, the castle, the royal servants, and the ball. However, in many respects this tale is typically Andean in its pairing of complementary and opposing elements (i.e., Andean dualism) and its allusion to the three (Christian) "worlds." Moreover, the wearing of animal "skins" (although not human skin) is an ancient Andean practice. According to some Spanish colonial chronicles, the Inca ruler put on puma skins before he engaged in battle,[114] and Inca farmers put on fox skins to ward off birds and other animals from their cultivated fields.[115] It is also well known that the Incas made war drums, called *runa tinya*, out of the skins of their defeated enemy leaders, especially if the warriors had shown great courage in battle.[116] This is particularly important in view of the title of this story, which is strongly suggestive of animal skins.[117]

Therefore, one way to look at the "skin" in which Bernarda is wrapped is as a symbol of power and courage, much like the puma skin that the Inca ruler wore into battle. This may represent the personal power and courage that Bernarda needed to confront her "adversary"—the sexual trauma—and, even more importantly, the strength and bravery required to overcome the pain, anxiety, and guilt associated with the trauma. Also, like the human skin Inca warriors used to make war drums to celebrate their military victories, the shedding of the skin that once enveloped

Bernarda may signify her personal victory over her psychosexual struggle. As previously noted, perpetrators of incest in the Andes are believed to change into condemned souls in the afterlife as punishment for their sins. Curiously, condemned souls are also often associated with "felines" (the *achachi* or *tigre otorongo* [scientific name *leo oncaperuvianus*] and also jaguars, tigers, lions, pumas, etc.) that, according to Andean lore, have a predilection for the "soft parts" of their victims' bodies, including tongues and female breasts.[118] It is significant, then, that Bernarda wore a dead skin, much like the skin the Inca ruler wore into battle, which was flayed from a dead puma. Accordingly, the skin disguising Bernarda may also metaphorically interconnect her body, the puma (in its symbolic role as the condemned soul), and the sinful act of incest.

Another possible interpretation is that the skin, much like the skin of the fox worn by Inca farmers, is the skin Bernarda used to ward off birds or pests (like her father) from continuing to "steal" her "seed," or feminine sexuality. Land in the Andes is also strongly associated with the feminine principle, due to its identification with the ancient female deity Pacha Mama, who is worshipped as the mother of agriculture, feminine occupations, topography, and humanity. Foxes, on the other hand, are often depicted in Andean stories as masculine tricksters who fall in love with native women and try to lure them away.[119] If the skin Bernarda wore is connected with this ancient practice of wearing fox skins to protect the cultivated fields, one may observe that the masculine, in this case the fox skin, is protecting the feminine, Bernarda, just as the fox skins protected the "feminine" land from seed-stealing birds. Another metaphoric interpretation is that Bernarda was wearing the skin of an animal known to court women and to lure them away; thus, when the young woman finally shed the skin, she also metaphorically cast off the hold such an "animal" had over her.

Finally, from a structuralist perspective it is readily apparent that the tale of Mama Little Skin is a repeating story. Many elements in the first and second half of the story are essentially identical. Bernarda in part I is identified with Mama Little Skin in part II; the father in part I becomes the prince in part II; the father's servants, who are looking for Bernarda in part I, become the prince's servants who are looking for the beautiful unknown woman in part II, and so forth. Present in the story are also various dualities or oppositions: young and old, male and female, parent and child, abusive and kind, high (status) and low (status), beggars and royals, tattered rags and fine clothing, above ground (the castle) and below ground (the cellar), and so forth. These contrapositions serve to accentuate the notion of Andean dualism present in all Native Andean tales.

CHAPTER SUMMARY

The pairing of sexuality and guilt is evident in the tale of Mama Little Skin, the origin myth of The Islands of Pachacamac, and other similar Andean stories. This appears to be a modern phenomenon, for prior to the Spanish Conquest, the pre-Columbian peoples of the Andes enjoyed a greater degree of sexual freedom. For the colonial Spaniards, however, this sexual freedom was tantamount to barbarism and licentiousness. Even today the Native Andean communities engage in controversial practices such as trial marriages, ritual robbing of women, and dances that culminate in sexual intercourse between men and women, which undoubtedly contravene Christian dogma. The tension between this more permissive view of sexuality and the more restrictive teachings of the Catholic Church is evinced in many contemporary Native Andean folktales, which struggle to resolve these conflicting moral codes. Nonetheless, addressing societal suppression of instincts, Freud stated: "It is certain that we do not feel comfortable in our present-day civilization, but it is very difficult to form an opinion whether and in what degree men of an earlier age felt happier and what part their cultural conditions played in that matter."[120]

In connection with this theme, we have explored the psychological dimension of Andean tales and examined the latent and symbolic imagery associated with sexuality in Native Andean stories, and the incest taboo in particular. We have observed that in Andean stories the trauma of incest is often disguised and expressed in symbolic form, and that more "acceptable" and remote images, such as a wedding proposal or ring, often substitute for the more "unacceptable" and inappropriate sexual act. Moreover, the guilt, repression, and dissociation of identity, which may accompany the incest, may also be depicted symbolically in the story as, for example, when a main character, an incest survivor, takes to wearing a disguise to shield or conceal his or her true identity from others.

8

SUPERNATURAL BEINGS

Land of Ecological Extremes

It is difficult to contemplate the magnificence of the Andean landscape without noticing that part of its beauty derives from the juxtaposition of ecological extremes. It is a land of sharp contrasts and striking variations, the most notable of which are five distinct geophysical divisions: desert coast, bordering on the Pacific Ocean; *sierra* or *cordillera* ("mountain range" or mountainous highlands); *altiplano* ("high plain" or "high plateau"); *yungas* (the warm lowland valleys, also known as *montaña*); and *selva* (Spanish for "jungle," referring to the true tropical rainforests of the Amazon). The striking topography of the Andes brings together some of the most rugged and inhospitable regions of the world; in the pre-Columbian era, great Andean civilizations arose in this area, a testament to human innovation and mastery over environmental extremes.

Using the country of Peru as our initial point of reference, to the far west of the Andes Mountains one encounters the Pacific Ocean, which the Quechua peoples affectionately call *Mama Qocha* (also spelled *Mama Qucha* or *Mama Cocha*, meaning "Mother Sea"). At any given moment *Mama Qocha* may peacefully and quietly rest, but more often than not, she rumbles from the strong southeast trade winds agitating her waters and the upwelling currents rising from her depths. These currents bring to the surface a variety of fish, marine plants, and other marine animals, which are the mainstay of many Andean coastal peoples. The cold currents of *Mama Qocha*, together with the southeast trade winds and the coastal mountains that deflect the rainfall, create barren coastal deserts like Chile's Atacama, which receives rainfall maybe once or twice every century, making it one of the driest places on earth.

Mama Qochaq Patan ("Mother Coast") suffers from lack of rainfall. The coastal Andean desert is a lonely and solitary place of grayish and brownish hues, which suffers from extreme dryness and heat. According to archaeologist Michael Moseley, "Whereas the littoral waters [of the Pacific Ocean] can be fished, very little of the desert can be farmed. Even with the largest irrigation systems in the Cordillera less than 10 percent of the coast is arable; and self-watering river floodplains are few."[1] Luckily, there are pockets of fertile ground bathed by the sacred waters flowing from the mountains, which many Andean peoples attribute to the benevolence of the *Wamanis* or *Apus* (Quechua deities of the mountains and high mountain lakes) or to the *Achachilas* or *Mallkus* (surrounding mountain deities, considered ancestors or godparents of the Aymara people). These runoff waters are formed by thawing glaciers on the western slopes of the Andes, forming rivers and streams and bringing much-needed irrigation water to the communities living and farming below. Some of these drain into large valley oases, where crops can be grown year round. In ancient times, these same river valleys gave rise to many great Andean civilizations that effectively employed irrigation and other technological measures to maximize agricultural production. However, today there is ample evidence that global warming is, at least in part, causing these mountain glaciers to evaporate at an alarming rate; so the future of the Andean communities that depend on these glaciers for their irrigation and drinking water, as well as their electrical needs, is uncertain.[2]

From the coastal valleys, the land rapidly ascends to the majestic and dry ecological zone of the *sierra* or *cordillera* ("mountain range," or mountainous highlands). From the perspective at the base of the mountains, the lofty *sierra* appears to touch the clouds. On the way up, the terrain is steep and tortuous; the ground is dusty brown with little vegetation, except for wild grasses and the occasional forbs and shrubs. However, out of the dust and dryness one witnesses an occasional miracle. Beautiful and oddly shaped cacti dot the barren landscape. Sometimes, amidst their shriveled and spiny surfaces, purple, red, and yellow flowers peer out curiously into the sun in defiance of the rain gods.

The difficult terrain of the *sierra* or *cordillera* is also home to the Andean camelids—the llama, the alpaca, the guanaco, and the vicuña—known throughout the world for the fine quality of their wool. Domesticated camelids are used as pack animals and as sources of meat and wool in the Andes. Llama fat and blood are often used in Andean agricultural and fertility rituals, and llama dung is burned as fuel and used as an organic fertilizer. In some parts of the Andes llamas are associated with water. For example, some Native Andeans believe that camelids originated from highland lakes and lagoons, so their birth parallels that of humans who emerged from their *paqarinas*, or sacred places of origin.[3] The Incas also made sacrifices of llamas during fixed intervals of the agricultural cycle. In October, the beginning of the Andean rainy season, black llamas in particular were tied to posts in the main square and deprived of food and water so they could cry out to the gods to induce them to produce rain.[4] Among the contemporary Aymaras, there is also a legend that llamas descended from a cluster of stars that fell to earth from the heavens. In honor of this legend, they celebrate a dance called *The Llamerada* ("Dance of the *Llameros* or Llama Herders") in which men and women, coupled in rows, dance in intricate formations, creating figures of stars and other shapes with the slings they carry in their hands. The movements of the dance imitate the traditional roundup of llamas and alpacas to sheer the animals' wool.[5]

On the way up to the top, one passes through a "rolling, transitional landscape of steppe covered with grasses and groves of trees," which is "more heavily watered . . . [and] gives way to multiple intermontane basins hemmed in by the two great mountain chains that form the Andes."[6] In these high mountainous valleys, one observes vestiges of the great Andean past in the rows and rows of agricultural terraces constructed on the slopes of the mountains. In these terraces, the past and the present converge. The Native Andeans of today witness the agricultural accomplishments of their pre-Columbian ancestors, who created flat, step-like farming platforms on the slopes of the mountains to maximize cultivation. Often these were connected to irrigation channels coming from higher elevations. Although many ancient terraces have been abandoned, some are still in use today and are an impressive sight. No doubt they also impressed the Spanish conquerors, who called them *andenes* ("platforms" for cultivation). This transitional zone formed the heart of a number of pre-Columbian Andean civilizations, including the Inca, which first settled in the high fertile valley of Cuzco, Peru, situated at about 3,400 meters (approximately 11,000 feet) above sea level.

Upon reaching the summit, one appreciates the imposing presence and power of the Andean mountain ranges—known as the *Cordillera Oriental* ("Eastern Mountain Range"), *Cordillera Real* ("Royal Mountain Range"), and *Cordillera Occidental* ("Western Mountain Range")—which reach their widest separation in Bolivia. Nestled between them is the high *altiplano* (in some parts also called the *puna*), the elevated plateau of the Central Andes, which occupies southeastern Peru, western Bolivia, and parts of northern Chile and Argentina. The altiplano stands at approximately 3,600 to 3,800 meters (11,800 to 12,500 feet) above sea level, and runs about 160 kilometers (about 100 miles) across and over 800 kilometers (about 500 miles) from north to south.

In the ancient past, the altiplano was the site of numerous lakes and waterways. Today, only two large lakes remain: Lake Titicaca on the Peruvian-Bolivian border and Lake Poopó in west-central Bolivia. More than twenty-five rivers empty into Lake Titicaca, which is home to more than forty islands, some densely populated. However, its southern neighbor, Lake Poopó, is slowly drying, and dying, of evaporation.[7] In recent years, even Lake Titicaca has experienced a dramatic decline in water levels under the combined influence of evaporation, diminished rainfall, human water removal (for drinking, irrigation, and industrial use), and the rapid melting of Andean glaciers feeding the inflow network of the lake.[8]

Lake Titicaca, situated at over 3800 meters (more than 12,500 feet) above sea level, is the highest navigable lake in the world. Arriving at the lake, one comes to the meeting place between earth and sky. It is so high that on certain days the clouds appear to be floating on the water. At night the stars hang above the lake like twinkling Christmas ornaments in a clear black sky, due to the absence of light pollution from surrounding areas. The lake below is generally calm and peaceful, except when *Wayra Tata*, the Aymara wind god, becomes angry. According to the beliefs of the Aymaras, who live in communities in and around the lake, Wayra Tata is the consort or spouse of *Pacha Mama*, the Andean Earth Mother. The Bolivian folklorist Antonio Paredes-Candia describes Pacha Mama as "the female [counterpart] of the wind because he makes her fecund by snatching up the waters of Lake Titicaca, suspending them in the skies, and later letting them fall in the form of rain."[9] By all accounts, Wayra Tata is very possessive and mistrustful of Pacha Mama. When he is irritated and jealous, he causes hurricanes and violent winds over land and lake. Occasionally he gets so agitated by Pacha Mama's real or imagined infidelities that he creates waterspouts and whirlwinds that capsize boats and rafts sailing on the lake. However, the Aymaras assure that when Pacha Mama lies by his side, and he is pleased with her, he relaxes and quietly goes to sleep at the bottom of the lake. They maintain that Wayra Tata is as powerful, if not more powerful, than the Sun god, *Inti*.[10] According to Aymara folklorist Germán Villamor, Wayra Tata "tends to overcome Inti in bloody combats."[11]

Despite the high altitude and the volatile nature of Wayra Tata, the mild temperatures surrounding Lake Titicaca allow for cultivation that yields many beneficial crops, including *oca* (a tuber), *quinua* (a high-protein pseudo-cereal), *tarwi* (a legume), and more than forty varieties of potatoes. Likewise, the sacred waters of the lake also supply their own gifts: a great variety of fish, edible reeds, ducks, flamingos, and other migratory animals. In ancient times, the pre-Columbian cultures of the altiplano also developed sophisticated methods for high altitude agricultural production, some of which are still used today.

Descending the eastern slopes of the Andean *cordillera*, one cannot help but intuit that Mother Earth is *alive*. Raging rivers cut and shape the rock as impassioned sculptors chiseling and molding their clay. The *huacas* (spirits) of natural springs and waterfalls break the silence of the mountains as they tempestuously drop their waters to earth, resounding like bombs bursting into explosion. If one continues the descent, one enters a realm of forested slopes that are lush and green, watered by the rain winds from the Atlantic Ocean. The further one descends, the more humid the air becomes until reaching the *yungas*, or warm Andean lowlands. According to anthropologist Alan Kolata, "the *yungas* are a zone of radical landscape transition, of movement from the dry, frozen edge of glaciated tundra where biological activity seems virtually paralyzed, dispersed, and energy conserving, to the suffocating humid heat of the tropical forest swarming with insects and redolent with the organic smells of decaying plant and animal tissue."[12]

In the Andean oral tradition, the yungas are also where the Sun god Inti gave his people the gift of the sacred coca plant. According to a well-known Andean legend about the origin of the coca plant, Inti delivered this message to an Inca priest during the Spanish Conquest.

> Do you see those small plants with green and oval leaves? I have made them grow for you and your brothers. They will perform the miracle of putting your sadness to sleep and will allow you to withstand fatigue. It will serve as an invaluable talisman for those bitter days. Tell your brothers that they should pick the leaves and then dry them, without damaging the stems. Then they should chew them. The extract from these plants will be the best remedy for the immense sadness in your souls.[13]

It is interesting to note that this centuries-old legend concerning the origin of the sacred coca plant also prophesied the misuse of the plant. In the legend, the Sun god foreshadowed the abuse of coca-derived narcotics.

> And when the white man wishes to do the same as you, and dares to use the [coca] leaves as you do, he will experience the contrary effects. The [coca] extract that will give you strength and life, for [the white man] will become a repugnant and degenerating vice.[14]

Although coca production has caused much controversy in recent decades, it is an integral part of the life of the Native Andean people, who use the coca leaf for social, medicinal, and religious purposes.[15] What has concerned many world leaders, including the United States government, is the illicit production of coca for conversion into coca paste, the essential ingredient in illegal street narcotics, such as cocaine and crack. It follows that one of the primary goals of the U.S. government, in conjunction with some of the Andean governments, has been the massive eradication of Native Andean coca fields. It is often the case, however, that when policymakers consider ways to eradicate the coca plant, seldom are the Native Andean cultural traditions and belief systems taken into account in developing such policies. Moreover, recent statistics demonstrate that cooperative methods with the indigenous communities are as effective, if not more, in diminishing coca production.[16]

Beyond the *yungas*, one enters the *selva*, the hot, tropical rain-forests of the Amazonian basin. Although there is some evidence to suggest that the ancient Andeans traded with the Amazonian peoples, the Incas encountered great resistance when they set out to conquer them. The Incas defined the Amazonian piedmont as the edge of the known world, beyond which there lay "a barbaric, inchoate world of true savages."[17] Though it took many centuries to dispel such myths, even centuries ago it was recognized that the Amazon basin was teeming with biodiversity and life. The ancient Andeans hankered for the multicolored feathers of the macaws, parrots, toucans, and kingfishers native to the Amazonian piedmont. They also valued the exotic pelts of the jaguars and ocelots. No doubt they had also heard stories about man-constricting snakes and man-eating piranhas. Some ancient Andean communities worshipped these animals as *huacas*. It is important to consider that even today investigators do not know exactly how many species of fish thrive in the Amazon basin, or how many species of plants flourish in this region. Several pharmaceutical companies are currently studying the flora of this area to determine their potential medicinal and commercial uses.

Upon reaching the hot lands of the *selva*, our Andean journey comes to an end. At the conclusion of the journey across five geophysical zones, each with its own distinctive characteristics, one thing is perfectly understandable: why the Native Andeans since ancient times have viewed nature as *alive* and imbued with life, anima, and spirit. Moreover, amidst the beauty and challenge of the Andean landscape, another factor is clearly evident—the human factor. Although the Native Andean peoples have for millennia developed creative ways to adapt and thrive in these ecological extremes, they are also subjected to constant stresses from living at the top of the world. According to Moseley, "for the majority, who traditionally [reside at] above 3,000 [meters], the corollaries of high altitude include elevated solar radiation, cold, high winds, rough terrain, limited farm land, poor soils, aridity, erratic rainfall, short growing seasons, diminished nutrition, and hypoxia [low levels of oxygen due to decreases in barometric pressure]."[18]

Andeans also suffer from the volatility and unpredictability of the landscape: earthquakes, mudslides, floods, volcanic eruptions, "El Niño" events, and other natural disasters, which are part of the day-to-day vicissitudes in the Andes. This is perhaps why the Native Andeans have such a healthy respect for *Pacha Mama*. Nature is both to be admired and feared, both respected and appeased. To those challenges, one must add the long list of social ills that have plagued the Native Andeans since the European conquest: poverty, disease, illiteracy, racism, and social and economic exclusion, to name a few.

BELIEF IN THE SUPERNATURAL

Many Native Andeans, especially in rural communities, believe that weather, topography, and natural phenomena are created by supernatural beings and forces that share their vivified landscape. As previously discussed, indigenous Andean communities continue to worship some pre-Columbian deities in rituals combining both Christian and animistic traditions. For the most part, these deities are associated with the topography or landscape—rocks, earth, mountains, rivers, lakes, caves, and so forth—and meteorological forces such as rain, thunder, snow, lightning, and wind.[19]

Some Native Andean groups also attribute diseases and pain to supernatural deities, and there is also a widely held belief that there are *lugares encantados* ("enchanted places") and *lugares malos* ("evil or bad places") that can bewitch, make ill, or engulf an individual or a group. Many Andeans are also familiar with *lugares pesados* ("heavy places"), where *almas en pena* ("souls in sorrow" or souls in Purgatory) and sometimes *almas condenadas* ("condemned souls") are purported to dwell. Additionally, some Native Andeans describe encounters with *huacas*, such as mountain deities, that may adopt human or animal forms, or supernatural beings and spirits, both benevolent and malevolent, which they believe walk the earth and partake of their sacred geography. These supernatural beings go by various names and interact with human beings in unexpected and often unsettling ways.

These beliefs are so numerous that it would be impossible to describe them all in a single chapter. For this reason, in this chapter we will focus mainly on supernatural beings *other* than deities or places which, according to Native Andean beliefs, appear in the living and dynamic landscape of the Andes. For purposes of this discussion, we will highlight some of the common beliefs of the Quechuas, the Aymaras, and their Andean neighbors, the Kallawayas,[20] concerning these supernatural beings.

It is important to keep in mind that few of these beliefs are purely of indigenous or pre-Columbian origin; rather, most express a blend of European, Native Andean, and African traditions that have coexisted and coalesced in the Andes over five centuries to form a widespread *mestizo*, or mixed, folklore. This folklore subsumes elements from many cultural and linguistic traditions, evincing its own local particularities depending on the place, time, language, and region of its source. Moreover, the Native Andean communities seldom live in isolation; they also interact with and borrow from one another, which may explain the occurrence of many common and shared beliefs. However, it is crucial to point out that these beliefs are not static or unchanging; they comprise a *fluid* system for each ethnic group or community that is subject to modification and change due to external influences, such as the arrival of new immigrants from other regions, contact and exchange of information with other groups or communities, and political, social, and economic factors.

Let us also preface this discussion by pointing out that the word "supernatural" is a culturally loaded term. Western definitions of the supernatural may include adjectives such as abnormal, unexplainable, invisible, occult, eerie, or miraculous, suggesting that encounters with the supernatural are extraordinary, mysterious, and perhaps even frightening. Native Andeans, however, especially in rural communities, have a much broader conception of reality than Westerners. Their reality incorporates many beings, spirits, and supernatural phenomena beyond our (Western) sensory experience. In other words, what may seem supernatural to us may seem perfectly natural to them. So, for purposes of this discussion, I am using the term supernatural to help the reader understand that the beings described here are outside the purview of *our* Western, observable, ordinary experience. By contrast, for many Native Andeans these beings exist within a broader framework of reality that often does not clearly distinguish between mind and body or immaterial (spiritual) and material. Theirs is a much more integrated view of a multidimensional reality, incorporating many worlds and many layers of meaning and experience. By the same token, some Native Andean groups, such as the Aymaras and the Kallawayas, have a very different conception of spirit or soul that does not readily conform to the teachings of Judeo-Christian and Western traditions.[21]

The reader may also observe that the number of malevolent beings in Andean folklore (collectively known in the Andes as *malignos*, or "evil ones") far exceeds the number of benevolent beings. This is not a mere coincidence. For many Native Andeans, especially in rural areas, the world is a frightening and unpredictable place, where natural disasters occur frequently and unexpectedly; death from disease, poverty, drought, and natural calamities is a common occurrence. In order to make sense of these apparently random and disturbing events, many Native Andeans attribute them to supernatural beings and forces, an imbalance of *ayni* (reciprocity) or *yanantin* (complementary duality), or sometimes even to black magic or sorcery. To counteract these supernatural forces and restore cosmic equilibrium, the Native Andeans have developed elaborate customs and rituals to ward off evil and misfortune. They also regularly practice different forms of divination to obtain advance warning of imminent hardships or, conversely, to receive welcoming news of upcoming good fortune.

Additionally, most Andeans, irrespective of social and economic class, recognize or are at least familiar with some of these supernatural notions, and they would probably think twice before dismissing them as mere superstitions. For example, many Andean families own a statuette of an *eqeqo* (also spelled *ekheko*)[22]—the Andean idol of good fortune, happiness, and abundance—and proudly display it in their homes. According to some Andean folklorists, the veneration of the *eqeqo* has pre-Columbian roots and only later incorporated mestizo and European elements.[23] Also, few Andean children have not heard the frightening stories about the *Cuco* or *Cucu* (the Andean "boogey-man"), who whisks children away in the middle of the night if they do not behave. Many Andeans also believe in *almas condenadas* ("condemned souls"), *almas en pena* ("souls in sorrow" or souls in Purgatory), and *almas santas* ("holy souls"), clearly illustrating the influence of Roman Catholicism on Native Andean folklore.[24]

We will begin our discussion of supernatural beings with the Andean legend of the *pishtaco* (also spelled *pistaku*) or *sacamanteca*, which is found in many regions throughout the Andes.

The Legend of the Pishtaco

The *pishtaco* or *sacamanteca* is a supernatural being who appears in legends throughout the Andes. The word *pishtaco* may derive from the Quechua word *pishtay*, which means "to cut into strips" or "to behead." The Spanish term *sacamanteca* means "he who takes, or extracts, fat." Aside from *pishtaco* and *sacamanteca,* he also goes by many other names, such as *llik'ichiris* and *ñak'aq* ("executioner") in Quechua,[25] *kharisiri* ("decapitator") in Aymara, and *degollador* ("decapitator") in Spanish. However, irrespective of the name assigned to this malevolent being, the image he brings to mind is virtually the same in every region of the Andes: a white, mestizo (mixed race), or foreign man who preys on unsuspecting humans and then extracts their body fat and blood to use for nefarious purposes.

In 2009 a team of suspected *pishtacos* made international news when Peruvian police captured a band of criminals who were allegedly killing people, extracting their body fat, and selling bottles of it to cosmetic companies in Europe through intermediaries in Lima.[26] In the face of mounting evidence that the story was a fabrication to explain murders that the police had failed to solve, the Peruvian chief of police was forced to step down. Nevertheless, the fact that the police would try to deceive the Peruvian public by deliberately playing on this old Andean tale, and that some Peruvians would find it credible, demonstrates the wide acceptance and strength of this legend.

The following is a typical Andean tale about the depraved *pishtacos*.

The Pishtacos

(Quechua)

They say that a long time ago, at about the time of the beginning of our republic, a group of individuals walked about the outskirts of the towns killing people in the countryside. They especially liked plump people with good singing voices, because they said that the blood and fat of those people were good for casting bells. They said that the better the voice, the better the bell would chime. That's how these bloodthirsty men came to be so feared by the villagers.

Regarding this belief, there's a story in the town of San Buenaventura that proves the existence of these so-called pishtacos.

In those days there was a close-knit bond or [spirit of] fraternity among members of the same community. When it came to doing their work, they were like one big family—so much so that if, for instance, a person was building a house, everyone helped in its construction. So the day came when one of them decided to build a house, and as usual, everyone—men and women alike—went to help him. All that was left to make was the roof, which was made out of straw. So [the workers] agreed to look for straw in the mountains. They left on the designated day, and since it was far, midway along the road they sat down to rest and have some fiambre. That's what they call a cold lunch that you take along with you. For their lunch they took toasted corn, cheese, beef jerky, fried potatoes, toasted green beans, and more.

They were calmly eating their lunch when they were surprised by the unexpected appearance of some strangers, who feigned sincere friendliness. The strangers shared with them some of their lunch, which consisted only of cracklings (pieces of fried meat). But these cracklings contained a narcotic. The wives of the men who had gone in search of straw [suddenly] realized that the strangers [conversing with their husbands] were pishtacos. They tried to signal to their husbands to not eat the meat. But the husbands didn't pay much attention to the women's signals and they continued eating. After lunch, the strangers retired. They probably went to hide, waiting to see the effects of their craftiness. A few minutes later all of the men fell into a deep sleep. So the desperate wives carried them, as best they could, and hid them in nearby caves or covered them with straw to keep them from being seen by the pishtacos. Then they returned to town as fast as they could to report this to the authorities and to the rest of the people who had remained behind.

The townspeople took to the mountains armed with axes, knives, and machetes. But when they arrived at the spot where the men were hidden, two men were missing. Everyone was distressed on account of the disappearance of their friends and relatives, so they went to look for the pishtacos who had committed this crime. About two or three kilometers away, they finally reached a cave where, at first glance, they discovered the bodies of the missing men. The bodies were beheaded and hanging by their feet from pins that were secured to the rocks forming the cave. Below the bodies there was a pot that collected the blood from the stiff corpses.

Horrified and indignant, the villagers went searching for the bandits. A few meters away from the cave, one of the villagers discovered one of the pishtacos sleeping peacefully after [completing his beastly] task. He approached the pishtaco very carefully, and with the axe he carried in his hand, he struck the neck of the pishtaco with such force that the head rolled away to one side. However, the pishtaco's reaction was so quick that his headless body made an abrupt move and managed to stand up [on its two feet]. But it couldn't stay up, and it fell again, dead. Upon hearing all the noise, the other pishtacos escaped without being seen.

The village men picked up the bodies of their dead relatives and brought them back to the town for burial. They left behind the body of the dead pishtaco so the crows would eat it.

[As I said before,] the [other] pishtacos fled. Unhappy about what had just occurred, they went in search of new victims. Walking, they reached the house of an elderly woman who had two little grandchildren. The pishtacos surrounded the house and were about to enter, when they heard the elderly woman utter these words: "Janampa, janampa, chaita, chaita, uraypi, uraypi!" Believing that the elderly woman was crying out for help, or that she might be a witch casting a spell on them, the pishtacos left and never returned. But actually, the elderly woman was showing her grandchildren how they should scrub their backs and was unaware of everything that was going on outside. She was saying to her grandchildren in Quechua, "Up, up! Down, down! There, there!" so that they would know where to scrub. In this way, she managed to save herself; otherwise, she would have been beheaded by the pishtacos.[27]

~~~

The Legend of the Pishtaco is well known throughout the Andes and has evolved over time. In folktales of the Spanish colonial period, the pishtaco often appeared as a knife-carrying priest, seeking human fat to melt and cast into church bells or to make holy chrism, the consecrated anointing oil used in Roman Catholic rituals.[28] Later, the pishtaco adopted other forms. For instance, sometimes he is portrayed as a *patrón* or an *hacendado*, the master and owner of a landed estate, who uses his position of authority to cut and steal the fat from his unsuspecting victims. On occasion he also assumes the image of a white or mestizo military man, intent on extracting the fat from the common people. He then hands the fat over to the government, which in turn sells it to foreign enterprises to lubricate their machinery, especially airplanes, or uses it to pay off the country's external debt.

Recently, with the advent of technology and economic flight from the countryside to the cities, the pishtaco has also metamorphosed into an evil doctor, an organ trafficker, or a medical technician who plucks out the eyes or surgically removes the organs of his innocent victims and then sells them to foreign markets.[29] The one who extracts the eyes of his victims is appropriately named *el sacaojos* in Spanish ("he who plucks out the eyes"). Most commonly, *el sacaojos* is described as a tall, white, and blondish stranger with light eyes, sometimes sporting a beard, who speaks with a distinctly foreign accent. He wears everything from a black overcoat to jeans and a woolen cap. According to anthropologist Mary Weismantel, the pishtaco is portrayed as "the quintessential foreigner from Europe or the United States... whitened by his sexual aggressivity, and masculinized by virtue of his whiteness."[30]

As is evident, the pishtaco generally assumes the form of the historical enemies of the Native Andeans.[31] The pishtaco priest, for instance, may represent the Catholic Church, whose followers set out to destroy the Native Andean belief systems during the colonial Extirpation of Idolatries and sanctioned, perpetrated, or turned a blind eye to the egregious abuses that the Native Andeans endured during the Spanish Conquest and colonial period.[32] Similarly, he may also embody the *hacendado* who, before the advent of agrarian reform, kept the Native Andeans as indentured servants or slaves on his land and became wealthy through exploitation of their labor.[33] In some regions of the Andes this repressive institution still exists today.

The pishtaco with the foreign accent also exposes the deep feelings of resentment that some Native Andeans harbor against white Europeans or North Americans presently living and working in Latin America. The stereotype among these Native Andeans is that such a *gringo* (a white foreigner) works for a multinational corporation, lives in a fancy house, and gets paid in euros or dollars while the people working for him or his company eke out a meager existence. Likewise, the relationship between the military and the Andean indigenous people has always been a tenuous one, especially in places and situations where military involvement has ignored and even violated their human rights.[34] Thus, at first blush The Legend of the Pishtaco appears to be a tale of social protest against the historical oppressors of the Native Andeans over the last five hundred years.

However, Weismantel challenges this interpretation. She delves into the strange "familiarity" that the victims feel upon encountering this stranger.

The old man immediately recognized a foreigner looking for the schoolteacher as the evil being who had recently killed two people in his neighborhood; the young woman recognized a stranger seen from a distance as a pishtaco. Employing the perfect tautology of myth, both speakers knew the pishtaco precisely because they had never seen him before. Upon recognizing him, they became afraid—and it was by their fear that they recognized him.[35]

Weismantel proposes that the *pishtaco* is not an unknown stranger but rather a figure that was "*once known*, but [is] now deliberately hidden—estranged—from conscious awareness."[36] This would explain why he appears to be strangely familiar to the Native Andean people; his dreaded countenance causes not only fear and consternation, but also psychological conflict in the complex racial milieu of the Andes. Again quoting Weismantel, "conceived as a picture of the racial enemy, [the] image [of the *pishtaco*] constantly threatens to resolve itself into something more intimate."[37]

Put differently, the telling of these legends has a dual significance. On the one hand it is a conscious expression of the racial division, mistrust, and segregation that typify Andean history and culture after the Spanish Conquest; on the other hand, it intimates an unconscious acknowledgment on the part of the Native Andean peoples of the Western and European acculturation that has occurred in the region over five centuries. This *foreign* aspect, even if overtly rejected, suffuses almost every aspect of Native Andean life: food, clothing, language, economics, and religion, to name a few. Despite recent efforts by some groups to "decolonize" Native Andean customs, traditions, education, and beliefs, and liberate them from Western values, it is difficult to discard five hundred years of miscegenation, cultural exchange, and forced assimilation of Western culture without causing some cognitive and cultural dissonance in the collective native identity.

The adoption of Western values and apparent loss of indigenous identity have also given way to accusations in certain Aymara villages that members of their own communities have become *kharisiris* (the Aymara term for *pishtacos*).[38] These indictments are launched against Aymaras who refuse to meet their community obligations, such as participating in mandatory communal work or properly discharging their religious duties. The label of *kharisiri* is also branded on Aymaras who behave like city dwellers, work as contractors on Western operations (e.g., hydroelectric projects), or make public displays of money without any apparent source of income. In each case, the fear underlying these grave accusations, which may lead to mistrust, shunning, or even death in some instances, is that these Native Andeans have lost or forgotten their traditional values, making them "strangers" and "foreign" to their communities.

In view of the foregoing, let us now attempt to decode The Legend of the Pishtacos.

With respect to the setting, it is interesting to note that this legend takes place "at about the time of the beginning of our republic." This is a Peruvian version of the legend, and thus the time frame stipulated by the storyteller is around 1821, when Peru declared its independence from Spain and became its own separate republic. Remarkably, Peru's movement toward independence was not launched by the indigenous masses, but rather by the landowning classes and their forces, who were mostly of Spanish descent and were tired of the economic and social constraints placed on them by the Spanish Crown. At that time many South American elite also became enamored with the ideas of the Enlightenment; notable South American liberators such as Simón Bolívar, Bernardo O'Higgins, José de San Martín, and others had been educated in Europe and regularly maintained correspondence with the European intelligentsia.[39] In the same way that Peruvian nationalists, including Native Andeans, overcame their European adversaries, the Indian villagers in our story ultimately overcome some of the crafty (and presumably white) "strangers," the pishtacos, who "feigned sincere friendliness" but concealed their evil and selfish motives.

The allusion to Spanish colonialism cannot be ignored in this account. The setting of the tale points to a time when all Peruvians—whites, mestizos, blacks, and Native Andeans alike—claimed victory over their Spanish overlords and declared their lands independent from Spanish rule. However, myth and history often present conflicting accounts. According to historian E. Bradford Burns, "The actual consummation of independence in Latin America only affected a minority of the area's inhabitants. The masses, composed primarily of Indians, blacks, mestizos, and mulattoes, played an ambiguous role ... [and] gained little."[40] Thus, in terms of history, the South American wars of independence were not Indian victories per se, because the Native Andean masses in general benefitted little from these conflicts.

It is also curious that in this pishtaco tale the strangers are not expressly characterized as white or foreign. However, "whiteness" is one of the most salient physical characteristics of the pishtacos, although there are some pishtaco legends in which the antagonists are mestizos. Nonetheless, The Legend of the Pishtaco is so widespread in the Andes that it is reasonable to assume that listeners familiar with these tales would probably *assume* these strangers were white or mestizo, unless otherwise expressly noted by the storyteller.

In this particular version, the narrator elaborates on the communal spirit that existed at the commencement of the republic among the Native Andean villagers. Specifically, the spirit described is a concept of work where the villagers operated as "one big family"—so much so that if, for instance, "a person was building a house, everyone helped in its construction." This spirit of community is still present among many contemporary Native Andean peoples, especially in the countryside. The Native Andeans have a formalized concept of community called *ayllu* (meaning "family" or "lineage" in Quechua), which promotes cooperation and embraces the notions of unity, integration, and kinship. The ayllu is a cohesive social and organizational unit, in which members forge strong bonds of solidarity based on religious and territorial ties as well as kinship and communal work. The concept of ayllu originated among the pre-Columbian Andean cultures and is part of the indigenous legacy of the Andes. Additionally, today Native Andeans often form temporary labor allyus (*mitmaq ayllu* or *minka*), such as the one described in this legend, to perform individual and community service projects like the construction of housing and irrigation canals. I am personally familiar with a small indigenous village near Ica, Peru, where the mayor stands on a high hill and, without the aid of a loudspeaker, calls for the community to work on building a particular house, or repairing a particular irrigation ditch, or constructing a particular wall, on such and such day. On the specified day, the labor ayllu assembles and works on the designated project. Just as described in the legend, ayllu members work together in the spirit of solidarity for the benefit of the entire community.

Given that the ayllu is still alive and well in many regions of the Andes, particularly in rural areas, it is surprising that the narrator speaks almost nostalgically about what was commonplace in the past when he states, "in those days, there was a close-knit bond or [spirit of] fraternity among members of the community." Let me offer two possible reasons: (1) This story is being told to city dwellers who may be less familiar with the ayllu concept; and (2) There is a genuine fear on the part of the storyteller that the ancient Native Andean traditions and values, of which the ayllu is a part, are gradually disappearing in the modern world and being replaced by Western traditions and values.

Both inferences may be true. This version of the pishtaco legend originated near the Peruvian city of Lima, possibly confirming the first option. Yet today there is also a genuine concern, especially among native elders in rural communities, that their children and grandchildren are losing the "old ways" of the Native Andean peoples. For instance, many Quechua elders comment that their family members no longer wish to speak Quechua; they speak only in Spanish, especially in the cities and large urban centers, where the predominant language is Spanish. Some compilers of Andean folktales and myths have also noted that in some Quechua-speaking regions, Spanish structure, terminology, and syntax are infiltrating the Andean oral tradition, especially in lowland regions where the indigenous peoples have more frequent contact with Spanish-speaking outsiders.[41] Some indigenous leaders are also concerned that storytelling and other traditional forms of communal fellowship and entertainment are competing against, and possibly being supplanted by, Western television, video games, and computers. One might even say that the pishtacos themselves represent the external forces of Westernization, urban living, foreign cultural influences, and so on, that are robbing the Native Andeans of their native languages, belief systems, and traditional values. In so doing, they are extracting the blood and fat (in Quechua *yawar* and *wira*, respectively)—the symbolic life and energy principles[42]—of the Native Andeans peoples.

This story also suggests that the Native Andeans have nothing to gain from their interaction with these malevolent strangers. The storyteller makes it evident that the Native Andeans are people blessed with plentiful resources. They eat toasted corn, cheese, beef jerky, fried potatoes, toasted green beans, and other foods for lunch—a diversity of foodstuffs produced by Mother Earth. By contrast, the pishtacos simply eat meat cracklings, or *chicharrón*, and this is the only food they share with the villagers whom they meet. This would imply that they have more limited resources, or a more limited availability of resources, because their meal consists of only one thing. They have less to give to the villagers than the villagers have to give to them. This asymmetrical and unbalanced arrangement is reminiscent of many Spanish colonial institutions and their modern-day progeny, in which Europeans and their descendants benefitted unilaterally from their relationship with the indigenous peoples.[43] From an indigenous perspective, the pre-Columbian Andean institutions were not always equitable and fair, but they were far more symmetrical and balanced than their European counterparts, because they were founded on principles of mutual reciprocity.[44]

At this juncture in our analysis, special mention must be made of how meat cracklings are prepared. According to Webster's dictionary, a crackling is "the crisp remainder left after the fat has been separated from the fibrous tissue (as in frying the skin of pork)."[45] Here we see a foreshadowing of the pishtacos' pernicious intentions to separate the fat from the fibrous tissue of their human victims. Also, there is an uncanny resemblance in the story between the way animal carcasses are generally hung to dry, and the way the bodies of the victims were found hanging in the cave after being beheaded by the pishtacos. According to the legend, "the bodies [of the villagers] were beheaded and hanging by their feet from pins that were secured to the rocks forming the cave. Below the bodies there was a pot that collected the blood from the stiff cadavers." This passage adumbrates an additional possibility: that after separating the fat and leaving the corpses to dry, the pishtacos intended to use the human skin and flesh of their victims for making cracklings. This would explain why the visiting strangers had only meat cracklings for lunch; this was the only "food" they had available because it was the only food they ordinarily consumed. Hence, this imagery intimates that the pishtacos were not only murderers but also cannibals. Moreover, in sharing their "human" cracklings with the villagers, they were also enticing others into unwittingly participating in a cannibalistic ritual.

In many regions of the Andes, the pishtacos are also believed to consume human blood. One Aymara dictionary describes the pishtaco or *kharisiri* (meaning "decapitator") as follows: "The kharisiri walks by night in search of human fat. If he finds you asleep, he will suck your blood, and you will die shortly afterward because there is no remedy that will cure you."[46] This predilection for human blood is also evidenced in the story in the description of the pot that was found inside the cave, which "collected the blood from the stiff corpses." Although the story does not explain how this blood was to be used, one possibility is that the pishtacos intended to consume it. So in addition to being cannibals, the pishtacos are hematophagous beings.

In this story the wives take their sleeping husbands, drugged by the pishtacos, to some nearby caves in the hope that they might "keep them from being seen by [them]." Of course their efforts fail, and the villagers later find the dead men hanging from the roof of the cave. The image of the cave conjures the representation of a *huaca* as a mediating space or a portal between the supernatural and natural worlds, or a space where such worlds meet. Therefore, one might speculate whether the pishtacos emerged from the supernatural world and entered the human world through the portal of the cave. This "crossing over" is reminiscent of other Andean myths, discussed in previous chapters, in which mountain-dwelling spirits or *huacas* enter or exit this mediating space, or receive offerings from the human world at the entrance of the cave, sometimes identified as a "door" into the supernatural realm of the mountain.[47] According to Andean legend, other supernatural beings that kill and prey on innocent victims in a manner similar to the pishtacos also purportedly live in caves[48] and, sometimes, in cemeteries,[49] again conjuring up the image of a place "between worlds."

Finally, at the end of the story a grandmother and her grandchildren escape the fate of the other victims at the depraved hands of the pishtacos who had survived the villagers' reprisal and were "in search of new victims." In a humorous twist, the *pishtacos* abandon their plan to kill the family, "believing that the elderly woman was crying out for help, or that she might be a witch casting a spell on them." In actuality, the grandmother was simply giving her grandchildren bathing instructions in Quechua. Echoing the advice of other indigenous elders, this part of the story intimates that the language and traditions of the past may be able to "save" the Native Andean people from the physical or symbolic death of their culture. The grandmother herself may be viewed as a symbol for reclaiming the traditions of the Native Andean past, because her utterances in the Quechua language—the language inherited from her Inca ancestors—save her and her grandchildren from the malevolent strangers.

THE MALIGNOS OR "EVIL ONES"

Many Quechuas, Aymaras, Kallawayas, and other Andean ethnic groups believe in malevolent beings or evil spirits, collectively known as *malignos* ("evil ones"), who deceive, defraud, injure, and harm individuals and communities. These malignos are often blamed for causing death and disease and bringing ill fortune to the native communities. From the descriptions that follow, the reader may observe that the malignos are usually physically gruesome or deficient in some way with oversized or disproportionate body parts, reversed feet or hands, upward-facing kneecaps, missing limbs, and so forth. Often they also lack the capacity for human speech and move awkwardly by jumping, hopping, or crawling on all fours. Black sorcerers in the Andes are believed to derive their power from malignos, as well as from demons and devils (*saqra* or *supay*). The belief in certain malignos is very widespread, whereas others are confined to more specific localities.

Among the Quechuas, Aymaras, and Kallawayas, there is a pervasive belief in an evil being known as the *anchanchu* (sometimes spelled *achanchu*), whose physical description varies somewhat from one community to the next. The *anchanchu* is often described as a small, wicked old man, or a "big-bellied dwarf with a big bald head, disproportionate to its body, a sly expression and...a fascinating smile."[50] Reportedly, he lives in isolated places, such as caves and empty riverbanks, and uninhabited dilapidated or abandoned houses. The Kallawayas also call him *janchcho-janchus*.[51] In communities where the Spanish language predominates, they often refer to him as a *duende*, a Spanish term that subsumes many magical creatures.

The anchanchu is jovial and friendly by nature, and his greatest weapon is his overwhelming charm, which he uses to attract unsuspecting people with the intention of killing them. He dotes on and flatters his victims to earn their trust, but he harbors ulterior motives for doing so. Once he earns the trust of his victims and they let their guard down, he develops a plan to kill them slowly and painfully. That is why Andean villagers warn against sleeping in abandoned and isolated places—these are places where the anchanchu tends to appear and murder innocent victims.

According to anthropologist Alison Spedding who conducted a study in the Southern Yungas of Bolivia, the anchanchu is often associated with red or reddish-colored dogs that appear at about one or two in the morning.[52] The color of the dog is especially significant. In this region black dogs are considered benevolent, whereas reddish dogs are considered malevolent. This is based on the belief that "after death, when one has to cross a deep lake, the black dogs help us by carrying us on their backs, whereas the red dogs try to block the way."[53] Both Aymaras and Quechuas affirm that in order to scare away the anchanchu, one must invoke the protection of Pacha Mama and the guardian spirits of the mountains.[54]

In the Southern Yungas, which is mostly comprised of Aymara and Spanish-speaking peoples, the locals also believe that malignos, such as the anchanchu, have the ability to change shapes. For example, Spedding informs that some villagers reported seeing malignos assume the form of domestic animals such as roosters, cats, dogs, horses, and bulls.[55] Moreover, she recounts a story from another Andean area called Inquivisi, where the father of one of her informants reportedly witnessed a certain maligno, known by its Spanish name *fantasma* (meaning "ghost" or "phantom"), transform into a dozen pigs.

When they lived in Lakalaka, above the deep gorge where the river of Inquivisi joins the Cotacajes, the father of an informant was returning from the front at night. At a distance he saw a white spot near one of the two community springs. He thought his wife had washed some sheets and had forgotten one [at the spring]. As he got closer, he saw the same spot coming toward him, floating in the air.

It came closer and closer, and at the last minute, he blessed himself [by making the sign of the Christian cross]. Perhaps because of this he was taken. His brothers, [who are] evangelists, say that one should not bless oneself. The white thing wrapped around him and made him lose consciousness. [When he came to,] he turned around and ran downhill like a madman. The sound of his footsteps woke up the dogs—he was near the houses now—and they began to bark and go after him. Their owner came out, and when the dogs had nearly reached the fleeing man, he saw the phantom detach itself from the man and transform into twelve red pigs that scattered and headed for the hills. Meanwhile, the man fell down and lost consciousness, and was cured only after many treatments. It's apparent that this "maligno" was especially dangerous, because it assumed the form of not only one animal, but a dozen animals.[56]

Similarly, she also cites a number of other instances in which villagers encountered black cats, barking dogs, crowing roosters, and other animals that, according to them, turned out to be malignos.[57]

On occasion, malignos may also assume human form to sexually seduce men and women. For instance, the Kallawayas believe in the existence of the *pilulo*, a maligno who kills his victims through overwhelming sexual pleasure. Often he appears on carnival days with a "spirit band" of musicians between midnight and two o'clock in the morning.[58] When he spots a desirable female, he appears as a flirtatious and seductive young man who lures the woman with his looks and false promises of a good time. Then he takes the woman to an isolated location and has sexual relations with her. During the sexual experience, the woman dies from an exaggerated sexual climax, or contracts a terrible illness, from which she dies afterward. To attract a man, the *pilulo* transforms into a coquettish woman of extraordinary beauty who lures the man by appearing half-naked, revealing her tantalizing breasts. Then, flirting and smiling, she leads the man to a remote area, where she sexually overpowers him and he dies from a violent orgasm.

The Kallawayas also fear another sexual predator, a maligno known as the *purun runa* (also spelled *purun runa*, meaning "wild or savage man" in Quechua). The *purun runa* is a male being "with long hair, a tanned face, and herculean features," who walks about naked, exhibiting an erect penis.[59] He is very handsome and has a sweet and melodious voice that he uses to attract and lure women to his isolated cave. Legend has it that if a woman looks at his male member, she experiences overwhelming and uncontrollable sexual arousal, and her fate is sealed. When the woman reaches his cave, the purun run'a sexually abuses her until she is dead. Afterward, he regrets the murder and "cries and howls like a monkey, [but] after getting bored with crying, he goes in search of other women."[60] Interestingly, the purun run'a displays both animal and human characteristics. On occasion he walks on two legs like a human, but at other times he crawls on all fours like an animal.

The female counterpart of the purun run'a in Kallawaya lore is the *mealla*, who also suffers from an insatiable sexual appetite. She is blonde with copper-colored skin, and her feet are positioned backwards, with heels in front and toes facing back.[61] Just as her malevolent male counterpart, the *mealla* goes in search of unwary victims to satisfy her sexual lust. She tempts men by walking around naked, with her long and flowing hair barely covering her genital area. Unfortunately, her victims suffer the same fate as the victims of the purun run'a—they endure a sexually violent death.

In like manner, the Quechuas and the Aymaras also believe in malignos who sexually prey on innocent men and women. Both the Quechuas and Aymaras acknowledge the existence of the *juppiñunu* (also spelled *happiñuño* or *japiñuñu*).[62] The *jappiñunu* is a maligno who sometimes assumes the form of a flying woman with long, provocative breasts. She flies on dark and silent nights with her breasts hanging, almost reaching the ground. Her breasts squash everything in their path and often carry off unsuspecting victims. Other accounts reveal that the jappiñunus disguise themselves "as beautiful women who attract men ... [with] their beautiful breasts engorged with delicious milk. They invite the young men to drink from them until they lose their reason; [then] they pull out their soul, leaving behind a skinny body like a skeleton."[63]

The Quichuas and mestizos of the north-central highlands of Ecuador also describe another maligno, the *chuzalongo*, a sexual predator who inflicts pain and misfortune. The chuzalongo is typically described as a child, about six years old, born of an incestuous union between a parent and child or between a brother and sister.[64] He has no home, so he is said to live in the forests with the wild animals. His most salient physical characteristic "is the enormous size of his genitals, which he drags along the floor, in the same way as his umbilical cord. His male member is so extremely long that he can wrap it around his neck."[65] He is also endowed with extraordinary strength and is sometimes described as having backward-facing feet with which he taunts and confuses his pursuers.

The chuzalongo uses his gigantic penis to rape and kill his victims, who are primarily women. Using his childlike cuteness, he attracts women who often find him wandering alone and feel the urge to adopt him or protect him. When the women take him home and embrace him in their arms, he rapes and kills them, or he cuts open their bodies and pulls out their uterus, "leaving them bloody and mortally wounded."[66] The chuzalongo adopts a different behavior with men. Sometimes he kills them with his evil stare or challenges them to a rock-lifting competition in which he uses his phenomenal strength to defeat and eventually kill his opponent.

Another maligno that provokes great fear among the Aymara communities is the *mekhala* (also spelled *miqhala* or *mikhala*).[67] Physically, the *mekhala* looks like an old skinny witch with unkempt hair, pointy teeth, and a fiery tail like a comet. She has an awkward and unusual jump or hop in her step, which is common among malignos. She dresses in a long red tunic covered with pockets. When she hops into orchards and cultivated fields, she steals fruit and stuffs it in her pockets, which widen and grow indefinitely to accommodate the stolen items. When she visits animal herds, she sucks the blood and life out of the youngest animals, which allegedly are her favorites. If she enters a child's bedroom, she takes away the child's brain and soul and stows them in her pockets. Often she also comes to the aid of evil sorcerers, who enlist her help in causing grave misfortune. They bargain with her and agree to make her offerings in exchange for her assistance in carrying out their dark arts.

In some regions of the Andes, they also claim the mekhala flies naked at night and plucks out her eyes, placing lit candles into her empty eye sockets.[68] To protect themselves against the mekhala, the Aymaras place an image of *Mama Sara* (the Andean Maize Mother) in their cultivated fields and also ask for help from the *Khonapas* (guardians of the home) and Pacha Mama.[69] The witch-like character of the mekhala also resembles the *warmi volajun* (meaning "flying woman" in Hispanicized Quechua) or *voladora* ("flying woman" in Spanish) found in the folktales of the Ecuadorian highlands. Sometimes she is also referred to as the *bruja voladora* (in Spanish "the flying witch"). Just as the mekhala of the Bolivian and Peruvian altiplano, the *voladora* is often a sinister woman who flies from the rooftops at night, with or without a broom, and engages in satanic or dark magic rituals that incorporate some element of "the black kiss" (in Spanish *el beso negro*), a kiss involving the hind quarter of a male goat.[70] In some stories she is a shape-shifter and turns into an owl at night. She is best known for an incantation that allegedly gives her the power to fly: *"De villa en villa y de viga en viga sin Dios ni Santa María"* ("From town to town and from rafter to rafter, without God or the Holy Mary").[71]

Although the "black kiss" of the Andean voladora suggests bestiality, some Andean malignos are reportedly guilty of, or the product of, incest—a strong cultural taboo among the Native Andean peoples. For example, as the chuzalongo is both the offspring of an incestuous union and also the lover and killer of his adoptive mother, his gruesome condition may be viewed as a punishment for incest. Similarly, in the southern and central highlands of Ecuador, people who commit incest are purportedly transformed into dog-like supernatural creatures known as *gagones* or *ingagos*. The name *gagón* derives from the Spanish word *gago* or *gangoso*, which means "nasal" or "speaking through one's nose." The term is also onomatopoeic in that it describes the sound the gagón reportedly makes, which is "nga, nga, nga," similar to the cry of a newborn baby.[72]

Ecuadorian villagers usually describe the gagón as a whitish dog with long front legs, a long tail, a very long neck, and no hind legs. As punishment for committing incest, it also loses its capacity for human language.[73] They claim that gagones usually appear in pairs, as incestuous couples usually band together. According to Andean folklorist Manuel Espinosa Apolo,

> Gagones appear at night and at times one finds them running and jumping around or simply crying near the house where the incestuous couple lives. Gagones are accustomed to jumping on the legs of those who find them and biting their knees to take out their kneecaps. Where they run they generally leave a trail of foul-smelling worms, and unless one makes the sign of the [Christian] cross, the worms climb up into the body and provoke an insatiable sexual desire. It is said that if one manages to catch one of the gagones and places a black carbon stain above its eyes, the next day the stain will appear on the forehead of [the incestuous person who is] cohabiting with another.[74]

The notion that the spirits of people involved in incestuous relationships embody an animal form by night and reassume their human form by day is commonplace throughout the Andes. In Peru, Bolivia, and other Andean regions, these supernatural beings are known by various names, including *qarqarias* (also *qarqachas*) in Quechua, and *qhach'us* in Aymara. The Quechuas believe that qarqarias may transform into llamas, mules, and other animals, usually with long necks.[75] The Aymaras go so far as to say these creatures can also bring misfortune to the entire community; for instance, qhach'us are sometimes blamed for crop failures and poor harvests.[76]

As discussed in previous chapters, there is also a widespread belief that incestuous people become *almas condenadas*, or "condemned souls," wandering spirits who are trapped between life and death. Condemned souls are reported to adopt many different forms, but they all share one thing in common—their fate results from a depraved or morally sinful act they committed during their lifetime, typically incest. Although not technically considered malignos, condemned souls often share some of the unusual physical characteristics ascribed to malignos.

Like malignos, condemned souls are sometimes described as human or humanlike, whereas at other times they are believed to adopt the form of animals. For instance, a condemned soul may appear in the form of a monk or priest sporting a brown, black, or white tunic and "fire" boots floating above the ground. In some parts of Bolivia, the condemned soul is believed to have "a skeleton [skull] instead of a head, and feet like the hooves of a mule, reminiscent of the descriptions of the qarqacha, incestuous people who become fire-breathing mules or llamas at night."[77] Condemned souls are often described as having crooked hands facing backward, and kneecaps facing upward. Some Andeans report hearing the rattling of chains or the sound of animal hooves when condemned souls are present. In some parts of Ecuador, the locals insist that only animals can see them, not humans. Typically, the condemned souls are reported to dwell in cemeteries or caves, and they may also become "attached" to specific places (*lugares pesados*, or "heavy places"). In Andean festivals and dances the condemned soul is represented by a male dancer dressed as a friar or priest, sporting a long brown robe that is tied at the waist with a long cord; he moves rhythmically but awkwardly, hopping and jumping in pursuit of his widow.[78]

As is apparent from these descriptions, malignos are usually portrayed as physically deficient or gruesome in some way. They also walk or jump awkwardly and sometimes lose their capacity for language (assuming they once had it). The *anchanchu* has a disproportionate head in relation to his body and has the ability to transform into an animal; the *gagón* is missing its hind legs and has lost its capacity for human speech; the *purun runa* howls like a monkey and sometimes crawls on his hands and knees; the *mealla* has reversed feet with heels facing forward and toes facing backward; the childlike *chuzalongo* exhibits an extraordinarily large penis and is sometimes described as having backward-facing feet; the *mekhala* has an awkward hop and a comet for a tail; the *jappiñunu* has unusually enlarged or engorged breasts; and so forth. In many respects the malignos are intermediary beings that embody what anthropologist

Lévi-Strauss aptly describes as "negativized being"—intermediary characters that because of their deficiencies personify modes of mediation or transition between two full or complete states, such as life and death, or health and disease.[79]

The reversal of the feet in some malignos, with the toes pointing backward and the heels facing forward, also suggest a return to the pre-Columbian past and ancient Andean belief systems, which may have incorporated some of these supernatural beings. The European conquerors and colonists who arrived in the Andes five centuries ago regarded these indigenous beliefs as pagan, idolatrous, and often monstrous. The native peoples were forced to convert to Christianity and separate themselves from their ancient religions. For this reason, these grotesque and malevolent creatures, which, incidentally, are also part "human," may externalize this ambivalence about the past and perhaps even the internal conflict concerning the practice of syncretistic religions. On the one hand, like the Andeans themselves, these supernatural creatures are very human; on the other hand, they belong to a set of ancient practices and beliefs that even today are considered barbaric, unsavory, and uncivilized by Western and Christian institutions.

The malignos may also express a reversion to an earlier state of human development in which humankind lacked the capacity to communicate through language and walk linearly and upright. From a modern perspective, the human body had not yet attained its proper and balanced proportions; some body parts were oversized and disproportionate. As is suggested in some Andean origin myths, sexuality may also have been exaggerated, excessive, and uncontrolled, mirroring the predatory behavior of some of these malignos. These malevolent beings also display supernatural powers—shape-shifting, flying, bewitching, soul snatching, and so forth—that are not part of "this world." Thus, the malignos of Andean lore closely straddle the division between the past and the present; between nature ("wildness") and culture; and between the natural and supernatural realms.

Chapter Summary
The Andean region is a land of ecological extremes. Although the Native Andean peoples have for millennia adapted and thrived in these conditions, they are also subjected to constant stresses from living at the top of the world: extreme temperature fluctuations, solar radiation, hypoxia (oxygen deficiency), high winds, aridity, poor farming soil, short growing seasons, erratic rainfall, earthquakes, mudslides, floods, volcanic eruptions,

"El Niño" events, rough terrain, and many other natural impediments. To this list we must add all the social ills that the Native Andeans have experienced since the European Conquest: poverty, disease, illiteracy, racism, and social and economic marginalization, among others.

Given the day-to-day vicissitudes of Andean life, especially in rural communities, it is not difficult to see why many Native Andeans believe that weather, topography, and natural phenomena are created and controlled by supernatural beings and forces that share their vivified landscape. There is also a widely held belief among Native Andeans that diseases, pain, injury, destruction, and sometimes death are caused by malevolent beings, known as *malignos* ("evil ones"), which deceive and harm individuals and communities.

In this chapter we have described only some of the many *malignos* and other supernatural beings that form part of the belief systems of the Native Andean peoples. Moreover, we have focused exclusively on supernatural beings, other than deities and places, which form part of the cultural traditions of the Quechuas, the Aymaras, and the Kallawayas. But there are innumerable others. Although some of these beliefs date back to the pre-Columbian era, they have also been greatly influenced by Spanish culture and religion, as well as African traditions, which have coexisted and coalesced in the Andes for nearly five centuries. As such, they may be rightfully described as mestizo, or culturally mixed, beliefs, which today are shared by some non-Native Andeans as well.

The malignos presented in this analysis tend to be physically deficient or gruesome in some way. Although most display some human physical characteristics, some have disproportionate body parts or enlarged sexual organs, which they use to harm human beings. Their movements and body parts are also awkward: they hop, jump, or walk on all fours; and they have crooked hands, upward-facing kneecaps, or reversed feet with heels facing forward and toes facing backward. Most malignos also demonstrate supernatural powers, such as the ability to transform into an animal or a male or female figure at will. They may also be able to steal a human soul, or bewitch an individual, or drive a person to madness, among other abilities.

It is possible that these portrayals of malignos may be expressing a reversion to an earlier state of human development, when human beings lacked the capacity to communicate through language and walk linearly and upright, and when the human body had not yet attained its proper size and proportion. However, symbolically they may also be externalizing an internal ambivalence about the practice of a syncretistic religion.

On the one hand the Native Andeans have accepted Catholicism, which characterizes these beliefs as pagan, idolatrous, and even monstrous; on the other hand, these beliefs, like the reversed feet, "point to" and have their roots in the pre-Columbian past and form part of the ancient traditions of the Native Andean peoples.

This chapter has also highlighted The Legend of the Pishtaco—a white, mestizo, or foreign man—who preys on unsuspecting humans and then extracts their body fat and blood for nefarious purposes. Sometimes he uses the human fat from his victims to melt and cast into church bells, to lubricate his machines, especially airplanes, or to pay off the country's external debt. More recently, the pishtaco has also metamorphosed into an evil doctor, organ trafficker, or medical technician who plucks out the eyes or surgically removes the organs of his victims and sells them to foreign markets. Although this legend has evolved over time, one element remains constant: the pishtaco generally assumes the form of the real or imagined historical enemies of the Native Andeans, be they priests, landlords, military men, government officials, organ traffickers, or *gringos* (white foreigners).

It is hard not to see the connection between the extraction of human fat and the historical exploitation of the native peoples for their physical labor in the Andes. So in many respects The Legend of the Pishtaco may be viewed as a tale of social protest against the historical oppressors of the Native Andeans during the last five hundred years. However, The Legend of the Pishtaco expresses much more than that. The "whiteness" of the pishtaco is a conscious expression of the racist attitudes, mistrust, and exclusionary practices that have marginalized the Native Andeans for centuries after the Spanish Conquest. It is also an unconscious acknowledgement and recognition of the Native Andeans' own European or Western acculturation process that has occurred over five centuries following the Conquest. This "foreign" aspect, even if overtly rejected, suffuses almost every aspect of Native Andean life, and yet is "estranged" from the Native Andean identity.

9

SOCIAL PROTEST

THE RISE OF ANDEAN INDIGENOUS MOVEMENTS

In the late 1970s and early to mid 80s, when many Andean countries were transitioning from military to civilian rule, the Native Andean people joined social movement organizations that opened up new opportunities for them to influence national legislative agendas. In the 80s they made impressive strides, but "most substantive gains were not achieved until the 1990s, after indigenous social movements [were formed and] had devised networks and strategies capable of mounting widespread protests and marches lasting weeks or even months."[1] Since then, aided by constitutional reforms and coalition building, the Andean political and cultural landscape has steadily transformed in favor of granting greater equality and social and economic justice to the Native Andean peoples.

Although indigenous uprisings have occurred in the Andean region of South America since the colonial period, the contemporary Andean indigenous movements have been instrumental in advancing many constitutional, social, and political reforms granting the native peoples greater territorial rights, access to bilingual education, and more decision-making authority over their own lives. Princeton professor Deborah Yashar remarks that the Latin American "[indigenous] movements have played a key role in discussions about land reform, land use, bicultural education, and census taking, among other issues."[2] However, the struggle for equality and civil rights is far from over. Today social exclusion and racial discrimination, a legacy from the colonial era, are still rampant in the Andes, often disguised as regionalism, pro-democracy concerns, anti-communism, economic and educational disparity, social class issues, and so forth. According to political scientist Donna Lee Van Cott, an expert on indigenous movements, "regional identities may [also] mask ethnic and racial identities that are not expressed because such identities are considered incompatible with national myths about *mestizaje* (racial mixing)."[3] Although many Andean nations have large mestizo (mixed) populations, according to Van Cott, "the intensity and depth of ethnic and racial cleavages distinguish the Andean region from other regions of Latin America.... A serious crisis of representation exists in the Andes."[4]

For centuries indigenous peoples across the Andes have been marginalized and excluded from meaningful participation in government and in the formation of policies that directly affect them. This fact was brought home to me in 2006 when I attended a conference in Washington, D.C. concerning coca policy in the Andes. Many embassy personnel, academics, and political leaders were in attendance, each discussing and sharing views on coca policy in the region. I invited a Native Andean community leader to attend the event, as the topic was one that affected his people directly in a Bolivian coca farming community. Aside from a single indigenous speaker—a recently elected female senator from Bolivia—the room had no other indigenous representation except for my friend, who made a very impassioned and eloquent comment about the sacred meaning of the coca plant to the Native Andean people and explained why they were against forced coca eradication policies. In a room full of dozens of policymakers and advisors, my friend and the indigenous senator were the lone voices speaking on behalf of the Native Andean peoples, whose daily lives were directly impacted by these policies. Curiously, my friend was also the only person in the room among dozens of Westerners whom the moderator asked to identify himself, perhaps questioning his right to be there. (Luckily, he had registered for the event in the same manner as everyone else.)

Even though this conference took place outside the Andean region, it sensitized me to the issues of lack of representation and consideration for the views of indigenous peoples, even when discussing and formulating policies that have a direct bearing on their lives. The intensity of racial divisions cuts deeply into the cultural and political fabric of the Andes; yet, despite centuries of social marginalization and overt racial discrimination, indigenous peoples are steadily gaining access to the political and social institutions that were once (and in most cases still are) bastions of elitism and conservatism.

It is important to keep in mind that in the Andes, indigenous peoples are by no means a monolithic group. The category of "Indian" (*indio*) was artificially imposed by the colonial powers, which agglomerated all native peoples into one general category without recognizing the great diversity among indigenous communities and ethnic groups, nor the historical affinity or animosity among them.[5] Moreover, the classification of "Indian," or indigenous, depends in large measure on self-identification based on census data or primary language use.[6] It is possible that many self-identified mestizos are also predominantly of indigenous descent.

For centuries the Native Andeans have been encouraged to adopt the dress, manner, education, and religion of a Europeanized society and assimilate into a mestizo culture. According to Deborah Yashar, "to avoid [racial] discrimination and to increase chances for social mobility, many (but not all) Indians appeared to follow the state's lead."[7] *Indios* are also primarily identified with the rural countryside and farming; for this reason, the term *indios* and *campesinos* ("country people" or "peasants") are often used interchangeably by many nonindigenous Andeans. Even some Native Andeans have internalized this notion. For instance, when working with Andean indigenous groups, I asked several Native Andeans whether they considered Alejandro Toledo—former president of Peru (2001–2006)—to be an Indian. Toledo had initially campaigned as an *indio* but later clarified that he considered himself a *mestizo* or *cholo*, a person of mixed Native Andean and European ancestry. My Native Andean coworkers explained, "Toledo has never planted coca, or maize, or potatoes. He is a product of Western institutions, so he is not *un indio verdadero* ('a real Indian') in our eyes."

However, as more and more Native Andean families have moved to the cities in search of work, and are engaged in many different kinds of economic activities, this description no longer fits the reality of the Indian urbanites. Because native people in the city suffer extreme discrimination, they often adopt a Western lifestyle and Western dress and encourage their children to speak only Spanish. These native migrants are often referred to as *cholos*.

In order to combat these exclusionary practices, as previously discussed, the Andean indigenous peoples joined social movement organizations, but these organizations suffered from internal racism of their own and failed to directly address cultural and land reform issues that were viewed as uniquely indigenous. Consequently, the Native Andean peoples launched their own indigenous organizations to promote their own interests in defending their languages, preserving their cultures, and conserving their territorial integrity. Today, some of these organizations wield a great deal of influence. For instance, in June 1990 Native Ecuadorians launched an unprecedented uprising or *levantamiento* spearheaded by CONAIE (*Confederación de Nacionalidades Indígenas del Ecuador,* or "Confederation of Indigenous Nations of Ecuador"), a powerful native organization with twenty-six organizational affiliates. CONAIE organized a historical revolt in which indigenous peoples banded together and took to the streets, blocking roads and the major Pan-American Highway that runs north and south, preventing trucks and food supplies from reaching the major cities, thereby effectively paralyzing the nation.[8] The Ecuadorian government had no alternative but to negotiate with the Native Andeans about the issues they wanted to address, namely, land reform, ecological concerns, bilingual education, and a new Ecuadorian constitution. Similarly, in 1997 and 2000 the Ecuadorian indigenous peoples took to the streets and successfully toppled two different presidents.

A turning point in Ecuadorian politics occurred when the Ecuadorian indigenous peoples decided to enter into the political arena and founded their own political party called *Movimiento Unidad Plurinacional Pachakutik—Nuevo País* ("Pachakutik Plurinational Unity Movement—New Country") in 1995–1996. As discussed in previous chapters, the term *pachakutik* (a variant spelling of *pachacuti*) means "the revolution, inversion, or turning around of the world." This term aptly describes what was happening in Ecuadorian politics at the time, as some Native Andeans decided that the best way to turn their world around and gain momentum for their own causes was to compete with the established, traditional parties and put forward their own candidates to run for political office. According to Ecuadorian expert Marc Becker, *Pachakutik* represented "a new political movement in which Indigenous peoples and other sectors of Ecuador's popular movements organized together as equals in a joint project to achieve common goals."[9] The new party was internally divided, so it made only modest inroads into the Ecuadorian political system; still, in 1998, having earned a fairly strong presence in the Constitutional Assembly, it pushed for a new Ecuadorian constitution, among other reforms.

Over a decade later, in 2008, a new Ecuadorian constitution was approved by public referendum. It recognized for the first time in world history the legal "rights of nature" (*derechos de la naturaleza*), identified as "nature or *Pacha Mama*"[10] (the Andean Earth Mother), making evident the influence of its indigenous communities. It also expressly prohibited racism of any kind against the native peoples and purported to give indigenous communities "an imprescriptible property [right] in their community lands, which are inalienable, not subject to seizure, and indivisible."[11] However, it was more nebulous with respect to the rights of indigenous peoples in the natural resources found on their lands.[12] Today this issue strikes at the heart of many indigenous communities, including the Ecuadorian Amazonian peoples, who are presently employing civil disobedience, mass demonstrations, court actions, and other methods in a herculean effort to prevent foreign oil companies from exploiting, destroying, and polluting their territories.[13]

Just as in Ecuador, in my own native land of Bolivia, indigenous, labor, and other social organizations employed similar tactics, such as blockades and mass demonstrations, and ousted a sitting president in October 2003. Nineteen months later, they also forced the resignation of his successor. During this tumultuous period, Bolivia narrowly averted a civil war. Tens of thousands of people, mostly Quechua, Aymara, and mestizo farmers, teachers, miners, and workers, participated in massive nationwide strikes, demonstrations, and road blockades that, according to some sources, were rapidly crippling the national economy. Their demands were many: the nationalization of the gas and oil industry, early elections to elect a new president, and the immediate formation of a Constitutional Assembly to redraft the Bolivian constitution, granting greater rights to the indigenous peoples.

In December 2005 Bolivia elected its first Native Andean president, Evo Morales Ayma. This was an unprecedented and historic moment in Bolivian history, as a Native Andean for the first time was elected to the highest leadership position in a nation where in 2001 approximately 62 percent of the population identified itself as indigenous. (In a subsequent 2012 census, conducted in a different manner, that figure dropped to 40 percent.) Morales won by an overwhelming majority, receiving more than 50 percent of the vote nationwide, and over 60 percent of the vote in predominantly indigenous departments such as La Paz, Oruro, and Cochabamba. In a boost to democracy and universal suffrage, more than two hundred international observers deemed the national election a fair and legitimate one.

Morales was an unlikely candidate for the presidency because he had openly campaigned as an *indio* ("Indian") and was of humble indigenous origin.[14] He received his higher education "in the University of Life," as he is so often quoted as saying. Prior to his election, Morales had been a *diputado* (an elected delegate, similar to a U.S. congressman) in the Chamber of Delegates, a syndicate leader who helped organize marches on behalf of coca producers (*cocaleros*), and a political activist who fought for indigenous rights and helped to win the "water war" in Cochabamba in 2000.[15]

Overseas, Andean policy experts viewed the election of Morales as a "mandate for change" in Bolivia,[16] particularly with respect to the rights of the indigenous peoples. Whereas newspapers and other media often portray Morales, who is a socialist, as a threat to democratic institutions, some political analysts regarded his election as strengthening democracy in Bolivia.[17] Sixty years ago a Native Andean could not have been elected president of Bolivia due to the extreme racism and prejudice against the indigenous peoples. Moreover, many Native Andean peoples were excluded from the voting process altogether by literacy and property requirements that, fortunately, were abolished in 1952. Yet "despite different periods of social upheaval and political polarization, Bolivia has experienced uninterrupted democratic rule since 1982."[18]

During his first term as president, Morales renationalized Bolivia's natural resources, continued to expand some of the land reform policies of his predecessors, launched a massive literacy campaign, helped create a new Bolivian Constitutional Assembly, and enacted a new Bolivian constitution that was ratified by popular referendum in February 2009. The new constitution describes Bolivia as a unified, "plurinational" and secular state, and it designates Spanish and the languages of all its indigenous nations and peoples as the official languages of the nation.[19] It also recognizes departmental and regional autonomies[20] and guarantees protection of numerous indigenous rights: the right to collective title to property; the right to a multilingual education; the preservation of indigenous cultural identity, religious beliefs, and native customs; and many others.[21] Despite a vocal and relentless opposition, primarily from groups in the wealthier eastern departments of Bolivia where most of the oil and natural gas reserves are located, Morales handily won reelection in December 2009 with more than 63 percent of the national vote, and he was elected to a another term in October 2014 with over 61 percent of the vote. A public referendum was held in February 2016 which, if approved, would have amended the Bolivian constitution to permit Morales to run for a third consecutive term (his first term was considered only partial); the measure was defeated by a 51 percent majority.

In other Andean countries, the changes have been less dramatic, but meaningful nonetheless. Peru, for example, experienced a social revolution, including land reform, from 1968 to 1975 under the leadership of Peruvian president, General Juan Velasco Alvarado. But many of these efforts were later reversed and may have created the conditions that gave rise to *El Sendero Luminoso* (the "Shining Path"), a violent Maoist guerrilla revolutionary movement that was founded in Peru in the 1960s and reached its height in the 1980s and early 90s.[22] According to economist John Sheahan, "the frustrations aggravated by the aborted effort at national transformation may well have contributed to the support the Shining Path was able to capture as it launched its murderous campaign of revolutionary violence in the 1980s."[23]

The Shining Path was an offshoot of the Communist Party of Peru and was the brainchild of a former philosophy professor named Abimael Guzmán, whose *nom de guerre* was "Presidente Gonzalo." Guzmán followed militant Maoist doctrine and his followers practiced guerrilla warfare and used killings, bombings, public executions, and other forms of violence to spark a cultural revolution and create what they called a "New Democracy." The name of the Shining Path was derived from a quote by Peruvian writer and philosopher, José Carlos Mariátegui, the founder of the Peruvian Communist Party in the 1920s. Mariátegui wrote: "*El Marxismo-Leninismo abrirá el sender luminoso hacia la revolución.*" ("Marxism-Leninism will open the shining path toward revolution.") Shining Path militants purported to follow Marxism, Leninism, Maoism, and *Pensamiento Gonzalo* ("Gonzalo Thought"). Their base of operations was the Ayacucho region of Peru in the Education Department of the San Cristóbal of Huamanga University, where Guzmán had been a professor. The group was also, according to some accounts, quite successful in recruiting women, who found greater gender, economic, and racial equality in the movement than in their own Andean society.[24]

The Shining Path took root in the Ayacucho region of Peru and rapidly gained control over a number of highland areas, where it initially gained support from the *campesinos* (countryside "peasantry"). It is worth noting that the Shining Path was not an indigenous-led movement, but rather a mestizo-led movement. Most members of the movement's Central Committee and leadership, including Guzmán, were *mistis*, the Peruvian term for privileged or educated whites or mestizos. Moreover, although the movement purported to organize indigenous peasants, "it reject[ed] demands or agendas emanating from indigenous identity," and therefore could not properly be considered an indigenous movement.[25]

Although the Shining Path initially had widespread support among the indigenous populations because it purported to be acting on behalf of the peasantry and the poor, its support dwindled as Indian communities got caught in the crossfire between the Shining Path and the Peruvian military, and were victimized by both.[26] Some native communities also learned that some of their union leaders, local politicians, and community leaders were targeted by the Shining Path for not supporting and sympathizing with the movement. At the time, the Peruvian government also granted the military plenary authority to detain persons suspected of being *senderistas* (Shining Path militants). In many instances the military used its power heavy-handedly by arresting, raping, and even torturing suspects (many indigenous), who in many cases were innocent. The Peruvian military forces and the police also carried out several massacres, causing greater conflict, turmoil, and instability in the region. Caught between the military forces and the Shining Path, many indigenous communities found themselves in a difficult no-win situation; some even formed their own militias to protect their villages. Finally, in 1992 Peruvian police captured Abimael Guzmán and a number of other Shining Path leaders. Although the Shining Path is still sporadically active, today it wields only a fraction of the influence it once had in the 1980s and early 1990s. The capture of its leadership essentially marked the collapse of the movement in Peru.

Interestingly, Peru—the birthplace of José Carlos Mariátegui, José María Arguedas, María Jesús Alvarado Rivera, and other social transformers—has not been at the vanguard of the Andean indigenous movement. That is not to say that indigenous activism does not exist in Peru—it does; however, Peruvian indigenous peoples have not organized and mobilized as effectively as those in other Andean nations, and a nationwide indigenous movement has yet to emerge in Peru.[27] Many reasons have been suggested for this disparity, including the political violence and social upheaval created by the guerrilla war in the 80s involving the military and the Shining Path; the "history of repression and organization of and by the army"[28]; the lack of political leadership among the native populations; and the misconception that "an urban Indian does not exist in Peru."[29] As these reasons are not mutually exclusive, it is possible that a confluence of factors have inhibited the emergence of a Peruvian indigenous movement.

Elsewhere in the Andes, indigenous peoples are also protesting and mobilizing to protect their rights. In Colombia the armed conflicts among the military, paramilitary, narcotraffickers, and leftist guerrillas have displaced many indigenous communities from their homes. Although the government of Colombia "only acknowledges 2.6 million internally displaced refugees in Colombia...human rights organizations claim that there are over 4 million."[30] The native peoples have also been the victims of countless human rights abuses and massacres, perpetrated by armed forces from both the left and the right.[31] According to the National Indigenous Organization of Colombia, over twelve hundred indigenous Colombians were murdered in the countryside from 2002 to 2008.[32] The violence against the indigenous peoples of Colombia is so widespread that observers from the United Nations have raised the specter of "genocide and ethnocide" of the native peoples.[33]

In some areas thousands of native Colombians are marching for greater territorial autonomy and self-determination, the right to learn and use indigenous languages in school, and an end to the violence against their communities and leaders.[34] In spite of the bloodshed in the countryside, some progress has been made. For instance, in the 70s and 80s the Colombian legislature granted the indigenous peoples "collective and inalienable indigenous titles to land,"[35] and there are now several hundred indigenous reservations (*resguardos*) operating in Colombia. In the early 90s, the indigenous communities also reached an agreement with the Colombian government granting them greater rights of self-determination. Consequently, the Colombian Constitution of 1991 establishes that indigenous territories will be "self-governing autonomous entities, authorized to devise, implement, and administer internal social, economic and political policies in accordance with indigenous customary law."[36]

Nevertheless, a recent report from Professor James Anaya, former special rapporteur of the United Nations on the situation of human rights and fundamental freedoms of the indigenous peoples, is troubling. According to Professor Anaya, "despite the significant level of attention [given] from the State of Colombia to indigenous issues," there exists in Colombia "an extremely worrying situation of violence and other crimes against indigenous people, as well as forced displacement and confinement, which threatens the physical and cultural survival of [the] indigenous people of the country."[37] For this reason, the special rapporteur recommended that "a Special Adviser for the Prevention of Genocide be watchful of the situation in that country."[38]

The special rapporteur of the United Nations also criticized the mistreatment of the Mapuche people of Chile.[39] Just as many other indigenous groups in South America, the Mapuches are fighting political, economic, and social exclusion, and they are intent on preserving their territorial integrity, their language known as Mapudungun (meaning "Language of the Land"), and their cultural traditions. In recent years, violence has escalated among some Mapuche communities. According to news reports, in December 2009 Mapuche activists, claiming their lands had been illegally seized for forestry operations, "engaged in a wave of arson attacks. Their assaults—torching forests, hijacking forestry trucks, seizing rural ranches... created Chile's worst security crisis in decades."[40] In response, the Chilean government reactivated a controversial antiterrorism law that had been developed during the dictatorship of former president Augusto

Pinochet to prosecute the Mapuches.[41] The antiterrorism law accords the accused few due process rights, allows for extended prison terms, broadens the enforcement powers of the police and the judiciary, and permits accusations "by anonymous and masked witnesses."[42] Richard Caifal, a Chilean human rights lawyer, remarked, "This law is an abomination…and the government is using it in a discriminating way, only against Mapuches."[43]

Since implementation of the law, the Chilean national police have been accused of countless acts of brutality, even against children.[44] Professor Anaya, the U.N. special rapporteur, recognized that the issue of the Mapuche has "historical roots and structural dimensions," and he called on the government of Chile to pay special attention to the human rights violations committed against Mapuche children in its southern territories.[45] Anaya commented that "children deserve special protection, and the [Chilean] State should be very cautious."[46]

The recent developments in Chile, Bolivia, Ecuador, Colombia, and Peru underscore the deeply entrenched racial issues that characterize and divide most Andean nations, and their concomitant social, economic, and political consequences. Yet they also demonstrate the growing power of the Andean indigenous movements that are galvanizing reforms in the region, and in the language of *pachacuti*, creating an "inversion" of the established order. These social protest themes are also communicated, expressly or symbolically, in some Andean stories, many of which criticize the unfair treatment of the native peoples and the power of Western institutions over their lives. In the following sections, we will discuss the historical roots of racism in the Andes and then proceed to analyze some contemporary Andean folktales embodying and exhibiting social protest themes.

COLONIAL INSTITUTIONS
AND HISTORICAL RACISM IN THE ANDES

Racism is not new to the Andes. The colonial Spaniards developed a very complex system of socio-racial nomenclature, often termed *sociedad de castas* ("society of castes"), with many regional variants, but which in all cases placed the Spaniards and their Andean-born children at the top of the social ladder and Indians and blacks at the very bottom.[47] During the colonial period, the Spaniards demonstrated great contempt for the Native Andean peoples and exploited their labor. The native peoples were considered savage, barbaric, inferior, and even expendable. The Native Andeans were forced to work in the mines, for little or no pay, and also on the Spanish *encomiendas* (landed estates; the term literally means "entrustments"). Although the *encomenderos* (landowners) were obliged to Christianize and protect "their Indians" in exchange for exacting tribute and labor from them, these obligations were seldom enforced.[48] The native peoples were also uprooted and displaced for the purposes of facilitating evangelization and providing physical labor in a draft system known as *repartimiento* ("distribution"). The system of *repartimiento* assured that Native laborers were always available to work in the mines and other labor-intensive projects. According to some historians, in the most infamous draft of the mid-1570s, about 16 percent of all indigenous men in the towns situated between Cuzco, Peru, and Potosí in present-day Bolivia were transplanted to work in the mines.[49] Moreover, the conditions in the mines were inhumane.

> Forced to work without rest, the Indians died of exhaustion inside the [mine] tunnels, without ever seeing the light of day. Some mine veins were only accessible by children, whom they obligated to slip through the cracks between the rocks. Sometimes parents preferred to maim the legs of their newborns so that being lame or crippled, their children would be exempt from mandatory labor.[50]

Although it is difficult to prove causation, there is little doubt that the physical exploitation and psychological demoralization the Native Andean peoples endured during the Spanish colonial period also contributed to the demographic disaster of the indigenous peoples in this region of the Americas.[51]

Today, in terms of race relations, the Andean region still suffers from the psychological effects of the Spanish Conquest and the Spanish colonial period. Even though laws in many Native Andean countries expressly prohibit discrimination and racism against Native Andeans, these laws are seldom enforced socially, legally, or politically, because their enforcement is dependent on magistrates, politicians, and judges who are overwhelmingly from the ruling white and mestizo social classes. These classes enjoy the greater share of economic wealth, power, education, and opportunity in the Andes. Native Andeans are openly discriminated against and relegated to the lowest stratum of the Andean social structure. The result is that the Native Andean peoples have been marginalized for nearly five hundred years and have been denied equal access and full participation in the social, political, and economic institutions of the Andean nations. As previously discussed, this has generated political mobilization and unrest among the Native Andean peoples, who are intent on reversing this historical legacy and obtaining parity with nonindigenous Andeans.

One of the effects of racism and marginalization is that Native Andeans comprise a great majority of the Andean people living in poverty. Based on a 1995 report on poverty in South America funded by an agency of the Swedish government, 11 percent of Bolivians, 16 percent of Peruvians, 20 percent of Ecuadorians, and 11 percent of Colombians live in *extreme* poverty, on less than one U.S. dollar per day.[52] Moreover, of those living in poverty in Peru and Bolivia, Native Andeans comprise 79 percent and 64 percent, respectively.[53] The report also observes that "material deprivation tends to be accompanied by lack of power and voice in society, as expressed in low social status and exposure to neglect or bad treatment by institutions of the state as well as civil society."[54] In other words, marginalization and poverty are intimately related.

Although the tide is gradually turning in the Andean region with the growing influence of indigenous movements, the Native Andean peoples, marginalized and poor, have historically had little or no voice in the affairs of their nations and societies. It is no wonder, then, that they have found other means of expressing their discontent, their opposition, their struggle, and their pain. Although "resistance has assumed multiple forms[,] ... everyday forms of resistance [are] embedded in dances, stories, and rituals that are an integral part of indigenous communities."[55] Along with other modes of expression, storytelling in the Andes has evolved into a socially acceptable mechanism for criticizing the institutions, groups, beliefs, and practices associated with the dominant culture and a means of extolling the virtues of indigenous culture. Some of these stories also plant the seeds of political protest, mobilization, and rebellion, although this call for action is often disguised in symbolic imagery. In the following tales, the Native Andean *cuentistas* ("storytellers") overtly or implicitly criticize the Andean social structure, foreigners, the Catholic Church, and other elements of Western society that they identify with the dominant white and mestizo culture. Collectively, these tales may be designated as stories of social protest.

THE POWER OF THE DOMINANT CULTURE

As previously discussed, a paramount issue facing the Andean nations today is the systematic racism and discrimination waged against the native peoples (and Afro-Andeans), which gives rise to many other corollary issues such as poverty, unemployment, political/social/economic marginalization, and so forth, all of which, from my perspective, are symptomatic of this much broader issue. The issue of racial discrimination in the Andean social hierarchy is also addressed in the Native Andean oral tradition. Many Andean stories allude to the power of whites and mestizos over the Native Andeans and the control they exert over their lives. The Legend of the Deer is one such story. Although on the surface the story appears to communicate a moral lesson about the virtue of generosity, on a more recondite level it criticizes the asymmetrical power structure and racial stratification that characterize Andean society.

The Legend of the Deer

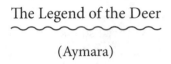

(Aymara)

There were two brothers in a family: one was a shepherd and the other was a farmer.

One day, the younger brother was grazing his sheep on a mountain far away from home. A man came over and introduced himself. He was also an Indian, of very poor and humble appearance. The man asked if he could stay and chat with him for a while, and the shepherd accepted. Since the shepherd agreed, the man sat down next to him. The shepherd shared his lunch with the stranger, offering it with courtesy and expecting nothing in return. After the meal and the conversation were done, the stranger said, "I have also brought something to eat." He took from his pocket a handful of white maize, and another of yellow maize, and handed it to the shepherd. The shepherd made a bundle to put it in and saved it for the evening.

When the shepherd came home that evening, he sat with his family next to the firebox. He opened his bundle and discovered, much to his surprise, that the grains of white and yellow maize the stranger had given him had turned into kernels of silver and gold!

After witnessing such a miracle, the brother farmer got up the next morning, and while his brother was still asleep, he put on his shepherd brother's clothes and set out very early to graze the sheep. He arrived at the mountain at the usual time, and a misti [an upper class white or mestizo] appeared and introduced himself. Just as had occurred with his brother, the stranger asked the brother farmer to share his food and his company. But the alleged shepherd turned him down and pushed him aside, because he was expecting to encounter a humble, poor man, just as his brother had described.

Witnessing such bad behavior, the misti cursed him and told him he would grow a head full of antlers and that his wife would throw him out of the house. He also said his own children and parents would fail to recognize him. When the brother farmer returned home that evening, everything came to pass just as the man had predicted. Since then, the farmer roams about the plains and the mountains in the form of a deer.[56]

~~

It is clear that this legend espouses certain moral values that are important to the indigenous communities: generosity and kindness, for example, as exhibited by the shepherd toward the humble Indian stranger, as opposed to the greed and selfishness demonstrated by his farmer brother upon encountering the *misti*. In the spirit of generosity, the shepherd is courteous to the stranger and shares his food and company willingly. He also reaps an unexpected reward for his generosity—the white and yellow grains of maize given to him magically turn into silver and gold kernels. In short, the shepherd's charitable and unselfish spirit is unwittingly rewarded with material wealth.

Generosity and kindness are universal virtues that also coincide with the communal values of many Native Andean peoples. Due to long-standing communal traditions and the hardships of daily life, especially in the countryside, Native Andeans tend to emphasize cooperation over competition, generosity over selfishness, and the welfare and gain of the community over the welfare and gain of the individual. Hence, in every respect, the opportunistic behavior of the farmer brother and his selfish and material pursuits are at odds with traditional Native Andean values. So on its face, the legend appears to be an allegory extolling the virtues of kindness and generosity.

However, if we look more closely, this story communicates other essential lessons concerning the reality of the Native Andean people in the Andean social structure, where they are controlled and overpowered by the dominant white and mestizo culture. Let us break down this story into its basic elements and examine it more carefully.

In the first instance, the stranger who appears to the shepherd is a poor Indian. By contrast, the stranger who appears to the farmer brother is a *misti*, a term that often refers to an upper class white or mestizo in Andean culture. The shepherd is courteous and generous with the Indian, whereas the farmer brother behaves rudely and selfishly toward the misti. The Indian shepherd is rewarded by the Indian stranger, who turns the shepherd into a wealthy man; the Indian farmer is punished (cursed) by the misti, who transforms the farmer into a four-legged animal, a deer.

This begs the question: Why did the misti transform the farmer into a deer? Because the farmer would not share his food and his company ("The stranger [had] asked the brother farmer to share his food and his company. But the alleged shepherd turned him down and pushed him aside"). So not only was the Indian farmer selfish, he was also assertive and uncooperative, unlike his more humble and servile brother.

But what would have happened if the shepherd had encountered the white or mestizo stranger in the same manner as his farmer brother? Would he also have been as courteous and generous? Would he also have shared his food and company? Most of us would probably answer "yes," because the farmer's behavior would, in all likelihood, be consistent with that of a giving person. Most of us assume that an authentically generous person would be generous with everyone, not just with a select few.

On the other hand, the Indian farmer in the tale is more selective. The story leads us to believe that had he met up with a humble Indian, just as his shepherd brother had described, he would also have been courteous and generous, albeit for selfish reasons. This is insinuated in the second part of the passage: "But the alleged shepherd turned him down and pushed him aside, because he was expecting a humble and poor man just as his brother had described." Instead, the brother farmer encounters a white or mestizo man and decides he does not wish to be generous. He decides *not to cooperate*, and, in fact, is openly defiant. And what happens to the uncooperative and defiant Indian? He is cursed and treated with disdain, and transformed into a four-legged animal!

This intimates that severe punishment awaits the Indian who does not cooperate and serve the dominant white or mestizo man. It also alludes to the great, even supernatural power that the misti has to determine the fate of the Indian. If the Indian is defiant and uncooperative, the misti can relegate him to a status of a lower animal. Metaphorically, the misti can transform him into a wild beast, a nonhuman entity. Even worse, the curse of the misti extends further—he can have the defiant Indian "throw[n] out of [his] house" and made practically "unrecognizable" to his wife, parents, and children. The Indian will be forced to roam about, without a home, in the wilderness of life—a very scary prospect, which according to the story, would inevitably "come to pass."

Had this simply been a story lauding the virtues of kindness and generosity, the Andean storyteller would have had no need to introduce the character of the misti. The farmer brother could just as easily have been punished by another humble Indian, the same Indian, or even by a wealthy but offended Indian. However, the Andean narrator intends, consciously or not, to introduce the element of race into this story to communicate additional and perhaps more subtle lessons readily recognized by Native Andean listeners. Thus, although on one hand The Legend of the Deer is indeed a didactic and morally instructive story, it is also a story of social protest challenging the inequities of Andean society. It recognizes the social inequality between whites or mestizos and Native Andeans, and it draws attention to the overwhelming—almost supernatural—power exerted by the mistis and the dominant culture over the fate of the Native Andeans. Although the issue is complex, this disparity is, in whole or in part, the result of almost five centuries of racial oppression and exclusion in the Andes, which in response has spawned powerful yet disguised stories of social protest. The Legend of the Deer is but one such story; there are countless others.

In keeping with the social protest theme, we will now examine another body of myths regarding "supernatural" foreigners, often depicted as *gringos*, which criticizes the power and influence of Western strangers over the Native Andean communities. In the following section we will discuss the "gringo menace" who appears in many forms and disguises in contemporary Andean folktales. Typically in these stories the gringo threatens the livelihood and very existence of the Indian.

The Gringo Menace

There are numerous stories in the Andes about a character generically described as a *gringo* who, much like the *pishtaco* described in previous chapters, is a white foreign intruder who threatens to buy, steal, devour, victimize, or destroy people, animals, or things that are valuable to the Native Andeans. Although gringo is a term often used in the Andes to denote a person, even an Andean, who is blond or fair-skinned (my mother had a blond cousin whom relatives affectionately called "El Gringo"), in this case gringo is used as a derogatory term to mean a light-skinned foreigner who fits the Native Andean stereotype of a North American or European. In some cases the gringo appears to be something other than human, endowed with animal-like and predatory characteristics; in other cases he is simply human, driven by greed, ignorance, and arrogance.

I have included the gringo tales among the stories of social protest because of the social and cultural criticisms they express, directly or indirectly. From a close observation of the gringo's stereotypic conduct in these stories, it is clear the Native Andean storytellers are commenting on what would be considered unacceptable behavior in Native Andean society. Moreover, the contrast between the gringo's comportment and that of the Native Andean characters in these tales reveals valuable information to the reader about what Native Andeans consider contrasting Western and indigenous values.

In particular, these stories speak to the Native Andean's intimate relationship with and respect for nature, and the "horizontal" view of her role and place in nature, in contrast to the gringo's (Western) "vertical" view of man's dominion and control *over* nature. Furthermore, the Native Andean criticizes the gringo's ignorance about the workings of nature and his blatant disregard for the destruction of animals, plants, and the natural environment. Moreover, the Native Andean criticizes the gringo's insatiable appetite for buying things and indiscriminate use of money to try to purchase what is most precious to the Native Andean. Finally, these tales touch on the Native Andean's deepest fear about the "predatory" activity of the gringo: that through his actions, power, and influence, the gringo will destroy the traditional lifestyle to which the Native Andean is accustomed, a mode of life that was bequeathed and handed down to her from her pre-Columbian ancestors.

We will begin our analysis of this type of tale with the well-known legend of *Atoqhuarco*, which means "Hanging Fox" in the Quechua language.

Atoqhuarco (Hanging Fox)

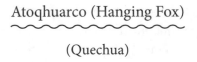

(Quechua)

Atoqhuarco is a very dangerous place, where the road bends twice as one enters and leaves the wooden bridge extending over the river. This is a foretaste of the dangerous Huallaga River, with its large and tumultuous flow, which runs between extremely high and jagged rocks. If the traveler looks up at the rocks, he will see in the highest part of the cliffs the figure of a petrified fox hanging by its neck, as if an amazing sculptor had carved it out of the hard rock.

If you ask about the origin of this figure, they will tell you this story.

One day, a being arrived at a village of shepherds. He was foreign, white-skinned, blond, large—a Gringo. No one knew where he came from, but they did know he spent his time robbing chickens and the most tender lambs to feed himself. He lived in a nearby cave and spread terror among the villagers, who called him Atoq, meaning fox.

Among all the young shepherdesses, the most beautiful was Mariacha. She was young, joyful, and pretty. She was also the one who was most frightened by the Atoq, who chased after the village girls.

One afternoon, when Mariacha was returning from shepherding her flock, at a moment when she least expected it, she bumped into the Gringo on a very narrow mountain path. Full of fear, she began to run every which way, on no apparent course. Seeing that the Gringo was following her, she strayed from the road and reached the edge of a cliff. She looked back and saw the sweaty Atoq, whose features were contorted from exertion. He was pleased to see that his prey was cornered. He delighted in this, for there was no escape. She would fall right into his hands.

Without a thought, the shepherdess let out a loud scream that the villagers confused with the howling of the wind. At the precise moment the Gringo was about to grab her, she let herself drop into the abyss. The Gringo also lost his balance and slid toward the edge of the cliff. He fell off the cliff and got stuck, hanging by his neck from some bramble bushes growing there.

As time went by, the Gringo could feel he was transforming into a fox whose body was gradually changing into stone. Meanwhile, multicolored garments floated in the river below, belonging to Mariacha, the most beautiful young woman among the shepherdesses of the village.[57]

~~~

It is interesting to observe in this story that the gringo is described not as a person, but as a "being," which in many Native Andean stories is a term usually reserved for supernatural beings, such as *huacas* (spirits or "animas" of nature) or *malignos* (malevolent spirits), among others. In other words, the foreigner is an It, not a He, creating the illusion that the character is not a member of this world, or at least not of the Andean world, the *Kay Pacha* (Quechua) or *Aca Pacha* (Aymara). The term gringo is also used interchangeably with *atoq* (Quechua for "fox") throughout the story, implying that the fox and the gringo have the same identity.

The narrator also tells us that the gringo has a penchant for chickens, which he robs from the local villagers, much like a fox, and also for "the most tender lambs," perhaps like a larger predator. Although, arguably, human beings also consume smaller animals, a being that spends most of "his time robbing [animals] . . . in order to feed himself" is displaying behavior characteristic of a predatory animal. Thus, the *atoq-gringo* may be characterized as an animal-like predator, whose feeding habits resemble those of lower animals. Final confirmation of this similarity comes at the end of the story when the gringo is transformed into a petrified fox, hanging by its neck from the bramble bushes.

The site of the gringo's dwelling is also revealing. The story informs that the gringo "lived in a nearby cave," presumably away from the village community. Mountain caves, as described in a previous chapter, are sometimes considered entrances or portals to the supernatural world,[58] and they are also often associated with the underworld (the World Below, or the Interior World). Thus, the gringo could be said to live on the edge of This World and the supernatural world, or between This World and the Interior World. Consequently, he cannot be human, because he is a being who lives in between worlds.

Additionally, the atoq-gringo in this story is not content with stealing animals to feed himself; he is also intent on capturing the native women, although it is not clear whether he intends to eat them or have sexual relations with them. The story informs that the atoq-gringo pursues the village women, since the beautiful Mariacha is described as the shepherdess "who was most frightened by the Atoq who chased after the village girls." However, when Mariacha is cornered, she does not submit to her pursuer. Rather than become prey to the atoq-gringo, Mariacha chooses to throw herself over the cliff and end her life instead. It is clear from the text that this is a volitional act, for the woman "let herself drop into the abyss." Like a warrior who chooses suicide instead of capture or death by the enemy, Mariacha, in an act demonstrating personal power and courage, chooses to end her own life instead of letting herself be victimized by the white-skinned predator.

Unfortunately, Native Andean women know too well what it means to submit to the white-skinned predator. The colonial indigenous chronicler Felipe Guaman Poma de Ayala vividly describes how Spanish conquistadors, landowners, administrative officials, bureaucrats, and even clergymen raped and enslaved Native women during the colonial period.[59] In some of the most egregious cases, parish priests would impregnate their female servants and then refuse to grant them absolution from their "sins" through the sacrament of confession.[60] In other instances, native women, many of whom had already converted to Christianity, were told by the predator priests and friars that they were already living "in sin" as their concubines, and were therefore not free to leave or receive any remuneration for their services.[61] Thus, the victimization of Native Andean women during the Spanish colonial period was both physical and psychological.

After the colonial period, the *hacendados* (owners of landed estates, called *haciendas*) often took advantage of their Native Andean servants, and women working on their lands, much like some white plantation owners in the North American South took advantage of their black female slaves. Of these unions, a significant number of mestizos were born, many of whom were never recognized as the children of the *patrones* (the masters of the *hacienda*). The fate of these children was often determined by the shade of their skin. The lighter-skinned children (often female) were sometimes sent to live and work in a different locality, where they might escape the probing eyes of those who recognized them as the patrones' children; the darker-skinned children remained on the hacienda to work alongside their native mothers and "adopted" native fathers and siblings.

White missionaries and priests also fathered many children. In an indigenous community near my hometown of Cochabamba, one priest alone had fathered so many children with local Native Andean women that all of his children were humorously known by the last name of "Alleluia." There are many anecdotes of this kind among the Native Andean communities in virtually all regions of the Andes, a testament to the pervasiveness and authenticity of this experience among Native Andean women.

This is but one of the fears that fuels the stereotype of the white atoq-gringo alluded to in this story. However, there are others.

Today, there are many concerns among the indigenous communities that whites and foreigners are robbing them of their livelihood and natural resources. This is exemplified in the story by the atoq-gringo "robbing" the villagers of their chickens and most tender lambs, and also going after the native women. The stereotypical notion is that once the gringo sets his eyes on something he wants (usually belonging to the native peoples), he doesn't stop until he gets it. Andean stories also sometimes humorously describe how the gringo inevitably gets what he wants and then, ironically, doesn't know what to do with it once he gets it. Yet another stereotype is that the gringo wants everything in large quantities (e.g., food, drink, or material possessions) and has trouble setting limits on his covetous impulses. The aphorism popularized by Mae West on the silver screen—"Too much of a good thing can be wonderful"—is often playfully refuted in many Andean stories. The following comical tales poignantly illustrate these points.

The Gringo and the Little Goats

(Quichua)

They tell that a Gringo was walking along the slopes of Mount Chimborazo. He was looking for turtledoves [and] animals big and small.

When the Gringo was walking through those parts, he saw in the distance a woman who was milking a goat at the bottom of a cliff.

From the edge of the cliff, he shouted, "Miss! Sell me a glass of milk!" Without hesitating, the young woman immediately sold him a glass of milk.

After drinking the milk, the Gringo said to the girl, "This milk is delicious! Sell me this little goat!"

The young woman responded, "I can't. She's the only female goat I have." But the Gringo insisted, "Miss, sell me this little goat."

Faced with his insistent demands, the young woman finally said, "I have a male goat, but I don't have a female goat to sell." The Gringo responded to her, "It doesn't matter!" And he bought the little goat for a lot of money; that is to say, for millions.

So even though the young woman warned him she only had male goats, that didn't seem to matter much to the Gringo.

The Gringo took the little goat from Chimborazo to Quito. He even transported it by plane. Then he took it from Quito to the United States.

Once in the United States, the Gringo, excited, tried to milk the little goat. He grabbed it by the testicles and said, "Raise it, you fool. Raise it, you fool." But nothing happened.

The disillusioned Gringo returned to Chimborazo from the United States to return the little goat to the young woman. In the midst of all these comings and goings he thought to himself, "I can't get any milk from this little goat! Even worse, his testicles almost broke off. I wonder why no milk comes out?"

The Gringo arrived at the house of the young woman who had sold him the little goat, hoping that if he gave her back the goat, she would return his money. But the young woman didn't want the little goat back, nor did she want to return the money the Gringo had given her. And she added, "Ha! You yourself bought it from me. I didn't want to sell it. You insisted that I sell it to you! We Indians say things once, and that's it." And she didn't give him back the money.

In view of this response, the Gringo marched off very angrily and headed toward a man who was standing at the foot of a ladder. He immediately told the man everything that had happened.

The man said to him, "Why didn't you come here before? I have lots of female goats here."

The Gringo instantly took a little goat. He pulled it by its udder and left it dead on the spot.[62]

What the Gringo Ate

(Quechua)

They say that a Gringo arrived on horseback. A lady was selling fried breaded frogs' legs, very well prepared. The Gringo ate two or three platefuls until he was stuffed. "How delicious, Ma'am!" he exclaimed. The Gringo ate really well! After he was done, he rode off on his horse.

Along the way, he saw a whole bunch of toads piled up by the river. The Gringo gathered them up until he filled his saddlebag. Then the Gringo arrived at the house where he was lodging.

He lit his little [kerosene] stove and coated the toads with flour. Then he fried them and ate the meat. But later that night, after eating them, he became gravely ill. The Gringo was really sick. When he was on the verge of death, he called for the landlady, the owner of the place where he was lodging. "Ma'am, I'm leaving!" he called out.

The landlady said to herself, "Ah, who cares if he goes! So long as he pays me. He's crazy if he thinks I'm getting out of bed. So be it. Let him leave!"

Again, he called for her, "Ma'am, I'm leaving!"

"Jeez! What am I supposed to do? I don't care if he doesn't pay me."

He called out to her one final time. It was the third time he had called for her. "Ma'am, I'm leaving!"

"Well then, just go!" shouted the landlady.

In the morning, the landlady got up. And when she got up, she saw that the Gringo's horse was still there. It turns out the Gringo was dead.

The landlady got to keep all of the Gringo's money. She even kept his horse, and there wasn't anyone to complain for the Gringo.[63]

It is hard to miss the irony and wit in these entertaining stories: the incongruity between what the gringo wants and what he ultimately gets; the gringo's ignorance of the process and functioning of the natural world, even though he clearly understands the power and workings of money. There is also an implication that the gringo knows no bounds; if he sees (or tastes) something he desires, he covets *all* of it at once and doesn't consider the consequences.

The Andean storytellers also perceive and express in an ingeniously humorous manner one of their darkest and deepest fears: that the white-skinned foreigner will make every attempt to *buy* what the Indian has—be it animals, land, or other natural resources—and that he will inevitably misuse it or abuse it because of his ignorance. This proposition is emphasized most vehemently at the end of The Gringo and the Little Goats when the gringo finally gets the female goat he wants, and then "pull[s] it by its udder and [leaves] it dead on the spot."

From a Native Andean perspective, what one "has" is much more than what one owns. Although contemporary Native Andeans clearly understand entrepreneurship and economic capitalism (*BloombergBusiness* recently featured an article on Bolivia's "new psychedelic mansions" in El Alto, an indigenous city), the concepts of individual ownership and personal property were notions first introduced in the Andes by the individualistic and gold-seeking Spanish conquistadors. Prior to the arrival of the Spaniards, the Inca state had a centralized economy based on collective labor and the collection of tribute. The state also regulated the distribution of all products. At the heart of its economy were the local *ayllus*, or communities, that specialized in producing different crops and goods that were collected and turned over to the state, which later redistributed them to other regions. Any surpluses were stored for future use and were available to the people in times of need.

The Native Andeans of today, especially in the countryside, still embrace the notion of *ayllu* and share a much broader and perhaps more egalitarian notion of property and possession than their Western counterparts. For example, recently an ancient Andean *khipu*—a pre-Columbian recording device used in the Andes, composed of knotted strings and colored cords—was returned to a small Bolivian Quechua community because the community successfully alleged that the individual who sold the item to a European collector was not the rightful "owner" of such property, which belonged to the community as a whole. Moreover, with respect to land, in many *ayllus*, the land is worked in common by a designated task group, composed of some or all members of the community; thus, in theory, *all* such members could probably lay claim to these communal lands and the crops and fruits they produce.

Perhaps it is for this reason that our Western notions of individualism and competition do not appeal to many rural Native Andeans, who value their collective identity far more than their individual identities, and extol the virtues of cooperation over competition. From their perspective, the welfare of the community in the aggregate far outweighs the well-being and success of any single individual. The rural Native Andeans also share an intimate, cooperative, and personal connection with nature, which they perceive as animate and life-giving. Moreover, nature does not favor one person over another, but rather shares equally and judiciously with all. Ricardo Sánchez, an Andean practitioner and teacher of the ancient Inca traditions, eloquently describes this notion in one of his writings.

> *Tayta Inti* or Father Sun shines equally on all of us. He doesn't discrim-inate among us and he doesn't fail us for a single day. He doesn't judge anyone. He is the unrivalled example of equality and liberty. Giver of life and energy, of universal and unconditional love, we stopped worshipping Him from the moment our attention was diverted to the Western God and to the other god called money.
>
> The ancestral knowledge is within the reach of everyone at every moment. The word "ancestor," in indigenous terms, does not mean solely human relatives, but also the great community—*Ayllu* of all creation in the eternal present (or the *Taytas* and *Mamas* of all the ages). We can learn from the role fulfilled by the birds, the harmony of the sun, the water, the wind, the land, worms, and insects in the life cycle of the maize, etc. This is how our Inka ancestors obtained the wisdom to guide their society, whilst maintaining an optimal equilibrium with nature.[64]

Living in the Andes, one is also witness to the strong emotional bonds forged between Native Andeans of the countryside and the animals and land that sustain them. A typical postcard or photograph from the Andean region often depicts the taciturn figure of a Native Andean followed by his or her llama herd against the silent and scenic backdrop of colossal, snow-capped mountains. The Native Andean treats the llama more as a friend than an animal. The llama is a faithful and constant companion; it is a dutiful servant, who hauls goods to market and back home again, always willing to lend a helping hand. The llama freely and generously gives of its fine wool for spinning and weaving clothing. Sometimes it even gives up its life to provide meat for the family or to serve as a sacrificial offering in important Andean rituals designed to secure the welfare of its human family and the larger *ayllu*, or human community. Legend has it that llamas were born from high mountain lakes or lagoons, or that they originated as stars that fell to earth from the heavens. As in colonial times, many Native Andeans also believe that each animal on earth has a patron star that guards over each member of its species.[65]

It is important to remember that in practically all Native Andean belief systems, the divinized Earth Mother, *Pacha Mama*, is considered a living, sentient, and knowing being. It is difficult to describe in Western terms the depth of the relationship between Native Andeans and their Mother, and the selfless devotion with which they care for the "offspring" (crops) of Mother Earth. The profound reverence, veneration, and respect the Native Andeans bestow upon the land also extend to other gifts of the land, including natural resources.

Aside from economic considerations, it is this extreme devotion and ardent desire to preserve the sanctity and integrity of the living earth and its many natural gifts that is at the root of the Native Andeans' grievances about paying for natural resources, such as water, and exporting natural products, such as gas, minerals, petroleum, and other natural resources to foreign lands and permitting foreigners (gringos) to "buy" them. Many Native Andeans characterize exports to foreign nations, such as gas, minerals, and petroleum, as "plunder" (*saqueo*) of their natural resources. Although the conflict is seldom depicted as a clash between different perspectives, Western and indigenous, these divergent worldviews are often contraposed in Native Andean stories.

These differences are also accentuated in stories, such as Atoqhuarco and The Gringo and the Little Goats, in which predatory forces are depicted as either robbing the Native Andeans of what is most precious to them or using the influence of money to obtain what, from an indigenous perspective, rightfully belongs to the Andean peoples. Both stories also express the fear that the white man will abuse or destroy those things that are of value to the indigenous peoples. One could even say that these white, predatory forces are not limited to the foreign interests of the gringos, as depicted in these stories, but also include the white, Westernized institutions that today control and dominate Native Andean life and often work in conjunction with foreign powers.

One such example is the U.S.-backed coca eradication policy carried out by Andean governments, working in collaboration with U.S. drug enforcement agencies. As previously discussed, this policy has failed to take into account Native Andean customs, traditions, and beliefs. The coca plant has been cultivated in the Andes for centuries and is used for chewing (in a manner similar to tobacco), brewing *mate de coca* (coca tea), and medicinal purposes such as treating stomach and intestinal afflictions and *soroche* ("high-altitude sickness"). According to Native Andean legend, the coca plant was given to the Native Andean peoples by the Sun god *Inti* as a lenitive for their pain and suffering during the Spanish Conquest, and as a means of warding off hunger, cold, and fatigue.[66] In the Andes coca leaves have a strong religious significance. They are used in ritual offerings for *Pacha Mama*, the mountain deities, and other *huacas*; in divination ceremonies performed by Native Andean healers and diviners, known as *yatiris* and *paqos*; in fasting and other forms of religious observance; as a ritual incense; and in burial ceremonies for the dead.

Eradication of the coca fields will not extirpate these indigenous beliefs that have survived the brutal Spanish Extirpation of Idolatries, and which are deeply rooted in pre-Columbian indigenous belief systems and cosmologies that predate the arrival of the Europeans by thousands of years. Whereas in the United States eradicating vineyards of grapes that might be used to make wine for Christian religious ceremonies would undoubtedly create a fundamental rights issue, the Native Andean rights have largely been ignored in the formulation of these U.S.-backed policies in the Andean nations. This is one example of the *atoq-gringo* policies to which the Native Andean stories might be referring. Thus, one possible interpretation is that the *atoq-gringo* of Native Andean stories represents the various white, Western, foreign, and/or domestic elements (the "It") that are robbing the Native Andeans of those things most precious to them and that threaten to alter the natural balance of their lives: the land on which they plant crops and raise animals; the resources (plant, animal, and mineral) that sustain their livelihoods; and the belief systems, languages, and values that constitute their ways of life.

Like Mariacha, the young shepherdess in the story of Atoqhuarco, the Native Andeans also find that their children are being victimized by the atoq-gringo, who is stealthily impinging upon their young lives. For example, more and more Native Andean children are refusing to speak their native languages and are adopting the language of the dominant culture, which is Spanish. (In my personal experience, many city-dwelling Native Andeans do not even admit to speaking an indigenous language for fear of racial discrimination.) In school native children learn, for the most part, about European and colonial history; the formidable accomplishments of their pre-Columbian ancestors are often overlooked or ignored. Some Native Andean children keep their animistic religious traditions secret, because the Catholic Church has deemed such practices pagan and bar-baric. Young Native Andeans have also taken to wearing Western clothing, such as t-shirts and blue jeans, instead of their traditional indigenous clothing. They are using computers, playing video games, and watching Western TV shows, all of which exalt the "foreign," the "white[-skinned]," the "large," and the "blond" stereotypically embodied by the atoq-gringo.

Curiously, the word *huarco* (also spelled *warkhu*), which derives from the Quechua word *warkhuy*, meaning "to hang," is also very close in pronunciation to the Quechua word *warku*, which means "peso" or "coin."[67] Thus another possibly disguised translation of *Atoqhuarco* might be "Money-Fox," which also coincides with the stereotype of the atoq-gringo, who robs from the Native Andeans "in order to feed himself" (possibly with money), and the gringo in the Little Goats story who throws his money around, believing this will get him whatever he wants. This might also be an accidental or intentional allusion in the story to a satiric illustration in the colonial chronicle of Felipe Guaman Poma de Ayala. In the drawing, the artist-chronicler depicts an Inca man sitting across from a greedy Spanish conquistador who, presumably, is asking for more gold. "Do you eat this gold?" the Inca asks in Quechua. The conquistador replies, "Yes, we eat gold."[68] Hence, the greedy conquistador is portrayed as the consummate atoq-gringo.

It is important to note that in both stories the Native Andeans do not succumb to the white gringo. In the first story, the beautiful Mariacha chooses to die instead of falling prey to the atoq-gringo. Even in the face of death, the shepherdess recognizes she has a choice: live and be victimized by the white predator, or die and be free of him altogether. Mariacha chooses to commit suicide by throwing herself off the cliff and, paradoxically, dying as a free woman. Similarly, in the second story the young native woman stands up to the gringo. When he returns to get his money back because he had erroneously purchased a male goat in spite of the young woman's admonitions, the native woman refuses. She states, "You yourself bought it from me. I didn't want to sell it. You insisted that I sell it to you! We Indians say things once, and that's it." Hence, there is an attitude of defiance present in both stories, which also hints at resistance and noncompliance, similar to that of the farmer brother in The Legend of the Deer.

Finally, in the story of The Gringo Who Ate Too Much, one notices an overt disdain for the gringo that borders on cruelty, and is perhaps more openly expressed in this story than in many other Andean tales. After the gringo dies, the landlady keeps his money, keeps his horse, and "there wasn't anyone to complain for the gringo." It is as if the storyteller is saying that the gringo got his just desserts, not only for eating too many poisonous toads but also for his ignorance, stupidity, and inability to set limits and consider the consequences of his actions. These criticisms are also echoed in The Gringo and the Little Goats where the gringo shows his denseness and experiences the aftereffects of his poor judgment.

Clearly, the Native Andean characters in these stories demonstrate an attitude of defiance, contention, and even haughty contempt for the gringo. Could the seeds of resistance and noncompliance have been intentionally planted in these and other similar Andean stories to foment native mobilization and rebellion? Or do these stories merely express strong and latent desires for Native Andeans to stand up for their rights and become more resilient, courageous, and unswerving in the face of the white gringo predator?

The answers to these questions are buried in the hearts and minds of the Native Andean storytellers and in indigenous writings of recent years that—for the first time, after centuries of cultural, political, and religious inhibition—are singing the praises of Native Andean cultures and exalting the virtues of indigenous beliefs. Most telling is that the contemporary speakers, writers, and leaders of reform are no longer "enlightened" whites and idealistic mestizos, as in prior generations, but a new generation of Native Andeans and mestizos who embrace the indigenous traditions and practice them with reverence, as demonstrated by the following powerful excerpt from a recent Quechua publication by Peruvian *paqo* ("healer"), Ricardo Sánchez.

A Meditation on the Indigenous Spiritual Vision

(Quechua)

Every Andean or foreigner who comes into contact with a true runa [Native Andean] agrees that to be indigenous is synonymous with humility and generosity. The Indian is that man who "having nothing" shares every- thing. He shows a deep respect for others. Without knowing a visitor, he greets him with "Imaynallan kashanki tatay/mamay,"[69] and lowers his head, showing reverence, tremendous nobility, and immense heart. He doesn't search for happiness because he is immersed in it—and without a cent in his pocket. His emotions and feelings are transparent in the eternal present. He sings, laughs, dances, or cries without fear or shame of anything, because his heart is pure. He doesn't harbor resentment or malice, despite five centuries of neglect.

Many criollos [descendants of the European conquerors] and Westerners criticize or mock the runa for not being like them, for not "being up to date," for being "left behind," or for being poor. But what they don't realize is that the runa, or the Indian, is the carrier of knowledge, and the keeper of the key that will detoxify this world from the works which have been carried out in the name of greed and personal power; in other words, the ego.

In his natural state, the runa is of a pure heart, just like the condor, the eagle, or the maize. He doesn't know the ego. The ego is not a fruit sown by Pachamama, nor a part of our ancient culture. All fruit of creation, in its natural or native state, is born without ego.

The characteristics of a person without ego are best demonstrated by a being who has been raised to show respect and harmony in both horizontal and vertical fashion; that is to say, in a great physical and spiritual circle that unites all of creation and is vertically aligned with our three Pachas.[70] In this creation one finds Great Spirit, Wiraqocha (Tunupa) [the Andean Creator], Pachakamaq, etc. for the Andeans; Wakan Tanka for the Sioux; Quetzalcóatl for the Aztecs; Kukulcán for the Maya, etc. Our cultures of Abya Yala (America)... represent the Great Spirit, not as a human, male, white, and bearded deity, as portrayed in the Judeo-Christian religions, created primarily in the characteristic vertical image of a human being, but as a divinity which brings together all different forms of life in the universe. For example,... the image of Wiraqocha... is formed by condors, pumas, serpents, symbols that represent the air, water, crops, fish, in addition to the balance of living energies of the universe or Kawsay Pacha.[71]

In societies that are predominantly vertical by "nature," one tends to live in hierarchies; even among relatives and friendships, a man is forced to look for his place within the hierarchy. The tool that facilitates his placement in the hierarchical structure is the ego. One has to show that he or she is "superior" to his peers in order to feel good about himself or herself, or to be accepted at the next, higher level. Something similar occurs in their hierarchical religious environs. God is accorded the highest position, and the rest of the world is positioned beneath HIM. At his side, the left side is empty. And in the lowest position, opposite to God, is the devil. On the one hand, those closest to God are "saved"; on the other hand, those possessed by the devil are punished with eternal terror. The horizontal aspect of the religions created by Western man is mutilated because they regard only the right side as important ("seated at the right hand of the Father").[72] This brings with it an endless array of mistaken notions at political, economic, and cultural levels, such as the old belief that everything created with the left hand is "bad." What would happen if one said, "is seated at the left hand of the Father"? We need two feet to walk; we need both left and right aspects of our surroundings in order to live and to communicate. The absence of feeling for the horizontal explains in part the lack of respect for the rest of nature, and why the Western world pollutes the environment in such an alarming way. The concern is for climbing "up," based on the fear of falling "down."

The indigenous cultures and the Inka culture in particular attained an optimal harmony with nature, far closer than any other culture or human civilization. It was the fruit of a cultural, scientific, social, and spiritual synergy that culminated after thousands of years of civilization in the Andes. In four centuries of existence as a confederation,[73] the Inkas applied the law of Yanantin,[74] or law of complementary duality, not only at the ritualistic level, but also at the governmental level—a key element in achieving global harmony. Examples of Yanantin include the application of masculine and feminine energy, left and right, vertical and horizontal vision, giving and receiving (Ayni[75]), individual and community (Ayllu[76]), thinking and feeling. However, this does not mean one versus another, or one OVER the other. The runa incorporated Yanantin since the early ages of the Andes. Our ancestors desired that there would always exist an acknowledgement of the presence of two different parts of equal importance, necessary for attaining harmony in any task undertaken. The belief existed that if something was not created in conformity with Yanantin, it was poorly made and unbalanced; that sooner or later it would lapse into chaos.

For the indigenous peoples the concepts and terms for God, the devil, exorcism, ego, saints, hell, etc., arrived on European ships five centuries ago.... The indigenous peoples did NOT create religions, nor did they bestow human attributes on the Great Spirit. They merely preserved and continued the spirit of natural harmony that gave birth to the creation. They know that the Great Spirit is neither man nor woman, neither white, copper-skinned, nor black; it is much more immense, something which is impossible to express in words or "sacred scriptures" written by man.

With good reason, the indigenous peoples of the pre-Columbian Andes did not develop writing. The indigenous peoples understood that the word is a limited form of communication among men.... Emotion is the language of spirit, and for the indigenous peoples EVERYTHING made by the Creator is imbued with spirit and energy. The language of this creation is expressed in forms that go beyond simple words—in music and sacred dances, intimate communion with plants, animals, and mountains, and through meditation and ritual. This level of holistic communication in large measure is misunderstood and misinterpreted by Westerners in their chronicles, and in present-day "discoveries" and scientific and anthropological investigations. Even so, the West labeled the Indian as an illiterate, without knowledge, when precisely the opposite was true.

Indigenous thought and emotion defend the Cosmic Rights of ALL: animals, plants, rivers, the environment, and humankind. One of the Andean festivals that Westerners had given up for gone has returned with strength and vigor. The feast of Pawkar Raymi ["Feast of the Blossoming" or "Feast of the Flowering" (of the earth)]... has just been celebrated in many communities of the Andes. In addition to rendering homage to Pachamama and Tata Inti [Father Sun] in celebration of a new agricultural cycle, this is a holistic feast shared with our Taytas and Mamas[77] in recognition of our union with [all of] creation.

It is time to "de-Colonize" [de-Westernize] our vision of the world— Pacha[78]—so that this way we may clearly understand the knowledge inherited from our ancestors, preserved not only in our oral tradition, but also in other forms of communication of greater content, such as symbols, rites, meditation, dances, wakas,[79] plants, and music.

It would not be just to describe Christianity, Judaism, or Islam using attributes and terminology foreign to its culture of origin. Each culture is sacred; each culture has its own vision of the world. It is only fair that the vision, cosmology, cosmogony of the indigenous world... be respected. It is time to show respect among cultures, to respect the liberty of belief that "democracy" proclaims applies to all faiths but which favors the Christian missionaries. The era of the "evangelization of the Indian"—equivalent to a lack of cultural respect—must also come to its final conclusion.

We can feel the arrival of the new Pachakuti[80]; we can feel a new dawn for all of humanity.[81]

~~~

CRITICISM OF THE CATHOLIC CHURCH

The relationship between Native Andeans and the Catholic Church, as with other Western institutions, has been an uneasy and conflicting one from the moment Christianity was imported from Europe to colonial South America in the sixteenth century. Charged by the Spanish monarchy with the immense task of augmenting the Christian faith and bringing "eternal salvation" to the indigenous peoples, the Church not only set out to Christianize and save the souls of the Native Andean peoples, "but also to draw them within the pale of empire, that is, to make them loyal subjects to their Most Catholic Majesties."[82] It relied on the untiring zeal of its spiritual soldiers—mostly Jesuit, Dominican, and Franciscan priests—not only to educate the Native Andeans in Catholic doctrine, but also to systematically eradicate all pre-Columbian rites, rituals, customs, and beliefs that were considered pagan and barbaric.

Starting with the First Council of Lima in 1551, the Church declared that all Indians who had died before the Spanish Conquest were condemned to burn in the eternal fires of hell. The Second Council of Lima in 1557 established the strict and systematic methods by which the clergy would destroy or "extirpate" idolatries that in colonial philosophic imagination were identified as "demonic frauds and delusions" perpetrated by the devil, "thanks to [the] perceived cultural backwardness and lack of intellectual talent" of the Indians.[83]

The Catholic Church attacked the native religions on many fronts. It sought to locate, dismantle, and destroy all indigenous *huacas*—generally temples, shrines, oracles, and objects venerated by the Native Andean religions—and to erect Christian crosses on or above natural *huacas*, such as rivers, mountains, and springs, that were considered sacred by the indigenous peoples. Also, in an effort to eliminate the religious and historical ties between the Native Andeans and their ancestors, and to eradicate the Andean ancestral cults, the Church tried to locate and destroy all *mallquis*—mummies and remains of venerated pre-Columbian ancestors. However, according to some colonial chroniclers, the mummies of some Inca kings were spared this destruction and were instead ceremoniously buried. Legend has it that some of the Inca faithful found the head of their ruler and worshipped it in secret.[84]

Finally, the Church sought to exterminate all indigenous rites, rituals, beliefs, customs, and practices associated with the Native Andean religions and all objects, including *khipu* (knotted records), that the Spaniards claimed were "instruments of pagan idolatry."[85] With the loss of many pre-Columbian *khipu*, which according to some colonial sources contained religious and other cultural information, present-day scholars are heavily dependent on the writings of Spanish colonial chroniclers for information about pre-Columbian Andean religions that, naturally, impose numerous impediments on scientific investigation. Although some of the chroniclers were of mestizo or Native Andean heritage, "no one, not even a handful of Andeans who wrote in the 16th and 17th centuries [and] set pen to paper, wrote explicitly as adherents of the ancient religious beliefs and practices of the Andes."[86] Thus, studies of pre-Columbian Andean beliefs have inevitably been perceived, influenced, and limited by Western European and Christian concepts and ideologies that are alien to Native Andean cultures and cosmologies.

In the absence of any existing literary *khipu*, the most meticulous accounts of pre-Columbian Andean myths were recorded by the colonial priests who were intent on destroying the ancient stories and beliefs as part of the Extirpation of Idolatries. Ironically, mythologists, ethnohistorians, theologians, and other scholars are indebted to the Catholic extirpators for preserving the scanty details known today about pre-Columbian Andean religions, rituals, and practices in the sixteenth and seventeenth centuries. In addition to keeping detailed records of almost every aspect of pre-Columbian religions, the Church sought to facilitate conversion of the native peoples by setting up schools to teach Catholic doctrine (the Church had a monopoly over education), ordaining Andean priests, converting the indigenous elite to Christianity, translating manuals of Christian doctrine into indigenous languages, superimposing Catholic churches on top of Native Andean temples and shrines, erecting Christian crosses over Native Andean holy sites, and so forth. Some of these methods had also been employed in the Iberian Peninsula during the forced conversion of the Moors.

However, the method that proved by far the most effective in Christianizing the Native Andeans was the colonial institution known as *la reducción* ("the reduction"). The reducción was the brainchild of Francisco de Toledo, a notorious Spanish colonial viceroy, known for his ruthlessness and cruelty against the Native Andeans and who from a Spanish perspective was one of the most effective colonial leaders. Reducciones were agglomerations of Indians of diverse ethnic backgrounds into a single village community or settlement, at the center of which was a central plaza surrounded by a church, administrative buildings, school, living quarters, and warehouses.[87] Usually, the reducción was constructed in conformity with a quadrangular layout, where streets were straight and parallel to one another, both vertically and horizontally, and crossed at right angles.

This colonial resettlement practice served various purposes, both religious and secular. First, it facilitated religious instruction of the Native Andeans. In the reducción, the Native Andeans could be educated en masse under the watchful eye of the missionaries; every aspect of their lives was regimented and carefully controlled. Second, the system of reducción reduced the risk of native revolts and rebellion by diluting local and ethnic allegiances through multiethnic groupings. It was difficult to organize and rebel against the Spaniards if the natives gathered in the reducción spoke different languages and lacked a sense of ethnic cohesion. Third, as in Western North America, the Catholic missions protected distant frontiers of the colony from foreign intrusion. This freed up the Spanish soldiers to deal with other matters that required military intervention.[88] Fourth, the reducción also served an economic function by establishing a ready reserve of Native Andean labor to feed the colonial draft labor system, or *repartimiento*. This meant that there was always an easily accessible and available supply of native laborers to toil in the mines and work on agricultural and construction projects.

The reducción also had a psychological effect on the Native Andeans. Although some Native Andeans were appointed as functionaries in the reducciones, "the churchmen in the final analysis rigidly controlled their charges. It was not a simple figure of speech when they spoke of the [Native Andean] neophytes as 'their children,' for that was exactly how they regarded them."[89] Aside from the physical displacement caused by forced relocation, the system of reducción also contributed to the breakdown of the Native Andean traditions and communal way of life.

> The reducciones distort[ed] the agricultural traditions of the [Native] Andeans by obligating the Indians to live in villages, newly founded, and not in their own lands. They lost their sown fields, their grazing lands, their poultry yards. They moved away from their springs and rivers, from their irrigation systems, from their Andean traditions.... The reducciones fracture[d] what was most important of the communal system. And the Indians [went] either to the reducciones or to the inhospitable [regions] of the highlands. Others [became] vagabonds. A third of them took to the Inca roads carrying tribute [for the Spaniards], heading for the mines, looking for a city in which to raise their claims, or, simply, running away from the Spaniards.[90]

There is also a common misconception in the Andes, often taught in schools, that the Native Andeans did not resist the Extirpation of Idolatries and readily converted to Christianity. Nothing could be further from the truth. Seeing their temples and idols destroyed, the practitioners of the indigenous religions worshipped the reconstituted or broken pieces. Secretly, they prayed for their *huacas* to come and obliterate the Spaniards. Many of them kept their homes immaculately clean in the event the *huacas* needed a place to stay upon their arrival.[91] As the pieces of their idols were repeatedly destroyed, and in some cases burned or discarded into the ocean or rivers, a new wave of religious resistance took hold in the Andes, represented by the indigenous movement of the late sixteenth century known as *Taqui Onqoy* ("Dancing Sickness," "Singing Sickness," or "Dance of the Pleiades").

From the Spaniards, the Native Andean priests adopted the concept of the Holy Spirit that "enters" the body, and they claimed that their sacred huacas had abandoned the broken idols and taken up residence inside the bodies of their indigenous priests. In a trancelike state, thousands of Native Andeans from Cuzco in Peru, to Sucre in present-day southern Bolivia, took to dancing the *Taqui Onqoy* in the streets and praising the huacas living inside the human body. In a role reminiscent of the pre-Columbian era, the Native Andean priests, now speaking for their huacas, assumed the role of intermediaries between the Andean deities and their devotees. They called upon the huacas to initiate a *pachacuti* by creating a natural catastrophe—be it flood, earthquake, deluge, or other cataclysmic event—in order to destroy the Spaniards, expel the Christian God, and reinstate the pre-Columbian indigenous religions.

Its primary spokesman, Juan Chocne, recharacterized the Spanish Conquest in terms of Andean cyclical notions of time, promising his followers that, unlike what transpired during the Conquest, this time the native huacas or deities would triumph over the Christian God, marking the end of Spanish rule and bringing in a new age for the Native Andeans.[92] Although the movement was deemed heretical and its followers were persecuted, short of killing thousands of people, it was nearly impossible to destroy the belief in the *living* huacas. It required very aggressive and often ruthless measures by the colonial authorities and Catholic Church over an extended period of time to finally put an end to the *Taqui Onqoy*. Even after its demise Native Andeans continued to worship their native huacas under the guise of worshipping Roman Catholic saints. To some extent, this practice continues to this day.

There are many regions of the Andes that still commemorate the *Taqui Onqoy*. In Andamarca, Peru, for example, during the annual water festival, two rival groups of villagers dance with antique scissors in a manner mimicking the *Taqui Onqoy*. "Promenading through unpaved streets... [the] dancers—scissors clanging away—[move] in long, quick strides broken by pirouettes and heel-clicking kicks."[93] To the sounds of violins and harps playing traditional *huaynos* (Native Andean dance music), the dancers, dressed in multilayered outfits decorated with colorful ribbons, tassels, and mirrors, and inebriated with *chicha* (maize beer), dance the *Taqui Onqoy*, just as their ancestors did centuries ago in a bold attempt to resist the Extirpation of the Native Andean religions. "In the swirling delirium [of the dance], the dancers take on the spirits of the *wamanis* [Andean mountain spirits] ... [acting] as intermediaries between Andean deities and townspeople."[94] It is not clear why the dancers use antique scissors (some colonial representations depict dancers carrying hatchets), but it is clear that the more they dance, the more dangerous their moves become. Some of the dancers inevitably cut and puncture their bodies; some perform daring and sometimes grotesque feats, such as eating live frogs, consuming pieces of a live boa, and tying live chickens to their body cuts. Ironically, the festival ends when the dancing procession reaches the village (Catholic) church, and the dancers descend from a tight rope, which runs down from the bell tower.

Perhaps the wounds inflicted during the (contemporary) *Taqui Onqoy* in Andamarca, Peru, and elsewhere in the Andes, are emblematic of the pain and suffering endured by the Native Andeans during the Extirpation of Idolatries; or maybe they are intended as blood offerings to the mountain deities or Pacha Mama. As previously discussed, many Native Andeans today practice a syncretistic version of Christianity, which incorporates Christian and pre-Columbian elements. However, given the tumultuous history and relationship between the Native Andeans and the Catholic Church, it is not surprising that Native Andean folktales express ambivalence toward this Western institution, introduced by the European conquerors. Catholic priests are often negatively portrayed in Andean stories, and there are some Native Andean beliefs that priests are associated with evil omens. For instance, if a priest or friar appears in a dream or unexpectedly arrives at one's dwelling, generally it is considered to be a sign of impending misfortune.[95]

The stereotype of the priest in many Native Andean stories is of a self-indulgent character who uses his influential position to lure or attract women with the promise of pleasure, reward, or salvation. However, the stories soon reveal his primary objective, which is to have sexual intercourse with the women. But the women whom the priest pursues are not always innocent victims. Sometimes they willingly succumb to the priest's advances; other times they are tricked into performing sexual acts. Both scenarios are presented in the following Andean stories.

The Priest, Juanito, and Maria

(Quichua)

This is a very old story. In the past, anyone before dying had to ask the priest for forgiveness. For that reason, Juanito, who didn't feel very well, went to ask the priest for forgiveness.[96]

"Padrecito,[97] forgive me," he said.

The priest was surprised by the confession. He began to observe Juanito and thought to himself, "Juanito is tall and handsome, and has been a good man." After looking at him attentively, the priest asked Juanito the following question: "What is your wife's name?"

The clever man answered him, "Her name is Maria."

The priest asked him again, "And what is your name?"

Juanito responded, "My name is Juanito."

The priest continued questioning him and said one more time, "What is it that you want?"

Timidly, Juanito replied, "Padrecito, I want your forgiveness and salvation for my soul."

After Juanito had made his request, the priest said, "Fine, my son. And what is your wife like?"

Juanito answered him, "My wife is beautiful, plump, good, rosy-faced, large, and friendly."

Upon hearing this, the priest said to him, "Good, my son. You have already confessed. Go in peace."

Feeling reassured after having asked the priest for forgiveness, Juanito was heading home, but the priest called him back again and said to him, "My, I had almost forgotten. I had almost forgotten something very important. Tell me again, what is your wife's name?"

Juanito repeated it three times, "Maria, Maria, Maria."

Then the priest said to him, "Go on, go on, my son." He then directed that when Juanito should die, his friends should bring his body to the church.

Three weeks went by and the body of Juanito failed to arrive. So the priest said, "Bloody hell! What happened? The man hasn't died. Bloody hell!"

Early one morning, the priest got out of bed and went to the church. While in the church, he saw some people bringing the body of the deceased Juanito. Quickly, the priest put on his vestments, went up to the main altar, and stood there waiting. Meanwhile, the relatives of the deceased arrived with the corpse and placed it in front of the priest. The priest remained standing for a long while without saying a word.

The priest was dead silent, and the people complained, "Quickly, quickly celebrate the mass!" Still, the priest didn't open his mouth.

Finally, after a long while, the priest exclaimed, "Where is the wife? Let the widow weep!"[98]

The widow immediately began to weep. Mournfully, she cried, "Ay! Dear husband, love of my life…! Ay! He's died on me…! Ay! Dear husband, love of my life…! He's died on me…!"

The relatives and the other participants also began to cry. Immediately afterward, the people accompanying the funeral procession said to the priest, "Hurry and celebrate the mass!" But the priest would not do it.

After he remained standing for a while longer, the priest thought and said, "Don't cry, Mariaaa…. I will give you bayeta, rebozo, and shiny anaco[99] [Andean fabric and clothing]…. Mariaaa…!"

"Ay, thank you, padrecito…. Ay, husband, love of my life…. Ay, may God repay you, padrecito…. Ay, may God repay you, padrecito…. Ay, husband, love of my life! Ay! Thank God that you're dead!"

Afterward, the priest ordered that the pallbearers carry the body of the deceased and bury it. When they all arrived at the cemetery, the priest whispered something to the widow, and later on, he asked her to leave with him. And that's where this story ends.[100]

The Priest and the Sexton

(Quechua)

They say there was a priest. There was also the sexton's wife, who was good-looking. She was so good-looking the priest wanted to be with her.

One day, the priest said to her, "Daughter, come over to my house for confession."

Before going to confession, the sexton's wife said to her husband, "Father priest has asked me to go to confession. I'll confess all of my sins to him." And she left.

The priest began to win the heart of the sexton's wife. She was pregnant. So the priest said, "The baby in your womb doesn't have any ears."

"Really?" It frightened the woman.

"Yes, really. But I'm going to give it some ears."

The woman accepted, and the priest gave the baby ears. When the woman returned to her house, she told the sexton, "It seems our baby didn't have any ears, but the priest put some ears on it."

"How could he have?" The sexton was very angry. Then he thought, "I wonder what I can do to get back at the priest."

One day the priest asked him nicely, "Hurry, take my horse to drink some water."

The sexton remembered what the priest had done to his wife but obeyed him anyway.

He took the horse to the river and there he cut off its ears. Afterward, he let the horse drink some water and then walked him back to the priest's house.

The next day, the priest took a look at his horse and began to reflect on what to do. "What am I going to do?" he thought.

He ordered the sexton to come for confession on such and such a day.

The sexton obeyed. Once inside the confessional, the priest ordered him to pray. The sexton prayed.

Then the priest said, "Tell me your sins! Why did you cut off my horse's ears?"

The sexton responded, "Well, just put some ears on him, since you already know how!"

The priest pretended that he was having some trouble hearing in the confessional. "What did you say?" he mumbled.

"From where I am, I can't hear you, doctor," said the sexton.

"Let's see...come," said the priest. "Talk to me from my place in the confessional."

The sexton took the place of the priest in the confessional and from there he repeated, "Just put some ears on him, since you already know how!"

The priest was sitting where the sexton had been before. "Ah, yes, you're right," he said, "one can't hear anything from here."

The priest couldn't say anything to him about the horse's ears. He also couldn't do anything to punish him. What could he have done? It's not like he could hit him, right? What could he have done? The priest had to swallow his anger and not say anything. He couldn't say, "I have helped your wife," or "I put some ears on your child" after the sexton had already cut off the ears of the horse. That's all.[101]

~~~

In these two Andean folktales, one can easily detect the feelings of ambivalence that characterize the relationship between the Native Andeans and the Catholic Church, and between the Native Andeans and the clergy in particular. Although these tales are couched in humor and amusing dialogue, they nonetheless express hostility toward the Church and question the morality of the clergy.

For instance, in The Priest, Juanito, and Maria, the honest and humble character Juanito goes to see the local priest to ask for "forgiveness." Juanito obviously misinterprets the Catholic sacrament of confession, or reconciliation, in which the priest is believed to act only as an intermediary between the penitent and God. According to Catholic doctrine, although the penitent "confesses" his sins to the priest, it is not the priest, but God, of whom the sinner asks forgiveness. Juanito, however, mistakenly believes he must ask for forgiveness from the *padrecito*.

During the alleged "confession," Juanito plainly states that he seeks forgiveness and salvation for his soul; yet, the priest is much more interested in learning about Juanito's wife than Juanito's sins. He repeatedly asks Juanito to tell him his wife's name, and he even inquires about her physical attributes and disposition. (At least this is the way Juanito interprets the question.) Honest and unassuming Juanito describes his wife as "beautiful, plump, good, rosy-faced, large, and friendly," piquing the interest of the priest.

As in many Native Andean folktales, the priest in this story is portrayed as clever, devious, scheming, and unapologetic. He clearly has designs on Juanito's wife and is anxiously waiting for the poor man to kick the bucket. In fact, when Juanito's body is not immediately brought to the church, the priest gets angry and restless ("Bloody hell! What happened? The man hasn't died. Bloody hell!"). When the body is finally delivered, the priest goes through the motions of putting on the appropriate vestments to celebrate the burial mass, yet the "priest remained standing for a long while—and didn't open his mouth." Nevertheless, the clever priest identifies the widow by instructing her to engage in the customary weeping, which is traditional at funerals in many parts of the Andes. He asks, "Where is the wife? Let the widow weep!"

After the widow initiates the weeping, relatives and friends begin to cry. The participants urge the priest to hurry and celebrate the mass, "but the priest would not do it." Instead, he uses his time at the altar to offer gifts to Juanito's widow. In an outlandish series of statements, he offers her clothing instead of condolences. He states, "Don't cry, Mariaaa....I will give you *bayeta*, *rebozo*, and shiny *anaco*." So if the priest's offer is taken literally, he is offering to dress Juanito's widow in fine Andean garments. However, figuratively the priest could also be offering to "wrap" or "cloak" the Native woman in wealth, comfort, and protection, or else provide adequate "cover" for a prospective illicit relationship. In any case, it is clear the priest is attempting to lure Juanito's widow into a prohibited relationship.

What is most salient in this account is the priest's utter indifference and disregard for Juanito's physical and spiritual welfare and mental state. He never probes into Juanito's concerns regarding his health, never counsels him, and never offers spiritual guidance or advice. More importantly, the priest shows complete disregard for the Christian sacraments and lack of respect for the fiduciary and moral obligations he vowed to uphold as a member of the priesthood. Juanito's confession is a sham, as is his subsequent burial mass. In a sense, the priest in this story is making a mockery of the Church, its teachings, and the Andean community he promised to serve.

Similarly, in The Priest and the Sexton, the priest ignores his vow of chastity and has a sexual affair with the sexton's pregnant wife, tricking her into committing adultery. In many respects, this story and the tale of Juanito are typical of many other Andean stories that criticize the power and corruption of the Church. In most of these stories, the priests have the upper hand and manipulate and mistreat the Native Andean people. In many cases, they also take advantage of women through trickery and deception, abusing the power vested in their office.

TOWARD AN INTEGRATED IDENTITY

Native Andean cultures are not static and have experienced enormous changes in the five centuries since the Spanish Conquest. Most Native Andeans are Christian, although some practice a syncretistic version of Christianity infused with pre-Columbian elements. Native Andeans are no longer predominantly rural, as many have moved to the cities and large urban centers in search of employment, education, and better economic opportunities. Native Andeans have intermarried with whites, mestizos, blacks, new immigrants from Europe, Asia, and the Middle East, other indigenous groups, and so forth, giving rise to a racially mixed Andean population and a pluralistic society. They have also been educated, acculturated, and, some would say, indoctrinated in the dominant Eurocentric culture that is largely Spanish speaking and Christian with a generally favorable view of Western institutions. This acculturation process has also inculcated certain values and psychological perceptions that have, for the most part, been detrimental to the Native Andean.

Native Andean history taught in the classroom is often misleading and exalts the accomplishments of the conquerors. Although many Native Andean schoolchildren learn about and take pride in the accomplishments of the former Inca Empire, they often learn false and misleading information about their Inca ancestors. For instance, as a child in a Bolivian history class I was taught that the Spaniards easily conquered the Inca Empire because the Incas were a peace-loving and submissive people! We were not taught that the Incas were formidable warriors. Even in more contemporary Andean textbooks, there is precious little written about the brilliance of Inca statecraft, for example, and the military genius of Inca emperors such as Pachacuti Inca Yupanqui, Tupac Inca Yupanqui, and Huayna Capac, who in less than one hundred years conquered a territory that nearly spanned the length of western South America. Although there have been some changes in recent years, traditionally, most Andean history readers designed for elementary education devote most of their pages to colonial history and very little (if any) pages to pre-Columbian indigenous cultures other than the Inca.

There are also numerous myths about the Spanish Conquest and the Extirpation of Idolatries that are repeated even by educated adults in Andean society. One huge misconception is that the Conquest saved the Native Andeans from their "barbarism" and introduced "culture" to Andean South America. This notion emanates from misguided European colonial suppositions concerning the superiority of Western European culture and the inferiority of Native Andean cultures and beliefs.[102] This sentiment still persists in many segments of Andean society, contributing to racial and cultural discord among Andean populations. Another frequently cited myth is that a handful of Spaniards, armed with superior weaponry, conquered the entire Inca Empire in a short period of time, with little or no native resistance. Although it is true that Inca clubs, slings, bolas, axes, lances, and spears, designed for hand-to-hand combat, were no match for the Spaniards' iron-tipped lances, steel swords, horses, firearms, and arquebuses, there is mounting evidence that the Spaniards did not fight their battles alone but were aided by native enemies of the Incas, who outnumbered the Spanish forces by many hundreds to one.[103] To this one must also add the devastating effect of European diseases to which the Native Andeans had no resistance; disease alone was probably the Spaniards' greatest weapon of conquest.

Even after the capture and execution of the last Inca emperor, Ata-hualpa, in 1533, the Native Andeans launched a systematic and organized resistance against the Spaniards for nearly four decades from their secret holdout in Vilcabamba, which was finally seized in 1572. As described in previous chapters, this period of native resistance subsided with the death of Tupac Amaru I, who was publicly beheaded in Cuzco in 1572, but again regained momentum with the Indian rebellions of the eighteenth century, "which constituted the most serious challenge to Spanish colonial authority in South America during the long colonial period."[104] Adding to these misconceptions, there is also a widespread myth that the Native Andeans did not resist the Extirpation of their native religions and, in fact, willingly accepted Christianity. As was previously discussed, history does not bear this out. Yet the persistence of these fallacies—which cut through the heart of Andean culture—has resulted in the social exclusion and marginalization of the Native Andean peoples for nearly five centuries, denying them parity and full participation in the social, economic, and political affairs of their nations.

Perhaps the most notable effect of perpetuating these misconceptions is the loss or diminished sense of identity experienced by many Native Andeans, which has produced a backlash against Eurocentric education by some indigenous and nonindigenous activists and educators.[105] This ambivalence concerning conflicting racial, cultural, and religious identities on the part of Native Andeans and also mestizos is often revealed surreptitiously in Andean stories. The following short yet symbolic tale is an example of this cultural ambiguity.

The Man Asleep

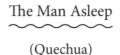

(Quechua)

On the road to Jesus,[106] there is a mountain where one can see a man who appears to be sleeping. His [condition] arose in the following way:

An Indian warrior rebelled against the Inca. Seeing that he was being pursued, he wanted to escape, so he took the road that leads to Jesus. But since the road was very long with no end in sight, the Indian was overcome by fatigue and fell asleep on the lower slope of the mountain.

Since he had offended the Inca, he was punished by his Father, the Sun, who submersed the rebel in an eternal sleep.

That's why many people who head toward the great terminal fountain of Jesus can observe this Indian lying on the slope of the mountain where he appears to be resting after a long walk.[107]

～～

This legend appears to be both a reference to a Peruvian town by the name of Jesus and also a symbolic reference to the European evangelization that, after the Spanish Conquest, put the Native Andeans "on the road to Jesus." Interestingly, the Inca ruler was considered *intip churin*—the son of the Sun god—and the Sun's divine representative here on earth. Likewise, the Christian conception of Jesus is that He is also the Son of God and begotten of the Father, inseparable from Him in the Catholic faith. In cosmological terms, Jesus could thus be viewed as an intermediary between God and man, and between heaven and earth. Likewise, the Inca ruler was also viewed as an intermediary between the Sun god and man, and perhaps between the Upper World (*Hanan Pacha*) and This World (*Kay Pacha*).

The focal point of The Man Asleep is the native rebel who falls asleep on the lower slope of the mountain on the road to Jesus. He has "rebelled against the Inca" and tries to escape his pursuers by taking the road that leads to Jesus. In many respects, this journey is analogous to the Christianization of the Native Andeans, who at first had to openly reject and defy their Inca and other native religions—which were perceived as instruments of the devil—in order to be put on the "right path" to Christianity as advocated by the European conquerors and later their mestizo and white descendants. In addition to religion, many other aspects of their native cultures were also discarded at the insistence—and often coercion—of the dominant culture, including their native dress, languages, customs, and traditions.

However, as the legend aptly describes, the road to Jesus has "no end in sight," and the Indian grows weary along the way. Metaphorically, the process of acculturation by the dominant Europeanized society is also interminable and the Native Andean can never completely get there. In many respects he shares this problem with some Andean mestizos, who may have completely assimilated the culture and values of "white" society and yet are not completely accepted as "white" because of arbitrary racial distinctions and hardened exclusionary practices observed (but often not admitted) by the white Andean elite.

Consequently, the Native Andean is weary of the long journey toward racial and social equality that has consumed his energies for nearly five hundred years. Yet the symbolism in this story also suggests that Native Andeans, and possibly mestizos, feel some guilt or anger about relinquishing their indigenous cultural identity, represented by the Inca ruler and his father, the Sun god, in the story. According to the tale, the native rebel has "offended the Inca [ruler]," and in retribution, the Sun god punishes him and "submerses [him] in an eternal sleep." Although not expressly stated in the story, the punishment meted out by the Sun god is petrification—one of the typical mythical punishments dispensed by the Andean deities—as the rebel eternally sleeps and permanently becomes part of the mountain. The curious passersby later observe him in a state of uninterrupted sleep "lying on the slope of the mountain."

A "petrified" rebel cannot move; The Man Asleep is immobilized for eternity. Yet in this story he has become part of the mountain, a remnant of the past, observed by those who are walking in the present. The present may be symbolized by the "many people who head toward the great terminal fountain of Jesus." Unlike the sleeping rebel of the past, the passersby of the present are mobile and heading toward the terminal fountain of Jesus—the final destination, unreachable in the past. Some might view "the great terminal fountain of Jesus" as a symbolic allusion to the baptismal waters of Jesus, and as an allegory of salvation through the adoption of Christianity. However, there is also another interpretation that is equally plausible in this context.

"On the road to Jesus" might well be the path toward self-hood or self-realization described by the psychologist, Carl Jung, as *individuation*.[108] According to Jungian theory, through the process of individuation, a person may eventually arrive at an integration of the Self, or the symbolic Christ, by embracing all aspects—even the repressed and rejected aspects ("Shadow" aspects)—of one's identity.[109] This process culminates in Jesus the Christ as an archetype or symbol of the integrated Self, the *imago dei* ("the image of God" or "the God within").[110] It is this integrated Self that might be epitomized in this story as the "great terminal fountain of Jesus [the Christ]," the final, and previously unattainable, destination.

Jung might predict that at the end of "the road to Jesus" the Native Andean, the mestizo, or any "passerby" will find psychological and spiritual restoration and wholeness. However, he or she must first find the courage to face and embrace the repressed and forgotten aspects of the Shadow, including any unconscious rejection of an indigenous identity, which is "submersed . . . in an eternal sleep" and languishing in the oblivion of the unconscious mind. Perhaps the fear of facing the Shadow is what caused the Indian warrior to rebel and flee from the mighty Inca in the first place, a symbolic escape from his discarded identity.

Ideally, from a Jungian perspective, the Andean passersby will observe the Man Asleep—their indigenous past—and continue onward toward the terminal fountain of Jesus (the Christ as Self). Upon arrival, they will no longer feel a need to rebel and run from their indigenous legacy. On the contrary, they will embrace and take pride in their native heritage, despite any racism or prejudice to which they might be subjected.

There is evidence that this is already occurring in the Andes. In my own homeland of Bolivia, the Native Andeans, together with a significant number of middle class mestizos, have determined that an indigenous person is worthy of being elected president, that one of their own shall lead their country. In a number of other recent presidential elections in South America, the majority of voters are also breaking with tradition and elite-driven politics by calling for more inclusive and participatory democracies that focus on the needs of the poor, the working classes, and the marginalized segments of society.[111] Irrespective of one's political leanings, it is important to recognize that these are pivotal events that are shaping the future of the Andean nations. For the Native Andean peoples, especially, these are decisive steps leading toward the terminal fountain of self-knowledge, self-realization, and self-determination.

Social protest is not just an external and collective expression of dissent and objection to the status quo; it is also an *internal* and individual avowal of the need for change, together with the requisite self-esteem to bring about such change. These are but a few of the underlying currents that form the fluid body of the Native Andean oral tradition. This tradition predates the arrival of the Europeans in the Andes, and to this day it continues to move in one direction or another, sometimes changing its course and revealing an infinite stream of fears, hopes, and dreams of contemporary Native Andeans, combined with the timeless voices of their indigenous ancestors who have long since returned to the womb of *Pacha Mama*.

Chapter Summary
We started this chapter by describing the rise of the Andean indigenous movements and the social and political reforms they are helping to bring about in the Andean region. In many respects, their ascent and the call for greater indigenous participation in the social, economic, and political life of the Andes are a strong indication that The Man Asleep has awoken

from his centuries-old slumber since the colonial uprisings. Indigenous movements of the past few decades have been instrumental in advancing constitutional, social, political, and economic reforms granting the Native Andean peoples greater territorial rights, access to bilingual education, greater community rights, and more decision-making authority over their own lives. Although the process is far from complete, their efforts have dramatically transformed the cultural landscape in the Andes, helping reverse centuries of discrimination and exclusionary practices that have marginalized and disempowered the Native Andean peoples.

As discussed, the roots of racism in the Andes began with the complex system of socio-racial nomenclature, or castes, developed under Spanish colonial rule, which placed Spaniards and their Andean-born children at the top of the social ladder and Indians and blacks at the bottom. The Spanish colonial institutions such as *encomienda* ("entrustment"), *repartimiento* ("distribution"), and *reducción* ("reduction"), implemented with the aid of the Catholic Church, had the intended effect of uprooting and displacing the native communities and breaking down their traditional values. Although it is difficult to prove causation, there is little doubt that the physical exploitation and psychological trauma of the Conquest contributed to the demographic disaster of the indigenous people in this region of the Americas.

To express dissatisfaction with the Western institutions and social classes that have denied them full participation in Andean life since the time of the Conquest, storytelling has evolved among Native Andeans into a socially acceptable mechanism for airing grievances and criticizing the dominant white and mestizo culture and foreign influences that exert control over their lives. It is also an avenue for extolling the traditional virtues and values of Native Andean cultures.

In this chapter we have explored how socially unacceptable forms of political and cultural expression find their way into the Andean oral tradition, disguised as more palatable, acceptable, and sometimes humorous stories containing benign and unobjectionable images. For instance, in The Legend of the Deer, a *misti* curses a Native Andean farmer by turning him into a deer. Although at first blush the tale appears to communicate a moral lesson about the virtue of generosity, on a more recondite level the story criticizes the asymmetrical power structure of Andean society, where a misti has the supernatural ability to turn an Indian into an animal and make him unrecognizable to his family.

Likewise, many *gringo* tales humorously criticize the stereotypic white foreigner for being too greedy, too ignorant, or too arrogant and causing his own demise. In some cases, he robs the villagers of their animals and chases after their women (Atoqhuarco). He may also set his eyes on something he wants (usually belonging to the Native Andeans), and he doesn't quit until he gets it. However, even if he inevitably gets what he wants, he doesn't know what to do with it once he gets it (The Gringo and the Little Goats). Yet another stereotype is that he covets everything in large quantities and has trouble setting limits on his covetous impulses (What the Gringo Ate). Although in the end the gringo usually gets his just desserts or is outsmarted by the Native Andeans, nonetheless, these stories imply that he is a threat to the Native Andean community, robbing it of its livelihood, possessions, and natural resources. The behavior of the gringo in the tale of Atoqhuarco is a poignant reminder of this threat. Throughout the story, the Atoq-Gringo is characterized as a superhuman predator, whose feeding habits resemble those of lower animals. Moreover, he traps a beautiful village girl and precipitates her untimely death. In other words, he is a menace who preys on the Native Andean community.

Similarly, we have also analyzed several Native Andean stories that criticize the behavior of Catholic priests. These wayward priests are typically selfish, self-indulgent, and not very concerned with the welfare of their flock. In fact, they usually use their power and influence to lure women for sexual purposes. This is not surprising, given the long and conflicting history of the Native Andeans and the Catholic Church. These stories are couched in humor and witty dialogue, yet they are obviously protesting the systematic abuses committed by members of the clergy.

NOTES

Chapter 1: Introduction

1. The author is Bolivian by birth and of mixed Spanish and indigenous ancestry. During her childhood, her caregivers were primarily Native Andean (Quechua) women who expounded on many of the topics covered in this book and told her many Andean stories. Later, her family moved to the United States where she completed her education. For fifteen years she taught Spanish and Latin American Studies at a university in Washington, D.C., and, as a U.S. lawyer, she has worked closely with Native Andean organizations seeking equal opportunity and social justice for the indigenous peoples of South America.

2. See Paul M. Lewis, ed., *Ethnologue: Languages of the World,* 16th ed. (Dallas, TX: SIL International, 2009), 234–35, 254, 257, 262, 299–302. According to *Ethnologue,* there are more than forty regional variations of the Quechua language, each with its concomitant local dialects. In Peru, Ayacucho Quechua (900,000 speakers), Cuzco Quechua (1,500,000 speakers), Huaylas Ancash Quechua (336,000 speakers), and Puno Quechua (500,000 speakers) are the most widely spoken. In Ecuador, Quechua is known as "Quichua" (also spelled "Kichwa") and also has several regional variations. Of these, Cañar Highland Quichua (100,000 speakers), Chimborazo Highland Quichua (1,000,000 speakers), and Imbabura Highland Quichua (300,000 speakers) are the most prevalent. The Quechua spoken in Bolivia is divided, geographically and linguistically, into North Bolivian Quechua (116,000 speakers) and South Bolivian Quechua (2,780,000 speakers). South Bolivian Quechua is also spoken in Argentina (855,000 speakers), with possibly 70,000 speakers in the northwestern Salta Province, where it is generally known as "Northwest Jujuy" or "Colla." Other variant forms of Quechua include Chilean Quechua (8,200 speakers), which may be similar to or the same as South Bolivian Quechua, and Santiago del Estero Quichua (60,000 speakers), spoken in north-central Argentina. In Colombia, "Inga," another variant form of Quechua, has about 12,000 speakers and appears to be partially intelligible with Imbabura Quichua (also known as "Otavalo Quichua") spoken in the northern highlands of Ecuador.

Quechua is also spreading to some non-Quechua-speaking areas where
Andean highland workers converse in their native tongue. For instance,
it is estimated that 500,000 immigrant workers living in Buenos Aires
speak South Bolivian Quechua (ibid., 232).

Additionally, there are three regional variants of Aymara in
the Andes: Central Aymara (2,262,900 speakers), Southern Aymara
(219,000 speakers), and Jaqaru (740 speakers). Central Aymara is
spoken in the "whole altiplano west of [the] eastern Andes" and the
Lake Titicaca region of Peru and Bolivia (ibid., 234). It is also spoken in
the extreme northern highlands of Chile (Tarapacá, Arica, Parincota,
and Iquique). Jaqaru has fewer than 1,000 speakers in the Tupe and Ca-
tahuasi districts of the Peruvian Yauyos Province (Lima Department).
Moreover, the Jaqaru dialect known as "Kawki" (or "Cauqui") is nearly
extinct, with only 11 remaining adult speakers. Central Aymara has also
been brought to Argentina (30,000 speakers) by immigrant workers and
others looking for employment (ibid., 232).

3. Although the Incas probably recognized themselves as a distinct ethnic
    group several hundred years prior to the Empire Period, it is generally
    accepted that they did not undertake any real conquests before 1438.
    It appears that they started as one of numerous highland groups living
    in the Cuzco valley in the thirteenth century, led by one or more local
    chieftains. During this formative period they pillaged and sacked neigh-
    boring areas but did not annex any territory. See Nigel Davies, *The Incas*
    (Niwot, CO: University of Colorado Press, 1995), 25–29. There is also
    some debate, especially among South American scholars, as to whether
    the Incas attained consolidation at the state level, and whether they
    achieved a cohesive and unified state identity. For the most part this
    argument is based on the fact that the localities that comprised the Inca
    nation retained a great deal of administrative and religious autonomy.
    For example, Peruvian scholar María Rostworowski de Diez Canseco
    maintains that the only centralizing measure imposed by the Incas was
    a common language, whereas the localities ("macroethnic groups")
    achieved cohesion through "a common mythical origin—the *pacarina*;
    a common language or dialect spoken by the group; a common identi-
    fying form of dress; and finally, economic and political unity." See María
    Rostworowski de Diez Canseco, *Historia del Tahuantinsuyu* (Lima:
    Instituto de Estudios Peruanos, 1999), 314 (my translation).

4. See Michael E. Moseley, *The Incas and their Ancestors: The Archaeology
    of Peru* (London: Thames and Hudson, 1992), 65; Gary Urton, *Inca
    Myths* (Austin: University of Texas Press, in cooperation with the British
    Museum Press, 1999), 24.

5. The Royal Road, carved out of treacherous mountain walls, covered
    about 3,250 miles (5,230 km), from Ecuador to Argentina. The Coastal

Highway ran the length of the Peruvian coast for approximately 2,520 miles (4,055 km). Additionally, 400 miles (644 km) of lateral roads traversed these great highways. For more in-depth information about Inca roads, see John Hyslop, *The Inka Road System* (Orlando, FL: Academic Press, 1984).

6. See Cristóbal de Molina, *Fábulas y mitos de los incas*, edición de Henrique Urbano y Pierre Duviols (Madrid: Historia 16, 1988), 60. (The original text is generally known as *Relación de las fábulas y ritos de los incas*; hereinafter all references to this chronicle will refer to this edition, unless otherwise noted.) See also Bernabé Cobo, *History of the Inca Empire: An Account of the Indians' Customs and their Origin Together with a Treatise on Inca Legends, History and Social Institutions*, translated and edited by Roland Hamilton, foreword by John Rowe (Austin: University of Texas Press, 1979), 133–34; Pedro Sarmiento de Gamboa, *Historia de los incas* (Madrid: Miriguano Ediciones y Ediciones Polifemo, n.d.), 87; Joan de Santacruz Pachacuti Yamqui Salcamaygua, *Relación de antigüedades deste reyno del Pirú*, in *Tres relaciones de antigüedades peruanas*, 207–81 (Asunción: Editorial Guaranía, 1950), 237. (Some versions allege that it was the Creator god, *Viracocha*, instead of the Sun god, *Inti*, who appeared to Pachacuti. Hereinafter all references to Santacruz Pachacuti's chronicle refer to this edition, unless otherwise noted.)

7. Santacruz Pachacuti, *Relación*, 238; Sarmiento, *Historia*, 88–89. See also Juan de Betanzos, *Narrative of the Incas*, translated and edited by Roland Hamilton and Dana Buchanan (Austin: University of Texas Press, 1996), 30.

8. Bernabé Cobo, *Inca Religion and Customs*, translated and edited by Roland Hamilton, foreword by John Rowe (Austin: University of Texas Press, 1990), 35–36.

9. El Inca Garcilaso de la Vega, *Comentarios reales de los incas (Tomos I y II)*, edición, índice analítico y glosario de Carlos Araníbar (México DF: Fondo de Cultura Económica, 1991), 593 (hereinafter "Araníbar edition"). See also El Inca Garcilaso de la Vega, *Comentarios reales*, introducción de José de la Riva-Agüero (México DF: Editorial Porrúa, 2000), 400–1 (hereinafter "Riva-Agüero edition").

10. Sarmiento, *Historia*, 149.

11. Molina, *Fábulas*, 62–63; Garcilaso, *Comentarios reales* (Riva-Agüero edition), 251.

12. Molina, *Fábulas*, 63; Garcilaso, *Comentarios reales* (Riva-Agüero edition), 252.

13. Alan Kolata, *The Tiwanaku: Portrait of an Andean Civilization* (Cambridge, MA: Blackwell Publishers, 1993), 86.

14. See Garcilaso, *Comentarios reales* (Araníbar edition), 634–44 (citing Agustín de Zárate).

15. See Molina, *Fábulas*, 55–56; Sarmiento, *Historia*, 41–42.
16. The name of this shrine may be derived from both the Quechua and Aymara languages. The Quechua term *wari* derives from Aymara and means "autochthonous" or "native" in both languages. See *Simi Taqe*: *qheshwa-español-qheshwa* (Diccionario quechua-español-quechua), *Qheshwa Simi Hamut'ana Kurak Suntur* (Academia Mayor de la Lengua Quechua), 2nd ed. (Cusco, Perú: Gobierno Regional Cusco, 2005), 724 (hereinafter "*Simi Taqe*"). *Wilka* or *willka* (also spelled *villca*) is an antiquated Aymara term, signifying "a shrine dedicated to the sun [god], or other idols." P. Ludovico Bertonio (1612), *Vocabulario de la lengua aymara, parte segunda*, compuesto por el P. Ludovico Bertonio, publicado de nuevo por Julio Platzmann (Leipzig: B. G. Teubner, 1879), 386 (my translation). Thus, combining the Quechua and Aymara term for "native" (*wari*) and the Aymara term for shrine (*wilka, willka*, or *villca*), one possible translation of *Wariwilka* is "native shrine."

    The colonial Italian priest Ludovico Bertonio (1612) developed one of the first dictionaries of the Aymara language. According to Bertonio, the term *wari* (also spelled *huari*) signifies "a liquid, not thick: it is used to refer to the *mazamorras* [liquids or soups made of a maize mixture], and things like that" (ibid., 151; my translation). Since the ancient site of *Wariwilka* is also known for its sacred spring, which supplies water to the surrounding valley, another possible translation may be "liquid [water] shrine."
17. Wanka (or "Wanca") Quechua encompasses both Jauja Wanka Quechua, spoken in the Jauja Province of the Junín Department of Peru, and Waylla Wanka Quechua, spoken in Huancayo and Concepción Provinces of the Junín Department. North Junín Quechua is a dialect of Jauja Wanka Quechua, but "with considerable phonological differences," and Waycha (or Central Huancayo), East Waylla, and West Waylla are dialects of Waylla Wanka Quechua (Lewis, *Ethnologue*, 301).
18. *Webster's College Dictionary* (New York: Barnes & Noble Books, by arrangement with Federal Street Press, a division of Merriam-Webster, 2003), 344.
19. Ibid., 586 (under "myth").
20. Generally speaking, *huacas* are animals, objects, and places venerated by the Native Andean religions. They may be natural or human-made. The subject of *huacas* will be treated thoroughly in a subsequent chapter.
21. Joseph W. Bastien, *Mountain of the Condor* (Prospect Heights, IL: Waveland Press, 1978), glossary, 211. (*Llaqta ayllu* is spelled *llahta ayllu*; *hatun ayllu* is spelled *jatun ayllu*; and *mitmaq ayllu* is spelled *mitmaj ayllu* in the original text.)
22. Constance Classen, *Inca Cosmology and the Human Body* (Salt Lake City: University of Utah Press, 1993), 14.

23. R. Cerrón-Palomino, "Language Policy in Peru: A Historical Overview," *International Journal of the Sociology of Language*, 77 (1989): 11–33.

24. Arguedas' most important works include *Warma Kuyay* (1933), *Agua y otros cuentos* (1935), *Yawar Fiesta* (1941), *Canciones y cuentos del pueblo quechua* (1949), *La novela y la expresión literaria en el Perú* (1950), *Diamantes y pedernales* (1954), *Los ríos profundos* (1959), *El sexto* (1961), *La agonía de Rasu Ñiti* (1962), *Todas las sangres* (1965), *El sueño del pongo* (1965), *Amor mundo y otros cuentos* (1967), and *El zorro de arriba y el zorro de abajo* (1971, published posthumously).

25. José María Arguedas and Francisco Izquierdo Ríos, eds., *Mitos, leyendas y cuentos peruanos* (Lima: Casa de la Cultura, 1970; first edition, 1947). See also José María Arguedas and Francisco Izquierdo Ríos, eds., *Mitos, leyendas y cuentos peruanos*, nota a la edición de Sybila Arredondo de Arguedas, Biblioteca de Cuentos Populares, no. 11 (Madrid: Ediciones Siruela, 2009). Hereinafter 2009 edition.

26. See José María Arguedas, ed., *Mitos, leyendas y cuentos peruanos* (*Colección escolar peruana, vol. 4*), selección y notas de José María Arguedas y Francisco Izquierdo Ríos (Lima: Ediciones de la Dirección de Educación Artística y Extensión Cultural, 1947).

27. José María Arguedas, *Canciones y cuentos del pueblo quechua* (Lima: Editorial Huascarán, 1949).

28. Luis Valcárcel and José María Arguedas, eds., *Narraciones y leyendas incas* (Lima, Perú: Editorial Latinoamericana, 1958).

29. See José María Arguedas, *El zorro de arriba y el zorro de abajo* (Buenos Aires: Editorial Losada, 1971).

30. As of the date of this writing, Lara's Quechua–Spanish dictionary is in its fifth edition of publication. See Jesús Lara, *Diccionario queshwa-castellano, castellano-queshwa*, 5th ed. (La Paz and Cochabamba, Bolivia: Editorial "Los Amigos del Libro," 2001).

31. Lara's most important compilations include *Leyendas quechuas* (1960), *Mitos, leyendas y cuentos de los quechuas* (1973), *Poesía quechua* (1947), and *Poesía popular quechua* (1956). Lara's other major works include *Repete* (1937), *Surumi* (1943), *Ollanta* (1967), *Inkallajta-Inkaraqay* (1967), *Sujnapura* (1973), *Yahuarwinchij* (1973), and many others.

32. See Jesús Lara, ed. and trans., *Tragedia del fin de Atawallpa (Atau Wallpaj p'uchukakuyninpa wankan)* (Cochabamba, Bolivia: Editorial "Los Amigos del Libro," 1989; first edition, 1957).

33. It would be virtually impossible to cite all of Antonio Paredes-Candia's major works, but here is a brief list: *Literatura folklórica; Cuadernos de folklore boliviano; Vocablos aymaras en el habla popular paceño; El folklore en la ciudad de La Paz; Antología de los cuentos de folklore boliviano; Folklore en el valle de Cochabamba; Artesanías e industrias populares en Bolivia; Brujerías, tradiciones y leyendas; La danza folklórica en Bolivia;*

Cuentos populares bolivianos; La fiesta folklórica en Bolivia; Diccionario mitológico de Bolivia; Leyendas de Bolivia; Tradiciones y leyendas; Las mejores tradiciones; Tradiciones paceñas; Diccionario de saber popular; Folklore de Potosí; Leyendas de Bolivia; and *Antología de tradiciones y leyendas bolivianas.*

34. See Claude Lévi-Strauss, *Myth and Meaning: Cracking the Code of Culture,* with a foreword by Wendy Doniger (New York: Schocken Books, 1979), 8. See also Edith Kurzweil, *The Age of Structuralism: Lévi-Strauss to Foucault* (New York: Columbia University Press, 1980), 19.

35. See Sigmund Freud, *The Interpretation of Dreams,* translated by Dr. A. A. Brill (New York: First Modern Library Edition, Random House, 1950). See also Sigmund Freud, *On Dreams,* translated and edited by James Strachey, with a biographical introduction by Peter Gay (New York and London: W. W. Norton & Company, 1952).

36. See Sigmund Freud, *Totem and Taboo: Resemblances between the Psychic Lives of Savages and Neurotics,* authorized translation with an introduction by A. A. Brill (New York: Vintage Books, a division of Random House, 1918).

37. See Christopher Monte, *Beneath the Mask: An Introduction to Theories of Personality* (New York: Praeger Publishers, 1977), 135.

38. The author recognizes that there are many criticisms that can be made of Jungian, Freudian, structuralist, and symbolist theories; however, addressing these in detail would be well beyond the scope of this book and would weigh it down for the reader. Generally, these theories assume the existence of unconscious psychic processes that critics claim are not subject to empirical observation.

39. See Garcilaso, *Comentarios reales* (Araníbar edition), 132, 238, 279, 286, 340, 344–48; Felipe Guaman Poma de Ayala, *Nueva corónica y buen gobierno (Vol. 75 and 76),* transcripción, prólogo, notas y cronología de Franklin Pease (Caracas: Biblioteca Ayacucho, 1980), 75:183, 260–65 (hereinafter "Pease edition"). See also Bernabé Cobo, *Historia del nuevo mundo,* in *Obras del P. Bernabé Cobo,* vol. 2, 7–275, estudio preliminar y edición del P. Francisco Mateos, Bibilioteca de Autores Españoles, vols. LXXXXI and LXXXXII (Madrid: Ediciones Atlas, 1964), 141–44.

40. The *khipu* has long been considered a strictly mnemonic device, with its various constituent parts serving as stimuli to trigger or jog the memory of the *khipucamayoc* (also spelled *khipukamayoq*), one of the interpreters and "keepers of the khipu" in the Inca empire; however, that longstanding theory has recently been called into question. See Jeffrey Quilter and Gary Urton, eds., *Narrative Threads: Accounting and Recounting in Andean Khipu* (Austin: University of Texas Press, 2002); Gary Urton, *Signs of the Inka Khipu: Binary Coding in the Andean Knotted-String Records* (Austin: University of Texas Press, 2003).

41. For a more detailed discussion concerning some of these limitations, see Rostworowski, *Historia,* 14–17; Davies, *Incas,* 1–7; R. Tom Zuidema, *Inca Civilization in Cuzco,* translated from French by Jean-Jacques Decoster, foreword by Françoise Héritier-Augé (Austin: University of Texas Press, 1990), 1–3.

42. Frank Salomon, introductory essay to the Huarochirí Manuscript, in *The Huarochirí Manuscript: A Testament of Ancient and Colonial Andean Religion,* translation from the Quechua by Frank Salomon and George L. Urioste, transcription by George L. Urioste (Austin: University of Texas Press, 1991), 1.

43. José María Arguedas, ed. and trans., introduction to *Dioses y hombres de Huarochirí,* nota a la edición por Ángel Rama, introducción y prólogo de José María Arguedas, apéndice por Pierre Duviols (Lima: Museo Nacional de Historia e Instituto de Estudios Peruanos, 1966), 9–18.

44. Ibid., 15 (my translation).

45. Ibid., 11 (my translation).

46. See Sarmiento, *Historia,* 22–24, 39, 42, 171.

47. For example, Garcilaso argued that the Incas believed in an invisible Creator god, *Pachacámac,* whom "they held in greater veneration inwardly than the sun [god]." Garcilaso (Aranibar edition), *Comentarios,* 70 (my translation). He likened this god to the Christian conception of an omniscient, omnipresent god ("the real God, our Lord") (ibid.), alleging he "was invisible and would not let himself be seen. And for that reason they did not build him any temples nor offer sacrifices [to him] like to the sun" (ibid., 392; my translation). He also maintained that the Incas had "attained" the conceptions of the immortality of the soul and of universal resurrection (ibid., 85). And, in contrast to other colonial chroniclers, he stated that the Incas did not worship the moon as a deity, but rather that they "entered her room [in the temple] to visit the moon and entrust themselves to her, because they regarded her as the sister and wife of the sun and mother of the Incas and of all [subsequent] generations. They did not offer sacrifices to her, as they did to the sun" (ibid., 191; my translation). Similarly, he denied the statements made by other chroniclers that the Incas considered the stars, thunder-lightning, and the rainbow as deities. He contended that the Incas considered these to be "servants" of the sun god, but not divinities in their own right (ibid., 122, 191). Furthermore, he asserted that some historians falsely attributed to the Incas practices that were not their own. For instance, he argued that the Incas did not practice human sacrifice, as did some of the cultures they subjugated and brought under their dominion (ibid., 88–89, 93–94). This assertion has been refuted by a number of archaeological findings, which will be discussed more fully in a subsequent chapter.

48. Ibid., 40.
49. See Rolena Adorno, introduction to the second edition of *Guaman Poma: Writing and Resistance in Colonial Peru* (Austin: University of Texas Press, 2000), xliv. Adorno categorizes Guaman Poma as an *indio ladino*, meaning one who is Indian by birth but is "presumably proficient in Castilian, Christian in belief, and Hispanicized in custom" (ibid). Often mistaken as a *mestizo* chronicler because of his surname "de Ayala," Guaman Poma explains that his father saved the life of a Spaniard, Luis de Ávalos de Ayala, father of Guaman Poma's half brother, Martín de Ayala, at the Battle of Huarina. This apparently earned his father the right to bear the Spanish surname "de Ayala" in addition to his own Quechua name. See Felipe Guaman Poma de Ayala (circa 1615), *El primer nueva corónica y buen gobierno*, edición crítica de John V. Murra y Rolena Adorno, traducciones y análisis textual del quechua por Jorge L. Urioste, 3rd ed. (México DF and Madrid: Siglo Veintiuno, 1992), 11–12.
50. Manuel M. Marzal, *Historia de la antropología indigenista: México y Perú* (Barcelona: Anthropos, and Mérida, Spain: Editora Regional de Extremadura, 1993), 243.
51. Guaman Poma, *Nueva corónica* (Murra, Adorno, and Urioste edition), 4 (my translation).
52. Ibid., 11.
53. See Guaman Poma, *Nueva corónica* (Pease edition), 75:362–429, 76:10–104, 306–11.
54. Francisco Carrillo Espejo, ed., *Cronistas indios y mestizos II: Guaman Poma de Ayala* (Lima: Editorial Horizonte, 1992), 43 (my translation).
55. See Guaman Poma, *Nueva corónica* (Pease edition), 76:336–57. See also Carrillo, *Guaman Poma*, 47–53.
56. Lévi-Strauss, *Myth and Meaning*, ix.

CHAPTER 2: ANDEAN ANIMISM

1. Paul R. Steele, with the assistance of Catherine J. Allen, *Handbook of Inca Mythology* (Santa Barbara, CA: ABC-CLIO, 2004), 24–25.
2. See Billie Jean Isbell, *To Defend Ourselves: Ecology and Ritual in an Andean Village* (Prospect Heights, IL: Waveland Press, 1985), 59, 256 (glossary); Moseley, *Incas and Ancestors*, 55.
3. The *altiplano* is "a high Andean plateau [with an elevation of about 12,500 to 13,000 feet, or about 3,800 to 4,000 meters], located between the eastern and western mountain ranges of Peru and Bolivia." Bastien, *Mountain of the Condor*, 211 (glossary). Most of the Aymara-speaking communities are situated in this region.
4. See Kolata, *Valley of the Spirits*, ix, 10; Jan van Kessel, "La organización tempo-espacial del trabajo entre los aymaras de Tarapacá: La

perspectiva mitológica," in *Etnicidad, economía y simbolismo en los Andes*, 267–97, Silvia Arze, Rossana Barragán, Laura Escobari, Ximena Medinaceli, compiladoras, II Congreso Internacional de Etnohistoria, Coroico (La Paz, Bolivia: Instituto Francés de Estudios Andinos, Sociedad Boliviana de Historia, Antropólogos del Sur Andino, and Instituto de Historia Social Boliviana, 1992), 270.

5. Isbell, *To Defend Ourselves*, 59.

6. This is an allusion to the main character of the play "Don Juan Tenorio," by the Spanish dramatist and poet José Zorrilla (1817–1893). In the play, Don Juan Tenorio is a notorious womanizer. In English we describe this kind of person as a "Don Juan."

7. Luis Bolívar Zaruma, "Taita Bueran imashina cashcata inishcamanta" ("Creencias del Taita Buerán") and "Taita Bueran urcumanta imalla parlashcacunamanta" ("La leyenda del Taita Buerán"), in *Los pueblos indios en sus mitos, no. 5: Cañari (Tomo I)*, 2nd ed. (Quito: Ediciones Abya-Yala, 1993), 43–47 (my translation).

8. Alan L. Kolata, *Valley of the Spirits: A Journey into the Lost Realm of the Aymara* (New York: John Wiley & Sons, 1996), 11.

9. Ibid. (italics added).

10. The Urus (or Uros) live on forty-two floating islands off the shores of Puno, Peru, in Lake Titicaca. These islands are human-made and are constructed using *totora* reed—a form of bulrush sedge—that grows abundantly and is indigenous to the lake. The Urus fashion their huts and *balsas* (reed boats) from the *totora*, and they also chew the *totora* pulp to supply much-needed iodine in their diet. The Urus survive on fishing, hunting birds, and trading and bartering with the mainland and other Uru islands. Some of the islands have also introduced tourism and the sale of local arts and crafts. In recent years Urus have also sought and found employment on the mainland. Although some schooling is available on the islands, older Uru children tend to go to school on the mainland. This continuous interaction with the mainland has brought the Urus into close contact with the land-dwelling Aymaras, resulting in intermarriage between the two ethnic groups. Today only a few words of the original language of the Urus (possibly Pukina, or a branch of Pukina) survive in the daily vocabulary of the island dwellers. Most Urus off the coast of Puno speak only Aymara and, in some cases, Spanish.

11. Nathan Wachtel, "Men of the Water: The Uru Problem (Sixteenth and Seventeenth Centuries)," in *Anthropological History of Andean Polities*, 283–310, edited by John V. Murra, Nathan Wachtel, and Jacques Revel (Cambridge, UK: Cambridge University Press, 1986), 284.

12. Bastien, *Mountain of the Condor*, 43.

13. Ibid., 37 (italics added).

14. Ibid., 51–81.

15. Ibid., 45.

16. Ibid.

17. See Bastien, *Mountain of the Condor*, 43–45. See also Javier Lajo, *Qhapaq Ñan: La ruta inka de sabiduría*, 2nd ed. (Quito: Ediciones Abya-Yala, 2006), 60–61.

18. The term *Kolla* (also spelled *Colla*) is derived from the Inca term for the southwestern quarter of their empire, known as *Collasuyu* or *Collao* (land or quarter of the predominant ethnic group known as the *Colla*). In the pre-Columbian era, the Kollas were fiercely independent warriors who fought bravely against the Incas to keep their sovereignty. Although they were finally overcome by the Incas, the Incas were forced to reconquer them several times because of their ongoing revolts to reclaim their independence. The land of the former Kollas encompassed the region in the proximity of Lake Titicaca, which is the home of the present-day Aymaras, many of whom consider themselves descendants of the Kollas.

19. Antonio Paredes-Candia, "Leyenda kolla de la creación del mundo," in *Leyendas de Bolivia*, 3rd ed. (La Paz, Bolivia: Librería Editorial "Popular," 1998), 104–8 (my translation).

20. See William J. Schull and Francisco Rothhammer, eds., *The Aymara: Studies in Human Adaptation to a Rigorous Environment* (Dordrecht, Netherlands: Kluwer Academic Publishers, 1990), 4; Robert B. Kent, *Latin America: Regions and People* (New York: Guilford Press, 2006), 135.

21. See Xavier Albó, "Preguntas a los historiadores desde los ritos andinos actuales," trabajo presentado al encuentro "Cristianismo y Poder en el Perú Colonial," 1–34, Fundación Kuraka, Cuzco, Perú, June 2000, 6. See also van Kessel, "Los aymaras," 270–82; Kolata, *Valley of the Spirits*, 11–12.

22. Centuries ago, the Incas conquered and occupied the land of the Aymaras and superimposed the Inca religion, whose principal deities included the Sun (*Inti*), the Creator (*Viracocha*), and the Thunder and Lightning god (*Illapa*). It is generally believed that after the Inca conquest, the local ethnic groups then worshipped the Inca gods, in addition to their own local deities. The same phenomenon occurred after the Spanish Conquest. For that reason, the *Alax Pacha* (World Above or Upper World) of the Aymaras is also described as the realm of the "foreign" gods. See van Kessel, "Los aymaras," 274; Albó, "Preguntas a los historiadores," 5–6.

23. van Kessel, "Los aymaras," 275. See also Domingo Llanque Chana, *Ritos y espiritualidad aymara* (La Paz, Bolivia: ASET, IDEA, and Centro de Teología Popular [CTP], 1995), 17–18; Luis Jolicoeur, *El cristianismo aymara*, "Cultural Heritage and Contemporary Change," Series V, Latin

America, vol. III (Cochabamba, Bolivia: The Council for Research in Values and Philosophy and Universidad Católica Boliviana, 1997), 38–39.

24. Ibid.

25. van Kessel, "Los aymaras," 275.

26. In 1551, the Council of Lima issued an edict informing the native populations, through their Catholic missionaries and priests, that their unbaptized, non-Christian ancestors were condemned to eternal damnation. See Carmen Bernand, *Los incas, el pueblo del sol*, traducción de Mari Pepa López Carmona, coordinación de José Manuel Revuelta (Madrid: Aguilar, 1991), 167 (citing Pierre Duviols, *La lutte contre les religions autochtones dans le Pérou colonial*). Moreover, the priests were instructed to "tell them how their ancestors and their [former] sovereigns found themselves in this abode of suffering because they had not known God, nor had they worshipped Him, but instead worshipped the Sun, the rocks and other creatures" (ibid.; my translation). This had the effect of demonizing the ancestors and separating the native peoples from their ancestral religions. It was also a strong political statement, declaring the victory of the Christian God over the pre-Christian *mallkis* (ancestors) and *huacus*. Karen Spalding, *Huarochirí: An Andean Society under Inca and Spanish Rule* (Stanford, CA: Stanford University Press, 1984), 245.

27. Kolata, *Valley of the Spirits*, 12.

28. van Kessel, "Los aymaras," 272 (my translation).

29. Ibid., 273.

30. Ibid., 273–74.

31. This Quechua cosmological realm is also sometimes known as *Awa Pacha* or *Jawa Pacha*, meaning "Outer World" or "Exterior World."

32. See John Earls and Irene Silverblatt, "La realidad física y social en la cosmología andina," in *Actes du XLIIᵉ Congrès International des Américanistes, Vol. IV, Paris, 2–9 Septembre 1976*, 299–325 (Paris: Société des Américanistes, 1978), 211–14.

33. The colonial mestizo chronicler Garcilaso de la Vega related that the Incas divided their cosmos into three worlds: *Hanan Pacha* ("Higher World"), *Hurin Pacha* ("Lower World"), and *Ucu Pacha* ("the center of the earth that means Lower World Down There"). Garcilaso, *Comentarios reales* (Araníbar edition), 85 (my translation). However, Garcilaso offered a more "Christianized" description of these worlds, where *Hanan Pacha* was analogous to the Christian concept of heaven "where [the Incas] said that good people went to be rewarded for their virtues," and *Ucu Pacha* was analogous to the Christian concept of hell "where they said that the bad people ended up" (ibid). No doubt this bolstered his argument, presented elsewhere in the text, that the Incas had nearly

arrived at the Christian conception of the immortality of the soul and universal resurrection.

34.   Isbell, *To Defend Ourselves*, 211. See also Isbell, "La otra mitad esencial: Un estudio de complementariedad sexual en los Andes," *Estudios Andinos*, Año (Year) 5, vol. 5, no. 1 (1976): 37–56.

35.   See Santacruz Pachacuti, *Relación de antigüedades*, 217, 227–28.

36.   The name of the river *Pillcumayo* (also spelled *Pilcomayo* or *Piscumayo*) has been translated in various different ways: the "River of Many Colors" from the Quechua word for "river" (*mayo* or *mayu*) and "many colors" (*pillku, pillcu,* or *pillqo*); the "Red River" from a legend that a prince from the Gran Chaco died there, killed by his brother, and the blood pouring from his heart turned the river waters red (in Quechua, *pillku* also means "red" and is synonymous with *puka* [Lara, *Diccionario queshwa-castellano*, 177]); "River of the Birds" from the Quechua word for "bird" (*piscu* or *pisqu*) and "river" (*mayo* or *mayu*); and the "River of the Pillcu Birds," based on Garcilaso's description of the *Pillcumayo* as a place where many indigenous birds, called *pillcus*, gathered in its upper region. See Ramón Lista, "El Pilcomayo o Río de los Pillcus," in *Boletín del Instituto Geográfico Argentino (Tomo XVIII)*, 583–600, editado por Francisco Seguí (Buenos Aires: Imprenta Buenos Aires, 1897), 583.

37.   Steele and Allen, *Inca Mythology*, 147. In the Huarochirí Manuscript, "[w]ater is often male, especially storm water and downward-flowing water… [and the] hydraulic embrace of moving water and enduring earth was imagined as sex." Salomon, introduction to *Huarochirí Manuscript*, 15.

38.   Steele and Allen, *Inca Mythology*, 148.

39.   The Inca ruler was considered the "sun of the Sun" (*intip churin*) and led his people in worship at all major festivals and ceremonies dedicated to the Sun god. According to many colonial chroniclers, "there was no other god [except the Sun god] to whom so many and such magnificent temples were dedicated" in the Inca Empire. Cobo, *Inca Religion and Customs*, 25–26 (Hamilton translation). The Creator and the Thunder–Lightning god were also important Inca deities. In most major public rituals of the Inca religion, the idols of the Sun, the Creator (*Viracocha*), and Thunder–Lightning always appeared together in the presence of the Inca (ibid., 24, 32). The Rainbow (*Cuichu* or *Cuychi*) was also part of the Inca pantheon and had his own alcove for worship in the Temple of the Sun in Cuzco. It was also one of the royal insignias of the Inca. Garcilaso, *Comentarios reales* (Araníbar edition), 192.

40.   Among some contemporary Quechua communities, the term *choquechinchay* describes the movement and ascent of vapors from the ground when it is loosened and opened in February and August in preparation

for planting. "This is known as a dangerous and crazy (loco) time. The vapor rises, that is, the cat springs from inside the earth and ascends." Steele and Allen, *Inca Mythology*, 148. See also Isbell, *To Defend Ourselves*, 150, 210. *Choquechinchay* is described as a *ccoa* (or *qoa*) cat, which in some parts of the Andes is believed to be a dangerous spirit that assumes the form of clouds and emerges from the highland springs during the rainy season. Its weapon is lightning, with which it attacks crops and unsuspecting people. See Inge Bolin, *Rituals of Respect: The Secret of Survival in the High Peruvian Andes* (Austin: University of Texas Press, 1998), 237; Regina Harrison, *Signos, cantos y memoria en los Andes: Traduciendo la lengua y la cultura quechua* (Quito: Ediciones Abya-Yala, 1994), 94. Because *choquechinchay* connects the Lower World (underground) and the Upper World (air or sky), it is often considered an intermediary between the two.

41. See Santacruz Pachacuti, *Relación de antigüedades*, 226; also described in Isbell, *To Defend Ourselves*, 208–9, and Steele and Allen, *Inca Mythology*, 147–48.

42. With respect to the significance of "still" water, see Isbell, *To Defend Ourselves*, 210; Steele and Allen, *Inca Mythology*, 147; Salomon, introduction to *Huarochirí Manuscript*, 15. In reference to the Inca worship of *Mama Cocha*, see Cobo, *Inca Religion and Customs*, 33 (Hamilton translation).

43. Cobo, *Inca Religion and Customs*, 29.

44. Irene Silverblatt, *Moon, Sun, and Witches: Gender Ideologies and Class in Inca and Colonial Peru* (Princeton, NJ: Princeton University Press, 1987), 47.

45. Isbell, *To Defend Ourselves*, 207, citing R. Tom Zuidema, "Inca Kinship," in *Andean Kinship and Marriage*, 240–81, edited by R. Bolton and E. Mayer (Washington, D.C.: American Anthropological Association, Special Publication No. 7, 1977).

46. Silverblatt, *Moon, Sun, and Witches*, 41, citing Samuel La Fone, "El culto de Tonapa," in *Tres relaciones de antigüedades peruanas*, 287–353 (Asunción: Editorial Guaranía, 1950), 306. See also Santacruz Pachacuti, *Relación de antigüedades*, 226.

47. Isbell, *To Defend Ourselves*, 207.

48. Ibid., 211–14.

49. As in the Inca diagram, the child's drawing depicted the sun, *Inti*, and his sister-wife, the moon, known in Quechua as *Killa* or *Quilla*. However, the orientation of the child's images was opposite to that depicted by Santacruz Pachacuti. Isbell explains the opposing orientation by proposing that the child's images were presented from an observer's point of view instead of a participant's point of view. Also,

as in the child's drawing two stars appeared in the Inca model, which were similarly labeled "grandfather" and "grandmother" in Quechua, and were identified as the Morning Star and Evening Star (of Venus). Thus, Isbell concluded that the "child's version of the Upper World is a simplified version of Pachacuti Yamqui's elaborate model." Isbell, *To Defend Ourselves*, 208–9, 211–12.

50.   Isbell speculates that the father was omitted from the girl's drawing because of the "extreme sexual parallelism" in the Andes, whereby young girls and women identify only with women in every aspect of their life—social, ritualistic, language usage, and otherwise. Isbell, *To Defend Ourselves*, 211.

51.   Ibid.

52.   Ibid. (my italics).

53.   Ibid., 211, 214.

54.   See Isbell, *To Defend Ourselves*, 214; van Kessel, "Los aymaras," 270, n. 7. See also Luis Leoncio Flores Prado, *El Quishpi cóndor: Danza milenaria* (Callao, Perú: Instituto del Libro y la Lectura, 2005), 21.

55.   Note on the translation: At this point in the original story the narrator switches from the past tense to the present tense in Spanish. However, for the sake of consistency, I have continued to use the past tense for the remainder of the story.

56.   Arguedas, "El joven que subió al cielo," in *Canciones y cuentos del pueblo quechua*, 105–14 (my translation). It is common in Andean stories for the narrator to end the story in the first person (voice), and to interpose himself or herself in the plot at the end of the tale. This implies that the storyteller has a personal connection with the events portrayed in the story as a participant in, or a witness to, those events.

57.   Garcilaso, *Comentarios* (Araníbar edition), 76.

58.   Ibid., 59, 62.

59.   Earls and Silverblatt, "Cosmología andina," 301.

60.   Sarah Lund Skar, "Andean Women and the Concept of Space/Time," in *Women and Space: Ground Rules and Social Maps*, 31–45, edited by Shirley Ardener, 2nd ed. (Oxford: Berg Publishers, 1997), 32 (my italics).

61.   Salomon, introduction to *Huarochirí Manuscript*, 14.

62.   See Rafael E. Núñez and Eve Sweetser, "With the Future Behind Them: Convergent Evidence from Aymara Language and Gesture in the Cross-linguistic Comparison of Spatial Construals of Time," *Cognitive Science* 30, issue 3, (May 2006): 401–50. For Quechua, see Wolfgang Wölk and Clodoaldo Soto, "The Concept of Time in Quechua," paper presented at the Symposium of Andean Time, American Anthropological Association Meetings, New Orleans, LA, 1973, cited in Earls and Silverblatt, "Cosmología andina," 302.

CHAPTER 3: INTERMEDIARIES

1. Briefly, the theory of structuralism assumes that certain universal structures underlie human mental processes and are discoverable through forms of cultural expression, including myth, language, and kinship. For structuralists, human cognition is understood in terms of binary processes or dichotomies, such as high–low, dark–light, good–evil, raw–cooked, and so forth. The French-Belgian anthropologist and ethnologist, Claude Lévi-Strauss, was influenced by the application of structuralism to the study of language. He tried to systemize the study of myth and demonstrate that the same rational principles could be applied to mythology. "The quest," of structuralism, he stated, is to search "for the invariant, or the invariant elements, among superficial differences." Claude Lévi-Strauss, *Myth and Meaning*, 8. According to Lévi-Strauss, what is invariant in mythology is the underlying "structure" of the myth that is revealed through "mythemes"—the "bundles of relations" occurring in the myth through the grouping of ideas, images, and elements. He argued that the notion of underlying universal structures explained the similarity of myths across different cultures. He reasoned that although myth is "language," it operates on a more complex level than language, because it can be translated, reduced, paraphrased, and acted upon, without losing its essential structure. See Claude Lévi-Strauss, *The Raw and the Cooked: Mythologiques, Volume One*, translated by John and Doreen Weightman (Chicago: University of Chicago Press, 1983); Edith Kurzweil, *Age of Structuralism*, 13–34.

2. See Lévi-Strauss, *The Raw and the Cooked*, 53, 62–63, 68. However, according to Lévi-Strauss, the intermediary can never resolve the conflict or dichotomy posed by the myth, for although "each dualism (such as male/female) produces a tension that seems to be resolved by the use of a mediating term (such as *androgyny*), . . . that new term turns out to be one-half of a new dualism (such as androgyny/sexlessness) [and so forth] *ad infinitum*." Thus, "every myth is driven by the obsessive need to solve a paradox *that cannot be resolved*." Wendy Doniger, foreword to Lévi-Strauss, *Myth and Meaning*, vii, x (italics in original).

3. Throughout this chapter, *hanan* and *hurin*, spelled in lowercase letters, are not meant to be equivalent to *Hanan Pacha* (Upper World) and *Ukhu Pacha* (also called *Hurin Pacha*, or Lower World). Instead, they designate the relative positions of above (upper) and below (lower). For instance, the sky is *hanan* (above) with respect to the earth, and the earth is *hurin* (below) with respect to the sky; the highlands are *hanan* with respect to the valley, and the valley is *hurin* with respect to the highlands, and so forth. However, when we speak in terms of the three worlds of Quechua cosmology, the surface of the earth and all

its inhabitants are considered part of *Kay Pacha* (This World) and not *Ukhu Pacha*.

4.   For a good example of this kind of tale, see Buenaventura Rocca Molina, "Ukuku" ("The Man-Bear"), in *She-Calf and Other Quechua Folk Tales*, compiled, translated, and edited by Johnny Payne (Albuquerque: University of New Mexico Press, 2000), 132–39. For useful discussions on this topic, see also Gary Urton, "Animal Metaphors and the Life Cycle in an Andean Community," in *Animal Myths and Metaphors in South America*, edited by Gary Urton, 251–84 (Salt Lake City: University of Utah Press, 1985), 270–72.

5.   Ronald M. Nowak, *Mammals of the World*, vol. I, 6th ed. (Baltimore, MD: The Johns Hopkins University Press, 1999), 680.

6.   In Andean lore, condemned souls (*almas condenadas*) are wandering spirits who are forced to walk the earth after their physical death to expiate their sins. They are neither living nor dead and can neither enter heaven nor hell. Condemned souls allegedly appear in many different forms, but they all share one thing in common—their fate usually results from a grave sin, typically incest. Their physical appearances also vary; sometimes they are described as human or humanlike, whereas at other times they are believed to adopt the form of animals. For instance, a condemned soul may appear in the form of a monk or a priest sporting a brown, black, or white tunic and "fire" boots floating above the ground. In some parts of Bolivia, the condemned soul is believed to have "a skeleton [skull] instead of a head, and feet like the hooves of a mule, reminiscent of the descriptions of the *qarqacha*, incestuous people who become fire-breathing mules or llamas at night." Spedding, "Almas, anchanchus y alaridos," 319 (my translation). Others say they have crooked hands, facing backwards, and kneecaps facing upward. [Ibid., 320.] Still others report hearing the rattling of chains or the sound of animal hooves when condemned souls are present. In some parts of Ecuador, the locals insist that only animals can see the condemned souls. Typically, they are reported to dwell in cemeteries or caves. In Andean festivals and dances, the condemned soul is represented by a dancer dressed as a friar or a priest, sporting a long brown robe tied at the waist with a long cord, hopping and jumping awkwardly in pursuit of his widow. See Espinosa Apolo, *Duendes, aparecidos*, 25–28; Ansión, *Desde el rincón de los muertos*, 165–73; Spedding, "Almas, anchanchus y alaridos," 319–21. See also Ranulfo Cavero Carrasco, *Incesto en los Andes: Las llamas demoníacas como castigo sobrenatural* (Ayacucho, Perú: Consejo Nacional de Ciencia y Tecnología, 1990).

7.   The narrator at this point introduces this "helper," but oddly, the character does not play a role in the subsequent plot and simply vanishes from

the story. This is a reminder that oral stories are like imperfect puzzles—sometimes all the pieces do not fit neatly together.

8. One possible interpretation of this passage is that the "death" of the condemned soul rids the community of this dangerous menace and protects others from potential harm, even death, that the being may inflict. The condemned soul may also view his destroyer as a "savior," because upon his (second) "death," the condemned soul is "saved" from an eternity of wandering. In other words, he is no longer eternally bound to exist "in between" worlds; he is finally free to "die" and leave this world.

9. In this passage, the transfer of "keys" lets us know that after the Boy-Bear kills the condemned soul, the Boy-Bear will own the condemned soul's former property in the depopulated village. This will enable the *ukuku* to become "lord of the manor," which is consistent with the ending of many other Andean *ukuku* tales. See Steele and Allen, *Inca Mythology*, 106.

10. Santos Pacco Ccama, "Ukuku uñamanta" ("El hijo del oso"), in *Karu Ñankunapi*, compiled, edited, and translated by César Itier (Cuzco, Perú: Centro de Estudios Regionales "Bartolomé de las Casas," 2004), 40–45 (my translation).

11. This passage illustrates the kind of religious syncretism that often occurs in modern Andean stories, merging Christian and Native Andean beliefs. Here the dove (Christian symbol of the Holy Spirit; sometimes interpreted as a symbol for the human soul) is bound for the (Christian) heaven; yet, concurrently with the dove, the "body" is also headed to the afterlife. Although many Native Andean peoples are aware of the Christian conception of the Resurrection, in many pre-Columbian Andean religions, the afterlife was considered corporeal; hence, one needed a body for the afterlife, just as one needed a body here on earth. In this instance, the storyteller may be covering all grounds by having both the soul and the body leaving together.

12. According to Andean lore, if a death is unresolved, or the soul has left unfinished business on earth, the soul or spirit of the dead may remain "attached" to the place where the death occurred, in which case the site becomes *un lugar malo*, an evil place where supernatural and harmful events take place. In this case, it seems that the storyteller is letting his listeners know that both the Boy-Bear (after his death in the future) and his victim did not become "attached" to the *pascana* (the lodging where the bones came together), thereby preventing the site from becoming haunted. See Gerald Taylor, comp., ed., and trans., *La tradición oral quechua de Chachapoyas* (Lima, Perú: Instituto Francés de Estudios Andinos, 1996), 87n13; Paredes, *mitos, supersticiones y supervivencias*, 386.

13. Patricio Gónaz Más, "Juan Oso," in *La tradición oral quechua de Chachapoyas*, compiled, edited, and translated by Taylor, 83–87 (my translation).

14. Urton, "Animal Metaphors," 272.
15. Ibid.
16. Ibid.
17. Ibid.
18. Steele and Allen, *Inca Mythology*, 105, citing Catherine J. Allen, "Of Bear-Men and He-Men: Bear Metaphors and Male Self-Perception in a Peruvian Community," *Latin American Indian Literatures* 7, no. 1 (1983): 38–51.
19. For a thorough description of the Oedipus complex and the mechanism of repression, see Christopher Monte, *Beneath the Mask*, 52–55, 66–68.
20. Sigmund Freud, *The Interpretation of Dreams*, 242.
21. However, only "memories, thoughts, ideas that are somehow connected to impulses or wishes *that are unacceptable to the individual's conscious ethical standards* are capable of the intense anxiety needed to trigger repression." Monte, *Beneath the Mask*, 53 (italics in original).
22. Asunción Lavrin, ed., *Sexuality and Marriage in Colonial Latin America* (Lincoln: University of Nebraska Press, 1989).
23. Payne, *Quechua Folk Tales*, 131.
24. Repression requires an expenditure of psychological energy and only works so long as there is a continuous expenditure of energy to keep the repressed material in the unconscious. Nonetheless, the individual has no "memory" of these desires. "When repression operates, the individual is not aware that he is avoiding certain thoughts or impulses. In fact, we could say along with R. D. Laing, that when an individual represses an idea, he 'forgets' it and then 'forgets' that he forgot it." Monte, *Beneath the Mask*, 53, citing R. D. Laing.
25. Ibid.
26. The Andean notion of a condemned soul is described more fully in note 6.
27. Steele and Allen, *Inca Mythology*, 107.
28. Attached souls are discussed more fully in note 12.
29. See Juan M. Ossio, *Los indios del Perú*, 2nd ed. (Quito: Ediciones Abya-Yala, 1995), 252n4.
30. Steele and Allen, *Inca Mythology*, 107.
31. Due to concerns about the rapid melting of Andean glaciers, Peruvian authorities have now banned this practice. The *ukukus* participating in the festival can no longer hack off chunks of ice from the glaciers and haul them down the mountain.
32. Teodora Paliza, "Wakacha" ("The She-Calf"), in *Quechua Folk Tales*, compiled, edited, and translated by Payne, 42–55.
33. Ibid., 50.
34. See Jesús Lara, "El lagarto," in *Mitos, leyendas y cuentos de los quechuas* (La Paz, Bolivia: Editorial "Los Amigos del Libro," Werner Guttentag, 2003),

334–38. See also Agustín Thupa Pacco, "Waka wawamanta" ("El hijo del toro"), in *Karu Ñankunapi*, compiled, edited, and translated by Itier, 140–45.

35. See Itier, *Karu Ñankunapi*, 145.

36. Paliza, "Wakacha" ("The She-Calf"), in *Quechua Folk Tales*, compiled, edited, and translated by Payne, 50.

37. Payne, *Quechua Folk Tales*, 41.

38. Ibid., 44.

39. "The Mouse Husband," in *Black Rainbow: Legends of the Incas and Myths of Ancient Peru*, edited and translated by John Bierhorst (New York: Farrar, Straus & Giroux, 1976), 115–17.

40. Ibid., 117.

41. Mercedes Cotacachi (versión quichua), *Huaca pachamanta causashca rimai (Los cuentos de cuando las huacas vivían)*, traducción al castellano por Ruth Moya, compilado por estudiantes de la Promoción 1991–1992 en el Taller de Quichua dirigido por Fausto Jara, Licenciatura en Lingüística Andina y Educación Bilingüe, Facultad de Filosofía, Letras y Ciencias de la Educación, Universidad de Cuenca, Ecuador (Quito: Ediciones Abya-Yala, 1993), 97n1 (my translation).

42. In the countryside, Native Andeans are accustomed to calling any kind of feline a "tiger," whether a mountain lion, puma, jaguar, ocelot, or any other type of wildcat.

43. See Paredes-Candia, "Leyendas del tigre," in *Leyendas de Bolivia*, 62.

44. Ibid., 61 (my translation).

45. Spedding, "Almas, anchanchus y alaridos," 315.

46. Paredes-Candia, *Leyendas de Bolivia*, 61 (my translation).

47. See van Kessel, "Los aymaras," 277–78; 278n24, in reference to both the Aymaras and the Quechuas.

48. See Carmen Escalante and Ricardo Valderrama, "Apu kunturmanta" ("Apu cóndor"), in *La doncella sacrificada: Mitos del valle de Colca* (Arequipa, Perú: Universidad Nacional de San Agustín and Instituto Francés de Estudios Andinos, 1997), 153–54.

49. van Kessel, "Los aymaras," 287n24.

50. See Paredes-Candia, "Cóndor jipiña," in *Leyendas de Bolivia*, 7–11.

51. See Rubila Chamorro, "Warmi kuyay kuntur" ("El cóndor que amaba a una mujer"), in *Relatos quechuas (Kichwapi Unay Willakuykuna)*, con un estudio sobre la narrativa oral quechua por Crescencio Ramos Mendoza (Lima, Perú: Editorial Horizonte, 1992), 72–75; Gloria Tamayo, "Kuntur" ("Cóndor"), in *Cuentos cusqueños*, compiled, edited, and translated by Payne, 30–33; Jesús Lara, "El cóndor raptor," in *Mitos, leyendas y cuentos de los quechuas*, 320–24; Agustín Thupa Pacco, "Sipasmantawan Kunturmantawan" ("La joven y el cóndor"), in *Karu Ñankunapi*, compiled, edited, and translated by Itier, 35–39.

52. In some parts of the Andes, villagers share the belief that there are "bad or evil places" (*lugares malos*) where the earth or evil spirits known as *malignos* may gobble up human beings, especially children. There are also places where one can contract *uraqui*, the "illness of Pacha Mama," and as a result, one may also die. See Spedding, "Almas, anchanchus y alaridos," 300–10.

53. This is mimicking the whirring sound made by the Hummingbird, or *kkenti* (also spelled *q'ente* or *q'enti*, in Quechua), as it rapidly flaps its wings to fly in place.

54· In this case, the Hummingbird is heckling the Condor using exclamatory remarks in Quechua, such as *jajaulla!* and *ajajaulla!* (in some regions, also *jajayllas!* and *ajayllas!*) to show that he is not intimidated by the large bird. These interjections are similar to the English expressions "hurrah!" or "hurray!," but aside from expressing triumph or joy, they also mock the intended recipient and communicate a degree of haughtiness or indifference. Since these words are very difficult to translate without losing their intended effect, I have left them exactly as they appear in the text. For purposes of pronunciation, the letter "j" in both Romanized Quechua and Spanish is pronounced similarly to the letter "h" in English.

55. See note 54.

56. This appears to be a blending of the Spanish interjection "*Ja, ja!*" ("Ha, ha!") and Quechua ending (*-y*) to form a combined word (*jajay!*); so, in this case, the Hummingbird is mocking and laughing at the Condor. In addition to the comments made in the previous notes, in this instance there also appears to be a play on words. Although clearly the Hummingbird's remarks are intended to heckle the Condor, the term *jaya* (also spelled *haya*) in Quechua means "spicy." Therefore, the Hummingbird's choice of words here, with a slight transposition of letters, may also foreshadow his intention to use hot chili pepper to irritate the Condor's eyes later in the story.

57. José María Arguedas, "La amante del cóndor," in *Narraciones y leyendas incas*, edited by Valcárcel and Arguedas, 41–52 (my translation).

58. See Cecilia Granadino and Cromwell Jara, *Las ranas embajadoras de la lluvia y otros relatos: Cuatro aproximaciones a la isla de Taquile* (Lima, Perú: Minka, Embajada Real de los Países Bajos, Kollino Taquile), 1996. See also Juan Carlos Godenzzi, *Tradición oral andina y amazónica: Análisis e interpretación de textos* (Cuzco, Perú: Centro de Estudios Regionales Andinos "Bartolomé de las Casas," 1999), 94.

59. Steele and Allen, *Inca Mythology*, 256.

60. Gary Urton, *At the Crossroads of the Earth and the Sky: An Andean Cosmology* (Austin: University of Texas Press, 1981), 180–81. See also Steele and Allen, *Inca Mythology*, 256–57.

61. *Chachapoya*, also spelled *Chachapuya*, may be an adulterated form of *Sacha Puyu*, which derives from the Quechua word for tree (*sacha*) and the Quechua term for cloud (*phuyu* or *puyu*). Thus, loosely translated, the name of this culture could mean "cloud tree" or "cloud forest."

62. Milagros Palma, *El cóndor: Dimensión mítica del ave sagrada* (Managua, Nicaragua: Editorial Nuestra América, 1983), 78.

63. Ibid., 79.

64. Donald A. Proulx, *A Sourcebook of Nasca Ceramic Iconography: Reading a Culture Through Its Art* (Iowa City: University of Iowa Press, 2006), 79.

65. See, e.g., Alan R. Sawyer, "Painted Nasca Textiles," in *The Junius B. Bird Pre-Columbian Textile Conference: May 19th and 20th, 1973*, 129–50, edited by Ann Pollard Rowe, Elizabeth P. Benson, and Anne-Louise Schaffer (Washington, D.C.: The Textile Museum and Dumbarton Oaks, Trustees for Harvard University, 1979), 131–33.

66. Proulx, *Sourcebook of Nasca Ceramic Iconography*, 134.

67. John E. Staller, "Dimensions of Place: The Significance of Centers in the Development of Andean Civilization: An Exploration of the *Ushnu* Concept," in *Pre-Columbian Landscapes of Creation and Origin*, 269–314, edited by John Edward Staller (New York: Springer Science and Business Media, 2008), 302.

68. See van Kessel, "Los aymaras," 270n7.

69. *Simi Taqe*, 137–38 (my translation).

70. See Godenzzi, *Tradición oral andina y amazónica*, 94.

71. Cobo, *Historia del nuevo mundo*, 228 (my translation).

72. See Paredes, *Mitos, supersticiones y supervivencias*, 33–34, 38; Demetrio Roca Huallparimachi, "El sapo, la culebra y la rana en el folklore actual de la pampa de Anta," in *Folkore: Revista de Cultura Tradicional 1*, July, 41–66 (Cuzco, Perú: Editorial Garcilaso, 1966), 45; Efraín Cáceres Chalco, *Si crees los Apus te curan: Medicina andina e identidad cultural* (Cuzco, Perú: Centro de Medicina Andina and Centro de Investigación de la Cultura y la Tecnología Andina, 2002; first edition, 1988), 67–68, 77.

73. Paredes, *Mitos, supersticiones y supervivencias*, 38; Cáceres, *Apus*, 67–68.

74. Cáceres, *Apus*, 67–68.

75. Paredes, *Mitos, supersticiones y supervivencias*, 34–37.

76. van Kessel, "Los aymaras," 278n24.

77. Harrison, *Signos, cantos y memoria*, 140 (my translation).

78. Urton, *Crossroads*, 180, citing Roca Huallparimachi, "El sapo, la culebra y la rana," 45.

79. Eugenia Condori Mita, "La fauna de los vertebrados de la cuenca del río Desaguadero y sus presagios," 1–23, resumen de un trabajo más extenso de la autora que se titula *Léxico-semántico de la fauna andina: Vertebrados de la cuenca del río Desaguadero*, Tesis de Licenciatura

en Lingüística e Idiomas, Universidad Mayor de San Andrés, La Paz, Bolivia, 2005, 18 (my translation).

80.   Urton, *Crossroads*, 180.

81.   Ibid., 181, citing Roca Huallparimachi, "El sapo, la culebra y la rana," 58–59 (Urton translation).

82.   Kolata, *Valley of the Spirits*, 36–37.

83.   Ibid.

84.   Elizabeth P. Benson, with a foreword by Susan Milbrath, *Birds and Beasts of Ancient Latin America* (Gainesville, FL: University Press of Florida, 1997), 78.

85.   The Nazca culture (circa 200–600 AD) was a pre-Columbian Andean civilization that developed in the south coastal region of Peru. It is known for having created giant animal, insect, and geometric lines and figures in the coastal desert readily visible only from the air. There are various theories about the significance of these, including the notion that they may have had calendrical or ritual significance for these ancient Native Andeans.

86.   Benson, *Birds and Beasts*, 78 (fig. 57).

87.   See Inés Callali, "Uvijiramanta k'achay-k'acha waynawan" ("La ovejera y el joven elegante"), in *Cuentos cusqueños*, compiled, edited, and translated by Payne, 44–45. An ancestor poses as an elegant young man to seduce a young shepherdess, who becomes pregnant with his child. Later, she insists he stay the night, and his skeleton shatters at the break of dawn. She gives birth to a skeleton. See also Arguedas, "La amante de la culebra," in *Canciones y cuentos del pueblo quechua*, 95–104. A young woman becomes the lover of a shape-shifting snake that lives under a grinding stone. Upon the advice of a shaman, the family and hired hands kill the "demon" snake. The young woman spontaneously aborts a multitude of little snakes that are born alive but are subsequently killed by the woman's family and friends.

88.   See "The Handsome Fox," as retold by María Eugenia Choque, Carlos Mamani C., and Raquel Condori, *Tiwulan panichasitapa (El zorro galán)* (La Paz, Bolivia: Ediciones Aruwiyiri and Taller de Historia Oral Andina, 1997). In this story, a fox assumes the form of a young man and falls madly in love with a woman. He courts her and then proposes marriage. During the wedding ceremony the guests discharge some firecrackers, which make very loud noises that alarm the fox. He jumps over the guest table, changes back into a fox, and immediately scampers away with his tail between his legs.

89.   See "The Fox's Wedding" ("Tiwulan Kasarasitapa"), grabado [recorded] en el Taller de Historia Oral Andina, cuentos recopilados por La Unidad de Asesoramiento y Servicio Técnico, en el Primer Encuentro Andino Amazónico de Narradores Orales Indígenas, La Paz, Bolivia, 1992, y

el Segundo Encuentro Nacional de Narradores Orales, Cochabamba, Bolivia, 1993. In this tale, a fox alters his appearance and becomes human to win the love of a shepherdess, whom he later marries. The jealousy and possessiveness of the fox drive him to kill an ex-suitor of his wife.

90. See "The Fox That Fell from Grace" ("Qamaqin Chijir Puritapa"), grabado [recorded] en el Taller de Historia Oral Andina, supra at note 89. In this story, a malicious fox adopts a human form to entice a married woman to become his lover. When the adultery is discovered, the fox escapes and hides among a herd of cattle. His mockery incites a bull to gore the fox and hurl him to his death.

91. Susana Colque Fernández, "El zorro que se convertía en hombre," in *Cuentos andinos de montaña*, Víctor Alanes Orellana, Carla Bracke, Hernán Condori Condori, Nelson Contreras, et al., compiladores, Centro de Ecología y Pueblos Andinos, Concurso de Cuentos de Montaña, Oruro, Bolivia, 2002 (Oruro, Bolivia: Latinas Editores, 2003), 161–63.

92. Paliza, "She-Calf," in *Quechua Folk Tales*, compiled, edited, and translated by Payne, 42–55.

93. Lajo, *Qhapaq Ñan*, 81–85.

94. Verónica Salles-Reese, *From Viracocha to the Virgin of Copacabana: Representation of the Sacred at Lake Titicaca* (Austin: University of Texas Press, 1997), 118.

95. Tristan Platt, "Mirrors and Maize: The Concept of *Yanantin* among the Macha of Bolivia," in *Anthropological History of Andean Polities*, 228–59, edited by John V. Murra, Nathan Wachtel, and Jacques Revel (Cambridge, UK: Cambridge University Press, and Paris: Maison des Sciences de l'Homme, 1986), 248.

96. José Yánez del Pozo, *Yanantin: La filosofía dialógica intercultural del manuscrito de Huarochirí* (Quito: Ediciones Abya-Yala, 2002), 25 (my translation).

97. Platt, "Mirrors and Maize," 245.

98. Garcilaso, *Comentarios* reales (Pease edition), 222 (my translation).

99. For example, the Quechua term *churi*, meaning "son," is still primarily used by a father in reference to his son, or by a son in reference to his filial relationship with his father; however, the word *wawa* (also spelled *guagua*) has been broadened to include a son *or* a daughter in relation to *either* his or her father or mother. See *Simi Taqe*, 78, 731.

100. Urton, *Crossroads*, 22 (italics and parentheticals added).

101. Ibid. (italics added).

102. Platt, "Mirrors and Maize," 232.

103. Ibid., 233.

104. Ibid.

105. Guaman Poma, *Nueva corónica* (Pease edition), 75:227.
106. Ana María Mariscotti de Görlitz, *Pachamama Santa Tierra: Contribución al estudio de la religión autóctona en los Andes centro-meridionales* (Berlin: Ibero-Amerikanisches Institut, 1978), 227–28.
107. Ibid., 223.
108. Salomon, *Huarochirí Manuscript*, 15.
109. Isbell, *To Defend Ourselves*, 138–43.
110. Ibid., 143.
111. Platt, "Mirrors and Maize," 241.
112. Ibid., 233.
113. Ibid., 236.
114. According to Isbell, productivity and fertility of both land and women are an overriding concern in these rituals. Isbell, *To Defend Ourselves*, 14, 138, 143, 163, 199.
115. Olivia Harris, "From Asymmetry to Triangle: Symbolic Transformations in Northern Potosí," in *Anthropological History of Andean Polities*, 260–79, edited by John V. Murra, Nathan Wachtel, and Jacques Revel (Cambridge, UK: Cambridge University Press, and Paris: Maison des Sciences de l'Homme, 1986), 266.
116. Repetition of words, phrases, and passages is part of the Andean oral tradition. The storyteller narrates these stories orally and therefore has little opportunity to edit or self-correct. Sometimes words and phrases are also repeated intentionally to emphasize or highlight important aspects of the story.
117. Teodora Paliza Torres, "Wayna uywaq aguilakuna" ("Las águilas que criaron a una niña"), in *Cuentos cusqueños*, compiled, edited, and translated by Payne, 12–17 (my translation).
118. In the Inca Empire, for instance, gold was associated with the Sun god (male) and silver with the Moon goddess (female). According to Garcilaso de la Vega, the *Coricancha* (also spelled *Qorikancha*, meaning "Golden Enclosure"), the most important and sacred temple of the Inca Empire, housed a number of different rooms or shrines dedicated to each of the Inca deities. The shrine dedicated to the Sun god had walls and niches lined with heavy gold plates that sparkled in the sunlight. In this shrine the Incas placed a thick, round gold disk that resembled a male human face, whose image was encircled by golden "flames" (sun rays). This idol represented their anthropomorphized vision of the Sun god. In like fashion, the shrine dedicated to the Moon was covered with large, light-reflecting silver plates, and the idol of the Moon was made entirely of silver and shaped in the form of a round female face. See Garcilaso, *Comentarios reales* (Araníbar edition), 188–92.

CHAPTER 4: PACHACUTI

1. See Guaman Poma, *Nueva corónica* (Pease edition), 75:20–28. See also, Santacruz Pachacuti, *Relación*, 209–11; Molina, *Fábulas* (Urbano and Duviols edition), 50–53.

2. Led by Bolivian president Victor Paz Estenssoro of the MNR party ("Movimiento Nacional Revolucionario," or "Nationalist Revolutionary Movement"), the Bolivian Revolution of 1952–1964 made sweeping and violent changes. The government established universal suffrage and abolished literacy and property requirements for voter eligibility. It nationalized tin production and made far-reaching agrarian reform by mobilizing and arming peasant militias and taking land away from the predominantly white and mestizo elite and redistributing it among the *campesinos* (peasants), who were predominantly Native Andean. There is much controversy as to whether the Bolivian Revolution was successful; however, many Native Andeans regard it as the starting point for greater indigenous participation in government and in the social and economic affairs of their nation. From their perspective, it produced cataclysmic changes in their lives, synonymous with *pachacuti*. For an informative discussion about the Bolivian Revolution, see Thomas E. Weil, Jan Knippers Black, Howard I. Blutstein, Hans J. Hoyer, Kathryn T. Johnston, and David S. McMorris, *Bolivia: A Country Study*, Country Studies/Area Handbook Series, sponsored by the U.S. Department of the Army (Washington, D.C.: Federal Research Division, U.S. Library of Congress, 1986–1998).

3. See van Kessel, "Los aymaras," 289n35. See also Juan van Kessel, "La cosmovisión aymara," in *Culturas de Chile, Etnografía: Sociedades indígenas contemporáneas y su ideología*, 169–88, edited by Jorge Hidalgo L., Virgilio Schiappacasse F., Hans Niemeyer F., Carlos Aldunate del S., and Pedro Mege R., in collaboration with La Fundación Andes, and sponsorship from the Universidad de Tarapacá, Sociedad Chilena de Arqueología, Museo Chileno de Arte Precolombino, and Archivo Nacional (Santiago: Editorial Andrés Bello, 1996), 186.

4. See "La nación dejó de ser clandestina: Afirman que éste es un hito histórico no sólo en Bolivia, sino en América Latina," *El Diario*, La Paz, Bolivia, January, 22, 2006; Wilson García Mérida, "Más noticias sobre la profecía del Pachacuti," *Indymedia: Qollasuyu Ivi Iyambae Bolivia*, Cochabamba, Bolivia, July 3, 2006, accessed September 5, 2006, http://sucre.indymedia.org/es/2006/01/25994.shtml.

5. Cobo, *Inca Religion*, 29 (Hamilton translation).

6. Garcilaso de la Vega, *Comentarios reales* (Riva-Agüero edition), 85 (my translation).

7. In his *Royal Commentaries* Garcilaso explains that the Incas believed the moon was especially fond of dogs. The Incas apparently whipped their

dogs so that the moon would take pity on them and stay awake. They
feared that if the moon went to sleep on account of her "illness," she
would never wake up again (ibid).

8.   Ibid. (my translation).

9.   Guaman Poma, *Nueva corónica* (Pease edition), 75:168–81. With respect
to disease, the Incas were on the mark. Disease came close to becoming a *pachacuti* by wiping out Native Andean populations, and other
indigenous populations elsewhere in the Americas, during the demographic disaster that occurred shortly after the Europeans landed on the
shores of the New World. The Native Americans had no immunity to
smallpox, measles, syphilis, influenza, or other European diseases, and,
as a result, millions died, and some indigenous groups were completely
extinguished. Disease also played a major role in the Conquest of Peru,
because it claimed the life of the Inca emperor Huayna Capac, who
ruled over a unified empire but died without leaving a successor. His
premature death sparked rivalries between two of Huayna Capac's sons
(by different mothers), Huascar and Atahualpa, who divided the empire
and engaged in a six-year civil war that claimed the lives of many
people, including Inca nobles responsible for administering the empire.
By the time the Spaniards arrived, Atahualpa had emerged victorious
but ruled over a war-weary and divided empire. Atahualpa himself may
have been the victim of a European disease. Some accounts of the Conquest state that he was an elegant man but that his scarified face bore
the pockmarks of a European disease. See Raúl Porras Barrenechea, *Los
cronistas del Perú (1528–1650) y otros ensayos*, Biblioteca Clásicos del
Perú, no. 2 (Lima: Banco de Crédito del Perú y Ministerio de Educación,
1986), 549.

10.   Cobo, *Inca Religion*, 112.

11.   Ibid., 8–9; Molina, *Fábulas y ritos* (Urbano and Duviols edition), 122.

12.   There is no agreement as to the literal or figurative meaning of *Tiahuanaco* (also spelled *Tiwanaku* or *Tiahuanacu*), the name of a formidable
Andean pre-Inca civilization that developed in the Andean altiplano
from about 500 to 1000 AD and exerted great cultural and religious influence over the entire region for many centuries. The Incas conquered
this region and were so impressed with the accomplishments of the
Tiahuanacotas that they may have altered their mythology to claim as-
cendency and connection with the great *huacas* of this region, including
Lake Titicaca. In one version of the Inca creation story, recorded during
the Spanish colonial period, the Inca Creator god, *Viracocha*, emerged
from Lake Titicaca and created the sun, the moon, and the stars, and
then created people at Tiahuanaco "from stone as a kind of model of
those that he would produce later." Afterward, he and his companions
dispersed and walked in different directions, traversing all the provinces

and summoning the people that *Viracocha* had created to come out of the caves, rivers, springs, and mountains to populate the land. After this was done, *Viracocha* and his companions reconvened at Puerto Viejo, on the shores of the Pacific Ocean, and they walked out into the sea, "[walking] on water as if on land," and the people never saw them again. Betanzos, *Narrative of the Incas*, 7–11 (Hamilton and Buchanan translation).

13. Cristóbal de Molina (1573), *Relación de las fábulas y ritos de los incas*, edición de Horacio H. Urteaga y Carlos Alberto Romero, Colección de libros y documentos referentes a la historia del Perú, Tomo I (Lima: Imprenta y Librería Sanmartí y ca., 1916), 4–6 (my translation and capitalization; italics added). (Hereinafter, "Urteaga and Romero edition.")

14. Genesis 6:17–22, 7:1–24, 8:1–5.

15. Ibid., 2:7 (Roman Catholic edition). The King James version of the Bible varies slightly and states that God formed man "of the dust of the ground and breathed into his nostrils the breath of life; and man became a living soul."

16. Sabine MacCormack, *Religion in the Andes: Vision and Imagination in Early Colonial Peru* (Princeton, NJ: Princeton University Press, 1991), 100.

17. The pre-Columbian Andean cultures described multiple creations as different "suns" and "ages" of the world. See Guaman Poma, *Nueva corónica* (Murra and Adorno edition), 40–97. See also Garcilaso, *Comentarios reales* (Araníbar edition), 805. In this case, the duality of *hanan* ("above") and *hurin* ("below"), written in lowercase letters, should not be confused with the Quechua and Inca cosmological concept of the existence of three worlds: *Hanan Pacha* ("Upper World"), *Kay Pacha* ("This World"), and *Ukhu or Hurin Pacha* ("Lower World" or "Interior World").

18. Relative to the "first ages" of the Andean world, Guaman Poma contended that the Indians of these ages, prior to the Incas, did not worship false idols or demon *huacas*. Although they had not heard the Gospel of Christ, they worshipped one Creator and practiced mercy, compassion, and charity. Guaman Poma, who was a convert to Christianity, urged his Christian readers to learn from these Indians about the meaning of true faith, devotion, and service to God. Guaman Poma, *Nueva corónica* (Murra and Adorno edition), 40–61. By contrast, the mestizo colonial chronicler Garcilaso de la Vega maintained that the first epoch, before the time of the Incas, was characterized by barbarism and idolatry: "They could not raise their thoughts to invisible things—they worshipped what they saw...without considering those things they worshipped, [and] whether they were worthy of being worshipped.... There was no animal too vile or filthy that they could not

worship as a god." Garcilaso, *Comentarios reales* (Aranfbar edition), 29 (my translation).

19. See Sarmiento (1572), *Historia de los incas*, 51–64; Cieza (1550), *Señorío de los incas*, 42–50; Betanzos (1551), *Narrative of the Incas*, 13–18. See also Gary Urton, *History of a Myth: Pacariqtambo and the Origin of the Inkas* (Austin: University of Texas Press, 1990). Other possible translations of *Pacariqtambo* include "Inn of Dawn," "Inn of Production," or "Place of Origin." See Urton, *History of a Myth*, 19; Rostworowski, *Historia del Tahuantinsuyu*, 38; also refer to the endnotes for the chapter on *Huacas*.

20. MacCormack, *Religion in the Andes*, 13.

21. Ibid.

22. See Arthur Demarest, *Viracocha: The Nature and Antiquity of the Andean High God*, Peabody Museum Monographs, no. 6 (Cambridge, MA: Peabody Museum of Archaeology and Ethnology, Harvard University, 1981).

23. See Cobo, *Inca Religion*, 3, 8. See also MacCormack, *Religion in the Andes*, 7, 55–63, 85–98, 183; Carmen Bernand, *Los incas*, 73–91.

24. The Wankas were probably the original inhabitants of the Valley of Jauja or Mantaro in the central highland region of Peru in the present-day department of Junín. According to local accounts, the Wankas were a bellicose people, contemporary of the Incas, who were eventually conquered by them during the reign of the Inca emperor Pachacuti Inca Yupanqui. Seeking their independence, the Wankas fought with the Spaniards against the Incas during the Spanish Conquest of Peru. Later, the Spaniards, in their attempts to Christianize the Wankas, partially destroyed their most important temple, Wariwilka, which is mentioned in this origin myth. Francisco Pizarro designated the town of Jauja, located in this valley, as the first provisional capital of Peru in 1534 and also had the first Christian cathedral built on this site. Later, the Peruvian capital was moved to Lima.

25. According to José María Arguedas, this term "is derived from [two] words: *wari*, [meaning] hiding place that has not been defiled, which keeps something or a sacred being [inside]; and *puquio*: "spring" [of water]." Arguedas, comp. and ed., "Aparición de los seres humanos sobre la tierra," in *Mitos, leyendas y cuentos peruanos*, Colección Escolar Peruana, vol. 4, n. at 66 (my translation). Another possible translation is "native spring" from the Quechua and Aymara term *wari*, meaning "native" and the Quechua term *puquio* (also spelled *pukyu* or *pujyu*), signifying "spring." *Simi Taqe*, 407; Lara, *Diccionario qheshwa-castellano*, 179, 382.

26. "La aparición de los seres humanos sobre la tierra," in Arguedas and Ríos, eds., *Mitos, leyendas y cuentos peruanos* (1970 edition), 65–66 (my

translation and capitalization). The unedited version of this story was recorded by Nelly Valle, a student at Colegio Nacional Miguel Grau de Magdalena Nueva, Lima, Peru, in or before 1947, when the first edition of this book was published. It is from the Junín region of Peru. This story also appears in a recent edition of this compilation. See Arguedas and Izquierdo Ríos, eds., *Mitos, leyendas y cuentos peruanos* (2009 edition), 44 (hereinafter "2009 edition").

27. For a discussion about the meaning and translation of the name of this shrine, refer to the notes in the *Introduction*.

28. Lawrence E. Sullivan, "Above, Below, or Far Away: Andean Cosmogony and Ethical Order," in *Cosmogony and Ethical Order: New Studies in Comparative Ethics*, 98–131, edited by Robin W. Lovin and Frank E. Reynolds (Chicago: University of Chicago Press, 1985), 104.

29. Ibid., 105.

30. Nevado del Ruiz is an active Andean stratovolcano that lies about 130 kilometers (approximately 80 miles) west of the city of Bogotá in the Tolima department of Colombia. Its "relative," Nevado Tolima, part of the Ruiz-Tolima volcanic massif, is a stratovolcano located to the south of Nevado del Ruiz in the same department. The dome-peaked Nevado Santa Isabel is a shield volcano, no longer eruptive, which lies on the boundary of three Colombian departments, Tolima, Caldas, and Risaralda, and it is located to the southwest of the Nevado del Ruiz volcano.

31. See "El cóndor de oro," in Palma, *Cóndor*, 57–58; María Acosta, "La bola de oro del cóndor," in *Cuentos y leyendas de América Latina: Los mitos del sol y la luna* (Barcelona: Editorial Océano Ámbar, 2002), 96–97.

32. Palma, *Cóndor*, 57 (my translation).

33. Ibid., 58 (my translation).

34. Ibid. (my translation).

35. van Kessel, "Los aymaras," 270 (my translation).

36. The *precordillera* is a Spanish term that literally means "before the mountain range." In this case, it is used to describe an ecological zone, comprised of hills and mountains, lying to the west of the higher Andean mountains and to the east of the Chilean coastal range in a mountainous depression.

37. van Kessel, "Los aymaras," 271.

38. Ibid.

39. Earls and Silverblatt, "Cosmología andina," 314–15.

40. Ibid., 314.

41. Ibid. (my translation).

42. Ibid. (my translation).

43. Ibid. (my translation).

44. Bolin, *Rituals of Respect*, 208.

45. See Urton, *Crossroads*.

46. Urton, *Crossroads*, 109.
47. Ibid., 109, 170.
48. Few species of snakes are indigenous to the Andean highlands, and none are as large or as deadly as some of the Amazonian varieties. However, Urton proposes that the Incas were familiar with large Amazonian reptiles, because Inca subjects who lived in the jungle lowlands east of Cuzco brought these animals to the Inca ruler as tribute (tax). Moreover, the Urubamba River may have facilitated trade between highland and lowland natives, so the highland peoples may have seen or heard of these impressive reptiles. Urton presents further evidence that the *Amaru* in Quechua meteorology is the multicolored rainbow, which is conceived by the Quechua as a giant serpent. *Machácuay*, on the other hand, is a dark cloud constellation and possibly the "dark" counterpart of the *Amaru*. Since *Machácuay* ("the dark cloud Serpent") is visible only during the rainy season, Urton argues that this may represent the same astronomical "complex of associations" that exists among the Guaraní Indians of Amazonia. The Guaraní associate celestial serpents with "rainbows (water), dark clouds in the Milky Way, and…the rainy season." Urton, *Crossroads*, 172, 177–80.
49. Ibid., 172.
50. Cobo, *Inca Religion*, 31 (Hamilton translation).
51. Ibid.
52. Ibid.
53. Cristóbal de Albornoz (1584), *Instrucción para descubrir todas las guacas del Pirú y sus camayos y haziendas,* edición de Henrique Urbano y Pierre Duviols (Madrid: Historia 16, 1988), 174–75 (my translation and capitalization; italics added).
54. Urton, *Crossroads*, 178.
55. The Moche or Mochica culture (200–850 AD) developed along the Peruvian north coast and was renowned for its impressive three-dimensional pottery and metallurgy, which was highly standardized and crafted in the service of the Moche state. Moche art often depicted anthropomorphic and zoomorphic creatures, and Moche murals sometimes portrayed double-headed snakes and double-headed birds growing out of a stylized human or crablike figure. A recurring image in Moche ceramics was "a double-headed rainbow arching over a central figure." Steele and Allen, *Inca Mythology*, 96. This figure has sometimes been described as an "arching mythical Sky Serpent" similar to an *Amaru*. Izumi Shimada, *Pampa Grande and the Mochica Culture* (Austin: University of Texas Press, 1994), 236, citing Dorothy Menzel, *The Archaeology of Ancient Peru and the Work of Max Uhle* (Berkeley: R. H. Lowie Museum of Anthropology, University of California, 1977), 34.

56. Chimor, also known as Chimú, was a kingdom that ruled the northern coast of Peru during the Late Intermediate Period (circa 1000–1470 AD) and was subsequently conquered by the Incas. It was the second largest pre-Columbian Andean civilization to develop in South America, and its capital of Chan Chan was located in the Moche River valley. The artisans of Chimor were known for their expert craftsmanship, especially in metalwork and luxury items made of gold, copper, bronze, and silver. In fact, some scholars speculate that the opulence and luxury we have come to associate with the Inca Empire derives from the Chimor influence on the Inca court. See Rostworowski, *Historia del Tahuantinsuyu*, 126. Some of the significant figures in Chimor iconography include a person known as "wrinkle face," an anthropomorphic iguana, marine birds, fish and other sea animals, and a two-headed rainbow-serpent. Moseley, *Incas and Ancestors*, 215; Urton, *Inca Myths*, 23.

57. *Yayamama* culture and art may have developed in the Lake Titicaca basin as early as 800 BC and continued until 200–400 AD, or even later, until the formative transformation of the Tiahuanaco culture (circa 500–700 AD). In 2008 Bolivian locals accidentally stumbled upon the remains of some *Yayamama* sculptures while clearing the ground to build a market in Copacabana, a scenic town located on the shores of Lake Titicaca. These carved stone sculptures included a male and a female figure, two-headed snakes, and geometric shapes. Sergio Chávez, the archaeologist in charge of the dig, reported that some of these artifacts were approximately 3,000 years old. See David Mercado, "Ancient Ruins Found in Bolivia," *Vancouver Sun*, Vancouver, British Columbia, Canada, July 10, 2008. For descriptions of *Yayamama* construction and iconography, see William H. Isbell and Patricia J. Knobloch, "Missing Links, Imaginary Links: Staff God Imagery in the South Andean Past," in *Andean Archaeology III: North and South*, 307–51, edited by William H. Isbell and Helaine Silverman (New York: Springer Science+Business Media, 2008), 319; Charles Stanish, *Ancient Titicaca: The Evolution of Complex Society in Southern Peru and Northern Bolivia* (Berkeley: University of California Press and Regents of the University of California, 2003), 132.

58. Garcilaso, *Comentarios reales* (Riva-Agüero edition), 86.

59. Ibid. (my translation).

60. Garcilaso, *Comentarios reales* (Riva-Agüero edition), 86.

61. Albornoz, *Instrucción*, 175.

62. Steele and Allen, *Inca Mythology*, 96.

63. Urton, *Crossroads*, 179.

64. Ibid.

65. Freud, *Interpretation of Dreams*, 242.

66. For a more detailed discussion of Andean dualism and the cosmological

concept of *yanantin* (complementary duality, or the union of equal and harmonious complementary principles), refer to the chapter on *Intermediaries*.

67.   See Garcilaso, *Comentarios reales* (Araníbar edition), 132–33, 344–48; Guaman Poma, *Nueva corónica* (Pease edition), 75:183, 260–65; Cobo, *Historia del nuevo mundo*, 141–44.

68.   See Guaman Poma, *Nueva corónica* (Pease edition), 75:260 ("cuentan en tablas, numeran de cien mil, y de diez mil, y de ciento, y de diez, hasta llegar a uno"); Garcilaso, *Comentarios reales* (Araníbar edition), 344 ("Por los colores sacaban lo que se contenía en aquel tal hilo, como el oro por el amarillo y la plata por el blanco y por el colorado la gente de guerra"). See also Leslie Leland Locke, *The Ancient Quipu or Peruvian Knot Record* (New York: The American Museum of Natural History, 1923; supplementary notes published in 1928).

69.   Traditionally, investigators considered the *khipu* a strictly mnemonic device, with its various constituent parts serving as stimuli to trigger or jog the memory of the *khipucamayocs*, or "keepers of the *khipus*"; however, recent scholarship has called into question that longstanding assumption. See Quilter and Urton, eds., *Narrative Threads*, and Urton, *Signs of the Inka Khipu*, full citations in the *Introduction*. It is also important to highlight that the colonial Spaniards destroyed the vast majority of Inca *khipus* during the Extirpation of Idolatries, alleging that they were instruments of the devil. Consequently, today there are only about six hundred surviving *khipus* housed in museums and private collections around the world.

70.   For a more complete description of these limitations, see text and notes in the *Introduction*.

71.   I hesitate to call this manuscript "mythology," because it is written with great precision, immense ethnic pride, and profound reverence for an ancient religion that collided with and, ultimately, was overthrown by Christianity. In this I am reminded of the words of the philosopher and poet, James K. Feibleman: "A myth is a religion in which no one any longer believes."

72.   One of the limitations of the Spanish colonial chronicles is that many of the chroniclers' informants belonged to the Cuzco elite, thus furnishing accounts from the perspective of the (former) Inca capital instead of from the outlying (or conquered) provinces. They also disproportionately represented the upper classes of Inca society and thus could not adequately relay the experiences of the *hatun runa* (commoners), who constituted the overwhelming majority of the Inca population.

73.   Arguedas, introduction to *Dioses y hombres*, 9–18. For a thorough discussion of the role Avila played in editing, summarizing, and possibly

ordering the preparation of the manuscript, see Salomon, introductory
essay to *Huarochirí Manuscript*, 24–28.

74. Albornoz, *Instrucción,* 195–96 (my translation; parentheticals added).
75. Ibid., 196 (my translation).
76. Salomon, introductory essay to *Huarochirí Manuscript*, 24.
77. Arguedas, *Dioses y hombres*, 15 (my translation).
78. Ibid., 11.
79. Salomon, introductory essay to *Huarochirí Manuscript*, 1.
80. Salomon and Urioste, *Huarochirí Manuscript*, 51.
81. Ibid.
82. Ibid., 53.
83. Ibid.
84. Ibid., 113.
85. M. Lemlij, L. Millones, M. Rostworowski, A. Péndola, and M. Hernández, "Las cinca ñamcas: Aspectos de lo femenino en ritos y tradiciones de Huarochirí recogidos por Francisco de Avila," in *Mitos universales, americanos y contemporáneos: Un enfoque multidisciplinario*, vol. I, 129–35, Moisés Lemlij, comp., y Giuliana Falco, ed. ejecutiva (Lima: Sociedad Peruana de Psicoanálisis, 1989), 129.
86. Ibid.
87. For a thorough discussion of the language substrates and non-Quechua influences on the text, refer to Salomon's introductory essay to the *Manuscript of Huarochirí*, 30–31.
88. *Huillcacoto* may also be spelled *Willkaqoto, Willkaqotu,* or *Villa Coto. Willka* means "sacred" or "divine" in Quechua; it also means "lineage" (*Simi Taqe*, 746). *Willka* also means "sun" in antiquated Aymara, but most contemporary Aymaras prefer to use the Quechua term *inti* in reference to the sun. *Qoto* or *qotu* means a small "heap" or "pile" in both Quechua and Aymara languages, as in *papa qoto* (Quechua) or *amka qutu amkaqä* (Aymara), "a small pile of potatoes." This suggests that at one time *qoto* or *qutu* might have referred to a small "mound" or a small mountain in the Huarochirí region. Consequently, there are various possible translations for the name of the mountain *Huillcacoto* or *Willkaqoto*, including "Sacred Mount," "Sun Mount," or "Lineage Mount." Today there is a mountain called *Villca Coto* located "12 km northwest of San Damián, between modern Huanre and Surco," in the department of Lima, Peru. Salomon and Urioste, *Huarochirí Manuscript*, 51n75, citing John Treacy, "A Preliminary Chorography of the Waru Chiri Myths," unpublished paper, Madison, University of Wisconsin, 1984, 18.
89. "Cómo pasó antiguamente los indios cuando reventó la mar. En esta parte volveremos a las cosas que cuentan los hombres muy antiguos," in Arguedas, ed. and trans., *Dioses y hombres*, 32 (my translation).

90.   The Qero people live in remote areas of the Andes east of Cuzco, Peru, at elevations higher than 13,000 feet. The Qeros believe that during the Spanish Conquest their Inca ancestors fled and hid in the mountains; thus, they were able to keep their pre-Columbian rituals and traditions relatively intact. The Qeros are best known for their healing practices and mysticism, as well as their high-quality textiles.

91.   Matthew 27:45, Mark 15:33, and Luke 23:44.

92.   This is probably a misspelling of *mutca, mutcca,* or *mut'ka,* which means "mortar" in both Aymara and Quechua languages.

93.   The Spanish word is *batanes,* which are grinding stones used in the Andes, generally shaped like a half moon.

94.   "Cómo el sol se desapareció cinco días. Y ahora vamos a contar cómo murió el día," in Arguedas, ed. and trans., *Dioses y hombres,* 34 (my translation).

95.   Bastien, *Mountain of the Condor,* 49, 214.

96.   Arguedas, *Dioses y hombres,* 35.

97.   The distinction between a hawk and a falcon may not be significant in this case, as the Spanish term *halcón* and the Quechua term *waman* (also spelled *huaman*), both often translated as "falcon," may also refer to various species of hawks.

98.   Arguedas, *Dioses y hombres,* 42.

99.   Salomon and Urioste, *Huarochirí Manuscript,* 54–57 (English translation), 162–65 (Quechua transcription).

100. Bastien, *Mountain of the Condor,* 49.

101. Ibid., 50.

102. Ibid., 51.

103. Ibid.

104. Ibid., 65.

105. Ibid., 45, 49 (citing lecture delivered by George Urioste at Cornell University, Ithaca, NY, in November 1971).

106. See Arguedas, *Dioses y hombres,* 24, 26–48, 51–61. The translation of *Huallallo Carhuincho* (also spelled *Wallallo Carwancho*) derives from Salomon and Urioste, *Huarochirí Manuscript,* 61.

107. Guaman Poma, *Nueva corónica* (Pease edition), 75:26, 39–57. See also Guaman Poma, *Nueva corónica* (Murra and Adorno edition), 25, 41–61.

108. The name of this age of the world is spelled *Uari Uira Cocha Runa* or *Vari Vira Cocha Runa* in the original text. *Runa,* in Quechua, signifies "man" (generically), "men," "humankind," or "people." *Wari* (spelled *Uari* or *Vari* in the original text) means "autochthonous" or "primitive" in modern Quechua. *Simi Taqe,* 724. *Viracocha* (also spelled *Wiracocha, Wiraqucha,* or *Uira Cocha*) is the name of the Andean Creator god, which is usually translated as "Sea Foam" or "Sea Fat." In this case, however, it refers to the term that the Incas ascribed to the conquering

Spaniards upon meeting them (*wiracocha* or *viracocha*), because physically they resembled the white-bearded Creator god of their mythology, who had promised that one day he would return. The Spaniards took advantage of their status as "gods" to facilitate their meetings with the Inca emperor Atahualpa and later to plunder and pillage the Inca temples. During the colonial period and centuries afterward, the Native Andeans continued to refer to white and mestizo men of European descent as *wiracochas*. Although the term is falling into disuse, it is still sometimes used, especially in the countryside, as a substitute for the word "sir," when addressing an important or respected man of European descent. And the term is still defined as such in some modern Quechua dictionaries (*Simi Taqe*, 752). Given Guaman Poma's explanation for naming these original peoples *Wira Cocha* because of their alleged "Spanish" descent, and the fact that even today such a term refers to a man of European descent, then it is reasonable to conclude that *Wari Wira Cocha Runa* means "Primitive People [who descended from the] Wira Cocha [European men or Spaniards]."

109. Guaman Poma, *Nueva corónica* (Murra and Adorno edition), 41 (my translation and capitalization).
110. Ibid., 42 (my translation).
111. Guaman Poma uses the more Hispanicized spelling, *uno yaco pachacuti* (ibid., 42). *Yaco* or *yaku* in Quechua means "water," but when used in conjunction with the word *uno* or *unu* it usually refers to "sacred water" as opposed to "secular water." In this case the water is sacred, because it is associated with the Creator or Judeo-Christian God referenced in the Holy Bible who, according to Guaman Poma, instigated the Deluge.
112. Ibid. (my translation).
113. Ibid., 46 (my translation).
114. Ibid.
115. As previously stated, *runa*, in Quechua, refers to "man" (generically), "men," "humankind," or "people." *Purun* is a Quechua adjective meaning "wild, savage, or uncivilized" (*Simi Taqe*, 414), as in the Quechua expression *purun runa*, which refers to an uneducated or simple rustic person, or in other words, a "country bumpkin." Since Guaman Poma, in this instance, is referring to the third age of the world when, presumably, humankind is only beginning to develop culture, it is reasonable to describe this age as that of "Uncivilized People." *Purun* can also be used to refer to uncultivated, desolate, wild, or barren lands (*Simi Taqe*, 414; Lara, *Diccionario queshwa-castellano*, 182), so another possible translation of *Purun Runa* is "People of the Wilderness."
116. Guaman Poma, *Nueva corónica* (Murra and Adorno edition), 48.
117. Ibid., 48–50.
118. Ibid., 50 (my translation).

119. Ibid., 52 (my translation).

120. Ibid., 52–53.

121. Ibid., 54 (my translation).

122. Ibid., 63 (my translation).

123. Carlos Araníbar, analytical index and glossary, in Garcilaso, *Comentarios reales, Tomo II* (Araníbar edition), 805 (my translation).

124. Steele and Allen, *Inca Mythology*, 227.

125. Arguedas, *Dioses y hombres*, 35.

126. Ibid.

127. Urton, *Inca Myths*, 73.

128. Inkarrí is a composite name derived from the Quechua word *Inka*, meaning "Inca," and the Spanish word *rey*, meaning "king."

129. Urton, *Inca Myths*, 44, 73-75.

130. Guaman Poma, *Nueva corónica* (Pease edition), 75:334 (my translation).

131. Bernand, *Los incas*, 52.

132. Ibid.

133. Condorcanqui was allegedly the great-grandson of Juana Pilco Huaca, daughter of Inca Tupac Amaru I, who was executed by the Spaniards in 1572.

134. José Yánez del Pozo, *Aztlan y el Incarrí: Dos mitos sobre nuestra América* (Quito: Ediciones Abya-Yala, 2000), 48 (my translation).

135. Bernand, *Los incas*, 51; Urton, *Inca Myths*, 74.

136. Some Native Andeans believe that water that flows down from the mountain or springs forth from the earth is the blood which flows through the "veins" of the *Wamani*, or spiritual embodiment of the mountain. Other Native Andeans believe that water originating in the ground is the "sweat" of *Pacha Mama*, the Andean Earth Mother.

137. *Yaku* and *unu* both mean "water" in Quechua, and *agua* means "water" in Spanish. However, *yaku* is the secular word for water, whereas the combined phrase *unu yaku* or *unu agua* (sometimes also written as *aguay unu*) has a spiritual or religious connotation, which could be defined as "sacred water" or "holy water." The term, however, conveys much more than that. As described in this myth, *unu yaku* or *unu agua* is considered a gift from the *Wamanis* or *Apus*, the deified Quechua mountain spirits, better described as the spiritual embodiment of the mountain peaks. *Unu* water is the fertilizing blood (in Quechua, "*yawar*") flowing through the "veins" (waterways) of the mountain spirits. Whereas some Quechuas perceive the rain falling from the sky as a gift from the [Christian] God, *unu* water is a gift from the *Wamanis* or *Apus* because it springs forth from the earth. Felipe Guaman Poma de Ayala also uses a similar distinction when he describes normal irrigation water as *yaku* but the Flood or Deluge water mentioned in the Bible as *unu yaku pachacuti*, ascribing to it a religious or spiritual quality.

According to anthropologist Juan M. Ossio, *unu yaku* or *unu agua* embodies notions of divinity, unity, vitality, fertility, and sanctity. See Juan M. Ossio, "El simbolismo del agua y la representación del tiempo y el espacio en la fiesta de la acequia de la comunidad de Andamarca," in *Actes du XLIIᵉ Congrès International des Américanistes, Paris, 2–9 Septembre 1976*, 377–96 (Paris: Société des Américanistes, 1978), 379–81.

138. *Wanakupampa* is a region located in the vicinity of the mountain of *Osqonta* (also spelled *Osk'onta*), (see subsequent notes). The toponym *Wanakupampa* derives from the Quechua word *wanaku* (in Spanish, *guanaco* or *huanaco*), the name of a brown Andean camelid, which is mostly undomesticated and a relative of the domestic llama. *Wanaku* wool is highly prized and considered second in quality only to that of the smaller *vicuña*. According to Edmer Calero del Mar, the word *pampa* in the name *Wanakupampa* is not associated with the low South American lowlands but rather with the ecological zone known as *salqa*, encompassing the puna and the mountainous highland peaks. Edmer Calero del Mar, "Dualismo estructural andino y espacio novelesco arguediano," *Boletín del Instituto Francés de Estudios Andinos* 31, no. 2 (2002). 162n14–15.

139. Viviano Wamancha, "El mito de Inkarrí," in Virgilio Roel Pineda, *Cultura peruana e historia de los incas* (Lima: Fondo de Cultura Económica and Universidad Alas Peruanas, 2001), 570–72 (my translation).

140. For a detailed explanation of these terms, see previous notes.

141. *Osqonta* (also spelled *Osk'onta*) is an Andean mountain located in the province and district of Cuzco, approximately 1,100 kilometers (about 690 miles) from Lima, Peru. The name for this mountain probably derives from the Quechua name for a South American wildcat, indigenous to the Andes, known by various common names, including *osqhollo*, *oskollo*, *osjollo*, *osqo misi*, *osjo*, and others, with an added Quechua ending *–nta* meaning "through" or "between, among." Calero del Mar, "Dualismo estructural andino," 162n15. In Spanish this mountain cat is generally known as *gato de las peñas*, *gato montés*, or *gato lince*. Depending on the region, this wildcat belongs to one of three different species of felines—*orealirus jacobita*, *oncifelis colocolo*, or *oncifelis geoffroyi*—all of which are considered endangered. See Pedro Clemente Perroud and Juan María Chouvenc, *Diccionario castellano-kechwa, kechwa-castellano: Dialecto de Ayacucho* (Santa Clara, Perú: Seminario San Alfonso de Padres Redentoristas, 1970), under entries for *oskollo* and *Osk'onta*; for a description and list of the common Andean wildcat names, see L. Villalba, M. Lucherini, S. Walker, D. Cossíos, et al., *The Andean Cat: A Conservation Action Plan* (La Paz, Bolivia: Alianza Gato Andino, 2004), 15–16.

142. The *intiwatana* (also spelled *intihuatana*) is a ritual multifaceted stone, analogous to an astronomical calendar or a sundial, which marks the dates of the annual solstices and other astronomical events. On June 21 the *intiwatana* is precisely aligned with the sun's position in the sky and casts a long shadow on its southern side. Conversely, on December 21 it casts a short shadow on its northern side. On midday November 11 and January 30, the sun stands directly above the stone and casts no shadow at all. When the sun cast no shadow at all, the Incas believed the Sun was in full glory and tied, or hitched, to the rock.

143. Alejandro Ortiz Rescaniere, *De Adaneva a Inkarrí: Una visión indígena del Perú* (Lima: Editorial Retablo de Papel, 1973), 139 (my translation).

144. Ibid., 148 (my translation).

145. Ibid.

146. For an informative discussion on the use of writing as an instrument of power in postconquest Latin America, see Hans-Joachim König, ed., in collaboration with Christian Gros, Karl Kohut, and France-Marie Renard-Casevitz, *El indio como sujeto y objeto de la historia latinoamericana: Pasado y presente* (Frankfurt: Vervuert, 1998), 53–67. See also Lydia Fossa, *Narrativas problemáticas: Los inkas bajo la pluma española* (Lima: Instituto de Estudios Peruanos Ediciones and Pontificia Universidad Católica del Perú—Fondo Editorial, 2006.)

147. Expressing this widespread sentiment among Native Andeans, Bolivian Foreign Minister David Choquehuanca, a native Aymara, made headlines in 2006 when he boldly stated, "I don't read books anymore; only the wrinkles in my elders' faces." This statement has been interpreted to mean that Western-style Andean education largely ignores traditional non-Western forms of knowledge derived from pre-Hispanic cultures. See Sergio Arispe B., Graciela Mazorco I., and Maya Rivera M., "Dicotomías étnicas y filosofías en la lucha por la descolonización," *Polis*, Revista Académica Universidad Bolivariana, no. 18, Santiago, Chile, November 30, 2007, accessed February 14, 2009, https://polis.revues.org/4012. This mistrust of Westernized schooling also impacts educational discourse in certain Andean countries about what constitutes appropriate educational policy. See María Elena García, "The Challenges of Representation: NGOs, Education, and the State in Highland Peru," in *Civil Society or Shadow State? State/NGO Relations in Education*, edited by Margaret Sutton and Robert F. Arnove (Greenwich, CT: Information Age Publishing, 2004), 45–70.

148. Sullivan, *Andean Cosmogony*, 105, citing William H. Isbell, "Cosmological Order Expressed in Prehistoric Ceremonial Center," in *Actes du XLIIᵉ Congrès International des Américanistes, Vol. IV, Paris, 2–9 Septembre 1976*, 269–98 (Paris: Société des Américanistes, 1978).

149. Betanzos, *Narrative of the Incas*, 74. Pumas are indigenous to South America, and *puma* is a Quechua word. Since pumas were unfamiliar to the Europeans, the Spanish colonial chroniclers often referred to them as *leones* ("lions"), as in this case.

150. Bastien, *Mountain of the Condor*, 43.

151. Ibid., 37, 45, 51–81.

152. Betanzos, *Narrative of the Incas*, 62 (Hamilton and Buchanan translation). See also Cobo, *Inca Religion*, 129, 149.

153. Thérèse Bouysse-Cassagne, "Urco and Uma: Aymara Concepts of Space," in *Anthropological History of Andean Politics*, edited by J. Murra, N. Wachtel, and J. Revel, 201–27 (Cambridge, UK: Cambridge University Press, 1986), 214.

154. Molina, *Fábulas* (Urbano and Duviols edition), 123.

155. Betanzos, *Narrative of the Incas*, 46 (Hamilton and Buchanan translation; italics in original text).

156. Bouysse-Cassagne, "Urco and Uma," 213. In the absence of a maternal uncle, some sources inform that the maternal grandfather or another maternal male relative may also perform the functions of a *lari*.

157. Ibid., 214 (italics in original).

158. See Yánez del Pozo, *Aztlán y el Incarri*, 47, citing Alberto Flores Galindo, *Buscando un Inca: Identidad y utopía en los Andes* (Lima: Instituto de Apoyo Agrario, 1987), 47.

159. Ibid. (my translation).

160. Ibid., 53–54 (my translation).

161. Ibid., citing Flores Galindo, *Buscando un Inca*, 23.

162. Ibid., citing Manuel Espinoza Tamayo, *Los mestizos ecuatorianos* (Quito: Trama Social Editorial, 1995), 227 (my translation).

163. Ortiz Rescaniere, *Adaneva a Inkarrí*, 139 (my translation).

CHAPTER 5: HUACAS

1. See Hugo Boero Rojo, *Discovering Tiwanaku* (Cochabamba and La Paz, Bolivia: Editorial Los Amigos del Libro, 1980), 22.

2. Salomon, Introductory essay to the *Huarochirí Manuscript*, 16.

3. Ibid., 17. See also Garcilaso, *Comentarios reales* (Araníbar edition), 76–78.

4. Salomon, Introductory essay to *Huarochirí Manuscript*, 17 and 112n557.

5. Garcilaso, *Comentarios reales* (Piñuela edition), 96–98 (my translation; italics added).

6. Garcilaso, *Comentarios reales* (Araníbar edition), 76, 87–88.

7. See Cobo, *History of the Inca Empire*, 237; Guaman Poma, *Nueva corónica* (Pease edition), 75:175, 181, 183–92; Cobo, *Inca Religion*, 8, 54, 58–60, 67, 70–73, 80–82, 89, 99, 151, 154–57, 170, 237–38.

8.   See Johan Reinhard, "Peru's Ice Maidens: Unwrapping the Secrets," *National Geographic*, June 1996, 62–81; Johan Reinhard, "At 22,000 Feet Children of Inca Sacrifice Found Frozen in Time," *National Geographic*, November 1999, 36–55; Peter Gwin, "Peruvian Temple of Doom," *National Geographic*, July 2004, 102–17. See also Johan Reinhard, *The Ice Maiden: Inca Mummies, Mountain Gods and Sacred Sites in the Andes* (Washington, D.C.: National Geographic Society, 2005); Walter Alva and Christopher B. Donnan, *Royal Tombs of Sipan (Tumbas reales de Sipán)*, 2nd ed. (Los Angeles: Fowler Museum of Cultural History, Regents of the University of California, 1994).

9.   Bastien, *Mountain of the Condor*, 174–75.

10. See Ibid., 51–83; Isbell, *To Defend Ourselves*, 137–65.

11. Santacruz Pachacuti, *Relación de antigüedades*, 244–45 (my translation). Note on the translation: Some verb inconsistencies were adjusted to the make the English translation more comprehensible, and the word *temerario* was interpreted to mean *temeroso* ("frightening" or "causing terror"), in concordance with the chronicler's intended meaning.

12. See Víctor Manuel Nivelo, "Jadan Llagtapi Tiyan Ushug Urcumanta" ("Leyenda del cerro de Ushug de la Parroquia Jadán"), and "Urcu Yayamanta Parlashca" ("El Urcu Yaya"), in Zaruma, *Cañari*, 67, 95–97. The first legend describes the friendship of two mountain *huacas*, one of whom wears different colored garments that signal climatic changes or seasons. The second describes a mountain *huaca* named "Father Mountain" who appears as a blond man wearing a large hat, a red poncho, and yellow shoes. The *huaca* shares his medicinal secrets with a humble and worthy man whom he encounters along a road. See also "Huaca raimimanta" (La fiesta de las huacas"), in Cotacachi, *Huaca pachamanta causashca rimai*, 178–85, in which a *huaca* pays two musicians in gold and silver corncobs to entertain at a party of *huacas* at the bottom of a lake. See also Santacruz Pachacuti, *Relaciones*, 239–40, where Pachacuti Inca Yupanqui encounters *huacas* and demons in the form of *curacas* or local chieftains, whom he sentences to work on the construction of the great fortress of Sacsahuaman and later building vantage points overlooking the sea.

13. The *lúcuma* or *lucmo* tree (scientific name *Pouteria lucuma*; formerly *Lucuma obovata*) is a South American fruit tree indigenous to the Andean valleys of Peru, Chile, and Ecuador. It produces an oval-shaped, fuzzy-textured fruit, similar to an eggfruit, which is covered in thin green or orange-brown skin with a sweet, soft, and aromatic yellowish pulp. Its durable wood is also used in construction.

14. The author transposed the last two sentences in this paragraph to clarify the sequence of events in the story.

15. Some Native Andean peoples share the belief that anyone guilty of speaking disparagingly about the puma will be punished. The puma, in retribution, will take away that person's flock or domesticated animals and eat them (Urton, *Animal Myths and Metaphors*, 259).

16. *Pachacamac* was a pre-Inca deity from the coastal region of Peru, whose cult had a profound influence on many Andean pre-Columbian cultures. A shrine, which goes by the same name and was dedicated to this deity, was built to the south of present-day Lima in a region known as the Lurín Valley. The shrine served as an important oracle to many pre-Columbian Andean cultures, including the Incas, who considered it one of their empire's holiest shrines. See Moseley, *Incas and Ancestors*, 16, 18–19, 159, 184–85, 246. See also Bierhorst, *Black Rainbow*, 10.

17. Cómo sucedió Cuniraya Viracocha en su tiempo y cómo Cahuillaca parió a sus hijo y lo que pasó. Vida de Cuniraya Viracocha," Arguedas, ed. and trans., *Dioses y hombres de Huarochirí*, 26–31 (my translation).

18. The name of the god *Cuniraya Viracocha* (also spelled *Cunirayu Wiraqucha* or *Coniraya Viracocha*) is a blended name, probably associated with the ancient Peruvian coastal deity *Con* or *Cun* and the Inca creator deity *Viracocha* (also spelled *Wiraqocha* or *Wiraqucha*) or *Con Tici Viracocha* (Steele and Allen, *Handbook of Inca Mythology*, 149). According to legend, "Con was a formless figure, without bones or joints, who came from the north, and was a child of the sun and the moon. After walking up and down the coast, shaping the land and creating all things in it, he disappeared into the sea and ascended into the sky" (David M. Jones, *The Myths and Religion of the Incas* [London: Southwater, an imprint of Anness Publishing, 2008], 62). Quechua linguist Celso Macedo y Pastor indicates that monosyllabic adjectives are almost nonexistent in Quechua, so he proposes that the proper adjective modifying the name of the deity is not *con* but *coni*, or rather, *koñi* (also spelled *q'oñi* or *kuñi*), meaning "hot" or "warm" in Quechua. See Celso Macedo y Pastor, "La esfinge: Coñi Illa Tijsi Wirakocha, Pacha Camaj, Pacha Yachachij, Tijsi Capaj: A la luz de la ciencia lingüística," *Revista histórica; órgano del Instituto Histórico del Perú*, dirigido por Carlos Alberto Romero, Tomo IX, Entrega IV, 357–80, Lima, Perú, 1935, 365–66. See also *Simi Taqe*, 503. Thus, the word *con* appears to be "indicative of heat, energy, and creation" (Jones, *Myths and Religion of the Incas*, 62). *Viracocha*, whose name in Quechua means "Sea Foam" or "Sea Fat," was the supreme creator deity of the Incas. The Incas built him a temple at Quishuarcancha in Cuzco, where they placed a golden statue of a ten-year-old boy, representing the deity. He also had a shrine in the *Coricancha* ("Golden Enclosure"), the most important Inca temple, with an idol made of mantles (Cobo, *Inca Religion and Customs*, 24).

19.   There is very little known about the origin of the name of this female divinity. *Caui* (also spelled *qawi*) in Aymara means "sweet" and is also used to describe a process by which oca (the Andean tuber *oxalis tuberosa*, also known as "oka" and "New Zealand yam") is sweetened by exposure to the sun. In his *Vocabulario de la lengua aymara* ("Vocabulary of the Aymara Language"), published in 1612, Ludovico Bertonio defines *Caui* as "sweet potatoes exposed to the sun" ("Apillas passadas al sol"); elsewhere he also defines *Caui* as "sweet" ("Dulce"). See Bertonio, *Vocabulario de la lengua aymara, parte segunda*, 223, 302. According to Bertonio, *llaca*—the second part of *Cauillaca's* name—signifies "a thin feather found in the wings of a vulture, and other birds" ("Pluma delgada que ay en las alas del Buytre, y otros paxaros") (ibid., 198).

20.   For instance, in some North American Indian myths from the Pacific Northwest, the trickster raven impregnates a young woman by turning himself into a pine or a hemlock needle, which finds its way into her drinking water. See Richard Erdoes and Alfonso Ortiz, eds., "Raven Lights the World," in *American Indian Trickster Tales* (New York: Viking Penguin, a member of Penguin Putnam, 1998), 259–65; Mary Helen Pelton and Jacqueline DiGennaro, "Raven Steals the Light," in *Image of a People: Tlingit Myths and Legends* (Englewood, CO: Libraries Unlimited, 1992), 47–50. In Aztec mythology, the goddess *Coatlicue* ("She of the Serpent-Woven Skirt") is impregnated by an obsidian knife, and later, by wearing a ball of feathers with the seed of *Huitzilopochtli* ("Hummingbird on the Left or South" or "Left-Handed Hummingbird"). See Karl Taube, *Aztec and Maya Myths* (Austin: University of Texas Press, 1993), 45–47; David Adams Leeming, *Creation Myths of the World: An Encyclopedia, Second Edition* (Santa Barbara, CA: ABL-CLIO, 2010), 55; Louis Herbert Gray and George Foot Moore, eds., with Hartley Burr Alexander, *The Mythology of All Races—Volume XI, Latin American* (Boston: Marshall Jones, 1920), 60.

21.   See Monte, *Beneath the Mask*, 150.

22.   Carl G. Jung, with M. L. von Franz, Joseph L. Henderson, Jolande Jacobi and Aniela Jaffé, *Man and His Symbols*, edited by Carl G. Jung (New York: J. G. Ferguson Publishing, 1964), 112.

23.   Jones, *Myth and Religion of the Incas*, 67–68, in reference to the Andean creator gods *Viracocha* and *Pachacamac*, who are said to have traveled in the guise of beggars.

24.   See Barbara Bode, "Disaster, Social Structure, and Myth in the Peruvian Andes: The Genesis of an Explanation," *Annals of the York Academy of Sciences* 293 (1977): 261.

25.   See Marie-France Souffez, "El simbolismo del piojo en el mundo andino," in *Anthropologica*, Departamento de Ciencias Naturales, Pontificia Universidad Católica del Perú, 3 (1985): 171–202.

26. Ibid., 198 (my translation).
27. Bierhorst, *Black Rainbow*, 20.
28. Ibid., 21.
29. In support of this argument, we can refer to the Inca origin myth retold by Garcilaso de la Vega, in which the first Inca queen Mama Ocllo instructs women "in the feminine occupations," which are described as spinning, weaving, and making clothing for their families. See Garcilaso, *Comentarios reales* (Porrúa edition), 32.
30. Bierhorst, *Black Rainbow*, 21.
31. Ibid.
32. Ibid.
33. Marco Antonio Ribeiro, "Formal Analysis of Myth of Maire-Pochy and of Cuniraya Viracocha," unpublished notes, September 1998. A similar argument also appears with respect to the myth of "Maire-Pochy" in Claude Lévi-Strauss, *The Story of Lynx (Histoire de Lynx)*, translated by Catherine Tihanyi (Chicago: University of Chicago Press, 1995), 45–53. Levi-Strauss affirms that "the myth methodically exploits a system of multidimensional oppositions," including "celestial/terrestrial," and that one of the structural themes of the narrative concerns "the sun pushed back to a safe distance" (ibid. 51).
34. Bierhorst, *Black Rainbow*, 20.
35. Claude Lévi-Strauss, *Structural Anthropology*, translated by Claire Jacobson and Brooke Grundfest Schoepf (New York: Basic Books, a Member of Perseus Books Group, 1963), 229.
36. Ribeiro, "Formal Analysis," September 1998.
37. I have adopted the terms "burnt world" and "world of rottenness" from the structural anthropologist Claude Lévi-Strauss. According to Lévi-Strauss, too much sun, or overexposure to the sun, can lead to a burnt world, whereas too little sun, or the absence of the sun, can lead to a world of rottenness and disease. The goal, then, for the myth is to find the appropriate balance between these two extremes through the introduction of "a mediating term conjoining extremes and making them indistinguishable, or coming between them to prevent them from growing closer." Lévi-Strauss, *Story of Lynx*, 8.
38. Garcilaso, *Comentarios reales* (Porrúa edition), 86 (my translation).
39. Ribeiro, "Formal Analysis," September 1998.
40. The whereabouts of *Cuniraya Viracocha* in this section of the myth is derived from the location of the pre-Columbian temple of Pachacamac, near the Peruvian coast, at the mouth of the Río Lurín, just south of present-day Lima. See Moseley, *Incas and Ancestors*, 16, 18–19, 184–85, 246. See also note 16, supra.
41. Diego González Holguín (1608), *Vocabulario de la lengua general de todo el Perú llamada lengua Qquichua o del Inca*, edición y prólogo de

Raúl Porras Barrenechea (Lima: Universidad Nacional Mayor de San Marcos, 1952), 125–26, digitalizado por *Runasimipi Qespisqa* Software para publicación en el Internet, 2007, accessed July 27, 2007, http://www.illa-a.org/cd/diccionarios/VocabvlarioQqichuaDeHolguin.pdf, under definitions for *huac*. Some examples that illustrate the notion of "double, apart, or other" include *huac sonco* [*sonqo*] (double-hearted, double-dealing, or duplicitous); *huacpi* ("apart in a different location, or place, or by itself"); and *huacruna* ("The one from over there, or that other [person] from over there") (ibid., my translations).

42. The Quechua dictionary of González Holguín (1608) also provides many examples of how *huaca* (also spelled *huacca*) can signify a "split" in relation to body parts. For instance, *huacca virpa* [*wirp'a*] means "split lip" and *huacca cinca* [*sinqa*] means "broken [or split] nose." The birth of twins is also described as *huacca huachassca*. González Holguín, *Lengua Qqichua*, 126 (my translations).

43. Classen, *Inca Cosmology*, 14.

44. *Shishu* or *shizhu* is the Quichua variant of the Quechua word *chichu*, meaning "pregnant." Thus, Mount *Shishu* means "Pregnant Mountain."

45. Zaruma, "Shizhu Urcumanta Parlascha" ("La leyenda del Shishu"), in *Cañari*, 91–92 (my translation).

46. *Curi* means "gold" and *taqui* "granary" in Quichua, the Ecuadorian variant of Quechua. Thus, *Curitaqui* signifies "Golden Granary" or "Granary of Gold."

47. José Nicolás Qhishpi, "Curi Taqui Shuti Urcumanta" ("Leyenda del Cerro Curitaqui"), in Zaruma, *Cañari*, 125–26 (my translation). Note on the translation: After the family receives the gold corncobs in exchange for the child, the narrator inexplicably switches from third person plural ("they") to third person singular ("he"), perhaps referring to the head of the family. So for purposes of clarity and consistency, I continue to refer to the family as a whole instead of a single individual. Such grammatical and narrative inconsistencies are quite common in extemporaneous storytelling.

48. "Mount Tepal is situated next to the Parish of Santa Ana in the canton of Cuenca, [Ecuador]." Zaruma, *Cañari*, 127.

49. "Tepal Urcumanta" ("Leyenda del Cerro Tepal"), ibid. (my translation).

50. The author takes note that the division between the natural and supernatural worlds is a Western construct that has no place in the indigenous cosmologies of the Andes, which tend to view the world as a unified whole and single reality. However, this artificial division is made here in order to facilitate the Western reader's understanding of the complexities of Native Andean myths and rituals, bearing in mind that for the native peoples of the Andes this separation may not exist.

51. See Reinhard, "Peru's Ice Maidens," 62–82. See also Reinhard, "At 22,000 Feet Children of Inca Sacrifice," 35–55.

52. See Guaman Poma, *Nueva corónica* (Murra and Adorno edition), 241.

53. See Arguedas and Ríos, ed., *Mitos, leyendas y cuentos* (2009 version), 38, 50–51, 68–69. In "El pozo encantado" ("The Enchanted Well"), a beautiful young woman appears from the interior of an enchanted well and offers thirsty travelers a drink of water. If they drink this water, the travelers disappear without a trace, along with the beautiful young woman. In "El cerro encantado" ("The Enchanted Hill"), inside an enchanted hill lives a golden bull that opens a silver path to come out and drink water at night; the silver path closes when he has finished. In "Una ciudad de enanos" ("A City of Dwarves"), a poor and hungry woman inadvertently enters a cave with a long tunnel and finds a large and beautiful city at the end of the tunnel inhabited by dwarves. The dwarves invite her and her family to live with them, saving the family from starvation. When the woman shares the good news with family and friends, so many townspeople try to cross the tunnel that it eventually closes.

54. Douglas Sharon, "The Return to Origins in North Peruvian and Huichol Pilgrimages," in *Actes du XLIIe Congrès International des Américanistes, Vol. IV, Paris, 2–9 Septembre 1976,* 397–403 (Paris: Société des Américanistes, 1978), 401.

55. Ibid.

56. This term is often mistranslated as "Sweet Mass" based on the Aymara word *muxsa,* which means "sweet," and the Spanish word *misa,* which means "mass." However, monolingual Aymara speakers do not distinguish between the "i" and "e" vowel sounds, as do Spanish speakers, so often they say *misa* instead of *mesa* ("table" in Spanish). Therefore, the correct translation of this syncretistic term is "Sweet Table" or "Sweet Table [Offerings]."

57. Kolata, *Valley of the Spirits,* 41–47.

58. William E. Carter and Mauricio Mamani, *Irpa Chico: Individuo y comunidad en la cultura aymara* (La Paz, Bolivia: Librería-Editorial "Juventud," 1982), 296.

59. *Gloria,* or the Upper World of the Kallawaya cosmology, is described in Gernando Fernández Juárez, *Testimonio Kallawaya: Medicina y ritual en los Andes de Bolivia,* serie "Hombre y Ambiente," Número Monográfico 44–45 (Quito: Ediciones Abya-Yala, 1997), 52–53.

60. Gerardo Fernández Juárez, *Los kallawayas: Medicina indígena en los Andes* (Cuenca, Spain: Ediciones de la Universidad de Castilla-La Mancha, 1998), 55.

61. Kolata, *Valley of the Spirits,* 44–45.

62. Fernández Juárez, *Los kallawayas,* 55–56 (my translation).

63.   Kolata, *Valley of the Spirits*, 44. See also Fernández Juárez, *Los kalla-wayas*, 53–56.

64.   Kolata, *Valley of the Spirits*, 44.

65.   Ibid.

66.   Ibid., 23, 53–54.

67.   Ibid., 42 (italics added), 45.

68.   Ibid., 44.

69.   See Sarmiento de Gamboa, *Historia*, 51–52. The indigenous colonial chronicler Santacruz Pachacuti Yamqui Salcamaygua also mentions these three "windows" in relation to the origin of the Inca ancestors. Santacruz Pachacuti, *Relación de antigüedades*, 217–18.

70.   There are various possible translations of this place name: "Inn of Dawn," "Place of Origin," "Inn of Production," "House of the Hidden," or "Hiding Place." See Urton, *History of a Myth*, 19. See also Rost-worowski de Diez Canseco, *Historia del Tahuantinsuyu*, 38 (my trans-lations); Lara, *Diccionario qheshwa-castellano*, 174 (my translation). Other possible translations include "Lodging [of that which] Awakens, Is Created, or Is Born" or "Lodging [of whom] Awakens, Is Created, or Is Born." These latter definitions derive from the Quechua verb *paqariy*, meaning "to appear, to be created, to originate, or to be born," and *pacha paqariy*, "to awaken" (*Simi Taqe*, 384). The Quechua word for "lodging" or "inn" is *tambo, tampu,* or *tanpu*. For alternate spellings of *Pacariqtambo*, see the Glossary.

71.   *Qhapaq,* or *capac,* was an honorific term used in the Inca Empire to denote a lord of high status or an Inca of royal blood who presided over an entire province or region of the empire. It was also used to denote anything noble, illustrious, magnanimous, powerful, or eminent, usually associated with the Inca royal family. In modern Quechua, the term has also come to mean rich, powerful, privileged, and opulent (*Simi Taqe,* 478). Thus, one possible translation of the term *qhapaq t'oqo,* or *capactoco,* is "Window (or Cave) of the Noble or the Powerful." Because the term *capac* first appeared in the Spanish colonial chronicles, which used Romanized spelling of Quechua words, it may also refer to the Quechua term *k'apak,* which means precise, exact, or just. In such case, *k'apak t'oqo* could signify "Window (or Cave) of the Just."

72.   Rostworowski de Diez Canseco, *Historia del Tahuantinsuyu*, 37–38.

73.   Sarmiento de Gamboa, *Historia*, 52.

74.   Cobo, *Inca Religion and Customs*, 17.

75.   Ossio, "El simbolismo del agua," 380.

76.   Ibid.

77.   Sharon, "Return to Origins," 400–403.

78.   Ibid.

79.   Ibid., 401.

80. See Cotacachi, "Huaca raimimanta" ("La fiesta de las huacas"), in *Huaca pachamanta*, 179–85. Two musicians are invited to play for a *huaca* party below the surface of a lagoon. The *huacas* pay the musicians with white and yellow corncobs that later transform into corncobs made of silver and gold. In Zaruma, "Shug C'ujumanta" ("El cuento de la sapita"), in *Cañari*, 201–9, the slowest of three brothers wins the heart of a frog-woman living in a lagoon. She finds a magical way to become a land-bound woman, marry the slow brother, and make him wealthy.

81. Arguedas and Izquierdo Ríos, eds., "Yanacocha," in *Mitos, leyendas y cuentos peruanos* (2009 edition), 51–52.

82. Ibid., 52 (my translation).

83. Arguedas and Izquierdo Ríos, eds., "La laguna de León Cocha," in *Mitos, leyendas y cuentos peruanos* (2009 edition), 66.

84. Arguedas and Izquierdo Rios, eds., "La laguna de las campanas encanta-das," in *Mitos, leyendas y cuentos peruanos* (2009 edition), 64–65.

85. Arguedas and Izquierdo Ríos, eds., "Los baños de Piquilhuanca," in *Mitos, leyendas y cuentos* (2009 edition), 59 (my translation).

86. Ibid. (my translation).

87. See Cotacachi, "Huacayashca cuitsa" ("La joven encantada"), in *Huaca pachamanta*, 175–77, where a water *huaca* rapes a young woman who gives birth to golden snakes. In Zaruma, "Culebrillas Cuchamanta Parlashca" ("La legendaria laguna de culebrillas"), in *Cañari*, 113–18, a married woman is kidnapped by a water *huaca* living in a lagoon. Even though she is rescued, the woman gives birth to twelve little snakes.

88. Cotacachi, *Huaca pachamanta*, 177n3 (my translation). See also van Kessel, "Los aymaras," 271.

89. Zaruma, "Culebrillas Cuchamanta Parlashca" ("La legendaria laguna de culebrillas"), in *Cañari*, 113–18 (my translation; italics added).

90. A typical description of this phenomenon is found in the Andean tale of "La laguna encantada" ("The Enchanted Lagoon"), in Arguedas, *Mitos, leyendas y cuentos peruanos* (Colección escolar peruana, 1947 edition), 43. In the story, "no one can swim [in an enchanted lagoon], because a strange animal comes out in the middle of the lagoon, and starts to spin around, *creating foam*" (ibid., my translation; italics added). Anthropologist Regina Harrison also argues quite convincingly that foam is a strong symbol of sexual power in the Andes and Amazonia, and that sex is often represented symbolically by the violent actions of water, such as where streams and rivers forcibly hit rocks, uniting the forces of earth and water. See Regina Harrison, *Signs, Songs, and Memory in the Andes: Translating Quechua Language and Culture* (Austin: University of Texas Press, 1989), 163. It is also interesting to note that the Quechua name of the Inca Creator god *Viracocha* (also known by various other names such as *Con Ticci Viracocha*, *Thunapa Viracocha*, and *Viracocha*

Pachayachachic) has been translated to mean "Sea Fat" or "Sea Foam," perhaps underscoring his masculine sexual energy.

91.   Salomon, introductory essay to *Huarochirí Manuscript*, 15.

92.   Ibid.

93.   For example, among the Cañari people of Ecuador several versions exist of an origin myth that describes the Cañari people as the offspring of a snake that emerged from, or submerged in, the water of a sacred lake. For this reason, the ancient Cañaris made offerings of silver and gold artifacts at these sacred sites, which were considered *huacas*. For useful discussions on this subject, see Marco Robles López, *Viaje al mito cañari y nociones filosóficas en el mundo andino*, serie "Mito y filosofía en el mundo andino," no. 17 (Azogues, Ecuador: Casa de la Cultura Ecuatoriana "Benjamín Carrión" Núcleo del Cañar, 2004), 77–78. In some versions of this origin myth, a water-dwelling snake brings a young maiden named Chobshi into his lake and asks her to become his spouse and the mother of his children. Their union begets three daughters and three sons, who become the ancestors of the Cañari people. See Edna Iturralde, *Los hijos de la guacamaya* (Quito: Editorial Alfaguara, Grupo Santillana, 2007.) Conversely, in a pre-Columbian Chibcha origin myth from Colombia, in what might be described as a return to origins or a return to the primordial matrix, a woman named Bachúe ("The Fertile One" or "The Large Breasted") and her husband-son, considered the mythological parents of the Chibcha people, submerge in the waters of Lake Iguaque, their sacred place of origin, and transform back into snakes at the end of their human life. See Repollés, "El dios Bochica de los chibchas," in *Las mejores leyendas mitológicas*, 379–80.

94.   Sigmund Freud, "An Outline of Psychoanalysis," in *The Standard Edition*, vol. XXIII (London: Hogarth Press, 1964), 193.

95.   See Sigmund Freud, "The Psychoanalytic View of Psychogenic Disturbance in Vision," in *The Standard Edition*, vol. XI (London: Hogarth Press, 1957), 24. See also Sigmund Freud, "A Note on the Unconscious in Psychoanalysis," in *The Standard Edition*, vol. XII (London: Hogarth Press, 1958), 263–64.

96.   For a comprehensive description of Jungian archetypes and the collective unconscious, see Carl G. Jung, "Archetypes of the Collective Unconscious," and "The Mother Archetype," in *Basic Writings of C. G. Jung*, translated by R. F. C. Hull and selected and introduced by Violet S. Laszlo (Princeton, NJ: Princeton University Press, 1990), 299–348.

97.   Jung, *Man and His Symbols*, 154.

98.   Ibid.

99.   Jung makes a similar argument concerning the Greek god Hermes, a mediator between two worlds. Hermes is the messenger of the gods and "the leader of souls to and from the underworld." He carries the

chthonic symbol of a caduceus, dual snakes twined around a staff (which later becomes the winged staff of the Roman god, Mercury). He also sports a winged hat and winged sandals, ascribing to him the "birdlike" qualities of transcendence. Thus, according to Jung, Hermes is a god of the crossroads between two worlds who manifests "the full power of transcendence from underworld snake consciousness, passing through the medium of earthly reality…to superhuman or transpersonal reality of winged flight" (ibid., 155–56).

100. There are numerous hypotheses about the origin of the name of this Andean Creator god, who appears to have a blended name, combining the names of the pre-Inca coastal deity *Cun* or *Con* and the Inca creator deity *Viracocha* (also spelled *Wiracocha* or *Wiraqucha*). The definition of the term *con* or *cun* is also in dispute, but it may be indicative of heat and energy. See note 18, supra. It has also been proposed that *Contiti* or *Contici* may be associated with the "cult of the setting sun," because *conti* (also spelled *qonti*, *cunti*, or *kunti*) signifies "west" in Quechua. See Clements R. Markham, "The Inca Civilization in Peru," in *Narrative and Critical History of America: Aboriginal America*, vol. I, 209–82, edited by Justin Winsor (Boston: Houghlin, Mifflin and Company, 1889), 222n1. See also *Simi Taqe*, 874. *Tici* (also spelled *Titi*, *Ticsi*, *Tecci*, or *Teqsi*) means founder, foundation, primal beginning, and origin in Quechua, and *Illa* (another term often associated with this god) means "light." Therefore, the complete name of this god, which sometimes appears as *Con Illa Ticsi Wiracocha*, might be translated as "Creator/God, Origin or Foundation of Heat and Light." For helpful analyses of these terms, see Macedo y Pastor, "La esfinge," 366–67; Markham, "Inca Civilization," 222n1; *Simi Taqe*, 179; and Jones, *Myths and Religion of the Incas*, 66.

101. "Que trata del Con Tici Viracocha (a), que ellos tienen que fué el Hacedor, é de cómo hizo el cielo é tierra é las gentes indios destas provincias del Perú," in Juan de Betanzos (1551), *Suma y narración de los incas, que los indios llamaron Capaccuna, que fueron señores de la ciudad del Cuzco, y do todo lo à ella subjeto*, edición de Marcos Jiménez de la Espada (Madrid: Imprenta M. G. Hernández, 1880), 1–3 (my translation). This version of the chronicle gives the publication date of 1576, the year of Betanzos's death. The date of 1551 derives from another transcription of the chronicle edited by María del Carmen Martín Rubio. See Juan de Betanzos, *Suma y narración de los incas*, transcripción, notas y prólogo por María del Carmen Martín Rubio, estudios preliminares de Horacio Villanueva Urteaga, Demetrio Ramos y María del Carmen Martín Rubio (Madrid: Ediciones Atlas, 1987).

102. Other versions include those recorded by the colonial chroniclers Bernabé Cobo (1653), Pedro Sarmiento de Gamboa (1572), and Cristóbal de Molina (1573). See Cobo, *Historia del nuevo mundo*, in *Obras*,

62–63. See also Sarmiento de Gamboa, *Historia*, 40, 42–46; and Molina, *Fábulas* (Urbano and Duviols edition), 50–54.

103. Kolata, *Tiwanaku*, 302.

104. See Garcilaso, *Comentarios reales* (Araníbar edition), 39–45.

105. Ossio, "El simbolismo del agua," 379–80.

106. Ibid. (my translation; italics in original). For use of the term *aguay unu* in a religious and mythological context, see also José María Arguedas, *Formación de una cultura nacional indoamericana*, introducción de Ángel Rama, 6th ed. (México DF and Madrid: Siglo Veintiuno Editores, 1998), 49–51.

107. See "Vichama, the Demigod," in *Myths of Ancient Peru*, compiled and translated by Oscar Espinar de la Torre, with the assistance of Quinn Meyer (Cuzco, Perú: Editorial Anka, n.d.), 60–61. The Creator god *Pachacamac* creates vegetables and grains from the body parts of a creature he has buried. From his teeth, he makes corn; from his bones, yucca; from his flesh, cucumbers, sweet potatoes, peppers, and other crops. In other versions of this tale, *Pachacamac* plants or buries his *brother's* body parts. In "The Legend of the Potato," (ibid., 76), a mortal falls in love with a goddess who lives on an isolated island. He swims out to see her and the gods, outraged, bury him in the soil, covering his body with eyes and turning him into a potato. In "Quinacha" ("La quenita," or "The Little Quena"), in Payne, *Cuentos cusqueños*, 32–33, the youngest of three brothers is murdered by his older brothers and is buried in a ravine, where he turns into a reed used for making a *quena*, a traditional Andean flute. In "La qantuta y la quiñwa" ("The Khantuta and the Quinoa"), in Edgar Quispe Chambi, ed. and trans., *Traducción de cuentos y tradiciones orales en aimara: Diseño educativo para culturas de tradición oral* (Puno, Perú: Academia Peruana de la Lengua Aymara, Instituto del Bien Común, 2004), 15, two young people, who belong to feuding communities, fall in love. Responding to prayers from the girl's father and the young man, the mountain spirits turn one young lover into a qantuta plant (also spelled khantuta or kantuta) and the other into a quiñwa tree (also spelled quinoa or quinua).

108. See Antonio de la Calancha (1637), *Crónica moralizada del orden de San Agustín en el Perú con sucesos ejemplares en esta monarquía: Volumen I*, 620–23, texto digitalizado por *Scribd.com* para presentación en el Internet, April 4, 2010, accessed January 28, 2012, https://www.scribd.com/collections/3170153/La-Cronica-Moralizada-de-Fray-Calancha.

109. Ibid.

110. For more about this Andean high god, see note 100, supra.

111. César Toro Montalvo, *Mitos y leyendas del Perú* (Lima: A.F.A. Editores Importadores, 2003), 129–30.

112. "Leyenda de la papa," in Paredes-Candia, *Leyendas de Bolivia*, 88–93.

113. See Antonio Díaz Villamil, "La khantuta tricolor," in *Leyendas de mi tierra*, 29–46 (La Paz, Bolivia: Librería Editorial "Juventud," 1993), 45 (my translation). The bell-shaped *khantuta* (also spelled *khantuta* or *qantuta*; scientific name *cantua buxifolia*) is a member of the Polemoniaceae family of wildflowers, indigenous to the Andes. It is also commonly known as the "magic flower" and the "sacred flower of the Incas." Because of its beauty and abundant growth in the Andes, the *khantuta* has been adopted as the national flower of both Bolivia and Peru. The Bolivian national flower is a tricolored variety comprised of red petals, a yellow floral tube, and a green calyx, mirroring the three colors of the Bolivian flag.

114. See Díaz Villamil, "La leyenda de la coca," in *Leyendas de mi tierra*, 105–15; Paredes-Candia, "Leyenda de la coca," in *Leyendas de Bolivia*, 17–21.

115. Roberto Levillier, *Don Francisco de Toledo*, vol. 2 (Buenos Aires: Espasa-Calpe, 1940), 172.

116. See *Simi Taqe*, 459, 478; Lara, *Diccionario qheshwa-castellano*, 215.

117. In "The Art of Moche Politics," Garth Bawden makes a similar argument with respect to the human sacrifice ceremony of the Moche (or Mochica), an advanced pre-Columbian civilization from north coastal Peru. He writes, "Blood, regarded as life force in earlier periods, as in contemporary ritual, was the most powerful category of gift. It follows that in the crucial event that ensured continuing social vitality, the life essence of elite human warriors [offered up as human sacrifices] would be the most fitting gift possible. Blood was offered to Pachamama with the expectation that an equally powerful life-giving substance—water—would be returned in the form of mountain rains, this reciprocal transaction ensuring fecundity for the earth and social balance for humanity." Garth Bawden, "The Art of Moche Politics," in *Andean Archaeology*, 116–29, edited by Helaine Silverman (Malden, MA: Blackwell Publishing, 2004), 126.

CHAPTER 6: THE ORIGIN OF CULTURE

1. Quichua (spelled with an "i") is a variant form of the indigenous language Quechua (spelled with an "e"), which is widely spoken in Ecuador and has a distinctive pronunciation and spelling. However, in spoken language Quechua speakers do not make the i/e distinction, as do Spanish speakers. The vowel sounds "i" and "e" are phonemic in Spanish but not in Quechua, where monolingual speakers often hear them as variant forms of the same sound. For that reason, Quechua speakers sometimes refer to their own language as Quichua or Quechua, interchangeably, depending on the region.

2. For a comprehensive description of the Cañari belief system, see Vicente Zaruma Quizhpilema, *Wakanmay, aliento sagrado: Perspectivas de*

teología india; una propuesta desde la cultura cañari (Quito: Ediciones Abya-Yala, 2006), 94–114. See also Bolívar Zaruma, *Cañari*, in dedication and 14.

3.   Bolívar Zaruma, *Cañari*, in dedication (my translation).

4.   The Spanish colonial chronicles describe the lurid details of how the last Inca emperor, Atahualpa, massacred the Cañaris after they switched sides to join Atahualpa's half brother, Huascar Inca, during the Inca Civil War, which immediately preceded the Spanish conquest of Peru. See Betanzos, *Suma y narración* (Rubia edition), 215–16; Garcilaso, *Comentarios reales (Tomo II)*, (Araníbar edition), 643–44; Pedro de Cieza de León (1550), *El señorío de los incas*, edición de Manuel Ballesteros Gaibrois (Madrid: Historia 16, 1985), 204.

5.   Molina spells the name of the mountain as *Huacaynan* or *Huaynan*, but the preferred modern spelling is *Huacayñan* or *Wakayñan*, which means "Trail of Tears" or "Road of Tears" in Quichua.

6.   Molina, *Fábulas* (Urteaga and Romero edition), 12–13 (my translation; italics added).

7.   Cobo, *Historia del nuevo mundo*, 152; also cited in Bolívar Zaruma, *Cañari*, 24–26.

8.   Federico González Suárez, *Estudio histórico sobre los cañaris, antiguos habitantes de la provincia del Azuay en la República del Ecuador* (Quito: Imprenta del Clero, por José Guzmán Almeida, 1878), 11.

9.   María Rostworoski de Diez Canseco, "Mitos andinos relacionados con el origen de las subsistencias," *Boletín de Lima* 37 (January 1985): 34 (my translation).

10.   Lévi-Strauss, *Raw and Cooked*, 65.

11.   Ibid., 142.

12.   Ibid.

13.   Ibid.

14.   Ibid.

15.   See Arguedas, "La amante de la culebra," in *Canciones y cuentos del pueblo quechua*, 95–104; Arguedas, "La amante del cóndor," in Valcárcel and Arguedas, eds., *Narraciones y leyendas incas*, 41–52; Bierhorst, "The Mouse Husband," in *Black Rainbow*, 115–17.

16.   See Bierhorst, "The Mouse Husband," in *Black Rainbow*, 115–17; Inés Callali, "The Shepherdess," in Payne, *Quechua Folk Tales*, 90–93.

17.   The biological anthropologist William H. Durham and his research assistants "spent over 2,500 hours in the course of two years studying both the myths and incest taboos of…sixty culture populations" from around the world. Among these populations, it was commonly believed that incest caused physical deformities and death (stillbirth) due to mystical sanctions and punishments imposed by the gods, who had the power to mold the human fetus in defective ways. In some cases

the perpetrators of incest were also believed to cause death to the clan by "sexual cannibalism," or sexual "self-consumption," making women infertile or unable to produce healthy children. See William H. Durham, *Coevolution: Genes, Culture, and Human Diversity* (Stanford, CA: Stanford University Press, 1991), Appendix A, 510–18.

18. In his collection of essays entitled *Totem and Taboo: Resemblances between the Mental Lives of Savages and Neurotics*, Sigmund Freud discusses the "dread of incest" among certain aboriginal peoples, which, he postulates, forms the basis for strict cultural prohibitions against marrying inside one's totem or clan. According to Freud, the rule is that "members of the same totem are not allowed to enter into sexual relations with each other; that is, they cannot marry each other" (Freud, *Totem and Taboo*, 7). In such cases, the totemic group or clan requires the individual to marry outside his or her own group—a concept known as exogamy—in order to prevent incest. Furthermore, this prohibition applies even if the man or woman is not a blood relative of everyone in the totemic group, because all members of the group are treated like blood relations (ibid., 9). This notion, however, is too limiting when applied to Andean origin myths, because one detects instances of both exogamy, as in the Cañari origin myth, and endogamy (sexual union or marriage inside the totemic group), as in the Inca, Chibcha, and other origin myths. This suggests that a number of Andean origin myths fall outside the purview of the exogamous prescription. Perhaps a way to reconcile these differences is to go beyond the exogamy/endogamy distinction and to recognize that in these and other examples, a new Andean culture or ethnic group arises from a culturally improper union or a prohibited sexual relationship—a cultural taboo—such as bestiality or incest.

19. Céline Geffroy Komadina, "El cuerpo abierto," in *Colección Aalten*, no. 817, 1–13 publicación del Instituto de Estudio de la Cultura y Tecnología Andina, Iquique, Chile, (2004).

20. This topic will be addressed more fully in the chapters on *Sexuality and Guilt* and *Supernatural Beings*.

21. On the custom of Inca princes marrying their sisters, and the reasons for doing so, see Garcilaso, *Comentarios reales (Tomo I)* (Araníbar edition), 217–18. For other accounts of incestuous practices among the Incas, see Cobo, *Inca Religion and Customs*, 209 (Hamilton translation); Betanzos, *Narrative*, 119–20, 122, 181, 204; Cobo, *History of the Inca Empire*, 142; Garcilaso, *Comentarios reales (Tomo II)* (Araníbar edition), 511–12.

22. Garcilaso, *Comentarios reales (Tomo I)* (Araníbar edition), 40 (my translation).

23. In the original text, the description of the staff actually appears in the next sentence, but here it is placed earlier for greater clarity and to avoid run-on sentences, which were quite common in colonial Spanish.

24. "El origen de los Incas, reyes del Perú," in El Inca Garcilaso de la Vega, *Primera parte de los Comentarios Reales* (Madrid: Imprenta de los Hijos de Doña Catalina Piñuela, 1829), 46–49 (my translation; italics added). (Hereinafter "Piñuela edition.")

25. Here Garcilaso uses the Spanish phrase "excelencias y preeminencias." The term *excelencias* literally means "excellencies" or "honorific treatment"; the term *preeminencias* means "preeminences" or "superior treatment." From this, it is understood that the inhabitants of Upper Cuzco were not intended to enjoy greater privileges, preferential rights, or superior treatment than those of Lower Cuzco.

26. *Aillu* (also spelled *ayllu*), in this instance, means "lineage group."

27. "La fundación del Cozco, ciudad imperial," in Garcilaso, *Comentarios reales* (Piñuela edition), 49–52 (my translation; italics added).

28. "Lo que redujo el primer Inca Manco Cápac," ibid., 52–53 (my translation; italics added).

29. Garcilaso understood the plight of the Native Andeans all too well. His mother, Ñusta Chimpu Ocllo, was an Inca woman of noble birth, first cousin to the Inca emperor, Atahualpa. His father, Sebastián de la Vega y Vargas, was a Spanish captain, also of noble lineage. During his childhood, Garcilaso was raised in the manner of a Spanish noble in Cuzco, along with many other children of the first generation after the Conquest who were of mixed Spanish and indigenous heritage. He was given a first-class education by the Spanish priests and was well versed in numerous academic disciplines, including the classics. However, after the arrival of Spanish women in the New World, the Catholic Church encouraged Spaniards to abandon their native (common-law) wives, with whom the Church claimed the men lived "in sin," in favor of marrying European women. Garcilaso's father contracted matrimony with a Spanish woman, Doña Luisa Martel de los Ríos, which effectively reduced Garcilaso's social status to that of an illegitimate child and also divested him of any hereditary rights. To add insult to injury, Garcilaso's mother was married off to a Spaniard of lowly birth. I believe these experiences caused irreparable trauma in Garcilaso's life. Although he loved his father dearly, by all accounts Garcilaso had a difficult relationship with his stepmother, and his keen intellect must have also made him acutely aware of the disparities created by these racially discriminatory colonial practices. After his father's death, to further his education Garcilaso traveled to Europe, where he wrote the *Royal Commentaries of the Incas* and many other literary works. Perhaps in an effort to reclaim and memorialize his indigenous identity, in Europe Garcilaso added the title "El Inca" to his Christian name. For a thoughtful discussion of Garcilaso's childhood, see Harold V. Livermore's introduction to *Royal Commentaries of the Incas and General History of Peru (Part One)*, by

El Inca Garcilaso de la Vega, translated by Harold V. Livermore, with a foreword by Arnold J. Toynbee (Austin: University of Texas Press, 1966), xx–xxii. See also José de la Riva-Agüero, introduction to Garcilaso's *Comentarios reales* (Riva-Agüero edition), x–xvii.

30.   Livermore, introduction to *Royal Commentaries*, xxii.

31.   Ibid., xxvii.

32.   When the Spaniards first arrived in Peru, they attributed almost everything they saw to the Incas, when in fact the Inca civilization represented the culmination of thousands of years of cultural experimentation in the Andes by many diverse and formidable Andean civilizations, many preceding the Inca. More often than not, "the institutions of statecraft that culminated in Tahuantinsuyu [the Inca Empire] were ancient ones employed by earlier states." Moseley, *Incas and Ancestors*, 65.

33.   MacCormack, *Religion in the Andes*, 404.

34.   The effort to reconcile these world visions was so strong on the part of Garcilaso that at times he distorted the reality of Inca religious practices to make them appear more Christian-like than they were. For example, Garcilaso denied the existence of human sacrifice among the Incas, a fact that has long been contradicted by archaeological evidence. He also adhered to the notion that the Incas came close to understanding the Christian concept of one omniscient, omnipresent, and invisible God. See citation notes in *Introduction*.

35.   Livermore, introduction to *Royal Commentaries*, xxii and xxiv (italics added).

36.   Garcilaso, *Comentarios reales (Tomo I)* (Araníbar edition), 218.

37.   Ibid. (my translation).

38.   Ibid.

39.   Hamilton, introduction to Betanzos, *Narrative of the Incas*, xiii.

40.   See Betanzos, *Narrative of the Incas*, 105 (Hamilton and Buchanan translation); Cobo, *History of the Inca Empire*, 142; Cobo, *Inca Religion*, 209. See also note 21 earlier.

41.   Hamilton, introduction to Betanzos, *Narrative of the Incas*, xiii.

42.   Garcilaso, *Comentarios reales (Tomo II)* (Araníbar edition), 511–12. See also Cobo, *History of the Inca Empire*, 163, implying that Huascar was born of incest because his rival half brother, Atahualpa, was "the second-born brother on the father's side only."

43.   Garcilaso, *Comentarios reales (Tomo I)* (Araníbar edition), 381.

44.   Ibid., 225 (my translation).

45.   Ibid., 97. Also, according to Felipe Guaman Poma de Ayala, the Incas punished idleness and lack of hygiene with "one hundred lashes"; moreover, the culprit was forced to swallow in public two urns filled with urine and excrement. See Guaman Poma, *Nueva corónica* (Pease edition), 75:224.

46.　In the dying declaration of the great Inca emperor, Pachacuti Inca Yupanqui, the aging ruler apparently instructed his lords that since "previously idle people tore the nation apart, they should tolerate no idleness in their nation or in the other nations and provinces, but, rather, all should work and practice all kinds of activities." Betanzos, *Narrative of the Incas*, 129 (Hamilton and Buchanan translation).

47.　Rostworowski, *Historia del Tahuantinsuyu*, 37.

48.　Ibid.

49.　See Sarmiento (1572), *Historia de los incas*, 51–64; Cieza (1550), *Señorío de los incas*, 42–50; Betanzos (1551), *Narrative of the Incas*, 13–18.

50.　There are multiple spellings of *Pacariqtambo* (see *Glossary*), which is commonly translated from the Quechua as "Inn of Dawn," "Inn of Production," "Place of Origin," "House of the Hidden," or "Hiding Place." Garcilaso's translation is "Shelter or Rest House of the Dawn." It may also mean "Lodging of That Which Rises, Awakens, or Is Born." See Urton, *History of a Myth*, 19; Rostworowski, *Historia del Tahuantinsuyu*, 38. See also *Simi Taqe*, 384.

51.　*Tampu T'oqo* is also spelled *Tambotoco* (for other alternate spellings, see *Glossary*). *T'oqo* means "window" or "hole" in Quechua and is thus referring to each mountain "cave."

52.　González Holguín, *Lengua Qquichua*, 56.

53.　Rostworowski, *Historia del Tahuantinsuyu*, 31.

54.　Ibid. (my translation).

55.　*Simi Taqe*, 677 (my translation).

56.　Rostworowski, *Historia del Tahuantinsuyu*, 32.

57.　Many traditional Andean home remedies include the use of chili peppers, which are believed to have curative properties against coughs, colds, intestinal problems, and joint and muscular pains caused by rheumatoid arthritis. Chili peppers are also considered effective treatments against lice and various kinds of insect bites. Additionally, they are often used to speed up the drying and healing of wounds.

58.　The translations of this name are derived from Steele and Allen, *Handbook of Inca Mythology*, 57.

59.　Sarmiento, *Historia de los incas*, 58.

60.　*Mama Ocllo* may also be spelled *Mama Uqllo* or *Mama Uqllu* in Quechua (see *Glossary* for additional alternate spellings). The possible meanings of her name are derived from Steele and Allen, *Handbook of Inca Mythology*, 57. In some Inca origin myths she is also called *Mama Huaco*, and in others she goes by the combined name *Mama Ocllo Huaco*.

61.　Guaman Poma, *Nueva corónica y buen gobierno* (Pease edition), 75:58.

62.　Rostworowski de Diez Canseco, *Historia del Tahuantinsuyu*, 38, citing Max Hernández, Moisés Lemlij, Luis Millones, Alberto Péndola and

María Rostworowki, *Entre mito y la historia: Psicoanálisis y pasado andino* (Lima: Imago Editores, 1987) (my translation).

63. According to the colonial priest-chronicler Bernabé Cobo, "marriages were prohibited with ancestors and descendants.... These restrictions were so strong that not only were such marriages unprecedented, but the death penalty was designated for anyone who committed such offense." Cobo, *Inca Religion and Customs*, 209 (Hamilton translation).

64. Betanzos, *Narrative of the Incas*, 105 (Hamilton and Buchanan translation).

65. Leo Estel, "The Mosca (Chibcha)," *Ohio Journal of Science*, no. 58, issue 4 (July 1958): 235.

66. Isbell, *To Defend Ourselves*, 203.

67. Arguedas, "La amante de la culebra," in *Canciones y cuentos del pueblo quechua*, 95–104 (my translation).

68. See Garcilaso, *Comentarios reales (Tomo II)* (Araníbar edition), 514–15.

69. Garcilaso, *Comentarios reales (Tomo I)* (Araníbar edition), 122.

70. Sullivan, "Andean Cosmogony," 103.

71. Ibid., 104.

72. Ibid., 105.

73. For a comprehensive description of the Moche "Warrior Narrative" and concomitant human sacrifice ceremony, see Christopher B. Donnan, *Moche Portraits from Ancient Peru* (Austin: University of Texas Press, 2004), 113–40. See also Walter Alva and Christopher B. Donnan, *Royal Tombs of Sipán*, 2nd ed. (Los Angeles, CA: Regents of the University of California and Fowler Museum of Cultural History, 1994).

74. See Cobo, *History of the Inca Empire*, 237. See also Cobo, *Inca Religion*, 54, 58–60, 67, 70–73, 78, 80–82, 89, 99, 151, 156, 170. Each describes human sacrifice rituals performed at various local *huacas* or shrines for the welfare of each region and community. See also Guaman Poma, *Nueva corónica* (Pease edition), 75:183–92. In each section, Guaman Poma describes the offerings, including human, made to the Inca *huacas* and to other major regional *huacas* of the empire.

75. Garcilaso, *Comentarios reales (Tomo I)* (Araníbar edition), 121–22 (my translation).

76. Guaman Poma, *Nueva corónica* (Pease edition), 75:164, 168 (my translation). Break in page numbers is due to illustrations.

77. Cobo, *Inca Religion*, 29 (Hamilton translation; parentheticals added).

78. For a comprehensive summary of the Electra complex, see Monte, *Beneath the Mask*, 68–70. See also *The Freud Encyclopedia: Theory, Therapy, and Culture*, edited by Edward Erwin (New York: Routledge, 2002), 179–80, 402–3, 410–11.

79. Monte, *Beneath the Mask*, 53–54; Erwin, ed., *Freud Encyclopedia*, 478–90.

Chapter 7: Sexuality and Guilt

1. Sarmiento, *Historia de los incas*, 23 (my translation).
2. Pedro de Cieza de León (1553), *La crónica del Perú*, edición, introducción y notas de Manuel Ballesteros (Madrid: Historia 16, 1984), 196–97 (my translation).
3. Guaman Poma, *Nueva corónica* (Pease edition), 75:374, 423, 425; 76: 10, 12–13, 15, 20–23, 26, 29, 33, 41–42.
4. See Cobo, *Inca Religion*, 204–10. See also Harold Osborne, *Indians of the Andes: Aymaras and Quechuas*, Routledge Library Editions, Anthropology and Ethnography (London: Routledge & Kegan Paul, 1952), 89, 98; Gordon F. McEwan, *The Incas: New Perspectives* (New York: Norton, 2006), 105.
5. Cobo, *Inca Religion*, 204–5. See also Rostworowski, *Historia del Tahuantinsuyu*, 249; Silverblatt, *Moon, Sun, and Witches*, 82; McEwan, *Incas*, 105.
6. Cobo, *Inca Religion*, 208.
7. For instance, the Spanish priest-chronicler Bernabé Cobo speaks of the custom among Native Andean men of cohabiting with a woman and "trying [her] out" ("amancebar con ella primero y tenerla en prueba") for a few months, or even years, before deciding whether to marry her. If he was satisfied with the woman, he would marry her; if he was dissatisfied with her, he was free to choose another woman. Cobo, *Historia del nuevo mundo*, 22.
8. See Paredes, *Mitos, supersticiones y supervivencias*, 219. See also Jorge A. Lira, *Diccionario kkechuwa español* (Tucumán, Argentina: Universidad Nacional de Tucumán, 1945), 921.
9. Cobo, *Historia del nuevo mundo*, 22 (my translation).
10. Many colonial chroniclers devoted a great deal of time in their narratives trying to prove the "legitimacy" or "illegitimacy" of the Inca kings and their wives. See Sarmiento, *Historia de los incas*, 167–70; Cobo, *Inca Religion*, 207–10. For instance, according to some of the chroniclers, Atahualpa Inca was not the "legitimate" ruler of the Inca Empire, because he was the son of the Inca emperor, Huayna Capac, and a secondary wife from Quito (Garcilaso, *Comentarios reales [Tomo II]* [Araníbar edition], 636). According to Spanish law, the legitimate ruler would need to be the son of the Inca emperor and his primary (or "legitimate") queen-wife. Likewise, the European notion of primogeniture would allow only the firstborn son to inherit and rule the kingdom of his parent(s) to the exclusion of all others. However, if this rule had been in place during the Inca Empire, this would have disqualified a younger Inca son, such as Tupac Inca Yupanqui (considered the Alexander the Great of Inca history), from ever assuming the throne in lieu of his older brother. Additionally, in at least one case cited in the chronicles, the Inca ruler

selected an "illegitimate" son to be his successor to the throne (Cieza, *Señorío de los incas*, 137–38). This has led some historians to conclude that the Spaniards were so "imbued with the principles of primogeniture, legitimacy, and royal succession, according to European models" that they may have overlooked "Andean customs such as the right of the election of the 'most able' to the offices of Inca and local lord." Rostworowski, *Historia del Tahuantinsuyu*, 16 (my translation).

11. See Rostworowski, *Historia del Tahuantinsuyu*, 16.

12. See Asunción Lavrin, ed., *Sexuality and Marriage in Colonial Latin America* (Lincoln, NE: University of Nebraska Press, 1989).

13. Sigmund Freud, *Civilization and Its Discontents*, translated and edited by James Strachey, with a biographical introduction by Peter Gay (New York: Norton, 1961), 52.

14. Antonio Paredes-Candia, *Folklore de Potosí* (La Paz, Bolivia: Ediciones ISLA, 1980), 13.

15. Ibid., 14.

16. For a very detailed and informative description of the courting custom and musical tradition of the *tuta qhaswa* (also spelled *tuta kashwa* or *tuta q'ashua*), see Thomas R. Turino, "The Charango and the *Sirena*: Music, Magic, and the Power of Love," *Latin American Music Review* (*Revista de Música Latinoamericana*), edited and published by University of Texas Press, vol. 4, issue 1 (Spring-Summer 1983): 81–119.

17. The *pinkuyllu* (also known as a *pinkillo* or *pinkullo*) is a large Andean flute, which measures over a meter in length, and is typically made of cane or bone and sometimes wood. It is difficult to maneuver because it has a tipped bevel and sometimes requires musicians to bow their head as they play. Its large size also requires musicians to stretch their fingers a great distance between the holes as they wrap the thumb around the wide girth of the flute. The Aymaras and Quechuas characterize the *pinkuyllu* as a "male" woodwind and strongly associate it with fertility and reproduction. See José María Arguedas, *Indios, mestizos y señores* (Lima: Editorial Horizonte, 1985), 41. See also Carlos Huamán, *Pachachaka, puente sobre el mundo: Narrativa, memoria y símbolo en la obra de José María Arguedas* (México DF: El Colegio de México and Universidad Nacional Autónoma de México, 2004), 280–82.

18. Paredes-Candia points out, however, that *khalas* (a slang Quechua word for *cholos*, or "half-breeds") sometimes take advantage of this practice, and "disguised in native dress and under the cover of night, practice *rumitankhay*," about which the native women complain, "*Cholo tankhaycu*" ("The half-breed has pushed me"). Ibid. (my translation; italics added).

19. Paredes, *Mitos, supersticiones y supervivencias*, 215 (my translation).

20. Ibid.

21. According to Paredes, the Aymara term *tincarjaciña* means "to get on" or "to get along" (*congeniar* in Spanish). Just as the Quechua term *sirwanakuy*, the Aymara term *sirvisiña* is believed to derive from the Spanish verb *servir*, which means "to serve." Ibid.

22. Ibid., 216.

23. María Dolores Castro Mantilla, "Los determinantes socioculturales en la salud sexual y reproductiva de mujeres indígenas," *Umbrales: Revista del Postgrado en Ciencias del Desarrollo*, Universidad Mayor de San Andrés, La Paz, Bolivia, edición de Cecilia Salazar, no. 18 (November 2008): 219.

24. Ibid., 219–20.

25. M. Lemlij, L. Millones, M. Rostworowski, A. Péndola, and M. Hernández, "Las cinco ñamcas: aspecto de lo femenino en ritos y tradiciones de Huarochirí recogidos por Francisco de Ávila," in *Mitos universales*, 133.

26. See Salomon and Urioste, *Huarochirí*, 78 (description of male *huaca*, "Rucana Coto").

27. For a description of Chaupi Ñamca and the dances and festivals dedicated to her, see ibid., 77–78. The cited quote is on p. 78.

28. In various pre-Columbian myths, the characters engage in premarital and extramarital sex, incest, rape, sodomy, polygamy, and sex with multiple lovers. According to the catechism of the Catholic Church, "Sexual pleasure is morally disordered when sought for itself [and] isolated from its procreative and unitive purposes" (CCC 2351). Therefore, under Catholic doctrine, these acts would be considered "grave offenses against the dignity of marriage" (CCC 2400) and characterized as "mortal" sins. A "mortal sin is sin whose object is [a] grave matter and which is also committed with full knowledge and deliberate consent" (CCC 1857). Unlike a "venial" sin that "does not break the covenant with God" and which is "humanly reparable through God's grace" (CCC 1863), a mortal sin must be absolved through the sacrament of reconciliation; otherwise, one is eternally separated from God, and dies "in a state of mortal sin," descending into the "eternal fire" of hell (CCC 1035). See *Catechism of the Catholic Church* (*Second Edition*), publication granted by Amministrazione del Patrimonio della Sede Apostolica, case number 130389, Saint Charles Borromeo Catholic Church, Picayune, MS, modified on September 8, 1997, to harmonize with the official Latin text promulgated by Pope John Paul II on the same date, accessed July 12, 2009, http://www.scborromeo.org/ccc.htm.

29. See Sigmund Freud, *Civilization and Its Discontents*, in *Freud Reader*, 757.

30. Ibid.

31. Ibid.

32. Ibid., 758.

33. For a comprehensive discussion of the latent and manifest content in dreams from a psychoanalytic perspective, see Monte, *Mask*, 84–85.
34. Ibid., 84.
35. Ibid., 85.
36. Freud, *Interpretation of Dreams*, 455.
37. Freud, *On Dreams*, 62.
38. Monte, *Mask*, 85.
39. Freud, *Interpretation of Dreams*, 239.
40. Arguedas, "Las islas de Pachacamac," in *Mitos, leyendas y cuentos perua-nos* (colección escolar), 41–42 (my translation; italics added). The uned-ited version of this story was recorded by Hortensia Lizárraga, a student at Colegio Nacional Miguel Grau de Magdalena Nueva, Lima, Peru, in or before 1947, when the first edition of this book was published. It is from the Pachacamac district in the province and department of Lima, Peru.
41. Freud, *On Dreams*, 71.
42. Freud, *Interpretation of Dreams*, 242.
43. Ibid., 241–42.
44. Freud, *Civilization*, 85–86
45. Ibid., 100.
46. Ibid., 100–101.
47. Freud, *Interpretation of Dreams*, 245.
48. Ibid.
49. For example, the *diuca* is a type of South American finch that is found in Chile, Bolivia, Argentina, Brazil, and Uruguay. In the Andean region, the term *diuca* is often used as a slang term for penis, along with another bird-related term, *pico* (meaning "beak"). In some parts of the Andes, the male sexual organ is also sometimes referred to as *pajarito* (the Spanish diminutive form of "bird"), but in the Caribbean, *pájaro* refers to a male homosexual. In several Latin American countries, *paloma* ("dove") and *turca* (a small mustached perching bird endemic to South America) are also used as slang terms for the male sexual organ.
50. Freud, *Interpretation of Dreams*, 242.
51. Freud, "An Autobiographical Study," in *Freud Reader*, 23.
52. Monte, *Mask*, 95.
53. See Freud, *Civilization*, in *Freud Reader*, 758.
54. Ibid., 272.
55. Freud, "The Neurosis of Defence (A Christmas Fairy Tale)," in *Freud Reader*, 91.
56. Freud, *Interpretation of Dreams*, 455 (italics deleted from original text).
57. See "Huacayashca cuitsa" ("La joven encantada"), in Cotacachi, *Huaca pachamanta*, 174–77. See also "Cómo sucedió Cuniraya Viracocha en

su tiempo y cómo Cahuillaca parió a su hijo y lo que pasó," in Arguedas, *Dioses y hombres*, 26–31.

58. See Teodora Paliza, "Patera payacha" ("La vieja paterita"), in Payne, *Cuentos cusqueños*, 18–22. In this story the incest is disguised as a wedding ring that the young woman puts on but cannot take off.

59. See Garcilaso, *Comentarios reales (Tomo I)* (Araníbar edition), 41–45.

60. Garcilaso, *Comentarios reales (Tomo I)* (Araníbar edition), 218; Cobo, *Inca Religion*, 25.

61. Cobo, *History of the Inca Empire*, 187. See also Davies, *Incas*, 158–59.

62. Garcilaso, *Comentarios reales (Tomo I)* (Araníbar edition), 218.

63. For example, according to the Spanish colonial chronicler Juan de Betanzos, both Tupac Inca Yupanqui and his older brother, Yamque Yupanqui, married their full-blooded sisters. Betanzos, *Narrative*, 119–20, 122. See also Cobo, *History of the Inca Empire*, 142. Also, according to Garcilaso, the emperor Huayna Capac married both his full-blooded sister and his first cousin. Garcilaso, *Comentarios reales (Tomo II)* (Araníbar edition), 511–12. Atahualpa, the last pre-Conquest Inca emperor, broke with this tradition   when he apparently married his first cousin as his principal wife. See Betanzos, *Narrative*, 181, 204.

64. Garcilaso, *Comentarios reales (Tomo I)* (Araníbar edition), 218.

65. See Betanzos, *Narrative*, 119. See also Cobo, *History of the Inca Empire*, 142.

66. Hamilton, in introduction to Betanzos, *Narrative*, xiii.

67. For example, most colonial writings concur that the Inca emperor Huayna Capac was the son of Tupac Inca Yupanqui and his sister-queen, Mama Ocllo. See Betanzos, *Narrative*, 123. See also Cobo, *History of the Inca Empire*, 142. According to most chronicles, Huascar Inca was also the son of Huayna Capac with his full-blooded sister, Raua Ocllo. See Garcilaso, *Comentarios reales (Tomo II)* (Araníbar edition), 511–12. See also Cobo, *History of the Inca Empire*, 163, wherein it is implied that Huascar is born of an incestuous union because Atahualpa, his rival, is "the second-born brother on the father's side only." Additionally, the Inca rulers bore children with other close relatives. Garcilaso recounts that Huayna Capac also had a child with his third wife, Mama Runtu, who was his first cousin. Garcilaso, *Comentarios reales (Tomo II)* (Araníbar edition), 512.

68. Spedding, "Almas, anchanchus y alaridos," 319.

69. Ibid., 321.

70. According to my native informants, this is a widespread belief among the indigenous peoples of the Mantaro Valley in the department of Junín, Perú. The native peoples of the Huancavelica region of Peru, located to the south of Junín, also share similar beliefs, particularly in the Tayacaja province to the north.

71. See Ranulfo Cavero Carrasco, *Incesto en los Andes: Llamas demoníacas*

como castigo sobrenatural (Ayacucho, Perú: Consejo Nacional de Ciencia y Tecnología, 1990). See also Ansión, *Desde el rincón de los muertos*, 153–58.

72. Spedding, "Almas, anchanchus y alaridos," 319.
73. "Caralla Mamamanta" ("Mama Pellejita"), in Zaruma, *Cañari*, 225–33 (my translation). Although this folktale hails from the Cañar province of Ecuador, other versions of this tale are also popular in the Cuenca canton, Azuay province of Ecuador.
74. See Freud, "The Neuroses of Defence (A Christmas Fairy Tale)," in *Freud Reader*, 91.
75. Freud, "Repression," in *Freud Reader*, 569–70 (italics deleted from original text).
76. Briefly, interpersonal psychology was a psychiatric theory developed by Harry Stack Sullivan, a medical doctor who worked extensively with schizophrenic patients. Unlike psychoanalysis, interpersonal psychology emphasizes the individual and his or her relationship to the environment, as well as the individual's interpersonal relationships, especially in early childhood. Unlike Freud, Sullivan believed that personality was not a product of unconscious and conscious forces battling in the human psyche, but rather, a constellation of long-term patterns developed in response to the individual's interpersonal relationships. As such, interpersonal psychology gives preeminence to the human social environment in forming normal and abnormal modes of behavior. See Harry Stack Sullivan, *The Interpersonal Theory of Psychiatry* (New York: Norton, 1953). See also F. B. Evans III, *Harry Stack Sullivan: Interpersonal Theory and Psychotherapy* (New York: Routledge, 1996).
77. Monte, *Mask*, 241, citing Harry Stack Sullivan, *Schizophrenia as a Human Process* (New York: Norton, 1962), 19.
78. Ibid., 246.
79. Ibid.
80. Freud's concept of the unconscious enfolds many subtleties and dimensions that cannot be adequately discussed in a single work. Generally, however, his concept of the unconscious is mostly personal in nature. For Freud, the unconscious acts as a kind of psychic repository of repressed, unacceptable feelings, instincts, and ideas that conflict with the individual's sense of morality and ethics. Nevertheless, Freud explains that the unconscious has a "wider compass"; he notes that "everything that is repressed must remain unconscious...but that the repressed does not cover everything that is unconscious." Thus, Freud opens the door but does not fully elaborate on the notion of a broader unconscious. See Freud, "The Unconscious," in *Freud Reader*, 573.
81. Jung, "Archetypes of the Collective Unconscious," in *Basic Writings* (1993 edition), 359.

82. Ibid. (italics in original).

83. Ibid.

84. Ibid., 359–60.

85. Jung, "On the Nature of the Psyche," in *Basic Writings* (1993 edition), 105–6.

86. Jung, "Archetypes of the Collective Unconscious," in *Basic Writings* (1993 edition), 361.

87. Jung, "On the Nature of the Psyche," in *Basic Writings* (1993 edition), 107. In some respects, the notion of collective archetypes reminds us of Plato's philosophical notion of the Forms. Plato's Forms are abstract entities that manifest their true form in the World of the Ideas, much like the Jungian archetypes in the collective unconscious. However, in our world, which Plato calls the World of the Appearances, we see only semblances or "shadows" of these true Forms. In much the same way, Jung envisioned the archetypal images and ideas that appear in human consciousness as only semblances and imperfect copies of the primordial archetypes found in the collective unconscious.

88. Jung, "Archetypes of the Collective Unconscious," in *Basic Writings* (1993 edition), 362.

89. Jung, et al., *Man and His Symbols*, 287.

90. Jung, "The Relations Between the Ego and the Unconscious," in *Basic Writings* (1993 edition), 175 (italics in original text).

91. Ibid.

92. Ibid.

93. Ibid., 179.

94. Ibid.

95. Ibid., 179–80.

96. Ibid., 81.

97. Ibid.

98. Monte, *Mask*, 163.

99. Jung et al., *Man and His Symbols*, 161.

100. For Jung, the Shadow embraces more than just negative aspects. It also contains motives, ideas, tendencies, and desires that have been repressed, irrespective of whether they are assigned a positive or negative value. The Shadow is both a product of individual creation and the effects of the creative unconscious. In many respects, this archetype is analogous to the Freudian concept of the "personal unconscious." Monte, *Mask*, 150–51.

101. Jung, "The Relations Between the Ego and the Unconscious," in *Basic Writings* (1993 edition), 183.

102. Jung, et al., *Man and His Symbols*, 196. Other archetypes of the Self include the image of the Christ, who according to Jungian theory is "the supreme

personification of [the divine] man," and the mandala or magic circle, which generally symbolizes integration or wholeness. Ibid., 215, 238.

103. Ibid., 196.

104. Ibid., 177, 189.

105. Monte, *Mask*, 151.

106. See Jung et al., *Man and His Symbols*, 191.

107. Ibid.

108. Ibid.

109. Ibid., 193.

110. For a lengthy and analytic interpretation of the tale of "Beauty and the Beast," see Jung, et al., *Man and His Symbols*, 137–40.

111. van Kessel, "Los aymaras," 273.

112. Ibid., 272.

113. Other examples of this theme are "The Cinder Maid," "The Little Glass Slipper," "Aschenputtel," "Kari Trestakk," "Pepelyouga," "Rashin-Coatie," and many others.

114. See Cieza, *El señorío*, 139.

115. Guaman Poma, *Nueva corónica* (Pease edition), 75:254 (illustration), 255, 469, 470 (illustration).

116. Martín de Murúa, *Historia general del Perú*, edición de Manuel Ballesteros (Madrid: Historia 16, 1986), 90, 129; Sarmiento, *Historia de los incas*, 131, 146; Guaman Poma, *Nueva corónica* (Pease edition), 75:224, 241.

117. The Quichua word *caralla* is derived from the word *cara* (also spelled *qara*), which means both human and animal "skin" (as in sheep skin, for example); it also means a "shell," a "covering," or a "wrapping." The suffix –*lla* in Ecuadorian Quichua is often used as a diminutive, similar to –*ito* and –*ita* in Spanish. It is for this reason that the Andean narrator translates the Quichua title of the story *"Caralla Mamamanta"* as *"Mama Pellejita"* in Spanish, meaning *"Mama Little Skin"* in English. The Spanish word *pellejita* is the feminine diminutive form of the Spanish word *pellejo* or *pelleja*, which, again, signifies "hide" (pelt) or "skin." The choice of terms may be purposely ambiguous in this case to denote both the "human" covering described in the story and the traditional "animal" coverings used in the pre-Columbian era.

118. Spedding, "Almas, anchanchus, y alaridos," 315.

119. See the Aymara tales of "Tiwulan panichasitapa" ("The Handsome Fox"), "Titulan Kasarasitapa" ("The Fox's Wedding"), and "Qamaqin Chijir Puritapa" ("The Fox that Fell from Grace"), described in the notes for chapter 3.

120. Freud, *Civilization*, in *Freud Reader*, 736.

CHAPTER 8: SUPERNATURAL BEINGS

1. Moseley, *Incas and Ancestors*, 102.

2. Alexandre Kiss, "Public Lectures on International Environmental Law," in *The Law of Energy for Sustainable Development*, 6–34, IUCN Academy of Environmental Law Research Studies Series, edited by Adrian J. Bradbrook, Rosemary Lyster, Richard L. Ottinger, and Wang Xi (Cambridge, UK: Cambridge University Press, 2005), 13. See also Mónica Machicao and Eduardo García, "Global Warming Melts Andean Glaciers," *Reuters*, June 7, 2007, accessed August 4, 2007, http://uk.reuters.com/article/uk-climate-bolivia-glaciers-idUKN0725512820070607; Carolyn Kormann, "Retreat of Andean Glaciers Foretells Global Water Woes," *Environment 360*, a publication of Yale School of Forestry and Environmental Studies, April 9, 2009, accessed April 30, 2009, http://e360.yale.edu/feature/retreat_of_andean_glaciers_foretells_global_water_woes/2139/.

3. Steele and Allen, *Handbook of Inca Mythology*, 116.

4. Bolin, *Rituals of Respect*, 57. See also Gary Urton, "Animals and Astronomy in the Quechua Universe, *Proceedings of the American Philosophical Society* 125, no. 2 (April 30, 1981): 122–23.

5. María Herrera-Sobek, ed., *Celebrating Latino Folklore: An Encyclopedia of Cultural Traditions*, vol. I (Santa Barbara, CA: ABC-CLIO, 2012), 129.

6. Kolata, *Tiwanaku*, 43.

7. As the waters decrease in Lake Poopó on account of evaporation, the salt concentration in the lake increases. Over time, the salt will crystallize completely, turning the lake essentially into a salt marsh. This has already occurred with other Andean lakes, such as Coipasa and Uyuni. For a more complete description of these processes, see Kolata, *Tiwanaku*, 43–44.

8. See "Threatened Lake of the Year 2012: Lake Titicaca in Peru and Bolivia," *Global Nature Fund*, accessed May 25, 2012, https://www.globalnature.org/35755/Living-Lakes/Threatened-Lake-2016/Threatened-Lake-2012/resindex.aspx; "Lake Titicaca Water Level Drops 2.6 Ft. This Year," *Peruvian Times*, November 13, 2009, accessed May 25, 2012, http://www.peruviantimes.com/13/lake-titicaca-water-level-drops-2-6-ft-this-year/4235/ .

9. Paredes-Candia, *Diccionario mitológico de Bolivia*, 64 (my translation).

10. *Inti* is the Quechua name for the Andean Sun god that centuries ago was the central figure in the Inca religion. The Aymaras had their own name for the Sun god—*Willka*—that probably fell into disuse after the Inca conquest of their region. In reference to the use of this term, Bertonio's colonial Aymara dictionary (1612) states the following: "*villca* [alternative spelling of *willka*]: The sun as they called him in the olden days, and now they call him *inti*." Bertonio, *Lengua aymara, parte primera*, 386 (my translation; italics added).

11. Villamor, *Moderno vocabulario del quechua y del aymara*, 152 (my translation).

12. Kolata, *Tiwanaku*, 48.

13. Díaz Villamil, "La leyenda de la coca," in *Leyendas de mi tierra*, 112 (my translation).

14. Ibid., 114 (my translation).

15. For example, the coca plant is used in religious offerings to the Andean Earth Mother, *Pacha Mama*, and other *huacas*. In Native Andean funerary rites, it is also the custom to place coca leaves in the mouth of the deceased. In many regions of the Andes, and mining areas in particular, the coca leaf is chewed to ward off hunger and fatigue. In such cases, the leaf extract acts as an analgesic for relieving the pain and fatigue caused by endless hours of labor, and it silences the hunger pains resulting from lack of food. Coca tea, called *mate de coca*, is also used as a remedy for high altitude sickness (*soroche*) and for treating many other ailments. The Native Andeans also look to the coca leaf in divination rituals to determine the health and well-being of their communities.

16. See "New Estimates Show Coca Rising in Colombia, Despite Record Year for Fumigation," Press Release, *Washington Office on Latin America*, Washington, D.C., June 5, 2007. See also John M. Walsh, "Reality Check: The Latest U.S. Coca Cultivation Estimates Make One Thing Clear: There Is Plenty of Coca," Report of the *Washington Office on Latin America*, Washington, D.C., June 11, 2007. Compare with 2006 statistics from Bolivia, after the Bolivian government instituted cooperative coca reduction methods: Kathryn Ledebur and Coletta A. Youngers, "ONDCP [Office of National Drug Control Policy] Reports No Increase in Coca Cultivation in Bolivia in 2006," Joint Report of *Andean Information Network* and *Washington Office on Latin America*, Washington, D.C., May 23, 2007. Since 2007, coca production in Colombia, Peru, and Bolivia, the three largest Andean coca producers, appears to be leveling off. However, according to a U.S. government report, Colombia showed a significant increase in 2014, likely due to several factors, "including increased cultivation in areas off limits to aerial eradication." See "Coca in the Andes," *Office of National Drug Control Policy*, The White House, n.d., accessed March 2, 2016, https://www.whitehouse.gov/ondcp/targeting-cocaine-at-the-source. Of all three countries, however, Bolivia, which expelled the U.S. Drug Enforcement Agency (DEA) in 2009 and has the lowest manual eradication figures, continues to exhibit the lowest coca cultivation production (in hectares) and the lowest coca production potential (in metric tons) (ibid.).

17. Kolata, *Tiwanaku*, 50.

18. Moseley, *Incas and Ancestors*, 27.

19. Aymara cosmology in particular is intimately connected with topographical and meteorological forces. The Aymaras venerate the *Achachilas* or *Mallkus* (guardians of the mountains who are considered

the ancestors or godparents of their people); *Wayra Tata* (god of wind and hurricanes) and his wife or consort, *Pacha Mama* (Mother Earth); *Kjunu Tata* (god of ice and snow); *Yaurinkka* (god of earthquakes, tremors, and other seismic forces, usually described as a giant black boa that undulates beneath the ground); *Santiago* ("St. James," closely associated for historical reasons with the Andean god of thunder and lightning, *Illapa* or *Illapu*); and many others. See Paredes, *Mitos, supersticiones y supervivencias populares de Bolivia*, 30–31, 58–60, 107–8; Paredes-Candia, *Diccionario mitológico*, 12, 64–65, 103–4, 148; Villamor, *Moderno vocabulario del quechua y del aymara*, 147, 152, 158; Spedding, "Almas, anchanchus y alaridos," 301, 308–10.

20.   The Kallawayas are neighbors of the Aymaras and reside in the Bautista Saavedra province in the westernmost region of the department of La Paz, on the border between Bolivia and Peru. For many centuries they have been recognized as great healers and herbalists—the peripatetic "doctors" of the Andes. Their ancestors were the physicians of the Inca royalty, and today their vast medicinal knowledge is still being transmitted orally from father to son (women are excluded) and from one generation to the next. The Kallawayas have knowledge of nearly a thousand medicinal herbs and plants that they use in their healing practices and traditional rites and rituals. Some elements of the Christian faith also appear to have been incorporated into their contemporary cosmology. In 2003, UNESCO declared that the Kallawaya cosmovision constitutes part of "The Oral and Intangible Heritage of Humanity" See "Masterpieces of the Oral and Intangible Heritage of Humanity: Proclamations 2001, 2003, and 2005," Report of the *United Nations Educational, Scientific and Cultural Organization (UNESCO)*, Intangible Heritage Section, Division of Cultural Heritage, Paris, 2006. Because they often travel from town to town offering their medical services, the Kallawaya men are often multilingual and speak Aymara, Quechua, and Spanish. The secret language they employ in their healing rituals appears to combine elements of a now-extinct pre-Columbian Andean language known as Pukina (also spelled "Puquina") with Quechua endings. Louis Girault, *Kallawaya: guérisseurs intinérants des Andes*, editions de L'Orstom (Paris: Institut Français de Recherche Scientifique pour le Développement en Coopération, 1984), 37.

21.   For example, the Aymaras believe in a tripartite soul called the *Ajayu*. The first part of the soul, called the *Jacha Ajayu* (or "Great Spirit"), exists only in human beings and is the most vital part of the soul. Its separation from the body leads to eventual death. The second part of the soul, known as the *Jiska Ajayu* (or "Little Spirit"), exists in both humans and lower animals and is expended during the course of one's lifetime. A person leaves bits of his or her *Jiska Ajayu* in everything that he or she

owns, touches, or handles (personal belongings, pets, parts of the home, etc.). Bits of the *Jiska Ajayu* also attach themselves to places where one visits and through which one travels, especially unfamiliar places. The third part of the soul, called the *Khamasa* or *Chchihui* (the "Shadow"), projects a person's individual personality, personal presence, or emotional state, which may vary from one day to the next. Paredes-Candia, *Diccionario mitológico*, 15–16, 75, 77, 79.

The Kallawayas also believe in an *Ajayu*, which is described as the "spirit or divine breath of Pachamama, which transmits the faculties of thought, sensitivity, and movement" (ibid., 22, citing Enrique Oblitas Poblete, *Cultura callawaya* [La Paz, Bolivia: Empresa Industrial Gráfica E. Burrillo y Cía., 1957], my translation). According to a Kallawaya priest whom I had the pleasure of meeting on the Island of the Sun, a person could live without his or her *Ajayu*, but he or she would be like the "living dead." The medicinal practices of the Kallawayas include the use of medicinal herbs and religious rituals and offerings designed to heal the person's *Ajayu*, or in some cases return it to the body. The Kallawayas do not distinguish among physical, mental, and emotional illnesses, as in Western medicine. All illnesses are treated as afflictions of the *Ajayu* often brought on by malignant spirits.

22. The *eqeqo* (also spelled *ekheko, ekeko,* or *iqiqu*) is a small ceramic male doll with a jovial face who carries all kinds of miniature merchandise pinned or hanging from his body: pots and pans, necklaces, cash, coca, cars, houses, credit cards, and anything else a devotee desires for a comfortable and prosperous life. Although the doll is dressed in the manner of a Native Andean man, its light complexion and moustache appear more European.

23. Paredes, *Mitos, supersticiones y supervivencias*, 78–84; Paredes-Candia, *Diccionario mitológico*, 50, 52.

24. For a discussion of the differences among these spirits or souls, see Espinosa Apolo, *Duendes, aparecidos, moradas encantadas y otras maravillas*, 25–28; Ansión, *Desde el rincón de los muertos*, 165–73; Spedding, "Almas, anchanchus y alaridos," 319–21.

25. Efraín Morote Best, "El degollador (Ñakaq)," in *Tradición: Revista Peruana de Cultura*, Cuzco, Perú, IV, no. 11 (1952), 67–91.

26. See Rory Carroll, "Alleged Killers Who Harvested Human Fat Arrested in Peru," *Irish Times*, November 21, 2009, accessed December 17, 2009, http://www.irishtimes.com/news/alleged-killers-who-harvested-human-fat-arrested-in-peru-1.775910; Arthur Brice, "Arrests Made in Ring That Sold Human Fat, Peru Says," *CNN*, November 21, 2009, accessed December 17, 2009, http://www.cnn.com/2009/WORLD/americas/11/20/fat.dead.humans.peru/index.html?eref=rss_crime; "A Peruvian Black Market in Human Fat? Medical Experts Dispute

Lima Police Claims That Gang Murdered Victims, Drained Fat from Bodies to Sell to Cosmetic Makers," *CBS News World*, November 21, 2009, accessed December 17, 2009, http://www.cbsnews.com/news/a-peruvian-black-market-in-human-fat/.

27. Arguedas and Ríos, eds., "Los pishtacos," in *Mitos, leyendas y cuentos peruanos* (1970 edition), 163–66 (my translation; italics added). The unedited version of this story was recorded by María del Socorro Dextre, a student at Colegio Nacional Miguel Grau de Magdalena Nueva, Lima, Peru, in or before 1947, when the first edition of this book was published. It is from the district of San Buenaventura, province of Canta, department of Lima, Peru.

28. Bolivian ethnographer M. Rigoberto Paredes offers an interesting explanation about why Catholic priests, and friars in particular, came to be associated with the *kharisiri* (another term for *pishtaco*) in the colonial era. He remarks that Native Andeans witnessed a great number of decapitations and dismemberments of prisoners and rebels during that period and came to the conclusion that the hooded executioner of these victims was a supernatural being, a *kharisiri* (meaning "decapitator") who feasted on human flesh, fat, and blood. As a Catholic priest was always present at these executions, he too, over time, became associated with the *kharisiri*, and eventually the distinction between priest and executioner disappeared. This association was strengthened by the observation that priests often traveled alone in remote and deserted areas of the countryside. Paredes, *Mitos, supersticiones y supervivencias*, 43–44.

29. Mary Weismantel, *Cholas and Pishtacos: Stories of Race and Sex in the Andes* (Chicago: University of Chicago Press, 2001), 3. See also Gonzalo Portocarrero Maisch, *Sacaojos: Crisis social y fantasmas coloniales* (Lima: Tarea, 1991).

30. Weismantel, *Cholas and Pishtacos*, xl.

31. Ibid., 7, 16.

32. For detailed accounts of these abuses, see Guaman Poma, *El primer nueva corónica y buen gobierno*, 533–661.

33. For a discussion of the *hacienda* system, see Peter Flindell Klarén, *Peru: Society and Nationhood in the Andes* (New York: Oxford University Press, 2000), 78, 208–9.

34. According to the Center for Justice and Accountability, "from 1980 to 2000, some 70,000 Peruvians, the majority of them indigenous, died in fighting between government forces and guerrillas. Both sides of the civil war committed systematic human rights atrocities. The number of dead and disappeared surpasses the casualties of all other wars in modern Peruvian history." ("Peru—The Struggle for Accountability: Civil War Atrocities," *The Center for Justice and Accountability*, San

Francisco, CA, 2011, accessed January 8, 2013, http://www.cja.org/
article.php?list=type&type=255). For a more general view on how security forces and civilian-elected governments, in conjunction with their
war on drugs, exacerbate political violence and human rights violations
in Andean countries, see Coletta A. Youngers, "Collateral Damage: The
U.S. 'War on Drugs' and its Impact on Democracy in the Andes," in *Politics in the Andes: Identity, Conflict, Reform*, 126–45, edited by Jo-Marie
Burt and Philip Mauceri (Pittsburgh, PA: University of Pittsburgh Press,
2004).

35. Weismantel, *Cholas and Pishtacos*, 11.
36. Ibid. (italics added).
37. Ibid., 15.
38. Gerardo Fernández Juárez, "Kharisiris de agosto en el altiplano aymara
    de Bolivia," *Chungará*, Revista de Antropología Chilena 38, no. 1 (2006):
    51–62.
39. E. Bradford Burns, *Latin America: A Concise Interpretive History*, 2nd
    ed. (Englewood Cliffs, NJ: Prentice-Hall, 1977), 69.
40. Ibid., 81.
41. Escalante and Valderrama, *La doncella sacrificada*, xiii–xiv.
42. Bastien, *Mountain of the Condor*, 45.
43. These institutions are described more fully in the chapter on *Social
    Protest*.
44. Bernand, *Incas*, 164–69, citing Nathan Wachtel, *The Vision of the Van-
    quished*, translated by Ben Siân Reynolds (New York: Barnes and Noble,
    1977).
45. *Webster's College Dictionary* (2003), 207.
46. Villamor, *Moderno vocabulario del quechua y del aymara*, 148.
47. See chapter on *Huacas*.
48. See Espinosa Apolo, *Duendes, aparecidos, moradas encantadas y otras
    maravillas*, 152 (in reference to *Espíndola*); Zaruma, *Cañari*, 103–9 (in
    reference to *Espíndola*); Arguedas and Izquierdo Ríos, *Mitos, leyendas y
    cuentos*, 96–97 (in reference to *Atoqhuarco*); Paredes-Candia, *Diccionar-
    io mitológico*, 109 (in reference to the *purun runa*).
49. Paredes-Candia, *Diccionario mitológico*, 84.
50. Paredes, *Mitos, supersticiones y supervivencias*, 94 (my translation). See
    also Carter and Mamani, *Irpa Chico*, 292.
51. Paredes-Candia, *Diccionario mitológico*, 76.
52. See Spedding, "Almas, anchanchus y alaridos," 304.
53. Ibid. (my translation).
54. Villamor, "Sueños, mitos, creencias y supersticiones," 150.
55. Spedding, "Almas, anchanchus y alaridos," 302.
56. Ibid. (my translation).

57. Ibid., 302–3.
58. Paredes-Candia, *Diccionario mitológico*, 107.
59. Ibid., 109 (my translation).
60. Ibid. (my translation).
61. Ibid., 95.
62. In Quechua, the verb *jappi* or *jap'iy* (also spelled *hap'iy*) means "to hold," "to seize," or "to capture"; in Aymara *japiraña* means "to catch" or "to trap." Ñuñu means "breast" or "tit" in both languages. Thus, *jappiñuñu* means "to hold, seize, capture, or trap [with] the breast or tit." And that is indeed what happens to the victims of the *jappiñunu*.
63. Villamor, "Sueños, mitos, creencias y supersticiones," 151 (my translation). See also José Felipe Costas Arguedas, *Diccionario del folklore boliviano (Tomo II)* (Sucre, Bolivia: Universidad de San Francisco Xavier, 1967), 21.
64. Espinosa Apolo, *Duendes, aparecidos*, 34–35.
65. Ibid., 34 (my translation).
66. Ibid., 35 (my translation).
67. See Paredes, *Mitos, supersticiones y supervivencias*, 96–97; Paredes-Candia, *Diccionario mitológico*, 95–96; Luisa Valda de Jaimes Freyre, *Cultura aymara en La Paz: Tradiciones y costumbres indígenas* (La Paz, Bolivia: Imprenta y Librería Renovación, 1972), 100.
68. Spedding, "Almas, anchanchus y alaridos," 316.
69. Paredes, *Mitos, supersticiones y supervivencias*, 96. See also Villamor, "Sueños, mitos, creencias y supersticiones, 150–51.
70. Zaruma, *Cañari*, 269.
71. Espinosa Apolo, *Duendes, aparecidos*, 82.
72. Ibid., 43.
73. Ibid., 42.
74. Ibid., 41 (my translation).
75. See Cavero Carrasco, *Incesto en los Andes*, 125, 176, 181; Ansión, *Desde el rincón de los muertos*, 154; Ossio, *Los indios del Perú*, 252.
76. Xavier Albó and Mauricio Mamani, *Esposos, suegros y padrinos entre los aymaras* (La Paz: Centro de Investigación y Promoción del Campesinado, 1976), 17.
77. Spedding, "Almas, anchanchus y alaridos," 319 (my translation).
78. For more detailed descriptions of *almas condenadas*, or condemned souls, and other supernatural beings guilty of incest, see Espinosa Apolo, *Duendes, aparecidos*, 25–28; Ansión, *Desde el rincón de los muertos*, 165–73; Spedding, "Almas, anchanchus y alaridos," 319–21. See also Ranulfo Cavero Carrasco, *Incesto en los Andes: Las llamas demoníacas como castigo sobrenatural* (Ayacucho, Perú: Consejo Nacional de Ciencia y Tecnología, 1990).
79. Lévi-Strauss, *The Raw and the Cooked*, 53.

CHAPTER 9: SOCIAL PROTEST

1. Donna Lee Van Cott, "Latin America's Indigenous Peoples," *Journal of Democracy* 18, no. 4 (2007): 131.

2. Deborah J. Yashar, *Contesting Citizenship in Latin America* (Cambridge, NY: Cambridge University Press, 2005), 4.

3. Donna Lee Van Cott, "Turning Crisis into Opportunity: Achievements of Excluded Groups in the Andes," in *State and Society in Conflict: Comparative Perspectives on Andean Crises*, 157–88, edited by Paul W. Drake and Eric Hershberg (Pittsburgh, PA: University of Pittsburgh Press, 2006), 157.

4. Ibid.

5. Yashar, *Contesting Citizenship*, 10.

6. Ibid., 19n22.

7. Ibid.

8. See Wilma Roos and Omer van Renterghem, *Ecuador: A Guide to the People, Politics and Culture*, edited by James Ferguson and Paul van der Boorn, translated by John Smith (Northampton, MA: Interlink Publishing Group, 2006), 42; Kintto Lucas, *We will not dance on our grandparents' tombs: Indigenous uprisings in Ecuador*, translated by Dinah Livingstone (London: Catholic Institute for International Relations, 2000), 3.

9. Mark Becker, "Pachakutik and Indigenous Political Party Politics in Ecuador," in *Latin American Social Movements in the Twenty-First Century: Resistance, Power, and Democracy*, 165–80, edited by Richard Stahler-Sholk, Harry E. Vanden, and Glen David Kuecker (Lanham, MD: Rowman and Littlefield Publishers, 2008), 165.

10. Ecuadorian Const. of 2008, Chap. 7, Art. 71–74 (my translation).

11. Ibid., Chap. 4, Art. 57(2) and 57(4) (my translation).

12. The Ecuadorian constitution provides that native peoples are permitted to participate in "the use, usufruct, administration, and conservation of renewable natural resources that are found on their lands," and may be "consulted" with respect to nonrenewable resources on their lands. But if the Ecuadorian government cannot reach an agreement with the native communities with respect to the latter, the constitution states that the government "will proceed in accordance with the Constitution and the law" (Ibid., Art. 57[6] and Art. 57[7], my translation). This suggests that the interests of the government—contractual and otherwise—in exploiting nonrenewable natural resources located in community lands override whatever interests these communities have in keeping their territories intact and their culture guarded against the threat of environmental pollution, soil destruction, and territorial displacement.

13. I am most familiar with the plight of the Sarayacu, a Quichua-speaking Amazonian community of about two thousand people, who have

been defending their territory from intrusion since 1989. The Sarayacu employ civil disobedience to prevent oil exploitation in their territory. For example, when the Ecuadorian government sent military guards to protect oil company workers who were entering Sarayacu territory without consent from the community, the Sarayacu women scolded and shamed the soldiers into giving up their guns. Sarayacu community members regularly patrol their borders and are presently considering building a "wall of flowers" to dissuade others from encroaching upon their territory. They are also very media savvy and have taken their message overseas. They have created videos documenting their encounters with government representatives, armed military guards, and oil company personnel, and they are advocating for their right to peaceably defend their lands and way of life. Community members have also recorded and distributed music with lyrics promoting their ecological and cultural message. (Personal communications with Mr. Elvis Toala, a spokesperson for the Sarayacu community in the United States from 2005–2009.) Many other native communities in South America are actively engaged in similar efforts.

14.   Although many former Bolivian presidents had acknowledged their indigenous roots, including Andrés de Santa Cruz, Mariano Melgarejo, René Barrientos Ortuño, and others, Evo Morales (affectionately dubbed "Evo" by the Bolivian people) was the first to openly identify himself as an *indio* ("Indian") and to rise to power from the ranks of the *campesinato* ("Indian peasantry"). Morales was born of a humble Aymara family in Orinaca, Oruro, a mining area in a predominantly indigenous department in western Bolivia. During his youth he worked as a farmer, a llama herder, a sheep shearer, and as technical director of a soccer team and organizer of soccer championship tournaments. In the early 80s his family moved to the Chapare, a lowland province in the northern region of Cochabamba, where they became coca farmers. It was through his work with the coca growers that, within a decade, Morales held several leadership positions representing the coca growers, and in 1993 he was elected president of the Andean Council of Coca Producers and leader of the Confederation of Coca Producers from Cochabamba in 1994. He started his political career in 1997 as a *diputado* (an elected position similar to a U.S. congressman), running under the banner of *Izquierda Unida* ("The Left United"), a left-wing political party. In 1999 he decided to form his own political party called MAS (*Movimiento al Socialismo*, or "Movement toward Socialism"), and he was the presidential candidate for MAS in the 2002, 2005, 2009, and 2014 general elections.

15.   The "water war" was an indigenous-led effort in Cochabamba that forced the Bolivian government to end a contract for the privatization

of water with "Aguas del Tunari," a consortium of multinational private investors that held a forty-year contract to deliver water service and sanitation in Cochabamba. Through mounting pressure from blockades, strikes, and protests, which claimed the lives of six people and injured more than a hundred others, the Aguas del Tunari contract was finally cancelled in April 2000, and control of the service was transferred to a coalition organization headed by the protest leaders. See "Water Privatization Case Study: Cochabamba, Bolivia," *Public Citizen,* 2001, accessed March 15, 2009, https://www.citizen.org/documents/Bolivia_(PDF). PDF.

16. See Jeffrey Vogt, "MAS Victory in Bolivia Signifies Mandate for Change," *Cross Currents,* Newsletter of the *Washington Office on Latin America* (WOLA), vol. 8, no. 1, March 2006, 2–3, 11.

17. See Evan Cuthbert and Kathryn Ledebur, "A New Constitution for Bolivia: The History and Structure of the Constitutional Assembly," Report of the *Andean Information Network,* Cochabamba, Bolivia, June 28, 2006.

18. George Gray Molina, "The United States and Bolivia: Test Case for Change," in *The Obama Administration and the Americas: Agenda for Change,* 167–82, edited by Abraham F. Lowenthal, Theodore J. Piccone, and Laurence Whitehead (Washington, D.C.: The Brookings Institution, 2009), 172.

19. Bolivian Constitution of 2009, Part I, Title I, Chap. 1, Art. 1 and 5; see also Part I, Title I, Chap. 1, Art. 4 and Part I, Title II, Chap. 3, Sec. 1, Art. 21(3).

20. Ibid., Part III, Title I, Chap. 2 and 3, Art. 280–82.

21. Ibid., Part I, Title II, Chap. 4, Art. 30–32.

22. For a collection of essays on the Shining Path, see Steve J. Stern, ed., *Shining and Other Paths: War and Society in Peru, 1980–1995* (Durham, NC: Duke University Press, 1998). For a revealing account of the devastating effects of the war between the Shining Path and the Peruvian military on a Quechua community in the Ayacucho region, and especially the women raped and victimized by soldiers, see the fictionalized ethnography, *Finding Cholita,* based on factual testimonies collected by anthropologist Billie Jean Isbell (Urbana: University of Illinois Press, 2009).

23. John Sheahan, "The Andean Economies: Questions of Poverty, Growth, and Equity," in *State and Society in Conflict,* 99–133, supra, 123.

24. Author, journalist, and human rights researcher Robin Kirk wrote a provocative book about the women who joined the Shining Path entitled *The Monkey's Paw: New Chronicles from Peru* (Amherst: University of Massachusetts Press, 2004). Through a series of interviews with former Shining Path members, Kirk learned that women played

a prominent role in the Shining Path movement. In fact, she stated that "in no other modern guerrilla movement have women played such a prominent role. According to Peru's penal authorities, a third of the people held on terrorism charges related to the Shining Path are women" (ibid., 63). The Shining Path also actively recruited women and put them in positions of power. Kirk stated that by joining the Shining Path, some women "went from the bottom of Peru's social pyramid to the top of the Shining Path's" (ibid., 79). They trained, planted bombs, killed, and even commanded forces, just like their male counterparts. One of their magazines apparently boasted that economic and gender equality would automatically be achieved through a successful and victorious Peruvian Maoist revolution led by the Shining Path (ibid).

25.   Yashar, *Contesting Citizenship*, 26.

26.   As one of my native informants from Ayacucho explained, "The Shining Path would come to our village and demand food and provisions at gunpoint. If we didn't want to die, we had no choice but to give them food and supplies. Then the military would come in and accuse us of being allied with the *senderistas* [Shining Path militants], and we were harassed, beaten, and sometimes killed for that" (my translation).

27.   Misha Kokotovic, *The Colonial Divide in Peruvian Narrative: Social Conflict and Transculturation* (Eastbourne, Great Britain: Sussex Academic Press, 2005), 198; Orin Starn, "Villagers at Arms: War and Counterrevolution in the Central-South Andes," in *Contemporary Indigenous Movements in Latin America*, 135–68, edited by Erick D. Langer with Elena Muñoz (Wilmington, DE: Scholarly Resources, 2003); Yashar, *Contesting Citizenship*, 26.

28.   Starn, "Villagers at Arms," 135.

29.   The argument here is that in countries like Bolivia and Ecuador, the concept of an urban Indian has been central to the notion of a collective indigenous identity, and therefore to the rise of "indigenism as a political alternative." By contrast, in Peru indigenous migrants to the cities become *cholos* and thus assume an identity that is "perceived as something other than indigenous" (Kokotovic, *Colonial Divide*, 198, citing Nelson Manrique).

30.   Rachel Wood, "Overview of the Colombian Conflict from a Human Rights-Based Methodological Perspective," Press Release of the *Council on Hemispheric Affairs* (COHA), Washington, D.C., July 28, 2009.

31.   The indigenous peoples of Colombia are often caught in the crossfire between the FARC (Revolutionary Armed Forces of Colombia), a leftist guerrilla group, and the Colombian military and paramilitary forces. In February 2009, in the southern Pacific region of Nariño, twenty-seven indigenous people were killed by the Colombian military and the FARC, and one hundred twenty were apprehended against their will. According

to statements made by the Awá, the native people of the region, and
other indigenous organizations, military forces entered the homes of the
Awá, mistreated them, and obligated them to give up information about
the location of FARC guerrillas. A few days later the FARC arrived in
their community and attacked the Awá in retaliation ("Comunicado a
la opinión pública nacional e internacional: a un año de la masacre en
Tortugaña Telembí," Report of *Organización Unidad Indígena del Pueblo
Awá* (UNIPA), San Juan de Pasto, Colombia, February 3, 2010; Mary
Tharin, "Awá Massacre Highlights Desperate Need for Fresh Approach
to Drugs in Colombia," Press Release of the *Council of Hemispheric
Affairs* [COHA], Washington, D.C., February 25, 2009). Some sources
report that the paramilitary groups have been the primary perpetrators
of human rights abuses against civilians, although the FARC are not far
behind. From 1993–95, the paramilitaries perpetrated about 300 human
rights abuses annually. In 1997 this figure rose to 800 abuses, and then
to 1200 abuses in 2001. The FARC committed 180–220 abuses between
1992 and 1995, 600 in 1999, and 1100 in 2002 (Wood, "Overview of the
Colombian Conflict," par. 3).

32. Jennifer Acosta, "Colombia's Indigenous March for Justice," Report of
the *Council on Hemispheric Affairs* (COHA), Washington, D.C., November 7, 2008, par. 11.

33. See Bartolomé Clavero, "Alerta por Genocidio en Colombia" (Report
of a Permanent Member of the United Nations Forum on Indigenous
Issues), *Coordinadora Andina de Organizaciones Indígenas* (CAOI),
Lima, Perú, January 21, 2010.

34. For instance, on February 4, 2010, ten thousand Indians from the Cauca
region walked the Pan-American Highway to the administrative capital
of the department, Popayán, demanding differential education (to
include indigenous languages), respect for their territorial autonomy,
and a halt to violence against their communities ("Colombia: Diez
mil indígenas marchan en el Cauca," Report of *Coordinadora Andina
de Organizaciones Indígenas* [CAOI], Popayán, La Arcada, Colombia,
February 2010). Similarly, indigenous communities embarked on a
three-day march in Santander de Quilichao, which drew an astonishing
60,000 people "condemning the aggressions committed against indigenous people" and protesting unfavorable constitutional reforms (ibid.,
par. 6, my translation).

35. Kay B. Warren and Jean E. Jackson, eds., *Indigenous Movements,
Self-Representation and the State in Latin America* (Austin: University of
Texas Press, 2002), 27.

36. Acosta, "Colombia's Indigenous March for Justice," par. 4.

37. "United Nations Special Rapporteur on Indigenous People Releases
Report on His Visit to Colombia in the Context of Follow Up to the

Recommendations Made by His Predecessor," Report of the *United Nations Office of the High Commissioner for Human Rights*, New York, January 11, 2010.

38.   "Rights Violations of Indigenous Peoples 'Deep, Systemic and Widespread': Special Rapporteur Tells United Nations Permanent Forum," Report of the *United Nations Economic and Social Council HR/5016*, Permanent Forum on Indigenous Peoples, Ninth Session, sixth and seventh meetings, New York, April 22, 2010.

39.   "Relator Anaya critica trato a mapuches en Chile," *Centro de Políticas Públicas*, Santiago, Chile, May 4, 2010. The Mapuches are descendants of the Araucanos, who boldly resisted repeated attempts by the Incas to conquer them in the fifteenth century, and fended off the Spanish invasion in some areas for over three hundred years. In fact, some Araucano victories were so decisive, the Spaniards did not return to those territories until the late nineteenth century. Today many Mapuches reside in southern Chile in a region known as Araucanía, lying between the rivers Biobío and Toltén, and bordered by Argentina to the east and the Pacific Ocean to the west. Although Mapuches still reside in their ancestral territories, a significant number have also migrated to cities, such as Santiago, Concepción, and Valparaíso, looking for better economic opportunities.

40.   Jonathan Franklin, "Prosperous Chile's Troubling Indigenous Uprising," *Time.com*, December 12, 2009, par. 1, accessed April 11, 2010.

41.   Ibid., par. 2.

42.   Ibid.

43.   Ibid.

44.   According to several sources, including UNICEF and the International Federation of Human Rights, Chilean police assaulted a school in Araucanía in October 2009, injuring many children. They have also subjected Mapuche children to physical and psychological abuse, and they have repeatedly detained children to question them about Mapuche activists. See "Organizaciones denuncian escalada de violencia contra menores mapuche," *Amnesty International—Chile*, Santiago, Chile, April 26, 2010 (citing original article in Radio Universidad de Chile); "Niño mapuche en clandestinidad es buscado por 'la justicia,'" *El Mercurio Digital*, escrito por Equipo de Comunicación Mapuche, April 27, 2010, posted in Spain on May 4, 2010; "UNICEF Urges the Chilean Government to Protect Mapuche Children," *Nationalia—Forum Social Mundial*, October 28, 2009; "Unicef pide imparcialidad en las indagaciones por violencia contra unos niños mapuche," *Agencia EFE*, Spain, October 26, 2009; personal e-mail correspondence with Lonko Juan Domingo Coñoman Quiñones, Mapuche political leader, in 2009 and 2010.

45.   Relator Anaya critica trato a mapuches en Chile, supra, par. 2, 4.

46. Ibid., par. 2.
47. Bernand, *Los incas,* 159–60. See also Peter Wade, *Race and Ethnicity in Latin America* (London: Pluto Press, 1997), 29.
48. Bakewell, *A History of Latin America,* 193.
49. Ibid., 194.
50. Bernand, *Los incas,* 70–71 (my translation).
51. Klarén, *Peru: Society and Nationhood,* 49.
52. See Stefan de Vylder, "Poverty Reduction in South America: The Millennium Goal Within or Beyond Reach?", report commissioned by the Swedish International Development Cooperation Agency (SIDA), Department for Latin America, June 20, 1995, 9. These statistics were expressed in terms of "ppp" dollars. "One ppp dollar" is equivalent to one U.S. dollar per person per day, adjusted for differences in prices between different countries. The World Bank recalibrated this figure in 2005 to $1.25 per person per day.
53. Ibid., 8.
54. Ibid., 7.
55. Yashar, *Contesting Citizenship,* 14. See also Sara Castro Klarén, "Dancing and the Sacred in the Andes: From the Taqui Oncoy to Rasu-Ñiti," in *New World Encounters,* 159–76, edited by Stephen Greenblatt (Berkeley: University of California Press, 1993); Marcia Stephenson, *Gender and Modernity in Andean Society* (Austin: University of Texas Press, 1999), 168–72 (in reference to the Aymara myth of Chuqil Qamir Wirnita).
56. María Luisa Valda de Jaimes Freyre, "La leyenda del venado," in Antonio Paredes-Candia, *Antología de tradiciones y leyendas bolivianas, Tomo III,* edited by Germán Villamor Lucía (La Paz, Bolivia: Librería-Editorial "Popular," 1990), 217–18 (my translation).
57. Arguedas and Izquierdo Ríos, eds., "Atoqhuarco," in *Mitos, leyendas y cuentos peruanos* (1970 edition), 96–97 (my translation and capitalization). The unedited version of this story was recorded by Carmen Ibazeta, a student at Colegio Nacional Miguel Grau de Magdalena Nueva, Lima, Peru, in or before 1947, when the first edition of this book was published. It originated in Pasco, Peru.
58. See chapter on *huacas.*
59. Guaman Poma, *Nueva corónica* (Pease edition), 75:374, 423, 425; 76:10, 12–13, 15, 20–23, 26, 29, 33, 41–42.
60. Ibid., 76:22 (illustration), 23.
61. Ibid., 76:11 (illustration), 12.
62. Mercedes Cotacachi, "Gringopac chitacunamanta" ("El gringo y los cabritos"), in *Huaca pachamanta causashca rimai,* 150–55 (my translation and capitalization).
63. Miguel Huaman, "Gringup mikhusqan" ("Lo que comió el gringo"), in Payne, *Cuentos cusqueños,* 74 (my translation and capitalization).

64. Ricardo Sánchez, "Lecciones del Sol y Comercio Justo," in *E-Chaski: Boletín quincenal sobre la cultura Quechua*, a publication of *Quechua Network*, April 27, 2005 (my translation).

65. This notion also appears in some Spanish colonial chronicles. See Cobo, *Inca Religion*, 30.

66. See Antonio Díaz Villamil, "La leyenda de la coca," in *Leyendas de mi tierra*, 105–15.

67. Lara, *Diccionario queshwa–castellano*, 284. See also *Simi Taqe*, 725.

68. Guaman Poma, *Nueva corónica* (Pease edition), 75:267 (illustration).

69. Quechua greeting, meaning "How are you?" *Tatay*, meaning "father," and *mamay*, meaning "mother," are often used as terms of respect when addressing another individual.

70. The three worlds of Quechua and Inca cosmology are *Hanan Pacha* (Upper World, sometimes also Outer World), *Kay Pacha* (This World), and *Hurin Pacha* or *Ukhu Pacha* (Lower World or Inner/Interior World).

71. In some Quechua cosmologies, it is believed there is a bubble of living energy around every human being, plant, animal, object, community, natural feature (e.g., mountain, spring, river, etc.), and all of creation. That is why the world or the cosmos is conceived as *Kawsay Pacha*, a "world of living energies" or "the energy universe."

72. The Andean concept of *yanantin* expresses the harmonious union of opposite or complementary elements or principles. In the dualistic cosmology of many Native Andean peoples, each gender, element, and principle has a necessary complement, and together both the element and its complement are essential to the continuity and integrity of the cosmos. In this particular case, the author is noting the absence or omission of "the left" in relation to the biblical reference that God the Son (Jesus) is "seated at the right hand of the father." By leaving "the left side empty," this passage violates the Andean law of *yanantin*, which requires inclusion of both *left* and *right* to attain integrity, continuity, and balance in the cosmos.

73. In this case, the commentator is referring to the notion proposed by some Andean scholars that the Incas did not form an empire, but rather a loosely held confederation of multiple ethnic groups, in which each ethnic group was allowed a great deal of local governmental and religious autonomy. Rostworowski, *Historia del Tahuantinsuyu*, 314. The Inca Empire lasted for a period of only one hundred years; so the reference to four hundred years might include the prior "formative" centuries in which it is speculated that the Incas identified as a distinct ethnic group in the Central Andes.

74. See note 72.

75. *Ayni* is the Andean notion of reciprocity, which is expressed in ritual, economics, and human relations.

76. Often translated as "community," an *ayllu* is a Native Andean organizational or administrative unit that binds the individual to the community by religious or territorial ties, by permanent claim to land and lineage, communal work, or symbolic ties to the land. It may also refer to a kin collective, an extended family, a lineage group, or several lineage groups that claim a common ancestral origin.

77. *Tayta* (meaning "Father") and *Mama* (meaning "Mother") are reverential terms used by the Native Andean peoples to show their spiritual kinship with and respect for nature. Often, the *huacas* (or *wakas*) of their religions are addressed as *Taytas* or *Mamas*. For example, *Tayta Buerán* ("Father Buerán") is an important Ecuadorian mountain; *Inti Tatay* ("My Father Sun") is a universal expression used throughout the Andes to render homage to the Sun; and *Mama Killa* ("Mother Moon") is a term of endearment used in Inca times and still used today to greet the Moon.

78. Loosely translated as "time-space," "world," "age," or "earth," *Pacha* is an untranslatable Andean term that expresses the concurrence, convergence, or integration of "time"—considered cyclical and astronomical—with physical or terrestrial "space." The peoples of the pre-Columbian Andes did not conceive of time in linear or chronological terms, but rather in cyclical terms in relation to agricultural, astronomical, hydraulic, and other natural cycles.

79. *Wakas* (also spelled *huacas* or *wak'as*) are sacred objects, animals, people (ancestors), and places venerated by the Native Andean communities. *Wakas* may be human-made (e.g., shrines, sanctuaries, or idols) or naturally occurring in nature (e.g., mountains, caves, springs, lakes, etc.), provided they have a religious or cosmological significance to a Native Andean group.

80. *Pachakuti* (also spelled *pachacuti*) is a cyclical Andean concept, which means "inversion of time-space/world" or "revolution of time-space/world." The cycle of *pachakuti* is usually initiated by a cataclysmic event (earthquake, deluge, volcanic eruption, etc.) that destroys the existing world and gives rise to a new creation or a new "age" of the world. In recent decades, the Native Andeans have also employed the term *pachakuti* to describe momentous historical events, such as the Spanish Conquest of Peru, or the Bolivian revolution of 1952–1964, which brought about significant and compelling changes in their lives and social conditions.

81. Richardo Sánchez, "Una reflexión sobre la visión espiritual indígena," in *E-Chaski: Boletín quincenal sobre la cultura Quechua*, a publication of *Quechua Network*, March 31, 2005 (my translation).

82. Burns, *Latin America*, 57.

83. MacCormack, *Religion in the Andes*, 8.

84. Bernand, *Los incas*, 52.
85. The destruction of these *khipu* was a great loss to humanity, for, according to some colonial sources, certain *khipu* contained narrative information about Inca religion, ritual, calendar, history, astronomy, poetry, and even law. See Guaman Poma, *Nueva corónica* (Pease edition), 75:183, 260; Garcilaso, *Comentarios reales* (Araníbar edition), 132, 346–48.
86. MacCormack, *Religion in the Andes*, 5.
87. Burns, *Latin America*, 58; Bernand, *Los incas*, 58.
88. Burns, *Latin America*, 59.
89. Ibid.
90. Carrillo Espejo, *Cronistas indios*, 42–43 (my translation).
91. MacCormack, *Religion in the Andes*, 183 (citing Cristóbal de Molina).
92. Raquel Chang-Rodríguez, *Hidden Messages: Representation and Resistance in Andean Colonial Drama* (Cranberry, NJ: Associated University Presses, 1999), 48.
93. Drew Benson, "Dancing with Scissors," *Washington Times*, December 9, 2003.
94. Ibid. For a comprehensive overview of the history, ethnography, and content of the scissors dance, contextualized within a study of urban growth in Lima, see Lucy Núñez Rebaza, *Los dansaq* (Lima: Museo Nacional de la Cultura Peruana, 1990).
95. See Spedding, "Almas, anchanchus y alaridos," 301; Villamor, "Sueños, mitos, creencias y supersticiones," 148.
96. This is a common misinterpretation of the Catholic sacrament of confession, or reconciliation, in which the priest acts only as an intermediary between man and God. According to Catholic doctrine, although a person "confesses" to the priest, it is not the priest but God of whom the sinner asks forgiveness.
97. *Padrecito* is a term of endearment that the Native Andeans often use in addressing a Catholic priest. In Spanish *padre* means "father," and when it is used in its diminutive form, *padrecito*, it could be translated as "dear father," denoting affection. Unfortunately, *padrecito* was also a term widely used during the Spanish colonial period, in which the Native Andeans were treated as though they were "children" or neophytes who needed to be counseled and guided by the fatherly priests. Thus, the term *padrecito* often evokes mixed emotions in the Andes.
98. Among the Native Andeans, it is customary for women to participate in ritual weeping at a funeral. Occasionally, professional mourners are also hired to weep. In this case, the priest is inviting the wife to initiate the customary weeping.
99. *Bayeta* is typically a handwoven fabric made of loosely woven wool with a coarse flannel-like texture that can be dyed in various different colors. The weave is usually made of handspun sheep wool, but it may

also be blended with other wool fibers, such as alpaca. *Rebozo* is a wide and long shawl, worn over the shoulders, that covers a woman's front and back. In many parts of the Andes, how the wrap is worn designates a woman's marital status. If it is worn folded over the left shoulder, this indicates the woman is single and available. If it is worn open or pinned shut, this shows the woman is married. *Anaco* (also known as *aksu* or *aqsu*) is a woman's robe, tunic, or dress made of uncut fabric and secured by pins.

100. Mercedes Cotacachi, "Taita cushipata, mama María, Juanchumantapas" ("El cura, Juanito y María"), in *Huaca pachamanta causashca rimai*, 196–201 (my translation; italics added).

101. Agustín Thupa Pacco, "Kuramantawan Sacristanmantawan" ("El cura y el sacristán)," in Itier, *Karu Ñankunapi*, 229–33 (my translation).

102. See Cobo, *Inca Religion*, 3–10. See also Sarmiento, *Historia de los incas*, 17–25, 39, 42, 46, 50–51, 171.

103. See Matthew Restall, *Seven Myths of the Spanish Conquest* (New York: Oxford University Press, 2003), 44–63. Archaeologists have also recently uncovered mass graves and forensic evidence of Andean natives fighting alongside the Spaniards during the Spanish Conquest of Peru. Thomas H. Maugh II, "Inca Warrior's Wound Tells Another Tale of Conquest," *Los Angeles Times*, June 20, 2007. Native allies also accompanied the Spaniards on other expeditions of conquest. For example, the Spanish conquistador Diego de Almagro and later Diego de Valdivia set out to conquer Chile "with 150 Spaniards and some 1,000 Indians from Peru in January 1540." George Childs Kohn, *Dictionary of Wars*, 3rd edition (New York: Facts on File, Inc., 2007), 518.

104. Ward Stavig and Ella Schmidt, eds. and trans., *The Tupac Amaru and Catarista Rebellions: An Anthology of Sources*, with an introduction by Charles F. Walker (Indianapolis, IN: Hackett Publishing Company, 2008), xiii.

105. See José Luis Saavedra, "Descolonizar e indianizar la universidad," *Pukara: Cultura, sociedad y política de los pueblos originarios*, year 1, vol. 5, March 7–April 7, 2006, La Paz, Bolivia, 4–5. See also Catherine Walsh, Álvaro García Linera, and Walter Mignolo, *Interculturalidad, descolonización del estado y del conocimiento* (Buenos Aires: Ediciones del Signo, 2006).

106. Jesús, in this case, is the name of a Peruvian town and also the site of a well-known fountain. The symbolism, however, is inescapable.

107. Arguedas and Izquierdo Ríos, eds., "El hombre dormido," in *Mitos, leyendas y cuentos peruanos* (2009 edition), 46. The unedited version was recorded by Delma Pacheco, student of the Colegio Nacional Miguel Grau de Magdalena Nueva, Lima, Peru, in or before 1947, when the first edition of this book was published. It originated in Arequipa, Peru.

108. Jung, *Basic Writings* (1993 edition), 181.

109. For Jung, the Shadow archetype embodies the dark, or negative, unconscious aspects of the personality and, occasionally, the repressed *positive* aspects of the personality. The Shadow aspects "have an emotional nature" and tend to have a "possessive quality" that controls the individual where weakest. On the road to self-realization, Jung recognizes that the individual must make considerable effort to embrace the Shadow and make it conscious, even though it creates considerable conflict in the ego-personality. See "Aion: Phenomenology of the Self," in Carl G. Jung, *The Portable Jung*, edited with an introduction by Joseph Campbell, translated by R. F. C. Hull (New York: Viking Penguin, 1971), 145–46.

110. According to Jung, the Christ symbol speaks to "the most highly developed and differentiated symbol of the Self," because it combines the antithetical qualities of wholeness and individuality. See Jung, "Introduction to the Religious and Psychological Problems of Alchemy," in *Basic Writings* (1993 edition), 556–58.

111. See Nadia Martínez, "Political Upheaval: Latin America Challenges the Washington Consensus," *These Times*, April 5, 2006. See also William M. LeoGrande, "U.S. Insecurity in Latin America: Radical Populism," *Cross Currents*, Newsletter of the *Washington Office on Latin America* (WOLA), March 2006, 1, 10.

GLOSSARY

The following italicized terms are introduced and discussed more fully in the book chapters and endnotes. The bracketed letters denote a Quechua or Quichua [Q], Aymara [A], Spanish [S], or Kallawaya [K] term. If a word exists in more than one contemporary language, such as in Quechua/Quichua and Aymara, that is also noted within brackets, as are loan words that may have a blended or mixed linguistic origin.

To date, there is no universally accepted spelling of Quechua and Aymara words, so whenever possible, alternate spellings of each term have been provided in the corresponding language. As often occurs in spoken syncretistic Quechua and Aymara, Spanish plural endings [-s or -es] replace the corresponding plural endings in Quechua [-kuna] and Aymara [-naka]. As this is not a linguistic but rather a cultural text, the familiar spellings and usages have been retained.

Achachilas [A]: Spirits or deities of the mountains and high mountain peaks which surround the Aymara communities and are believed to be responsible for the production and dispensation of water needed for irrigation and other community uses. They are also considered to be the ancestors or godparents of the Aymara people, as well as the guardians of their animals and crops. Also known as *Mallkus* or *Mallcus*.

Aca Pacha [A]: "This World." In Aymara cosmology, the surface and the world above the surface of the earth and all its inhabitants, including flora, fauna, and humanity. It is also considered a neutral space where all three worlds, or *pachas*, converge. Alternate spelling: *Aka Pacha*.

aguay unu [blended S and Q]: See *unu*.

Alaj Pacha [A]: The "World Above" or "Upper World." In Aymara cosmology, the space of luminosity occupied by foreign (Inca and Spanish) deities, including the sun (closely associated with the Creator), moon, thunder/lightning, planets, stars and constellations, in addition to God the Father (*Dios Awki*), Jesus, the Virgin Mary, the apostles, the angels, and the Catholic

393

saints. Today it is equated with the Christian Heaven and beneficent forces. The *Achachilas* or *Mallkus* also belong to the realm of *Alaj Pacha*. Alternate spellings: *Araj Pacha, Alax Pacha*.

allpa [Q]: "Earth" or "ground." Denotes the earth or the ground in a secular context (e.g., a cultivated field), as opposed to *pacha*, which describes the earth or the world in a religious or spiritual context (e.g., *Kay Pacha*, "This [cosmological] World").

almas condenadas [S]: "Condemned souls." In Andean lore, wandering spirits or supernatural beings who are forced to walk the earth after their physical death in order to expiate some grave or mortal sin, such as incest, committed during their lifetime. Sometimes also known as *kukuchis* or *kukus*.

almas en pena [S]: "Souls in sorrow." Wandering or lost souls, or souls in purgatory, who left unfinished business on earth before they died and are in need of prayers. These souls may dwell in and become attached to *lugares pesados* ("heavy places"). See also **lugares pesados**.

almas santas [S]: "Holy souls." Souls in purgatory who are often represented in Andean processions and, according to the Catholic faith, are in need of redemption and prayers. Some Andeans believe they cluster around churches and other holy sites and may perform miracles on behalf of the faithful.

altiplano [S]: "High plain" or "high plateau." The high west-central Andean plateau situated between the eastern and western mountain ranges of the Peruvian and Bolivian Andes, as well as parts of northern Chile and Argentina. Its average altitude is about 12,300 feet (3,750 meters) above sea level. In rural areas, the primary economic activities are mining and herding animals; in the urban centers, service industries and manufacturing. Sometimes also called *puna*.

Amaru [Q, A]: A mythical zoomorphic creature that is part serpent, or a two-headed or bifurcated serpent, often depicted as a rainbow with a head at each end. It is strongly associated with the economy and dispensation of irrigation water, explosive forces, and *pachacuti*-like events. Also known as *Katari, Hatun Mach'aqway* (or *Mach'acuay*), and *Yakumama*. Alternate spellings: *Amalu, Amaro*.

anchanchu [Q, A, K]: An evil spirit or malevolent being who is often described as a small, wicked old man or a big-bellied dwarf with a captivating smile. His greatest weapon is his overwhelming charm, which he uses to attract unsuspecting victims and later kill them. Also known as *janch-cho-janchus* [K] and *duende* [S]. Alternate spelling: *achanchu*.

andenes [S]: "Platforms" or "[agricultural] terraces." Farming platforms or agricultural terraces constructed by pre-Hispanic cultures on the slopes of the Andean mountains to create cultivable hillsides and to maximize agriculture. A great number of these are still in use today.

Apus [Q]: Spirits or deities of the mountains and high mountain lakes venerated by the Quechua peoples and believed to be responsible for the production and dispensation of water needed for irrigation and other community uses. Their power is also presumably based on the relative height of their peaks—the higher the mountain, the more powerful its guardian spirit. Also known as *Wamanis*.

atoq [Q]: "Fox." In Andean folktales, the fox generally plays the role of a shape-shifting trickster who deceives others into doing his bidding. It is also the name of a "dark cloud constellation" (*yana phuyu*) visible in the Milky Way. See also ***yana phuyu***. Alternate spellings: *atuq, atuj*.

auca [Q]: "Enemy," "adversary," "rival," "traitor." Also "warrior," "rebel," "savage." One of the mythical ancestors of the Incas, the *Ayar* brothers, was known as *Ayar Auca*. Alternate spellings: *auka, awqa, auqa*.

Auca Runa or ***Auca Pacha Runa*** [Q]: "Warlike People" or "People of the Age of War." According to Felipe Guaman Poma de Ayala, this was the fourth age of the world, which preceded the age of the Inca, when the natives lived in fortified settlements, waged war with advanced weapons, and worshipped their creator without engaging in idolatry.

Ayar [Q]: "Wild quinoa." Name of the male mythical ancestors of the Inca— *Ayar Mango* (or *Manco*), *Ayar Cachi, Ayar Uchu,* and *Ayar Auca*—who emerged out of the mountain of *Tampu T'oqo* at *Pacariqtambo*. Also describes a form of wild quinoa, probably *Chenopodium quinoa,* which was strongly connected with Andean origins.

Ayar Mango [Q]: One of the male mythical ancestors of the Inca who emerged out of the mountain of *Tampu T'oqo* at *Pacariqtambo*. *Ayar* means "wild quinoa," and *mango* may be related to an ancient Andean grass (scientific name *Bromus mango*) used to make flour and *chicha,* and which, until recently, was considered extinct. Alternate spelling: *Ayar Manco*. See also ***Manco Capac.***

ayllu [Q]: A Native Andean organizational or administrative unit that binds the individual to his or her community by religious and territorial ties, permanent claim to land and lineage, communal work, or symbolic ties to the land. It may also refer to a kin collective, an extended family, a lineage group, or several lineage groups that claim a common ancestral origin. Alternate spellings: *ayllo, aillu*.

ayni [Q]: "Reciprocity." A mutual exchange of goods or activities, or an even exchange of labor. In a religious context, making sacrifices or offerings to *Pacha Mama,* the *Apus, huacas,* or other divinities also constitutes *ayni* because it is expected that the deities will appreciate these gestures and confer benefits in return.

batán [S]: "Grinding stone." Typically used only by women, the Andean grinding stone consists of two pieces: a flat rectangular stone slab, which forms the base, and a second smooth-bottomed stone, sometimes called the *una*, shaped like a thick crescent moon. The user grinds the seed or food by rocking the "moon stone" back and forth.

cacique [S; may be of Caribbean or Central American origin]: "Chieftain" or "overlord." A Spanish colonial term used to denote the status of indigenous local leaders who were responsible for the political oversight and administration of their communities.

Caja Rueda [S]: "Box Wheel" or "Box Round." A Native Andean nocturnal dance that takes place every night during the carnival season in February and is followed by a sexual custom of overtaking women. See also *rumitankhay*.

capac [Q]: "Powerful," "illustrious," "rich," "noble," "magnanimous," "mighty." During Inca times, this term was used as an honorific title denoting a lord of high status, or an Inca of royal blood, who presided over an entire province or region of the empire. It was usually reserved for royal Incas and Incas by privilege whose rank was higher than the secondary (local) nobility. Alternate spellings: *qhapaq, qapaq, qhapaj*.

capac cocha or *capac hucha* [Q]: Usually translated as "royal obligation" or "opulent prestation"; may also signify "royal lake [of human blood]." Human sacrifice ceremony of the Incas, usually performed during the most important religious festivals dedicated to the Sun god, the coronation of a new emperor, before important military campaigns, after the occurrence of natural disasters, and during times of great famine, hunger, and disease. Alternate spellings: *qhapaq qocha, qhapaq hucha, capac hucha*.

Capac Toco [Q]: "Window or Cave of the Noble" or "Window or Cave of the Powerful." According to some Inca origin myths, one of the three caves in the mountain of *Tampu Toqo* at *Pacariqtambo* from which the first Inca ancestors—the Ayar brothers—emerged and begat their royal lineage. Alternate spelling: *Qhapaq Toqo*. See also *Pacariqtambo*.

chacara [Q]: "Cultivated field," "sown field," "planted field." According to some colonial accounts, this was also the name of an Inca temple dedicated to the worship of snakes. Alternate spellings: *chacra, chakra*.

ch'allakuy [Q]: Andean custom or ritual act of spilling, spraying, or sprinkling a little bit of liquid, usually *chicha*, on the ground, or on one's body, house, or animals as an offering to the Andean Earth Mother, *Pacha Mama*. Also known as *challa*.

chicha [Q, A; possibly of native Panamanian origin]: Corn beer or any of several varieties of alcoholic beverages made in the Andes by fermenting maize, grains, fruits, roots, or seeds. It is used as a libation and religious offering. Nonalcoholic varieties also exist.

chicharrón [S]: "Pork rind" or "meat crackling." In the Andes, a dish usually made of fried pork rinds or pork ribs, with added seasonings and lemon juice. In Andean stories cracklings made of human flesh are often considered the "food" of the malevolent *pishtacos*. See also **pishtaco**.

cholo(a) [S]: "Half-breed." Denotes an indigenous person who has moved to the city and adopted Western manners and modes of dress, an upwardly mobile Native Andean, or a *mestizo(a)* with distinctive Native Andean features. In a pejorative sense, it may also be used as a racial slur implying that a person is ill-mannered, lower class, or cannot be trusted.

choquechinchay [Q]: A mythical Andean cat, associated with the Andean *ccoa*, *k'oa*, or *qoa* cat, that is believed to assume the form of clouds and vapor emerging from highland springs or from the ground when it is loosened and opened up for planting. It is often considered an intermediary connecting the Lower World underground and the Upper World of air or sky.

chuño [Q, A, adopted into S]: Freeze-dried potatoes, prepared by a method of alternate freezing and drying. Also called *ch'umi*. Alternate spellings: *ch'uñu*, *ch'uño*.

churi [Q]: "Son." Usually refers only to a man's son. In the pre-Columbian era, the Inca ruler was called *intip churin*, meaning "son of the Sun."

ch'uwa khiwxata [A]: "Calling for rain, or clear liquid, from afar." An Aymara rain-calling ritual in which community religious leaders climb to the summit of a mountain and make offerings to *Pacha Mama*, the Andean Earth Mother, and to *Qarpa Achachila*, the guardian spirit of irrigation, imploring them to bring rain.

chuzalongo [Q]: An evil spirit or malevolent being of Andean lore who is often described as a sexual predator or seducer. He is characterized as a small child with long (often blond) hair, white skin, and blue eyes, endowed with an enormous penis that he uses to rape and kill unsuspecting women who want to protect or adopt him. Legend has it that he is the offspring of an incestuous union.

coca [S, Q, A]: A plant or shrub in the family *Erythroxylaceae*, native to the Andean region, which is considered sacred by the Native Andean peoples. The Native Andeans have chewed coca leaves for hundreds of years for their stimulating effects and to ward off hunger and fatigue. They also use it as a religious offering and for social and medicinal purposes, such as treating high altitude sickness (*soroche*). Alternate spellings: *kuka*, *qoqa*, *qoka*.

cocha [Q]: "Lake," "lagoon," "sea," "ocean." Alternate spellings: *qocha*, *qucha*. See also **Mama Cocha**.

collca [Q]: An Inca "storehouse" or "warehouse." Today it also means "silo," "granary," or other storage facility. Also, "The Pleiades." Alternate spellings: *qolqa*, *colca*, *qollqa*.

Con [Q]: May derive from Quechua, *coni*, *koñi*, *q'oñi* or *kuñi*, meaning "hot" or "warm." Name of an ancient Peruvian coastal creator deity, who was the child of the sun and moon. Some myths describe him as a god who came from the north, walked all along the coast, shaped the topography of the region, and then disappeared into the sea, never to be seen again. Alternate spellings: *Cun, Kon, Kun, Qon.*

Coniraya Viracocha [Q]: See ***Cuniraya Wiracocha.***

Con Ticsi Wiracocha [Q]: "Universal or Fundamental Creator ["Sea Foam" or "Sea Fat"] [associated with] Heat or Warmth." One of the several names of the Inca Creator god. Alternate spellings: *Contiti Wiracocha, Conticsi Wiracocha, Contiksi Wiracocha, Con Ticci Wiracocha, Con Teqse Wiracocha, Con Teqsi Wiracocha, Con Ticze Wiracocha, Con Ticsi Wira Cocha.*

cordillera [S]: "Mountain range" or "mountainous highlands." See also ***sierra***.

Coricancha [Q]: "Golden Enclosure." The most sacred and important temple of the Incas, located in the city of Cuzco, the imperial capital. Each Inca divinity had its own room or chamber in the *Coricancha*, which housed its corresponding idol. Alternate spellings: *Koricancha, Qorikancha, Qurikancha.*

coya [Q]: "[Inca] queen," "empress," or principal wife of the Inca ruler. Alternate spellings: *quya, qoya, koya.*

cuentista [S]: "Storyteller," "narrator." May also be called *narrador* or *narradora, cuentacuentos,* and *versero* or *versera.*

Cuychi [Q]: "Rainbow." One of the Inca divinities, which was also represented on royal banners, *keros* (ritual drinking vessels), and the headdress of the Inca ruler (*maskaypacha*). In the diagram of the Inca cosmos reproduced by the colonial indigenous chronicler Joan de Santa Cruz Pachacuti Salcamaygua, Lord Earth, or *Camac Pacha,* is depicted with an arching rainbow above him. Alternate spellings: *Cuichu, K'uychi, Coichi.*

cumbi [Q]: A cloth or garment made of very fine wool, typically vicuña, intended for the Inca or his royal family, or as an offering to the Inca gods.

Cuniraya [Q]: Name of a male divinity, or *huaca,* associated with the sun, who appears in the *Huarochirí Manuscript.* He travels disguised as a beggar and impregnates a female *huaca* named *Cauillaca,* who flees from him with her child and escapes by plunging into the sea. See also ***Cuniraya Viracocha***.

Cuniraya Viracocha [Q]: One of the several names of the Inca Creator god. His name appears to be a composite of *Cuniraya* (see ***Cuniraya*** **and *Con***) and *Viracocha* or *Wiracocha,* meaning "Sea Foam" or "Sea Fat." The Incas built a temple dedicated to him at Quishuarcancha in Cuzco, where they placed a golden statue of a ten-year-old boy representing the deity. He also had a temple in the *Coricancha* with an idol made of mantles. Alternate spellings: *Cuniraya Wiraqucha, Coniraya Viracocha.* See also ***Wiracocha***.

curandero(a) [S]: "Healer." Usually refers to a native healer, herbalist, shaman, or medicine man/woman.

Cuzco [Q]: "Navel [of the world]", "Boundary Stone(s)," "Piles of Earth and Stone." Capital city of the Inca Empire. Only the Inca nobility could live there. At one time it may have been called *Aqhamama* ("Mother Chicha"). Today it is the name of a city, a department, and a region in southeastern Peru. Alternate spellings: *Cusco, Qosqo, Qusqu*.

despacho [S]: "Remittance." Typically refers to a religious offering that is burned or buried and is made to the Andean Earth Mother, *Pacha Mama*, the mountain spirits or deities (*Apus/Wamanis* or *Achachilas/Mallkus*), and the Native Andean ancestors. Alternate spelling: *dispachu*.

encomendero [S]: The recipient or holder of an *encomienda*.

encomienda [S]: "Entrustment." An early Spanish colonial institution that conveyed land and Indians to a Spanish overlord in recompense for his services to the Crown. The Indians working the land were required to pay tribute to the Spanish overlord in the form of labor, and he in turn was responsible for their physical and spiritual well-being, or Christianization. In practice, this system created an unbalanced and exploitive relationship in which the Spanish overlords benefitted unilaterally from native labor.

eqeqo [A]: An Andean idol of good fortune and a minor god in Aymara mythology who represents abundance. He is usually depicted in the form of a small ceramic male doll with a jovial, light complexioned face who carries all kinds of miniature merchandise hanging from his body: pots and pans, necklaces, cash, bags of coca, cars, houses, credit cards, and anything else a devotee desires for a comfortable and prosperous life. Alternate spellings: *ekeko, ekhekho, iqiqu*.

Españurri [S with Q pronunciation]: "Spanish king." From Spanish, *España*, meaning "Spain," and *rey*, meaning "king," mispronounced as *rri*. A character who often appears in Andean *Inkarrí* myths, usually in opposition to his "brother," the messianic Andean hero *Inkarrí*. He personifies Spanish, European, or Andean Europeanized culture that relies on the printed word and records made of pen and paper (i.e., "writing"). See also **Inkarrí**.

gagones [S]: From Spanish, *gago* or *gangoso*, meaning "nasal," "speaking through one's nose," "stammering," or "stuttering." Human beings, guilty of incest, who according to Andean highland lore transform into dog-like supernatural creatures at night. They are usually described as whitish dogs with long front legs and tails, very long necks, and no hind legs. Also known as *ingagos*.

gentiles [S]: "Gentiles." Non-Christian ancestors, their mummies, or their spirits. See also **mallqui**.

gringo [S]: A derogatory term used to describe a foreigner, usually a North American, or a person from an English-speaking country. It may also refer to a person with light-colored hair who may not be foreign.

guacamaya [S]: A female "macaw." In some Cañari origin myths a macaw-woman, or in some versions two macaw-women, is considered the progenitor(s) of the Cañari people and culture.

hacendado [S]: "Landowner." A person who owns or holds a large landed estate, or *hacienda*.

hacienda [S]: A large landed estate used for farming or ranching. Modern progeny of the colonial *encomienda* system. Also known as *finca*. See also **encomienda**.

hanan [Q]: "Above" or "superior," relative to a lower or inferior point or position. The term may also refer to the upper moiety or subdivision of a Native Andean town, province, or community.

Hanan Pacha [Q]: "The Upper World" or "World Above." In Quechua cosmology, the space of luminosity occupied by the sky beings: the sun, moon, thunder/lightning, planets, stars and constellations, Milky Way, and Creator. After the Spanish Conquest, it also became equated with the Christian heaven and beneficent forces. Sometimes known as *Awa Pacha* or *Jawa Pacha*, "The Outer World" or "The Exterior World," as opposed to *Ukhu Pacha*, "The Inner World" or "The Interior World." Alternate spellings: *Hanaq Pacha, Janan Pacha, Janaq Pacha*.

hanp'atu [Q]: "Toad" and other related species of anurans. The common Andean toad (scientific name *Bufo spinulosus*), native to the Andean highlands, that hibernates underground or under rocks during the dry season and reemerges above ground during the rainy season. Because of its dual nature, it acts as a mediator between the Lower World and this one. Also the name of one of the "dark cloud constellations" (*yana phuyu*) of the Milky Way. See also **yana phuyu**. Alternate spellings: *hanpatu, anpatu, janp'atu, janpato, jambatu, jambatyuj*.

hatun runa [Q]: "Citizen," "citizenry," or "common people." From Quechua, *hatun*, meaning "extensive" or "large," and *runa*, meaning "man," "person," or "people." Name assigned by the Inca nobility to the common people of the Inca Empire.

huaca [Q]: Any object, animal, person (ancestor), or place venerated by the Native Andean religions of the past or present, including temples, idols, and shrines, and animas or spirits associated with aspects of nature (mountains, caves, springs, rocks, etc.). The term may also describe a portal or crack between the natural and supernatural worlds, or a sacred space that exists simultaneously in both worlds. Alternate spellings: *guaca, waka*, or *wak'a*.

huaman [Q]: "Hawk" or "falcon." May also appear in traditional Quechua names, such as Felipe *Guaman* Poma de Ayala, the Andean colonial indigenous chronicler. Alternate spellings: *waman, guaman*.

Huanacauri [Q]: Probably an adulterated form of the Quechua term *Wayakawri* or *Huayacauri*, meaning "Rainbow." A sacred hill on the southeast side of the Cuzco Valley and one of the most important Inca *huacas*, or sacred shrines. According to legend, this was the place where *Manco Capac* and *Mama Ocllo*, the mythical ancestors of the Incas, thrust their golden

staff into the earth and founded their imperial city. In other versions of
the Inca myth, one of the Ayar siblings, ancestors of the Incas, turned into
stone at the top of the hill and remained there as an idol. Alternate spellings: *Wanakawri, Wanakaure, Guanacauri, Huanacaure.*

huarachico [Q]: Male maturity rites ceremony of the Incas that took place
during the December solstice festival dedicated to the Sun god (*Capac Inti
Raymi*). During this ceremony teenage boys of noble lineage participated in downhill races, slingshot competitions, and tests of hand-to-hand
combat; they also underwent several religious rituals, including one at the
top of Mount *Huanacauri*. At the conclusion of the ceremony, the boys had
their earlobes pierced and inserted with golden earplugs, a mark of Inca
nobility. Alternate spellings: *guarachico, warachicuy, warachicu.*

Huarochirí Manuscript [written in Q]: An important colonial document,
composed at the turn of the seventeenth century, that recorded a pre-Columbian Andean religious tradition in a Native Andean language. It
was probably written by native informants from the highland region of
Huarochirí, to the east of present-day Lima, Peru, by order of the Spanish
extirpator and priest, Francisco de Ávila. Alternate spellings: *Waruchiri,
Waru Chiri.*

Huayra Tata [Q, A]: See **Wayra Tata**.

hurin [Q]: "Lower" or "inferior," relative to a higher or superior point or position. The term may also refer to the lower moiety or subdivision of a Native
Andean town, province, or community.

Hurin Pacha [Q]: "The Lower World," "The World Below," "The Inner World,"
or "The Interior World." The term is often used in contemporary Andean
texts as a synonym for *Ukhu Pacha*, the "Lower" or "Interior" World of
Quechua cosmology, but some colonial chronicles suggest that the Incas
differentiated between the two. Also considered an entryway to the realm
of the dead or an inverted version of "This World" (*Kay Pacha*).

Illapa [Q, A]: "Lightning." Also known as *Apu Illapa* or *Apu Illapu* ("Lord
Lightning"). A principal Andean meteorological deity who embodies both
Thunder and Lightning. The Incas imagined that *Illapa* was a man who
lived in the sky whose garment was made of stars. He held a war club in
his left hand and sling in his right hand, which he cracked when he wanted
it to rain. Alternate names: *Liviac* or *Libiac, Chuki Illa*. Alternate spelling:
Illapu.

incarismo [S]: A utopian doctrine that exalts the positive aspects associated
with Inca rule, prior to the arrival of the Europeans, when the Native
Andeans allegedly lived without hunger, oppression, or exploitation, and
they were free to organize and govern themselves.

indio [S]: "Indian," "Native American," "indigenous person." A Native Andean
or member of any Native American ethnic group. In the Andes it is often
used interchangeably with *campesino* (a person from the countryside).

Depending on the context, it may also be employed as a racial slur to
describe a person as ill-mannered, low class, uneducated, or untrustworthy.

Inkarrí [blended S and Q]: "Inca King." From Spanish, *rey*, meaning "king," and
Quechua, *Inka*, meaning "Inca." A messianic hero of Andean mythology,
whose legend foretells he will one day return to reinstate the Inca and put an
end to European domination. Many of these stories maintain that the buried
head of *Inkarrí* is looking for its body, and when the body becomes whole
again a *pachacuti* will take place, ushering in a new age for the descendants
of the Inca. Alternate spellings: *Inkarri, Inkari, Incarrí, Incarri*.

Inti [Q]: "Sun." A major Inca deity who had numerous idols, the most prominent housed in the *Coricancha* ("Golden Enclosure") in Cuzco. The most
important Inca festivals were dedicated to this deity, who was considered
the mythical father of all the Inca rulers. Today many Native Andean
religions also venerate the Sun, who is often paired or coupled with the
Moon (*Killa*).

intip churin [Q]: "Son of the Sun." Used in reference to the Inca emperor, who
was considered the son of the Sun god and his representative on earth.
Alternate spelling: *inti churin*.

jappiñunu [Q, A]: "To hold, seize, capture, or trap [with] the breast or tit."
An evil spirit or malevolent being of Andean lore who assumes the form
of a flying woman with long, provocative breasts that destroy everything
in their path, or of a beautiful woman with tantalizing breasts, engorged
with delicious milk, who causes men to lose their reason and die. Alternate
spellings: *japiñuñu, happiñuño*.

jurq'u [Q]: A male mountain peak in Macha cosmology. Each is paired with a
female mountain spring, or *warmi jurq'u*, who is considered his wife.

kantuta [Q, A]: A bell-shaped Andean wildflower (Scientific name *Cantua
buxifolia*) that grows in the high valleys and is the national flower of both
Peru and Bolivia. Legend has it that the flower sprouted from the blood
of two warring princes, who were mortally wounded in battle and finally
made their peace moments before their deaths. Also known as *qantu*,
qantus, or *flor del inca* ("flower of the Inca"). Alternate spellings: *cantuta,
khantuta, qantuta*.

Kawsay Puriq [Q]: "Circulating Life"; often translated as "Path of Living
Energy." A Native Andean belief system that ascribes a "living energy"
to each rock, plant, animal, mountain, person, community, and being in
the universe. Together all these entities interact in the "World of Living
Energies," or *Kawsay Pacha* (also spelled *Kausay Pacha*). Alternate spelling:
Kausay Puriq.

Katari [Q, A]: See **Amaru**.

Kay Pacha [Q]: "This World," "This Time," or "This Epoch." In Quechua cosmology, the surface and the world above the surface of the earth and all its
inhabitants, including flora, fauna, and humanity. It is considered a neutral

space where all three worlds, or *pachas*, converge. This World is also impacted by conflicts between Upper World (*Hanan Pacha*) forces and Lower World (*Ukhu Pacha*) forces. Alternate spellings: *Kai Pacha, Cai Pacha*.

k'ayra [Q]: "Frog." An edible Andean highland frog with smooth skin often linked to rainwater and to the common Andean toad, or *hanp'atu*. Also known as *k'ayrankulli* or *ch'eqlla*. Alternate spellings: *k'aira, kaira*.

khantuta [Q]: See **kantuta**.

Killa [Q]: "Moon" or "month." Also known as *Mamakilla* or *Mama Killa* ("Mother Moon"). Name of the Inca moon goddess. In Inca cosmology, she was the sister-wife of the Sun and symbolic mother of the Inca people, and her silver idol was housed in the *Coricancha* ("Golden Enclosure"). Today she is still venerated in Native Andean religions and is usually paired or coupled with the Sun god (*Inti*). Alternate spelling: *Quilla*.

khipu [Q]: "Knot" or "to knot." A three-dimensional ancient Andean recording system consisting of colored strings and knotted cords used to encode statistical and mathematical information and, possibly, narrative information. Most of the *khipu* were destroyed after the Spanish Conquest. Alternate spellings: *quipu, quipo, kipu*.

Kjunu [A]: "Snow." Also known as *Kjunu Tata* ("Father Snow"). Aymara god of ice and snow. The Aymaras imagine him as an old man with a long white beard who lives on the mountaintops and carries two large bags of snow, which he empties on the ground from time to time, creating frost, ice, and snow. In some Aymara or Kolla creation myths, he empties snow from his bags and covers the entire earth with a white mantle of death, contributing to its destruction. Alternate spelling: *Khunu*.

kkenti [Q]: "Hummingbird." In Aymara, it is *qinti* or *luli*. Alternate spellings: *kenti, q'enti, q'ente*.

kuntur [Q]: "Condor." Scientific name *Vultur gryphus*. Guardian of the Andes. In Andean mythology, he often acts as a mediator between This World and the Upper World, or as an earthly messenger to the gods. In Quechua folktales he usually plays the role of a shape-shifting trickster who adopts the form of a human to woo and bed a human woman. Alternate spelling: *kundur*.

layqa [Q]: "Sorcerer" or "witchdoctor." A person who specializes in the dark arts and can cast spells designed to bring harm, disease, and even death to others. Alternate spellings: *layqaq, layja*.

llama [S, Q]: "Llama." Scientific name *Lama glama*. A domesticated Andean camelid used since pre-Inca times as a beast of burden, a source of wool, and, to a lesser extent, a source of meat. Llama fat and blood are often used in Andean agricultural and fertility rituals, and llama dung is burned as fuel and used as an organic fertilizer. In Aymara, the most common name for the llama is *qawra* or *qarwa*. Also the name of a "dark cloud constellation" (*yana phuyu*) in Quechua astronomy.

lliklla [Q, A]: A woven mantle or shawl worn by Native Andean women in the highlands. It is often brightly colored with rows of geometric designs. Alternate spellings: *lliclla, llijlla, liclla.*

lugares encantados [S]: "Enchanted places." In Andean lore, places that may charm or bewitch a person, such as a magical lake, cave, mountain, or volcano. In Andean stories these places are usually inhabited by a supernatural being who enchants unsuspecting individuals and brings them under his or her control.

lugares pesados [S]: "Heavy places." In Andean lore, places where "souls in sorrow" or souls in purgatory (*almas en pena*), and sometimes condemned souls, are believed to dwell. Wandering or lost souls purportedly become attached to these places when they fail to find their way to the afterlife.

lugares malos [S]: "Bad or evil places." In Andean lore, evil or harmful places where the earth or malevolent spirits known as *malignos* may hurt or swallow human beings, especially children. They may also be places where humans can contract *uraqui*, the "illness of *Pacha Mama*," resulting in an untimely death.

Mach'ácuay [Q]: "Serpent" or "Snake." The name of one of the "dark cloud constellations" of the Milky Way (see ***yana phuyu***), whose appearance is correlated with the coming of the rainy season. The Incas worshipped *Mach'ácuay* as the patron of snakes, serpents, and vipers, and they assigned this name to some of their principals. In a generic sense, it is also known as *amaru, mach'awara, wata puñuq*. Alternate spellings: *Mach'acuay, Mach'aqway, Machaway, Machaqwa, Mach'aqwa.*

machu [Q]: "Old," "ancient," "of great age." Term may also refer to the survivor of a previous world age.

malignos [S]: "Evil ones," "malicious ones," "malevolent ones." Evil spirits who are believed to cause injury, disease, and even death among the native populations. Most are described as physically deficient or gruesome in some way with oversized, reversed, or disproportionate body parts. Often, they also lack the capacity for human speech and move awkwardly by jumping, hopping, or crawling on all fours. Black sorcerers in the Andes are believed to derive their power from these *malignos*, as well as from demons and devils (*saqra* or *supay*). Also known as *fantasmas* [S].

Mallkus [A]: Spirits or deities of the mountains and high mountain peaks which surround the Aymara communities (see ***Achachilas***) and are symbolically represented in ritual by the condor (A: *kunturi*), which inhabits these Andean peaks. The honorary title of *mallku*, or *apu mallku*, is also given to an important Aymara political authority, or a significant political figure, who presides over a region (*marka*) or a network of Andean communities (*ayllus*).

mallqui [Q, A]: A non-Christian ancestor, mummy, or spirit. Also a "sapling," "branch," or "young tree," or a plant or tree in general. Ancestors are also known as *gentiles*. Alternate spelling: *mallki*.

Mama Cocha [Q]: "Mother Ocean" or "Mother Sea." Inca goddess of the sea who had dominion over all bodies of water, including oceans, lakes, and lagoons. Natural fountains and springs were also considered her children. In some Andean mythologies, she was also considered the wife of the Inca Creator god *Wiracocha*. Alternate spellings: *Mama Qocha, Mama Qucha, Mama Jocha, Mama Kucha.*

Mama Qochap Patan [Q]: "Mother Coast." Usually denotes the dry Andean coastal desert that suffers from lack of rainfall. Even with large irrigation systems constructed in the adjoining *sierra* or *cordillera*, it is estimated that only 10 percent of the Andean coast is arable.

Mama Huaca [Q]: Loosely translated as "Divine Mother" or "Mother Divinity." In Cañari mythology, a supernatural being or *huaca* who has supernatural powers and inhabits the interior of the mountains, which are believed to be enchanted realms of magical fruits and crops, such as gold corncobs and gold peas. She is usually characterized as having long blonde hair, dressing in a long tunic, and possessing the power to bewitch or enslave human beings.

Mama Huaco [Q]: Often translated as "Vigorous Woman," "Great Grandmother," or "Mother Who Shows Her Teeth." Mythical female ancestor of the Incas and sister-wife of *Ayar Mango* (or *Ayar Manco*), who emerged from the center cave, called *Capac Toco* in the mountain of *Tampu T'oqo* at *Pacariqtambo*, along with three other sister-wives of the male *Ayar* brothers. Her identity is sometimes separate from but more often merged with *Mama Ocllo* (see ***Mama Ocllo***). She is strongly associated with the maize plant and its cultivation. Alternate spellings: *Mama Wako, Mama Guaco.*

Mama Ocllo [Q]: "Shapely Mother" or "Plump Mother." Also known as *Mama Huaco* or *Mama Ocllo Huaco*. Mythic female founding ancestor of the Incas, who according to legend either emerged from a cave in the mountain of *Tampu T'oqo* at *Pacariqtambo* or appeared on the Island of the Sun at Lake Titicaca. Like her husband-brother *Manco Capac*, according to Garcilaso she was the daughter of the Sun and the Moon and founder of Cuzco. She, along with her brother, introduced the civilizing arts in this region of the world, including those associated with the "feminine" occupations. Alternate spellings: *Mama Oqllo, Mama Oqllu, Mama Uqllu, Mama Occlo.*

Mama Sara [Q]: "Maize Mother." Andean goddess and guardian of grains and cultivated fields. She is associated with maize that grows in multiples. Alternate spellings: *Mamasara, Mamazara, Saramama.*

Mama Raywana [Q]: "Mother Furrow." A pre-Inca deity or *huaca* whose myths concern the emergence of agriculture and the origin of food in the Andes. In these myths she loses her son, through no fault of her own, and his dismembered body parts give rise to maize, potatoes, oca, yucca, beans, peas, and other crops and plants.

Manco Capac [Q]: "Powerful, Noble, Rich, Illustrious, Mighty, Magnanimous, or Noble [Lord] Manco." Mythical first ruler and founding ancestor of the Incas, who according to legend either emerged out of a cave in the mountain of *Tampu T'oqo* at *Pacariqtambo* or appeared on the Island of the Sun at Lake Titicaca. According to Garciluso, he was the son of the Sun and the Moon and brother of *Mama Ocllo*, his sister-wife. He and his queen founded Cuzco and introduced the civilizing arts in this region of the world. Also known as *Ayar Mango* or *Ayar Manco*. Alternate spellings: *Mango Capac, Manko Qhapaq, Manq'hue Qhapaq, Manqu Qhapaq.*

Manqha Pacha [A]: "The World Below," "The Lower World," "The Inner World," or "The Interior World." In Aymara cosmology, the space associated with the subterranean world or underworld, minerals and their guardian spirits, darkness, the inside of mountains, dark interior spaces like caves, caverns, and mines (the "bowels" or "entrails" of the earth), and the black arts. After the Spanish Conquest it also became associated with the Christian inferno, demons, and malevolent forces. In some Aymara communities it is also linked to the cult of the ancestors and ancestral deities.

mayu [Q]: "River" or "water current" of great volume. Alternate spelling: *mayo*.

Mayu [Q]: Celestial "River." Quechua name for the Milky Way, which in the Andes is associated with agricultural and hydraulic cycles. Alternate spelling: *Mayo*.

mealla [K]: Often translated as "satyr." An evil female spirit or malevolent being who purportedly suffers from an insatiable sexual appetite. In Andean lore she is often depicted as a copper-skinned blonde woman with backward-facing feet who walks around naked, her long flowing hair barely covering her genitals. She attracts the attention of unwary victims and then takes them back to her lair, where they endure sexually violent deaths.

mekhala [A]: A malevolent being or evil spirit whom the Aymaras describe as an old, skinny witch with unkempt hair, pointy teeth, and a fiery tail like a comet. Some say she flies naked at night and plucks her eyes out, placing lit candles into her empty eye sockets. Others maintain she dresses in a long red tunic with ever-expanding pockets that she fills with stolen food, animal parts, and the brains and souls of children she has consumed. Often she comes to the aid of evil sorcerers, who enlist her help in causing grave misfortune. Alternate spellings: *miqhala, mikhala*.

mesa [S]: "Table." Also pronounced *misa* by some Aymara, Quechua, and Kallawaya speakers. Usually refers to a ritual table, surface, or space where a religious ceremony is performed and religious offerings are made. See also **Muxsa Misa**.

mestizaje [S]: "Racial mixing" or "miscegenation."

mestizo [S]: "Mixed race." A person of mixed European and Native American ancestry. This term is used throughout Latin America, including the Andean region.

misterios [S]: "Mysteries." Multicolored chalky rectangular candies used in *Muxsa Misa* and other *mesa* rituals. These sweets are embossed with images of the sun, moon, stars, planets, signs of the Zodiac, the Virgin Mary, and other images carefully chosen by the celebrants, depending on the purpose of the ritual. See also *Muxsa Misa*.

misti [S]: Short for *mestizo*. Used primarily in Peru to denote a non-Indian or an upper-class white or *mestizo*. See also *mestizo*. Alternate spelling: *mizti*.

mitimaes [Q]: Hispanicized plural of Quechua term *mitma*, *mitmaq*, or *mitmashka*, meaning "foreigner," "stranger," or a colonist from another region or another place of origin. The Incas established a practice of colonization in which they moved entire communities or ethnic groups, often sympathetic to the Incas, from one region of the empire to another. These colonists spread Inca religion, language, and culture and defended the imperial frontiers. On occasion it was also used as a punitive measure to isolate insurgent groups with separatist tendencies.

Muxsa Misa [Blended A and S]: "Sweet Table," often mistranslated as "Sweet Mass." Also known as *Muxsa Mesa* or *Tulsi Misa*. An Aymara and Kallawaya ritual in which sweet offerings, invocations, and prayers are offered up to *Pacha Mama*, the Virgin Mary, the Christian saints, the mountain spirits, and the spirits of the earth and sky to invoke their blessings and protection. The sweet offerings are always paired and placed on a ritual surface or *mesa*, which is emblematic of the sacred space or the sacred geography where various cosmological worlds come together.

Ñawpa Machu [Q]: "Ancient Old Man." A character or being of Andean mythology who lived in the *Ñawpa Pacha*, an early pre-Christian age of the world. In contemporary Andean stories, *Ñawpa Machu* lives in a mountain called School and is often portrayed as an ally of Jesus, who is intent on eating the children of the Inca and *Pacha Mama*, and who also confuses them with "writing." Alternate spelling: *Ñaupa Machu*.

Ñawpa Pacha [Q]: "Ancient, Remote, or Previous Time[s]" or "Ancient, Remote, or Previous World." In the *Huarochirí Manuscript*, the pre-Christian world before the arrival of the Spaniards, from which the scribes of the *Manuscript* claimed they derived their rites, rituals, and customs. This epoch coincides with the mythic times of the Huarochirí peoples. Alternate spelling: *Ñaupa Pacha*.

Pacárec Tampu [Q]: See *Pacariqtambo*.

Pacarimoc Runa [Q]: "People of the Dawning" or the "Original Peoples." According to Guaman Poma, these are all the succeeding generations of Indians who descended from the *Wari Wira Cocha Runa*. See also *Wari Wira Cocha Runa*.

Pacariqtambo [Q]: Commonly translated as "Inn of Dawn," "Inn of Production," "Place of Origin," "House of the Hidden," "Hiding Place"; Garcilaso's translation is "Shelter or Rest House of the Dawn"; may also mean

"Lodging of That Which Rises, Awakens, or Is Born" or "Lodging of Whom Rises, Awakens, or Is Born." Site of a holy cave and the mythical place of origin, or *paqarina*, of the Incas. It was from here that according to some Inca origin myths the Ayar brothers emerged, each with a sister-wife, and set out to find a permanent homeland. The original location may have been at *Mawk'allaqta* ("Ancient Place") in the Espinar province, Cuzco region, but a town named *Paqaritambo* was also founded during the Spanish colonial period in the province of Paruro, also in the Cuzco region. Alternate spellings: *Pacaritambo, Paqaritampu, Paqariqtambo, Pacarictambo, Paqariq Tanpu, Paqareqtambo, Paucari Tampu, Pacaritampu, Pacárec Tampu.*

pacha [Q, A]: "Time-space," "world," "age," "earth." An untranslatable Andean term that expresses the concurrence, convergence, or integration of time—which is cyclical and astronomical—with physical, or terrestrial, space. It may also signify earth in a religious or spiritual context, as opposed to a nonreligious or secular context (*allpa*).

Pachacamac [Q]: Often translated as "Lord Earth," "Earth Maker," "Earth Shaker," or "World Creator." His name also suggests that he was the *camac*, or vitalizer, who infused time-space (*pacha*) with energy and procreative essence. Name of a pre-Inca creator deity from the coastal region of Peru. A temple complex, which goes by the same name and was dedicated to this deity, was built in the Lurín Valley, to the southeast of present-day Lima, Peru, and served as an important oracle and shrine to a number of Andean pre-Columbian cultures, including the Inca. Myths concerning this god often relate to the emergence of agriculture and the mythical origin of certain crops, fruits, and plants from the dismembered body parts of his brother. Alternate spellings: *Pacha Camac, Pachakamaq, Pacha Kamaq, Pachacaman, Camac Pacha.*

pachacuti [Q, A]: "The inversion or turning over of time-space or world." Derived from the union of the word *pacha*, signifying "time-space," "age," "world," or "earth," and *cuti* (also spelled *kuti*), meaning "revolution," "inversion," or "turning over, around, or upside down." A cycle of destruction and creation, precipitated by a cataclysmic event, such as a flood or an earthquake, that destroys the existing world but then allows for the creation of a new one, marking a new age of the world or a new "sun." It may also refer to a cataclysmic historical or cultural transformation, such as the Spanish Conquest, that dramatically changed the lives of the Native Andean people (symbolic or historical *pachacuti*). Alternate spelling: *pachakuti.*

Pacha Mama [Q, A, K]: "Mother Earth" or "Mother World." The divinized earth, one of the most important deities of the Native Andean religions. She is considered the mother of crops, humanity, topography, and all feminine occupations and is strongly associated with fertility and fecundity. She is worshipped at all major agricultural festivals in the Andes and receives a variety of community offerings and *despachos*. Alternate spelling: *Pachamama*.

Pacha Tata [Q]: "Father Earth." In Macha cosmology, he is the husband or consort of *Pacha Mama* ("Mother Earth").

pachawawa [Q]: "Child or children of the earth." An alternate name for the Andean toad, or *hanp'atu*, and other related species of anurans. See also **hanp'atu**.

pago [S]: "Payment." An offering made to any Andean *huaca* or divinity, consisting of food, coca, *chicha*, figurines, wool, crops, shells, flowers, candies, animals (principally guinea pigs, sheep, rabbits, llamas and other camelids), animal fat, llama dung, and many other items available to a community.

Pajsi [A]: "Moon" or "month." According to Aymara or Kolla mythology, one of the two "suns" created by *Wiracocha*, the Andean Creator god, to illuminate the world. Alternate spelling: *Phaxsi*.

pan de San Nicolás [S]: "Bread of Saint Nicholas." A sweet circular cookie used in *Muxsa Misa* and other *mesa* rituals. It is embossed with the image of a star or the Virgin Mary. See also **Muxsa Misa**.

paqarina [Q]: From *paqariy*, meaning "to dawn," "to be born," "to appear," or "to originate." A sacred place of origin, usually a place in nature such as a cave, mountain, lake, or spring, from which the first ancestors of a Native Andean ethnic group are believed to have emerged and later founded their culture. It may also be considered a crack or mediating space between the world of the ancestors and this world. Also a *huaca*. See also **huaca**. Alternate spellings: *pakarina, pacarina*.

Paqariqtambo [Q]: See **Pacariqtambo**.

paqo [Q]: "Diviner," "prognosticator," "healer," "wise man," "shaman." A Native Andean priest in charge of making offerings and performing rituals and healings. He may also be a diviner who can foretell the future using coca leaves and other methods. Also known as *hanpiq, hanpiko, hapeq, hanpikoq,* or *janpiri* [in Q]; *yatiri, luktiri, uñiri,* or *yati* [in A]. Alternate spellings: *paqu, paku*.

Pariacaca [Q, A, K]: "Igneous Rock." Name of a mountain and a fivefold deity in the *Huarochirí Manuscript*, whose worship unified various ethnic and kinship groups. He was born of five eggs that then became five falcons (or five hawks) and five men, the founding ancestors of human groups. He is also symbolically reborn as the mountain-body when different lineage groups and ecological levels come together in kinship and ritual. Alternate spellings: *Pariya Qaqa, Paria Caca*.

pascana [Q]: "Lodging" or "resting place" along an Inca road, or any traveler's road, especially in the mountains. It may also signify the end of a journey, when one finally gets a chance to stop and rest. Alternate spelling: *paskana*.

pilulo [K]: An evil Andean spirit or malevolent being who kills his victims through overwhelming sexual pleasure. According to Kallawaya beliefs, victims of this *maligno* die from an exaggerated sexual climax, or they contract some terrible illness from which they never recover.

pirac [Q]: From *piray*, meaning "to mark with blood." Also known as *pirani*. An Inca ritual in which the faces of people or religious idols were marked with animal or human blood, creating a symbolic facial geometry. According to some Spanish colonial accounts, *pirac* took place during the male maturity rites ceremony of *huarachico* or *warachicuy*, and during the coronation of a new Inca ruler. Today similar rituals are practiced in some Andean communities. See also *sucullu*.

pishtaco [Q]: May derive from *pishtay*, meaning "to cut into strips" or "to behead." A mythical character depicted in Andean stories as a white, *mestizo* (mixed race), or foreign man who preys on unsuspecting Andeans by extracting their body fat and blood to use for nefarious purposes. Typically, he assumes the form of priests and friars, *patrones* (masters), *hacendados* (landowners), military men, *gringos* (white foreigners), and, more recently, organ traffickers and eye pluckers. Also known as *ñak'aq* and *llik'ichiris* [in Q]; *kharisiri* [in A]; *degollador, sacamanteca*, and *sacaojos* [in S]. Alternate spellings: *pistaco, pistaku, pishtaku*.

precordillera [S]: "Before the mountain range." An ecological zone or geographical area comprised of hills and mountains lying before a greater Andean mountain range or *cordillera*.

puma [Q, adopted into S]: "Mountain lion." According to some archaeologists, the metaphoric body of the Inca capital, Cuzco. In Inca times, the Inca ruler was believed to be the "head" of the puma. Also a traditional Quechua name, as in Felipe Guaman *Poma* de Ayala.

puna [Q, adopted into S]: The highest inhabitable Andean ecological zone, from 12,000 to 14,000 feet above sea level (from about 3,600 meters to 4,200 meters in altitude), where the people tend to live in small isolated communities and engage in pastoralist activities. Also known as *sallka* or *salqa* [Q] or *suni* [A].

puquio [Q]: "Spring" or "fountain." Alternate spellings: *pukio, puqyo, puquiu*. Also known as *pujyu*.

purun runa [Q, K]: "Wild man" or "savage man." An evil spirit or malevolent being who bewitches women with the mere sight of his male sexual organ, which causes overwhelming and uncontrollable sexual arousal. In Andean lore he is often described as a handsome tanned-face male with long hair and a herculean physique, who sometimes walks on two legs like a human and at other times crawls on all fours like an animal. He lures women back to his cave and then sexually abuses them until they die. Alternate spelling: *purun run'a*.

Purun Runa [Q]: "Uncivilized People" or "People of the Wilderness."

According to Guaman Poma, this was the third age of the world, which was inhabited by native people who developed a more complex culture than their predecessors. They promulgated laws, improved agricultural methods, built roads, walls, and enclosures out of stone, and mined "native" silver and gold (*purun cullque* and *purun cori*). During this time, according to the chronicler, a pestilence broke out that claimed the lives of many people.

Qarpa Achachila [A]: Aymara guardian spirit of irrigation. He is one of the deities who is invoked in the rain-calling ritual of ch'uwa khiwxala. See also **ch'uwa khiwxala**.

qarqacha [Q]: An incestuous person who, according to Andean lore, becomes a fire-breathing mule, llama, or other animal at night. During the day, however, the spirit repossesses its body and reassumes its human form. Also known as *qarqaria* and *joljolia*.

qarqaria [Q]: See **qarqacha**. Also known as *quach'us* [A]. Alternate spelling: *jarjaria*.

qhapaq [Q]: See **capac**.

quinua [Q, A, adopted into S]: A nutritious pseudocereal and a species of goosefoot, scientific name *chenopodium quinoa*, which is cultivated at high and low altitudes throughout the Andes. It was also an important part of the diet of pre-Columbian civilizations. Alternate spellings: *quinoa, kinua, kinwa, quiñwa*.

quispia [A]: A sexual custom among the Aymaras that involves the ritual robbing of women of marriageable age during the first harvest and animal marking festival of *Anata* (meaning "Game") or *Marqha Phajjsi*, beginning on February 16 and ending on March 17, a period which marks the transition into autumn and the Andean dry season.

Qoyllur Rit'i [Q]: "Starry Snow" or "Shining Snow." A traditional three-week festival and pilgrimage in the Cuzco region of Peru, which takes place in late May or early June, leading up to the Christian celebration of Corpus Christi. The festival centers around an image of Christ ("the Lord of the Snow Star"), painted on a rock, under which, according to legend, is buried the body of a young native herder who experienced a miraculous encounter. The festival partakes of Catholic masses and prayers and other Christian elements, but it also includes other rituals and customs with pre-Columbian roots, such as the inclusion of various kinds of dancers who embody the duality or opposing complementarity of lowland and highland groups. Alternate spelling: *Quyllur R'iti*.

q'uwa [Q]: An intensely aromatic herb that is often used in Native Andean rituals as an incense, or to fragrance a burnt offering, or is sometimes mixed with llama fat (*wira*) to create handmade effigies in the form of llamas and other animals, which are later burned as ritual offerings. Alternate spellings: *k'oa, q'oa*.

reducción [S]: "Reduction." A Spanish colonial resettlement practice in which native peoples of different ethnic groups were uprooted, grouped, and "reduced" into a single community or territory, typically laid out in a grid pattern around a central plaza, surrounded by administrative buildings and a church. This system was designed to forestall rebellion by diluting ethnic identity, establish a ready reserve of labor for the *repartimiento* system, and facilitate evangelization and control over the native populations.

repartimiento [S]: "Distribution," "partition," "division." A Spanish colonial institution that permitted the temporary assignment of a certain number or percentage of native workers to do unpaid or low-paid work, particularly in the mines, on farms, or on public construction projects. This was a forced labor system in which many Indians worked in deplorable conditions, particularly in the mines, and were subjected to physical punishments, exploitation, and, often, death.

rumitankhay [Q]: "Stone pushing." A sexual custom associated with a Native Andean dance called *Caja Rueda* (S: "Box Wheel" or "Box Round"), in which adolescent males finish the dance and go in search of young females to "take them" (sexually speaking) with or without their consent. The male participants see the act of sexually overcoming the women as analogous to drilling and blasting holes in the ground. See also **Caja Rueda**.

runa [Q]: "People," "man," or "human being." Refers to a person of indigenous origin. In the Inca Empire, the common people were called *hatun runa*.

Runa Rurac [Q]: "Maker of Man or Humankind." A reference to the Andean Creator god, *Wiracocha*. See also **Wiracocha**.

Runa-Tigre [blended Q and S]: "Man-Tiger." From Quechua, *runa*, meaning "man," and Spanish, *tigre*, meaning "tiger." A shape-shifting character in Andean folktales who is often considered a man with the ability to change into a tiger or other feline. In Andean lore he is said to victimize women and exhibit a predilection for eating their "soft parts," such as tongues and breasts. In many parts of the Andes, priests or shamans are believed to possess this power of transfiguration.

Santiago [S]: "St. James." During the Spanish Conquest, the Native Andean peoples came to associate the thunderous sound of gunpowder and Spanish firearms, and the Spanish battle cries of "*Santiago! Y a ellos!*" (St. James! [And] at them!), with the Andean thunder and lightning god, *Illapa*, also known as *Liviac/Libiac* or *Chuki Illa*. Today some Native Andeans believe that if a person is struck by lightning and survives, he or she is "baptized by fire" and favored by St. James, who endows the person with the gift of clairvoyance and the power to ward off evil spirits. See also **Illapa**.

saqra [Q]: "Devil" or "demon." See also **supay**.

selva [S]: "Jungle" or "rainforest." One of the five geophysical divisions of Andean topography referring to dense equatorial forest or the true tropical rainforests of the Amazon.

sierra [S]: "Mountain range" or "mountainous highlands." Also known as *cordillera*. Refers to the Andean mountain range, one of the five geophysical divisions of Andean topography, that consists of a continual range of highlands extending along the western coast of South America, split into several branches intermittently separated by depressions. The average height of the *sierra* or *cordillera* is about 13,000 feet above sea level (approximately 4,000 meters), and its climatic conditions vary greatly depending on altitude, latitude, and proximity to water. The primary economic activities of the *sierra* center on mining, llama herding, and high mountain agriculture.

sirwanakuy [Q]: "Trial marriage." A Quechua couple contemplating matrimony enters into a trial marriage for a designated period before making a permanent commitment to each other. Alternate spelling: *sirvinakuy*. In Aymara it is called *tincarjaciña* or *sirvisiña*.

sucullu [A]: An Aymara rite of passage ceremony that takes place during the potato harvest and is intended to incorporate children, born in the preceding year, into the social order of the community. As part of the ceremony, each child's maternal uncle (*lari*) or other maternal male relative collects blood from a dead vicuña and smears the blood of the sacrifice across the child's face, making a horizontal line from cheek to cheek and thereby creating a sacred facial geometry.

supay [Q]: "Devil," "demon," Satan, or malignant spirit that resides in the Lower World. Also known as *saqra*. After the introduction of Christianity, all Native Andean *huacas* were considered works of the devil and therefore called *saqra* or *supay*. Also refers to the principal character in *La diablada*, or "Devil Dance," performed during the Andean carnival season in February, dedicated to *La Virgen del Socavón*, the "Virgin of Underground Mines" and patron saint of miners. Alternate spelling: *zupay*.

tampu [Q]: Lodging or shelter along an Inca road. It often had an adjacent storehouse. Alternate spellings: *tambo, tanpu*.

Tampu T'oqo [Q]: "Lodging Window," "Lodging Cave," "Lodging Hole," "Way-Station Window, Cave, or Hole." Sacred place, mountain, hill, or cave from which the first Incas—the *Ayar* brothers—emerged, each with a sister-wife at a site called *Pacariqtambo*. According to legend, these men and women emerged fully grown and were endowed with divine powers. Also spelled *Tambo Toco, Tambotoco, Tanput'oqo, Tampu T'oqo*. See also **Paqariqtambo**.

Taqui Onqoy [Q]: "Dance [of] Sickness or Ailment," "Dancing Sickness," or "Singing Sickness." Also sometimes translated as "Dance of the Pleiades." A millenarian resistance movement that took hold in the sixteenth-century Andes in defiance of Spanish culture and religion. Proponents of the *Taqui Onqoy* took to dancing in the streets in praise of their *huacas*, or native deities, the spirits of which, they claimed, were in possession of their bodies. They also invoked the *huacas* to initiate cataclysmic events that would put an end to Spanish rule and expel the Christian God from their lands. Alternate spellings: *Taki Onqoy, Takiy Onqoy.*

Tata Inti [Q]: "Father Sun." One of the many Quechua names for the Sun. In Quechua cosmology, he is often paired with *Mama Killa,* or "Mother Moon." See also **Inti**. For alternate spellings of *tata,* see **tayta**.

Tawantinsuyu (Q): "The Four Parts United or Integrated Together," often translated as "The Land of the Four Quarters." The name the Incas ascribed to their nation or imperial state that, viewed from the Inca capital at Cuzco, was divided into four regions or quarters: *Collasuyu* (southeast), *Antisuyu* (northeast), *Chinchasuyu* (northwest), *Cuntisuyu* (southwest). Alternate spellings: *Tahuantinsuyo, Tahuantinsuyu, Tawantinsuyo.*

tayta [Q]: "Father." In Aymara, it is *tata* or *tataku.* Alternate spellings: *taita, tata.*

Tiahuanaco [undetermined name origin]: See **Tiwanaku**.

Ticsi Wiracocha [Q]: "Universal Creator," "Fundamental Creator," "Base Creator," "Beginning Creator." Also known as *Illa Ticsi Wiracocha* ("Fundamental Creator [of the] Light"). Another name for the Inca Creator god. According to Guaman Poma, this was also one of the names that the ancient *Wari Wira Cocha Runa* assigned to the Creator, in addition to *Runa Rurac* ("Maker of Man or Humankind"). Alternate spellings: *Ticci Wiracocha, Ticze Wiracocha, Tiksi Wiracocha, Teqse Wiracocha, Teqsi Wiracocha.* See **Wiracocha**; **Wari Wira Cocha Runa**.

Tiksi [Q]: "Universal/Fundamental/Base/Beginning [god]." A meteorological and creator god who appears in Wanka mythology and may have predated Inca mythology. Alternate spellings: *Ticci, Ticsi,* Ticze, *Tiksi, Teqse, Teqsi.*

tincarjaciña [A]: "To get on with." The Aymara concept of "trial marriage." Also known as *sirvisiña.* See also **sirwanakuy**.

titi [A]: "Wildcat," "mountain cat," "Geoffroy's cat," "puma." Generic name for Andean wildcats, but it also refers to the bits of puma skin that are used in Aymara and Kallawaya rituals.

Tiwanaku [undetermined name origin]: An advanced pre-Inca civilization that emerged in the Andean *altiplano,* south of Lake Titicaca, and served as the dominant political and religious force in that region from about 500 to 1000 AD. In one Inca creation myth, the Creator god *Wiracocha* created the peoples of the earth at *Tiwanaku,* summoning them from caves, rivers, springs, mountains, and other natural sites. Alternate spellings: *Tiahuanaco, Tiahuanacu.*

toq'o [Q]: "Window" or "hole"; may also denote a "cave." Also spelled *t'uqu* [Q] or *t'uxu* [A].

Tulunmaya [Q]: "Rainbow" deity of Wanka mythology. Alternate spellings: *T'ulunmanya, T'ulunmaya.*

tuta qhaswa [Q]: "Night dance." Name of a repetitive melody that acts as an invitation to courtship and lovemaking, and also a Quechua dance of pre-Columbian origin that represents the culmination of an elaborate courting and sexual custom in which eligible young men invite young women of marriageable age to participate in a nocturnal dance that ends in sexual encounters. Alternate spellings: *tuta kashwa, tuta q'ashua.*

uchu [Q]: Commonly called "chili pepper." Also known as *ají* [S]. The fruit of any of the different flowering plants in the nightshade family Solanacea (genus *Capsicum*). In the Andes it is used as a food flavoring and for medicinal purposes. One of the Inca ancestors, or *Ayar* brothers, was known by the name *Ayar Uchu*, suggesting that the name was also connected with the ontogeny of Andean crops. See also **Ayar**

ukuku [Q]: "Bear." In Andean folktales it refers to the Andean "Boy-Bear" or "Man-Bear," an anthropomorphic character who is half human and half bear and who exhibits both human and animal characteristics. The *ukuku* is also celebrated in Andean festivals and dances in which young highland men wear costumes and masks, representing the spirit of the Boy-Bear. Also known as *jukumari, ukumari, ucumari,* or *ukumali.*

Ukhu Pacha [Q]: "The Lower World," "The World Below," "The Inner World," or "The Interior World." In Quechua cosmology this space is associated with the subterranean world and with the interior or inner world that houses minerals and their guardian spirits, darkness, the inside of mountains, and dark interior spaces like caves, caverns, and mines (the "bowels" or "entrails" of the earth). After the Spanish Conquest, it also became associated with the Christian inferno, demons, and malevolent forces, as well as the practice of the black arts. For some Quechuas, it is also considered the realm of the dead and of "deep" worlds. Alternate spellings: *Uk'u Pacha, Ucu Pacha.*

unu [Q]: "Water" in a sacred, religious, or spiritual context, as opposed to a secular and nonreligious context (*yaku*). *Unu* water has also been described metaphorically as the fertilizing blood flowing through the veins, or waterways, of the mountain deities. Sometimes also called *yaku unu* [Q] or *aguay unu* [blended S and Q].

unu yaku pachacuti [Q]: "*Pachacuti* or cataclysm [caused by] sacred water." According to Felipe Guaman Poma de Ayala, the Indians used this term to describe the biblical Deluge or Flood. Alternate spelling: *uno yaco pachacuti.* See also **unu**.

Uñallamacha [Q]: "Baby Llama." One of the "dark cloud constellations" of the Milky Way. See also **yana phuyu**.

uraqui [A]: "Earth" or "land" in its material form. May also refer to an illness one may contract from *Pacha Mama*, the Andean Earth Mother.

Urcu-Yaya [Q]: "Father Mountain." In Cañari mythology, a masculine mountain deity, considered to be the "owner" of a particular mountain or its physical embodiment. He may adopt a human or animal form and may interact with humans in both positive and negative ways. Alternate spelling: *Urqu-Yaya.*

Urpayhuachac [Q]: "She Who Gives Birth to Doves." Breeder of fish and
  mother of two daughters of the god *Pachacamac* in the *Huarochirí Manuscript*. The male *huaca Cuniraya* seduces or rapes the first daughter and
  then tries to sleep with the second one. The second daughter narrowly
  escapes his advances by turning herself into a dove and flying away. In
  some Peruvian mythologies *Urpayhuachac* is also one of the five sisters of
  Pachacamac.

usuta [Q]: "Sandal." Also known as *ojota*. A simple Andean rubber sandal, at
  one time made of wool or coarse grass fibers, typically composed of three
  bands, one wrapping around and supporting the ankle and two others
  crossing over the instep, supporting the rest of the foot. Young men were
  required to show that they could make simple sandals during the Inca
  ceremony of *huarachico*, or male maturity rites, because warriors required
  strong footwear for their long military campaigns. Alternate spellings:
  husut'a, ushuta, ushut'a, ussuta, uxuta, juk'uta.

vicuña [Q, S]: Scientific name *Lama vicugna*. One of the two wild species of
  Andean camelids (the other is the *guanaco*) related to the *llama* and the
  alpaca, which lives at very high altitudes and is known for its very fine wool.
  In Inca times *vicuña* wool was woven into very fine garments called *cumbi*,
  worn only by the Inca and his royal family. Alternate spelling: *wikuña* [Q].

vilca [Q]: See **willka**.

Viracocha [Q]: See **Wiracocha**.

wakacha [Q]: "Calf" or "little cow." The term also refers to the "She-Calf" or
  "Calf-Girl" of Andean folktales, an anthropomorphic character who is part
  calf and part human girl.

Wamanis [Q]: See **Apus**.

warachikuy [Q]: See **huarachico**.

wari-puquio [Q]: "Native spring." Also known as *warina*. In Wanka origin
  myths, one such spring launched or gave birth to the first human couple,
  Mama and *Taita*, who constructed a temple called *Wariwilka* and founded
  the Wanka culture. Alternate spellings: *wari-pukyo, wari pukyo, wari pujyo*.

Wari Runa [Q]: "Primitive People." According to Guaman Poma, the second
  age of the world that was populated by Indians who worshipped the
  Creator and three aspects of the Thunder or Lightning god, which Guaman
  Poma equated with the Christian Trinity. These people dressed in animal
  skins, lived in rudimentary houses that looked like ovens, and developed
  agricultural techniques that included terrace farming and irrigation canals.

Wariwilka [Q, A]: "Native Shrine" or "Liquid [Water] Shrine." Temple
  constructed by the pre-Columbian Wanka culture, incorporating a sacred
  spring, with accompanying staircase, two or three pepper trees (*molle*), and
  a purification pool. According to Wanka origin myths, the ancestors of the
  first Wanka people emerged from this sacred spring. Alternate spellings:
  Wariwillka, Huarivillca, Huarivilca.

Wari Wira Cocha Runa [Q]: "Primitive or Autochthonous People [who descended from] the *Wira Cocha* [the Spaniards]." According to Guaman Poma, this was the first generation of Indians who descended from the Spaniards and who came out of Noah's ark after the Deluge in male and female pairs. They did not know how to make clothing or build housing, and they worshipped the Creator as their primary Lord. Alternate spellings: *Uari Uira Cocha Runa, Vari Vira Cocha Runa* (in original colonial text).

warmi jurq'u [Q]: A female mountain spring in Macha cosmology. Each is paired with a male mountain peak (*jurq'u*) and is considered his wife. Water that rises from one of these springs flows downward from the mountain.

warmi volajun [blended Q and S]: "Flying woman." From Quechua, *warmi*, meaning "woman," and Spanish, *volar*, meaning "to fly." A character appearing in highland Andean folktales who is often described as a sinister woman or a shape-shifter (woman/owl) who flies from the rooftops at night, with or without a broom, and engages in satanic or dark magic rituals and ceremonies. She is best known for an incantation that allegedly gives her the power to fly: "*De villa en villa y de viga en viga sin Dios ni Santa María*" (S: "From town to town and from rafter to rafter, without God or the Holy Mary"). Also known as *bruja voladora* (S: "flying witch").

Wayra Tata [Q, A]: "Father Wind." Andean god of wind and hurricanes, often considered the consort or spouse of *Pacha Mama*, the Andean Earth Mother. His quick temper allegedly gives rise to strong air currents and hurricanes that cause great damage on land and whirlwinds and waterspouts that agitate the high lakes, especially Titicaca. In some Aymara creation myths, *Wayra Tata* also initiates a world destruction at the behest of *Wiracocha*, the Andean Creator god, paving the way for a new creation and new age of the world. Alternate spelling: *Huayra Tata.*

wawa [Q, A, adopted into Andean S]: "Baby" or "child," either male or female. The term may be used by either a mother or a father. In Inca times, the term applied to any child before his or her naming ceremony. Alternate spellings: *huahua* or *guagua.*

werakkocha [Q]: See ***wiracocha*** (lowercase).

willka [Q, A]: "Sacred" or "divine." According to some colonial sources, anything regarded as a deity or *huaca*. Also the name of the Aymara Sun god, which probably fell into disuse after the Inca conquest of their region. It was also used as an Inca surname and designation for a member of the Inca priesthood. Alternate spellings: *wilka, villca, vilca, huillca, huilca.*

wira [Q]: "Fat." Considered the "energy principle" of Native Andean offerings, which is imbued in offerings made of animal fat.

wiracocha [Q]: "Gentleman," "sir," "don." In a case of mistaken identity, the Incas referred to the Spanish conquistadors as *wiracochas* or *viracochas.*

Today the Native Andeans still use the term, especially in the countryside, to address an important or respected man of European descent, but the term is falling into disuse. Alternate spellings: *wiraqocha, viracocha, wira-qucha, huiracocha, uira cocha, werakkocha.*

Wiracocha [Q]: "Sea Foam" or "Sea Fat." High Andean Creator god who is believed to have created the sun, moon, and the nations and peoples who populate the earth. His myths also allude to previous creations, inhabited by creatures he was forced to destroy because they failed to abide by his laws. In pre-Columbian Andean cultures, he may have been associated with a sky-god complex that included aspects of the sky, thunder, light-ning, and sun. He was one of the major Inca deities and was known by various other names in the central Andes, including *Wiracocha Yachachic* or *Wiracocha Yachachiq* ("Wiracocha the Teacher/Creator") and *Wiraco-cha Pachayachachic* or *Wiracocha Pachayachachiq* ("Wiracocha Teacher/ Creator of the World"). Alternate spellings: *Viracocha, Wiraqucha, Wiraqo-cha, Huiracocha, Uira Cocha, Werakkocha.*

yaku [Q]: "Water" used in a secular context, such as for drinking or irrigation, as opposed to water used in a religious or spiritual context (*unu*).

yaku unu [Q]: See **unu**.

yana phuyu [Q]: "Dark cloud." In Quechua astronomy, the dark clouds of interstellar dust, also known as "dark cloud constellations," that appear among the stars in the southern, star-dense, and brightest portion of the Milky Way. These dark cloud constellations include many animal names, such as "Toad" (*Hanp'atu*), "Fox" (*Atoq*), "Tinamou" (*Yutu*), "Llama," "Baby Llama" (*Uñallamacha*), and "Serpent" (*Mach'acuay* or *Mach'aqway*).

yanantin [Q]: Complementary duality, or the union of equal and harmonious complementary principles, such as masculine and feminine, day and night, wet and dry, and so forth. The Quechua ending *-ntin* denotes inclusion, to-tality, and union; therefore, *yanantin* also connotes integration. In Aymara, it is called *yanani*.

yatiri [A]: See **paqo**.

Yarqa Aspiy [Q]: From *yarqha* or *yarqa*, meaning "irrigation canal," and *aspiy*, meaning "to dig holes in the ground." A Quechua ritual, observed in September, that marks the beginning of the rainy season and involves community labor and the cleaning of irrigation canals. As part of the ritual, the community makes offerings at each of the irrigation sites to ensure abundant rainfall and a plentiful harvest. Alternate spelling: *Yarqha Aspiy.*

Yaurinkka [A]: Aymara god of earthquakes, tremors, and other seismic forces. He is often described as a giant black boa that undulates beneath the ground or hides at the bottom of lakes and lagoons. When he becomes ag-itated, his violent undulations purportedly cause tremors and earthquakes above the ground. Alternate spellings: *Yaurinka, Yawrinka.*

yawar [Q]: "Blood." Considered the "life principle" of Native Andean offerings, which is imbued in animal offerings. Figuratively, it also refers to bloodline, kinship, or lineage. Alternate spellings: *yahuar, yayar, yaár, llawar, ñahuar.*

ymaymana ñauraycunañawin [Q]: "Eyes of abundance" or "eyes of generosity," depicted in the Inca diagram of the cosmos reproduced by the colonial indigenous chronicler, Joan de Santacruz Pachacuti Yamqui Salcamaygua. These "eyes" have sometimes been compared to little stones called *inqaychus, inqa, illa,* or *conopa,* which modern Andean communities believe contain generative powers that increase the growth and success of their animal herds. Alternate spellings: *imaymana ñauraykunañawin, imaimana ñauraykunañawin.*

yungas [Q, adopted into S]: One of the five geophysical divisions of Andean topography, characterized by humid subtropical montane forest, or cloud forest, and warm lowland valleys. It is often described as a transitional zone between the highlands and the true rainforests. Also known as *montaña* [S].

works consulted

Acosta, Jennifer. "Colombia's Indigenous March for Justice." Report of the *Council on Hemispheric Affairs*. Washington, D.C., November 7, 2008.

Acosta, María. *Cuentos y leyendas de América Latina: Los mitos del sol y la luna*. Barcelona: Editorial Océano Ámbar, 2002.

Adorno, Rolena. *Guaman Poma: Writing and Resistance in Colonial Peru*. 2nd ed. Austin: University of Texas Press, 2000.

Alanes Orellana, Víctor, Carla Bracke, Hernán Condori Condori, Nelson Contreras, et al., compiladores. *Cuentos andinos de montaña*. Centro de Ecología y Pueblos Andinos, Concurso de Cuentos de Montaña, Oruro, Bolivia, 2002. Oruro, Bolivia: Latinas Editores, 2003.

Albó, Xavier. "Preguntas a los historiadores desde los ritos andinos actuales." Trabajo presentado al encuentro "Cristianismo y Poder en el Perú Actual," 1–34. Fundación Kuraka, Cuzco, Perú, June 2000.

Albó, Xavier, and Mauricio Mamani. *Esposos, suegros y padrinos entre los aymaras*. La Paz, Bolivia: Centro de Investigación y Promoción del Campesinado, 1976.

Albornoz, Cristóbal (1584). *Instrucción para descubrir todas las guacas del Pirú y sus camayos y haziendas*. Edición de Henrique Urbano y Pierre Duviols. Madrid: Historia 16, 1988.

Allen, Catherine J. *Foxboy: Intimacy and Aesthetics in Andean Stories*. With illustrations by Julia Meyerson. Austin: University of Texas Press, 2011.

———. *The Hold Life Has: Coca and Cultural Identity in an Andean Community*. Washington, D.C.: Smithsonian Institution Press, 1988.

———. "Of Bear-Men and He-Men: Bear Metaphors and Male Self-Perception in a Peruvian Community." *Latin American Indian Literatures*, 7. no. 1 (1983): 38–51.

Alva, Walter, and Christopher B. Donnan. *Royal Tombs of Sipan (Tumbas reales de Sipán)*. 2nd ed. Los Angeles: Regents of the University of California and Fowler Museum of Cultural History, 1994.

Ansión, Juan. *Desde el rincón de los muertos: El pensamiento mítico en Ayacucho*. Lima: Gredes, 1987.

Arguedas, José María. *Agua y otros cuentos indígenas*. Lima: Editorial Milla Batres, 1974.

421

———. *Canciones y cuentos del pueblo quechua.* Lima: Editorial Huascarán, 1949.

———. *Canto kechwa.* Lima: Compañía de Impresiones y Publicidad, 1938.

———. *Dioses y hombres de Huarochirí.* Edición y traducción de José María Arguedas. Nota a la edición por Ángel Rama, introducción y prólogo de José María Arguedas, apéndice por Pierre Duviols. Lima: Museo Nacional de Historia e Instituto de Estudios Peruanos, 1966.

———. *Formación de una cultura nacional indoamericana.* Introducción de Ángel Rama. 6th ed. México D.F.: Siglo Veintiuno Editores, 1998.

———. *Indios, mestizos y señores.* Edición de Sybila Arredondo de Arguedas. Lima: Editorial Horizonte, 1985.

———. *Mitos, leyendas y cuentos peruanos.* Colección escolar peruana, vol. 4. Selección y notas de José María Arguedas y Francisco Izquierdo Ríos. Lima: Ediciones de la Dirección de Educación Artística y Extensión Cultural, 1947.

———. "Mitos quechuas post-hispánicos: El mito de Incarrí y las tres humanidades." En *Ideología mesiánica del mundo andino,* 377–92. Edición de Ignacio Prado Pastor. Antología de Juan M. Ossio. Lima: Gráfica Morson, 1973.

———. "Voy a hacerles una confesión." En *Primer encuentro de narradores peruanos: Arequipa, Perú, 1965,* 36–43. Lima: Casa de la Cultura del Perú, 1969.

———. *El zorro de arriba y el zorro de abajo.* Buenos Aires: Editorial Losada, 1971.

Arguedas, José María, and Francisco Izquierdo Ríos, eds. *Mitos, leyendas y cuentos peruanos.* Lima: Casa de la Cultura, 1970. First published in 1947 by Ministerio de Educación Pública, Lima, Perú.

———. *Mitos, leyendas y cuentos peruanos.* Nota a la edición de Sybila Arredondo de Arguedas. Biblioteca de Cuentos Populares, no. 11. Madrid: Ediciones Siruela, 2009.

Arispe B., Sergio, Graciela Mazorco I., and Maya Rivera M. "Dicotomías étnicas y filosofías en la lucha por la descolonización." *Polis,* Revista Académica Universidad Bolivariana, no. 18, Santiago, Chile, November 30, 2007.

Ayala, José Luis. *Literatura y cultura aimara.* Lima, Perú: Universidad Ricardo Palma, Editorial Universitaria, 2002.

Bakewell, Peter. *A History of Latin America.* Oxford, U.K.: Blackwell Publishers, 1997.

Barney, E. G. "Native Races in Colombia, S.A." In *The American Antiquarian and Oriental Journal* 5, no. 2 (January–October 1883): 124–31. Edited by Stephen Denison Peet. Chicago: Jameson & Morse, 1883.

Barriga López, Franklin. *Los mitos en la región andina: Ecuador.* Quito: Instituto Andino de Artes Populares del Convenio Andrés Bello—Sede Central, 1984.

Bastien, Joseph W. *Healers of the Andes: Kallawaya Herbalists and Their Medicinal Plants.* With illustrations by Eleanor Forfang Stauffer. Salt Lake City: University of Utah Press, 1987.

———. *Mountain of the Condor.* Prospect Heights, IL: Waveland Press, 1978.

———. *People of the Water: Change and Continuity Among the Uru-Chipayans of Bolivia.* Salt Lake City: University of Utah Press, 2012.

Bauer, Brian S., and David S. P. Dearborn. *Astronomy and Empire in the Ancient Andes.* Austin: University of Texas Press, 1995.

Bauer, Brian S., and Charles Stanish. *Ritual and Pilgrimage in the Ancient Andes: The Islands of the Sun and the Moon.* Austin: University of Texas Press, 2001.

Bawden, Garth. "The Art of Moche Politics." In *Andean Archaeology*, 116–29. Edited by Helaine Silverman. Malden, MA: Blackwell Publishing, 2004.

Becker, Mark. "Pachakutik and Indigenous Political Party Politics in Ecuador." In *Latin American Social Movements in the Twenty-First Century: Resistance, Power, and Democracy*, 165–80. Edited by Richard Stahler-Sholk, Harry E. Vanden, and Glen David Kuecker. Lanham, MD: Rowman and Littlefield Publishers, 2008.

Benson, Drew. "Dancing with Scissors." *Washington Times*, Washington, D.C., December 9, 2003.

Benson, Elizabeth P. *Birds and Beasts of Ancient Latin America.* Foreword by Susan Milbrath. Gainesville, FL: University Press of Florida, 1997.

Bernand, Carmen. *Los incas, el pueblo del Sol.* Traducción de Mari Pepa López Carmona. Coordinación de José Manuel Revuelta. Madrid: Aguilar, 1991.

Bertonio, Ludovico (1612). *Vocabulario de la lengua aymara, parte primera y parte segunda.* Compuesto por el P. Ludovico Bertonio. Publicado de nuevo por Julio Platzmann. Leipzig: B. G. Teubner, 1879. First published in 1612 by La Compañía de Jesús, Juli Pueblo, Chucuito Province, Perú.

Betanzos, Juan de (1551). *Narrative of the Incas.* Translated and edited by Roland Hamilton and Dana Buchanan from the Palma de Mallorca manuscript. Austin: University of Texas Press, 1996.

———. *Suma y narración de los incas.* Transcripción, notas y prólogo por María del Carmen Martín Rubio. Estudios preliminares de Horacio Villanueva Urteaga, Demetrio Ramos y María del Carmen Martín Rubio. Madrid: Ediciones Atlas, 1987.

———. *Suma y narración de los incas, que los indios llamaron Capaccuna, que fueron señores de la ciudad del Cuzco, y do todo lo à ella subjeto.* Edición de Marcos Jiménez de la Espada. Madrid: Imprenta M. G. Hernández, 1880.

Bierhorst, John, ed. and trans. *Black Rainbow: Legends of the Incas and Myths of Ancient Peru.* New York: Farrar, Straus & Giroux, 1976.

———. *The Mythology of South America (with a new Afterword).* Oxford, U.K.: Oxford University Press, 2002. First published in 1988 by William Morrow and Company.

Bode, Barbara. "Disaster, Social Structure, and Myth in the Peruvian Andes: The Genesis of an Explanation." *Annals of the York Academy of Sciences* 293 (1977): 246–74.

Boero Rojo, Hugo. *Discovering Tiwanaku.* La Paz and Cochabamba, Bolivia: Editorial Los Amigos del Libro, 1980.

Bolin, Inge. *Rituals of Respect: The Secret of Survival in the High Peruvian Andes.* Austin: University of Texas Press, 1998.

Bolivian Constitution of 2009. Art. 1–5, 21(3), 30–32, 280–82.

Bouysse-Cassagne, Thérèse. "Urco and Uma: Aymara Concepts of Space." In *Anthropological History of Andean Polities*, 210–27. Edited by J. Murra, N. Wachtel, and J. Revel. Cambridge, U.K.: Cambridge University Press, 1986.

Brice, Arthur. "Arrests Made in Ring That Sold Human Fat, Peru Says." *CNN*, November 21, 2009.

Burns, E. Bradford. *Latin America: A Concise Interpretive History.* 2nd ed. Englewood Cliffs, NJ: Prentice-Hall, 1977.

Cáceres Chalco, Efraín. *Si crees en los Apus te curan: Medicina andina e identidad cultural.* Cuzco, Perú: Centro de Medicina Andina y Centro de Investigación de la Cultura y la Tecnología Andina, 2002.

Calancha, Antonio de la (1637). *Crónica moralizada del orden de San Agustín en el Perú con sucesos ejemplares en esta monarquía: Volumen I.* Texto digitalizado por *Scribd.com* para presentación en el Internet, 1–1107, April 4, 2010.

Calero del Mar, Edmer. "Dualismo estructural andino y espacio novelesco arguediano." *Boletín del Instituto Francés de Estudios Andinos* 31, no. 2 (2002): 153–81.

Carrillo Espejo, Francisco, ed. *Cronistas indios y mestizos II: Guaman Poma de Ayala.* Lima: Editorial Horizonte, 1992.

———. *Literatura quechua clásica.* Enciclopedia Histórica de la Literatura Peruana 1. Lima: Editorial Horizonte, 1986.

Carroll, Rory. "Alleged Killers Who Harvested Human Fat Arrested in Peru." *Irish Times*, November 21, 2009.

Carter, William E., and Mauricio Mamani. *Irpa Chico: Individuo y comunidad en la cultura aymara.* La Paz, Bolivia: Librería-Editorial "Juventud," 1982.

Castro Klarén, Sara. "Dancing and the Sacred in the Andes: From the Taqui Oncoy to Rasu-Ñiti." In *New World Encounters*, 159–76. Edited by Stephen Greenblatt. Berkeley: University of California Press, 1993.

Castro Mantilla, María Dolores. "Los determinantes socioculturales en la salud sexual y reproductiva de mujeres indígenas." *Umbrales: Revista del Postgrado en Ciencias del Desarrollo*, Universidad Mayor de San Andrés, La Paz, Bolivia, edición de Cecilia Salazar, no. 18, 205–35, November 2008.

Cathechism of the Catholic Church. 2nd ed. Publication granted by Amministrazione del Patrimonio della Sede Apostolica, case number 130389. Saint

Charles Borromeo Catholic Church, Picayune, Mississippi. Modified on September 8, 1997, to harmonize with the oficial Latin text promulgated by Pope Paul II on the same date.

Cavero Carrasco, Ranulfo. *Incesto en los Andes: Las llamas demoníacas como castigo sobrenatural.* Ayacucho, Perú: Consejo Nacional de Ciencia y Tecnología, 1990.

Cerrón-Palomino, R. "Language Policy in Peru: A Historical Overview." *International Journal of Sociology of Language* 77 (1989): 11–34.

Chang-Rodríguez, Raquel. *Hidden Messages: Representation and Resistance in Andean Colonial Drama.* Cranberry, NJ: Associated University Presses, 1999.

Choque, María Eugenia, Carlos Mamani C., and Raquel Condori. *Tiwalan panichasitapa (El zorro galán).* La Paz, Bolivia: Ediciones Aruwiyiri y Taller de Historia Oral Andina, 1997.

Cieza de León, Pedro de (1550). *El señorío de los incas.* Edición de Manuel Ballesteros Gaibrois. Madrid: Historia 16, 1985.

———. (1553). *La crónica del Perú.* Edición, introducción y notas de Manuel Ballesteros. Madrid: Historia 16, 1984.

———. *La crónica del Perú.* Madrid: Espasa-Calpe, 1962.

———. *The Discovery and Conquest of Peru: Chronicles of the New World Encounter.* Translated by Alexandra Parma Cook and David Noble Cook. Durham, NC: Duke University Press, 1998.

Classen, Constance. *Inca Cosmology and the Human Body.* Salt Lake City: University of Utah Press, 1993.

Clavero, Bartolomé. "Alerta por Genocidio en Colombia" (Report of a Permanent Member of the United Nations Forum on Indigenous Issues). *Coordinadora Andina de Organizaciones Indígenas* (CAOI), Lima, Peru, January 21, 2010.

Cobo, Bernabé (1653). *Historia del nuevo mundo.* En *Obras del P. Bernabé Cobo de la Compañía de Jesús,* vol. 2, 7–275. Estudio preliminar y edición del P. Francisco Mateos. Bibilioteca de Autores Españoles, vols. LXXXXI and LXXXXII. Madrid: Ediciones Atlas, 1964.

———. *History of the Inca Empire: An Account of the Indians' Customs and their Origin Together with a Treatise on Inca Legends, History and Social Institutions.* Translated and edited by Roland Hamilton. Foreword by John Rowe. Austin: University of Texas Press, 1979.

———. *Inca Religion and Customs.* Translated and edited by Roland Hamilton. Foreword by John Rowe. Austin: University of Texas Press, 1990.

"Coca in the Andes." Report of the *Office of National Drug Control Policy,* The White House, Washington, D.C., n.d.

"Colombia: Diez mil indígenas marchan en el Cauca." Report of *Coordinadora Andina de Organizaciones Indígenas* (CAOI), Popayán, La Arcada, Colombia, February 2010.

"Comunicado a la opinión pública nacional e internacional a un año de la masacre en Tortugaña Telembí." Report of *Organización Unidad Indígena del Pueblo Awá* (UNIPA), San Juan de Pasto, Colombia, February 3, 2010.

Condori Mita, Eugenia. "La fauna de los vertebrados de la cuenca del río Desaguadero y sus presagios," 1–23. Resumen de un trabajo más extenso de la autora que se titula *Léxico-semántico de la fauna andina: Vertebrados de la cuenca del río Desaguadero.* Tesis de Licenciatura en Lingüística e Idiomas, Universidad Mayor de San Andrés, La Paz, Bolivia, 2005.

Cornejo Polar, Antonio. *José María Arguedas: Antología comentada.* Serie Biblioteca Básica Peruana, vol. XII. Lima: Biblioteca Nacional del Perú, 1996.

Corr, Rachel. *Ritual and Remembrance in the Ecuadorian Andes.* First Peoples Series: New Directions in Indigenous Studies. Tucson: The University of Arizona Press, 2010.

Correa Rubio, François. "Mitología de los muiscas: el incesto primordial." *Universitas Humanística*, Pontificia Universidad Javeriana, Bogotá, Colombia, year XXXI, no. 59 (January 2005): 22–35.

Costas Arguedas, José Felipe. *Diccionario del folklore boliviano (Tomo II).* Sucre, Bolivia: Universidad de San Francisco Xavier, 1967.

Cotacachi, Mercedes (Versión quichua). *Huaca pachamanta causashca rimai (Los cuentos de cuando las huacas vivían).* Traducción al castellano por Ruth Moya. Compilado por estudiantes de la Promoción 1991–1992 en el Taller de Quichua dirigido por Fausto Jara, Licenciatura en Lingüística Andina y Educación Bilingüe, Facultad de Filosofía, Letras y Ciencias de la Educación, Universidad de Cuenca, Ecuador. Quito: Ediciones Abya-Yala, 1993.

Cuthbert, Evan and Kathryn Ledebur. "A New Constitution for Bolivia: The History and Structure of the Constitutional Assembly." Report of the *Andean Information Network*, Cochabamba, Bolivia, June 28, 2006.

Davies, Nigel. *The Incas.* Niwot, CO: University of Colorado Press, 1995.

Dávila Andrade, César, José de la Cuadra, Alejandro Carrión, Pablo Palacio, and Alicia Yánez Cossío. *Cuentos ecuatorianos.* Madrid: Editorial Popular, en colaboración con UNESCO, 1999.

Demarest, Arthur A. *Viracocha: The Nature and Antiquity of the Andean High God.* Peabody Museum Monographs, no. 6. Cambridge, MA: Peabody Museum of Archaeology and Ethnology, Harvard University, 1981.

Díaz Villamil, Antonio. *Khantutas: Cuentos bolivianos.* 2nd ed. La Paz, Bolivia: Librería y Editorial "Juventud," 1969.

———. *Leyendas de mi tierra.* La Paz, Bolivia: Librería y Editorial "Juventud," 1993.

"Dimension of Need: An Atlas of Food and Agriculture." Report of the *Food and Agriculture Organization of the United Nations*, Rome, 1995.

Donnan, Christopher B. *Moche Portraits from Ancient Peru.* Austin: University of Texas Press, 2004.

Durham, William II. *Coevolution: Genes, Culture, and Human Diversity.* Stanford, CA: Stanford University Press, 1991.

Duviols, Pierre. "Un mythe de l'origine de la coca (Cajatambo)." *Boletín del Instituto Francés de Estudios Andinos,* Lima 2, no. 1 (1973): 34.

Earls, John, and Irene Silverblatt. "La realidad física y social en la cosmología andina." In *Actes du XLII⁰ Congrès International des Américanistes, vol. IV, Paris, 2–9 Septembre 1976,* 299–325. Paris: Société des Américanistes, 1978.

Ecuadorian Constitution of 2008. Art. 57 (2–4) (6–7), 71–74.

Eliade, Mircea, ed. *The Encyclopedia of Religion,* vol. 10. New York: Macmillan Publishing Company, 1987.

Erdoes, Richard, and Alfonso Ortiz, eds. *American Indian Trickster Tales.* New York: Viking Penguin, 1998.

Erwin, Edward, ed. *The Freud Encyclopedia: Theory, Therapy, and Culture.* New York: Routledge, 2002.

Escalante Gutiérrez, Carmen, and Ricardo Valderrama Fernández. *La doncella sacrificada: Mitos del valle de Colca.* Edición bilingüe quechua y castellano. Prólogo de Martín Lienhard. Arequipa, Perú: Universidad Nacional de San Agustín, and Lima: Instituto Francés de Estudios Andinos, 1997.

Espinar de la Torre, Oscar. *Myths of Ancient Peru.* Compiled and translated by Oscar Espinar de la Torre, with the assistance of Quinn Meyer. Cuzco, Peru: Editorial Anka, n.d.

Espinosa Apolo, Manuel. *Duendes, aparecidos, moradas encantadas y otras maravillas.* "Colección Memoria," no. 2. Quito, Ecuador: Taller de Estudios Andinos, perteneciente a la Fundación Felipe Guaman Poma, 1999.

Espinoza Tamayo, Manuel. *Los mestizos ecuatorianos.* Quito: Trama Social Editorial, 1995.

Estel, Leo. "The Mosca (Chibcha)." *Ohio Journal of Science,* no. 58, issue 4 (1958): 235–44.

Estete, Miguel de (1533–1552). *Relación de la conquista del Perú.* En *Historia de los incas y la conquista del Perú.* Anotaciones y concordia con las crónicas de Indias por Horacio H. Urteaga. Lima: Imprenta y Librería Sanmartí y Ca., 1924.

Evans III, F. B. *Harry Stack Sullivan: Interpersonal Theory and Psychotherapy.* New York: Routledge, 1996.

Fernández Juárez, Gerardo. *Los kallawayas: Medicina indígena en los Andes.* Cuenca, Spain: Ediciones de la Universidad de Castilla-La Mancha, 1998.

———. "Kharisiris de agosto en el altiplano aymara de Bolivia." *Chungará, Revista de Antropología Chilena* 38, no. 1 (2006): 51–62.

———. *Testimonio Kallawaya: Medicina y ritual en los Andes de Bolivia.* Serie "Hombre y Ambiente," Número Monográfico 44–45. Quito: Ediciones Abya-Yala, 1997.

Flores Galindo, Alberto. *Buscando un Inca: Identidad y utopía en los Andes.* Lima: Instituto de Apoyo Agrario, 1987.

————. *In Search of an Inca: Identity and Utopia in the Andes*. Edited and translated by Carlos Aguirre, Charles F. Walker, and Willie Hiatt. Introduction by Carlos Aguirre and Charles F. Walker. New Approaches to the Americas Series. New York: Cambridge University Press, 2010.

Flores Lizana, Carlos. *El Taytacha Qoyllur Rit'i: Teología india hecha por comuneros y mestizos quechuas*. Sicuani, Perú: Instituto de Pastoral Andina, 1997.

Flores Prado, Luis Leoncio. *El Quishpi cóndor: Danza milenaria*. Callao, Perú: Instituto del Libro y la Lectura, 2005.

Fossa, Lydia. *Narrativas problemáticas: Los inkas bajo la pluma española*. Lima: Instituto de Estudios Peruanos Ediciones y Pontificia Universidad Católica del Perú—Fondo Editorial, 2006.

Francovich, Guillermo. *Los mitos profundos de Bolivia*. 2nd ed. La Paz y Cochabamba, Bolivia: Editorial Los Amigos del Libro, 1987.

Franklin, Jonathan. "Prosperous Chile's Troubling Indigenous Uprising." *Time.com*, December 12, 2009.

Freud, Sigmund. *Civilization and Its Discontents*. Translated and edited by James Strachey, with a biographical introduction by Peter Gay. New York: Norton, 1961.

————. *The Freud Reader*. Edited by Peter Gay. New York: Norton, 1989.

————. *The Interpretation of Dreams*. Translated by Dr. A. A. Brill. New York: First Modern Library Edition, Random House, 1950.

————. "A Note on the Unconscious in Psychoanalysis." In *The Standard Edition* XII. London: Hogarth Press, 1958.

————. *On Dreams*. Translated and edited by James Strachey, with a biographical introduction by Peter Gay. New York: Norton, 1952.

————. "An Outline of Psychoanalysis." In *The Standard Edition* XXIII. London: Hogarth Press, 1964.

————. "The Psychoanalytic View of Psychogenic Disturbance in Vision." In *The Standard Edition* XI. London: Hogarth Press, 1957.

————. *Totem and Taboo: Resemblances between the Psychic Lives of Savages and Neurotics*. Authorized translation with an introduction by A. A. Brill. New York: Vintage Books, a division of Random House, 1918.

Fuentes Roldán, Alfredo. *Quito tradiciones*. Quito: Ediciones Abya-Yala, 1996 (*Tomo I*) and 1999 (*Tomo II*).

García, María Elena. "The Challenges of Representation: NGOs, Education, and the State in Highland Peru." In *Civil Society or Shadow State? State/NGO Relations in Education*. Edited by Margaret Sutton and Robert F. Arnove. Greenwich, CT: Information Age Publishing, 2004.

García Mérida, Wilson. "Más noticias sobre la profecía del Pachacuti." *Indymedia: Qollasuyu Ivi Iyambae Bolivia*, Cochabamba, Bolivia, July 3, 2006.

Garcilaso de la Vega, El Inca (1609 and 1617). *Comentarios reales de los incas (Tomos I y II)*. Edición, índice analítico y glosario de Carlos Araníbar. México, D.F.: Fondo de Cultura Económica, 1991.

————. *Comentarios reales de los incas.* Introducción de José de la Riva-Agüero. México, D.F.: Editorial Porrúa, 2000.

————. *Primera parte de los Comentarios Reales.* Madrid: Imprenta de los Hijos de Doña Catalina Piñuela, 1829.

————. *Royal Commentaries of the Incas and General History of Peru (Parts One and Two).* Translated with an introduction by Harold V. Livermore and foreword by Arnold J. Toynbee. Austin: University of Texas Press, 1966.

Geffroy Komadina, Céline. "El cuerpo abierto." In *Colección Aalten,* no. 817, 1–13. Publicación del Instituto de Estudio de la Cultura y Tecnología Andina, Iquique, Chile, 2004.

Girault, Louis. *Kallawaya: guérisseurs intinérants des Andes.* Editions de L'Orstom. Paris: Institut Français de Recherche Scientifique pour le Développement en Coopération, 1984.

Godenzzi, Juan Carlos. *Tradición oral andina y amazónica: Análisis e interpretación de textos.* Cuzco, Perú: Centro de Estudios Regionales Andinos "Bartolomé de las Casas," 1999.

Gómara, Francisco López de (1551). *Primera y segunda parte de la historia general de las Indias.* Barcelona: Ediciones Iberia, 1954.

González Holguín, Diego (1608). *Vocabulario de la lengua general de todo el Perú llamada lengua Qquichua o del Inca.* Edición y prólogo de Raúl Porras Barrenechea. Lima: Universidad Nacional Mayor de San Marcos, 1952. Digitalizado por *Runasimipi Qespisqa* Software para publicación en el Internet, 1–426, 2007.

González Suárez, Federico. *Estudio histórico sobre los cañaris, antiguos habitantes de la provincia del Azuay en la República del Ecuador.* Quito: Imprenta del Clero, por José Guzmán Almeida, 1878.

Granadino, Cecilia, and Cromwell Jara. *Las ranas embajadoras de la lluvia y otros relatos: Cuatro aproximaciones a la isla de Taquile.* Lima, Perú: Minka, Embajada Real de los Países Bajos, Kollino Taquile, 1996.

Gray, Louis Herbert, and George Foot Moore, eds., with Hartley Burr Alexander. *The Mythology of All Races—Volume XI, Latin American.* Boston: Marshall Jones, 1920.

Gray Molina, George. "The United States and Bolivia: Test Case for Change." In *The Obama Administration and the Americas: Agenda for Change,* 167–82. Edited by Abraham F. Lowenthal, Theodore J. Piccone, and Laurence Whitehead. Washington, D.C.: The Brookings Institution, 2009.

Guaman Poma de Ayala, Felipe (circa 1615). *Letter to a King: A Peruvian Chief's Account of Life under the Incas and under Spanish Rule.* Arranged and edited with an introduction by Christopher Dilke and translated from *Nueva corónica y buen gobierno.* New York: E. P. Dutton, 1978.

————. *Nueva corónica y buen gobierno (vols. 75 y 76).* Transcripción, prólogo, notas y cronología de Franklin Pease. Caracas, Venezuela: Biblioteca Ayacucho, 1980.

―――. *El primer nueva corónica y buen gobierno.* Edición crítica de John V. Murra y Rolena Adorno. Traducciones y análisis textual del quechua por Jorge L. Urioste. 3rd ed. México D.F.: Siglo Veintiuno Editores, 1992.

Gwin, Peter. "Peruvian Temple of Doom." *National Geographic,* July 2004, 102–17.

Harris, Olivia. "From Asymmetry to Triangle: Symbolic Transformations in Northern Potosí." In *Anthropological History of Andean Polities,* 260–79. Edited by John V. Murra, Nathan Wachtel, and Jacques Revel. Cambridge, U.K.: Cambridge University Press, 1986.

Harrison, Regina. *Signs, Songs, and Memory in the Andes: Translating Quechua Language and Culture.* Austin: University of Texas Press, 1989.

―――. *Signos, cantos y memoria en los Andes.* Quito: Ediciones Abya-Yala, 1994.

Hemming, John. *Conquest of the Incas.* New York: Harcourt Brace Jovanovich, 1970.

Hernández, Max, with Moisés Lemlij, Luis Millones, Alberto Péndola, and María Rostworowki. *Entre mito y la historia: Psicoanálisis y pasado andino.* Lima: Imago Editores, 1987.

Hernández, Max et al. "Aproximación psicoantropológica a los mitos andinos." *Boletín del Instituto Francés de Estudios Andinos* 14, no. 3–4 (1985): 15–45.

Herrera-Sobek, María, ed. *Celebrating Latino Folklore: An Encyclopedia of Cultural Traditions,* vol. I. Santa Barbara, CA: ABC-CLIO, 2012.

Hertzler, Douglas. "Bolivia's Agrarian Reform Initiative: An Effort to Keep Historical Promises." Report of *Andean Information Network,* Washington, D.C., June 28, 2006.

Huamán, Carlos. *Pachachaka, puente sobre el mundo: Narrativa, memoria y símbolo en la obra de José María Arguedas.* México D.F.: El Colegio de México y Universidad Nacional Autónoma de México, 2004.

Hyslop, John. *The Inka Road System.* Orlando, FL: Academic Press, 1984.

Iglesias, Angel María. *Cañar: Síntesis histórica.* Serie "Las cien mejores obras de autores del Cañar," no. 16. Azogues, Ecuador: Casa de la Cultura Ecuatoriana "Benjamín Carrión," Núcleo del Cañar, 2004.

Isbell, Billie Jean. *Finding Cholita.* Interpretations of Culture in the New Millennium Series. Urbana, IL: University of Illinois Press, 2009.

―――. "La otra mitad esencial: Un estudio de complementariedad sexual en los Andes." *Estudios Andinos,* year 5, vol. 5, no. 1 (1976): 37–56.

―――. *To Defend Ourselves: Ecology and Ritual in an Andean Village.* Prospect Heights, IL: Waveland Press, 1985.

Isbell, William H. "Cosmological Order Expressed in Prehistoric Ceremonial Center." In *Actes du XLIIᵉ Congrès International des Américanistes, vol. IV, Paris, 2–9 Septembre 1976,* 269–98. Paris: Société des Américanistes, 1978.

Isbell, William H., and Patricia J. Knobloch. "Missing Links, Imaginary Links:

Staff God Imagery in the South Andean Past." In *Andean Archaeology III: North and South*, 307–51. Edited by William H. Isbell and Helaine Silverman. New York: Springer Science+Business Media, 2008.

Itier, César, ed., comp., and trans. *Karu Ñankunapi*. 2nd ed. Cuzco, Perú: Centro de Estudios Regionales "Bartolomé de las Casas," 2004.

Iturralde, Edna. *Los hijos de la guacamaya*. Quito: Editorial Alfaguara, Grupo Santillana, 2007.

Johnson, Allen W., and Douglass Price-Williams. *Oedipus Ubiquitous: The Family Complex in World Folk Literature*. Stanford, CA: Stanford University Press and the Board of Trustees of the Leland Stanford Junior University, 1996.

Jolicoeur, Luis. *El cristianismo aymara*. "Cultural Heritage and Contemporary Change," series V, Latin America, vol. III. Cochabamba, Bolivia: The Council for Research in Values and Philosophy and Universidad Católica Boliviana, 1997.

Jones, David M. *The Myths and Religion of the Incas*. London: Southwater, an imprint of Anness Publishing, 2008.

Jung, Carl G. *The Archetypes and the Collective Unconscious*. Translated by R. F. C. Hull. Princeton, NJ: Princeton University Press, 1968.

———. *The Basic Writings of C. G. Jung*. Translated by R. F. C. Hull and selected and introduced by Violet S. de Laszlo. Princeton, NJ: Princeton University Press, 1990.

———. *The Basic Writings of C. G. Jung*. Edited with an introduction by Violet Staub de Laszlo. New York: Modern Library Edition, Random House, 1993.

———. *The Essential Jung*. Selected and introduced by Anthony Storr. Princeton, NJ: Princeton University Press, 1983.

———. *Modern Man in Search of a Soul*. Translated by W. S. Dell and Cary F. Baynes. San Diego: A Harvest Book, Harcourt Brace & Company, n.d.

———. *The Portable Jung*. Edited with an introduction by Joseph Campbell. Translated by R. F. C. Hull. New York: Viking Penguin, 1971.

Jung, Carl G., with M. L. von Franz, Joseph L. Henderson, Jolande Jacobi, and Aniela Jaffé. *Man and His Symbols*. Conceived and edited by Carl G. Jung. New York: J. G. Ferguson Publishing, 1964.

Kapsoli Escudero, Wilfredo. *El retorno del inca*. Lima, Perú: Universidad Ricardo Palma, Centro de Investigación, 2001.

Kent, Robert B. *Latin America: Regions and People*. New York: Guilford Press, 2006.

Kiderra, Inge. "Backs To The Future: Aymara Language And Gesture Point To Mirror-Image View Of Time." *ScienceDaily*, June 13, 2006.

Kirk, Robin. *The Monkey's Paw: New Chronicles from Peru*. Amherst: University of Massachusetts Press, 2004.

Kiss, Alexandre. "Public Lectures on International Environmental Law." In *The Law of Energy for Sustainable Development*, 6–34. Series: IUCN Academy of Environmental Law Research Studies. Edited by Adrian J. Bradbrook, Rosemary Lyster, Richard L. Ottinger, and Wang Xi. Cambridge, U.K.: Cambridge University Press, 2005.

Klarén, Peter Flindell. *Peru: Society and Nationhood in the Andes.* New York: Oxford University Press, 2000.

Kohn, George Childs. *Dictionary of Wars.* 3rd ed. New York: Facts on File, Inc., 2007.

Kokotovic, Misha. *The Colonial Divide in Peruvian Narrative: Social Conflict and Transculturation.* Eastborn, Great Britain: Sussex Academic Press, 2005.

Kolata, Alan. *The Tiwanaku: Portrait of an Andean Civilization.* Cambridge, MA: Blackwell Publishers, 1993.

———. *Valley of the Spirits: A Journey into the Lost Realm of the Aymara.* New York: John Wiley & Sons, 1996.

König, Hans-Joachim, ed., in collaboration with Christian Gros, Karl Kohut, and France-Marie Renard-Casevitz. *El indio como sujeto y objeto de la historia latinoamericana: Pasado y presente.* Frankfurt: Vervuert, 1998.

Kormann, Carolyn. "Retreat of Andean Glaciers Foretells Global Water Woes." *Environment 360,* a publication of Yale School of Forestry and Environmental Studies, April 9, 2009.

Kurzweil, Edith. *The Age of Structuralism: Lévi-Strauss to Foucault.* New York: Columbia University Press, 1980.

La Fone, Samuel. "El culto de Tonapa." In *Tres relaciones de antigüedades peruanas,* 287–353. Asunción, Paraguay: Editorial Guaranía, 1950.

Lajo, Javier. *Qhapaq Ñan: La ruta inka de sabiduría.* 2nd ed. Quito: Ediciones Abya-Yala, 2006. First published in 2005 by Amaro Runa-CENES, Lima, Perú.

"Lake Titicaca Water Level Drops 2.6 Ft. This Year." *Peruvian Times,* November 13, 2009.

Lara, Jesús. *Diccionario queshwa-castellano, castellano-queshwa.* 5th ed. La Paz and Cochabamba, Bolivia: Editorial "Los Amigos del Libro," 2001.

———. *Leyendas quechuas: Antología.* La Paz, Bolivia: Ediciones y Librería "Juventud," 1960.

———. *La literatura de los quechuas: Ensayo y antología.* Cochabamba, Bolivia: Editorial Canelas, 1961.

———. *Mitos, leyendas y cuentos de los quechuas.* La Paz, Bolivia: Editorial "Los Amigos del Libro," Werner Guttentag, 2003.

———. *Poesía popular quechua.* La Paz and Cochabamba, Bolivia: Editorial Canata, n.d.

———. *Tragedia del fin de Atawallpa (Atau Wallpaj p'uchukakuyninpa wankan).* Cochabamba, Bolivia: Editorial "Los Amigos del Libro," 1989.

Lavrin, Asunción, ed. *Sexuality and Marriage in Colonial Latin America.* Lincoln, NE: University of Nebraska Press, 1989.

Ledebur, Kathryn, and Coletta A. Youngers. "ONDCP [Office of National Drug Control Policy] Reports No Increase in Coca Cultivation in Bolivia in 2006." Joint Report of *Andean Information Network* and *Washington Office on Latin America*, Washington, D.C., May 23, 2007.

Leeming, David Adams. *Creation Myths of the World: An Encyclopedia*. 2nd ed. Santa Barbara, CA: ABL-CIO, 2010.

Lemlij, M., L. Millones, M. Rostworowski, A. Péndola, and M. Hernández. "Las cinco ñamcas: Aspectos de lo femenino en ritos y tradiciones de Huarochirí recogidos por Francisco de Avila." En *Mitos universales, americanos y contemporáneos: Un enfoque multidisciplinario*, vol. I, 129–35. Moisés Lemlij, comp., y Giuliana Falco, ed. ejecutiva. Lima: Sociedad Peruana de Psicoanálisis, 1989.

LeoGrande, William M. "U.S. Insecurity in Latin America: Radical Populism." *Cross Currents*, Newsletter of the *Washington Office on Latin America*, March 2006, 1, 10.

Levillier, Robert. *Don Francisco de Toledo (vol. 2)*. Buenos Aires: Espasa-Calpe, 1940.

Lévi-Strauss, Claude. *Myth and Meaning: Cracking the Code of Culture*. Foreword by Wendy Doniger. New York: Schocken Books, 1979.

———. *The Raw and the Cooked: Mythologiques, Vol. One*. Translated by John and Doreen Weightman. Chicago: The University of Chicago Press, 1969.

———. *The Story of Lynx (Histoire de Lynx)*. Translated by Catherine Tihanyi. Chicago: University of Chicago Press, 1995.

———. *Structural Anthropology*. Translated by Claire Jacobson and Brooke Grundfest Schoepf. New York: Basic Books, a Member of Perseus Books Group, 1963.

———. *Tristes Tropiques*. Translated by John and Doreen Weightman. New York: Penguin Books, 1992. First published in 1974 in New York by Atheneum Publishers.

Lewis, Paul M., ed. *Ethnologue: Languages of the World*. 16th ed. Dallas, TX: SIL International, 2009.

Lira, Jorge A. *Diccionario kkechuwa español*. Tucumán, Argentina: Universidad Nacional de Tucumán, 1945.

Lista, Ramón. "El Pilcomayo o Río de los Pillcus." En *Boletín del Instituto Geográfico Argentino (Tomo XVIII)*, 583–600. Editado por Francisco Seguí. Buenos Aires: Imprenta Buenos Aires, 1897.

Llanque Chana, Domingo. *Ritos y espiritualidad aymara*. La Paz, Bolivia: ASET, IDEA, y Centro de Teología Popular (CTP), 1995.

Locke, Leslie Leland. *The Ancient Quipu or Peruvian Knot Record*. New York: The American Museum of Natural History, 1923. Supplementary notes published in 1928.

Lockhart, James. *Spanish Peru: 1532–1560, a Colonial Society*. Madison, WI: University of Wisconsin Press, 1968.

López-Baralt, Mercedes. *El retorno del inca rey: Mito y profecía en el mundo andino.* La Paz, Bolivia: Instituto de Historia Social Boliviana, 1989.

Lucas, Kintto. *We will not dance on our grandparents' tombs: Indigenous uprisings in Ecuador.* Translated by Dinah Livingstone. London: Catholic Institute for International Relations, 2000.

Lund Skar, Sarah. "Andean Women and the Concept of Space/Time." In *Women and Space: Ground Rules and Social Maps*, 31–45. Edited by Shirley Ardener. 2nd ed. Oxford, U.K.: Berg Publishers, 1997.

MacCormack, Sabine. *Religion in the Andes: Vision and Imagination in Early Colonial Peru.* Princeton, NJ: Princeton University Press, 1991.

Macedo y Pastor, Celso. "La esfinge: Coñi Illa Tijsi Wirakocha, Pacha Camaj, Pacha Yachachij, Tijsi Capaj: A la luz de la ciencia lingüística." *Revista histórica; órgano del Instituto Histórico del Perú*, dirigido por Carlos Alberto Romero, Tomo IX, Entrega IV, 357–80, Lima, Perú, 1935.

Machicao, Mónica, and Eduardo García. "Global Warming Melts Andean Glaciers." *Reuters*, June 7, 2007.

Mariscotti de Gorlitz, Ana María. *Pachamama Santa Tierra: Contribución al estudio de la religión autóctona en los Andes centro-meridionales.* Berlin: Ibero-Amerikanisches Institut, 1978.

Markham, Clements R. "The Inca Civilization in Peru." In *Narrative and Critical History of America: Aboriginal America*, vol. I, 209–82. Edited by Justin Winsor. Boston: Houghlin, Mifflin and Company, 1889.

Martínez, Nadia. "Political Upheaval: Latin America Challenges the Washington Consensus." *These Times*, April 5, 2006.

Marzal, Manuel M. *Historia de la antropología indigenista: México y Perú.* Barcelona: Editora Regional de Extremadura, 1993.

"Masterpieces of the Oral and Intangible Heritage of Humanity: Proclamations 2001, 2003 and 2005." Report of the *United Nations Educational, Scientific and Cultural Organization (UNESCO)*, Intangible Heritage Section, Division of Cultural Heritage, Paris, 2006.

Maugh II, Thomas H. "Inca Warrior's Wound Tells Another Tale of Conquest." *Los Angeles Times*, June 20, 2007.

McDonnell, Patrick J. "Bolivia nationalizes oil, gas industry: Populist leader vows to establish control of natural resources." *Boston Globe*, May 2, 2006.

McEwan, Gordon F. *The Incas: New Perspectives.* New York: Norton, 2006.

Menzel, Dorothy. *The Archaeology of Ancient Peru and the Work of Max Uhle.* Berkeley, CA: R. H. Lowie Museum of Anthropology, University of California, 1977.

Mercado, David. "Ancient Ruins Found in Bolivia." *Vancouver Sun*, July 10, 2008.

Molina, Cristóbal de (1573). *Destrucción del Perú y Fábulas y ritos de los incas.* Prólogo bio-bibliográfico por Carlos A. Romero, epílogo crítico bibliográfico por Raúl Porras Barrenchea. Anotaciones y comentarios por Francisco A. Loayza. Lima: Librería e Impresa Miranda, 1943.

———. *Fábulas y mitos de los incas*. Edición de Henrique Urbano y Pierre Duviols. Madrid: Historia 16, 1988. Original text is generally known as *Relación de las fábulas y ritos de los incas*.

———. *Relación de las fábulas y ritos de los incas*. Edición de Horacio H. Urteaga y Carlos Alberto Romero. Colección de libros referentes a la historia del Perú, Tomo I. Lima: Imprenta y Librería Sanmartí y ca., 1916.

Monte, Christopher. *Beneath the Mask: An Introduction to Theories of Personality*. New York: Praeger Publishers, 1977.

Morote Best, Efraín. "El degollador (Ñakaq)." *Tradición: Revista Peruana de Cultura, Cuzco, Perú*, IV, no. 11 (1952): 67–91.

Moseley, Michael E. *The Incas and their Ancestors: The Archaeology of Peru*. London: Thames and Hudson, 1992.

Murúa, Martín de (1613). *Historia general del Perú*. Edición de Manuel Ballesteros. Madrid: Historia 16, 1986.

"La nación dejó de ser clandestina: Afirman que éste es un hito histórico no sólo en Bolivia, sino en América Latina." *El Diario*, La Paz, Bolivia, January 22, 2006.

"New Estimates Show Coca Rising in Colombia, Despite Record Year for Fumigation." Press Release of *Washington Office on Latin America*, Washington D.C., June 5, 2007.

"Niño mapuche en clandestinidad es buscado por 'la justicia'." *El Mercurio Digital*, escrito por Equipo de Comunicación Mapuche, Spain, April 27, 2010.

Nowak, Ronald M. *Mammals of the World*, vol. I. 6th ed. Baltimore, MD: The Johns Hopkins University Press, 1999.

Núñez, Rafael E., and Eve Sweetser. "With the Future Behind Them: Convergent Evidence from Aymara Language and Gesture in the Crosslinguistic Comparison of Spatial Construals of Time." *Cognitive Science* 30, issue 3 (May 2006): 401–50.

Núñez Rebaza, Lucy. *Los dansaq*. Lima: Museo Nacional de la Cultura Peruana, 1990.

Oblitas Poblete, Enrique. *Cultura callawaya*. La Paz, Bolivia: Empresa Industrial Gráfica E. Burrillo y Cía., 1957.

Ocampo López, Javier. *El imaginario en Boyacá: La identidad del pueblo boyacense y su proyección en la simbología regional*. Bogotá: Universidad Distrital "Francisco José de Caldas," 2001.

"Organizaciones denuncian escalada de violencia contra menores mapuche." *Amnesty International—Chile*, Santiago, April 26, 2010.

Ortiz Rescaniere, Alejandro. *De Adaneva a Inkarrí: Una visión indígena del Perú*. Lima: Editorial Retablo de Papel, 1973.

Osborne, Harold. *Indians of the Andes: Aymaras and Quechuas*. Routledge

Library Editions, Anthropology and Ethnography. London: Routledge & Kegan Paul, 1952.

———. *South American Mythology*. Feltham, Middlesex, England: The Hamlyn Publishing Group, 1968.

Ossio, Juan M. *Los indios del Perú*. 2nd ed. Quito: Ediciones Abya-Yala, 1995. First published in 1992 by Ed. MAPFRE, S.A., Madrid.

———. "El simbolismo del agua y la representación del tiempo y el espacio en la fiesta de la acequia de la comunidad de Andamarca." In *Actes du XLIIᵉ Congrès International des Américanistes, vol. IV, Paris, 2–9 Septembre 1976*, 377–96. Paris: Société des Américanistes, 1978.

Palma, Milagros. *El cóndor: Dimensión mítica del ave sagrada*. Managua, Nicaragua: Editorial Nuestra América, 1983.

Paredes, Rigoberto. *Mitos, supersticiones y supervivencias populares de Bolivia*. Edición de Germán Villamor Lucía. 7th ed. La Paz, Bolivia: Ediciones ISLA, 1995. First published in 1920 by ARNO Hermanos—Libreros Editores, La Paz, Bolivia.

Paredes-Candia, Antonio. *Antología de tradiciones y leyendas bolivianas: Tomo I, Tomo II y Tomo III*. Edición de Germán Villamor Lucía. La Paz, Bolivia: Librería-Editorial "Popular," 1990.

———. *Diccionario mitológico de Bolivia: Dioses, símbolos, héroes*. 2nd ed. La Paz, Bolivia: Ediciones ISLA y Librería-Editorial Popular (Co-Editores), 1981.

———. *Folkore de Potosí*. La Paz, Bolivia: Ediciones ISLA, 1980.

———. *Leyendas de Bolivia*. 3rd ed. La Paz, Bolivia: Librería Editorial "Popular," 1998.

Payne, Johnny, ed., comp., and trans. *Cuentos cusqueños*. 3rd ed. Cuzco, Perú: Centro de Estudios Regionales Andinos "Bartolomé de las Casas," 2003.

———. *She-Calf and Other Quechua Folk Tales*. Albuquerque, NM: University of New Mexico Press, 2000.

Pease, Franklin G. *El dios creador andino*. Lima: Mosca Azul, Editores, 1973.

———. *El pensamiento mítico*. Lima: Mosca Azul, Editores, 1982.

Pelton, Mary Helen and Jacqueline DiGennaro. *Image of a People: Tlingit Myths and Legends*. Englewood, CO: Libraries Unlimited, 1992.

Perroud, Pedro Clemente, and Juan María Chovenc. *Diccionario kechwa-castellano, castellano-kechwa: Dialecto de Ayacucho*. Santa Clara, Perú: Seminario San Alfonso de Padres Redentoristas, 1970.

"Peru—The Struggle for Accountability: Civil War Atrocities." *The Center for Justice and Accountability*, San Francisco, CA, 2011.

"Peruvian Black Market in Human Fat? Medical Experts Dispute Lima Police Claims That Gang Murdered Victims, Drained Fat from Bodies to Sell to Cosmetic Makers." *CBS News World*, November 21, 2009.

Pizarro, Pedro (1571). *Relación del descubrimiento y la conquista del Perú*. Edición y consideraciones preliminares de Guillermo Lohnmann Villena y nota de Pierre Duviols. Lima: Pontificia Universidad Católica del Perú, Fondo Editorial, 1978.

Platt, Tristan. "Mirrors and Maize: The Concept of *Yanantin* among the Macha of Bolivia." In *Anthropological History of Andean Polities*, 228–59. Edited by John V. Murra, Nathan Wachtel, and Jacques Revel. Cambridge, U.K.: Cambridge University Press, 1986, and Paris: Maison des Sciences de l'Homme.

Porras Barrenchea, Raúl. *Los cronistas del Perú (1528–1650) y otros ensayos.* Biblioteca Clásicos del Perú, no. 2. Lima: Banco de Crédito del Perú y Ministerio de Educación, 1986.

———. *Mito, tradición e historia del Perú.* 3rd ed. Lima: Retablo de Papel, Ediciones, 1973.

Portocarrero Maisch, Gonzalo. *Sacaojos: Crisis social y fantasmas coloniales.* Lima: Tarea, 1991.

Proulx, Donald A. *A Sourcebook of Nasca Ceramic Iconography: Reading a Culture Through Its Art.* Iowa City: University of Iowa Press, 2006.

Quilter, Jeffrey, and Gary Urton, eds. *Narrative Threads: Accounting and Recounting in Andean Khipu.* Austin: University of Texas Press, 2002.

Quispe Chambi, Edgar, ed. and trans. *Traducción de cuentos y tradiciones orales en aimara: Diseño educativo para culturas de tradición oral.* Puno, Perú: Academia Peruana de la Lengua Aymara, Instituto del Bien Común, 2004.

Ramos Mendoza, Crescencio, comp., ed., and trans. *Relatos quechuas (Kichwapi Unay Willakuykuna).* Con un estudio sobre la narrativa oral quechua por Crescencio Ramos Mendoza. Lima, Perú: Editorial Horizonte, 1992.

Reinhard, Johan. "At 22,000 Feet Children of Inca Sacrifice Found Frozen in Time." *National Geographic*, November 1999, 36–55.

———. *The Ice Maiden: Inca Mummies, Mountain Gods, and Sacred Sites in the Andes.* Washington, D.C.: National Geographic Society, 2005.

———. "Peru's Ice Maidens: Unwrapping the Secrets." *National Geographic*, June 1996, 62–81.

"Relator Anaya critica trato a mapuches en Chile." *Centro de Políticas Públicas*, Santiago, Chile, May 4, 2010.

Repollés, José. *Las mejores leyendas mitológicas.* Barcelona: Editorial Optima, 1999.

Restall, Matthew. *Seven Myths of the Spanish Conquest.* New York: Oxford University Press, 2003.

Ribeiro, Marco Antonio. "Formal Analysis of Myth of Maire-Pochy and of Cuniraya Viracocha." Unpublished notes, Washington, D.C., September 1998.

"Rights Violations of Indigenous Peoples 'Deep, Systemic and Widespread': Special Rapporteur Tells United Nations Permanent Forum." Report of the *United Nations Economic and Social Council HR/5016*, Permanent Forum on Indigenous Peoples, 9th Session, 6th and 7th Meetings, New York, April 22, 2010.

Robles López, Marco. *Teogonía y demiurgos de la cultura cañar.* Azogues, Ecuador: Casa de la Cultura Ecuatoriana "Benjamín Carrión," Núcleo del Cañar, 1988.

——. *Viaje al mundo cañar y nociones filosóficas en el mundo andino.* Serie "Mito y filosofía en el mundo andino," no. 17. Azogues, Ecuador: Casa de la Cultura Ecuatoriana "Benjamín Carrión" Núcleo del Cañar, 2004.

Roca Huallparimachi, Demetrio. "El sapo, la culebra y la rana en el folklore actual de la pampa de Anta." En *Folklore: Revista de Cultura Tradicional,* Cuzco, Perú, Editorial Garcilaso, 1, (July 1966): 41–66.

Rodríguez Castelo, Hernán. *Leyendas ecuatorianas.* Guayaquil, Ecuador: Publicaciones Educativas "Ariel," n.d.

Roel Pineda, Virgilio. *Cultura peruana e historia de los incas.* Lima: Fondo de Cultura Económica and Universidad Alas Peruanas, 2001.

Rojas, J. Heriberto. *Reportajes cañaris andinos.* Azogues, Ecuador: Casa de la Cultura Ecuatoriana "Benjamín Carrión," Núcleo del Cañar, 2003.

Roos, Wilma, and Omer Van Renterghem. *Ecuador: A Guide to the People, Politics and Culture.* Edited by James Ferguson and Paul van der Boorn. Translated by John Smith. Northampton, MA: Interlink Publishing Group, 2006.

Rostworowski de Diez Canseco, María. *Historia del Tahuantinsuyu.* Lima: Instituto de Estudios Peruanos Ediciones, 1999.

——. "Mitos andinos relacionados con el origen de las subsistencias." *Boletín de Lima* 37 (January 1985): 33–37.

Saavedra, José Luis. "Descolonizar e indianizar la universidad." *Pukara,* year 1, vol. 5, La Paz, Bolivia, March 7–April 7, 2006.

Salazar, Ernesto. *Entre mitos y fábulas: El Ecuador aborigen.* Quito, Ecuador: Corporación Editora Nacional, 1995.

Salazar Bondy, Sebastián. *Poesía quechua.* Montevideo, Uruguay: Arca, 1978.

Salles-Reese, Verónica. *From Viracocha to the Virgin of Copacabana: Representation of the Sacred at Lake Titicaca.* Austin: University of Texas Press, 1997.

Salomon, Frank. *The Cord Keepers.* Durham, NC: Duke University Press, 2004.

——. *The Huarochirí Manuscript: A Testament of Ancient and Colonial Andean Religion.* Translated from the Quechua by Frank Salomon and George L. Urioste. Transcription by George L. Urioste. Austin: University of Texas Press, 1991.

Sánchez, Ricardo. "Lecciones del Sol y Comercio Justo." In *E-Chaski: Boletín quincenal sobre la cultura quechua,* a publication of *Quechua Network,* April 27, 2005.

——. "Una reflexión sobre la visión espiritual indígena." In *E-Chaski: Boletín quincenal sobre la cultura quechua,* a publication of *Quechua Network,* March 31, 2005.

Santacruz Pachacuti Yamqui Salcamaygua, Joan de (1613). *Relación de antigüedades deste reyno del Pirú.* In *Tres relaciones de antigüedades perua-nas*, 207–81. Asunción, Paraguay: Editorial Guaranía, 1950.

———. *Relación de antigüedades deste reyno del Pirú.* In *Tres relaciones de antigüedades peruanas. Publícalas el Ministerio de Fomento, con motivo del Congreso internacional de americanistas que ha de celebrarse en Bruselas el presente año*, 231–328. Madrid: Imprenta y Fundición de M. Tello, 1879.

Sarmiento de Gamboa, Pedro (1572). *Historia de los incas.* Madrid: Miriguano Ediciones y Ediciones Polifemo, n.d.

Saunders, Nicholas J., ed. *Icons of Power: Feline Symbolism in the Americas.* London: Routledge, 1998.

Sawyer, Alan R. "Painted Nasca Textiles." In *The Junius B. Bird Pre-Columbian Textile Conference: May 19 and 20, 1973*, 129–50. Edited by Ann Pollard Rowe, Elizabeth P. Benson, and Anne-Louise Schaffer. Washington, D.C.: The Textile Museum and Dumbarton Oaks, Trustees for Harvard Universi-ty, 1979.

Schull, William J., and Francisco Rothhammer, eds. *The Aymara: Studies in Human Adaptation to a Rigorous Environment.* Dordrecht, The Nether-lands: Kluwer Academic Publishers, 1990.

Sharon, Douglas. "The Return to Origins in Northern Peruvian and Huichol Pilgrimages." In *Actes du XLIIᵉ Congrès International des Américanistes, vol. IV, Paris, 2–9 Septembre 1976*, 397–403. Paris: Société des Américanistes, 1978.

Sheahan, John. "The Andean Economies: Questions of Poverty, Growth, and Equity." In *State and Society in Conflict: Comparative Perspectives on Andean Crises*, 99–133. Edited by Paul W. Drake and Eric Hershberg. Pittsburgh, PA: University of Pittsburgh Press, 2006.

Shimada, Izumi. *Pampa Grande and the Mochica Culture.* Austin: University of Texas Press, 1994.

Silverblatt, Irene. *Moon, Sun, and Witches: Gender Ideologies and Class in Inca and Colonial Peru.* Princeton, NJ: Princeton University Press, 1987.

Simi Taqe: qheshwa-español-qheshwa (Diccionario quechua-español-quechua). *Qheshwa Simi Hamut'ana Kurak Suntur* (Academia Mayor de la Lengua Quechua). 2nd ed. Cusco, Perú: Gobierno Regional Cusco, 2005.

Souffez, Marie-France. "El simbolismo del piojo en el mundo andino." *An-thropologica*, Departamento de Ciencias Naturales, Pontificia Universidad Católica del Perú, 3 (1985): 171–202.

Spalding, Karen. *Huarochirí: An Andean Society under Inca and Spanish Rule.* Stanford, CA: Stanford University Press, 1984.

Spedding, Alison. "Almas, anchanchus y alaridos en la noche: El paisaje vivificado en un valle yungueño." En *Etnicidad, economía y simbolismo en los Andes*, 299–327. Silvia Arze, Rossana Barragán, Laura Escobari, Ximena Medinaceli, compiladoras. II Congreso Internacional de Etnohistoria, Coroico. La Paz, Bolivia: Instituto Francés de Estudios Andinos, Sociedad

Boliviana de Historia, Antropólogos del Sur Andino, e Instituto de Historia Social Boliviana, 1992.

Spence, Lewis. *The Myths of Mexico and Peru*. New York: Dover Publications, 1994. First published in 1913 by George G. Harrap & Company, London.

Staller, John E. "Dimensions of Place: The Significance of Centers in the Development of Andean Civilization: An Exploration of the *Ushnu* Concept." In *Pre-Columbian Landscapes of Creation and Origin*, 269–314. Edited by John Edward Staller. New York: Springer Science+Business Media, 2008.

Stanish, Charles. *Ancient Titicaca: The Evolution of Complex Society in Southern Peru and Northern Bolivia*. Berkeley: University of California Press and Regents of the University of California, 2003.

Starn, Orin. "Villagers at Arms: War and Counterrevolution in the Central-South Andes." In *Contemporary Indigenous Movements in Latin America*, 135–68. Edited by Erick Langer with Elena Muñoz. Wilmington, DE: Scholarly Resources, 2003.

Stavig, Ward, and Ella Schmidt, eds. and trans. *The Tupac Amaru and Catarista Rebellions: An Anthology of Sources*. Introduction by Charles F. Walker. Indianapolis, IN: Hackett Publishing Company, 2008.

Steele, Paul R., with the assistance of Catherine J. Allen. *Handbook of Inca Mythology*. Santa Barbara, CA: ABC-CLIO, 2004.

Stephenson, Marcia. *Gender and Modernity in Andean Society*. Austin: University of Texas Press, 1999.

Stern, Steve J., ed. *Shining and Other Paths: War and Society in Peru, 1980–1995*. Durham, NC: Duke University Press, 1998.

Sullivan, Harry Stack. *The Interpersonal Theory of Psychiatry*. New York: Norton, 1953.

———. *Schizophrenia as a Human Process*. New York: Norton, 1962.

Sullivan, Lawrence E. "Above, Below, or Far Away: Andean Cosmogony and Ethical Order." In *Cosmogony and Ethical Order: New Studies in Comparative Ethics*, 98–131. Edited by Robin W. Lovin and Frank E. Reynolds. Chicago: University of Chicago Press, 1985.

Taller de Historia Oral Andina. Cuentos recopilados por La Unidad de Asesoramiento y Servicio Técnico en el Primer Encuentro Andino Amazónico de Narradores Orales Indígenas, La Paz, Bolivia, 1992, y el Segundo Encuentro Nacional de Narradores Orales, Cochabamba, Bolivia, 1993.

Tatzo, Alberto and Germán Rodríguez. *La visión cósmica de los Andes*. Quito: E.B.I. Proyecto de Educación Bilingüe Intercultural y Ediciones Abya-Yala, 1998.

Taube, Karl. *Aztec and Maya Myths*. Austin: University of Texas Press, 1993.

Taylor, Gerald. *Diccionario quechua Chachapoyas-Lamas*. Lima, Perú: Instituto Francés de Estudios Andinos, Instituto de Estudios Peruanos y Editorial Comentarios SAC, 2006.

————. *La tradición oral quechua de Chachapoyas*. Lima, Perú: Instituto Francés de Estudios Andinos, 1996.

Teología India, Memoria: Sabiduría Indígena, Fuente de Esperanza. III Encuentro, Taller Latinoamericano, Cochabamba, Bolivia, 24 al 30 de agosto, 1997. IDEA (Perú), CTP (Bolivia), IPA (Perú). Edición de Ramiro Argadoña (CTP), Diego Irarrázabal (IDEA) y María José Caram Padilla (IPA). Cuzco, Perú: Editorial Grafisol, 1998.

Teología India, II Parte: Sabiduría Indígena, Fuente de Esperanza: Aportes. III Encuentro, Taller Latinoamericano, Cochabamba, Bolivia, 24 al 30 de agosto, 1997. IDEA (Perú), CTP (Bolivia), IPA (Perú). Edición de Gisela Grundges (IPA). Cuzco, Perú: Editorial Grafisol, 1998.

Tharin, Mary. "Awá Massacre Highlights Desperate Need for Fresh Approach to Drugs in Colombia." Press Release of the *Council on Hemispheric Affairs*, Washington, D.C., February 25, 2009.

"Threatened Lake of the Year 2012: Lake Titicaca in Peru and Bolivia." *Global Nature Fund*, May 24, 2012.

Toro Montalvo, César. *Mitos y leyendas del Perú*. Lima: A.F.A. Editores Importadores, 2003.

Turino, Thomas R. "The Charango and the *Sirena*: Music, Magic, and the Power of Love." *Latin American Music Review (Revista de Música Latinoamericana)* 4, issue 1 (Spring–Summer 1983): 81–119.

"Unicef pide imparcialidad en las indagaciones por violencia contra unos niños mapuche." *Agencia EFE*, Spain, October 26, 2009.

"UNICEF Urges the Chilean Government to Protect Mapuche Children." *Nationaliu—Forum Social Mundial*, October 28, 2009.

"United Nations Special Rapporteur on Indigenous People Releases Report on His Visit to Colombia in the Context of Follow Up to the Recommendations Made by His Predecessor." Report of the *United Nations Office of the High Commissioner for Human Rights*, New York, January 11, 2010.

Untoja, Fernando, and Ana A. Mamani Espejo. *Pacha en el pensamiento aymara*. La Paz, Bolivia: Fondo Editorial de los Diputados, 2000.

Urioste, George, ed. *Hijos de Pariya Qaqa: La tradición oral de Waru Chiri (Vols. I and II)*. Foreign and Comparative Studies, Latin American Series, no. 6. Syracuse, NY: Syracuse University Maxwell School of Citizenship and Public Affairs, 1983.

Urton, Gary, ed. "Animals and Astronomy in the Quechua Universe." *Proceedings of the American Philosophical Society* 125, no. 2 (April 30, 1981): 110–27.

————. *Animal Myths and Metaphors in South America*. Salt Lake City: University of Utah Press, 1985.

————. *At the Crossroads of the Earth and the Sky: An Andean Cosmology*. Austin: University of Texas Press, 1981.

———. *The History of a Myth: Pacariqtambo and the Origin of the Inkas.* Austin: University of Texas Press, 1990.

———. *Inca Myths.* Austin: University of Texas Press, in cooperation with the British Museum Press, 1999.

———. *Signs of the Inka Khipu: Binary Coding in the Andean Knotted-String Records.* Austin: University of Texas Press, 2003.

Uther, Hans-Jörg. *The Types of International Folktales: A Classification and Bibliography. Based on the System of Antti Aarne and Stith Thompson. Parts I–III (FF Communications, Nos. 284, 285, 296).* Three Volumes. Helsinki: Suomalainen Tiedeakatemia, 2011.

Valcárcel, Luis. *Historia del antiguo Perú.* Lima, Perú: Editorial Juan Mejía Baca, 1964.

———. *Los siete hijos de Katu.* Lima, Perú: Vilock, 1966.

Valcárcel, Luis, and José María Arguedas, eds. *Narraciones y leyendas incas.* Lima, Perú: Editorial Latinoamericana, 1958.

Valda de Jaimes Freyre, Luisa. *Cultura aymara en La Paz: Tradiciones y costumbres indígenas.* La Paz: Bolivia: Imprenta y Librería Renovación, 1972.

Van Cott, Donna Lee. "Latin America's Indigenous Peoples." *Journal of Democracy*, 18, no. 4 (2007): 127–42.

"Turning Crisis into Opportunity: Achievements of Excluded Groups in the Andes." In *State and Society in Conflict: Comparative Perspectives on Andean Crises*, 157–88. Edited by Paul W. Drake and Eric Hershberg. Pittsburgh, PA: University of Pittsburgh Press, 2006.

van Kessel, Jan. "La cosmovisión aymara." In *Culturas de Chile, Etnografía: Sociedades indígenas contemporáneas y su ideología*, 169–88. Edited by Jorge Hidalgo L., Virgilio Schiappacasse F., Hans Niemeyer F., Carlos Aldunate del S., and Pedro Mege R., in collaboration with La Fundación Andes, and sponsorship from the Universidad de Tarapacá, Sociedad Chilena de Arqueología, Museo Chileno de Arte Precolombino, and Archivo Nacional. Santiago: Editorial Andrés Bello, 1996.

———. "La organización tempo-espacial del trabajo entre los aymaras de Tarapacá: La perspectiva mitológica." En *Etnicidad, economía y simbolismo en los Andes*, 267–97. Silvia Arze, Rossana Barragán, Laura Escobari, Ximena Medinaceli, compiladoras. II Congreso Internacional de Etnohistoria, Coroico. La Paz, Bolivia: Instituto Francés de Estudios Andinos, Sociedad Boliviana de Historia, Antropólogos del Sur Andino, e Instituto de Historia Social Boliviana, 1992.

———. "El zorro en la cosmovisión andina." *Volveré*, year IV, no. 21, December 2005.

Vega-Delgado, Gustavo, César Hermida Piedra, y Alberto Quezada Ramón. *El mundo mítico ritual y simbólico de la medicina y la salud: Mitos y leyendas en el Azuay.* Cuenca, Ecuador: Proyecto CONUEP y Universidad de Cuenca, Departamento de Difusión Cultural, 1995. Also known by the title

Mitos y leyendas: Sus correlaciones con la medicina y la salud: El mundo mítico, simbólico y ritual en las serranías del Azuay.

Villalba, L., M. Luchcrini, S. Walker, D. Cossíos, A. Iriarte, J. Sanderson, G. Gallardo, F. Alfaro, C. Napolitano, and C. Sillero-Zubiri. *The Andean Cat: A Conservation Plan.* La Paz, Bolivia: Alianza Gato Andino, 2004.

Villamor, Germán G. *Moderno vocabulario del quechua y del aymara y su correspondencia en castellano; sueños, mitos, creencias y supersticiones; conversaciones en ambos idiomas y su traducción al castellano.* 4th ed. La Paz, Bolivia: Librería-Editorial Popular, 1981.

Vogt, Jeffrey. "MAS Victory in Bolivia Signifies Mandate for Change." *Cross Currents, Newsletter* of the *Washington Office on Latin America,* March 2006, 2–3 and 11.

Vylder, Stefan de. "Poverty Reduction in South America: The Millennium Goal Within or Beyond Reach?" Report commissioned by the *Swedish International Development Cooperation Agency* (SIDA), Department for Latin America, June 20, 1995.

Wachtel, Nathan. "Men of the Water: The Uru Problem (Sixteenth and Seventeenth Centuries)." In *Anthropological History of Andean Polities,* 283–310. Edited by John V. Murra, Nathan Wachtel, and Jacques Revel. Cambridge, U.K.: Cambridge University Press, 1986.

———. *Sociedad e ideología: Ensayos de historia y antropología andinas.* Lima: Instituto de Estudios Peruanos, 1973.

———. *The Vision of the Vanquished.* Translated by Ben Sian Reynolds. New York: Barnes and Noble, 1977.

Wade, Peter. *Race and Ethnicity in Latin America.* London: Pluto Press, 1997.

Walker, Ernest P. *Mammals of the World.* Baltimore, MD: The Johns Hopkins University Press, 1964.

Walsh, Catherine, Álvaro García Linera, and Walter Mignolo. *Interculturalidad, descolonización del estado y del conocimiento.* Buenos Aires: Ediciones del Signo, 2006.

Walsh, John M. "Reality Check: The Latest U.S. Coca Cultivation Estimates Make One Thing Clear: There Is Plenty of Coca." Report of the *Washington Office on Latin America,* Washington, D.C., June 11, 2007.

Wamancha, Viviano. "El mito de Inkarrí." Transcribed by Josafat Roel Pineda and compiled by Virgilio Roel. In *Décimo pachakuty: De Túpac Amaru a Inkarrí o El anuncio del décimo pachakuty,* Movimiento Indio Peruano, April 13, 2006.

Warren, Kay B., and Jean E. Jackson, eds. *Indigenous Movements, Self-Representation and the State in Latin America.* Austin: University of Texas Press, 2002.

"Water Privatization Case Study: Cochabamba, Bolivia." *Public Citizen,* 2001.

Webster's College Dictionary. New York: Barnes & Noble Books, by arrangement with Federal Street Press, a division of Merriam-Webster, 2003.

Weil, Thomas E., Jan Knippers Black, Howard I. Blutstein, Hans J. Hoyer, Kathryn T. Johnston, and David S. McMorris. *Bolivia: A Country Study.* Country Studies/Area Handbook Series, sponsored by the U.S. Department of the Army. Washington, D.C.: Federal Research Division, U.S. Library of Congress, 1986–1998.

Weismantel, Mary. *Cholas and Pishtacos: Stories of Race and Sex in the Andes.* Chicago: University of Chicago Press, 2001.

Wölk, Wolfgang, and Clodoaldo Soto. "The Concept of Time in Quechua." Paper presented at the Symposium of Andean Time, American Anthropological Association Meetings, New Orleans, LA, 1973.

Wood, Rachel. "Overview of the Colombian Conflict from a Human Rights-Based Methodological Perspective." Press Release of the *Council on Hemispheric Affairs*, Washington, D.C., July 28, 2009.

Xerez, Francisco de (1534). *Conquista del Perú.* Badajos, Extremadura, España: Arqueros, 1929.

Yánez del Pozo, José. *Aztlán y el Incarrí: Dos mitos sobre nuestra América.* Quito: Ediciones Abya-Yala, 2000.

———. *Yanantin: La filosofía dialógica intercultural del manuscrito de Huarochirí.* Quito: Ediciones Abya-Yala, 2002.

Yashar, Deborah J. *Contesting Citizenship in Latin America.* New York: Cambridge University Press, 2005.

Youngers, Coletta A. "Collateral Damage: The U.S. 'War on Drugs' and its Impact on Democracy in the Andes." In *Politics in the Andes: Identity, Conflict, Reform*, 126–45. Edited by Jo-Marie Burt and Philip Mauceri. Pittsburgh, PA: University of Pittsburgh Press, 2004.

Zaruma, Luis Bolívar. *Los pueblos indios en sus mitos, No. 5: Cañari (Tomo I).* 2nd ed. Quito: Ediciones Abya-Yala, 1993. First edition published as *Mito y creencias de Hatun Cañar*, Radio de la Voz de Ingapirca, 1989.

Zaruma Quizhpilema, Vicente. *Wakanmay, aliento sagrado: Perspectivas de teología india; una propuesta desde la cultura cañari.* Quito: Ediciones Abya-Yala, 2006.

Zuidema, R. Tom. *The Ceque System of Cuzco: The Social Organization of the Capital of the Inca.* Leiden, The Netherlands: E. J. Brill, 1964.

———. *Inca Civilization in Cuzco.* Translated by Jean-Jacques Decoster. Foreword by Françoise Héritier-Augé. Austin: University of Texas Press, 1990.

———. "Inca Kinship: A New Theoretical Outlook." In *Andean Kinship and Marriage*, 240–81. Edited by R. Bolton and E. Mayer. Washington, D.C.: American Anthropological Association, Special Publication no. 7, 1977.

———. "Mito e historia en el antiguo Perú." *Allpanchis Phuturinga*, no. 10 (1977): 15–52.

———. "Myth and History in Ancient Peru." In *The Logic of Culture: Advances in Structural Anthropology and Methods*, 150–75. Edited by Ino Rossi. Hadley, MA: J. F. Bergin Publishers, 1982.

Index

Page numbers in *italics* indicate illustrations.